To Thomas P. Roche, Jr.
who made this book possible

≥ঌ

Essays in Medieval Culture

≥ঌ

Essays in
Medieval Culture

D. W. Robertson, Jr.

Princeton University Press
Princeton, New Jersey

Copyright © 1980 by Princeton University Press
Published by Princeton University Press, Princeton, New Jersey
In the United Kingdom: Princeton University Press, Guildford, Surrey

All Rights Reserved
Library of Congress Cataloging in Publication Data will be
found on the last printed page of this book

This book has been composed in VIP Bembo

Clothbound editions of Princeton University Press books
are printed on acid-free paper, and binding materials are
chosen for strength and durability

Printed in the United States of America by Princeton
University Press, Princeton, New Jersey

Contents

List of Abbreviations   ix

Author's Introduction   xi

I

Historical Criticism (1950)   3

The Doctrine of Charity in Medieval Literary Gardens
(1951)   21

Some Medieval Literary Terminology, with Special
Reference to Chrétien de Troyes (1951)   51

Some Observations on Method in Literary Studies (1969)   73

The Allegorist and the Aesthetician   85

II

Certain Theological Conventions in Mannyng's
Treatment of the Commandments (1946)   105

Frequency of Preaching in Thirteenth Century England
(1949)   114

III

Two Poems from the *Carmina Burana* (1976)   131

Five Poems by Marcabru (1954)   151

The "Partitura Amorosa" of Jean de Savoie (1954)   166

Chrétien's *Cligés* and the Ovidian Spirit (1955)   173

The Idea of Fame in Chrétien's *Cligés* (1972)   183

Love Conventions in Marie's *Equitan* (1953)   202

IV

The Pearl as a Symbol (1950)   209

The Heresy of *The Pearl* (1950)   215

The Question of Typology and the Wakefield Mactacio
Abel (1974)   218

V

The Historical Setting of Chaucer's *Book of the Duchess*
(1965)   235

The Concept of Courtly Love as an Impediment to the
Understanding of Medieval Texts (1968)   257

Chaucer's Franklin and his Tale (1974)   273

Some Disputed Chaucerian Terminology (1977)   291

VI

In Foraminibus Petrae: A Note on Leonardo's "Virgin of
the Rocks" (1954)   305

Sidney's Metaphor of the Ulcer (1941)   308

A Medievalist Looks at *Hamlet*   312

Pope and Boethius (1964)   332

Notes   341

Bibliography   383

Index   385

List of Abbreviations

ABR	American Benedictine Review
AR	Archivum Romanicum
CEMA	Les Classiques Français du moyen âge
CL	Comparative Literature
ELH	Journal of English Literary History
JEGP	Journal of English and Germanic Philology
JMRS	Journal of Medieval and Renaissance Studies
Mansi	J. D. Mansi, Sacrorum Conciliorum Novae Amplissima Collectio
MBP	Maximo Bibliotheca Veterum Patrum
MGH	Monumenta Germaniae Historica
MLN	Modern Language Notes
MLR	Modern Language Review
MP	Modern Philology
MS	Medieval Studies
MV III	Mythographus Vaticanus Tertius
PL	Patrologia Latina
RF	Romanische Forschungen
RPh	Romance Philology
SATF	Société des anciens textes français
SP	Studies in Philology
SQ	Shakespeare Quarterly
TLL	Thesaurus Linguae Latinae
TRHS	Transactions of the Royal Historical Society
ZFSL	Zeitschrift für Franzosische Sprache und Literatur
ZPR	Zeitschrift für Romanische Philologie

You then whose Judgment the right Course wou'd steer,
Know well each ANCIENT's proper *Character*,
His *Fable, Subject, Scope* in ev'ry Page,
Religion, Country, Genius of his *Age*:
Without all these at once before your Eyes,
Cavil you may, but never *Criticize*.

         —*Mr. Pope*

In Faith and Hope the world will disagree,
But all Mankind's concern is Charity:
All must be false that thwart this One great End,
And all of God, that bless Mankind or mend.

         —*Mr. Pope*

In foliis verba, in pomis intellige sensus,
 Haec crebro accrescunt, illa bene usa cibant.

         —*Theodulf of Orleans*

Words are like *Leaves*; and where they most abound,
Much *Fruit* of *Sense* beneath is rarely found.

         —*Mr. Pope*

The great Design of Arts is to restore the Decays
that happen'd to human Nature by the Fall, by
restoring Order.

         —*Mr. Dennis*

Author's Introduction

I SHOULD like to begin by thanking those who have helped me assemble this volume for the many hours of hard work they have devoted to it. The collection, which includes two hitherto unpublished
lectures, covers a span of almost forty years, but it is arranged in accordance with general topics rather than chronologically. At the beginning of each selection I have provided a note. These introductory
notes serve a number of functions. In some instances they call attention to what I now regard as errors in detail, or to details inadequately
supported. These revisions, however, do not in any instance affect the
general thesis being developed. In some instances further supporting
bibliography is suggested, but such references are suggestive rather
than exhaustive. Where the introductory notes are short this fact simply means that I wish the selection to speak for itself.

A few of the selections concern method or what might be called
"theory." Actually, the scholarly premises on which these selections
are based are extremely simple and not new. First, I am convinced that
the cultural products of any age, or for that matter its general history,
can be understood only in terms that would have been comprehensible
at the time. We may realize, for example, that the measures taken by
individuals to avoid the Plague in the fourteenth century were often
misguided, but our own more accurate understanding of the disease
does not explain the reactions of people in the fourteenth century.
Moreover, the introduction of a modern universe of discourse, especially that derived from the social sciences or from post-Crocean
aesthetics, in the analysis of earlier literature creates problems that
would have been meaningless or incomprehensible to people living at
the time. Chrétien de Troyes, Chaucer, Dante, Petrarch, Boccaccio,
Spenser, Shakespeare, Milton, and Pope have all been victimized by
analyses made in accordance with psychological and aesthetic theories
or general patterns of thought, like "binary" structures, for example,
appropriate only to a modern mass culture.

Thus it becomes necessary to resort to primary sources of all kinds
to understand a literary work produced in an earlier age. Without such
study it is impossible to understand the connotations of words, much
less the connotations of ideas. During the Middle Ages, and, indeed,

until the development of mass societies in the course of the eighteenth century educated persons in Europe were the inheritors of a large body of traditional beliefs based chiefly on the Bible and the Classics. It seems only reasonable, therefore, to determine as accurately as possible, and without modern prejudice, how the Bible and the Classics were understood in any given period. For this reason it is important for medieval scholars to study both Patristic and Medieval Scriptural exegesis, sermons, treatises on special subjects like Penance, standard texts like the *Glossa ordinaria* or the *Major glossatura* and the *Sententiae* of Peter the Lombard, as well as encyclopedias, mythographic manuals, and commentaries on the Classics. Some texts, like *The Consolation of Philosophy* of Boethius, were extremely influential from Old English times until the later eighteenth century, so that it is necessary for all scholars interested in the culture of this enormous span of years to understand them as accurately and sympathetically as they can.

To this endeavor the study of the visual arts affords an enormous asset, since the visual arts reflect, sometimes in obvious ways, the same figurative conventions that appear in literature. At the same time, because of the well-known phenomenon that readers tend to find in the texts before them what they expect to find, the visual arts afford extremely valuable clues to the nature of changing styles. Style in the arts, including literature, tends to change at roughly the same time in a given place, not because of any mystical principles but because changing styles reflect changes in the structure of society and consequent changes in human attitudes. In the Middle Ages, as in other periods, the analysis of stylistic change must make allowances for provincial or local differences, as well as for differences in the status of audiences being addressed. Thus an audience of burgesses or an audience of monks cannot be expected to have the same tastes exhibited by an audience made up of members of a royal court.

The medievalist should include among primary sources literary works used by the author being studied, like the *Roman de la rose*, for example, in the study of Chaucer. Literary traditions afford clues not only to attitudes, patterns of thought and action, and significant imagery, but also to the significance of "forms," like the dream vision. Again, they often offer a means of studying eloquence, or the changing techniques of effective verbal appeal. Although the essays included here do not make much use of them, ideas concerning such matters as astrology, cosmology, music, both theoretical and practical, logic, medicine, physiognomy, and other disciplines contemporary with the work being studied are extremely useful.

Finally, a literary work is shaped in many ways by the structure of the society that produced it and by the peculiar problems and interests of that society at the time the work was produced. To consider Chaucer, for example, ideas concerning fourteenth-century English society have undergone significant changes during the past forty years with the publication of court records, including those of the central courts, the rolls of the Justices of the Peace, coroners' rolls, records of courts holding the View of Frankpledge, borough courts, and manorial courts. These records offer many insights both into the general structure of English society and into the details of daily life. There have been in addition many fine studies of particular estates, of regions, and of individual manors, as well as histories of towns and accounts of trades and industries. These materials form a necessary adjunct to our understanding of Chaucer's treatment of the various characters in *The Canterbury Tales*. His reaction to them, and that of his audience, was probably affected by the rapid changes in English society after the Black Death. With reference to the ecclesiastical figures in the *Tales* there are also now available a variety of documents and studies that were unavailable forty years ago.

The same kind of progress has been made in the legal and social history of other periods in the Middle Ages and in the Renaissance. Scholars in these areas thus have a remarkable opportunity for fruitful research in a wide variety of fields. The requirements are, first of all, a healthy skepticism concerning accepted views, a willingness to endure the calumny that results from the questioning of such views, and the kind of dedication that stimulates hard work and that leads ultimately to the satisfactions of genuine achievement. If the materials collected in this volume stimulate further endeavor they will serve a useful purpose. Meanwhile, I look forward with pleasure to the modification, correction, or even rejection of my own views not on the basis of a self-protective resort to current fashions but on the basis of more thorough research and more adequate knowledge.

Readers may want to know whether these essays represent any underlying critical theories other than those suggested in the article "Some Observations on Method in Literary Studies" and in the two lectures "Historical Criticism" and "The Allegorist and the Aesthetician." Since others may be curious about the manner in which the ideas revealed there were generated, an autobiographical approach to the subject may be helpful. It will have at least some value as an empirical record, perhaps having the exemplary usefulness recommended by St. Augustine for such narratives.

In the beginning, so to speak, the directors of my master's thesis at the University of North Carolina, H. K. Russell and George R.

Coffman, insisted that I use original languages—Latin, French, German, Italian, and Spanish, in addition to English—in my survey of the controversy over "catharsis" in Aristotle's definition of tragedy (1937). I found it possible to assemble as many as three scholarly English translations of a passage from a Renaissance critic, all of which said different things, and none of which said what the original said. Ever since I have thought that learned journals and scholarly books should print quotations in their original languages, and that readers who cannot read these languages should simply avoid the subjects involved (an "incorrigible" attitude that wins small sympathy from editors). Later on, I found that translations of medieval documents could be equally misleading, even when they contained no "errors" identifiable in grammars and dictionaries. Although I have published translations myself, mostly for use in undergraduate courses, I am convinced that all translators, including me, are often inadvertent scoundrels.

A further observation that resulted from the preparation of the thesis was that theories of "catharsis" in a given period reflect certain common basic assumptions, even when on the surface they seem to be dramatically or even violently contradictory. Moreover, these basic assumptions were harmonious with similar assumptions in the literature and art of the same period. In other words, theories of "catharsis" reflected the trends of what I later learned to call "stylistic history."

Some years after the completion of my thesis, having in the meantime been inspired by the inimitable Urban T. Holmes to enjoy Old French literature and to relish the intricacies of Old Irish, I wrote a dissertation under the direction of Professor Coffman on Robert Mannyng's *Handlyng Synne* (1946), discovering in the first place that this work, based on an Anglo-Norman source, is a manual of confession for laymen reflecting the conventions already established in Latin manuals, and that many of the "reflections of daily life" it was said to contain actually represent traditions of pastoral theology sometimes extending back as far as the sixth-century sermons of St. Caesarius of Arles. Incidentally, I came to have an enormous respect for the eloquence of St. Caesarius; he was not only eloquent but, it seemed to me, intelligent and practical, although I was not especially religious. In general, my study convinced me that to understand any work written in the past it is necessary to discover and examine carefully relevant primary sources and intellectual traditions. However, in the preparation of the article on preaching in the thirteenth century written soon after I obtained my degree I discovered that primary sources could be deceptive also; that is, unless great care is taken they may be made to say exactly what one wants them to say. This is what the proponents of "rare sermons" in thirteenth-century England were doing with the materials they pretended to use with such "scientific" precision. Without mentioning names, I have noticed at least one instance recently in which a quoted Latin passage is made to say the opposite of what it obviously meant, simply by surrounding it with a convincing verbal context. I am afraid that we are all, like Chaucer's Chauntecleer, capable of this sort of thing.

When I arrived at Princeton, I met B. F. Huppé and discovered a common interest in *Piers Plowman*. We decided to devote a summer to the joint composition of a book on the poem, since we had some general ideas concerning a new interpretation. These ideas were soon forgotten, however, for early in our researches we decided to look up some of the scriptural quotations in the poem in medieval commentaries. Some of these quotations seemed puzzling as they stood, and we felt that some knowledge of medieval attitudes toward the scriptures might be useful in understanding them. Initial trials produced good results, and our office soon became crowded with volumes of the *Patrologia Latina*, which was then not much in demand in the Princeton library. As our work progressed we found that the commentaries shed light not only on the passages quoted but on other more indirect reflections of the scriptures in the text. The exegetes we read also taught us the importance of knowing as much as possible about patristic writings generally and in particular we were impressed by the enormous influence of St. Augustine. I still think that a careful and extensive study of St. Augustine's writings is a necessary preliminary to almost any study involving the traditions of medieval thought, and I have observed many instances in which a failure to conduct such a study has produced very misleading results. Moreover, the fundamental importance of charity or the New Law was everywhere apparent in the materials we studied, although we found that most professed Christians among our contemporaries were not very familiar with it. There was a widespread tendency to say that charity is simply one of the "three theological virtues." In any event, the result of our labors was *Piers Plowman and Scriptural Tradition* (Princeton, 1951) and the first draft of *Fruyt and Chaf* (Princeton, 1963).

Although the only "theory" we had in mind when we wrote our joint book on *Piers* was that one should consult relevant primary materials, our work produced an immediate furor of protest, largely because of the kind of primary materials we had used. We were called "neo-Augustinians" (actually rather complimentary, although not so intended), "neo-exegetes," and, since Professor Huppé left Princeton for administrative work elsewhere and I continued to lecture and publish, the term "Robertsonian" achieved wide currency, which, I am amused to say, it still has. We were falsely accused of wishing to read all earlier literature on "four levels," of neglecting later medieval exegetes, and sometimes justly of a variety of other sins. My efforts to publish articles on Old English literature using exegetical sources and works like *The Consolation of Philosophy* were completely unsuccessful, for editors insisted that Old English literature contained nothing but Germanic ideals of *comitatus* relationships, some gnomic wisdom, and a few pious interpolations. The general attitude was well expressed in George Anderson's *The Literature of the Anglo-Saxons* (Princeton, 1949): "We have tramped the fields of Old English poetry almost flat." My own department grew suspicious of me, and I abandoned my seminar in Old English. I continued to teach what I believed in other fields, however, and graduate students in due course came to publish for themselves, so that something known as "the Princeton school" of medievalists appeared. I hope that those who use this term realize that they are talking about nothing more than an emphasis on primary research. Moreover, I am happy to say that Old English studies have improved, that many scholars now use the *Patrologia Latina* with impunity, and that even a musicologist, untainted by me, can carefully explain the virtues of the *Glossa ordinaria* in print.[1]

Meanwhile, after a lecture delivered before the English Club at Princeton, my friend and colleague Carlos Baker castigated me for neglecting the Latin classics. Investigation demonstrated that medieval scholars had their own ideas about the classics, and their own methods of interpreting them, although most modern literary scholars tended to disregard what they said, or to treat it with contempt, preferring to think that our medieval ancestors read such things surreptitiously and then cooked up excuses for doing it. It also revealed that the late Charles G. Osgood of Princeton knew a great deal about these matters, and I was happy to initiate the republication of his excellent book, *Boccaccio on Poetry* (Library of Liberal Arts, 1956). I also discovered that certain historians of art were fully aware of the kind of adaptations medieval people made of classical materials for their own purposes.

While Professor Huppé and I were working on our two joint efforts, our friend John Weld used to admonish us that we ought to know something about art history, since art historians had done work very similar to what we were doing, notably Emile Mâle. He also urged us to consult the works of Bersuire, used effectively by art historians. My own interest in this pursuit was further stimulated by a conversation, very memorable to me, with Mrs. Kurt Weitzmann and the late Paul Frankl. A series of brilliant lectures on style delivered at Princeton by Meyer Schapiro for the Gauss Seminars reminded me of certain observations I had made in the course of writing my master's thesis and renewed my interest in "stylistic history," leading me to consult the work of Wölfflin, whose general conclusions (if not specific terms of analysis) seemed to me to be reinforced by the work of "psychological historians" like J. H. Van den Berg. These interests resulted in the elaborate illustrations for *A Preface to Chaucer* (Princeton, 1962), the introduction to that book and the chapter it contains on "Late Medieval Style." Later on, I sought to develop some of these ideas further in the second part of *Abelard and Heloise* (New York, 1972).

I now believe that styles change, with local variations, with a regularity somewhat like that proposed many years ago by the Young Grammarians in their theory of "the unexceptionability of phonetic law." That is, anyone who travels through the countryside of England can observe, sometimes painfully if he is a stranger from America, that "phonetic laws" do indeed have many exceptions. Nevertheless, no one in England speaks Old English, Middle English, Elizabethan English, or even the language of *Tom Jones*. I am old enough now, moreover, to have observed enormous changes in style in the popular arts, not to mention scholarship, criticism, and even "scientific law." For, with reference to the last, the "Laws of Nature" are actually constructions of the human mind, subject to continuous modification and improvement. "Style" is basically a way of doing something. And as ways of doing things change, social structures change, and with them those cultural attitudes that make up "human" as distinct from "animal" nature. For this reason, as I have frequently said, if we are to understand the literature of the past we must not impose our own attitudes, values, and ideals, which belong to a different universe of discourse, upon it. It is true, of course, that the imposition of currently fashionable attitudes upon the literature of the past, if eloquently managed, can make an enormous impression upon the unsuspecting public, on students, and even on university officials and government bureaucrats, who like relevance. The world, as someone once said, wishes to be deceived, and this deception is profitable. But I do not think it constitutes education.

In this connection I have often been accused of being too "moral." But up until roughly the end of the first half of the eighteenth century human conduct was understood conventionally in moral rather than in "psychological" terms. Scholastic "psychology" and Elizabethan "natural and moral philosophy" are basically moral in their implications, although they may contain physiological and medical material. Thus Thomas Wright, for example, in the third chapter of the first book of *The Passions of the Minde*, condemns self-love as the source of "all the euils, welnie, that pester the world," and goes on to cite St. Augustine (Enn. in Ps. 64) on the two lovers and the two "cities," affirming that charity is "the base and foundation of all goodnesse." There are more elaborate statements of these principles in Burton's *Anatomy* (3.1.1.2 and 3, and 3.4.1.1.), a fact that should not really surprise us. For as Francis Bacon tells us in his neglected essay *In Feliciam memoriam Elizabethae Angliae Reginae*, the good Queen and Shepherdess of her people "In Scripturis et patrum (praecipue beati Augustini) legendis, multum versata est." Later on, Mr. Pope, discussing the nature of man, could say, "all Mankind's concern is Charity." True "neo-Augustinians" as distinct from paltry observers like me make up a distinguished company. If individuals in earlier periods understood themselves and their fellows in moral terms, we should seek to understand the products of their culture in those terms also, regardless of whether we happen to agree with the moral principles they professed. Modern thinkers often identify themselves with those primitive cultures whose practices happen to coincide, for purely contingent reasons, with their own prejudices, at the same time refusing to recognize other principles no longer popular as they appear in the cultural products of our own past. Aleksandr Solzhenitsyn recently accused the American news media of blindly following current prejudices. It would be possible to level the same criticism at some American scholarship. In an editorial in *Science* (16 June 1978) Cyril Comar observes that "Bad science, being more newsworthy, will tend to be publicized and seized upon by some to support their convictions." This situation is even more acute in the humanities.

Most scholars in the humanities are very reluctant to recognize the fact that morality, as it was once understood, affords standards of values that make possible a sense of humor. Psychology, aesthetics, political ideology (a modern invention that has caused more misery and inhumanity than any other invention of the human mind), and romantic love are solemn subjects. Even sexual love, which used to be rather jolly, has become solemn and problematical, even a prescription, recommended for neurotic women by Dr. Freud, a sad substitute for Mr. Fielding's remedy for querulous wives. If we take into account the prevailing moral ideals of the Middle Ages much of the humor of medieval literature reappears. I have long thought that most of the literature rather indiscriminately labelled "courtly love" literature is actually moral and usually humorous. My attacks on "courtly love" have led to very strong reactions, and some venerable scholars have delivered vigorous lectures attacking me for "misleading the youth" about this matter. Indeed, I have found "courtly love" to be a many-headed monster that must be systematically extirpated in every alleged instance. The essays on Marcabru, Chrétien, Marie de France, and Latin poetry in the following pages are small efforts in this direction. There are further efforts in *A Preface to Chaucer*, but I realize that much more work needs to be done to destroy this treasured academic platitude. As my students are aware, I have pursued this task avidly in graduate seminars. I hope that even solemn modernists can soon be led to laugh again.

Exegetical and doctrinal materials are by no means the only kinds of primary materials that have suffered neglect among literary scholars. During the years since I was a graduate student there have been enormous advances in our knowledge of fourteenth-century life. Literary scholars have seldom kept pace with these advances, many of which appear only in highly specialized studies. Agrarian, local, and economic historians have taught us that medieval communities suffered a great deal of dislocation after the Black Death, and that the cloth industry, represented in Chaucer by the Wife of Bath, was flourishing. Disruptions of local communities closely knit by familial and other ties can have rather drastic effects on the lives and *mores* of the people involved, as even modern instances demonstrate.[2] Changes in English society and the decline of English chivalry after 1369 undoubtedly made an enormous impression on Chaucer. And these developments were probably responsible for his criticism, usually humorous, of his contemporaries, who were departing in one way or another from ideals that he revered. The demonstration of the immediate relevance of what he had to say to his contemporaries will, however, require a great deal of very careful research, both in primary materials like court records, borough records, manorial documents, and ecclesiastical records, as well as in recent secondary studies, some of which are extraordinarily rewarding. New approaches to historical sociology like those developed by J. A. Raftis and Peter Laslett, or to historical geography of the kind inspired by H. C. Darby, offer promising new avenues of study. I wish I had another forty alert and vigorous years, and the real privilege of spending them at Princeton.

Finally, I should like to thank the many students, both graduate and undergraduate, who have encouraged me or offered useful criticisms of my endeavors. A scholar alone without bright and alert students runs many risks. Some of my graduate students, and a few undergraduates, have bravely faced the onus of being "Robertsonians," a disability from which some still suffer. I wish I knew how to thank them for their faithfulness, not to me, but to their convictions, and, above all, for their courage. And I hope that they will correct, modify, and otherwise improve the conclusions of my own research.

For in the long run no one ever makes statements that cannot be improved. There will always be new frontiers to be explored, new directions to be tried, and new evidence to be developed, not on the basis of new "theories" concocted from abstractions, but on the basis of careful observation leading to working hypotheses. No field of the mind's explorations has been "tramped flat." There will always be means to improve our understanding of and appreciation for old statements, meanwhile, made by those who, like St. Augustine, for example, worked hard and earnestly to bring us a better knowledge of ourselves and of that odd little blue planet we currently inhabit.

I

Historical Criticism

❧

I am still of the opinion that "modern aesthetic systems, economic philosophies, or psychological theories," being features of the universe of discourse, and not of the realm of things, do not exist before they are formulated, and that their validity or "truth" is confined to fairly restricted areas of space and time. However, certain details in this essay need correction. I no longer think that charity and cupidity are "opposites," since love is basically a motion of the will toward something and varies in nature with the character of its object. Man's "quest," moreover, is not "eternal." The word levels applied to tropological, allegorical, and anagogical interpretations is convenient but misleading. The meaning ascribed to the primrose in "The Maid of the Moor" is perhaps dubious. The flower mentioned may simply be an early rose. The fact that the song was not relished by a Franciscan Bishop, adduced by opponents of this interpretation, does not convince me that it is "pagan," "lewd," or superstitious. Many Franciscans preferred literal piety.

❧

B Y "Historical Criticism" I understand that kind of literary analysis which seeks to reconstruct the intellectual attitudes and the cultural ideals of a period in order to reach a fuller understanding of its literature. In actual practice not much criticism of this kind has been written. Although the literary historian sometimes ventures into the realm of historical criticism, he is usually preoccupied with purely literary rather than with intellectual traditions. He seeks to establish texts, to date them, to attribute them to the proper authors, and to determine literary sources and influences. The historian of ideas frequently centers his attention on a single thought pattern so that his materials apply to literature either in a very general way or only to isolated passages. And in recent years the literary critic has tended to avoid historical materials altogether, reacting against the accumulation of historical information which sheds no immediate light on the texts he wishes to study. The historical critic, or at least the kind of historical critic I wish to speak of today, has a healthy respect for the work of the literary historian, which is a necessary basis for his own work. Unlike the historian of ideas, who centers on single topics, he attempts to form a workable conception of the intellectual background of a period as a whole, so that the various ideas he has to deal with may be considered in perspective. Meanwhile, he shares the respect of the literary critic for the artistic integrity of the works with which he has to deal, but he looks with some misapprehension on the tendency of the literary critic to regard older literature in the light of modern aesthetic systems, economic philosophies, or psychological theories. He feels that such systems, whatever their value may be, do not exist before they are formulated. In this paper I wish to discuss certain aspects of medieval intellectual history and literary theory and to show that a knowledge of these things contributes to a better understanding of medieval texts. Since this discussion must be presented in a relatively short time, I may be excused for a certain amount of oversimplification.

First of all, medieval literature was produced in a world dominated intellectually by the church. Too frequently, modern historians have tended to deplore this fact rather than to make a sincere effort to understand it. Neither the church nor the doctrine it sought to teach was exactly like anything existing in the world today, for the rigorous Augustinian Christianity of the Middle Ages has been softened and sentimentalized in almost all modern churches. Whatever it may mean to the historian, the dominance of the church in the Middle Ages considerably simplifies the task of the historical critic. Although the period witnessed an enormous theological development, especially after the middle of the twelfth century, certain doctrines remained constant, the common heritage of every civilized individual for more than a thousand years of European history. The most important of these constants is the doctrine of charity. Some knowledge of this doctrine is essential to an understanding either of medieval history in general or of medieval literature in particular. Since the word "charity" has lost most of its old content today, some explanation of it here may be helpful. Charity, briefly, is the New Law which Christ brought so that mankind might be saved. Under the Old Law, which Piers Plowman tears in half to the astonishment of literary historians, salvation was not possible. The New Law does not replace the Old Law, but simply vivifies it, and all of the Old Law is implicit in the New. It may be stated very simply, but like most simple statements it is not easy to understand. Love God and thy neighbor. For most of us, including myself, the love of God is a very difficult concept, and I shall not attempt to explain it except to say that, very roughly, the medieval love of God is the equivalent of a modern faith in the perfectibility of mankind. God, as St. John says, is charity. Love of one's neighbor does not imply love of man for his own sake, but love of man for the sake of

God, for his nobility in reason. Man should be loved for his humanity, and this humanity consists of that part of him which distinguishes him from the beasts, his reason. To be human and lovable in the Middle Ages was to be reasonable, for reason is the Image of God in man. It is vain to seek "humanism" of any other kind in medieval literature, except in that written by avowed heretics. To love a man for physical, romantic, or sentimental reasons is to indulge in the opposite of charity.

The opposite of charity is cupidity, the love of one's self or of any other creature—man, woman, child, or inanimate object—for the sake of the creature rather than for the sake of God. Just as charity is the source of all the virtues, cupidity is the source of all the vices and is responsible for the discontents of civilization. The two loves, both of which inflame, and both of which make one humble, are accompanied by two fears. Charity, like wisdom, begins with the fear of the Lord; and the fear of earthly misfortune leads to cupidity and ultimately to despair and damnation. These two loves and their accompanying fears are the criteria by means of which all human actions, individual or social, are to be evaluated. To use a common figure, charity builds the city of Jerusalem, and cupidity builds the city of Babylon. Man is a pilgrim or exile in a Babylonian world who should journey toward the eternal peace of Jerusalem. The world and the things in it are given to him to be used for the purposes of this journey or voyage; they are not to be enjoyed in themselves. Jerusalem was thought of as existing within the human heart, in the church or in society, and in the after life, and the pilgrimage of the spirit had to be made, as Will learns in *Piers Plowman*, first within one's self. It is frequently said that medieval man kept his eyes directed toward the after life, but this is an exaggeration. He did engage, or propose to engage, on an eternal quest for Jerusalem, but this quest was individual and social as well as other worldly. It is as if in the modern world we were able to discuss the goal of personal effort, of social effort, and of religious effort in a single terminology, and to come to an agreement about the general meaning of that terminology.

This opposition between the two loves, or the two cities, is fundamental to an understanding of medieval Christianity, throughout the thousand years of its history. Naturally, the specific elaborations and applications of this doctrine varied with the course of time, so that the historical critic finds it necessary to consider a given literary work in the light of contemporary theological developments. Thus, for example, the poem known as "The Debate of the Body and the Soul" was written as a part of a concerted effort to popularize the sacrament of

Penance, which began with the Fourth Lateran Council in 1215. A few books will establish a frame of reference for the most significant aspects of this development. Generally, for the earlier Middle Ages, the most useful works in which widely accepted doctrinal elaborations of charity may be found are the *De doctrina christiana* of St. Augustine, his *Civitas Dei*, and the *De clericorum institutione* of Rabanus Maurus. In addition, the *De consolatione* of Boethius contains what was throughout the entire course of the Middle Ages the most popular philosophical elaboration of Augustinian doctrine. This work has recently been called "the last purified legacy of the ancient world," but the ancient aspects of the book are merely formal. It is, rather, a section of the preface to the medieval world. Most of this preface was written not by Boethius, but by St. Augustine. For the later Middle Ages the most fundamental work is the *Sententiae* of Peter Lombard, which was for some four hundred years the standard textbook of theological study. The *De sacramentis* and the *Didascalicon* of Hugh of St. Victor contain many ideas which are highly significant to an understanding of both theological and literary developments. After the middle of the thirteenth century, it is necessary to follow three distinct types of theology: Dominican, Franciscan, and secular. Both the Dominicans and the Franciscans collected and wrote poetry, each order developing its own literary traditions. And the seculars inspired some of the most famous writers of the later Middle Ages, such as Jean de Meun, Chaucer, and the author of *Piers Plowman*. For Dominican attitudes nothing can replace the *Summa* of St. Thomas Aquinas, although this work should not be used as a guidebook to medieval theology generally. Franciscan attitudes are accessible in the works of St. Bonaventura, which are available in a magnificent modern edition. The secular theologians, who should be of special interest to students of English, are poorly represented in modern editions. William of St. Amour, the founder of the late secular tradition, has received little attention from modern scholars, but the *quodlibets* of one of his successors, Godefroid de Fontaines, are now available in an excellent edition published at Louvain. Meanwhile, the thirteenth century witnessed the growth of a large body of pastoral theology, surviving in records of church councils. Here it is possible to find the abstract principles of theology applied to the concrete realities of everyday life. A new edition of the English councils is now being prepared.

All of this theological activity centered on the study of the Bible, for the ultimate purpose of study of all kinds was either the interpretation of the Sacred text or the application of the principles it contains. Since the Bible was also a model and source book for literature, it is necessary for the historical critic of medieval literature to familiarize himself with the conventions of Scriptural exegesis. A few of the elementary principles may be examined here. In the first place, the Bible was said to teach nothing but charity and to condemn nothing but cupidity. But large portions of the Bible, especially the Old Testament, express the message of charity in an obscure way. When this message is not apparent on the surface, it was thought necessary to resort to interpretation. For the purposes of this task, various techniques were employed, some of them verbal and some of them physical. Names might be interpreted to imply a kind of word play. Thus, "Jerusalem" was said to consist of two elements meaning "City of Peace." Most of the names, both of persons and of places, which appear in the Bible were interpreted in this way, and in addition all the machinery of classical rhetoric was brought to bear on the text. The physical techniques are a little more difficult for us to understand. Numbers were thought to be signs of abstract concepts. Thus, "three" and "nine" are signs of the Trinity; "seven" is the number of life on earth or of the church; "eight" indicates the Resurrection or Christ. Many of the things mentioned in the Bible were thought of as signs of other things. Thus, a lion, not the word "lion," is a sign either of Christ or of Satan. As in this instance, such signs frequently embrace two opposites. A sign, as opposed to a verbal figure, might have tropological, allegorical, or anagogical values—sometimes one of these, sometimes two, and sometimes all three. In other words, a principle stated in signs or implied by a sign might apply to the individual, to society or the church, and to the after life. This procedure is not quite so "mystical" as it sounds. All that is meant by it ultimately is that a given precept or principle may apply equally well within man, within society, or within Heaven or Hell. A good example is afforded by "Jerusalem." Verbally, it means "City of Peace." But since Jerusalem is an actual city as well as a word, it is also a sign. As a sign it indicates the highest kind of human satisfaction, whether in the individual, in society, or in Heaven. The values of a given sign might be numerous. In the first place, a sign may have four levels of meaning. If we include the opposites, there are eight. And some signs might have several basic meanings, so that they imply several sets of eight somewhat different values. Theoretically an object may have as many meanings as it has characteristics in common with other objects in the universe, but practically the better known signs are limited by the contexts in which they appear in Scripture. For purposes of clarity, I shall speak of verbal symbols as "figures" and of physical symbols as "signs." The importance attached to this kind of analysis in the Middle Ages is attested by the fact that the *trivium* was devoted to the analysis of figures and the *quadrivium* to the analysis of signs. Medieval encyclopedias, the *De universo* of Rabanus Maurus, for example, are largely devoted to the exegetical meanings of figures and signs. And in the twelfth century, a number of exegetical dictionaries were published, giving the most common values for figures and signs in the Bible. One of these was written by a poet, Alanus de Insulis.

Much of the Bible was thus thought of as having a "cortex," or level of surface meaning, covering a "nucleus" of truth. The task of the exegete was to strip the cortex away by interpreting the figures and signs, so that the nucleus might be revealed. No one looked upon the obscurity of the Bible as an evil; on the contrary, it was thought to be highly advantageous. First, the determination of the inner meaning required an exercise of the mind which tends to discourage both contempt for the text and laziness. Again, one arrived at the nucleus with something of the pleasure of a discovery. To paraphrase St. Augustine on this point, that which is acquired with difficulty is much more readily and pleasurably retained. Finally, if the great truths of the faith were expressed too openly, the result might be to cast pearls before swine, or to enable the foolish to repeat without understanding. This reasoning is similar to that used in the Bible to explain why Christ spoke to the multitude in parables. These arguments in favor of obscurity, developed by St. Augustine and the early exegetes, are employed by Petrarch at the close of the Middle Ages to defend the obscurity of poetry.

The analogy between Scriptural techniques and poetic techniques was observed at a very early period. Scotus, for example, makes a direct comparison of the two. Christian thinkers were for the most part loth to part with their heritage of Classical literature, especially Latin literature. Since, however, it could not be enjoyed in itself, but was to be used for purposes of furthering charity, it was necessary to interpret it much in the same way that it was necessary to interpret the Old Testament. But in the interpretation of pagan literature only verbal techniques could be employed. Pagan authors might be capable of rhetoric and word play, but they could not be expected to understand the signs whose meanings are revealed only under the direct inspiration of the Holy Spirit. Moreover, pagan poetic narratives are not accounts of actual events. The *Aeneid* is not a history, but a lying fable. Beneath the lying cortex, however, diligent study may reveal a nucleus useful to the faith. The words "cortex" and "nucleus," together with a variety of synonyms for them, became popular literary terms as well as exegetical terms in the course of the Middle Ages. St. Augustine speaks of a poetic "tectorium"; Theodulph of Orleans uses the word "tegmen"; Alanus de Isulis uses "integumentum," "involucrum," and "pallium" as well as "cortex"; and Chaucer uses the words "fruyt" and "chaf" for "nucleus" and "cortex." A medieval Christian poem was like a pagan poem in that the external narrative was a lie. The poet combined things not found combined in nature so as to form an artificial "pictura." In the twelfth century, Alanus calls the process of combination "conjunctura," and Chrétien de Troyes speaks of his *Erec* as a "molt bele conjointure." But a medieval Christian poem differs from a pagan poem in that the author might employ signs as they are used in the Bible as well as figures. Thus, any of the multitude of Scriptural signs may appear in a medieval poem, and since these signs are things, the new poetic combination of them may not resemble verbally any passage in Scripture. For example, a Christian poem may contain a description of a garden based on signs taken from both Genesis and the Canticum and dressed up to suit the literary tastes of the poet's own audience. The result is a *pictura* which is fundamentally Biblical, but which does not resemble any Biblical scene and does not contain any Biblical phrases. There are gardens of this kind in Old English literature, in the romances, in the *Roman de la Rose*, in Chaucer, in *Piers Plowman*, and in a great many other places, but it is impossible to detect their existence except by the methods of historical criticism.

In the schools of the twelfth century any text, Biblical or profane, was read in three ways. First one read for the "littera," or the grammatical and syntactical construction. Next one proceeded to the "sensus," or obvious meaning. Finally, one sought to determine the "sententia," or doctrinal content. This last step was the end toward which all interpretation was directed, the first two steps being preliminary. The *littera* of the *Aeneid*, for example, would involve the kind of comments one still finds in textbooks for use in schools. The *sensus* would be the bare narrative without interpretation, and the *sententia* would consist of the kind of observations made in the twelfth century commentary by Bernard Silvestris. Marie de France seems to be aware of these three elements in the prologue to her *Lais*, and at the beginning of the *Chevalier de la charrette* Chrétien de Troyes says that his patroness gave him the matter and sense, or *sensus* of the story; he has added nothing but his own labor and "antancion," or *sententia*. Chaucer makes several references to "sentence," as he calls it, and Thomas Usk begins his *Testament of Love* with an observation to the effect that it is difficult to get one's "sentence" across to a dull audi-

ence. Most modern discussions of medieval literature have been concerned only with the *littera* and *sensus*. This is a restriction which
would have been most unsatisfactory to the medieval reader.

These remarks indicate that poetry during the Middle Ages was
thought of as being allegorical. If we take "allegoria" in the medieval
sense, saying one thing to mean another, this observation is very just.
Medieval Christian poetry, and by Christian poetry I mean all serious
poetry written by Christian authors, even that usually called "secular," is always allegorical when the message of charity or some corollary of it is not evident on the surface. As John of Salisbury asserts,
reflecting a very common attitude, nothing is worth reading unless it
promotes charity. The poet wished to make his message vivid and
memorable, and at the same time he did not want to cast pearls before
swine, so that his normal office was to construct obscure and puzzling
combinations of events; frequently involving tantalizing surface inconsistencies, in order to stimulate his audience to intellectual effort.

The *sententia* or *nucleus* of a poem arises from the figures and signs it
contains. It is thus obviously impossible to interpret medieval poems
without determining first what the figures and signs in it mean. In this
enterprise, the use of surface associations and of one's own knowledge
of Scripture is helpful, but not sufficient. A few of the signs still survive as secondary meanings of words. One of the values for "sleep,"
for example, was sexual embrace, and this notion still clings to the
word in certain contexts. Again, the modern phrase "at the eleventh
hour," meaning "at the last minute," stems from the medieval interpretation of the Parable of the Vineyard. But relics of this kind are
rare. No one today, I think, would be inclined offhand to associate a
worm with Christ or to guess that frost and ice are signs of Satan or of
the adversities he uses for purposes of temptation. To determine what
a sign means we must consult exegetical works of various kinds. In
this connection, there were some works, such as the commentaries of
Augustine, Bede, Gregory, and Rabanus, which remained standard
reference works throughout the Middle Ages. In the twelfth century
the *Glossa ordinaria* offered a convenient short cut to conventional interpretations, although these are often so abbreviated that it is necessary to look at the original commentaries as well. The exegetical
writings of Peter Lombard and Hugh of St. Victor were especially
influential. Later on, much of the exegetical work was done by friars,
but fraternal commentaries should be used only in the study of literature influenced by the fraternal orders. The commentaries of St.
Thomas are occasionally applicable to situations in *Piers Plowman*, but
this is true only because St. Thomas frequently reflects earlier tradi-

tions. The controversy between the friars and the seculars was very violent in the fourteenth century, and the friars were accused of interpreting the Bible to suit their own special interests.

Some specific applications of the principles we have outlined will indicate their usefulness. What has been said above, incidentally, constitutes only the barest outline, and it will be impossible to do more than to illustrate very briefly here. For the medieval interpretation of pagan poetry we may consult either the commentary on the *Aeneid* by Bernard Silvestris or the Old French *Ovide moralisé*, both of which have been edited in modern times. Scholars have been too ready to dismiss these commentaries with a contemptuous shrug. But these works and others like them show the principles of medieval poetic theory in operation and are good indications of the kind of interpretation a medieval poet might expect his own work to be subjected to. The better educated poets, moreover, did not hesitate to employ allegorical devices or figures from these commentaries in their poems, and they sometimes made their own reinterpretations of them. When Chaucer, for example, mentions Dido, we should not think of the *Aeneid* as we understand it, but as Chaucer must have understood it. But it is also clear that Chaucer's use of the story of Ceyx and Alcyone in *The Book of the Duchess* does not depend on the interpretation of that story given in the *Ovide moralisé*. Some of the Ovidian characters achieved fairly widespread conventional interpretations, as students of medieval art are aware. But others were subject to widespread fluctuations in meaning. In general, it is fortunate for the critic that Scriptural figures and signs are more common in poetry than are figures from the classics.

We may begin at the beginning, as it were, with a selection from Old English poetry. There has been a general tendency to think of this poetry as being at its best romantic after an exotic Germanic fashion and at its worst crude, barbaric, naïve, and incoherent. After reading a conventional history of the literature of ancient England one emerges with visions of rather stupid, but nevertheless heroic, Wagnerian figures looming on cold misty headlands or making their way through gloomy fens inhabited by old Germanic monsters. The flashes of obvious Christianity in this poetry are conventionally described as the work of monkish revisers or pious interpolators armed with what are called "sops." Recently the conception of the Old English poet has been gradually undergoing a change, and many scholars concede that the *Beowulf* poet was a well-educated man with fundamentally pious intentions. We might say as much, I think, for the author of *The Wanderer*, whose poem I wish to examine very briefly. Conventionally, although there have been voices to the contrary, the poem is regarded as a mixture of pagan and Christian elements arranged incoherently in the form of a dialogue which no one knows quite how to punctuate. The most recent history of Old English literature informs us that the obviously Christian ending has nothing to do with the body of the poem. Let us look for a moment at the opening lines, which I quote for purposes of clarity in R. K. Gordon's translation: "Often the solitary man prays for favor, for the mercy of the Lord, though, sad at heart, he must needs stir with his hands for a weary while the icy sea across the watery ways, must journey the paths of exile; settled in truth is fate!" On the surface we have a picture of a man sorrowfully rowing across icy seas with his hands, traveling in exile in a fashion said to be usual among the Germanic tribes. The speaker comments that fate is inexorable, an idea which is said to reflect the doctrines of Germanic paganism. However, the picture of the exile suggests at once one of the commonest of all Christian figures, the exile in the world who wanders in search of Christ, his Lord, in Jerusalem. And if we look in either Augustine, Gregory, or Bede, or even in Boethius, we find that the sea is a very common sign for the world in which the pilgrim makes his journey. The word "fate" represents Old English "wyrd," which is the term used in Old English to translate "Fortuna," the Boethian personification of the inexorable instability of the world. What the opening lines say, therefore, is that the pilgrim or exile in the world faces difficulties as he prays to God for mercy and confronts the trials of Fortune.

The poet tells us that the opening observation is made by a dweller on earth who is "mindful of hardships, of cruel slaughters, of the fall of kinsmen." Again, we think of the hardships of the old Germanic life, of battles and bloody wounds. On the surface, that is exactly what the poet was thinking of, but the wayfaring Christian is also a warfaring Christian, as students of Milton are uncomfortably aware. The battle of the Christian exile, concerning which St. Augustine wrote a book, is a battle against cupidity in himself and against heresy and the temptations of Fortune in the world. In a larger sense, it is the battle against Satan. And there are many who fall, a fact which disturbs the speaker in our poem. He is described later, for there is only one speaker, as a wise man who sits apart in thought. The poem itself constitutes the advice of this wise contemplative to his wayfaring and warfaring fellow Christians. Modestly, the poet does not offer this advice himself, but attributes it to someone else, a man who makes vivid reference to Scripture and to the observations of another wise man, Solomon.

The speaker continues by referring to his own troubles. He bewails them, he says, alone "at the dawn of each day." Why the dawn? Are troubles most oppressive at dawn, or was it at the dawn that the ancient Germanic peoples communed with their pagan gods of consolation? If we consult Gregory, we find that the dawn is a sign of the light of God's justice. In other words, the wise man considers his troubles alone in the light of Divine Providence, as Boethius learns to do in the *De consolatione*. He does not complain to his fellow men about them. Surely this must be a reference to some sort of pagan Stoicism. But let us hear Bede on this point. The Apostle James, he says (James 5)

> prohibits us from complaining to our fellows in adversity and shows what is to be done instead. If you happen to be deprived of anything in sorrow, or if other men injure you by force, or if you are wounded, or burdened by a family affliction, or if for any other reason you are made sorrowful, do not in that time complain to your neighbor and murmur against God's justice, but rather hasten to the Church and with bended knee pray to God that he may send you the gift of consolation, lest the sorrows of this world, which bring death [to the spirit], absorb you.

Christianity itself was not without its genuinely heroic virtues. The wise man continues, saying "Nor can the weary mood resist fate, nor does the fierce thought avail anything." The "weary mood" and the "fierce thought" are the twin evils of despair and overconfidence, which, as St. Augustine explains in one of his sermons, kill the souls of men. Our speaker describes his own exile, which began, as he says, with the burial of his "gold-friend." The meaning of this burial would have been clear, I believe, to the medieval audience, for as St. Paul says (Romans 6:3-6), baptism is a participation in the burial of Christ. And the exile of the Christian in the world begins with baptism, "the first raft after shipwreck." Having outlined his own search for Christ, the speaker cites the authority of the experienced man on the dangers and sorrows of the way. The pilgrim will avoid cupidity and the desire for gold. He will think of his one fleeting union with Christ at baptism and dream of embracing his Lord again when he finds him a King in Heaven as He was once a King on earth. But such visions do not last long, and the wayfarer must return again to the sterile ways of the world. There he finds little consolation in his fellow-pilgrims, for they, too, are subject to Fortune. The succeeding admonitions in the poem are orthodox enough. We are cautioned to be patient, for the Day of Doom will come, when the world and all its evils will disappear. Tokens of Doomsday are all about us in the ruins of once proud kingdoms. The Kings of the earth and all their trappings are ephemeral. Another token of Doom is the Flood, wherein the giants perished from the Earth. These giants, like some other giants in Old English literature, are only superficially, if at all, relics of Germanic superstitution. In the commentaries the giants in the earth are simply those who become monsters by destroying the Image of God within themselves by cupidity. They were destroyed in the Flood, but, as Bede assures us, they arose again afterward. One of these later giants was Grendel, in whose lair was found a sword used in the battle of giants and men before the Flood. The poem moves toward a close with a brilliant rhetorical expression of the lesson of Ecclesiastes. The world, with its cold northern storms of temptation, its darkness of sin, and its transient human inhabitants, is vain. The poet has already suggested the fate of those who embrace it. These are the observations of the wise man, who concludes: "Well is it for him who seeks mercy, comfort from the Father in Heaven, where for us all security stands." This is the nucleus of the poem, the lesson implicit under the cortex from the very beginning. The poet has commended the proper love, the love for the gold-friend Christ, and condemned as foolish the improper love of the world.

The traditional pattern of thought in this poem is the very essence of medieval literary expression. Our wandering pilgrim walks in all the varied costumes of the Middle Ages. Sometimes he achieves the company of his Lord, at least in spirit, as Ivain does in Chrétien's romance. At other times he runs with comic hilarity in the wrong direction, as does Aucassin. In *Piers Plowman* he travels in the guise of the human will seeking Truth in the confused field of the fourteenth-century church. And he is the prototype of these pilgrims to Canterbury who are actually pilgrims to Jerusalem, except for the Pardoner, as the "povre person" suggests when he speaks to them

> Of thilke parfit glorious pilgrymage
> That highte Jerusalem celestial.
> ("Parson's Prologue," 50-51)

In his ballade called "Truth" Chaucer advises us all to be pilgrims like the wanderer in the old poem. The problems which the wise man discusses in *The Wanderer* are the problems of every "poor wayfaring stranger" who must "travel through this world of woe." Nothing could be more mistaken than the usual notion that Old English literature exists in a kind of peculiar Germanic isolation from the rest of medieval literature. On the contrary, it is in Old English poetry that the grand themes and the poetic techniques of medieval literature are first established in a vernacular.

For a second illustration, I wish to consider a poem written in a lighter vein, the Middle English "Owl and the Nightingale." We shall have time to consider only a few of the key figures and signs in the poem. Neither the Owl nor the Nightingale is a Scriptural sign, but the two birds do have some meaning in literary traditions. An owl's cry was heard by Dido in the *Aeneid*, foretelling the evil fate of her love. As John of Salisbury puts it, making the time of the cry a little more crucial than Vergil makes it, "Bubonem Dido, dum misceretur Eneae, sensit infaustum." He also finds the owl to be a figure of foresight. Moreover, the owl was sacred to Minerva, the goddess of wisdom, and the wisdom of the owl is still proverbial. The nightingale, on the other hand, is frequently, although not always, associated with the wrong love. Thus, in Chrétien's *Cligés* it is the song of a nightingale which entices Fenice to her adulterous "deduit" in the garden constructed by Jehan. Another nightingale brings Iseut to meet Tristan under their pine tree. Again, the moralization of Chrétien's *Philomena* in the *Ovide moralisé* speaks of

> Philomena, qui signefie
> Amour decevable et faillie.

This evidence is admittedly scattered and unsatisfactory, but it points to a contrast between foresight, or wisdom, and the love of the world. In the poem itself, the Nightingale is said to dwell in a flowery hedge amidst tall grass. The Owl, on the other hand, occupies an old stock covered with ivy. The Nightingale associates itself with flowers and with springtime, but the Owl compares the Nightingale's dwelling unfavorably with his own. The ivy does not fade in either summer or winter, but the Nightingale's flowers and grass are transitory. The general features of these descriptions are, unlike the Owl and the Nightingale themselves, familiar Scriptural signs. In Isaiah 40:6-8, the transitory flower of the grass is contrasted with the Word of God. St. Jerome compares this flower with the beauty of a girl who attracts many followers, but who soon fades. It is the flower of the flesh, the flower of that greatest of all modern fictional women who said "We are flowers all." St. Jerome classes the admirers of this *flos feni* with those who bear the earthly image rather than the Image of God. In St. Augustine's commentary on the first Psalm, the flower of the grass is contrasted with the evergreen leaf of God's Word on the Tree of Life. This contrast is repeated by Bede, in his commentary on the Catholic

Epistles, where the evergreen tree of the just, in this instance a palm, is shown to be superior to the flower of cupidity, which withers in the sunshine of God's justice. Both the fading flower and the evergreen leaf appear in other parts of Scripture and in the work of other commentators. The old stock where the Owl resides thus appears to be an aspect of the Tree of Life, which may represent Christ, or the church, or the just. And the flowery hedge of the Nightingale is the fading glory of the flesh which the Nightingale encourages with his summery songs. At one point in his argument, the Nightingale says that he sings by the bower

> þar lauerd liggeþ & lauedi.
> (959)

He evidently means that he encourages legitimate wedded love. For the Owl replies that the Nightingale does not always further such love.

> Þu seist þu witest manne bures,
> þar leues boþ & faire flores,
> þar two iloue in one bedde
> liggeþ bi-clop & wel bi-hedde.
> Enes þu sunge, ic wod wel ware,
> bi one bure, & woldest lere
> þe lefdi to an uuel luue. . . .
> (Cotton Ms., ed. Wells, 1045-1051)

Here the bower of wedded love is appropriately characterized by the presence of both leaves and flowers, for it is there that the glory of the flesh is made harmonious with the Word of God. The debate in the poem is a cleverly disguised and humorous contest between the wisdom of the Owl and the fleshly love of the Nightingale. And there can be no doubt as to where the poet's sympathies lie. The Owl is confident that Master Nicholas, who will judge the debate, although he once affected nightingales and other "wiʒte gente & smale," is now "a-coled." The wintry sorrow associated with the Owl is the sorrow of the wanderer who finds the world a dark and frosty dwelling unworthy of confidence and enjoyment for its own sake.

An excellent example of poetic *aenigma* is afforded by the fourteenth-century poem called "The Maid of the Moor." The interpretation offered here was developed in collaboration with Bernard F. Huppé, who also shares responsibility for the approach as a whole. The poem is short enough to quote in its entirety.

Maiden in the mor lay,
  In the mor lay,
Seuenyst fulle, seuenist fulle,
Maiden in the mor lay,
  In the mor lay,
Seuenistes fulle ant a day.

Welle was hire mete;
  Wat was hire mete?
  Þe primerole ant the,—
  Þe primerole ant the,—
Welle was hire mete;
Wat was hire mete?—
  The primerole ant the violet.

Welle was hire dryng;
  Wat was hire dryng?
Þe chelde water of þe welle-spring.

Welle was hire bour;
  Wat was hire bour?
Þe rede rose an te lilie flour.
    (*Fourteenth Century Verse and
        Prose*, ed. Sisam, p. 167)

On the surface, although the poem is attractive, it cannot be said to make much sense. Why should a maiden lie on a moor for seven nights and a day? And if she did, why should she eat primroses and violets? Or again, how does it happen that she has a bower of lilies and roses on the moor? The poem makes perfectly good sense, however, if we take note of the figures and signs in it. The number seven indicates life on earth, but life in this instance went on at night, or before the Light of the World dawned. The day is this light, or Christ, who said "I am the day." And it appears appropriately after seven nights, or, as it were, on the count of eight, for eight is also a figure of Christ. The moor is the wilderness of the world under the Old Law before Christ came. The primrose is not a Scriptural sign, but a figure of fleshly beauty. We are told three times that the primrose was the food of this maiden, and only after this suspense are we also told that she ate or embodied the violet, which is a Scriptural sign of humility. The maiden drank the cool water of God's grace, and her bower consisted of the roses of martyrdom or charity and the lilies of purity with which late medieval and early Renaissance artists sometimes adorned pictures of the Blessed Virgin Mary, and, indeed, she is the Maiden in the Moor, the maiden who was at once the most beautiful of all women and the divinity whose humility made her the most accessible of all saints.

One final illustration from the works of Chaucer should serve to make at least part of the approach advocated here clear. Chaucer shows an awareness of the existence of *sententia* in its technical sense in the prologue to the Tale of Melibee. We should not be unjustified, therefore, in seeking this "sentence" in his works. Parenthetically, I believe that a failure to look beneath the surface of Chaucer's works has caused us to miss a great deal of the humor they contain. Chaucer's surface fun-making is obvious enough, but the spectacle of the pilgrim who leaves the true way in pursuit of some ephemeral satisfaction only to fall heels over head in the mire is one of the chief sources of medieval comedy. For the fall of man can be comic as well as pathetic or tragic. Be that as it may, let us consider briefly the key figure in the prologue to "The Legend of Good Women," the daisy. The daisy is not a Scriptural sign, but it has certain affiliations with some of the signs we found in "The Owl and the Nightingale." It is a flower

> Fulfyld of vertu and of alle honour,
> And evere ylike fayr and fresh of hewe,
> As wel in wynter as in somer newe.
> ("Legend of Good Women," 56-58)

Although the daisy is a flower of the grass, it is peculiar among such flowers in that it blooms in winter as well as in summer. Moreover, it has an affinity for the sun and is "afered of the nyght." Chaucer says that he has nothing to do with the contest between the flower and the leaf, since he is concerned with something which antedates that conflict. Now the conflict between the flower and the leaf began with the Fall, for it was then that the glory of the flesh was first opposed to the Word of God. These hints should make the meaning of the daisy clear. Since it survives the winter, it shares the characteristics of both flower and leaf. That is, it is like those bowers referred to by the Owl, where there are both leaves and flowers. Moreover, it has an affinity for the sun, which is a sign of God's justice. And the night which it fears is the night of sin, the night of the deed of darkness. Before the Fall the flower and the leaf were combined in the conjugal love of Adam and Eve, which was regarded during the Middle Ages as the type to be imitated by all good married couples. Thus, the daisy is an appropriate figure of conjugal love, a conclusion which is reinforced by the fact that it is identified with Alceste, who in both literary exegesis and in medieval art represents conjugal fidelity. In Chaucer's poem she wears the green robe of God's Word, and her crown is made of pearl, a Scriptural sign of innocence or freedom from sin. This crown is decorated with those legitimate flowers of the flesh which bloom only under the sacrament of wedlock. Married love looks to God's justice for its inspiration, is "afered" of sin, preserves the innocence of its participants, is harmonious with the Word of God, but fears neither the "heat o' the sun" nor the "furious winter's rages." This interpretation of the daisy receives further confirmation in a ballade by Trebor, where it is said that Jupiter espoused the daisy in Engedi. The reference to Engedi in the Canticum is a reference to the marriage of Christ and the church, a marriage used in the Epistles as a symbol for true human marriage. Chaucer's literary contemplation of the daisy and its beauties is neither mere poetic decoration nor irrelevant historical allegory, but a graceful and forceful tribute to one of the highest kinds of human affection and one of the most humanly accessible forms of charity. On the whole, I think that it is safe to say that Chaucer is seldom given either to airy flights of fancy or to superfluous verbiage. The details of his poetry are deliberate and meaningful contributions to his "sentence."

To conclude, I think it is obvious that interpretations of this kind, if they are worth making at all, cannot be made without a great deal of historical research. Since the illustrations used here are necessarily brief and lack full documentation, I shall ask you to suspend judgment concerning them until the publication of more thorough studies. In this paper I have not illustrated the necessity for an awareness of specific theological attitudes, since it seemed to me that the discussion of theological complexities might be inappropriate at this time. When the method is applied, however, literary works which have heretofore seemed incoherent or meaningless become consistent, meaningful, and aesthetically attractive. Whether similar methods, employing different background materials, might be fruitful in other periods, I am not prepared to say. But I am convinced that if we can achieve some understanding of and respect for the cultural ideals of the Middle Ages, we shall find the literature of the period much more fruitful than we have usually thought it to be. The allegorical character of medieval poetry made possible an almost unbelievable richness and subtlety of expression. And the ideals which that poetry reflects, although they may not be so romantically attractive as those of pagan literature, ancient or modern, are, after all, the ideals upon which Western civilization was founded.

Pedagogically speaking, it is, I think, our duty to inculcate in our students an admiration for the ideals which have enabled men to achieve cultural satisfaction in the past. It is only on the basis of a knowledge of these ideals that new ideals may be firmly established. In the sophisticated glitter of the modern world we have tended to forget the wise humility taught in the twelfth century by Bernard of Chartres, who said, "We are as dwarves upon the shoulders of giants." Moreover, our judgments of value are dependent not only on our own experience, but also on the conception we are able to formulate of the experience of humanity. The better we are able to understand our own history, the wiser we ourselves will be. Literature, regarded historically, is an excellent guide to this larger experience. Regarded historically, in short, it can provide the food of wisdom as well as more transient aesthetic satisfactions. To think of reasons for denying this is simply to think of reasons for shirking our own responsibilities.

The Doctrine of Charity in Medieval Literary Gardens: A Topical Approach Through Symbolism and Allegory

≈⁳

Once more charity and cupidity are treated as "opposites" forming a "polarity," but see A Preface to Chaucer *(Princeton, 1962), pp. 92, note 67, and 24-31. Love, the motivating force of human action, was thought to move the will toward either the lower or the higher parts of the hierarchy of being; but the various parts of an ordered hierarchy are not "polar opposites," being merely degrees in a scale, somewhat like "heat" and its absence, "cold." If this had not been true, a movement from the "lower" degrees of the scale to the "upper" such as that envisaged by St. Gregory in his commentary on the Can-ticum, or by Dante in the* Commedia, *or by Castiglione, would have been impossible. It is possible that the phrase "to corrupt the Image of God" in contexts after the middle of the twelfth century should be "to corrupt the like-ness of God," although earlier, and sometimes later, "image" was loosely used, as it is in the quotation included from St. Jerome on the fading beauty of a woman, where the "earthly image" is contrasted with the "celestial image." In connection with* Beowulf, *I now think it probable that the poet, for good reasons, intended his hero to fail before his final test. The remarks about An-dreas Capellanus are elaborated in* A Preface to Chaucer *(Princeton, 1962), pp. 391-448, and I am pleased that several prominent scholars now admit that Andreas had a sense of humor. The gardens in the* Roman de la rose *have now been carefully examined by John V. Fleming,* The Roman de la Rose: A Study in Allegory and Iconography *(Princeton, 1969); and there is an excellent annotated translation of the poem by Charles R. Dahlberg (Princeton, 1971). The echoes of the Canticum in the Merchant's Tale have been discussed at greater length by James I. Wimsatt, "Chaucer and the Can-ticle of Canticles," in* Chaucer the Love Poet *(Athens, Ga., 1973), esp. pp. 84-89. Similar echoes have been found by R. E. Kaske in the Miller's Tale, "The* Canticum Canticorum *and the Miller's Tale,"* SP, *59 (1962), 479-500.*

A T the heart of medieval Christianity is the doctrine of Charity, the
New Law which Christ brought to fulfill the Old Law so that
mankind might be saved. Since this doctrine has extremely broad implications, it cannot be expressed satisfactorily in a few words, but for
convenience we may use the classic formulation included in the *De doctrina Christiana* of St. Augustine: "Charitatem voco motum animi ad
fruendum Deo propter ipsum, et se atque proximo propter Deum:
cupiditatem autem, motum animi ad fruendum se et proximo et
quolibet corpore non propter Deum."[1] The opposite of Charity, as St.
Augustine describes it, is cupidity, the love of any creature, including
one's self, for its own sake. These two loves, Charity and cupidity, are
the two poles of the medieval Christian scale of values. For St. Augustine and for his successors among medieval exegetes, the whole
aim of Scripture is to promote Charity and to condemn cupidity:
"Non autem praecipit Scriptura nisi charitatem, nec culpat nisi
cupiditatem."[2] Where this aim is not apparent in the letter of the Bible,
one must seek it in the spirit beneath the veil of the letter. In the *De
doctrina* there is developed a theory of literary interpretation by means
of which one may remove the veil and effect the necessary discovery.

The obscurity of Scripture is useful, for it serves to exercise the intellect so that the truth may come to the reader in a pleasant and
memorable way: "Nunc tamen nemo ambigit, et per similitudines
libentius quaeque cognosci, et cum aliqua difficultate quaesita multo
gratius inveniri."[3] The pleasure accompanying the search for and the
discovery of Charity in the Bible is thus, as H.-I. Marrou has said, a
pleasure "d'ordre littéraire,"[4] so that reading the Bible confers aesthetic as well as spiritual rewards. To obtain these rewards, one must
not only be familiar with purely rhetorical devices but also with the
meanings of objects in the physical world: "Rerum autem ignorantia
facit obscuras figuratas locutiones, cum ignoramus vel animantium,
vel lapidum, vel herbarum naturas, aliarumve rerum, quae plerumque
in Scripturis similitudinis alicujus gratia ponuntur."[5] In other words,
one must be able to read the Book of God's Work in order to understand His Word. In the later Middle Ages, the *trivium* was devoted to
studies facilitating the literal reading of the Bible. It was for this purpose that one studied rhetoric. The *quadrivium* furnished the necessary
information about creation to enable one to discover allegorical and
tropological values, "in quibus constat cognitio veritatis et amor virtutis: et haec est vera reparatio hominis."[6]

The techniques of reading developed by St. Augustine were not
confined to the study of the Bible. Thus, Rabanus Maurus prefaces his
transcript of part of the *De doctrina* in the *De clericorum institutione* with

an indication that the methods described apply to the reading of profane as well as of sacred letters.[7] And in the *Didascalicon*, which is basically an elaboration of the *De doctrina*, Hugh of St. Victor describes a procedure for arriving at the underlying meaning of literature of any kind. One begins with the *letter*, or grammatical structure, turns next to the *sense*, or obvious meaning, and finally to the *sentence*, or doctrinal content, which furnishes the desired allegorical and tropological values.[8] Profane letters were thought of as being allegorical in much the same way as the Bible is allegorical. To quote Professor Charles G. Osgood, "This allegorical theory of poetry, deriving from the Ancients, and sustained in early medieval times by a naturally strong inclination to symbolism and allegory, supports the allegorical quality of literature and art from Prudentius to Spenser. Nor is it confined only to formal allegory such as the *Divine Comedy*, but suspects and seeks ulterior meaning in all art and poetry worthy of the name."[9] In this paper I wish to examine first some of the more obvious meanings of gardens and garden materials as they are explained in medieval commentaries and encyclopedias. The selection of this particular chapter from the Book of God's Work is purely arbitrary; similar studies might be made of names, numbers, animals, stones, or other things. When a sufficient background of meanings, presumably of the kind studied in the *quadrivium*, has been presented, I wish to show that the conventionally established meanings are relevant to the interpretation of natural and artificial gardens in medieval literature. When these conventional meanings are applied in "art and poetry worthy of the name" it becomes apparent, I believe, that medieval literary authors frequently share the primary aim of Scripture, to promote Charity and to condemn its opposite, cupidity. Not all medieval literary gardens may be included in a preliminary study of this kind, so that I have selected a few typical gardens from a wide range of literary types. At the same time, I have used illustrations which cover a very long period, from the early Middle Ages to the second half of the fourteenth century.

Many gardens are little more than groves of trees, and still others have a tree as a central feature. Some notion of the significance of the tree is still familiar, since it occupies a very important position in the story of the Fall, which involves the Tree of Knowledge of Good and Evil; and the Redemption involves another tree, the Tree of Life, or the Cross. In the Middle Ages, the very important position of these trees in Biblical narrative gave rise to an enormous complex of associations. Any tree may be considered as an aspect of one of the trees just mentioned, or as a transitional growth between the two extremes. A tree *per se* without further qualification suggests both of them. Any tree may have implications for the individual, for society, or for the afterlife. Thus the Tree of Life variously represents *sapientia*, the Cross, Christ, or the good Christian.[10] The Tree of Knowledge of Good and Evil was not evil in itself, since God put nothing evil in Paradise; but eating the fruit of the tree represents turning away from God in pride. When man suffered the consequences, he knew "quid intersit inter bonum quod deseruit, et malum in quod cecidit."[11] After they had eaten the fruit Adam and Eve concealed themselves "in medio ligni paradisi" (Genesis 3:8). St. Augustine comments: "Quis se abscondit a conspectu Dei, nisi qui deserto ipso incipit jam amare quod suum est? Jam enim habebant cooperimenta mendacii: qui autem loquitur mendacium, de suo loquitur (John 8:44). Et ideo ad arborem se dicuntur abscondere, quae erat in medio paradisi, id est ad seipsos, qui in medio rerum infra Deum et supra corpora ordinati erant."[12] To hide within the tree is to hide within oneself in self-love or cupidity. In one sense, the tree represents free will, and the eating of the fruit is the corruption of the will that follows abandonment of reason.[13] Theoretically, the reason is made up of three parts: memory, intellect, and will. When these parts are preserved in their proper hierarchy, with the will subservient to the other two, they reflect the Trinity and constitute the Image of God in man.[14] But when the will dominates in disobedience, the Image is corrupted. To eat the fruit of the Tree of Knowledge of Good and Evil is to corrupt the Image of God, and to hide under the tree is to seek protection in lying rationalization.

The shade of the tree where Adam and Eve sought refuge is frequently associated with *scientia* (as opposed to *sapientia*), for worldly wisdom is conducive to a false sense of security. This shade is vividly and eloquently described in a sermon by Hugh of St. Victor:

> Cave ergo ne et tu dum sub umbra, foliorum requiem quaeris, incipias pati caliginem. Nec possis in umbra positus clare discernere; quia imago quae apparet umbra, sola est, non veritas. Hanc ergo umbram foliorum suspectam habe, ne decipiaris. Quae sunt folia? Species rerum visibilium folia sunt; quae modo quidem pulchra et virentia apparent, sed cadent subito cum turbo exierit. Quae sunt folia? Domus, vineae, horti, piscinae, sylva lignorum, germinantium, familiae, possessiones, aurum, argentum, substantiae regum et provinciarum: lyrae, citharae, tibiae, organa, scyphi, et urcei, et vasa pretiosa divitiae et pompae, et gloria: omnia haec folia sunt. Quare folia? Quia vana, quia caduca, quia transitoria: ideo folia. Virent quidem modico tempore, sed cito arescunt et cadunt. Sed

tamen dum stant, umbram faciunt et habent refrigerium suum; sed est obscura umbra et inimica lumini. . . . Ideo dixi ut suspectam habeas umbram, qui te sub foliis positum confiteris. Sub foliis es, in umbra es, et sapientiam juxta te vides. Vide diligenter ne forte non sit sapientia, sed aliud aliquid latens sub specie illius. Quae est enim sapientia in umbra foliorum? Nam umbra foliorum delectatio est, et jucunditas in specie et pulchritudine rerum transitoriarum. Et habet ista sapientiam suam. Sic enim homines vocant sapientiam qua ista requies, et tranquilitas ista carnis callide et astute quaeritur, et prudenter conservatur . . . et lumen verae sapientiae, apud quam stultitia est sapientia ista, videre non possunt.[15]

Here the leaves of the tree are the objects of worldly vanity—wealth, physical beauty, music, and so on—and the shade is the deceitful comfort which things of this kind afford, a comfort fortified by a *scientia* which excludes true wisdom or *sapientia*. In the shade the image we see "sola est," without the higher meaning of Divine truth. But the leaves ultimately fall, leaving the person seeking shelter fully exposed to the heat and light from which he sought to escape. As we shall see, this light is the sunshine of God's justice. These transitory leaves should be contrasted sharply with the evergeen leaves of the Tree of Life, which represent the unfading and eternal Word of God. They offer true protection to those who seek solace beneath them.[16]

Tropological elaborations of the two trees as trees of the virtues and vices were extremely popular in the Middle Ages. Unusually fine specimens appear in the *De fructibus carnis et spiritus* printed by Migne among the works of Hugh of St. Victor. The edition in the *Patrologia* contains a schematic reproduction of the manuscript illustration which shows some of the wider implications of the trees very clearly. The evil tree on the left appears under the rubric *Vetus Adam*, or man unredeemed. The tree is rooted in *superbia* and its crowning fruit is *luxuria*. On branches which droop toward the ground are six other vices depicted as fruits surrounded by vicious leaves. The tree is prominently marked *Babylonia*. The good tree on the right appears under the rubric *Novus Adam* to indicate man redeemed and in a state of grace. It is rooted in *humilitas* and its crowning fruit is *caritas*. On ascending branches hang the other two theological virtues and the cardinal virtues surrounded by virtuous leaves. It is marked *Hierosolyma*.[17] Other fruits for these trees appear when they are considered on other levels. For example, when the good tree is the Cross, its fruit is Christ.[18] When the tree is Christ, its fruits are the Apostles and their successors;[19] when the tree is an individual its fruits may be good works.[20]

Anagogically, the fruit is eternal life.[21] In any event, the symbolic act of eating the fruit confers salvation on the individual. The fruit of the evil tree has corresponding and opposite values.

Some of this material may be clarified by reference to a simple example of the use of these meanings in art. The Ruthwell Cross, a stone monument probably dating from the first half of the eighth century, shows on its sides two panels covered with foliage. In the foliage are birds and beasts eating the fruit.[22] In the light of what has been said above, it is clear that the carvings are not merely decorative. The foliage is made up of the unfading leaves of the Tree of Life, and the birds and beasts are those who in the shelter of the Word of God eat the fruit of eternal life. Monuments such as this undoubtedly suggest to their creators various levels of significance. Thus in the Old English poem, *The Dream of the Rood*, part of which appears on the Ruthwell Cross, there is a clear reference to the tropological level of meaning. Referring to the Day of Judgment, the poet observes: "Ne þearf ðær þonne ænig   anforht wesan/þe him ær in breostum bereð beacna selest" (ll. 117-118). No one who has borne the Tree within him need fear at the Last Judgment. To live righteously is to live in the image of the Tree of Life, or in imitation of Christ. Then one bears the fruit of good works which assures the fruit of the anagogical tree and a place before it.

The author of the *De fructibus*, as we have seen, associates the two trees with Jerusalem and Babylon. To see the full implications of the trees, we must examine these concepts briefly. Jerusalem (*visio pacis*) implies tropologically virtue and spiritual peace, allegorically the Church of the faithful, and anagogically the Celestial City. Babylon (*confusio*) implies the opposites of these things. The two cities, as St. Augustine explains in the *De civitate Dei*, spring from two loves, Charity and cupidity. Properly, all Christians are strangers and pilgrims in the world: "Charissimi, obsecro vos tanquam advenas et peregrinos abstinere vos a carnalibus desideriis" (1 Peter 2:11). The manner of the voyage from Babylon to Jerusalem is succinctly described by Peter Lombard:

> Sciendum itaque est duas esse spirituales civitates in praesenti: unam malorum quae incoepit a Cain, et dicitur Babylonia; alteram bonorum, quae coepit ab Abel, et dicitur Jerusalem. Illius cives facit cupiditas, Jerusalem cives facit charitas. Quae licet sint mistae corpore, separatae sunt mente, quarum una peregrinatur in altera, et captiva tenetur. Quandiu enim sumus in hoc corpore, peregrinamur a Domino, qui de Babylonia ad Jerusalem suspiramus, id est de

saeculo et corpore peccati ad coelum. . . . De hac tamen captivitate incipit redire, qui incipit amare. Charitas enim ad reditum movet pedem.[23]

The direction of man's journey is thus dependent on the kind of love which moves in his will. Cupidity, which is the source of all of man's sins and hence of his discontents, makes a Babylon of the individual mind, a Babylon of society, and leads to an ultimate Babylon in eternal damnation. Charity brings the peace of Jerusalem to the mind, to society, and to the Celestial City where its radiance is all-pervasive. With these loves go two fears. Cupidity is accompanied by the fear of earthly misfortune, and Charity is accompanied by the fear of God which leads to wisdom. The supreme importance of this concept in Christian doctrine may be indicated with a brief quotation from Peter Lombard, who here reflects a traditional Augustinian position: "Omnia ergo peccata, duae res faciunt in homine, scilicet cupiditas et timor: sic econtra amor Dei et timor ejus ducunt ad omne bonum. Amas enim ut bene sit tibi; times ne male sit tibi. Hoc age in Deo, non in saeculo. Uterque amor incendit, uterque timor humiliat."[24] Both loves inflame, and both fears humiliate, but the two loves produce radically opposite results. These loves and fears are the key to the behavior of any individual, and the key to his destiny.

The fact that the word love (*amor*) could be used for either Charity or cupidity opened enormous possibilities for literary word-play. It is also, I believe, responsible for the manifest preoccupation with "love" in medieval literature. A certain very significant discrepancy between the scheme represented in the traditional Augustinian position just outlined and the scheme of the trees in the *De fructibus* is relevant in this connection. The crowning fruits of the trees are *caritas* and *luxuria* rather than *caritas* and *cupiditas*. Again, if we look in St. Bonaventura's magnificent account of the two cities in the Prologue to his comment on Ecclesiastes, we find the word *libido* used where we should expect *cupiditas*.[25] And in the treatise on the two loves written by Gérard of Liège the contrast is obviously one between the love of God and sexual love.[26] But this tradition is also Augustinian, for St. Augustine interpreted the word *fornicatio* in the Scriptures to mean not only illicit conjunction of the sexes, but also idolatry or any aspect of love of the world as opposed to the love of God.[27] When *luxuria* or *fornicatio* is used symbolically, either one well describes the sin of Adam and Eve and may be justly placed as the crowning fruit of the Tree of Babylon. The evil tree thus suggests idolatrous sexual love, an extreme form of cupidity and a reflection of the Fall.

Trees exist in various stages of development, and there are many widely different types of trees. For example, a tree appears with budding leaves at the approach of summer in Matthew 24:32-33: "Ab arbore . . . et folia nata, scitis quia prope est aestas; ita et vos, cum videritis haec omnia, scitote quia prope est in ianuis." The context shows that the budding tree is a promise of the second coming, which implies the Resurrection of the Just. The *Glossa ordinaria* contains the observation that the dry tree is revivified with faith and charity, and that the new leaves are the "verba praedicationis" which announce the summer of "aeterna serenitas."[28] On the other hand, in Jude 1:12 there are some "arbores autumnales, infructuosae bis mortuae, eradicatae." Bede explains that the autumnal trees bear either no fruit or evil fruit. They are individuals who perform no good works and who live in despair of salvation.[29] Among trees of various species, the palm has a prominent place. It is a symbol of the just, since its flowers of hope do not fall but produce the fruit of eternal reward. In contrast to the flower of the flesh, Bede explains, the palm flourishes in the sunshine of God's justice.[30] Generally, the good tree is a green tree. Thus in Luke 23:31 Christ exclaims: "Quia si in viridi ligno haec faciunt, in arido quid fiet?" The *Glossa ordinaria*, following Bede, identified the green tree with Christ and His elect, the dry tree with sinners.[31] Hence the willow, because of its persistent green foliage is sometimes identified with the just.[32] But much more commonly it represents those sterile in good works, since it bears no fruit, and it is associated with the waters of cupidity. In this sense, its green leaves are words of false piety.[33] An especially interesting variant of the Tree of Life is afforded by the sycamore. Its peculiarity arises from the story of Zacchaeus, who in Luke 19:4 climbs a sycamore in order to see Jesus. The sycamore's leaf resembles that of the fig, but its fruit is not attractive, so that it came to be called "ficus fatua." In the commentaries, however, it represents foolishness in the eyes of the world and wisdom in the eyes of God. Extending this concept, commentators associate it with faith or with the Cross, and they sometimes point out that the faithful will, like Zacchaeus, climb the sycamore.[34] Conversely, the sycamore may represent "vana scientia," but this meaning is rare.[35] St. Bernard divides evil trees into three classes: those which do not bear fruit, like the elm; those hypocritical trees which bear fruit that is not their own; and those trees which bear fruit too early so that it is destroyed before it ripens.[36]

This brief account of the higher meanings of the tree is by no means exhaustive. Trees may be manured, transplanted, pruned, blown by winds, burned, or otherwise affected in Scriptural contexts, with consequent modifications of their significances, and there are many varieties of trees with special subsidiary meanings. Enough material has been adduced, however, to afford an initial grasp of what a tree may involve, so that we may turn our attention to other garden materials. Flowers occur in great variety in the Scriptures, and although the flower does not have quite the central significance of the tree in Christian doctrine, the commentators devote a great deal of attention to it. Thus, for example, there is a long list of flowers together with their higher meanings in the *De universo* of Rabanus Maurus. The flowers of the palm have already been mentioned above. Some specific flowers, as we should expect, have both good and evil meanings of some importance. The rose, as Rabanus describes it, is an unfading flower of martyrdom in Ecclesiasticus 28:14 and 50:8.[37] On the other hand, in Wisdom 2:8, the heretics crown themselves with garlands of roses obviously associated with lechery and idolatry. Because of the direct Scriptural connection between the lily and Christ, the lily has customarily only a good meaning. It is well known that a combination of lilies and roses was used to show martyrdom and purity, Charity and innocence, or related ideas. Pictures of the Annunciation, like that by Filippo Lippi, sometimes show an angel presenting a lily to the Blessed Virgin Mary. In one sense, a picture of this kind is a picture of a lily and a rose. One Scriptural flower deserves special attention and emphasis, the *flos foeni*,[38] which represents the transitory glory of the flesh. In Isaiah 40:6–8, it is contrasted with the Word of God: "Omnis caro foenum, et omnis gloria eius quasi flos agri. Exsiccatum est foenum, et cecidit flos, quia spiritus Domini sufflavit in eo. Vere foenum est populus; exsiccatum est foenum, et cecidit flos; verbum autem Domini nostri manet in aeternum." In his comment on this passage, St. Jerome uses as an illustration of the transient flower the beauty of a girl, who, in her youth, attracts many followers. But her beauty soon fades. In the same way, those who bear the earthly image, serving vices and lechery, have but a transient glory. On the contrary, those who bear the Image of God and cherish it share the glory of the Word of God, which does not fade:

> Pulchra mulier quae adolescentulorum post se trahebat greges, arata fronte contrahitur; et quae prius amori, postes fastidio est. . . . Exsiccata est igitur caro, et cecidit pulchritudo, quia spiritus furoris Dei atque sententiae flavit in ea (ut a generali disputatione ad Scripturae ordinem revertamur), ejus qui portat imaginem terreni, et servit vitiis atque luxuriae, foenumque est et flos praeteriens. Qui autem habet atque custodit imaginem coelestis, ille caro est quae

cernit salutare Domini, quae quotidie renovatur in cognitionem
secundum imaginem Creatoris, et incorruptibile atque immortale
corpus accipiens, mutat gloriam, non naturam. Verbum autem
Domini nostri, et hi qui verbo sociati sunt, permanent in aeternum.[39]

The *flos foeni* appears elsewhere in Scripture and in the work of other
commentators. In James 1:10, 11, it is said that the rich man, or the
man who sets his heart on worldly treasure, "sicut flos foeni transibit;
exortus est enim sol cum ardore, et arefecit foenum, et flos eius decidit." Bede compares this flower, which may be fragrant and beautiful, but which is nevertheless transitory, with temporal felicity which
fades in the sunshine of God's justice.[40] The flower of the flesh was
not slow to appear in European poetry. For example, the epitaph attributed to Alcuin warns: "Ut flores pereunt vento veniente minaci/Sic
tua namque caro, gloria tota perit." This is not a mere simile. In Isaiah
and in the commentaries, the flower is contrasted with the Word of
God, which as we have seen, is represented by the leaf which does not
wither on the Tree of Life. An explicit contrast between the flower
and the leaf appears in a position of prominence at the beginning of the
most authoritative of all commentaries on the most widely read book
of the Bible, St. Augustine's commentary on the Psalms: "*Et folium
ejus non decidet*: id est, verbum ejus non erit irritum; quia *omnis caro
foenum, et claritas hominis ut flos foeni; foenum aruit, et flos decidit, verbum
autem Domini manet in aeternum.*"[41] To the fading flower of human
glory and radiance is here opposed the evergreen leaf of the Tree of
Life. This contrast is familiar in the vernacular literature of the later
Middle Ages.[42] Meanwhile, it should be noted that the *flos foeni* has
definite associations with feminine beauty, a kind of beauty which
sometimes tempts man to seek a deceptive shade.

Gardens frequently contain wells or streams by means of which the
trees and flowers are watered. Thus in Psalm 1:3, the Tree of Life
grows "secus decursus aquarum," and in Apocalypse 22:1-2 it stands
on either side of a "fluvium aquae vitae, splendidum tanquam crystal-
lum."[43] Again, in Genesis, the Tree is associated with a river which
flows away in four streams, usually said to be the cardinal virtues. The
Water of Life, which either flows by the tree or emanates from it,[44] is
variously interpreted as baptism, wisdom, true doctrine, *Christus irrigans*, Charity, or the Holy Spirit.[45] This water is contrasted with the
temporal water of cupidity offered by the Samaritan woman in John
4:13-14, which has opposite values. Either tree may be depicted beside

a river or shading a well or fountain. As we have already seen, the willow grows beside evil waters. In the later Middle Ages, the well beside the good tree also suggests the Blessed Virgin Mary, who was called "Well of Grace." Representations of the Cross standing beside a well were common in late medieval art. St. Augustine associates the Rock whence flow the Living Waters, a common Scriptural designation of Christ, with the Tree of Life.[46] The fountain or well under either tree may be thought of as coming from a rock or stone basin.

Many gardens offer protection to singing birds. The *De universo* of Rabanus supplies a list of various species with their higher meanings. Although the birds in Scripture frequently tend to have an evil significance, representing evil spirits, vices, and so on,[47] St. Ambrose describes the birds in the Garden of Eden at some length, showing that the song they sing is an inspiration to Charity. St. Gregory finds good birds in the parable of the Grain of Mustard Seed. The very small seed grows into a very large tree, in which the birds of the air find shelter. The seed is the seed of doctrine planted by Christ, the branches of the tree are holy preachers who have spread the doctrine throughout the world, and the birds who rest in the shade are pious spirits who desire to abandon terrestrial things and fly to celestial realms.[48] A more elaborate development of these ideas appears in Bede's comment on Matthew.[49] The tree itself is an aspect of the Tree of Life.

Having considered the most important elements which combine to form gardens, we may now examine complete gardens very briefly. To begin with, the Tree of Life stands in a *hortus deliciarum*. The garden surrounding the Tree and irrigated by its waters is interpreted in various ways. Usually, it symbolizes either the Church allegorically or the individual tropologically. Anagogically it is the New Jerusalem.[50] A garden with a *fons signatus*, this time called a *hortus conclusus*, also appears in the Canticum; and the commentators, in accordance with their usual practice, relate the two gardens. Like the Paradise of Genesis, the garden of the Canticum represents the Church or the individual, although it is sometimes used in praise of the Blessed Virgin Mary. The commentaries on it yield a wealth of values for trees and flowers.[51] An especially valuable tropological description of the garden may be found in Richard of St. Victor's sermons. We are shown in some detail how one may prevent or eradicate weedy vices and encourage the desirable plants. In this discussion the *fons* is the "anima devota," and the *puteus aquarum viventium* is the Holy Spirit.[52] The *fons* is to be associated with the well or fountain under the Tree of Life, but the appearance of the well here without the tree makes possible the literary or artistic use of wells and streams independently of the two trees. The meaning of the garden is general enough so that it may represent an individual, the world of men or the Church, or the next world. These meanings have considerably more force when we remember that Christ is described at one point in Scripture as a *Hortulanus*. The nature of any garden, that is, of any individual, any society of men, or any ultimate afterlife, is determined, in a given instance, upon whether Christ, or *sapientia*, is the gardener. When Christ is the gardener, the garden is ruled by wisdom and suffused with the warmth of Charity. Otherwise it is ruled by worldly wisdom or *scientia* and suffused with cupidity. To the medieval mind, cupidity or self-love can lead only to the discomfort and disaster of an unweeded garden.

We may conclude that the various meanings of trees, flowers, streams, and other features of gardens have a very wide scope, and that they suggest what were regarded in the Middle Ages as the most important doctrines of Christianity. In fact, their implications are wide enough so that it would be possible to use the two trees and their surroundings for a contrast just as fundamental and meaningful as that between the two cities which underlies St. Augustine's *De civitate Dei*. To rest comfortably in the shade of the wrong tree amounts to the same thing as to make a home in Babylon. If one wished to distinguish the two forms of expression, one might say that the garden suggests forcibly the truth as it is contained in Genesis and the Canticum, whereas the city suggests the truth as it is expressed in later Old Testament history and in the Psalms. Both devices appear in the Prophetic Books and in the New Testament. The garden image emphasizes the relationship between the sexes, which is apparent on the surface in both Genesis and the Canticum, so that it tends to be associated with idolatrous sexual love used as a symbol for extreme cupidity. The conventional associations of both the evil tree and the *flos foeni* reinforce this tendency. But, at the same time, the sexual relationship is not a necessary adjunct of the garden, since the Fall of Adam and Eve was only figuratively sexual, as is the relationship expressed in the Canticum. This is not to say that cities and gardens afford the only means of making the contrast between Charity and cupidity. Since all creation is meaningful in the same way, the number of ways of making the contrast is infinite. For, it should be recalled, it is not the words *tree* or *city* which are meaningful, but trees and cities themselves. Creation is an expression of God's infinite love, but to see it there, one must set aside the shell, which is in itself the object of scientific investigation, to find the kernel beneath, the food of wisdom and, in accordance with medieval doctrine, the source of the only true beauty human eyes may see.

The appearance of the higher meanings of garden materials in early vernacular poetry may be illustrated in *Beowulf*. Competent scholars now agree that the author of the poem was a man of considerable learning and that his basic intention was pious, although the "interpolator" still lingers in the background.[53] One scene in the poem appears to utilize certain features of the materials presented above, the picture of Grendel's mere. It has already been observed that a very similar description is used in one of the Blickling Homilies to suggest Hell,[54] which is simply the evil garden taken anagogically. As the *Beowulf* poet describes the scene, its general features at once suggest commonplace Scriptural associations: a stream makes a pool in a place surrounded by overhanging trees, and beside the pool is a rock. Certain attributes of the scene are extremely significant. In the first place, the pool is the dwelling of a giant, one of the generation of Cain. In Bede's *Hexaemeron* we find that the giants of Genesis 6:4 were "terrenis concupiscentiis adhaerentes" and that although they were destroyed in the Flood, they arose again thereafter.[55] Figuratively, the generation of Cain is simply the generation of the unjust to which all those governed by cupidity belong. They are monsters because they have distorted or destroyed the Image of God within themselves. Babylon, as we have seen, traditionally began with Cain, and it is maintained on earth by his generation. We may say as much for the evil garden. Thus Grendel is the type of the militant heretic or worldly man, and his dwelling is appropriately in the waters which are the opposite of those which spring from the Rock of Christ. It is pertinent also that Beowulf should find under these waters a sword which is a relic of the struggle between the giants and the just in the days before the Flood (ll. 1687-1693). The poet could hardly refer more specifically to the character of the pool and of its inhabitants. The relationship between the stream and the rock is not entirely clear in the poem, but the rock is a part of the traditional scenery, one of the elements associated with either garden. The trees overhang the pool in a manner suggesting that they shade it, excluding from it, or seeming to exclude from it, the sunshine of God's justice. This impression is reinforced by the fact that the pool suddenly becomes light when Beowulf kills Grendel's mother, who may be taken as the source of the evil which her offspring spreads throughout the world:

> Lixte se leoma,   leoht inne stod,
> efne swa of hefene   hadre scineð
> rodores candel.[56]
>
> (1570–1572a)

The trees are covered with frost, a feature which Professor Klaeber recognizes as being symbolic. On the word *hrinde* (l. 1363) he comments: "The epithet is eminently suitable symbolically. . . . It is not to be imagined that Beowulf found the trees covered with hoar-frost. He would not have sailed for Denmark in winter."[57] Implicit in these observations is the excellent principle that when a work by an obviously accomplished medieval poet does not seem to make sense on the surface, one must look beneath the surface for the meaning. Frost and ice are traditional symbols of Satan, whom God permits to tempt the human spirit to fall in cupidity.[58] Moreover, the chill of cupidity may be considered characteristic of the evil garden as opposed to the warmth of Charity in the good garden. The trees, the rock, and the pool all point strongly to the theory that what the poet had in mind was the evil garden of the Scriptures.

Grendel's mere has other attributes which tend to reinforce this interpretation. We are told that the hart pursued by hounds chooses rather to give up its life than to hide its head in the grove surrounding the pool. Literally, this description makes little sense, since a hart could hardly fear a fate worse than death. But the associations of Psalm 42 lead us to recognize in the hart the faithful Christian who seeks his Lord in the Living Waters. Thus Bede wrote in his poem on this Psalm:

> cervus ut ad fontes sitiens festinat aquarum,
> sic mea mens ardet te, conditor alme, requirens
> viventemque sitit te cernere libera lucem.

But the hart in *Beowulf* carefully avoids Grendel's waters, which he knows will not assuage his thirst. The example of Adam and Eve has warned him that this is not an effective hiding place. He prefers death to the eternal damnation which results from hiding under the wrong trees. We may see the opposite of the hart in the monsters which swim about in the pool or rest on its banks. The poet says somewhat cryptically of them,

> ða on undernmæl   oft bewitigað
> sorhfulne sið   on seglrade,
> wyrmas ond wildeor.
>
> (1428–1430a)

Professor Klaeber's note on this passage has a tone of despair: "In any case, consistency is not to be postulated in the descriptions of the scenery."[59] However, if we see in these monsters those who allow their spirits to be killed by Grendel, the sea voyage they make does not involve an actual sea, somehow contiguous with the pool, but is merely the last journey which leads, in this instance, to damnation. In so far as the epic as a whole is concerned, the interpretation of Grendel's mere as a reflection of the evil garden is consistent with the attitude toward the poem expressed in the introduction to Klaeber's most recent edition. The suggestion of Christ which Klaeber sees in Beowulf should lead us to expect further suggestions of the same kind consistently and thematically interwoven in the poem. Although it is obvious that Beowulf is not Christ historically, every true Christian lives in imitation of Christ, and there are certain virtues and abilities which a ruler must exhibit in the course of this imitation. In the Grendel episode Beowulf shows himself capable of purifying a society of men from the forces of cupidity. The fact that neither Christ nor the Tree of Knowledge of Good and Evil is mentioned in the poem is in keeping with the principles of Augustinian literary interpretation. An intellectual effort is necessary to discern Divine truth in the arrangement of materials in the poem, and it is from the fruitful pursuit of this effort, not from the decoration on the outer shell, that the poem's aesthetic value arises.

In *Beowulf* the evil garden is repulsive on the surface. But the shade of the tree undoubtedly seemed attractive to Adam and Eve, and, moreover, we who succeed them are also tempted by it. There is, thus, no reason why the evil garden should not be made to appear superficially attractive. A picture of a more attractive evil garden appears at the beginning of the Old English "Judgment Day II" or "Doomsday" based on the *De die judicii* attributed to Bede:

> Hwæt! Ic ana sæt   innan bearwe,
> mid helme beþeht,   holte tomiddes,
> þær þa wæ terburnan   swegdon and urnon
> on middan gehæge,   eal swa ic secge.
> Eac þær wynwyrta   weoxon and bleowon
> innon þam gemonge   on ænlicum wonge,
> and þa wudubeamas   wagedon and swegdon
> þurh winda gryre;   wolcn wæs gehrered,
> and min earme mod   eal wæs gedrefed.
>
> (1-9)

The poem goes on to express the speaker's fears concerning his state of sin and the coming of Doomsday, when the world and its garden will be no more. It should be noticed that the wood is "helme beþeht," indicating that the speaker is hiding from the sun of God's justice. He sits "holte tomiddes," *in medio ligni.* Beneath the trees in this "gehæge" bloom the flowers of the flesh watered by the streams of worldly wisdom. But a storm arises. That is, the wood where Adam and Eve sought protection, even though its flowers and rippling streams may seem attractive, will soon pass in the storm of God's wrath.[60] In spite of the flowers and murmuring streams, the speaker is not altogether comfortable. A famous successor to this poet also found himself uneasy in this grove:

> Nel mezzo del cammin di nostra vita
> mi ritrovai per una selva oscura,
> che la diritta via era smarrita.

A very suggestive picture of the good garden, rich in conventional detail, appears in the Old Irish *Saltair na Rann,* a verse paraphrase of Scripture. I quote the translation of the late Robin Flower, who observed justly that the words of the poem "remember an accumulated beauty of tradition."[61]

> The Tree of Life with bloom unchanged,
> Round it the goodly hosts are ranged,
> Its leafy crest showers dewdrops round
> All Heaven's spreading garden-ground.
>
> There flock bright birds, a shining throng,
> And sing their grace-perfected song
> While boundless mercy round them weaves
> Undying fruit, unfading leaves.
>
> A lovely flock! bright like the sun,
> A hundred feathers clothe each one,
> And pure and clear they chant together
> A hundred songs for every feather.

Here are the unfading flowers, leaves, and fruit of the commentaries, and the birds of the parable who sing the *canticum novum* of Psalm 32:3 and Apocalypse 14:3. The tree grows in the anagogical *hortus deliciarum,* freshening its surroundings with the Water of Life in the form of dew.[62] It is apparent from these illustrations that the various elements connected with the two gardens may be combined in a variety of ways to suit the needs of a given poet or audience, and that other materials, like frost or dew, may be associated with them. The Irish poet wished to convey the harmonious beauty of Charity in the Celestial Kingdom. Throughout these pieces there runs an implicit contrast between human cupidity and the ideal of Charity, and in all of them the intention is to make Charity understandable and desirable.

The literature to be examined now was written after the appearance of the *Didascalicon*, so that we may use the terminology of the three levels of interpretation—*letter*, *sense*, and *sentence*—with some justification. We have seen that the evil garden may be superficially attractive, as it is in the poem on Doomsday. For purposes of courtly irony and humor it was made even more attractive in the twelfth century. The *De amore* of Andreas Capellanus has been taken very seriously by a number of modern critics, who in this respect follow the example of Bishop Tempier, but through an examination of the garden in it we may be able to see that the author's intention was not actually very different from that of the *Beowulf* poet. An ironic presentation of the evil garden for purposes of satire has the same ultimate effect as a straightforward presentation to illustrate Christian heroism on the part of one conquering its evil. In the fifth dialogue of the *De amore* the nobleman who addresses a noble lady uses as a part of his seductive argument a description of a garden said to show the fates of lovers of various types.[63] This garden is divided into three sections. The central part, called Amoenitas, is covered by the branches of a tall tree bearing fruit of all kinds. From its base springs a fountain of clear water. Two thrones for a king and queen of love stand beside the fountain, very richly decorated. A great many couches are situated in this inner garden, and by each one flows a small stream from the fountain. When knights and ladies occupy the couches they are entertained by jugglers and by musicians playing on all kinds of instruments. The delights of Amoenitas are reserved for those women who "sapienter se amoris noverunt praebere militibus et amare volentibus cunctum praestare favorem et sub commento amoris subdole amorem petentibus digna praenoverunt responsa tribuere" (p. 96). They give their gifts freely, but with the restrictions necessary to true love. As Andreas explains in I, x, true love must center on a single object. The second garden area, surrounding the first one, is soggy and marshy with the waters of the fountain, which are here unbearably cold. Meanwhile, the sun pours down unmercifully, for this part of the garden is unshaded. It is occupied by women who "petentium omnium fuerunt annuentes libidini et nulli petenti suae ianuae negaverunt ingressum" (p. 97). These women, clearly, lack a certain kind of wisdom. Finally, the outer area is very dry and hot. The earth bakes in the sun, which burns terribly. Ladies in this area sit on bundles of thorns, which are obligingly revolved beneath them by attendants. These ladies are followers of the

God of Love who refused his knights altogether. A beautiful road stretches from the edge of this outer garden into the center, and on it no one feels any pain at all.

On the surface, or level of *sense*, this description seems to reinforce the nobleman's argument that the lady should submit to him, since the outer section of the garden seems rather uncomfortable, and he insists that she will occupy it if she does not submit. But underneath, on the level of the *sentence*, the description is perfectly harmonious with what Andreas says in Book III. The assorted fruit of the tree at the center of the garden suggest at once the hypocritical trees which do not bear their own fruit in St. Bernard's classification of evil trees, and the shaded atmosphere of temporal wealth and amusement closely resembles the shade described in the sermon by Hugh of St. Victor. The stream flows from this Tree of Knowledge of Good and Evil into the rivulets mentioned in "Doomsday." Beside the fountain stand the thrones which are the obverse of the *sede Dei et Agni* of Apocalypse 22:1. The presence of a god and goddess on these thrones simply emphasizes the idolatry to which cupidity may lead and which distinguishes "true" lovers from the merely lustful. To understand this distinction fully, we should remember that by medieval standards idolatrous love, whether it involves the act of fornication or not (whether it is "pure" or "mixed"), is a much worse sin than simple lechery. To love a woman more than one loves God is to abandon the faith completely in violation of the First Commandment, but the sin of simple fornication, although mortal, is not irremissible. The idolator in "pure" love is thus a much worse sinner than the peasant with occasional casual lapses. In the middle garden area, between the other two, the lustful but indiscriminate rest uneasily in the icy waters of Grendel's fenland, fully aware of their iniquity and unprotected from the sunlight of God's justice by any idolatrous delusions.[64] They have not been able to find a place of shelter *in medio ligni*. Finally, the situation of those in the outer garden area vividly illustrates the torments of *concupiscentia carnis*. Here the thorns of desire torment the flesh, but conscience prevents further progress in sin and leaves the occupants mercilessly exposed to the hot sun. The road from the area of concupiscence to the second area is an easy one, once conscience is subdued; and from there, with the hardness of heart that comes from indulgence, one may move readily to join the Old Adam in Amoenitas, that romantic day-dream which turns the lust of the flesh into a blind Babylonian paradise with its own "spiritual" trappings. The story does indeed show the fates of lovers and describes well their *hortus deliciarum*; but the catch in it is that it is not altogether necessary and certainly not reasonable to follow the God of Love at all. He may be the individual "per quem universus regitur mundus," but *mundus*, whether we call it Babylon or Fortuna, *transit*. There is another God and another garden, not quite so worldly. What is the effect of having the nobleman in his courtship solemnly and unwittingly recommend the wrong wisdom, the wrong love, and a destiny in Hell under the rule of Satan? Clearly, the effect is ludicrous. I suspect that Drouart la Vache and his friends found this dialogue especially amusing.

If Andreas' garden is ironic, it is possible that the first two books of his treatise are generally ironic. There is no space for a thorough examination of this possibility here, but a few remarks may be devoted to it in support of the interpretation of the garden presented above. In the first place, the opening definition is quite sound theologically as a definition of fleshly love: "Amor est passio quaedam innata procedens ex visione et immoderata cogitatione formae alterius sexus, ob quam aliquis super omnia cupit alterius potiri amplexibus et omnia de utriusque voluntate in ipsius amplexu amoris praecepta compleri" (p. 3). That fleshly love, as opposed to Charity which proceeds from reason, arises "ex visione" is well attested in Scripture and in doctrinal works.[65] The "immoderata cogitatione" is familiar in the Ninth Commandment and in its penitential elaborations. Again, the object of this love, for which Andreas uses the verb *cupio*, is certainly very similar to the supreme fruit of the tree of Babylon in the *De fructibus*. The definition itself thus not only makes it clear that Andreas proposes to discuss the wrong love, the *fornicatio* of the Garden of Eden, but it also shows that he knows what he is doing. To make his meaning unmistakable, he goes on at once to associate this love with the wrong fear, the fear of earthly misfortune: "Vulgi quoque timet rumores et omne, quod aliquo posset modo nocere; res enim imperfectae modica turbatione deficiunt. Sed et, si pauper ipse sit, timet, ne eius mulier vilipendat inopiam; si turpis est, timet, ne eius contemnatur informitas vel pulchrioris se mulier annectat amori; si dives est, praeteritam forte tenacitatem sibi timet obesse. Et, ut vera loquamur, nullus est, qui possit singularis amantis enarrare timores" (p. 4). Andreas explains that all those who are incapable of lechery or idolatry are disqualified. The true lover needs both. The old man over sixty cannot maintain the lechery necessary; and the boy under eighteen, although he may be physically able, tends either to be embarrassed or too inconstant for idolatry. The blind man cannot indulge in *concupiscentia oculorum* and so cannot get himself well under way, and the over-passionate lover will not pause for idolatry. It may be true that court poets wrote extravagant poems of love and admiration for their feudal overlords,

even when these overlords were ladies, but this kind of love is not Andreas' subject. His pictures of various types of people expressing their
cupidity in a foolishly inflated style are, I believe, deliberately solemn
but ludicrous nonsense, intended to be humorous. The transparent
flattery, hypocrisy, and sophistry in which the speakers indulge is en-
livened by bits of obvious perversions of doctrine like the denial of
free will in the seventh dialogue. And the ideas expressed are patent
comments on the lovers themselves. The doctrine of "service," for
example, of which much has been made by modern writers on
"courtly love," is a theological commonplace; all those who give
themselves up to the world in cupidity are in bondage. As Boethius
put it (III, Met. x):

> Huc omnes pariter uenite capti
> quos ligat fallax roseis catenis
> terrenas habitans libido mentis.

True freedom lies elsewhere (V, Pr. ii): "Humanas uero animas
liberiores quidem esse necesse est, cum se in mentis diuinae
speculatione conseruant; minus uero, cum dilabuntur ad corpora;
minusque etiam, cum terrenis artubus colligantur. Extrema uero est
seruitus, cum uitiis deditae rationis propriae possessione ceciderunt."
Or, to quote Peter Lombard again, "Uterque amor incendit, uterque
timor humiliat." When Gérard of Liège described carnal love, which
he contrasted with Charity, as a "miserable servitude," he was reflecting a traditional doctrine.[66] And this is exactly what Andreas refers to
when he says (I, iii), "Nam qui amat, captus est cupidinis vinculis
aliumque desiderat suo capere hamo" (p. 9). In literature, the servitude
is expressed in feudal terms, but subjection to God was also expressed
in feudal terms. God is the permanent Liege Lord of the feudal hierarchy, and it is from this fact that the feudal contract acquires its validity.
To serve a lady in self-love, to "goo hoodles to the Drye Se" for some
fair "piggesnye," is not only to make a ludicrous deviation from the
pilgrimage of man but also to make a ludicrous parody of the structure
of feudal society. Finally, if we take an attitude of this kind toward the
first two books, we have no need to seek "sources" for them in remote
and improbable areas like Bulgaria and Andalusia, nor are we obliged
to accuse Andreas of being a "dualistic" heretic. As for Bishop Tempier, I think everyone will agree that official condemnations of books
are not always based on an understanding of the books, or, to take a
more favorable attitude toward the bishop, that the best books may be
misused. Humor arises from an exaggerated departure from a standard of values. To see the humor in Andreas, we must first understand

the values from which his lovers depart. There is nothing illogical in the assumption that Andreas' purpose was to ridicule cupidity and to show by contrast the reasonableness of Charity.

Many specimens of the two gardens appear in the romances. Edmond Faral, commenting on a selection of these gardens, wrote: "Il est remarquable qu'à la base de ces descriptions se trouve le souvenir du paradis terrestre, décrit d'abord dans la *Genèse*."[67] To this we may add that the descriptions frequently also owe a great deal to the Canticum. Such a garden appears, for example, in Chrétien's *Cligés*. When Fenice is recovering from her "martire" in the tower prepared by Jehan, the voice of the nightingale is heard in the land. This sweet voice turns her thoughts once more in the direction of Amoenitas:

> Grant bien me feïst uns vergiers,
> Ou je me poïsse deduire.
>
> (6360-6361)

Characteristically, Jehan has already prepared a garden. We see it as Fenice enters:

> Par l'uis est antree el vergier
> Qui mout li pleist et atalante.
> Anmi le vergier ot une ante
> De flors chargiee et anfoillue,
> Et par desus iert estandue.
> Einsi estoient li raim duit,
> Que vers terre pandoient tuit,
> Et pres jusqu'a terre beissoient
> Fors la cime don il neissoient.
> La cime aloit contre mont droite.
> (Fenice autre leu ne covoite).
> Et desoz l'ante est li praiaus
> Mout delitables et mout biaus,
> Ne ja n'iert li solauz tant hauz
> A midi, quant il est plus chauz,
> Que ja rais i puisse passer,
> Si le sot Jehanz conpasser
> Et les branches mener et duire.
> La se va Fenice deduire,
> Et an sor jor i feit son lit,
> La sont a joie et a delit.
> Et li vergiers est clos antor
> De haut mur qui tient a la tor,

> Si que riens nule n'i antrast,
> Se par son la tor n'i montast.
> (6400-6424)

Here the tree is an "ante," a grafted tree which, if it bears fruit at all, does not bear its own.[68] The branches droop downward like those of the tree of the vices, and they are carefully arranged so as to exclude the rays of the sun. In the shade of the tree the lovers seek the "refrigerium" *in medio ligni* described in Hugh of St. Victor's sermon, keeping the *scientia* which sustains this shade by them in the person of Jehan. Although the wall is scientifically constructed so that no one may enter except through the tower,[69] it is at once surmounted by one Bertran, who

> Soz l'ante vit dormir a masse
> Fenice et Cligés nu et nu.
> (6450-6451)

Thus the elaborate worldly wisdom of Jehan proves of no avail to the lovers as they lie in spiritual oblivion.[70] Chrétien uses this Babylonian garden with its tree of cupidity not only to reinforce the irony of his story, but to contribute to its humor. The antics of his twelfth century Eve and Adam are a mockery not only of their love, but of those in the audience who would take them seriously.[71] In this connection, Fenice's insistence that she does not want to be another Yseut is simply a preposterous determination to make her submission to idolatry complete, and the ruse by means of which she accomplishes her purpose is in itself a laughable comment on the illusory character of the consummation she so persistently desires. *Cligés* is not an "anti-Tristan"; it carries the Tristan theme to an even greater extreme. If anything, it is a "super-Tristan." Chrétien's purpose, like that of Andreas, was to show the foolishness of idolatrous cupidity in an entertaining way that his audience could understand. Implicitly, he wished to promote the opposite of cupidity, Charity.

Other garden scenes in the works of Chrétien and his contemporaries immediately suggest themselves. One recalls, for example, an orchard where there is a pine tree shading a fountain, or the dark wood of Morois, or another nightingale. But I wish to show the appearance of these things in literature of other types. The works so far discussed are not formal allegories, and the analyses presented are not intended to show that they are. There is a difference between a work whose "symbolism" resides solely in the things referred to and a work which contains personified abstractions. I wish to examine one of the latter

type now, a poem which contains one of the most elaborate and influential gardens in medieval literature, the *Roman de la rose*. An analysis
of the opening description of the garden with the help of the background we have established may reveal things "apertement" that are
there, as in a dream, stated "covertement." The garden appears to the
dreamer "tot clos de haut mur bataillé," in the manner of Jehan's garden and its obverse in the Canticum. The wall is designed, like its various predecessors, to keep unsympathetic persons out. On it are depicted figures of various types to show who those are who may not
enter. Generally, they are those whom Andreas describes as being incapable of love.[72] The wall gives special assurance that the garden
within is a place "Ou onc n'avoit entré bergiers," for every successor
of the *pastor bonus* seeks rather the garden described by Genius much
later in the poem, presided over by a somewhat less romantic gardener. When the dreamer hears the sound of the birds within, who,
like Fenice's nightingale, represent the opposite of those admirable
birds in the *Saltair na Rann*, he wishes to enter the garden of love at
once and by any means. That is, the delight expressed by those who
enjoy Amoenitas awakens *concupiscentia carnis* in himself. With this
kind of love within him, he has no use for the *ostium ovium*, but finds
instead its opposite, a little door attended by a blonde, "gente e bele."
This lovely creature displays the typical symptoms of *accidia* and is
named Oiseuse. Her superficial splendor disguises a not very admirable character. Chaucer, seeing her through the eye of reason rather
than through the eyes of the flesh, calls her

> The ministre and norice unto vices,
> Which that men clepe in Englissh ydelnesse,
> That porter of the gate is of delices.

Without sloth the love awakened in the dreamer would die by "leveful
bisynesse," but sloth lets him into the garden of Deduit, an Amoenitas
which is appropriately planted with trees brought "de la terre as Sar-
radins." A grove of such trees, however it may appear to the fleshly
eye, can be nothing underneath but the frosty grove of Grendel's
mere.

Once inside, the dreamer is completely overcome. He feels that no
paradise could be better than this plantation of heresy:

> E sachiez que je cuidai estre
> Por voir en parevis terrestre;
> Tant estoit li leus delitables
> Qu'il sembloit estre espiritables;

Car, si come lors m'iert avis,
Il ne fait en nul parevis
Si bon estre come il fasoit
Ou vergier qui tant me plaisoit.
(635-640)

The fleshly delights are spiritual to the romantic eye of the dreamer. Various figures, who seem Angels to him, disport themselves within. With Deduit is sweet-singing Leece, and the folk generally are entertained by the musicians of Amoenitas. Dame Cortoisie with very polite seductiveness invites the dreamer to the dance, the "olde daunce" which he is eager to learn. Deduit wears the chaplet of roses he acquired in Wisdom 2. Leece, his love, like a "rose novelle," and "li deus d'Amours" accompany him. The dreamer, this time not altogether incorrectly, thinks of the latter as an Angel from Heaven. With the god is Douz Regarz, the stimulator of *concupiscentia oculorum*, bearing two bows with five arrows each. One set of arrows fosters idolatry, the other simple lechery.[73] Various fine ladies attend the god: Biautez, Richece, Largece, Franchise, and Cortoise, all described with humorous irony. Oiseuse and Jonece follow in the dance. The merrymakers approach the trees, where their delights are most compelling:

Les queroles ja remanoient,
Car tuit li plusor s'en aloient
O lor amies ombreier
Soz ces arbres, por doneier.
Deus! com menoient bone vie!
Fos est qui n'a de tel envie.
(1291-1296)

The dreamer has seen the joys which idleness and youth may follow *in medio ligni paradisi*. In this garden the trees are well adapted for excluding one's awareness of God's justice:

Mais li rain furent lonc e haut,
E, por le leu garder de chaut,
Furent si espès par deseure
Que li solauz en nesune eure
Ne pooit a terre descendre,
Ne faire mal a l'erbe tendre.
(1369-1374)

Moreover, there are shaded wells and streams to water the tender flowers of the flesh that grow under the trees.

In this garden, which Beowulf purified, and which Bede and Dante found uncomfortable, the dreamer finds himself situated pleasantly beside "une fontaine soz un pin," a scene vividly reminiscent of that with which the surviving portion of Beroul's *Tristan* begins. There Tristan and Yseut found their Amoenitas, like Adam and Eve "sub cooperimenta mendacii." The fountain issues from a marble stone, the rock of Grendel's pool seen from an attitude of luxuria. In the *Roman* of Guillaume the fountain is clearly identified as that beside which died "li biaus Narcisus," who, like Adam, is a very obvious type of the man who learns to love "quod suum est," except that, unlike Adam, Narcissus never repents. The legend of his death as it is told in the *Roman* is a vivid illustration of the absurd sterility of cupidity in general and of idolatrous love in particular. But the poet "covertement" draws another moral from the story, much in the same way that the noble suitor in the *De amore* drew a surface moral from his garden:

> Dames, cest essemple aprenez,
> Qui vers voz amis mesprenez;
> Car, se vos les laissez morir,
> Deus le vos savra bien merir.
> (1507–1510)

In other words, Eve should be less stingy with her apples. But the poem is, as Guillaume assures us, a presentation of the truth, and it is true "apertement" that if we take "morir" as a reference to the spiritual death resulting from idolatry, the dames who encourage it will, like Eve, merit God's wrath.

With some misgivings the dreamer looks into the well. There lie "deus pierres de cristal" which we should contrast with the carbuncle in the Well of Life as it is described later by Genius. These crystals enable the dreamer to see the garden on one side at a time. For they are the eyes of the flesh, the dreamer's own eyes, and to see all of the garden through them, he must turn his head. Having succumbed to *concupiscentia carnis*, the dreamer is now ready to indulge in *concupiscentia oculorum*, which leads, as St. Paul tells us, to pride of life. The wrong love, it will be remembered, proceeds "ex visione."[74] In the waters of Babylon the eyes of Narcissus betrayed him, for he fell into the net of Cupid or *cupiditas*; and so the dreamer is caught—"captus est in cupidinis vinculis"—for he sees "rosiers chargiez de roses," each one a fine specimen of St. Jerome's *flos foeni*. Among them, the dreamer prefers the buds, for the full blown roses last only a day, whereas the buds remain fresh a little longer:

> Les roses overtes e lees
> Sont en un jour toutes alees,
> Mais li bouton durent tuit frois
> A tot le moins deus jorz ou trois.
> (1645-1648)

"Qui portat imaginem terreni, et servit vitiis atque luxuriae, foenum-que est et flos praeteriens." The dreamer is not the man to linger in the wet garden of Andreas; having seen the delights of the shade, he soon centers his attention on one bud. So strong is his desire for this little "primerole" that he readily swears homage to the God of Love, who, as we should have no trouble seeing now, is Satan decked out in fine "humanistic" trappings. In the remainder of Guillaume's poem, which is not quite the "sentimental novel" one distinguished critic has accused it of being, Reason fights a losing battle to save the dreamer as he moves toward the consummation of his idolatry. The poem as a whole, including Jean de Meun's part, is a humorous and witty retelling of the story of the Fall, designed to impress the members of a courtly audience as they laughingly discern "apertement" what is presented "covertement." Under the inspiration of Guillaume de Saint Amour, Jean wishes to show that the Fall of man is in his day accomplished with the full cooperation of the fraternal orders.[75]

Jean de Meun, who was in a much better position than we are to understand Guillaume's garden, confirms in the observations of Genius the general interpretation here given to the garden:

> Pour Deu, seigneur, prenez ci garde:
> Qui bien la verité regarde,
> Les choses ici contenues,
> Ce sont trufles e fanfelues.
> Ci n'a chose qui seit estable,
> Quanqu'il i vit est corrompable.
> Il vit queroles qui faillirent,
> E faudront tuit cil qui les firent.
> (20349-20356)

Genius goes on to contrast this garden with another garden where there is a fountain of Living Waters which bestow eternal health and freedom from thirst (cf. John 4:13-14). It is watched over by a wise "bergiers," the *pastor bonus* whose successors, among whom Jean does not include the friars, are excluded by the wall from the garden of Deduit. The fountain produces the threefold but unified stream of the Trinity. Over it is a fruitful olive tree, much more glorious than the pine, bearing an inscription:

"Ci cueurt la fontaine de vie
Par desouz l'olive foillie
Qui porte le fruit de salu."
(20521-20523)

And beneath the tree "whose leafy crest showers dewdrops round" are truly unfading herbs and flowers of the virtues. In this fountain there are no deceiving crystals, but a great carbuncle glowing of its own light with undying splendor. This is the Image of God, reason with its three aspects—memory, intellect, and will—which in its proper harmony leads man to partake of *caritas* rather than *cupiditas*, and thus to partake of God, for as St. John says, *Deus caritas.*

Of the various gardens in Chaucer's works, the one in the Merchant's Tale affords perhaps the most suitable final example for this discussion, for it shows that the traditional materials we have been examining could appear in a fabliau. I assume here, perhaps rashly, that Chaucer's story is what Boccaccio thought of as "poetry worthy of the name" and not merely what the Nun's Priest calls "chaf." An old knight, Januarie, who has for sixty years enjoyed the pleasures of Andreas' wet garden, desires, with a great deal of amusing perversion of doctrine, to move over into the shade by marrying. "Nam umbram foliorum dilectio est et jocunditas in specie et pulchritudine rerum transitoriarum." The use of marriage for this purpose, "non propter Deum," is preposterous, but he convinces himself of the feasibility of this procedure with a great show of worldly wisdom. Thinking over the possibilities, he decides on a little bud named May, and while lying in bed stimulates himself "ex . . . immoderata cogitatione." After some indecision, in the course of which Chaucer makes the old knight's foolishness quite plain—except, that is, to Harry Bailey who sees in everything a reflection of his own marital difficulties—he does marry, showing meanwhile definite symptoms of Papelardie. But his squire, one Damyan, is overcome by *concupiscentia oculorum* when he sees May and takes to his bed with the lover's malady, an extreme form of *accidia*. The lady, who is not very well served, learns of Damyan's illness, and out of the truly modern sentimentality takes pity on him, for "pitie renneth soone in gentil herte," especially when one has the aid of Franchise. To increase and protect his Deduit, Januarie builds a *hortus conclusus*, in which there stands a laurel by a well. It is an attractive place:

So fair a gardyn woot I nowher noon.
For, out of doute, I verraily suppose

That he that wroot the Romance of the Rose
Ne koude of it the beautee wel devyse;
Ne Priapus ne myghte nat suffise,
Though he be god of gardyns, for to telle
The beautee of the gardyn and the welle,
That stood under a laurer alwey grene
                                                    (2030-2037)

The motivation underlying such gardens is somewhat cynically expressed in their "god," who here appears in a classical but transparent disguise. The references to Priapus, an obvious symbol of the painful frustration of cupidity which began with the Fall, and to the *Roman de la rose* are clear indications, I believe, that Chaucer had something more than the mere surface narrative in mind. In the garden the "married" couple disport themselves in summer:

And whan he wolde paye his wyf hir dette
In somer seson, thider wolde he go,
And May his wyf, and no wight but they two;
And thynges whiche that were nat doon abedde,
He in the gardyn parfourned hem and spedde.
                                                    (2048-2052)

We are, I think, in the garden of Deduit, under Tristan's pine tree, in the garden of Jehan, in Amoenitas, and beside Grendel's pool. Ultimately, we are back at Eve and Adam's *in medio ligni paradisi*, whence the river that feeds Januarie's well runs. The "laurer" is, in truth, "alwey grene," for the pattern of the Fall is perennial in human experience. Significantly, having built his *hortus deliciarum*, Januarie goes blind, a fact which emphasizes his spiritual blindness. Taking advantage of the literal blindness, May has a duplicate key to the "smale wyket" of the garden made, so that she and Damyan may use it. If Januarie's rationalizations and the ridiculous behavior of Damyan and May are amusing, what happens next reaches the apex of the comic, for Chaucer makes the underlying value from which his characters deviate quite plain:

But now to purpos: er that dayes eighte
Were passed, er the month of Juyn, bifil
That Januarie hath caught so greet a wil,
Thurgh eggyng of his wyf, hym for to pleye
In his gardyn, and no wight but they tweye,
That in a morwe unto his May seith he:
"Rys up, my wyf, my love, my lady free!

> The turtles voys is herd, my dowve sweete;
> The wynter is goon with alle his reynes weete.
> Com forth now, with thyne eyen columbyn!
> How fairer been thy breestes than is wyn!
> The gardyn is enclosed al aboute;
> Com forth, my white spouse! out of doute
> Thou hast me wounded in myn herte, O wyf!
> Ne spot of thee ne knew I al my lyf.
> Com forth, and lat us taken oure disport;
> I chees thee for my wyf and my confort."
>
> (2132-2148)

The veil is off. The garden of the lover is the garden of the *Canticum* turned upside down for purposes of ironic comedy. The Scriptural echoes in this passage are not mere literary decoration. They show the extreme foolishness to which cupidity like Januarie's may lead. For the doting knight, May represents what the lady in the *Canticum* represents to the faithful: she is his Holy Church, his Blessed Virgin, his refuge from the transitory world. The traditional nightingale, an obverse of the turtle, the spring atmosphere, and the beauty of the rose stand here undisguised. But the humor of Chaucer's story does not slacken. Januarie's wall affords no better protection than Jehan's, so that May, the "white spouse," is able to climb a tree to meet her Damyan in its branches. It is not a sycamore, but a pear tree, and the fruit it bears is in a very striking way the fruit which crowned the tree called *Vetus Adam* in the *De fructibus*. Januarie's garden is the garden which all those governed by cupidity think to build for self-concealment, and his fate is the fate of all those who try to make of wedlock the wrong kind of "paradys." In spite of Januarie's assertion to the contrary, a man may, as the Parson assures us, "sleen hymself with his owene knyf." And, as he continues, "Certes, be it wyf, be it child, or any worldly thyng that he loveth biforn God, it is his mawmet, and he is an ydolastre." To take this story as being merely an elaborate merry tale is to miss both the "sentence" and the best of the "solaas." To those who, like Chaucer, "lyve in charite," or at least attempt to do so, the behavior of others who hide under the Tree of Knowledge of Good and Evil is sometimes pathetic, and sometimes, when innocent victims fall also, it is tragic. But it can be uproariously comic as well, for cupidity often leads to ridiculous self-deception.

The works we have examined include a wide variety of types, from epic to fabliau, and they extend from our earliest non-celtic vernacular literature well into the latter fourteenth century. But in all of them,

from *Beowulf* to the Merchant's Tale, there is evidence for a real simi-
larity of attitude. The gardens which we have touched upon consistently enforce a single lesson. There is no evidence of pagan ideals or
superstitions in the picture of Grendel's mere, no evidence of any seriously maintained system of "courtly love" in Andreas' description of
Amoenitas, no sentimental naturalism in the gardens of the *Roman de
la rose*, and no "humanism" of the kind which exalts human flesh
above God, except as an object of satire, in the garden of the Merchant's Tale. On the contrary, all of these works either condemn or
satirize cupidity and hold forth Charity as an ideal either directly or by
implication. This is exactly what we should expect of Christian authors. Moreover, the assumption that the authors had in mind a series
of higher meanings seen in the light of wisdom tends to resolve apparent inconsistencies and contradictions in their works. In this respect,
this study supports the findings of a very early medievalist: "Miraris?
parum abest quin dicam theologiam poeticam esse de Deo: Christum
modo leonem modo agnum modo vermen dici, quid nisi poeticum
est? mille talia in Scripturis Sacris invenies que persequi longum est.
Quid vero aluid parabole Salvatoris in Evangelio sonant, nisi ser-
monem a sensibus alienum sive, ut uno verbo exprimam, alieniloquium, quam allegoriam usitatiori vocabulo nuncupamus? Atqui ex
huiusce sermonis genere poetica omnis intexta est."[76] The persistence
of the higher meanings involved in poetic allegory gives to the
thousand years of the medieval tradition a surprising unity and continuity. And this continuity is enforced by the attitude that Christ's
New Law is the ultimate expression of truth and the only source of
any real beauty.

Some Medieval Literary Terminology, with Special Reference to Chrétien de Troyes

Charity and cupidity are here again mistakenly called "opposites." Similarly, there is no "opposition" between the spirit and the letter.

IN an article which has become one of the classics of Arthurian scholarship, William A. Nitze offered an elaborate explanation of the terms *sens* and *matière* as they are used in the prologue to Chrétien's *Roman de la charrete*.[1] The second term, *matière*, presents little difficulty, since it is more or less the equivalent of the modern expression "subject matter," but the first term still lacks precise definition. Nitze defined *sens* as "signification" or "interpretation," and showed that in some contexts it is also the equivalent of "la *sciance* ou *sapiance* qui vient a Dieu."[2] Since this second meaning is not strictly literary, we may disregard it here. Technically, as Nitze indicated, *sens* is a term of scholastic origin, "essentiellement le produit des écoles monastiques du XIIᵉ siècle."[3] In literary discussions, Nitze maintained, it is analogous with *sensus*, used to indicate the higher meaning or "signification" of Scripture. This seems fairly clear and convincing. It has become customary to regard Chrétien's romances as stories with "theses" so that the term *sens* is useful in discussions of the distinction between subject matter and theme. But in a more recent study of the *Roman de la charrete* written by Tom Peete Cross in collaboration with Nitze, a somewhat different interpretation of the term was offered. The authors maintained that *sens* is the *interpretatio* or *expositio* of the narrative, and that this "consisted, in general, in saying the same thing in as many different ways as possible."[4] It is obvious that there is a decided difference between the higher meaning of a Scriptural passage or of a profane narrative on the one hand and diversified repetition on the other. A still further modification of the term *sens* was made by Eugene Vinaver, who found that it is "not the 'meaning' or *signification*, but the 'theme,' or 'purpose,' or 'intention' of a work; not part of a given matter, as a sense inherent in the story, but an idea brought in as it were from outside."[5] Vinaver wished to emphasize the fact that a literary narrative does not have a definite meaning inextricably involved in it and that the *sen* arises from the treatment of the narrative in a given instance. But this fact does not, as he indicates, eliminate the terms *meaning* or *signification* as equivalents for *sen*; for it is a matter of commonplace observation that a Scriptural story or a profane story such as an exemplum might be used by medieval authors with several different meanings or significations in varying contexts. As a matter of fact, St. Augustine regarded the possible variation in meaning of a Scriptural passage as a decided asset.[6] In a literary treatment of a story, as in a doctrinal treatment of a parable or exemplum, we may assume that the "meaning" and "intention" are the same, provided, of course, that the author has the ability to make himself clear. In effect, therefore, Vinaver's use of the term *sen* or *sens* is not very different from that first recommended by Nitze. One difficulty with all of these definitions arises from the fact that *sensus* in the twelfth century frequently did not mean "intention" or "significance" at all. A re-examination of the evidence and of certain related terms used by medieval literary theorists may serve to make our conception of *sens* more precise. Clues to the background of literary theory in which Chrétien worked may be found in the prologue to *Erec* as well as in the *Roman de la charrete* in which the terms *matière* and *sens* occur. In this paper I wish to examine the most significant features of this background very briefly.

Erec opens with an extended statement of purpose which reflects some pertinent literary conventions. The word *conjointure* in line 14 affords a key to the context of associations in which the prologue was written. Nitze translated line 14 "une tres belle combinaison," but did not find any authority for the Latin *conjunctura* upon which the word *conjointure* was based.[7] However, *conjunctura* was used as a literary term by Chrétien's contemporary, Alanus de Insulis, in the *De planctu naturae*. Nature replies to the dreamer's question concerning poets:

> At, in superficiali litterae cortice falsum resonat lyra poetica, sed interius, auditoribus secretum intelligentiae altioris eloquitur, ut exteriore falsitatis abjecto putamine, dulciorem nucleum veritatis secrete intus lector inveniat. Poetae tamen aliquando historiales eventus joculationibus fabulosis quadam eleganti fictura confoederant, ut ex diversorum competenti conjunctura, ipsius narrationis elegantior pictura resultet.[8]

On the outside, the fables of poets are false; but the reader should discover beneath the outer shell a kernel of truth. Poets compound their fictions of diverse elements, that from the juxtaposition of these elements a more elegant picture may result. It will repay us to make a rather thorough examination of the terms *cortex*, *nucleus*, and *pictura* before we consider the meaning of *conjunctura*.

The terms *cortex* and *nucleus* were borrowed from Scriptural exegesis, where the *cortex* is the literal or historical sense and the *nucleus* is the higher meaning, whether tropological, allegorical, or anagogical.[9] This distinction was crucial in medieval exegesis. Thus Rabanus, following St. Augustine, describes adherence to the letter as a miserable servitude:

> Nam in principio cavendum est, ne figuratam locutionem ad litteram accipias. Ad hoc enim pertinet quod ait Apostolus: *Littera occidit, spiritus autem vivificat*. Nulla mors animae congruentius appellatur, quam cum id etiam quod in ea bestias antecellit, hoc est intelligentia, carni subjicitur sequendo scilicet solam litteram. Qui enim sequitur litteram translata verba sicut propria tenet, neque illud quod proprio verbo significatur, refert ad aliam significationem. Et ea est miserabilis animae servitus, signa pro rebus accipere, et supra creaturam corpoream, oculum mentis ad hauriendum aeternum lumen levare non posse. Quae tamen servitus in Judaeo populo longe a caeterarum gentium more distabat, quandoquidem rebus temporalibus ita subjugati erant, ut unus eis in omnibus commendaretur Deus. Gentes autem simulacra manufacta deos habebant, et si quando aliqui eorum illa tanquam signa interpretari conabantur, ad creaturam colendam venerandamque referebant. Sed ab hac utraque servitute, veniens Christus veritatis suae luce illuminans, omnes in se credentes veraciter liberavit.[10]

The distinction between the literal and the allegorical meanings was thus associated with the Pauline distinction between the letter and the spirit, and the spirit underlying the letter was associated with Christ and the New Law. Not all of the Bible was thought to be allegorical, but to overlook allegory where it is present is to miss the essential message of Christianity, to react as an unreasoning animal rather than as a human being. For medieval thinkers, the problem of distinguishing allegorical from non-allegorical passages was relatively simple. All those passages which do not on the surface promote Charity are to be taken allegorically. Where the message of Charity, or the condemnation of its opposite, cupidity, is apparent on the surface, one may follow the letter with confidence. On this point we may again quote Rabanus, who combines several passages from St. Augustine's *De doctrina*:

Demonstrandus est igitur proprius modus inveniendae locutionis, propriane an figurata sit, et iste omnino modus est, ut quidquid in sermone divino neque ad morum honestatem, neque ad fidei veritatem proprie referri potest, figuratum esse cognoscas. Morum honestas ad diligendum Deum et proximum, fidei veritas ad cognoscendum Deum et proximum pertinet. . . . Non enim praecipit Scriptura nisi charitatem, nec culpat nisi cupiditatem; et eo modo informat mores hominum. Charitatem voco motum animi ad fruendum Deo propter ipsum, et se atque proximo, propter Deum. Cupiditatem autem motum animi ad fruendum se et proximo, et quoilibet corpore non propter Deum.[11]

Thus a *nucleus* beneath the *cortex* of Scripture was to be sought when the message of the New Law is not apparent on the surface or in the *cortex* itself. This is the theory which underlines the passage from the *Livre des reis* quoted by Nitze:

Fedeil Deu, entend l'estoire. Asez est clére, e semble nue, mais pleine est de sens é de meule. L'histoire est paille, le sen est grains; le sen est fruit, l'estorie raims.[12]

The exegetical meaning of *cortex* was reinforced by the usual interpretation of the story of Jacob's rods. Concerning it, Rabanus wrote:

Quid est virgas virides et amygdalinas atque ex platanis ante oculos gregum ponere, nisi per Scripturae seriem antiquorum Patrum vitas atque sententias in exemplum populis praebere? . . . Dumque ab ipsis cortex litterae subtrahitur, allegorice candor interior demonstratur.[13]

The same interpretation appears in a poem among those attributed to Hildebert:

Ut majora metas in Christo gaudia, rectis
  Scripturae verbis instrue, pastor, oves.
Non est mysterii candor quaerendus in illis,
  Non gaudent solo cortice verba foris.
Intimus est candor instructio mystica, cortex
  Exterior dici littera potest.[14]

In Scriptural exegesis, therefore, an opposition between *cortex* and *nucleus* is an opposition between the letter and the spirit, the literal and the allegorical, or, by association, between the Old Law and the New.

Poetry and theology were sometimes compared, since both reduce an obscure exterior to a comprehensible truth. Scotus Erigena, for example, wrote:

Quemadmodum ars poetica per fictas fabulas allegoricasque similitudines moralem doctrinam seu physicam componit ad humanorum animorum exercitationem, hoc enim proprium est heroicorum poetarum, qui virorum fortium facta et mores figurate laudant; ita theologica veluti quaedam poetria sanctam Scripturam fictis imaginationibus ad consultum nostri animi et reductionem corporalibus sensibus exterioribus, veluti ex quadam imperfecta pueritia, in rerum intelligibilium perfectam cognitionem, tanquam in quandam interioris hominis grandaevitatem conformat.[15]

And the term *cortex*, or synonyms for it, was applied to the allegorical shell of poetry as well as to that of Scripture. An examination of some of these terms in their context should make the underlying concept clear. St. Augustine condemns certain verses in these terms:

Haec siliqua intra dulce tectorium sonantes lapillos quatit; non est autem hominum, sed porcorum cibus. Novit quid dicam, qui Evangelium novit.[16]

The sweet shell, in this instance, contains no real nourishment, but only food for swine, or heretics. But St. Augustine did realize that in other instances the apparently mendacious *cortices* of poems might conceal germs of truth:

Nec apud auctores tantum saecularium litterarum, ut apud Horatium, mus loquitur muri, et mustela vulpeculae, ut per narrationem fictam ad id quod agitur, vera significatio referatur; unde et Aesopi tales fabulas ad eum finem relatas, nullus tam ineruditus fuit, qui putaret appellanda mendacia.[17]

Theodulph of Orleans used an argument involving the word *tegmen* to defend his reading of pagan literature:

Et modo Pompeium, modo te, Donate, legebam,
Et modo Virgilium, te modo, Naso loquax.
In quorum dictis quamquam sint frivola multa,
Plurima sub falso tegmine vera latent.[18]

A common synonym for *cortex* during the twelfth century was *integumentum*, which implied an obscure covering over an inner truth. At the beginning of his commentary on the *Aeneid*, Bernard Silvestris defined this term as follows:

Integumentum vero est genus demonstrationis sub fabulosa narratione veritatis involvens intellectum, unde et involucrum dicitur.[19]

Later on in this work, the term appears again in the gloss on *Aen.* VI, 88-100:

> Talibus ex adyto dictis Cumaea Sibylla
> Horrendas canit ambages antroque remugit,
> Obscuris vera involvens.

ambages quasi ambiguitates i.e. responsa integumentis involuta. . . . *Obscuris* integumentis. *Vera* veritatem enim per integumenta occultat. Intelligentia namque divina praecipue docet, divinis vero integumenta praecipue congruunt, quia ut ait Martianus cuniculis verborum divina sunt tegenda. Unde Plato et alii philosophi cum anima vel alio theologico aliquid dicunt ad integumentum se convertunt: ut Maro in hoc opere.[20]

The poetic obscurity of the *integumentum* is thus especially appropriate to divine subjects. Alanus uses both *integumentum* and *involucrum* in the *De planctu*, where he expresses bewilderment concerning the nature of Cupid:

> Quamvis enim plerique auctores sub integumentali involucro aenigmatum, ejus naturam depinxerint, tamen nulla certitudinis nobis reliquerunt vestigia.[21]

The word *aenigma* used here is also a literary term, applied to poetry by St. Augustine in a gloss on Numbers 21:27:

> *Propterea dicent aenigmatistae, Venite in Esebon,* etc. Qui sint aenigmatistae ideo non apparet, quia non sunt in consuetudine litteraturae nostrae, neque in ipsis divinis Scripturis fere alio loco reperitur hoc nomen: sed quia videntur quasi canticum dicere, quo cecinerunt bellum . . . non incredibiliter putantur isti aenigmatistae sic tunc appellati, quos poetas nos appellamus; eo quod poetarum sit consuetudo atque licentia miscere carminibus suis aenigmata fabularum, quibus aliquid significare intelligantur. Non enim aliter essent aenigmata, nisi illic esset tropica locutio, qua discussa perveniretur ad intellectum qui in aenigmate latitaret.[22]

Scotus uses the same term in speaking of Scriptural obscurity:

> Propterea decebat mystica eloquia veritatem supermundanorum intellectuum per aenigmata occultare.[23]

And Isidore of Seville makes a distinction between *aenigma* and *allegoria*:

Inter allegoriam autem et aenigma hoc interest, quod allegoriae vis gemina est res alias aliud figuraliter indicat; aenigma vero sensus tantum obscurus est, et per quasdum imagines adumbratus.[24]

Allegoria is defined as "alieniloquium. Aliud enim sonat, et aliud intel-legitur."[25] An enigmatic statement contains a *cortex* which is in itself obscure, whereas the *cortex* of an allegorical statement may be per-fectly clear. That is, *aenigma* is obscure *allegoria*. Thus Alanus com-plains in his query about Cupid that the descriptions of the god, al-though they contain a hidden truth, are obscure even on the surface. John of Salisbury twice uses *involucrum*, the accepted synonym for *in-tegumentum*, in the *Policraticus*. The Thebans, he says, are ridiculed by Athenians and Lacedemonians, but their fables contain an element of truth:

Riserunt eos Athenienses et Lacedemonii populi grauiores, his-toriarum gesta, naturae morumque mysteria uariis figmentorum inuolucris obtexentes. . . .[26]

Again, he defends Vergil in the following terms:

Si uerbis gentilium uti licet Christiano, qui solis electis diuinum et Deo placens per inhabitantem gratiam esse credit ingenium, etsi nec uerba nec sensus credam gentilium fugiendos, dummodo uitentur errores, hoc ipsum diuina prudentia in Eneide sua sub inuolucro fic-titii commenti innuisse uisus est Maro, dum sex etatum gradus sex librorum distinctionibus prudenter expressit.[27]

Finally, John of Garland defined *integumentum* as "veritas in specie fabule palliata,"[28] and called his own exposition of Ovid *Integumenta ovidiana*.[29]

The word *palliata* in John of Garland's definition suggests the re-lated noun *pallium*. Alanus uses it in speaking of Vergil:

Virgilii musa mendacia multa colorat,
Et facie veri contexit pallia falso.[30]

The *cortex* or *pallium* was frequently described contemptuously, as it is here, a fact which reveals an attitude parallel to the conventional at-titude toward the *cortex* of Scripture. Thus Baudri wrote of the super-ficial *garrulitate* of poets:

Ecce poetarum perlecta garrulitate
Investigamus quid latet interius.[31]

And Nigellus Wireker, in the prologue to the *Speculum stultorum*, warned:

> Saepius historiae brevitas mysteria magna
> Claudit, et in vili res preciosa latet.[32]

Underneath the "vile thing" which is the exterior fable the poet expressed his more precious doctrine. In the words of a vernacular poet, Jaufré Rudel (VI),

> Ni conois de rima co·s va
> Si razo non enten en si.

At the close of the Middle Ages, Chaucer expressed this attitude quite clearly, using for his purpose the imagery we found in the *Livre des reis*:

> Taketh the moralite, goode men,
> For seint Paul seith that al that writen is
> To oure doctrine it is ywrite, ywis;
> Taketh the fruyt, and lat the chaf be stille.[33]

We may conclude that the words *cortex* and *nucleus* in Alanus' description of poetry reflect a very widespread doctrine that poetry is by nature allegorical, so that it expresses a truth under an attractive but lying exterior. The terms *cortex*, *integumentum*, *involucrum*, and *pallium* are roughly synonymous. *Allegoria* implies the presence of a *cortex* and *nucleus*. And *aenigma* is a special kind of *allegoria*.

Before we proceed to a consideration of other terms, it is necessary to add that the *cortex* of a pagan poem differs fundamentally in structure from the *cortex* of Scripture. In the *cortex* of Scripture the things spoken of may be allegorical, as well as the words, whereas in a pagan poem the words only are allegorical. Since the medieval conception of the meaning of things is not only important but a little difficult for modern readers to understand, we may consider some of its principal features here. As Hugh of St. Victor explains it, the meanings of words are established by human convention, but the meanings of things are divinely established, representing, as it were, the voice of God speaking to men:

> Sciendum est etiam, quod in divino eloquio non tantum verba sed etiam res significare habent, qui modus non adeo in aliis scripturis inveniri solet. Philosophus solam vocum novit significationem, sed excellentior valde est rerum significatio quam vocum, quia hanc usus instituit, illam natura dictavit: haec hominum vox est, illa vox Dei ad homines.[34]

The allegory of Scripture is based on the nature of things, on the inner structure of creation as revealed by the Holy Spirit, whereas the allegory of pagan poetry is merely a matter of usage. Perhaps some over enthusiastic teachers in the twelfth century attempted to find the inner significances of things in pagan writings as well as in the Scriptures, for we have an objection to this error by John of Salisbury:

> Diuinae paginae libros, quorum singuli apices diuinis pleni sunt sacramentis, tanta grauitate legendos forte concesserim, eo quod thesaurus Spiritus sancti, cuius digito scripti sunt, omnino nequeat exhauriri. Licet enim ad unum tantummodo sensum accommodata sit superficies litterae, multiplicitas misteriorum intrinsecus latet et ab eadem re saepe allegoria fidem, tropologia mores uariis modis edificet; anagoge quoque multipliciter sursum ducit ut litteram non modo uerbis sed rebus ipsis instituat. At in liberalibus disciplinis, ubi non res sed dumtaxat uerba significant, quisquis primo sensu litterae contentus non est, aberrare uidetur michi aut ab intelligentia ueritatis, quo diutius teneantur, se uelle suos abducere auditores.[35]

John goes on to condemn specifically the allegorization of Porphyrio. As we have seen, he looks with approval on allegorical interpretations of the *Aeneid* and of pagan fables, so that this passage should not be taken as a condemnation of the allegorical theory of poetry or as evidence for an "opposition" between "poets and theologians." Verbal allegory characteristic of pagan writings was not susceptible of elaboration on the three higher levels: tropological, allegorical, and anagogical. For this kind of elaboration, wherein the word *allegoria* means "pertaining to the faith or to the church," the revealed meanings of things are required. And it would be futile to expect such meanings, except occasionally and by accident, in pagan writings. The pagans were not able, as Rabanus tells us, "oculum mentis ad hauriendum aeternum lumen levare."

The conception of an allegorical "thing" is not actually very difficult. St. Augustine calls such things "signs" in the *De doctrina*:

> Signum est enim res, praeter speciem quam ingerit sensibus, aliud aliquid ex se faciens in cogitationem venire: sicut vestigio viso, transisse animal cujus vestigium est, cogitamus.[36]

This kind of simple association must not be applied indiscriminately, however. A given statement may contain either things without further signification or things which are signs of other things:

> Omnis doctrina vel rerum est vel signorum, sed res per signa discuntur. Proprie autem nunc res appellavi, quae non ad significandum aliquid adhibentur, sicuti est lignum, lapis, pecus, atque hujusmodi caetera. Sed non illud lignum quod in aquas amaras

Moysen misisse legimus, ut amaritudine carerent [Exod. 15:25];
neque ille lapis quem Jacob sibi ad caput posuerat [Gen. 28:11];
neque illud pecus quod pro filio immolavit Abraham [Gen. 22:13].
Hae namque ita res sunt, ut aliarum etiam signa sint rerum.[37]

The values for things which are signs of other things in the Bible have
a kind of absolute quality, since the Bible is the Word of God. Ignorance of the nature of things was considered to be a major obstacle to an
understanding of obscure passages in Scripture:

Rerum autem ignorantia facit obscuras figuratas locutiones, cum
ignoramus vel animantium, vel lapidum, vel herbarum naturas,
aliarumve rerum, quae plerumque in Scripturis similitudinis alicujus
gratia ponuntur.[38]

To remedy this ignorance, books on the nature of things like the *De
universo* of Rabanus Maurus were written.

A further distinction was used to clarify the difference between divine and pagan writings. Hugh of St. Victor explains that the works of
God are twofold: *opus conditionis* and *opus restaurationis*. Divine writings concern themselves with the *opus restaurationis* and are thus distinguished in subject matter from other writings:

Duo sunt opera Dei, quibus consummantur omnia quae facta sunt.
Primum est opus conditionis, quo facta sunt quae non erant: secundum est opus restaurationis, quo reparata sunt quae perierant. Opus
conditionis est creatio mundi cum omnibus elementis suis. Opus
restaurationis est incarnatio Verbi cum omnibus sacramentis suis;
sive quae ante incarnationem praecesserunt ab initiio saeculi, sive
quae post subsequentur usque ad finem mundi. . . . Aliarum enim
Scripturarum omnium materia est in operibus conditionis, divinarum Scripturarum materia in operibus restaurationis constat.[39]

Not only do divine writings differ from others in material but also in
technique, for they employ the significances of things. One may arrive
at the meanings of words by applying the disciplines of the *trivium*, but
to determine the meanings of things, it is necessary to use the disciplines of the *quadrivium*:

Unde apparet quantum divina Scriptura caeteris omnibus scripturis
non solum in materia sua, sed etiam in modo tractandi, subtilitate et
profunditate praecellat; cum in caeteris quidem scripturis solae
voces significare inveniantur; in hac autem non solum voces, sed
etiam res significativae sint. Sicut igitur in eo sensu qui inter voces et
res versatur necessaria est cognitio vocum, sic in illo qui inter res et

facta vel facienda mystica constat, necessaria est cognitio rerum.
Cognitio autem vocum in duobus consideratur; in pronuntiatione
videlicet et significatione. Ad solam pronuntiationem pertinet
grammatica, ad solam significationem pertinet dialectica; ad pronuntiationem simul et significationem pertinet rhetorica. Cognitio
rerum circa duo versatur, id est formam et naturam. Forma est in
exteriori dispositione; natura in interiori qualitate. Forma rerum aut
in numero consideratur ad quem pertinet arithmetica; aut in propor-
tione ad quam pertinet musica; aut in dimensione ad quam pertinet
geometria; aut in motu ad quem pertinet astronomia. Ad interiorem
vero rerum naturam physica spectat.[40]

Things are more fruitful in meaning than are words, for a thing may
have as many meanings as it has properties in common with other
things:

Est etiam longe multiplicior significatio rerum quam vocum. Nam
paucae voces plusquam duas aut tres significationes habent; res
autem quaelibet tam multiplex potest esse in significatione aliarum
rerum, quot in se proprietates visibiles aut invisibiles habet com-
munes aliis rebus.[41]

Fortunately, however, the number of meanings for a given thing was
limited by the conventions of Scriptural interpretation, at least for
practical purposes. The higher meanings of Scripture, the tropological
and allegorical levels, arise only from the significances of things; it is
impossible to arrive at them through the disciplines of the *trivium*:

Ex quo constat quod omnes artes naturales divinae scientiae
famulantur; et inferior sapientia recte ordinata ad superiorem con-
ducit. Sub eo igitur sensu qui est in significatione vocum ad res, continetur historia; cui famulantur tres scientiae sicut dictum est, id est
grammatica, dialectica, rhetorica. Sub eo autem sensu qui est in significatione rerum ad facta mystica, continetur allegoria. Et sub eo
sensu qui est in significatione rerum ad facienda mystica, continetur
tropologia; et his duobus famulantur arithmetica, musica, geometria, astronomia et physica. Super haec ante omnia divinum illud est
ad quod ducit divina Scriptura sive in allegoria, sive in tropologia:
quorum alterum (quod in allegoria est) rectam fidem, alterum (quod
in tropologia est) informat bonam operationem: in quibus constat
cognitio veritatis et amor virtutis: et haec est vera reparatio
hominis.[42]

An examination of the meanings of words leads merely to an historical
interpretation, or, we may add, only to the solution of verbal allegory,

which may reveal useful moral principles but not the message of faith and good works necessary to salvation.

An illustration may clarify some of these principles. In Scriptural contexts, the hart is a sign either of Christ or of the faithful Christian, but we should not expect the hart to have these meanings in a pagan poem. Marie de France, for example, gives no such significance to the hart in her translation of the pagan fable *De cervo ad fontem*.[43] Again, the comments of Bernard Silvestris on the *Aeneid* are usually verbal. A typical example is afforded by the interpretation of the name *Theseus*: "dicitur Theseus divinus et bonus: theos enim deus, eu bonus."[44] Other glosses depend largely on the context of the interpretation. There are some references to the nature of things, but these things operate as figures of speech rather than as signs. Thus the notion that the Trojan horse represents "luxuria" is supported by the argument: "Equus ideo hanc habet figuram quia in hoc animali plurimum luxuria viget."[45] The observation is derived from Pliny, and although it happens that a horse may sometimes have a similar meaning as a sign in Scripture, that fact is an accident which does not indicate any special knowledge of revelation on the part of either Vergil or Pliny. It is true that the interpretation of *montes* is reinforced, as are certain other interpretations, by Scriptural references,[46] and that there are similarities between meanings given by Bernard to common objects, like the sea, and the traditional Scriptural meanings of these objects; but Bernard does not elaborate tropological, allegorical, and anagogical senses from his text. Usually, he simply says that in "philosophy" a given word has a certain meaning or series of meanings. If Apollo can stand for divine wisdom, certainly this fact is not based on the inner attributes of any "thing." In general, the *cortex* of a pagan poem is verbal, although a certain amount of scientific knowledge may be useful in the process of removing it. But the *cortex* of Scripture contains words for signs as well as words for mere things, so that the underlying *nucleus* may be revealed only by one familiar with the disciplines of the *quadrivium* as well as with those of the *trivium*. If pagan deities may sometimes stand for the divine beings of the Christian hierarchy, as they do in the *Ovide moralisé*, this fact is due to the simple device of *allegoria*, not to the inner structure of creation.

This distinction does not apply to the works of Christian poets, for it is obviously the function of the Christian poet to use as the matter of his work the *opus restaurationis* rather than the *opus conditionis*. The very fact of his Christianity in the Middle Ages was an indication that he had learned to avoid the error condemned by Rabanus, "signa pro rebus accipere." Thus the Scriptural sign of the hart is familiar in

Christian hagiography, iconography, and literature.[47] Poets like Prudentius do not hesitate to use "things" with the significances they have in the Bible, and their appearance is well attested in the Victorine sequences.[48] Alanus de Insulis demands that the readers of his *Anticlaudianus* seek tropological and allegorical as well as literal values in the poem, thus implying that the things in it are significant:

> In hoc etenim opere, litteralis sensus suavitas puerilem demulcebit auditum; moralis instructio proficientem imbuet sensum; acutior allegoriae subtilitas perficientem acuet intellectum.[49]

It is noteworthy here that the literal sense is not regarded very highly. In a poem by a well educated Christian author we should not be surprised to find an extremely complex *cortex* made up of signs stemming both from the traditions of Scriptural exegesis and from the traditions of literary exegesis. A poet might well use signs from Scripture and figures from conventional interpretations of Vergil and Ovid in the same poem. At the same time, there was nothing to prevent him from making new allegorical inventions of his own, based on etymologies, on conceptions of natural history, or on new combinations of traditional elements. His ingenuity and enterprise in this respect were limited more by the character of his audience than by any theoretical considerations.

In one way, however, the *cortex* of a poem, Christian or pagan, does differ essentially from that of most of the Scriptures. With the possible exceptions of the parables and prophetic visions, Scriptural narratives do not form *picturas*. The concept underlying the term *pictura* is made plain in Isidore's definition of the office of the poet:

> Officium autem poetae in eo est ut ea, quae vere gesta sunt, in alias species obliquis figurationibus cum decore aliquo conversa transducant. Vnde et Lucanus ideo in numero poetarum non ponitur, quia videtur historias conposuisse, non poema.[50]

The poet does not write histories which include events as they actually took place. Instead, he combines elements in ways in which they are not combined in nature. Unlike poetry, much of Scripture is made up of history.[51] When a Scriptural passage concerns actual events, the events themselves are significant, so that the allegory springs from them. But in a parable, the events are fictitious, like those of a poem. This fact does not prevent the things in the parable from being significant as things. If it did, it would be impossible to interpret parables on more than one level, but it is a commonplace that parables were given tropological, allegorical, and anagogical meanings. We must thus be careful not to confuse allegory arising from events with the concept of the allegory of things. A poem may contain things which are significant in spite of the fact that the events it describes are a mere *pictura* of something which never happened. The word *pictura* itself is used by Hugh of St. Victor in the *Didascalicon*. Here poems are classified along with pagan philosophical writings as "appendicia artium." These writings are not truly philosophical in themselves, but they may prepare the way toward philosophy. It is clear that Hugh is writing of pagan poetry, but the conception of the *pictura* applies to Christian poetry as well:

> huiusmodi sunt omnia poetarum carmina, ut sunt tragoediae, comoediae, satirae, heroica quoque et lyrica, et iambica, et didascalica quaedam, fabulae quoque et historiae, illorum etiam scripta quos nunc philosophos appellare solemnus, qui et brevem materiam longis verborum ambagibus extendere consueverunt, et facilem sensum perplexis sermonibus obscurare, vel etiam diversa simul compilantes, quasi de multis coloribus et formis, unam picturam facere.[52]

The poet is said here to bring together diverse things, or things not actually combined in nature, so that a *pictura* appears made up of many colors and forms. The *pictura* is essentially an artificial combination of elements. As is well known, the fables of poets are frequently called "lying" fables. The *pictura* is the lying configuration of the surface of a poem.

Alanus says that the *pictura* results from a *conjunctura*. The meaning of the term *conjunctura* should now be clear from the context. The *cortex* of a poem is false, but beneath the surface lies a *nucleus* of truth. The falsity of the exterior is due to the fact that the poet is not an historian. He uses diverse materials from various places. The persons, places, or events he describes may or may not be actual persons, places, or events, but the sequence in which he places them is his own. This new sequence is the *conjunctura*, which should be made, as Isidore says, with a certain perfection or attractiveness. When the *conjunctura* has been made "cum decore aliquo," an attractive *pictura* results. The *conjunctura* is thus the construction of the *cortex* of the poem, and it was conventionally made so that a *nucleus* of truth lay beneath it.

The materials assembled here may shed some light on the prologue to *Erec* as a whole. To facilitate reference, I quote here the first twenty-two lines:

> Li vilains dit an son respit
> Que tel chose a l'an an despit,

Qui mout vaut miauz que l'an ne cuide.
Por ce fet bien qui son estuide
Atorne a bien, quel que il l'et;
Car qui son estuide antrelet,
Tost i puet tel chose teisir,
Qui mout vandroit puis a pleisir.
Por ce dit Crestiens de Troies
Que reisons est que totes voies
Doit chascuns panser et antandre
A bien dire et a bien aprandre,
E tret d'un conte d'avanture
Une mout bele conjointure,
Par qu'an puet prover et savoir
Que cil ne fet mie savoir,
Qui sa sciance n'abandone
Tant con Deus la grace l'an done.
D'Erec, le fil Lac, est li contes,
Que devant rois et devant contes
Depecier et corronpre suelent
Cil qui de conter vivre vuelent.

When Chrétien says that his poem is "une mout bele conjointure," he implies (1) that it is a fable as opposed to an actual sequence of events, a *conjunctura* of events not joined in nature; (2) that this *conjunctura* is "bele," that is, that it is made "cum decore aliquo"; and (3) that this pleasing *cortex* covers a *nucleus* of truth. The third implication is reinforced by the prologue as a whole. At the beginning, it is said that many things commonly despised are actually worth more than they are usually considered to be worth. The thing of little value, in this instance, is the narrative of *Erec* as it is usually told by professional conteurs. Moreover, Chrétien continues, one does well who "son estuide atorne a bien," for otherwise he might conceal something pleasing. For this reason, Chrétien, who feels that everyone ought to speak and teach well, has brought forth from the little esteemed "conte d'avanture" a "mout bele conjointure." The spirit of this statement is quite similar to that of Nigellus Wireker's prefatory remark quoted earlier. The "conte" is the "vile thing" not much esteemed. But Chrétien, fulfilling his obligation to teach, has made of this "jangler's" story an attractive *conjunctura* "par qu'an puet prover et savoir" a *nucleus* of truth. And this *nucleus*, as he says, is the fact that it is foolish for one to refuse to use the wisdom which God has given him. Erec was *récréant*, that is, in much more than a social sense. The story, as Chrétien says, has been corrupted by professional entertainers. But his own *conjunctura* will be remembered "tant con durra crestiantez" (25). This is not a boast made in vanity, but a warning to the reader or listener that *Erec* does not rattle pebbles "intra dulce tectorium"; it is not mere "porcorum cibus."

In the *De planctu* Alanus uses the term *littera*: "in superficiali litterae cortice." It is implied here that *littera* and *cortex* are equivalents; and the poem attributed to Hildebert explicitly states "cortex exterior littera dici potest." In the *Livre des reis* the historical level, called "paille," is contrasted with the *sen*, called "grains." Thus the terms *littera* and *sensus* in these contexts have much the same force as *cortex* and *nucleus*. In the schools of the twelfth century, however, these terms had somewhat different meanings. Our authority for this terminology is the *Didascalicon* of Hugh of St. Victor, at once a reliable guide to twelfth century scholastic practice and a work of enormous influence.[53] Hugh describes the process of explaining a text as follows:

> expositio tria continet, litteram, sensum, sententiam. littera congrua ordinatio dictionum, quod etiam constructionem vocamus. sensus est facilis quaedam et aperta significatio, quam littera prima fronte praefert. sententia est profundior intelligentia, quae nisi expositione vel interpretatione non invenitur. in his ordo est, ut primum littera, deinde sensus, deinde sententia inquiratur. quo facto, perfecta est expositio.[54]

The term *littera* here refers merely to the grammatical and syntactical construction of the work being explained. When this has been understood, one proceeds to the *sensus* or obvious meaning. This is what we have been describing as the *cortex* or *pallium* and what Hugh of St. Victor and others after him call the *historia* or the "literal" sense. The higher meaning, toward which the exposition of a text is directed, is called the *sententia*. The procedure here described was used in the study of profane works. If the work examined were a pagan poem, let us say the *Aeneid*, the study of the *littera* would result in grammatical and rhetorical observations similar to those in the notes of modern school texts. These observations would enable one to see the obvious meaning or *sensus* and to learn the outline of the narrative. Finally, the *sententia* would involve the kind of observations made in the commentary of Bernard Silvestris. When Scripture was read, exactly the same general procedure was followed:

> Expositio tria continet: litteram, sensum, sententiam. in omni narratione littera est, nam ipse voces etiam litterae sunt, sed sensus et sententia non in omni narratione simul invenitur. quaedam habet lit-

teram et sensum tantum, quaedam litteram et sententiam tantum, quaedam omnia haec tria simul continet. omnis autem narratio ad minus duo habere debet.[55]

All Scriptural narratives contain at least two of these elements. In the first place, any piece of writing is made up of the first element, *littera*, so that it is common to all. When the passage being considered conduces to Charity without further interpretation, it contains the first two elements, *littera* and *sensus*. A passage may contain historical truth and allegorical truth at the same time, and, in this event, it contains all three elements. But there are passages in the Bible which employ *aenigma*, so that the level of *sensus* is meaningless. Such passages contain only *littera* and *sententia*. We may apply these same principles to Christian poetry, or, that is, to serious poetry written by medieval Christians, whether their work is now classified as "religious" or "secular." If a poem conduces to Charity on the surface, or level of *sensus*, and makes perfectly good sense on that level, no further interpretation is necessary. If it is clear on the surface but does not conduce to Charity on the level of *sensus*, then the poem is allegorical and it is necessary to determine the *sententia*. Whatever "poetic license" a poet may have had in the Middle Ages, the fact of his being a poet did not give him any license for heresy. Finally, if a poem is enigmatic on the surface, it contains only the two levels *littera* and *sententia*. In the category of "serious" poetry, however, we should not include occasional poems written either for political purposes or for the expression of personal feeling.

It may at first seem rash to assume that a poem must conduce to Charity in the sense that Scripture does, and to lay this principle down flatly is contrary to modern romantic notions of the poet; but medieval observations on the function of literature amply justify the principle. Poetry, as we have seen, was regarded as an adjunct to philosophy. As Bernard Silvestris puts it, "Sunt namque poetae ad philosophiam introductorii."[56] Philosophy, to the medieval mind, was not the academic exercise it has become today, but the study of and the love for Christian wisdom or *sapientia*. This wisdom could not be obtained without Charity. Thus Rabanus wrote:

> Quicunque igitur ad sapientiae culmen pervenit, ad fastigium charitatis perveniat necesse est, quia nemo perfecte sapit, nisi is qui recte diligit.[57]

Without Charity the ethics of the pagan philosophers were thought to be useless. Hugh of St. Victor says of pagan ethics:

Ethicam quoque scripserunt gentilium philosophi, in qua quasi membra quaedam virtutum de corpore bonitatis truncata pinxerunt; sed membra virtutum viva esse non possunt sine corpore charitatis Dei. Omnes virtutes unum corpus faciunt; cujus corporis caput charitas est. Nec possunt vivere membra corporis nisi sensificentur a capite.[58]

Since poetry is an adjunct of philosophy, therefore, it must also be an adjunct of Charity, which is the vivifying principle of philosophy. John of Salisbury, who was not an extremist, goes so far as to identify philosophy with Charity and to say further that any writings which do not conduce to Charity are but empty fables deserving the wrath of God:

Si enim secundum Platonem philosophus amator Dei est, quid aliud est philosophia nisi diuinitatis amor? . . . Qui uero philosophando caritatem adquirit aut dilatat, suum philosophantis assecutus est finem. Haec est itaque uera et immutabilis philosophantium regula ut sic in omnibus legendis aut discendis, agendis aut omittendis quisque uersetur ut proficiat caritati. . . . Quicquid aliorsum uergit in artibus siue quibuscumque scripturis, non philosophiae dogmata sed inanes fabulae sunt et figmenta eorum super quorum impietatem ira Dei de celo reuelatur [Rom. 1:18].[59]

This principle applies to pagan poetry as well as to Christian poetry, for it was the purpose of medieval interpretations of pagan poems to make them conform to Christian doctrine, at the center of which is, or was, the principle of Charity. We may conclude that to the medieval mind the *sententia* of any serious poem is a corollary of Charity, and that the word *sententia* in its literary use suggests Charity. It is true that the interpretation of a pagan poem leads to a *sententia* subsidiary to Charity, not to Charity itself; but the *sententia* of a Christian poem is always an aspect of Charity. When we recall that the complex theological developments of the Middle Ages are essentially elaborations of the New Law, we may well refrain from regarding this principle as a severe limitation on the aims of medieval literary art. To use a modern figure, the word *Charity* like the word *sea* is a little misleading. In both instances a single word stands for something of infinite and continuous elaboration and variation, for something which no human mind can grasp in its entirety. For Charity, like the sea, although fundamentally a constant, changes in its specific applications with time and person, with place and circumstance. It was the function of the medieval poet to keep this great civilizing concept alive and active for his own special audience, to prevent that audience from becoming a multitude of those who have ears and hear not.

That Chrétien de Troyes was generally familiar with these principles is evident in the prologue to the *Conte del Graal*. The prologue begins with a reference to the Parable of the Sowers. In this parable, which is interpreted in the Scriptures, the seed is said to be the *verbum regni*, the Word of God (Matthew 13:19). Chrétien associates his own romance with this seed:

> Crestiens seme et fet semance
> D'un romanz
>
> (7-8)

The implication is clear that the romance carries the message of Charity, which is the New Law, the Word of God. The poet is confident that this seed will fall on good ground, since it is written for Phillip of Alsace, a charitable man: *Que vero in terram bonam seminatus est, hic est qui audit verbum et intellegit.* The count is no hypocrite, but a man who lives in Charity,

> Charité, qui de sa bone oeuvre
> Pas ne se vante, einçois se cuevre
> Si que nus nel set se cil non:
> Qui Deus et charitez a non:
> Deus est charitez, et qui vit
> An charité, selonc l'escrit,
> Sainz Pols le dit et je le lui,
> Il maint an Deu, et Deus an lui.
>
> (43-50)

The seed which Christ sowed was presented *in parabolis*. In the same way, Chrétien presents the seed he wishes to sow in a "romanz," a story which must be interpreted if one wishes to find the *nucleus*. It will take root and grow only among those who not only hear but understand.

In a recent note, I suggested that the three elements of interpretation—*littera*, *sensus*, and *sententia*—are referred to in the prologue of the *Lais* of Marie de France. She employs the terms *lettre* and *sen* and a third term "surplus," which may, in this context, be a synonym for *sententia*.[60] It is possible that *sens* may be used in this way, rather than with its older meaning, in the prologue to the *Roman de la charrete*. There Chrétien says:

> Del chevalier de la charrete
> Comance Crestiens son livre;
> Matiere et san l'an done et livre
> La contesse, et il s'antremet
> De panser si que rien n'i met
> Fors sa painne et s'antancion.
>
> (24-29)

Cross and Nitze translate lines 26-29 as follows:

> Matter and meaning of it the Countess gives and delivers unto him;
> and he undertakes to direct his thinking so that he may add nothing
> to it except his own effort and understanding.[61]

Two words here may need reconsideration. In the first place, *san* may
indicate surface meaning, or, in this instance, the outline of the plot or
fable. The word *antancion* has always presented difficulties to those
who wish to make *san* mean *sententia* or its equivalent. The revised edition of the *Wörterbuch* glosses it "Anstrengung," but in other contexts
lists the more natural meanings "Zweck, Absicht, Meinung, Sinn."[62]
If *san* is taken to mean *sensus* with that word's usual twelfth century
implications, there is nothing discordant about the more usual meaning of *antancion*. With these changes, the passage might be rendered:

> The matter and the narrative (*sensus*) the Countess gives and delivers
> to him; and he undertakes to direct his thinking so that he may add
> nothing except his own effort and intention (*sententia*).

It is possible that the Countess was pleased by Chrétien's ability to
make "une mout bele conjointure" of unlikely materials. Certainly,
the story she proposed would make an excellent test of his skill. That
it was not considered impossible to obtain a message consistent with
Charity from a *cortex* having to do with adultery is attested by John of
Salisbury in a comment on the story of David and Uriah:

> Denique ad speciem facti quis Vria iustior? quis David nequior aut
> crudelior? quem decor Bersabee ad proditionem homicidium et
> adulterium inuitauit. Quae quidem omnia contrarium faciunt intel-
> lectum, cum Vrias diabolus, Dauid Christus, Bersabee peccatorum
> labe deformis ecclesia figuretur.[63]

There is not room for an interpretation of Chrétien's story here, and I
do not mean that such an interpretation should necessarily follow the
lines of John of Salisbury's exposition of the story just referred to; but
an interpretation which showed the "courtly love" in the *Roman* to be

merely a feature of the *cortex* would constitute an act of kindness to Chrétien and to his Lady, and it would also be much more consistent with medieval literary theory than the current one. As the matter now stands, among most critics, the poet is made out to be a heretic of a very peculiar kind, guilty of writing an empty fable which is indeed "porcorum cibus," and his Lady is accused of foisting upon him his rather silly heresy.

The language of the prologues here examined indicates that Chrétien was familiar with the poetic theory of his day. The poet was thought to be distinguished from the historian by the fact that he combined elements not found combined in nature (*conjunctura*). When this combination was made, there resulted a new configuration (*pictura*), preferably with a certain enjoyable perfection (*decor*). The poem might use one thing to indicate another (*allegoria*), or it might be obscure on the surface (*aenigma*). It had a lying surface meaning (*cortex*) covering an inner truth (*nucleus*). The surface meaning (*cortex* or *sensus*) might be interpreted to reveal a doctrinal truth (*sententia*) which was, in Christian poetry, always an aspect of Charity. If the poem were pagan in origin, one removed the *cortex* by applying grammar, rhetoric, and dialectic. If it were Christian, one needed to use the disciplines of the *quadrivium* as well, and tropological or allegorical levels of meaning might arise from the interpretation of the "things" mentioned in the poem. Among these terms, Chrétien uses equivalents for *conjunctura* and *decor* and quite probably also equivalents for *sensus* and *sententia*. The phrase "mout bele conjointure" in *Erec* is used in a context which strongly suggests the related terms *cortex* and *nucleus*, together with their usual associations; and the word *antancion* in the *Roman de la charrete* is a logical equivalent for *sententia* as opposed to *sensus*.

I append here a little glossary of the most important terms used in this discussion:

AENIGMA. An obscure statement, series of statements, or poem concealing an underlying truth, obscure allegory.

ALLEGORIA. The device of using one word or thing to mean another. In pagan literature *allegoria* is verbal; in Christian literature, it may be verbal, but it may also be based on the nature of things. SYN. *alieniloquium*.

CONJUNCTURA. The artificial combination of diverse elements characteristic of poems as distinguished from histories.

CORTEX. *Fig., usually pej.*, the outer covering of a poem which conveys its superficial meaning and appeal. SYN. *littera* 1, *pallium, tectorium, tegmen,* OF *paille,* ME *chaf.*

DECOR. The perfection or attractiveness of a poem, arising from a well made *conjunctura*.

INTEGUMENTUM. *Fig.*, a surface fable or history concealing a hidden truth. SYN., *involucrum*.

LITTERA. 1 the superficial meaning of a narrative. When opposed to *spiritus* the Old Law or heresy. SYN., *historia*. 2 In the schools of the twelfth century, the grammatical and syntactical construction of a text.

NUCLEUS. *Fig.*, the doctrinal truth in a poem, hidden in the *cortex*. SYN., *sensus* 1, *sententia*, OF *fruit, grains*, ME *fruyt*.

PICTURA. The attractive but lying configuration resulting from poetic *conjunctura*.

SENSUS. 1 the doctrinal content of a text. 2 In the schools of the twelfth century, the superficial meaning of a text. SYN., *cortex, historia, fabula*.

SENTENTIA. The doctrinal content of a text, its "theme" or "thesis"; the idea intended by the author. The *sententia* in Christian poetry is always an aspect of Charity. SYN., *nucleus, sensus* 1.

Some Observations on Method in Literary Studies

❧

This rather solemn performance was designed to promote interest in stylistic history. It seems to me that students are too often taught to be skeptical about the beliefs and ideals of the past without being taught also that current beliefs are equally contingent and transitory. This does not mean that verbal "truths," which always have a date and place, should not be respected when they have some operational validity, but that their contingent nature should be recognized, and their practical function (if any) in the society that produces them should be considered. If they are or were useful tools, they deserve the utmost respect. And this is true in spite of the fact that verbal formulations useful at some time in the past may no longer be useful.

❧

A WORK of literature, or, indeed, a work of architecture, a statue, or a painting is usually approached in either of two ways. It may be presented as a "work of art" embodying elements that appeal more or less spontaneously to the student. Its relevance may be explained on the basis of the insights of the teacher regarding form, structure, and techniques that are thought of as belonging to the province of all art. On the other hand, the student may be led to examine sources, traditions, historical information of relevance to the work in question, and other matters thought to have a subsidiary value in appreciating the work of art. Roughly, those who employ the first approach are called "critics" while those who employ the second are called "scholars." This difference has led to a great deal of debate.[1] To avoid the unpleasantness arising from controversy, and perhaps, with some sense of creating a kind of Hegelian "higher synthesis," many scholars now like to be thought of as "scholar-critics," and critics have in some instances made certain concessions to scholarship. Usually, the "scholar-critic" agrees with the critic that human nature is a constant and that there are qualities of art that may be said to have a universal appeal. The deliberate cultivation of exotic art, either as "primitive art," or as art from geographically remote places, during the early years of this century, together with an increasing interest in humanity for its own sake, regardless of its specific cultural traditions,[2] has given

Method in Literary Studies

a tremendous impetus to the study of all forms of human expression. Most recently, it has become fashionable to reduce works of art, literary or visual, to their elementary structures, regardless of content. These structures are felt to be somehow valuable in themselves, especially as "aesthetic" manifestations of a kind of universal human reality.

There is some evidence of a growing uneasiness with this posture. In the first place, an ingrained historical optimism has led many persons to assume that privileged men of the past "transcend" their time in such a way that they are able to "look forward" to ideas and attitudes we now think of as being more or less self-evident. The scholar has frequently adjusted his "history" in such a way as to make possible accolades of "great artists" in the past as prophets, and the critic has welcomed such interpretations as confirmation of universal human realities. Each new critical school has been quick to adopt all the more admirable artists of the past as worthy predecessors of its own views and attitudes. However, rapid changes in attitude since the early years of this century, in spite of the continuity of a certain substratum of opinion, make it clear that what was "self-evident" in 1920 is no longer "self-evident" today. Are the attitudes "self-evident" to Chaucer, Shakespeare, or Pope the attitudes of 1920 or those of 1968? It is clear that they cannot be both, and it is increasingly obvious that they cannot be either, and that, moreover, Chaucer, Shakespeare, and Pope did not share the same attitudes. Meanwhile, we have learned a great deal since 1920 about history, so that much of the historical reconstruction of the scholar-critics of a generation ago now seems naive and factually unacceptable. Not only that, but "aesthetic" ideas have changed as well, so that what appeared to be "universal art" in 1920 must now be made "universal" on quite other grounds, if, indeed, it is possible to formulate any such grounds at all.

Perhaps the first coherent solution to the problem was that advanced by historians of the visual arts, who have developed, chiefly under the guidance of Heinrich Wölfflin, a concept of "stylistic history."[3] The aims of stylistic history were at first rather modest: to study changing modes of apprehending the visual world. However, it was realized at the outset that these modes of vision imply "the bases of the whole world picture of a people," and it has become apparent that stylistic history does not lose its validity when the visual arts themselves abandon the "visual world" as it is ordinarily understood entirely. It became clear that what is "good" in terms of one artistic style is not necessarily "good" in terms of another, and, further, that each style representing the tastes of a given population at a given time has an appeal peculiar to certain specific attitudes and ideals, which are much more "basic" than the visual styles seem to be when we regard them in isolation from their cultural contexts. In so far as literary studies are concerned, various efforts have been made to demonstrate parallels between styles in the visual arts and styles in literature, but since the whole subject of stylistic history is still new, and since appropriate descriptions of specific stylistic periods are not always available, a great deal of work still needs to be done.[4]

A new impetus to sharper historical perspectives has arisen in two disciplines unrelated to art history. The fact that these disciplines seem at first unrelated to literary studies should not deter us from paying careful attention to their conclusions, since these conclusions will undoubtedly exert a profound effect on such studies in the future. In the first place, certain psychologists, who belong, roughly, to the "phenomenological school" in Europe, most notably Jan Hendrick van den Berg,[5] have developed a concept of "psychological history." Much of their work has a very sound basis in observation, and it is by no means necessary to be a disciple of Edmund Husserl in order to appreciate the value of some of their conclusions. Having observed that different social structures in the modern world profoundly affect the psychic constitutions of those who participate in them, these psychiatrists have reached the very plausible conclusion that historical changes in social structure produce marked alterations in "human nature." That is, "human nature" in one kind of social environment is likely to be very different from "human nature" in a second social environment differing significantly in structure from the first. This general conclusion has already influenced a number of historical studies.[6] Techniques for employing it vary among scholars, and the results have not always been convincing. Nevertheless, it is evident that the idea, here stated only in a very simple form, has enormous possibilities for development, and that its disciplined application will profoundly affect our attitudes toward the literature of the past.

Beginning with far different assumptions, largely derived from theories of "structural linguistics" first announced in Prague in 1928, anthropologists like Claude Lévi-Strauss and philosophers like Michel Foucault,[7] have sought to show that careful "synchronic" studies, or studies in depth of a given culture at a given time reveal adequate and reasonable "universes of discourse" suited to the structures of earlier or more primitive societies that should not be naively criticized from the point of view of our own, and, at the same time, that historical change is something far more complex than we had ordinarily assumed it to be. Again, the results of these studies may be appreciated even by those who do not share all of the assumptions upon which they are constructed. That is, the conclusions are not necessarily offensive to linguists trained in the school of the "Young Grammarians" who have learned to reverence scholars like Wilhelm Streitberg, Antoine Meillet, and Ernst Kieckers. The new studies have shown that a given idea or institution may play a far different rôle in one society than it does in one immediately preceding it or in one immediately following it in time. This fact becomes more apparent when a society is viewed as a "system," not, that is, as a rigorous artificial structure, but as an integrated whole in which the various "parts" are sufficiently interdependent so that a change in one implies concomitant changes in all the others. The metaphor "organic structure" has sometimes been used in this connection, but, although it may be revealing and helpful, it should be considered as a tool rather than as a descriptive epithet. Perhaps it is significant that these ideas are contemporary with "systems analysis" as it has been developed in other fields. In any event, the old attitude toward the "history of ideas" frequently oversimplifies or distorts the actual situation before us in the historical evidence, since it tends to neglect the shifting position of the ideas being studied within the social structure as a whole.

Disturbed by the usual naiveté of diachronic studies in this respect, Foucault has developed a concept of historical "archaeology." That is, he has set out to show, specifically on the basis of attitudes toward language and money, that a substratum of common assumptions underlies apparently divergent opinions set forth contemporaneously in a given society, and that this substratum undergoes radical shifts at certain periods in the course of history. Although the evidence adduced is sometimes rather fragmentary, especially in the treatment of the Renaissance, and Foucault is not always aware of the background of some of the ideas he adduces (like that, for example, of *convenientia*), the results are extremely impressive in a general way. He makes it obvious that "truths" concerning language and money in the nineteenth century are not the "truths" concerning these matters in earlier societies, and that we have no justification for projecting nineteenth-century "truths" about these matters on the Baroque or Renaissance past. Meanwhile, although he did not employ the evidence of stylistic history in any systematic way, the "periods," or chronological divisions of relative stability in the substratum of thought, that he proposes are roughly the same as those used by stylistic historians in the study of the visual arts. At the same time, with minor exceptions, they are generally consonant with conclusions we should expect from studies in "psychological history." That is, scholars interested in

stylistic changes, alterations in "human nature," and shifts in the substratum of thought are occupied with what are essentially similar
phenomena. In this connection, it is highly significant that similar
conclusions have been reached on the basis of very different kinds of
premises and working methods. It is obvious that, leaving aside all
quarrels about premises, definitions, and other features of what might
be called the tools of investigation, we shall, in the future, need to be
much more thorough in our synchronic studies of cultural structures
in the past. The integrity of past structures must be respected, and histories of isolated classes of phenomena must be written with a careful
eye to the shifting position of those phenomena within the structures
that produce them. Above all, it seems obvious that we shall need to
exhibit far greater reluctance than we have usually shown to impose
our own formulations about ideas and institutions on the structures of
the past as though they were universal truths.[8]

Perhaps the key to any helpful understanding of earlier cultural
structures is the realization that human formulations and institutions,
including our own, are contingent phenomena without any independent reality of their own. For example, language exists only in the presence of one human being addressing either another human being,
himself as though he were another human being, or an imaginary audience, including any inanimate objects to which he may choose to
speak. It has no reality beyond one of these situations, and it has no
"nature" independent of the nature imposed on it by the speaker and
his audience, real or imaginary. The sounds that are the vehicle for
language do not constitute its nature, since they have no significance as
language except by virtue of a common understanding between the
speaker and his audience, real or imaginary. If, as the psychological
historians insist, human nature undergoes changes, it is clear that language must undergo changes also, not only of the kind usually discussed under the heading "linguistic change," but also more profound
changes in its nature. Again, the nature of language in one society may
be quite different from its nature in another society. In connection
with this last consideration, Foucault seeks to show that Baroque language was essentially "representation," but that in the nineteenth century language became "expression." The only sane answer to the
question as to whether language *is* "representation" or *is* "expression"
must be that language was "representation" for speakers during the
Baroque period and was "expression" for speakers during the nineteenth century. To say that language *is* expression and has always been
expression, or, as more recent linguists are likely to say, language is "a
system that embodies a reproduction of reality" is to posit an inde-

pendent existence and nature for something merely contingent. It is also true that the assumption of any absolute stand on the nature of language will inevitably prevent us from understanding the language of the past as it survives in literary and other documents. This is not to say that formulations of the kind "Language is a system" are not useful. They may be very useful indeed so long as they are regarded as tools and not as absolutes. But in our studies of Chaucer, Shakespeare, or Pope (each of whom used a language appropriate to his time and place), we should constantly keep before us the fact that the language employed by any one one of them is not "the same thing" as the language we employ today. The tendency to read literary texts from the pre-nineteenth-century past as though the language in which they were written was essentially "expression" has given rise to enormous distortions in our criticism.

This caution concerning language should be extended to other ideas and institutions as well. For example, the Oxford neo-positivists have frequently adduced ideas from Hume, Kant, Hegel or other earlier philosophers as though those philosophers were writing today. This procedure simply fails to recognize the fact that a statement by Hume means quite a different thing taken in isolation today from what it meant in the context of the society to which Hume addressed himself. What is worse, the same neo-positivists have not infrequently subjected the terms used by earlier philosophers to semantic analysis in an effort to show that they are meaningless. It may be quite true that a term used by Hume or Kant has little meaning in the stylistic environment in which we move, but this does not imply that the term was meaningless at the time it was used. That is, a statement may be valid at one time and meaningless at another. Again, as I have sought to show elsewhere, the system of "principal vices" popular during the late Middle Ages may be largely irrelevant in the society of today, but it played a functional part in medieval society, where it had a genuine operational validity.[9] The same kind of considerations apply to more complex institutions like marriage. It is obvious that the institution of marriage plays an entirely different part in our society with its egalitarian ideals, where the sacramental value of the contract is usually merely formal and its function is largely personal, from that it played in an hierarchical society organized in small groups like that of the Middle Ages. Nevertheless, scholars have not hesitated to attribute "modern" attitudes toward marriage to Chaucer, who lived in a society where such attitudes would have been absurd.[10] The initial assumption that marriage is "the same thing" in the fourteenth century as it is today is, of course, erroneous.

Generally, the categories by means of which we analyze our own society may sometimes appear in earlier societies. When such coincidences occur, as they do in the examples cited above, we should be willing to recognize the fact that their significance in the past may be very different from their significance in the present, and, moreover, that their significance in the present will undoubtedly change in the future with changes in the structure of society and concomitant alterations in "human nature." That is, unless we take into account changes in the positions of institutions within the social structure in the course of time, our studies of subjects like "the history of marriage" are bound to be misleading. The common assumption that institutions, attitudes, and ideals display a "linear development" in the course of history has no justification in the evidence of history itself. And the further assumption that the present represents a kind of glorious fruition of linear developments amounts to nothing more than what might with some justice be called "historical anthropomorphism" inherited from romantic philosophers like Hegel.

In addition to preserving old categories, but in altered form, new societies construct new categories of their own. These new formulations are likely to appear in fairly large numbers at about the same time, and their appearance on a large scale is accompanied by "changes in style," or "changes in human nature," or, to put it in another way, "changes in the substratum of thought." Such changes occurred, for example, in the mid-twelfth century, in the fifteenth century, in the early seventeenth century, in the later eighteenth century, and at the beginning of the nineteenth century. It is possible, of course, and sometimes desirable to subdivide the "periods" thus established still further. Sometimes these periods coincide with periods of linguistic change as such change is described by historical linguists, although the significance of this coincidence has never been explored. The new categories developed during these periods of change are concomitant with changes in social structure and have little relevance to social structures preceding them. For example, the later eighteenth century developed a concept of "art" and "the artist" that has been continued and modified since. But neither the eighteenth-century concept nor its subsequent modifications have any relevance to earlier societies where "art" meant something entirely different and where the "artist" in the eighteenth-century sense did not exist. Thus for example, one student of the Gothic cathedral has seen fit to explain at some length that the cathedrals do not constitute what we call "art."[11] The same period witnessed the development of an idea of "personality," which was deepened and strengthened in the nineteenth and twentieth centuries, but this, too, was an idea suited to life within a new kind of social structure without relevance to life as it was lived in earlier centuries.[12] The usual assumption that "art" as we understand it, or "personality" has "always existed" even though people did not "talk about it" in earlier times makes an unwarranted universalization of purely contingent phenomena.

In general, new categories should not be imposed on the past. Freudian psychology, for example, represents a series of generalizations based on the effects of a kind of social structure that developed during the course of the later nineteenth century. The relevant social conditions together with certain concomitant attitudes toward sex did not exist in the eighteenth century, and are now rapidly disappearing. Hence efforts to analyze earlier cultural phenomena in Freudian terms inevitably lead to false conclusions. This is not to say that Freudian psychology is or was "wrong," but simply that its truths have a date and locale attached to them. To put this in another way, Freudian psychology is a part of a "universe of discourse" with a nexus of relationships to other elements in that "universe." To insert it into an earlier universe of discourse where no such nexus exists is to create absurdities. That is, Freudian "complexes" have about as much place in discussions of Shakespeare as have carburetors or semiconductors. It cannot be emphasized too urgently that any age in the past can be understood only when we analyze it in so far as is possible in its own terms. If we can begin to understand those terms in their own context, we can begin to understand the age, but if we impose our own terms on it, we might as well be studying ourselves rather than the past.

Changes in the structure of society and the nature of language frequently imply changes in very basic attitudes toward reality, toward the location of reality, and toward its relation to space and time.[13] Since the early nineteenth century, for example, there has been a very marked tendency to locate reality within the individual. Croce's "intuition," Ortega y Gasset's position that "Reality is my life," and Bishop Robinson's desire to locate God "in the depths of the personality," to cite only a few random examples, are all manifestations of a common "stylistic" or "archaeologically discernible" mode that is a more or less natural concomitant of a society in which the individual is isolated in a complex of large group structures. This mode, with its emphasis on inner reality, is at the same time conducive to expressionistic attitudes toward thought, language, and art, to subjective evaluations of space, and to a mistrust of the "past" and the "future."[14] But to impose various facets of this mode or its logically felt consequences on the past, as though it were generally characteristic of all humanity, is to invite serious misapprehensions concerning both ourselves and our ancestors.

In the course of the above discussion I have used "the past" simply as a convenient expression. Actually, we know very little about the past beyond the dubious evidence of our memories, which are always colored by the present. What we as students have before us instead of the past itself is a series of monuments, artifacts, and documents existing in the present, which are just as much a part of the present as are automobiles, neutrons, or cola beverages. The historian or the student of literature concerns himself with the order and significance of the detritus of the past in the present, not with the past itself, which is unapproachable. The works of Chaucer, or Shakespeare, or Milton exist today in libraries, in homes, or in the rooms of students. Why not treat them as though they were written within our own generation? The critic, or even the scholar-critic, often shows a marked inclination to do this, either by stating, in terms of some currently fashionable critical doctrine, that great art is universal, or by seeking to interpret the evidence of the past in such a way as to make it conform to the conventions of the present. If modern audiences cannot appreciate the music of Bach played in a Baroque manner on Baroque instruments, why not present symphonic arrangements of Bach that make Bach sound like Tchaikowsky?

There are a number of valid answers to this question, some of them quite simple. To begin with a simple one, it is fairly obvious that Tchaikowsky wrote much better music in his own style than Bach could, and that the efforts of an arranger of Bach are unlikely to equal the efforts of Tchaikowsky himself. If one wishes to listen to music in the style of Tchaikowksy, he would do much better to listen to Tchaikowsky's own compositions. The idea that Bach's music transformed for a modern symphony orchestra has a "cultural value" is, therefore, specious. Moreover, the unpleasant prospect looms that we shall some day hear Bach in the style of Webern, or the later Stravinsky, or even Stockhausen, as Bach keeps up with the times. Much the same criticisms may be made of Chaucer, or Shakespeare, or Milton transformed in the classroom into "modern" authors. They are less good at their newly imposed task than are modern authors themselves, and their "cultural" value becomes negligible. More seriously, the literary critic who customarily employs tools first created during the romantic movement now modified by Crocean aesthetics in its various modern forms, frequently commits historical blunders that are obvious to persons of no very great sophistication.[15] Crocean aesthetics is, actually, little more than a rationalization of the expressionistic style which seeks to turn all art into a lyrical expression of intuitively recognized inner truths. Although it is well suited to works produced in this style, it has no relevance to earlier styles consonant with social structures wherein the conditions necessary to produce expressionistic attitudes did not exist. If we are to compose valid criticism of works produced in earlier stylistic periods, we must do so in terms of conventions established at a time contemporary with the works themselves. If we fail to do so, we shall miss the integrity of the works we study, not to mention their significance, frequently profound, for their original audiences.

What we call the past is, in effect, a series of foreign countries inhabited by strangers whose manners, customs, tastes, and basic attitudes even partially understood widen our horizons and enrich our daily experience. Concealed self-study through the inadequate medium of the past only stultifies us within the narrow confines of our own naively envisioned perspectives. The specious and easy "relevance" achieved by positing "universal humanity" and then imposing our own prejudices on the past is not merely detrimental to understanding. It will soon become absurd in the light of a growing awareness of the complexity of historical processes. Finally, it is barely possible that the recognition of valid realities established by earlier generations may lead us at least one small step away from that rancid solipsistic pit into which the major tendencies of post-romantic thought have thrust us.[16]

Specifically, there are a number of ways in which literary studies might well be improved in the light of the above considerations. In the first place, the usual "diachronic" courses now offered in colleges and universities—courses in the history of the epic, the drama, the lyric, or other "genre" histories—should be recognized as being extremely artificial and misleading. The "lyric" is one thing in the thirteenth century and quite another in the nineteenth century. To present students with a "definition" of the lyric and then study its "history" from the thirteenth century to the present is to engage in a completely artificial exercise that has almost no educational value except that accidentally achieved by the presentation of occasional works that one student or another may, for a short time, enjoy. Similarly, to concoct a "definition" of tragedy, an exercise for which Aristotle offers an unfortunate precedent, and then to make all "tragedies"—Greek, Elizabethan, romantic, and modern—conform to the definition is not only to limit the understanding of the student but to distort the evidence of the past within a framework that has no intellectual respectability. If we are to make literary courses significant, genuinely stimulating, and indeed comparable in sophistication with courses now being offered by some historians of the visual arts, we shall need to emphasize "period" and "author" courses a great deal more, and to enrich these courses with more thorough and intellectually respectable considerations of relevant monuments from the visual arts, with descriptions of social institutions, and with efforts to evaluate the works being studied in a way that would have been comprehensible to their authors and their original audiences. The usual "genre" courses do not provide sufficient time for the development of an adequate background in the various styles encountered.

Diachronic studies of relatively brief periods in detail can be extremely helpful, since they reveal the gradual changes in attitude that culminate in more pronounced changes in style. However, such studies should not assume any kind of "progress" except that in time. As social institutions change there are concomitant changes in thought, language, and ideals, as well as changes in style. But these changes are better regarded as adaptations within a system than as illustrations of linear progress. Ideas and forms of expression appropriate to a later generation are not necessarily appropriate to an earlier generation, so that there are little grounds for thinking of them as "improvements." But such studies can show very clearly the interaction of various elements in a society that accompany changes in literary conventions. Studies of more extensive periods broken by major stylistic shifts, like the eighteenth century, for example, can serve to illustrate the kind of dramatic contrasts that may appear in the juxtaposition of two very different styles. Undergraduate "survey" courses afford a striking opportunity to present in a simplified fashion the integrity of various stylistic conventions and at the same time to clarify the essential peculiarities of the stylistic modes to which we are accustomed today. But in order to be effective, such courses need to concentrate on a few selected literary texts and to make far more use of the visual arts, music, and relevant historical sociology. Stylistic features are frequently more apparent in the visual arts than they are in literature, since it is always possible to read a text naively in terms of one's own stylistic attitudes.

All this implies, of course, a new professionalism in graduate training. Too frequently graduate students today are treated as though they were potential poets or novelists whose "sensibilities" need cultivating. There is undoubtedly a place for creative arts courses in a modern university, and certainly no one objects to cultivated sensibilities. However, if graduate schools in English are to be professionally effective, they must provide a more thorough grounding in period studies, with emphasis on primary sources in variety, and the cultivation of the kind of imagination that involves skepticism concerning accepted secondary formulations, the ability to see new relationships among primary materials, and the impulse to formulate relevant relationships between those materials and literary texts. The old system that required little more than the learning of a long series of secondary conclusions by rote, regardless of their value, is now long out of date, and its futility is obvious, even to the students themselves. It has led to academic conservatism of a most undesirable kind and to the unthinking repetition and transmission of outmoded generalizations on a large scale. Literary scholars must learn to welcome the prospect of new approaches and new ideas. At present no group of university men is more resistant to change or more antagonistic to new developments that do not serve to confirm attitudes previously learned than that made up of teachers of what are called the humanities.

The task of understanding a literary text from an earlier generation as it was initially presented is formidable. We cannot, on the basis of the evidence available reconstruct completely any period in the past, and our understanding will always be impeded to a certain extent by the conventions of our own times, which change continuously, but from which no one can escape entirely. But this fact should act as a stimulus rather than as a deterrent, since it means that there will always be something more to be done. The frontiers before us have no limit. And we may be consoled by the fact that the more accurately we can describe the detritus left to us by the past, the better able we shall be able to understand ourselves. And if the "humanities"—a nineteenth-century invention—can help us in this task, they will serve a useful and beneficial function in our society. Meanwhile, the realization that our own attitudes are, like those of the past, largely contingent may help to induce a certain equanimity and detachment. If literary studies are divorced from the larger concerns of cultural history they will eventually wither away.

The Allegorist and the Aesthetician

◦§

This essay was first delivered as a lecture to a group of teachers gathered at the University of York in England, where, it seemed to me, my references to childhood classics might be appreciated, as I am happy to say they were. Subsequently I discovered that many persons in American audiences were unfamiliar with them. I have decided, however, not to adorn them with footnotes, which would not actually help very much.

During my early years at Princeton I encountered very determined opposition from scholars with definite "Crocean" views, mostly adherents of the then fashionable "New Criticism." Today such attitudes are less systematic, but are still pronounced in certain circles. It seems to me salutary to consider some of their logical implications and to emphasize the basic difference between the idea of "art" that developed during the eighteenth century and the craftsmanship of earlier periods. It was once fashionable to ask whether medieval writers were "conscious artists." This question has no answer, since in the modern sense they were not artists at all.

◦§

THE two characters referred to in the title to this essay, "The Allegorist and the Aesthetician," have been placed in that somewhat uneasy juxtaposition for the very reason that they frequently engage in altercation. Their voices raised in unmannerly contention may be heard in academic halls, in the pages of learned journals, and even occasionally in those of critical reviews. The undoubted brilliance of the Aesthetician has won many allies for his cause, and has even enabled him to acquire positions of honor in our universities. In fact, it has become fashionable recently for a third character, the Conventional Scholar, grown somewhat bored with his conventional pursuits, to join forces with the Aesthetician, or even to claim that he is himself, by nature, an Aesthetician *par excellence*, and that, moreover, he already knows all there is to know about allegory. All this leaves the Allegorist in a rather lonely plight.

We shall hear from these characters in person later, but to put the matter simply and in non-allegorical language, my own interests have for a number of years centered on what medieval authorities call "allegory" in their discussions of medieval texts, and on what historians of art call "iconography," or the study of meaning, in the visual arts. At the outset, I had no intention of offending anyone. It simply seemed to me that in view of the extremely unsettled opinions regarding the meanings of medieval texts to be found in the writings of the Conventional Scholar, considerations of the kind I have mentioned might prove helpful. Like other human pursuits, the study of allegory and iconography is constantly subject to the enemies Error, Ignorance, and Stupidity; and I have not been able to avoid these enemies altogether. However, the reactions of both the Aesthetician and the Conventional Scholar to what I have said have been so violent, and at times so much more wrathful than anything required by the operations of the weaknesses above, to which they too are subject, that I feel that some answer to their attacks is appropriate. As a lonely Allegorist, I could quite properly retort, "You're another!" or words to that effect. But instead, I have decided to put on a new guise entirely. The retort suggested would only add fuel to the controversy and not resolve it. For the purposes of this paper, therefore, let me introduce a fourth character, the Stylistic Historian. It is in this august guise that I wish to address you here. Although my efforts in this direction have already provoked considerable animosity, I firmly believe that they offer the only suitable means of reconciling the Allegorist and the Aesthetician. Neither one is likely to regard the proposed solution with much sympathy at first, but I am determined to persevere, even though the result may be only a very lonely Stylistic Historian.

Let us begin with the Aesthetician. He has not been with us very long, but he has nevertheless made a very great impression, especially in academic circles, for which we must give him due credit. During the Middle Ages, he did not exist at all in his present form. When medieval authorities talk about the beautiful, and they are not simply talking about rhetoric: they seek to direct our attention to the realm of the intelligible, and they insist generally that the beauty of creation, whether natural or artificial, lies in a proportional order that is a reflection of the beauty of the Creator. On the infrequent occasions when they use a word related to the word *aesthetics*, they are obviously talking about mere sensory appeal. Thus John the Scot associates aesthetic sensitivity with effeminacy and sensuality, qualities that he regards with small patience, since they are unreasonable and misleading. It is not surprising, therefore, that the first modern discussion of aesthetics by Baumgarten, stemming from the mid-eighteenth century, should have continued more or less in the same vein, using the word *aesthetics* to refer to an inferior sensory knowledge.

The change in attitude toward aesthetics, deprecated, incidentally, in the New English Dictionary, is actually a product of the late nineteenth and early twentieth centuries. It is, moreover, largely the work of one man, Benedetto Croce, although its antecedents, in spite of Croce, are clearly visible in the critical utterances of the romantics. Croce's great contribution was to make aesthetics a separate and distinct discipline, with a proper realm of its own, and to suggest a series of principles capable of producing what seem to be more or less objective analyses. To remind ourselves of the basic nature of the Aesthetician, since it is not only Christians who sometimes forget the tenets of their faith—Allegorists and Aestheticians do the same thing—I should like to cite a few principles from Croce's lecture "What is Art," written for the inaugural ceremonies at Rice Institute (now Rice University) at Houston, Texas, in 1912.

In the first place, the Aesthetician set about creating a new reality. Physical facts, he said, "lack reality." But "art," he affirmed, "to which so many devote their whole lives and which fills everyone with heavenly joy, is *supremely real*."[1] I doubt that many contemporary academic aestheticians would go quite so far. They tend, like most of the faithful elsewhere, to cling to the physical world a little. Nevertheless, most of them are inclined to assert that art has a reality of its own. The view is, after all, common in romantic criticism, the traditions of which are still very strong. Croce goes on to tell us that "art considered in terms of its own nature has nothing to do with the *useful*, or with *pleasure* and *pain*, as such."[2] Again, we may find here an echo of Gautier, who told us long ago that beauty has nothing to do with utility. And again, the romantics insisted that the intense feelings in art might be either pleasurable or painful, so long as they were feelings, and intense. Feeling, indeed, is the basic reality to which Croce refers us. The agent that reduces feelings to art in the first place is something Croce calls "intuition," not a Bergsonian intuition fruitful in concepts, but an intuition that arises from feeling. Let us listen to Croce a moment:

> Intuition is truly such because it expresses an intense feeling, and can arise only when the latter is its source and basis. Not idea but intense feeling is what confers upon art the ethereal lightness of the symbol. Art is precisely a yearning kept within the bounds of representation. In art the yearning (for expression) is there solely for the

sake of representation, and representation solely for the sake of the yearning. Epic and lyric, or drama and lyric, are scholastic divisions of the indivisible. Art is always lyrical, or, if you like, the epic and drama of feeling.[3]

Aesthetics thus becomes a "science of expression," and the reality with which it is concerned is a reality based on feeling. It has, moreover, like Schlegel's romantic poetry, a "universal" character.

It is not difficult to see that this theory, in spite of Croce's attacks on romanticism, has clear romantic origins, and that it is essentially a rationalization for the style that has dominated a great deal of European thought, art, and politics since the mid-nineteenth century, the style usually called "Expressionism." One thinks immediately of Nietzsche and Wagner at the beginning of the expressionistic period, and of the variations on the same theme that have so far characterized twentieth-century thought. In the introduction to his little manual of *Twentieth-Century Painting* Hans L. C. Jaffé tells us that in the twentieth century painting "freed itself from all ties with religion, history, scholarship, and technical curiosity." Having lost, he says, "the security of religion, myths, and the hierarchic order," man is for the first time "confronted by reality." The artist, he continues, now views "the world in order to give an account of its reality content, its truth."[4] Needless to say, this bare reality has usually been found within the artist. Thus the variety of expressionism most popular between the two world wars, Surrealism, added the Subconscious Mind as a source of artistic material, a source that enabled the artist to think of himself as a kind of sacred magician, since he now had access to the innermost secrets of the psyche. To quote Wallace Fowlie, one of Surrealism's staunchest advocates,

> The artistic work might be compared to the "host" of sacramental Christianity which contains the "real presence." The poet then is the priest who causes the miracle by a magical use of words, by an incantation which he himself does not fully understand. And the work, thus brought into being, is a mystery which can be felt and experienced without necessarily being comprehended.[5]

My readers may recognize a certain affinity between this theory and the techniques displayed in one of the most celebrated poems of the twentieth century, T. S. Eliot's *Waste Land*.

Being a poet, however, Eliot does make use of myth, but in a magical way that supposedly taps certain reservoirs of the collective unconscious. If a myth of this kind is stripped of its surface features it be-

comes an archetype, and this in turn, like an electron, can be thought
of as an essential universal reality. Let us listen for a moment to one of
the greatest of our abstract painters, Mondrian:

> We desire a new aesthetic based on pure harmonies of pure lines
> and pure colors, since only pure harmonies among constructive
> elements can produce pure beauty. Today, not only is pure beauty
> necessary to us, but it is for us the only medium manifesting purely
> the universal force that is in all things. It is identical with that which
> is unveiled in the past under the name of Divinity, and it is indispen-
> sable to us, poor humans, so that we may live and find an equilib-
> rium; for things in themselves oppose themselves to us, and the
> matter most outside of ourselves makes war upon us.[6]

A great deal of abstract painting has been produced on the basis of
similar ideas, and one can well understand why certain painters wish
to use drugs to explore even more deeply that inner reality which is
presumably a key to universal truth. We should notice that in Mondrian the physical world, dismissed by Croce as being "unreal," has
become actively inimical.

Expressionism is, of course, not a style confined to literary and visual art. Croce's philosophy was, indeed, not simply an aesthetic, but
had a certain claim to being a general system. Our friend the Aesthetician has cousins among philosophers, psychologists, and even
theologians. For example, Bishop John A. T. Robinson recently made
quite a stir by re-locating God. He expressed dissatisfaction with St.
Paul for putting God "up there." Because the universe has changed
considerably since the days of St. Paul, most of us, Bishop Robinson
says, tend to locate God rather vaguely "out there." "Up and down"
make little sense astronomically, and the old "three-decker universe,"
as the Bishop calls it, where Heaven is "up," Hell is "down," and we
are "in between" has vanished. Bishop Robinson wishes to get God
out of the interstellar spaces altogether and to put Him "in the
depths," not in the depths of the earth, but in the depths of the personality. He tells us that "personality is of ultimate significance in the con-
stitution of the universe," and that "in personal relationships we touch
the final meaning of existence as nowhere else." What we are supposed to do in these relationships is, the Bishop assures us, taking a
sentence from St. Augustine out of context, love and do what we will.
I need not, perhaps, belabor the point that Bishop Robinson's God is
located in exactly the same place that Croce's or Mondrian's reality is
located, deep within ourselves, and that if this God is to be approached
in any way, we shall have to use something very like Croce's "intui-

tion" to get at Him. There is no indication that He will be conceptually fruitful. Meanwhile, we do not have to search far to find similar tendencies among thinkers of other kinds. Heidegger, for example, has sought very hard to "objectify" what is essentially subjective space, and the phenomenological psychologists, taking hints from Husserl, are daily uncovering more and more objective reality in realms heretofore considered to be purely subjective.

The Aesthetician thus has, like Rabbit, many friends and relations all pulling together. Together, they seem to have the world in hand, so that the poor Allegorist has small chance in it. Indeed, the Aesthetician rather easily brushed him off at the outset. "The insurmountable difficulties of allegory," said Croce, "are well known; so is its barren and anti-artistic character known and universally felt." He even takes away from it any real function in medieval art:

> Allegory met with much favor in the Middle Ages, with its mixture of Germanic and Romanic elements, barbarism and culture, bold fancy and subtle reflection. However, this was owing to a theoretical prejudice, and not to the actual reality of medieval art itself, which, wherever it is art, ejects allegorism from itself and resolves it from within.[7]

In other words, whenever medieval art is really art, it is not allegorical. Croce hastens to make a distinction between allegory and symbol, a distinction that appears in more familiar form in the pages of *The Allegory of Love* by C. S. Lewis:

> In symbol the idea is no longer thinkable by itself, separable from the symbolizing representation, nor is the latter representable by itself without the idea symbolized.[8]

That is, the idea and the material of the symbol fuse to form a new reality, irreducible to its components. As Lewis says, quite correctly, "the poetry of symbolism does not find its greatest expression in the Middle Ages at all, but rather in the time of the romantics; and this, again, is significant of the profound difference that separates it from allegory."[9] The symbol, then, is the product of the kind of intuitive magic of the feelings that produces what Croce described as the reality of art. Allegory, on the other hand, points to a conceptual realm that is alien to art.

At this point the meditations of the Stylistic Historian were interrupted by the Allegorist, who exclaimed,

"You *have* done it all with charms and incantations, and this, moreover, *is* a practical joke, and you have *not* made me very much run after!" He noticed, however, with some satisfaction, that neither one of his legs had grown any longer.

"*You* should talk about charms and incantations!" replied the Aesthetician. "If you had been more skilful with yours, I should not have had to make mine."

But the Stylistic Historian quickly and quietly calmed them, pointing out that it was now time to begin talking about the Allegorist, who, he hastened to add, was not really involved with Romanic and Germanic elements. Adjusting his mortar-board, and giving both the Aesthetician and the Allegorist a severe look, the Stylistic Historian resumed his discourse.

The Allegorist, unlike the Aesthetician, has been with us for a very long time. Indeed, he began talking about Homer as early as the sixth century B.C., and not without some justification. For it seems quite unlikely that either Homer or the members of his audience had any expectation of meeting characters like Pallas Athena in person wandering through the vineyards or among the goats on the hillsides. Nor is it likely that they had any nineteenth-century ideas about "myth." Claude Lévi-Strauss has recently suggested, or seems to have suggested, that even among primitive peoples what we call "myths" exist for very practical purposes. We should not expect the ancient Greeks to be any less practical. In the *Odyssey* it is obvious that careful attention to Pallas is desirable, and that this is what enables Odysseus to enjoy his success; but it is also obvious that devotion to Pallas implies the use of one's head to control both one's own passions and other men. The goddess serves to personify a kind of wisdom, which, in Homer, includes a certain wiliness; and devotion to her serves to protect men from something called the "wrath of Zeus." This rôle is even more pronounced, and considerably refined so as to remove the wiliness, when we come to the *Oresteia*, where Athena is able to transform the vengeful passions into instruments of civic tranquility. On the other hand, Athena is not a psychological attribute. Her wisdom is something outside of her worshipers that can be reflected in them only when they love her. The Greeks seem to have been deeply moved to create a world of conceptual realities thought of as existing outside of themselves, independent of them. Behavior was felt to be based on the manner in which one regarded those realities, rather than on the peculiar attributes of the personality. The Greeks, in fact, had no concept of personality. In Plato the realities become abstract, but there is a sense in which this means simply that they were divested of their human attributes and arranged in an abstract hierarchy of forms culminating in what Socrates, in the *Symposium*, calls "beauty absolute." Although

Plato seems to have felt that poetry is allegorical, he preferred the Naked Truth.

Plato's followers, however, were not quite so restrictive. As Jean Pepin has shown, there was considerable emphasis on allegorical interpretation, as well as on rhetoric, in classical education; and it is well known that the practice of allegorizing poetry reached a kind of climax in what might be called the Renaissance of the First Century B.C., when Platonists, Pythagoreans, and others set about interpreting Homer to support their own philosophical systems. Christianity, which substituted the Wisdom of Christ, *Sapientia Dei Patris*, for the wisdom of Pallas, born from the head of Zeus, brought with it a new realm of conceptual, and external, realities: the *invisibilia Dei*. At the same time, it introduced a new allegorical method. The *invisibilia Dei* were to be found, not in fabulous narratives, but in "the things that are made." This meant that not only the historical materials in the Old Testament were allegorical, looking forward to the New Testament, but that the created world itself could be turned into a vast allegory. Thus, in the twelfth century, Hugh of St. Victor can say that created things are "the voice of God speaking to man."

The nature and history of Scriptural exegesis during the Middle Ages need not concern us here. We have available at last a historian of the subject who understands it and regards it with some sympathy, Henri de Lubac. His monumental *Exégèse médiévale* (Paris, 1959-1964) is not only an indispensable guide to its special subject, but also an indispensable adjunct to the study of medieval culture generally. However, we might pause to consider a minor aspect of the subject briefly, its aesthetics, although this aesthetics is not a real aesthetics and will not have much interest for our friend the Aesthetician, who is concerned with a beauty that originates in feeling. The exegete, on the other hand, was concerned to discover a beauty outside himself, in the conceptual realm of the *invisibilia Dei*. It is true that if the exegete happened to be an Augustinian—and quite a few exegetes were—this beauty might indeed be found within; for the higher part of the reason was regarded as the *Imago Dei*, an image thought to exist in any man. However, it must be remembered that this inner illumination was a part of God, or at least a clear reflection of Him, and not a feature of the individual psychological make-up.

When St. Augustine himself talks about the attractiveness of the Scriptures, he does so in terms of their obscurity, as well as in terms of their rhetorical effectiveness. Perhaps the best statement of the principles involved appears in the second book of *On Christian Doctrine*. I shall quote the statement in full:

But many and varied obscurities and ambiguities deceive those who read casually, understanding one thing instead of another; indeed, in certain places they do not find anything to interpret erroneously, so obscurely are certain sayings covered with a most dense mist. I do not doubt that this situation was provided by God to conquer pride by work and to combat disdain in our minds, to which those things which are easily discovered seem frequently to become worthless. For example, it may be said that there are holy and perfect men with whose lives and customs as an exemplar the Church of Christ is able to destroy all sorts of superstitions in those who come to it and to incorporate them into itself, men of good faith, true servants of God, who, putting aside the burden of the world, come to the holy laver of baptism, and, ascending thence, conceive through the Holy Spirit and produce the fruit of a twofold love of God and their neighbor. But why is it, I ask, that if anyone says this, he delights his hearers less than if he had said the same thing in expounding that place in the Canticle of Canticles where it is said of the Church, as she is being praised as a beautiful woman, "Thy teeth are as flocks of sheep, that are shorn, which come up from the washing, all with twins, and there is none barren among them"? Does one learn anything else besides that which he learns when he hears the same thought expressed in plain words, without this similitude? Nevertheless, in a strange way, I contemplate the saints more pleasantly when I envisage them as the teeth of the Church cutting off men from their errors and transferring them to her body after their hardness has been softened as if by being bitten and chewed. I recognize them most pleasantly as shorn sheep having put aside the burdens of the world like so much fleece, and as ascending from the washing, which is baptism, all to create twins, which are the two precepts of love, and I see no one of them sterile of this holy fruit.[10] (2.6.7)

Now from the point of view of the Aesthetician all of this sounds very curious indeed. There seems to be nothing emotional about the process at all. The picture of a beautiful lady biting and chewing men who suddenly become sheep being dipped and bearing lambs is neither "terrible"—a favorite Aesthetician's word—nor sublime. Why did St. Augustine like it? He himself says,

But why it seems sweeter to me than if no such similitude were offered in the divine books, since the thing perceived is the same, is difficult to say and is a problem for another discussion. For the present, however, no one doubts that things are perceived more readily through similitudes and that what is sought with difficulty is discovered with more pleasure. (2.6.8)

In other words, we are tempted to say, St. Augustine liked to solve puzzles. But there is a great deal more to it than that. To solve a puzzle does give one a sense of achievement, but once the puzzle is solved we are left empty-handed. On the other hand, at the conclusion of his puzzle-solving St. Augustine had a cherished principle, a conceptual reality. As he tells us in one of his letters, those things that are stated figuratively, or allegorically, in the Scriptures move the mind from the terrestrial things used to make up the enigmatic statements to invisible things, and this motion, from a lower realm to a higher, inflames the mind with love for the invisible things so discovered. The solving of the puzzle thus leaves one not empty-handed, but moved toward the solution one has discovered by love.

We are accustomed in modern times to love our feelings, and, on occasion, the feelings of others, whose manifestations assure us that they are, like ourselves, human. But during antiquity and throughout the whole course of the Middle Ages men of all kinds loved ideas, not ideas regarded as being products of individual human cogitation, but ideas regarded as having a reality of their own, a reality stemming ultimately from God. This is, after all, the lesson of that favorite medieval book, *The Consolation of Philosophy* of Boethius, which inspired King Alfred, John of Salisbury, Dante, Chaucer, and even Queen Elizabeth I. When Jean de Meun, the author of a much maligned continuation of the *Roman de la rose*, sought to sum this book up in the preface to his French translation, he explained that sensible goods, or good things that appeal to the senses, attract man first. But since he is human, and a reasoning creature, his true good lies in the realm of the intelligible. *The Consolation of Philosophy*, he assured his royal patron, Philip the Fair of France, is the best among all books ever written to teach men to despise the false goods of Fortune, or goods available to the senses, and to seek instead true and immutable goods that will lead to happiness. This is indeed a fair summary of the *Consolation*, in spite of anything said about it in more recent times. It is a fable, not a piece of confessional autobiography, whose figurative devices as well as its explicit statements are designed to lead exactly to the end Jean de Meun described. To understand this is to understand also why Petrarch thought Horace to be a better teacher than Aristotle. Aristotle tells us very well what a virtue is, but Horace can lead us to love it.

In view of this attitude toward the nature of reality and its location, it is not surprising that medieval authorities insist from very early times down to the days of Boccaccio and Salutati that poetry is allegorical. What they mean by this is simply that poetry says one thing and means another. Poetry still does this. When Burns wrote "My love is like a red, red rose," he did not mean that the lass in question had petals like a flower. The difference lies in the kind of "other meaning" intended. During the Middle Ages, the "other meaning" is usually conceptual, whereas in modern times it usually belongs to the realm of feeling.

This fact is apparent in some remarks on poetry by that distinguished scholar Richard de Bury, whose influence, spread by his circle of friends, permeates much English thought during the second half of the fourteenth century. He is addressing lovers of Naked Truth like Plato or St. Bernard:

> All the various missiles by means of which those who love only the naked Truth attack the poets are to be warded off with a double shield, either by pointing out that in their obscene material a pleasing style of speech may be learned, or that where the material is feigned but a virtuous doctrine is implied, a natural or historical truth is enclosed beneath the figurative eloquence of fiction.
>
> Although almost all men by nature desire to know, not all of them are equally delighted by the process of learning; indeed, when the labor of study is tasted, and the fatigue of the senses is perceived, many throw away the nut unadvisedly before the shell is removed and the kernel obtained. For a double love is inborn in man, that is, a love of liberty in his own guidance, and a certain pleasure in work. For this reason no one subjects himself to the rule of others or willingly pursues a labor that involves any effort. For pleasure perfects work, just as beauty perfects youth, as Aristotle most truly asserts in the tenth book of the *Ethics*. Concerning this matter the prudence of the Ancients devised a remedy by means of which the wanton will of man might be captured as if by a certain pious fraud, when they hid away Minerva in secret beneath the lascivious mask of pleasure. We are accustomed to lure children with rewards so that they will wish to learn those things to which we force them, though unwilling, to apply themselves. For corrupted nature does not migrate toward virtues with the same impetus with which it supinely thrusts itself toward vices. Horace tells us about this in a little verse, when he is speaking of the art of poetry, saying,
> > Poets wish either to teach or to delight.
> He implies the same thing in another verse of the same book more openly, writing,
> > He hits the mark who mingles the useful and the sweet.[11]

The mask of pleasure that hides Minerva, or wisdom, is exactly the same thing that Petrarch described as the "poetic veil." If a man does not admire the beauties of Naked Truth, she can be usefully clothed in attractive garments. When the labor of removing these, revealing her charms one by one, is presented to the reader, he can be led to embrace her with more avidity.

The reaction to modern poetry is direct and spontaneous, but the labor of unveiling Truth might, in the Middle Ages, be considerable. Thus Boccaccio says that poetry makes "truths which would otherwise cheapen by exposure the object of strong intellectual effort and various interpretation, that in ultimate discovery they shall be more precious." This, he says, quoting St. Augustine, is the method of the Scriptures. If we wish to understand poetry, he says, we must "put off the old mind, and put on the new and noble," implying that only those who put off the Old Man with his fleshly lusts and put on the New Man as St. Paul admonishes will be able to understand it properly. The lessons of poetry are thus regarded as adjuncts to what John of Salisbury called "true philosophy," or the love of Christ. The intellectual effort involved in discovering these lessons may be very great indeed: "You must read, you must persevere, you must sit up nights, you must inquire, and exert the utmost power of your mind. If one way does not lead to the desired meaning, take another; if obstacles arise, then still another; until if your strength holds out, you will find that clear which at first looked dark. For we are forbidden by divine command to give that which is holy to dogs, or to cast pearls before swine."[12]

At this point the Conventional Scholar interrupted.

"It is just this sort of nonsense that has upset all my labors in the past. The Allegorist here has even been at *Beowulf*, which everyone knows is simply a convenient collection of three folktales about monsters, and at *Piers the Plowman*, which has nothing to do with that old business of 'four levels' I disposed of long ago, and now he is casting his eye on Chaucer, whom everyone recognizes as being a supreme realist. Just read my books!"

"Bah for books!" retorted the Allegorist. "All you do is repeat the same old platitudes originally cooked up in the nineteenth century, never looking again at primary sources or paying any attention to what we have learned about the few primary sources you once used long ago! With the aid of the Aesthetician here, you polish up the old ideas for the younger generation, decorating them with myths, archetypes, and other ghosts and fancies, borrowed, once they have become slightly stale and outmoded, from the pseudo-sciences."

The Aesthetician, who had not heard the remarks of Boccaccio because he was asleep, woke up upon hearing his name, yawned, and said ponderously, quoting the author of a mildly allegorical tale, "I had rather see the portrait of a dog I know than all the allegories you can show me."

"Tut, gentlemen," said the Stylistic Historian. "I have not quite finished, and since I have not much time left, you had both better listen carefully." He then resumed as follows.

What I have been discussing is actually a change in style, a change that has taken place in the course of the centuries both in the nature of reality and in its location. This change implies many concomitant changes in the arts, in philosophy, in political theory, and in thought and action generally. It is consistent with changes in the structure of the human community, and, as psychological historians like J. H. van den Berg have shown us, it implies changes in what we think of as "human nature." I shall have time for only a few brief points.

Perhaps the general idea may be made clear if we return for a moment to Bishop Robinson. I have no quarrel with his theology, which is good Expressionistic doctrine, but he should not have criticized St. Paul. The "up," "down," and "in between" of St. Paul and his successors have reference to an ideal hierarchy of conceptual realities, and nothing whatsoever to do with anything that may be seen through a telescope. Bishop Robinson has simply been rather naively literal-minded about this, although it is true that St. Paul was referring literally to conceptual realities. Again, the "personality" in which the good Bishop wishes to locate God is a modern invention. It was not until the latter eighteenth century that the word *personality* came to mean the sum of the peculiar traits of an individual, and "personality" did not acquire such things as "force" and "depth" until much later. No one in antiquity or the Middle Ages, or even in the Baroque period, either had a personality in this sense or accused anyone else of having one; and we should not look for personalities either in the artists of these periods or in the characters they portray in their works. The rise of the concept of personality is a part of the general shift of reality from a position outside of ourselves to a position within ourselves. When reality became firmly entrenched within, during the romantic period, it could be either a realm of ideas, as it is among German romantics and modern positivists, or a realm of feeling, as it is among aestheticians and some philosophers. This inner reality logically implies solipsism, whether it is a matter of ideas, of feelings, or of indistinguishable "reactions." But Rabbit and his friends and relations are uneasy solipsists desperately seeking a way out of the solipsistic bur-

rows to which they have retreated to find contacts with others, or proclaiming in disillusionment that the others, if they are really there, are
all enemies.

Hence the prevalence of the theme of loneliness in modern art. Wallace Fowlie has described the situation very vividly:

> The experience of solitude probably explains more about modern
> literature and art than any other single experience. . . . In his sol-
> itude, which is his inheritance, the modern artist has had to learn
> that the universe which he is going to write or paint is in himself.
> He has learned that this universe which he carries about in himself is
> singularly personal and unique as well as universal. To find in one-
> self what is original and at the same time what can be translated into
> universal terms and transmitted, became the anxiety and the occu-
> pation of the modern artist. The romantics held this belief partially
> and intuitively. The surrealists made it into a creed and a method.[13]

We may add that the existentialists have carried the creed even further.
The melancholy solitude of Rousseau, the lonely dreamer, has spread
and deepened with the years. Wordsworth wanders "lonely as a
cloud," Coleridge's Mariner is "all, all alone"; lonely figures in vast
seascapes or on monstrous barren mountains fill the canvases of the
romantic painters; and today characters in existentialist films are lost
in long, empty corridors with doors leading nowhere, or ascending
interminable spiral staircases. We are alone in a lonely crowd, lodged
on a minuscule planet fixed precariously in an arm of a whirling spiral
of countless stars. If reality is to be found in human terms, it must be
found within. It is not surprising that one of the most discerning of
our philosophers, Ortega y Gasset, should have said, "Reality is my
life."

As the locus of the real changed, the locus of the beautiful changed
with it. The beautiful is that which is desirable and worthy of worship.
Today, we worship ourselves, proclaiming a kind of humanistic piety,
and regard art as the free expression of the personality; during the
Middle Ages, art had nothing to do with personality. This difference
has led some scholars to say simply that medieval art is not art at all.
Thus, writing of the cathedral builders, Jean Gimpel, who admired
medieval cathedrals very much, wrote, "the word 'artist' is deliberately not used here, since it adds nothing to the greatness of the
cathedral builders and because its current meaning is essentially
foreign to the spirit of the Middle Ages."[14] The word *artist*, in a modern sense, he adds, first appears in the Dictionary of the French
Academy in 1762. The date is significant, for the traditions of ancient
and medieval art ended with the downfall of the Rococo style. The

delightful little allegory of Sylphs and Gnomes in Pope's *Rape of the Lock*, an allegory that Dr. Johnson and most of his successors failed to understand, is one of the last manifestations of the true allegorical manner in English.

Just a word in reply to the Conventional Scholar about "realism." It is obvious that the nature of "realism" depends on what one considers to be "real." But the term *realism* as an artistic criterion is a product of the mid-nineteenth century. The great romantic painter Delacroix, whose works look much more "realistic" than anything produced during the Middle Ages, said that he thought realism to be "the antipodes of art." But he nevertheless lived to see the first great realistic painting, Courbet's *The Artist's Studio*. The characters on either side of the artist in the painting, some of them very unsavory, and some of them making up a kind of Vanity Fair, represent types of the society that the artist, disillusioned by the middle-class triumph of the French Revolution, wished to criticize. They seem unaware of two figures immediately behind the artist, a child and a nude woman, who represent Innocence and Truth. Courbet's naked Truth, however, is not the Naked Truth represented in the famous statue by Bernini, an inviting wench who sits with her left foot on the globe of the world and a medallion of Apollo in her right hand. This is the same truth as that described by Richard de Bury, but Bernini has tried, quite successfully in his Italian Baroque manner, to make her look attractive without much of a poetic veil. Courbet's Truth is a sentimental Truth suggesting unsullied Nature, pure Womanhood, and the Eternal Feminine, regarded mystically. Meanwhile, the realistic figures in the remainder of the picture are true types, realities that we can recognize on the surface in the streets and drawing-rooms of his time.

Chaucer's portraits, on the other hand, are not "types" at all. The Friar, for example, as he appears in the General Prologue to *The Canterbury Tales* is not a "typical" friar. He is instead an exemplar of the weaknesses and vices commonly attributed to friars in the late fourteenth century. This or that friar on the streets of London might have one or two of them, but a great many friars had none of them. It is true that Chaucer's little portrait, which is essentially a collection of attributes, has considerable verisimilitude on the outside, just as the other collections of attributes we call "characters" in the General Prologue display a similar verisimilitude. But the verisimilitude simply serves to give the underlying concepts a local habitation and a name. The reality of these portraits is a conceptual reality, the reality of the virtues and vices depicted in them. In the fourteenth century, when people lived together in small tightly knit groups, this kind of reality was very practical indeed, the immediate and daily concern of everyone in Chaucer's audience. Perhaps I need not add that the friar and his companions do not have "personalities."

With the shift in the position of reality, time has changed also. Just as Heidegger's space, which, for all its technicality, reflects rather common attitudes, is different from the space of Gothic art, so also are there differences that have come with the years in human attitudes toward time. During the Middle Ages the cycles of time on earth were regarded as reflections of eternity, an idea that we can see implied, for example, in the Labors of the Months or the Signs of the Zodiac as they appear on the great cathedrals. This conception gave to the span of time confronting any man during his life a firm reality that he could contemplate with equanimity. Hence the popularity of the pilgrimage in life, in art, and in literature. Everyone had an opportunity to "stand upon the ways," as Chaucer's Parson advises, and to choose in leisurely fashion the best way for his journey. The flux of events approaching from the future could be read slowly and carefully; and the present, that imaginary point glimpsed fleetingly between the future and the past, rested firmly on a solid and stable foundation. An artist, a poet, or an architect had no need to present a configuration to his audience that could be gulped down in a moment. He could adorn his Truth with figures and icons to be contemplated at leisure.

As the years passed, however, and the Truth of eternity became more indistinct as men busily immersed themselves more and more in what Boethius called the realm of Fortune, the time line began to break down into segments. At first these are segments given meaning by sentiment. In Sterne's *Tristram Shandy*, or even in Fielding's *Tom Jones*, where the framework of the sequential pilgrimage is preserved, the authors concentrate on moments of sentiment and feeling. The old taste for the patient unraveling of a fruitful puzzle disappeared, and men found themselves moved instead by sentimental tableaux. The romantics shortened these segments of time even further so as to produce art in which the feelings and sensations of the eighteenth century gave way to deep emotions, emotions to be transformed by the Victorians into crises of sentimentality. Today, sentimentality has been refined still further to become intensity. We have little patience with time, but seek desperately in our art to plunge into the depths of the moment as though we had no confidence at all either in the past or in the future except as they may be used as adjuncts to our precipitous descent. Hence the instantaneous appeal of abstract art. The depths of the moment are also the depths of the personality. The symbol, the frozen archetype of Truth, has replaced the ancient Lady adorned with puzzling attributes.

"Sir," said the Stylistic Historian to the Allegorist, "henceforth I hope that you will confine yourself to areas usually referred to as Classical, Medieval, Renaissance, Baroque, and Rococo, leaving what has happened since strictly alone. Those ages may be somewhat musty, but they suit your disposition. And as for you," he continued, addressing the Aesthetician, "you have no business in those areas at all. If you tried to make a robe for Naked Truth, in whom you most emphatically do not believe, with those symbols of yours, which are truths themselves, you would only confuse matters horribly. And if you treat the old icons and attributes as symbols, you will simply be talking nonsense. Therefore, I urge you most seriously to keep to your own time."

At this point the Stylistic Historian turned abruptly away, saying, "I am the Stylistic Historian who walks by himself, and all places are alike to me." The tassel on his mortar-board waved disconcertingly from side to side as he strode toward the trees.

The Allegorist, the Aesthetician, and the Conventional Scholar, each remembering himself to be a Proper Man, promptly took off their shoes and threw them after him. Then the Scholar and the Aesthetician walked off arm in arm down the road, intent on a learned discussion of Freudian aspects of courtly love in Chaucer's *Troilus and Criseyde*. The Scholar was seen to reach into his pocket and take out a small object which he handed to the Aesthetician. The latter polished it a little with his magical puce-colored handkerchief and gave it back. It seemed to the Allegorist as he sat watching them depart that the object was a chestnut.

"Well," said the Allegorist to himself as he sat alone, looking owlish, on an old stump covered with fading ivy, "I am really getting too old for all that intense feeling advocated by the Aesthetician anyhow. Moreover, I cannot bring myself to believe in his magic, except, that is, when I have had a few drinks and am feeling most sentimental. And moreover, that expressionism of his has entered politics. I know that Croce did not like Mussolini, but the Duce's intuitive reactions and vigorous emotional expressions inducing intuitive responses in his followers put him firmly in Croce's camp. Much the same can be said for Hitler and Stalin, and even for the more benevolent Roosevelt. In any event, I have had enough of it, and of the later existentialists, who are among Rabbit's more dubious relations, and of all other varieties of moment-plunging as well."

With that, he reached for his copy of the *Glossa Ordinaria*, nodded for a few minutes over the long double columns of Latin in small print, and then, with the book open before him, fell asleep.

II

Certain Theological Conventions in Mannyng's Treatment of the Commandments

❧

I no longer believe in a "Marriage Group" in The Canterbury Tales, *in spite of Robert E. Kaske's spirited defense of the idea in* Chaucer the Love Poet *(Athens, Ga., 1973), pp. 45-65. Meanwhile, the persistence of basic doctrine during the Middle Ages is well illustrated in* Handlyng Synne, *of which, incidentally, a much needed new edition is now in preparation. The work is an excellent introduction to late medieval pastoral theology in England. Although Furnivall wrote in the Preface to his Roxburghe Club edition that Mannyng's "narrative power and versification" make him "the worthiest forerunner of Chaucer," he has been largely neglected by literary scholars.*

❧

THE section of *Handlyng Synne* dealing with the Ten Commandments frequently reflects commonplace patterns of medieval theology. It is the purpose of this article to call attention to certain of these patterns. No attempt is made to present a history of any given convention; I wish merely to show that the conventions existed. Their recognition, I believe, contributes materially to an understanding and appreciation of the text. For the purposes of this paper, matters pertaining to pastoral rather than doctrinal theology are deliberately disregarded.

Under the First Commandment, Mannyng included, in addition to the obvious sin of forsaking God, much material on witchcraft, superstition, and dreams. Indeed, most of his discussion is devoted to these matters. They had long been associated with the commandment when Mannyng wrote, so that he could not very well have omitted them. St. Augustine, for example, had been not only very explicit but peculiarly emphatic about this matter:

> Dicit tibi, *Unus est Deus tuus, unum Deum cole.* Tu vis dimisso uno Deo tanquam legitimo viro animae, fornicari per multa daemonia: et quod est gravius, non quasi aperte deserens et repudians, sicut apostatæ faciunt; sed tanquam manens in domo viri tui admittis adulteros: id est, tanquam christianus non dimittis Ecclesiam, con-

sulis mathematicos, aut aruspices, aut augures, aut maleficos; quasi
de viri domo non recedens, adultera anima, et manens in ejus con-
jugio fornicaris.[1]

In the thirteenth century, there were various ways of interpreting the
commandment. William Peraldus, author of the famous *Summa de
vitiis*, spoke of three ways in which one might violate it:

> *Tripliciter* autem facit quis contra Primum Mandatum. . . . *Primo*
> ille qui magis allii quam Deo, ut qui vetulis sortilegis magis credit
> quam ministro dei. . . . *Secundo* facit contra hoc praeceptum, qui plus
> confidit in creatura quam in creatore. . . . *Item* contra hoc praecep-
> tum faciunt qui plus amant aliquid terrenum, divitias vel delitias
> quam Deum.[2]

A similar threefold division, somewhat closer to the general pattern of
exposition in *Handlyng Synne*, appears in the *De decem praeceptis* of St.
Bonaventura:

> Dico igitur, quod in primo verbo: *Non habebis deos alienos coram
> me*, prohibentur omnes profanae *pactiones daemonum*, sive fiant per
> incantationes verborum, sive per inscriptiones characterum vel
> imaginum, sive per immolationes sacrificiorum. In istis tribus con-
> sistunt omnes partes artis magicae. . . . In secundo verbo: *Non facies
> sculptile*, prohibentur omnes falsae et superstitiosae *adinventiones er-
> rorum*. Et notandum hic, quod omnis error nihil aliud est nisi fictio
> mentis. Errorem autem facit phantasia obnubilans rationem et fa-
> ciens videri esse quod non est. . . . In tertio verbo: *Neque facies
> similitudinem eorum quae in caelis sunt* etc., prohibentur omnes perver-
> sae *appretiationes mundialium naturarum*.[3]

Some of the details of Mannyng's discussion may have been devised to
reflect local practices, but the general subject matter of magic, superstition, and *fictio mentis* was a part of traditional theology.

At the beginning of his discussion of the Second Commandment,
Mannyng makes a distinction between lying, which is sinful, and unwittingly transmitting an untruth, which is not sinful:

> Y aske 'wheþyr ys grettyr eye,
> A lesyng, or a fals tale seye.'
> Here mayst þou lerne a queyntyse,
> To knowe of boþe þe ryȝt asyse;—
> Þou mayst here and beleue a fals
> Þat is seyd of a-noþer als,
> And telle hyt forþ þe same wyse,

Ryght as he vn-to þe seyse,
And ȝyf þou wene þat þat sawe ys ryȝt
Þouȝt hyt be fals, þou hast no plyȝt;
For, þyn ynwyt, þe shal saue,
Þou wenyst to seye weyl, no plyȝt to haue.
    A lesyng haþ weyl wers wey:
Þe tokyn of a leysyng y shal þe sey.
whan ys a lesyng, but þan ys hyt
whan hyt ys seyd aȝens ynwyt;
Soþely to sey, a lesyng ys
whan þou wost þat þou seyst mys.
                              (617-634)[4]

The form of this passage obviously reflects a scholastic *quaestio*, but
the distinction itself is at least as old as St. Augustine, who was the
fountainhead of much medieval theology. He wrote:

Quid autem intersit inter falli et mentiri, breviter dico. Fallitur qui
putat verum esse quod dicit, et quia verum putat, ideo dicit. Hoc
autem quod dicit qui fallitur, si verum esset, non falleretur: si non
solum verum esset, sed etiam verum esse sciret, non mentiretur. Fallitur ergo, quia falsum est, et verum putat; dicit autem nonnisi quia
verum putat. Error est in humana infirmitate, sed non est in con-
scientiae sanitate. Quisquis autem falsum putat esse et pro vero as-
serit, ipse mentitur.[5]

Mannyng goes on to discuss false swearing and oaths, topics which
we should naturally expect to find under the Second Commandment,
but there is one passage which has nothing to do with these things:

Ȝyf þou trowest þat god was nat byfore
Or he was of þe maydyn bore;
Or ȝyf þou trowyst þat he was noght
Before or þe worlde was wroght;
Ȝyf þou wene þat verement,
Hyt ys aȝens þys comaundement.
God was euer wyþ outyn bygynnyng
Ar þe worlde, or man, or ouþer þyng.
    Ȝyf þou trowyst þat hys manhede
Haþ no powere with þe godhede,
Repente þe, þou art yn synne,
For ydylnes hast þou hys name ynne;
    Ȝyf þou trowest þat he may naght
Yn heuene and erþe hys wyl haue wroȝt,

þe manhede þat toke flesshe & bone,
Þat with þe godhede ys al one;—
But þou repente þe byfore þy fyn,
Þou mayst be lore, seyþ seynt Austyn.
(647-664)

Again, "seynt Austyn" furnishes the key to the matter:

Dicitur tibi, *Ne accipias in vanum nomen Dei tui.* Ne existimes
creaturam esse Christum, quia pro te suscepit creaturam; et tu con-
temnis eum qui aequalis est Patri, et unum cum Patre.[6]

Although this interpretation of the commandment may seem strange
to the modern reader, it was once quite common among theologians.
Thus Rabanus Maurus wrote:

Secundum praeceptum pertinet ad Filium, dum dicit: "Non as-
sumes. . . ." Id est, ne aestimes creaturam esse Filium Dei, quoniam
omnis creatura vanitati subjecta est, sed credas eum aequalem esse
Patri. . . .[7]

Almost the same words were employed by one of the earliest scholas-
tics, Anselm of Laon:

Secundum preceptum ad Filium [pertinet], quod tale est: Ne as-
sumas. . . . id est, ne credas Filium dei tantum esse hominem, quod
nomen dei in uanum assumere est.[8]

Hugh of St. Victor distinguished between the "literal" and the "mystic" or allegorical interpretations of the commandment:

Hoc [Exod. 20] ad simplicem litterae sensum taliter intelligi debet, ut nomen Dei homo in vanum non assumat, id est, vel ad mendacium confirmandum, vel ad idolum venerandum, scilicet, ut
neque idola nomine divino honoret, neque falsitati nomen Dei as-
societ. Mystice autem nomen Dei in vanum assumere, est Filium
Dei visibilem per humanitatem factum creaturam existimare. In
vanum quippe nomen Dei assumit, qui Filium Dei aeternum ex
tempore coepisse credit.[9]

The same distinction between the two interpretations appears in the
Sentences of Peter Lombard.[10] It is clear, then, that the passage just
quoted from *Handlyng Synne* is not a digression but an essential element in the theological interpretation of the commandment.

Under the Fifth Commandment, Mannyng discusses various kinds
of homicide. First, there are ways of actually bringing about death:

murder, imprisonment, mutilation. Then it is said that failure to feed the poor constitutes spiritual slaughter. False indicters, those whose counsel or command brings about death, and false judges are said to be murderers. Those who turn others from righteousness, detractors, and evil speakers are also guilty of homicide. What Mannyng says about detractors is especially interesting. The backbiter kills three persons at once:

> Bakbyter, þurgh ryght resun,
> Of þre mennys deþ ys enchesun.
> Þou wost weyl, with-outyn les,
> þe bakbyter fyrst hym self sles;
> He slekþ hym þat trowyþ hys lesyng,
> whan he forþ beryþ hys bakbytyng;
> And hym algate þat hyt ys on leyde,
> He ys slayn.
>
> (1523-1530)

That this was a popular theological cliché is attested by its appearance in a medieval *florilegium*, where it is attributed to St. Bernard:

> Lingua detractoris gladius triceps qui uno ictu tres animas inter-
> ficit, primo eum qui detrahit, secundo de quo detrahit, tertio eum
> qui libenter detractorem audit.[11]

But to return to the general content of this section of *Handlyng Synne*, it may be said that the materials employed by Mannyng fall readily into the conventional threefold division of the commandment. It was held that homicide may be committed in three ways: "*manu, lingua, consensu.*" In *Handlyng Synne* the order of the last two is transposed, but it is not difficult to see that these rubrics control the details. For a statement of the theological principle, we may again turn to Anselm of Laon:

> Manu fit, cum quis alium actualiter uita priuat, uel in locum mor-
> tis, ubi uita priuetur, precipitat, ut in carcerem, uel in alium quem-
> libet locum talem. Lingua fit duobis modis, id est, precipiendo uel
> suggerendo. . . . Consensu similiter duobus modis fit homicidium,
> uel dum mortem alterius desideramus et cupimus, uel dum eum a
> morte liberare possumus, uitam eius negligimus, id est, adiutorium
> non impendimus.[12]

The Sixth Commandment was customarily given a very general interpretation. For example, Peter Lombard wrote:

Tertium[13] est: *non moechaberis*, id est, ne cuilibet miscearis, excepto foedere matrimonii.[14]

That Mannyng's treatment of this matter is not full of rather shocking details is due to his expressed purpose to avoid *"priuites"* characteristic of some penitential works.[15] But in spite of this restriction, the very general character of the current theological interpretation allowed Mannyng, or the author of his source, considerable freedom in the choice of materials. The discussion opens with a problem which was later to receive much attention from Chaucer:

> God made womman man to gyue,
> To be hys helpe yn hys lyue;
> he made here nat, man to greue,
> No to be mayster, but felaw leue,
> No nat ouer logh, no nat ouer hy,
> But euene felaw, to be hym by;
> And he, mayster, lorde, & syre;
> To hys wyl she shal meke hyre.
>
> (1611-1618)

A certain ambiguity is evident in the passage: woman was made not too low, not too high, but equal; at the same time, her husband should always be "master, lord, and sire." Perhaps the contradiction is more apparent than real; in any case, I do not pretend to be able to solve it. It is easy to show, however, that both attitudes, if there are two attitudes, were theologically quite sound. The equality of woman, perhaps merely social, was thought to be evident in the procedure followed in her creation. As Peter Lombard tells us,

> cum vir dicit: ego accipio te in meam, non dominam, non ancillam, sed coniugem. Quia enim non ancilla, vel domina datur, ideo nec de *summo* nec de *imo* a principio formata est, sed de *latere* viri ob coniugalem societatem. Si de *summo* fieret, ut de capite, videretur ad dominationem creata; si vero de *imo*, ut de pedibus, videretur ad servitutem subiicienda; sed quia nec in dominam nec in ancillam assumitur, facta est de *medio*, id est de latere, quia ad coniugalem societatem assumitur.[16]

In the thirteenth century, we find similar reasoning in Robert de Sorbon's treatise on marriage:

> Dixit enim Dominus in Genesi, II . . . *simile sibi*; quod est relativum aequiparantiae. In quo notatur quod mulier debet esse aequalis viro suo, sive socia, non sub viro, non supra virum. . . .

Item, mulier facta fuit de costa viri, non de inferiori parte vel de superiori, sed de media, ut per hoc significaretur quod mulier debet esse aequalis viro suo.[17]

In spite of these manifestations of what some may regard as an enlightened attitude, there was no circumventing the Biblical text (Ephesians 5:22-24):

Mulieres viris suis subditae sint, sicut Domino: quoniam vir caput est mulieris: sicut Christus caput est Ecclesiae: ipse, salvator corporis eius. Sed sicut Ecclesia subiecta est Christo, ita et mulieres viris suis in omnibus.

It was not difficult, therefore, for Ivo of Chartres to assemble an imposing list of authorities to show that woman should be subject to man.[18] Indeed, Peter Lombard was able to make man and wife equal only in one respect. Although Mannyng does not comment on this exception to the general rule, it was to be transformed by his great successor as a teller of tales, Geoffrey Chaucer, into the very substantial figure of the Wife of Bath:

. . . cum in omnibus aliis vir *praesit* mulieri, ut caput corpori, est enim *vir caput mulieris*; in solvendo tamen carnis debito *pares sunt*.[19]

Perhaps the apparent ambiguity we have just observed had much to do with the appearance of a "marriage group" in the *Canterbury Tales*.

In this same section, after enumerating certain sins connected with troth, Mannyng calls attention to the example of Joseph and Mary, which, he says, shows that first troths are binding:

> Þe ferst womman þat þou ches
> Ys þy wyfe, with-oute les.
> Ensample haue we þerby,
> Of Iosep þat wedyd oure lady;
> Þere was verry matrymony,
> withþoute fleshly dede of any.
> By þys ensample mayst þou se
> þat þe fyrst womman þy wyfe shulde be.
> (1655-1662)

The reasoning in this passage is not very clear, but there is a fuller statement of the same argument by Isidore of Seville which illuminates Mannyng's text considerably:

Coniuges appellati propter iugum, quod inponitur matrimonio coniungendis. Iugo enim nubentes subici solent, propter futuram concordiam, ne separentur. Coniuges autem verius apellantur a

prima desponsationis fide, quamvis adhuc inter eos ignoretur
coniugalis concubitus; sicut Maria Ioseph coniux vocatur, inter quos
nec fuerat nec futura erat carnis ulla commixtio.[20]

Mannyng apparently ranks himself here among the followers of Lombard, who, opposing Gratian and his adherents, regarded consummation as unnecessary to *matrimonium ratum*.[21] The whole matter had violent repercussions in pastoral theology.

In his discussion of the Seventh Commandment, Mannyng includes, as one would expect, various kinds of theft, kidnaping,
churchbreaking, rape, unjust rents, usury, and so on. The topics developed fall under one or another of the three sins conventionally as-
signed to this commandment, and this threefold division was undoubtedly responsible for the variety of the details used. As Peter
Lombard put it:

> *Non furtum facies*; ubi *sacrilegium* et *rapina* omnis prohibetur. . . .
> Hic etiam *usura* prohibetur, quae sub rapina continetur.[22]

The sin of sacrilege is only touched upon in this part of *Handlyng
Synne*, probably because an entire section is devoted to it later; but various manifestations of the other two sins are elaborated.

Traces of a conventional theological division may also be seen in
Mannyng's treatment of the Eighth Commandment, which was said
to involve two major sins:

> Quintum[23] praeceptum est: *Non loqueris contra proximum tuum fal-
> sum testimonium;* ubi crimen *mendacii* et *periurii* prohibetur.[24]

The section of *Handlyng Synne* on the subject is devoted to manifestations of these two sins. It opens with a conventional definition of lying:

> who-so with hys mouþe, one, seys,
> And with hys herte þenkeþ ouþer weys,—
>   (2639-2640)

Again, the standard theological textbook of the time furnishes the
convention:

> Hoc enim malum est proprium mentientis, aliud habere clausum in
> pectore, aliud promptum in lingua.[25]

Mannyng goes on to enumerate various types of lies, warning his
readers repeatedly that lies involving "delyte" are especially deadly.[26]
That this warning was not a personal whim we learn from St.

Bonaventura, who tells us that certain venial lies may become mortal *"per libidinem magnam."*[27]

Among the various kinds of evil swearing described in *Handlyng Synne*, some are easily recognizable commonplaces, but one is especially interesting because of its specific character:

> ʒyt þer ys anoþer sweryng
> where-þurgh comþ ofte grete cumbryng,
> Þe whyche ys, an oþe oute of mesure,
> Þat he shulde haue a mysauenture
> On wyfe, and on chylde, to falle,
> And on hys ouþer godys alle,
> But he holde at hys myght
> hys oþe þat he swereþ to alle ryght.
> Swyche an oþe ys grete doute to swere,
> For chaunce comþ on many manere.
> Þou settest þy chylde to myche rewþe
> But þou holde þyn oþe to trewþe.
>
> (2765-2776)

At first glance, one might take this for one of the "reflections of daily life" so frequently seen by students of Mannyng's work. It may be, but it is something more besides; for Peter Lombard wrote, quoting St. Augustine:

> "Est etiam quoddam genus iuramenti gravissimum, quod fit per *exsecrationem*, ut cum homo dicit: si illud feci, illud patiar, vel illud contingat filiis meis." Secundum quem modum accipitur etiam interdum, cum aliquis iurando dicit: per salutem meam, vel per filios meos, et huiusmodi. Obligat enim haec Deo. Unde Augustinus: "Cum quis ait: per salutem meam, salutem suam Deo obligat. Cum dicit: per filios meos, oppignerat eos Deo, ut hoc eveniat in caput eorum, quod exit de ore ipsius: si verum, verum; si falsum, falsum. Et sicut per hoc iurans aliquando hoc Deo obligat, ita per Deum iurans ipsum adhibet testem."[28]

The passage in *Handlyng Synne* thus reflects a very old and very well known theological principle.

In general, further study of *Handlyng Synne* may reveal that it contains much less that is original than has commonly been supposed. If the selection and organization of its materials sometimes reflect conventional patterns of doctrinal theology, we may reasonably suppose that at other times—and perhaps more frequently, since the book is addressed to layman—the selection, organization, and even the details themselves, may reflect conventions of pastoral theology.[29]

Frequency of Preaching in Thirteenth Century England

Although the conclusions of this article have been widely accepted, the older view of G. G. Coulton and his followers still sometimes appears, as it does, for example, in Dorothy Owen's generally useful study, Church and Society in Medieval Lincolnshire *(Lincoln, England 1971).* Roger Weseham's Instituta, *mentioned here, is an early statement of Franciscan efforts to reach the minds and hearts of ordinary people that eventually resulted in Franciscan use of lyrics and even dramatic passages in their sermons, as well as* exempla. *See David L. Jeffrey,* The Early English Lyric and Franciscan Sprituality *(Lincoln, Neb., 1975), and his article, "Franciscan Spirituality and the Rise of Early English Drama,"* Mosaic, 8 (1975), 17-46. *For a general account of Franciscan literature and its ideals, see John V. Fleming,* An Introduction to the Franciscan Literature of the Middle Ages *(Chicago, 1977). Pecham's requirement that priests seek assistance in hearing confessions reflects an attitude that by the fourteenth century resulted in regular efforts on the part of some bishops to send out "penitentiaries," not all of whom were friars, for this purpose. See R. M. Haines,* The Administration of the Diocese of Worcester in the First Half of the Fourteenth Century *(London, 1965), 174-177.*

STATEMENTS to the effect that "a sermon was a rare event" in thirteenth-century England, indeed so rare that a typical parishioner heard one fewer than "the statutory four times a year" have become common in recent books about the Middle Ages.[1] It can be shown that such statements are unwarranted by the evidence at present available. The prevailing attitude is curious on the face of it when one considers the fact that across the channel, in France, the early thirteenth century witnessed a veritable renaissance of popular preaching, and that priests there, except in unusual circumstances, are thought to have delivered sermons regularly on Sundays and Holy Days, and in one diocese at least, on every single day of the year.[2] It is possible, of course, to dismiss this situation by alleging the cultural superiority of France, but I do not believe that this factor is sufficient to account for any such discrepancy.

Before considering the evidence which bears directly on the problem, it is necessary to formulate some conception of the nature and function of the conventional mediaeval sermon. In the first place, it was not ordinarily expected that the average parish priest should compose his own sermons. As early as the fifth century, Bishop Cyril of Alexandria wrote a series of homilies to be memorized and used by the Greek bishops. The practice of using official collections was approved by St. Augustine, fostered officially by Charlemagne, and encouraged by a long series of bishops in the Western church.[3] Thus in the late twelfth century, Maurice de Sully, Bishop of Paris, issued for the priests in his diocese a series of sermons which enjoyed wide popularity, not only in France, but in other countries as well, including England.[4] At the time he wrote, it was an established principle of canon law that every priest should have, among other books, *"omelie per circulum anni dominicis diebus et singulis festiuitatibus apte."*[5] In a typical thirteenth-century parish, therefore, we should expect, without direct evidence to the contrary, that the priest had for his use a collection of homilies for Sundays and Holy Days. These would be either sermons of the Fathers or more recent collections issued by enterprising bishops like Maurice de Sully. No special training in the art of preaching was necessary to adapt these sermons in the vulgar tongue for regular delivery. In England, there is some evidence, nevertheless, that prospective priests learned to use them in schools.[6]

It is sometimes said that ignorance of the Bible prevented regular preaching, but this notion rests on a mistaken conception of the function of the ordinary sermon. Except on special occasions, sermons were preached during the course of the Mass, usually following the reading of the Gospel. The essential function of the sermon *de tempore* was to explain the lesson for the day,[7] which had just been read, or to draw some conclusion from it, not to expatiate on random selections from Scripture. When additional Scriptural authority was needed, priests in the thirteenth century had available long collections of Scriptural quotations, arranged under subjects and sometimes cross-indexed, like that of John Pecham.[8] The *sermones festivales*, devoted to the saints, varied with local usage, but should not have required any extensive Biblical knowledge. And these two types made up "le domaine ordinaire de la chaire."[9] It is important to observe that this program of sermons based on the Gospel, Epistle, or on the characteristics of the saints, did not allow for extensive exposition of special subjects, such as the Commandments, the Creed, the Lord's Prayer, the *Ave*, the sins, or the sacraments. Series of sermons based on such subjects appear in thirteenth-century French collections, but are unusual: "elles ne convenaient pas plutôt dans une situation que dans l'autre."[10] It was, then, quite possible for a preacher to prepare vernacular sermons for all the Sundays and Holy Days without either a Bible or an extensive knowledge of theology. Moreover, we must be careful to avoid the conclusion that these facts point to sermons of poor quality, for the sermons of ordinary parishes were probably in many instances sermons of the Fathers, or sermons composed or collected by a prominent bishop.

We may admit, therefore, that the average parish priest had no Bible, knew little or no theology, and had no training in the art of preaching; but at the same time we may assume that he had the means at his disposal to deliver a respectable sermon on every Sunday and Holy Day of the year. What I wish to show in this paper is that there is nothing inconsistent with the hypothesis that he actually did deliver these sermons in the English episcopal decrees usually adduced to prove that he did not. Such a demonstration, if successful, will not prove that the sermons were actually delivered, but it will show that there is no particular reason for saying that they were not delivered.

It is difficult to evaluate developments in thirteenth-century ecclesiastical institutions in England without reference to the Fourth Lateran Council of 1215. The tenth canon of this council stressed the importance of sermons and stipulated that bishops should appoint suitable men to assist them in preaching and hearing confessions.[11] The first English decree of the thirteenth century concerning preaching was issued by Richard le Poore, who not only attended the Lateran Council, but was extremely influential in disseminating its decrees in England.[12] There is nothing in the decree to indicate the frequency with which sermons were preached in Richard's diocese; it demands merely that the priests explain a certain specified subject in the course of their sermons:

> Cum per ministerium nostrum ecclesiastica sacramenta debeant tractari et dispensari,[13] necessarium est vobis, filii carissimi, fidei catholicae agnitio et professio, quia 'sine fide impossible est Deo placere,' et 'sicut corpus sine spiritu mortuum est, ita fides sine operibus mortua est.' Propterea vobis praecipimus, quod bene vivendo fidem rectam teneatis, parochianos vestros in articulus fidei, sine qua non est salus, saepius instruentes; quod, ut melius et expeditius fiat a vobis, districte injungimus archidiaconis, quod in

capitulis suis expositionem catholicae fidei *in Generali Concilio pro-mulgatam*,[14] sane et simplicibus verbis sacerdotibus exponant: et sacerdotes, prout Deus eis inspirauerit, parochianos suos instruant, et eis illam expositionem frequenter domestico idiomate[15] sane inculcent.[16]

Although this decree has been cited as evidence of the "low standards of education among the clergy,"[17] perhaps because *"articulis fidei"* was taken to mean the Apostle's Creed, the words *"in Generali Concilio promulgatam"* indicate clearly that what Bishop Poore wanted explained in his dioceses was the profession of faith at the opening of the Fourth Lateran Council. In the Salisbury constitutions, the text of the first decree of the Lateran Council is quoted in full immediately after the above passage,[18] but in the reissue at Durham, which I quote below, only the beginning is given, evidently with the assumption that the archdeacons were familiar with the Lateran text:

> Firmiter credimus et simpliciter confitemur, quod unus est solus Deus verus, omnipotens, aeternus, immensus, immutabilis, incomprehensibilis, et ineffabilis; Pater, et Filius, et Spiritus Sanctus; tres quidem personae, sed una essentia, substantia, seu natura, simplex omnino, *prout in capitulo concilii continetur.*[19]

Far from indicating either ignorance or the infrequency of sermons, this decree asks the priests to add a new and important formulation of the faith to their regular course of teaching, whatever that may have been. It is significant that Innocent's words reached the parishes of an English diocese as quickly as they did.

One other feature of Bishop Poore's statutes deserves comment here. They contain a lengthy explanation of the seven sacraments.[20] This fact should not be taken as an indication that the priests in Salisbury were ignorant because they did not know the sacraments; there were no "seven sacraments" anywhere before *ca.* 1145.[21] The system of seven sacraments was popularized on the scholastic level by Peter Lombard in the *Sentences*, and did not reach the pastoral level until after the Fourth Lateran Council, which decreed as follows:

> Cum sit ars artium regimen animarum, districte praecipimus, ut episcopi promovendos in sacerdotes diligenter instruant et informent, vel per se ipsos, vel per alios viros idoneos, super divinis officiis, et ecclesiasticis sacramentis, qualiter ea rite valeant celebrare. . . .[22]

So far as I have been able to discover, Bishop Poore's decrees represent the very first recorded attempt to bring that system to the level of the ordinary parish priest.[23] It was not firmly established in the schools until after St. Thomas Aquinas had endorsed it.[24] When we find a thirteenth-century bishop instructing his priests to teach the seven sacraments, therefore, we should realize that he was promulgating a relatively new doctrine, not something that any parish priest might be expected to know. Specifically, when Bishop Simon of Exeter, or his successor William Brewer, demanded, sometime before 1237, that his priests teach the sacraments and the *formam symbolorum Lateran' concilii*,[25] he was asking for materials which the priests could not possibly find in their *omelie per circulum anni*. The old sermons *de tempore* and *de sanctis* were being supplemented with newer sermons designed to carry out the reforms instituted by Innocent III.

Before 1224 and 1237, Bishop Alexander Stavensby of Coventry, who had once been regent of theology at Toulouse,[26] issued a set of constitutions containing three parts: some decrees, a treatise on the vices, and a treatise on penance.[27] At the beginning of the treatise on the sins there is a statement which indicates that it was to be used for purposes of instruction in the vulgar tongue:

> Dicatur omnibus sacerdotibus, quando parochiani sui congregati sunt in ecclesia in dominicis diebus, vel in aliis festis; quod dicant haec verba, quae sequuntur. . . .[28]

What follows is by no means a simple enumeration of sins suitable for a primer, but a relatively sophisticated treatise, complete with scholastic definitions and "authorities." Again, it is obvious that this is not the sort of thing one would find arranged systematically in the homilies of the Fathers. It is true that the general principle underlying the seven criminal vices is as old as Gregory the Great,[29] but it was not until the twelfth century that a clear and consistent distinction was made between major sins and principal vices, or tendencies of the soul from which sins originate.[30] During the second half of the twelfth century, this distinction, together with its theological elaboration, became an integral part of the comprehensive system of theology worked out by Peter Lombard and his followers. Bishop Alexander, himself a theologian of some reputation, was attempting by means of his two treatises to bring certain fundamental elements of that system, still relatively new and not yet crystallized, to the level of the ordinary priest and his parishioners. There is no reason for interpreting his action to mean either that the priests in Coventry were woefully ignorant or that they did not customarily preach sermons.

Perhaps the most important decree concerning preaching issued in the thirteenth century appears in the constitutions of Walter de Cantilupe, Bishop of Worcester (1240).[31] It runs:

> Sciantque sacerdotes ea, quae exiguntur ad verae confessionis poenitentiae sacramentum. Et quia observatio decalogi necessaria est fidelibus ad salutem: exhortamur in Domino sacerdotes, et pastores animarum, ut sciant decalogum, id est, decem mandata legis Mosaicae, quae populo suo, sibi subjecto, frequenter praedicent, et exponant. Sciant quoque, quae sunt septem criminalia peccata, quae populo praedicent fugienda. Sciant etiam saltem simpliciter vii. ecclesiastica sacramenta, quae sunt. Habeat etiam saltem quilibet eorum fidei simplicem intellectum, secundum quod continetur in psalmo, qui dicitur "Quicunque vult," et tam in majori, quam in minori symbolo; ut in his plebem sibi commissam noverint informare.[32]

Here the priests are urged to know the sacraments and to preach concerning the ten commandments, the seven sins, and the elements of the faith as contained in the creeds. The expression *"frequenter praedicent"* should not be overlooked. Moreover, it should be observed that this is a demand for specified subjects, not necessarily with the implication that the priests were not carrying out their duty to explain the Gospel of the Mass and to discuss the virtues of the Saints. In order to understand the significance of the subjects demanded, however, it is necessary to know what purpose Bishop Walter had in mind when he formulated the decree. He wrote, immediately after the words quoted above:

> Ut autem sciant sacerdotes, quorum aliqui sunt simplices, pro quibus delictis superioribus sunt poenitentiae reservandae; ut sciant etiam parochianos suos instruere, quomodo debeant confiteri, necnon et eorum conscientias perscrutari, injunctionum etiam diversitates, quia non sanat oculum, quod sanat calcaneum, quendam tractatum de confessione fecimus, quem sciri ab omnibus capellanis praecipimus, et etiam observari in confessionibus audiendis, quia longum esset, ipsum in praesenti synodo publicare.[33]

It is significant that these materials, including the sacraments, are described as *"delictis"* and that they were to be presented to the people for the special purpose of teaching them *"quomodo debeant confiteri, necnon et eorum conscientias perscrutari."* It will be remembered that the Lateran Council had required bishops to find suitable men to assist them in hearing confessions as well as in preaching; Innocent III also stipulated that every one of the adult faithful should confess to his priest at least once a year on pain of minor excommunication.[34] Perhaps Bishop Walter's interest in confession had been further stimulated by the success of the Friars as confessors, for, as his contemporary, Bishop Grosseteste, put it, they were setting a good example for the parish clergy in both preaching and confessing.[35] At any rate, it is clear that Walter de Cantilupe desired his priests to present a systematic analysis of sinful conduct under the rubrics of the commandments, the sins, perhaps the sacraments, and the elements of the faith, so that their parishioners might more readily examine their consciences preparatory to confession. No such systematic analysis would have been available in the collections of homilies the priests were supposed to have, so that once more we need not conclude that the subjects demanded by the decree were the only subjects employed in sermons. In fact, in its intent to educate the laity as well as the clergy for confession, the decree goes a step beyond the Fourth Lateran Council;[36] it should be regarded, not as a "reform" but as an essentially progressive measure.

The importance of Walter de Cantilupe's decree is attested by its reappearance, with some variations, in the statutes of other bishops throughout the century.[37] Statutes based on it, directly or indirectly, were issued by Grosseteste (1240),[38] in some Norwich statutes of 1240-1243,[39] in some Ely statutes of 1241-1268,[40] by Walter de Kirkham of Durham (1258-1260),[41] by John Gervais of Winchester (1262-1265),[42] and by Peter Quivil of Exeter (1287).[43] The variant by John Gervais makes it clear that the priests were not only to know the sacraments but to explain them.[44] The Exeter version is the longest and most elaborate, and like Walter de Cantilupe, Bishop Quivil wrote a treatise to accompany it:

> Ut autem quilibet sacerdos, cui animarum cura incumbit, melius sciat et intelligat, qualiter debeat in ipsa versari; praecipimus, quod quilibet, cui parochialis ecclesiae regimen incumbit, quandam summulam plurimum utilem, immo verius necessarium a diversis tractatibus extractam sub compendio (quae summula sub eisdem verbis incipit, quibus et praesens synodus) citra festum Sti. Michaelis habeat scriptam, et ipsam sane intelligat, ac ea utatur sub poena unius marcae, loci archidiacono applicandae. Quam si archidiaconus remiserit, et ipsam, vel ipsius partem quandam levari poterit, et recipere praetermiserit, eundem archidiaconum in duabus marcis fabricae ecclesiae Exoniensi volumus obligari.[45]

The prologue to the *Summula*, which follows the constitutions, develops, in the style of a sophisticated academic sermon, the theme *Al-*

tissimus de terra creavit medicinam (Ecclesiasticus 38:4) to form, with a concordance of authorities,[46] the conclusion that sin is a malady, the Trinity a physician, and penance a medicine. It then continues:

> Haec ergo ego Petrus, Exoniensis presbyter, intime considerans, et insufficientia presbyterorum secularium confessiones audientium compatiens, quorum ignorantiam, proh dolor! saepissime sim expertus; praesentem summulam eisdem assigno, ut eam sciant ad utilitatem suam et confitentium.[47]

This is sufficient to indicate that what we have before us is not an exposition of "the rudiments of the Christian faith,"[48] but a treatise on confession.

In order to appreciate the contents of the *Summula*, it is necessary to know something of the history of penance.[49] After the adoption of secret confession by Theodore of Tarsus in the seventh century, penitentials, which had been developed as a type in the Celtic church, came into widespread use. These works were essentially lists of questions concerning specific sins which the priests followed as guides in the interrogation of penitents. In the twelfth century, when penance became a sacrament, the theology of confession underwent rapid expansion and refinement, so that it became possible, at the beginning of the thirteenth century, to abandon the penitentials and to substitute for them general principles by means of which a confessor could estimate the gravity of any sin confessed to him. The technique employed involved first a classification of the sins confessed under a standard rubric. Next the confessor considered the circumstances of the sin, frequently using for the purpose a principle originated by Hermagoras of Temnos and popularized in Ciceronian rhetoric.[50] On the basis of the circumstances, it was possible to estimate the degree of consent involved in the sin and hence its gravity.[51] Thus, the twenty-first canon of the Fourth Lateran Council stipulated, not that every priest should have a penitential, but that he should inquire concerning circumstances.[52] The bishops were confronted with an enormous task—to teach their parish priests, most of whom had little or no training in theology, how to make use of the techniques of confessional analysis developed in the twelfth-century schools and being constantly refined in the first half of the thirteenth century, especially by the Dominicans.[53] It should occasion no surprise that they frequently lamented the ignorance of the clergy. To implement this educational program, bishops and other authorities not infrequently issued confessional instructions, sometimes in the decrees of their councils,[54] and sometimes in treatises like those of Alexander Stavensby and Walter de Cantilupe mentioned above, the supplementary treatise on penance ascribed to William of

Auvergne, Bishop of Paris (1228-1249),[55] or the *De Confessione* of
Robert de Sorbon.[56] An examination of the *Summula* will reveal that it
is a treatise embodying relatively new principles of penitential theology.[57] Far from being an exposition of elementary matters for the unlearned, it is a manual of some sophistication designed to assist the
priests of Exeter in the administration of the most complex and difficult of all the sacraments, the sacrament of penance. In so far as preaching is concerned, it is evident that Bishop Quivil, like Walter de Cantilupe before him, desired that his priests prepare their parishioners for
self-analysis at confession. The success of the bishops in popularizing
confessional education among the laity may be judged by the success
of the *Manuel des péchés*, which was probably inspired by some variant
of the decree we have just been examining.[58]

Sometime between 1245 and 1254, Roger Weseham, Bishop of
Coventry, sent to the priests in his diocese a little treatise known as the
Instituta, which has been recently printed by C. R. Cheney.[59] Bishop
Roger was not only a learned man, reader in theology to the Franciscans at Oxford, but also a man of wide pastoral experience, having
been Archdeacon of Oxford (1236-1241) and Dean of Lincoln (*c.*
1241-1245).[60] The material on preaching in the *Instituta* is therefore
worthy of special consideration. The treatise opens with an elaborate
statement of the necessity for faith in Christ,[61] which is followed by
some instructions concerning preaching:

> Nos igitur qui racionem redditure sumus de animabus sub-
> ditorum nostrorum vocati sicut credimus et speramus per con-
> spiracionem divinam et ad curam et regimen animarum ipsarum,
> volumus, in visceribus Iesu Christi obsecramus, et desideramus
> quod fides Iesu Christi operans per dilectionem, sine qua quasi mor-
> tua est fides, per nos ac per vos pure, integre, et expresse subditis
> nostris innotescat, non solum in ydiomate latino, immo in proprio
> ydiomate sub verbis magis notis ac congruis prout deus vobis ac
> nobis inspiraverit. Volumus eciam quod de fide et de suis articulis
> fiant frequenter menciones in ecclesiis ad populum et predicaciones
> aliquando simpliciter et sine discucione, magis initentes exemplis
> quibus congrue possunt quam racionibus subtilibus vel in-
> quisicionibus vel discucionibus; fides cum sit principium chris-
> tianorum et supponenda est, non inquirenda nec discucienda, sed
> pro re notissima et certissima firmiter habenda et tenenda, iuxta
> illud Salomonis: Perscrutator maiestatis opprimetur a gloria; et in
> Ecclesiastico: Noli scrutari multipliciter, quod intelligendum est
> precipue de hiis que ad fidem pertinent. Possunt autem sicut cre-

dimus articuli subsequentes absque dubietate doceri de fide ac pre-
dicari, dummodo verbis congruis et simplicibus.[62]

There is nothing peculiar in a bishop's desiring, at any time, to have
faith preached in his diocese *"pure, integre, et expresse."* I take the
"ydiomate latino" to be a reference to the liturgy but not to sermons. As
to sermons, Bishop Roger seems to have been most deeply concerned
about the distinctions, subtle reasoning, and other academic devices
which he evidently heard in his diocese. Perhaps under the influence of
the Franciscans, who were officially instructed that their sermons be
"examinata et casta et cum brevitate sermonis," and directed *"ad utilitatem
et aedificationem populi,"*[63] he wished to have the faith preached in well
known words and illustrated with *exempla* and familiar allusions. Certainly this passage does not imply either that sermons were not being
delivered at all or that the priests were too ignorant to be capable of
preaching.

The list of the articles of the faith which follows the above passage
contains several suggestions for elaboration. For example,

Undecimus articulus est quod sacramenta ecclesie animas
sanctificant. Ad hunc articulum reducere possumus quod sacramenta nove legis efficiunt quod figurant; item quod extra
ecclesiam et absque sacramentis non est salus.[64]

These suggestions and the preceding general directions indicate that
what Bishop Roger wanted in his sermons was not a simple enumeration of the articles, but an illustrated and well developed discussion of
each one. We can only conclude that he had reason to think his priests
capable of composing such discussions for themselves. The *Instituta*
closes with a description of those things which oppose the articles of
the faith—heresies, witchcraft, magic, and so on—written, like the rest
of the treatise, with a dexterous interweaving of Scriptural authorities.[65]

The decree responsible for the notion that there were only four
"statutory" sermons a year is that issued by Archbishop Pecham in
1281. It runs:

Ignorantia sacerdotum populum praecipitat in foveam erroris; et
clericorum stultitia vel ruditas, qui de fide catholica mentes fidelium
instruere jubentur, magis aliquando ad errorem proficit quam doctrinam. Quidam etiam caeci praedicantes non semper loca visitant,
quae magis constat veritatis lumine indigere; testante propheta, qui
ait: quod "parvuli petiebant panem, nec erant qui frangerent": et
alio clamante: "quia egeni et pauperes quaerunt aquas, et lingua

eorum exaruit." In quorum remedium discriminum statuendo praecipimus, ut quilibet sacerdos plebi praesidens, quater in anno, hoc est, semel in qualibet quarta anni, die uno solemni vel pluribus, per se vel per alium exponat populovulgariter, absque cujuslibet subtilitatis textura fantastica, quatuordecim fidei articulos; decem mandata decalogi; duo praecepta evangelii, scilicet geminae charitatis; septem opera misericordiae; septem peccata capitalia, cum sua progenie; septem virtutes principales; ac septem gratiae sacramenta. Et ne quis a praedictis per ignorantiam se excuset, quae tamen omnes ministri ecclesiae scire tenentur, ea perstringimus summaria brevitate.[66]

There follows a very concise outline of the materials demanded; it is, as Pecham indicated, a brief summary, not a full exposition, so that it must be supposed that the materials were considerably elaborated for presentation in sermons.[67] The decree deserves analysis in some detail. The opening denunciation of ignorance obviously refers to theological ignorance, which we might expect, since the parish priests had only recently been introduced to the theology of the schools in any systematic way, and their slowness to grasp its ramifications must have been a constant source of episcopal annoyance. It should be remembered that two hundred years before Pecham wrote even a fairly well educated priest who regularly delivered his "statutory" sermon every two or three weeks[68] would have been necessarily even more ignorant in the same way. In his second sentence the Archbishop spoke of some of his priests as *"caeci praedicantes."* These men were not accused of neglecting to preach at all, but of getting their materials from the wrong places. That is, I believe, Pecham meant that they did not make adequate use of systematic theological information available to them. There follows an injunction that these men preach in a certain way four times annually about certain specified subjects. First, with regard to the manner, they were to preach *"vulgariter, absque cujuslibet subtilitatis textura fantastica."* Here we see the Franciscan influence at work again. Like Roger Weseham before him, Pecham disliked the subtleties of academic sermon style and wished the sermons delivered to the people to be popular in appeal, not learned. We may infer that some of the priests under his jurisdiction had been making their sermons ineffectual by exhibiting, perhaps with some vanity, too great a stylistic sophistication for their audiences. Finally, the tri-monthly sermons especially demanded were to explain fourteen articles of the faith, the ten commandments, the two precepts of the gospels, the seven works of mercy, the seven sins, the seven virtues, and the seven sacramental graces. The significant thing about this list is that it was not exactly commonplace at the time it was written. First, in popular instruction, there were usually twelve articles of the faith, not fourteen.[69] Moreover, this is the first demand, so far as I know, in English decrees of the period that the people be taught systematically the two precepts, the works of mercy, and the virtues. I have already shown that information about the seven sacraments was relatively new in the thirteenth century. Archbishop Pecham's decree, then, was a demand for special sermons to be delivered in a certain specified way on certain specified subjects at specified times. These sermons would not be available to the priests in their collections of sermons *de tempore* and *de sanctis*: "elles ne convenaient pas plutôt dans une situation que dans l'autre." There is no implication in the decree that the ordinary sermons were not delivered; on the contrary, it is implied that the ordinary sermons were becoming tainted with artificial subtleties.

A passage elsewhere in Pecham's writings confirms the attitude taken above toward his decree:

> Secundo, quod provideant fideliter gregi sibi commisso, in spiritualibus; ut pote in praedicatione verbi Dei et sacramentis ecclesiae dispensandis, et specialiter in confessionibus audiendis; et ubi ipsi non sufficiunt ad hoc, vocent in sui adjutorium viros sanctos ad hoc specialiter deputatos.[70]

The emphasis on the sacraments and on confession here makes it clear that the author's concern was with theological inadequacy. His attitude is typical of that of the more learned of the thirteenth-century bishops, who, in accordance with the program outlined by the Fourth Lateran Council, were anxious to bring the fruits of scholastic synthesis to the people. Both the inadequacy of the priests and the anxiety of the bishops must be considered in the light of contemporary theological progress.

I believe that the foregoing decrees, from that of Richard le Poore shortly after the Fourth Lateran Council to that of John Pecham in 1281, are the most important of those concerning preaching now in print to which attention is usually called. A passage in the *Rotuli* of Robert Grosseteste alleged to show the infrequency of preaching remains to be disposed of. It appears in a series of nine licences for private chapels granted in the diocese of Lincoln. The first of these stipulates that John Haunsard and his family may attend their chapel instead of the local parish church except "singulis annis die Natalis Domini, die Purificationis Beate Virginis, die Pasche, die Omnium Sanctorum, et die Assumptionis Beate Marie, die dedicationis ecclesie, et

dominicis diebus quibus predicatio fieri consuevit ad populum . . ."[71]
Another charter, after a similar list of solemn feasts, employs the expression ". . . et festivis quibus predicatio fieri consuevit."[72] At first
glance, this passage seems to indicate that the lords who received the
charters were required to attend the parish church only on rare occasions and seems to imply, moreover, that sermons were delivered at
the parish church only on certain exceptional Sundays and feast
days.[73] If the priests at the parish churches involved, however, were
delivering their regular sermons *de tempore* and *de sanctis*, there would
be a sermon every Sunday and on every solemn feast day, that is, on
every day of solemn celebration. But isn't that exactly what Grosseteste meant by listing certain solemn feasts and mentioning Sundays?
The lords were permitted to attend daily services in their chapels, but
on solemn feasts and on Sundays—when there were sermons—they
were required to go to the parish church. I think the texts of the other
seven charters support this interpretation. I quote the relevant passages, omitting the lists of feast days:

> . . . et singulis dominicis diebus et festivis quibus solempnes in ipsa
> [the parish church] fient predicationes.
> . . . et singulis diebus dominicis, et festivis quibus solemnes fiunt in
> ipsa predicationes.
> . . . et etiam in aliis diebus solempnibus et festivis quibus in eadem
> matrici ecclesie solempnes fiunt predicationes.
> . . . et exceptis singulis diebus dominicis et festivis quibus solempnes
> in dicta ecclesia de Hameldon fiunt predicationes.
> . . . et exceptis singulis diebus dominicis et festivis quibus solempnes
> in dicta ecclesia de Esteneston fiunt predicationes.
> . . . et singulis diebus dominicis et festivis quibus sollempnes in ipsa
> matrici ecclesia fient predicationes.
> . . . et singulis dominicis diebus et festivis quibus solempnes in dicta
> ecclesia de Hemelhamsted fiunt predicationes.[74]

There is no doubt that all Sundays and solemn festivals are excepted in
all of these seven charters but the third, where Sundays are not mentioned. But in all of them, including the third, the expression *solemn
sermons* is employed, indicating again that the author meant all days
of solemn celebration, implying, perhaps, that there may have been
sermons on other days not regarded as solemn. The lists of solemn
festivals vary somewhat. Since they are short, and since there was considerable local variation in solemn festivals, I take them to be merely
illustrative. When Bishop Peter Quivil, some years later, wished to
standardize the celebration of solemn festivals in his diocese, he listed

over forty "*festa solenniter celebranda.*"[75] It may be assumed, therefore, that the recipients of Grosseteste's charters went quite frequently during the year to hear sermons at their parish churches.

The purpose of this paper, as I said at the beginning, is to show that there is nothing inconsistent with the assumption that the average priest delivered his sermons *de tempore* and *de sanctis* in the decrees usually adduced to prove that he did not. I believe that this purpose has now been accomplished. In closing, I should like to quote two relevant decrees which are usually left unmentioned because they tend to show that the ordinary sermons for the year were actually delivered. The first occurs in some statutes dated 1237 in the *Concilia*:[76]

> Prohibeant etiam sacerdotes parochianis suis sub interminatione anathematis, ne diebus dominicis mercata frequentent, dismissis ecclesiis suis, apud quas debent convenire, maxime diebus illis, et orationi intendere, ac officium ecclesiasticum et verbum Dei audire; quod non faciunt aliquo die in septimana nisi rarissime, cum magnae fuerint festivitates. . . .[77]

The author of this decree, whoever he may have been, seems to have been confident that the parishioners who went to church on Sunday in his diocese would hear a sermon. Another bishop who expressed the same confidence in the same connection a little more explicitly was Bishop Peter Quivil:

> Tam veteris, quam novi testamenti pagina septimum diem ad humanam requiem deputavit; unde Judaei secundum literam, diem sabbatum, nos vero secundum literae intellectum, diem dominicum a manuali opere custodimus; quo in ecclesia conveniens populus christianus tam divina obsequia audiat, quam vivendi normam addiscat. Et quanto variae seculi operationes parochianos non sinunt caeteris diebus divinis officiis interesse; tanto his diebus singuli curiosus tenentur adesse, ut dum pro pane materiali, in singulos dies perituro sex diebus laboraverunt; septimo saltem die cibo spirituali, qui non perit, verbo scilicet praedicationis salubrius refocillentur.
>
> Idcirco parochialibus presbyteris praecipimus universis, ut parochianos suos moneant diligenter, et efficaciter inducant; ut ecclesiam suam festis diebus, praesertim dominicis, studeant frequentare, divinum officium audituri; et recte vivendi instructionem humiliter recepturi.[78]

The implication that sermons were delivered on Sundays for those who went to hear them is unmistakable. Thus, in two decrees, one from the first half of the thirteenth century and the other from the second, there is clear—although not necessarily conclusive—evidence to show that ordinarily regular Sunday sermons were actually delivered in English churches. Perhaps Bishop Quivil and his predecessor were somewhat optimistic; but, discounting certain isolated instances which they too probably knew about and recognized as atypical, we have no particular reason for concluding that their assumption was unjustified.

To conclude, the evidence concerning preaching in English episcopal decrees and in other documents of the thirteenth century does not indicate that "a sermon was a rare event." The decrees merely reflect an effort to incorporate in sermons what has been aptly described as "the large body of popular pastoral theology which was growing rapidly in this age."[79] Moreover, we do not lack evidence that, in the ordinary parish, sermons were regularly delivered on Sundays and on feast days. The quaint old thirteenth-century priest who fumbles through a rare sermon on the pages of certain modern historical writings may be considered a fiction.

III

Two Poems from the Carmina Burana

❧

To the reference to "sleep" in Romans 13:11-14 I should have added a reference to Psalm 118:28 involved in the illustration. The interpretation of "Dum Diane Vitrea" recently offered by Winthrop Wetherbee, "The Theme of Imagination in Medieval Poetry and the Allegorical Figure of 'Genius,'" Medievalia et Humanistica, *n.s. 7 (1976), pp. 54-55, seems to me puzzling.*

❧

I. "Dum Diane Vitrea"

WE owe to Peter Dronke an account of "Dum Diane Vitrea" that treats the poem as a whole, and not only provides a newly edited text but a new translation.[1] Dronke's attractive and gracefully written exposition envisions a rare form of "serenely perfect love" as the subject, although he finds that the poem is not a work of what he calls *amour courtois.* The more learned and elaborate poems in the *Carmina Burana* were clearly written for a rather sophisticated audience of clerks (or students) whose background and training involved texts no longer familiar today, so that their interpretation is difficult; and we must be careful not to substitute our own familiar background for theirs when we bring connotations to the language of the poems. Dronke in effect acknowledges this fact by introducing into his discussion a supporting quotation from Hildegard of Bingen. However, his conclusion seems strange at the outset since the poem near its beginning states that the joy of sleep is equal to the sweetness of love and concludes by emphasizing the uneasiness and discomfort of lovers. Perhaps the poem needs a more detailed examination.

It begins with a description of moonrise and its effect on mortal creatures. I have arranged the text here for ease of reference rather than in accordance with its poetic form:

> 1.1 Dum Diane vitrea
> sero lampas oritur,
> et a fratris rosea
> luce dum succenditur,

5   dulcis aura Zephiri
     spirans omnes etheri,
     nubes tollit,
     sic emollit
     vi chordarum pectora,
10   et inmutat
     cor, quod nutat
     ad amoris pignora.

The MS reading *spirant* is printed by Schmeller (37.6), but Schumann (62.6) and Dronke emend to *spirans*,[2] which seems necessary for coherence. In 9 the MS reading *vi*, echoed in the tavern-song parody (Schmeller 176.2.3), is retained by Schmeller but emended to *vis* by Schumann and Dronke. In 12 the MS reading *pignora* printed by Schmeller is emended to *pondera* by Schumann, but is felicitously restored by Dronke. The text above thus constitutes a compromise. Although everyone should understand that modern translations should be avoided except as very rough guides to twelfth-century texts, a tentative translation might run something like this:

> When the glass lamp of Diana rises late, and when it is illumined by the rosy light of her brother, the breeze of sweet Zephyrus fills all the heavens, removes the clouds, softens breasts in this way with the force of its music, and transforms the heart, which falters at the pledges of love.

The "clouds" are, figuratively, the cares that beset the mind, and the "music" of the soft breezes should probably be understood as a product of the natural harmony involved in the cycles of the sun and moon. We shall return to this concept later. Since the word *aura* could be used for gentle wind, light, or even tone, its appearance here is especially felicitous, for all three appear under the aegis of Diana. The soft light, the clear unclouded heavens, and the music of the breeze constitute the "pledges" or tokens of a love before which the heart falters or becomes calm in preparation for the fruit of that love, which is, as we soon learn, natural sleep.

It was said that Diana, in her manifestation as the moon, "rorem de se egerit et emittit,"[3] but here that function is performed by her assistant, Hesperus, the evening, whose gift removes cares, producing a sleep, the joy of which is equal to the sweetness of love:

2.1   Letum iubar Hesperi
      gratiorem
      dat humorem
      roris soporiferi

  5 mortalium generi.
3.1 O quam felix est
    antidotum soporis,
    quod curarum tempestates
    sedat et doloris!
  5 Dum surrepit clausis
    oculorum poris,
    ipsum gaudio equiperat
    dulcedini amoris.

It is important to notice that this sleep, unlike another kind of sleep soon to be described, removes worldly cares. Moreover, it steals into the channels of the eyes from without. The "medical" terminology some have found objectionable in the latter part of the poem actually appears first in 3.6.

Diana is further assisted by Orpheus, famous for his soothing melodies:

4.1 Orpheus in mentem
    trahit impellentem
    ventum lenem,
    segetes maturas,
  5 murmura rivorum
    per harenas puras,
    circulares ambitus molendinorum,
    qui furantur somno lumen oculorum.

The MS reading *Orpheus* in 4.1 was emended by Schumann to read *Morpheus*, but properly restored by Dronke.[4] The music of twilight sounds helps to darken the eyes in sleep in a stanza that will appeal to all of those once moved by "The Elegy in a Country Churchyard," although there is actually no taint of romantic melancholy in our poem. Here the mind is affected.[5]

Diana, Hesperus and Orpheus thus cooperate to bring relaxation and freedom from care in sleep to all those willing to accept Diana's tokens of love. The poet now turns to another kind of sleep brought on by Venus. This variety has nothing to do with the sleep we have just been discussing. Its inspiration and physiological processes are very different. The elaborate physiological description, which has repelled some readers of the poem, is actually couched in very commonplace terms, but it serves to emphasize the very distinctive qualities of this kind of sleep. Schumann relegated the text from here on to a note, since it did not seem to him to preserve the "wundervolle echt dichterische Stimmung" of the previous stanzas. However, the poet clearly wished to celebrate Diana and to deprecate Venus, so that we should assume that the offensive subject-matter served a deliberate purpose:

> 5.1   Post blanda Veneris conmercia
>   lassatur cerebri substantia;
>   hinc caligant
>   mira novitate
> 5   oculi nantes
>   in palpebrarum rate.
>   Hei quam felix transitus
>   amoris ad soporem,
>   sed suavior
> 10   regressus ad amorem!

Here the substance of the brain (or the understanding) is deprived of vigor, and the eyes, swimming in the eyelids, are darkened in a manner to be described in the next stanza. Both Whicher and Dronke translate 5.7-8 so as to indicate a transition from love to sleep, but the alternative possibility is probably better in the context of the poem: "O how happy is the passage to the sleep of love, but sweeter is the return to love!"[6] That is, the lover is torn between two pleasant choices: he enjoys the somnolence of amorous exhaustion, but he enjoys even more a return to amorous activity. In short, his sleep is not restful. Venereal activity begets a restless desire for itself.[7]

In connection with the above stanza, the verb *caligare* (5.3) and the noun from which it was derived, *caligo*, when associated with the eyes were sometimes medical terms indicating pathological blindness, mental or physical; and *novitas* (5.4) could mean "strangeness." Connotations such as these are reinforced by the language of the following stanza, which is clearly "physiological":

> 6.1   Ex alvo leta
>   fumus evaporat,
>   qui capitis tres
>   cellulas irrorat;
> 5   hic infumat oculos
>   ad soporem pendulos,
>   et palpebras
>   sua fumositate
>   replet, ne visus
> 10   exspacietur late;
>   unde ligant oculos

virtutes animales,
que sunt magis
vise ministeriales.

All the editors agree in emending the MS reading *me* in 6.9 to *ne*. From the pleasantly satisfied belly[8] a fume arises to bedew the three cells of the brain, or the faculties of imagination, reason and memory. In medieval texts the order of these faculties sometimes varies, but not their nature. The moisture here should be contrasted with the "humorem roris soporiferi" provided by Hesperus (2.3-4), which comes from without as a part of a natural series of ordered events rather than from within as a result of wilful superfluity. Gastric flatulence "smokes" or beclouds the eyes and makes the eyelids heavy with its fumosity so that the sight does not range very far. Thus the animal spirits blind the eyes. Dronke translates the last two lines "which specially in this show themselves our servants." It seems to me that a simpler and better rendition would be, "who are in a higher degree seen administrators," with the implication that the animal spirits, thought of in the twelfth century as administrators of the reigning soul, in their higher function nourish the sight rather than dim it. Sight was thought to be the chief gateway to the understanding, provided that the three cells of the brain function properly and are not, as they are here, beclouded. We should notice in this connection that whereas Diana removes clouds, Venus infuses them, producing what can justly be called in the terms of this poem stupefaction rather than natural drowsiness.

The activities of the animal spirits thus blind the eyes and lead to the usual garden of love, which is not a place but a state of mind conducive to Venereal pursuits and subsequent exhaustion. If we recognize the fact that gardens of this kind in medieval literature are often "inner" gardens, the visionary products of Venereal warmth, we have no difficulty in understanding the logical progression from stanza 6 to this one. Here the garden with its temptations is the product of the befuddled brain:

> 7.1 Fronde sub arboris amena,
>   dum querens canit Philomena,
>   suave est quiescere,
>   suavius ludere
> 5   in gramine
>   cum virgine
>   spetiosa.
>   Si variarum
>   odor herbarum

10   spiraverit,
      si dederit
      thorum rosa,
      dulciter soporis alimonia
      post Veneris defessa conmercia
15   captatur,
      dum lassis instillatur.

The reigning spirit of the garden is Philomena, singing her complaint against Tereus, who, as Ovid tells us (*Met.* 6.519-562), raped her, and then, alarmed by her threats of disclosure, pulled out her wrathful tongue with some tongs, cut if off with his sword, and left it to writhe and murmur on the ground.

> Hoc quoque post facinus, vix ausim credere, fertur
> saepe sua lacerum repetisse libidine corpus.
>
>   (6.561-562)

He sought to preserve the "secrecy of love," and to maintain his garden of delights in a hut, in which he imprisoned his beloved; but in due time he was discovered, with very unpleasant consequences for himself. Philomena and her "natural" surroundings represent an inauspicious attitude of mind produced by the Venerian befuddlement just described. The stanza moves from the self-induced stupor of the preceding stanza to a post-Venereal lassitude quite unlike the healthful and pleasant repose offered by Diana. The final stanza should thus come as no surprise:

8.1   O in quantis
      animus amantis
      variatur
      vacillantis!
5   Ut vaga
      ratis per equora,
      dum caret anchora,
      fluctuat inter spem
      metumque dubia:
10   sic Veneris milicia.

The figure of the wandering bark is reminiscent of Proverbs 23:33-34, and the hope and fear are precisely of the kind concerning which Boethius says (*Cons.* 1.m.7),

> Gaudia pelle,
> pelle timorem

spemque fugato
nec dolor adsit.
Nubila mens est
vinctaque frenis,
haec ubi regnant.

The clerical audience who first addressed themselves to this poem
would have been no strangers to classical myth. Diana, whose lamp
illuminates the first stanza, is, among other things, the goddess of
chastity, a huntress who (Ovid *AA* 1.261) "tela Cupidinis odit." She
reflects the light of her brother, Apollo, called "omnium creatorem,"
and the god of wisdom and medicine.[9] The healthful rest she offers her
followers permits the virtuous pursuit of ferocious beasts rather than
the Venerian pursuit of small creatures that turn their backs (Ovid
Met. 10.705-707). As a planet Hesperus, like Lucifer, is Venus in
another guise, its double appearance leading to the epithet "Paphiae."
But the mythological connotations of Hesperus are obscure and limited in scope, so that his appearance here is probably, as suggested earlier, no more than a reinforcement of the idea of order. The conception
is well expressed by Boethius (*Cons.* 1.m.5):

> O stelliferi conditor orbis
> qui perpetuo nixus solio
> rapido caelum turbine uersas
> legemque pati sidera cogis,
> 5 ut nunc pleno lucida cornu
> totis fratris obuia flammis
> condat stellas luna minores,
> nunc obscuro pallida cornu
> Phoebo propior lumina perdat,
> 10 et, qui primae tempore noctis
> agit algentes Hesperos ortus,
> solitas iterum mutet habenas
> Phoebi pallens Lucifer ortu.

The appearance of Hesperus driving the cold stars before him is thus a
token of that divine order from which, as the meter goes on to say,
men somehow deviate. Orpheus, who, as the speaker in the tenth
Book of Ovid's *Metamorphoses*, was no friend to Venus, produced a
music of wisdom and eloquence, one function of which was to control
passion.[10] Finally, Venus was the goddess of either proper or improper love, although in our poem even her proper function as an assistant to Nature in generation is denied her.[11] The improper "milicia

Veneris" mentioned in the last line was almost universally ridiculed in both Classical and medieval sources.[12]

Medieval readers and audiences were quite likely to have seen further more specifically Christian implications in the text. The moon is a well-attested figure for the Church, illumined by the light of Christ,[13] which offers to its lover the "dew" of grace and the "sleep" of contemplation,[14] often induced by the harmonious wisdom and eloquence of a good preacher, or Orpheus.[15] The passions of worldly concern, typified by Venus, lead to a "sleep" from which all Christians are urged to awaken (Romans 13:11-14). The coherence of these connotations in the poem strongly suggests that they were intended. However, the poem is, even without these connotations, a plea for continence and freedom from the uneasiness of self-indulgence. It is pleasant to think, although rash to conjecture, that the clerk who wrote it may have had lodged somewhere in his memory the little poem by Statius, "Somnus" (*Silv.* 5.4). The speaker cannot sleep, although the morning and evening stars have passed seven times, and the dew wafted from Tithonia's whip (the light of the moon) as she chases the stars before her has moistened him as often. He asks a boon:

> at nunc heu! si aliquis longa sub nocte puellae
> 15 brachia nexa tenens ultro te. Somne, repellit,
> inde veni. . . .

He and his audience together undoubtedly did remember the great hymn of St. Ambrose, the memory of which brought peace to St. Augustine after the death of his mother:

> deus creator omnium
> polique rector, vestiens
> diem decoro lumine,
> noctem soporis gratia.
>
> artus solutos ut quies
> reddet laboris usui,
> mentesque fessas allevet,
> luctusque solvat anxios.

II. "Si Linguis Angelicis"

In his *Medieval Latin and the Rise of European Love Lyric*, Peter Dronke, who is frequently perceptive, describes "Si linguis angelicis" from the *Carmina Burana* as a poem "grounded in a unity of experience which can affirm divine love and every nuance of human love without setting up dichotomies." The "liturgical allusions" in the poem are said to be used "not to establish an incongruity but to overcome one."[16] This rather improbable and romantic eventuality has been challenged by James I. Wimsatt, who finds in the poem "a witty tale of how an infatuated lover got his lady despite himself."[17] The perception of wit in the poem seems to me worthy of elaboration, although the lover does not, actually, "get his lady," a fact that adds substantially to the humor. The following brief discussion, which is not exhaustive, adds more detail than Wimsatt was able to supply in an even briefer treatment contributing to the larger purposes of his essay. The humor of medieval literature, like the wit of Ovid, often escapes modern critics, and it is not always easy to describe in print.

"Si linguis" is generally thought of as a poem or song written in a clerical environment, perhaps by a clerk in a cathedral school. Among the poems in the *Carmina Burana* there are a number that reveal unusual learning and subtlety. It is probable that these, some of which used to be attributed to Abelard, were written by masters for the benefit of their students to exemplify points of grammar for them and to test their skill at "exposition," which included the discovery of the doctrinal content of the texts provided.[18] Once mastered, texts such as this one might be sung with appropriate spirit on festive occasions. Material for exposition was ordinarily supplied by the inclusion of figurative language based on the Scriptures, the Latin classics, and on other works frequently studied in schools, like the *De nuptiis Philologiae et Mercurii* of Martianus Capella. We can see this technique clearly exemplified in the poems of Bernard Silvestris and Alanus de Insulis, so that we should not be surprised to find it applied in lighter poems as well. If poems composed as texts for students could be made amusing as well as instructive, their effectiveness could be enhanced. The general aim of education was to teach eloquence combined with wisdom,[19] and the wisdom involved was derived from the philosophy of the New Testament, appropriate principles from the Old Testament, especially the sapiential books, the Fathers, and from classical writers whose works could be adapted for Christian use. The *Moralium dogma philosophorum*, which was sufficiently popular to warrant a French translation, illustrates the kind of classical materials that could be used directly, and the commentaries of writers like William of Conches and Arnulf of Orléans together with the works of the mythographers furnished guides to interpretation as well as much useful figurative language derived from exposition. The original readers of "Si linguis" must have been either students or former students, for no one else at the time could have read or understood the poem at all.

In either event, those readers would have also had some training in dialectic, or the art of probable argument, as an essential part of their study of eloquence. We should add that gross errors in probable argument provide a fertile source of humor, especially when they emanate from the mouths of vain and pretentious persons. Finally, the popularity of Ovid and the frequency with which language from the Canticle of Canticles appears in the Latin poetry of the time attest to the fact that humorous or even "lascivious" subjects were not considered to be impediments to the pursuit of wisdom. In largely agricultural societies, where the behavior of domestic animals is open to the scrutiny of everyone from childhood, a knowledge of sexual activity in great variety is commonplace. Stallions are often spectacularly instructive in this respect. In addition to this fact, we should also remember that medieval residences afforded little privacy. "Man and Nature," so to speak, coexisted with relative equanimity.

The speaker in our poem, who should be distinguished carefully from the author, since the day when poems were considered to be sincere outpourings of personal emotion had not yet arrived, begins,

> 1.1   Si linguis angelicis   loquar et humanis
>   non valeret exprimi   palma, nec inanis,
>   per quam recte preferor   cunctis Christianis,
>   tamen invidentibus   emulis prophanis.

The first line is an obvious echo of 1 Corinthians 13:1: "Si linguis hominum loquar, et angelorum, charitatem autem non habeam, factus sum velut aes sonans, aut cymbalum tinniens." The context of this very famous verse would not have escaped medieval students, and it would be grossly unfair not to remind modern students of its import. St. Paul goes on to say that neither prophecy, knowledge, faith, almsgiving nor martyrdom is worth anything without charity. Moreover,

> Charitas patiens est, benigna est: Charitas non aemulatur, non agit perperam, non inflatur, non est ambitiosa, non quaerit quae sua sunt, non irritatur, non cogitat malum, non gaudet super iniquitate, congaudet autem veritati: omnia suffert, omnia credit, omnia sperat, omnia sustinet. (1 Corinthians 13:4-7)

Charity is, of course, the love of God and of one's neighbor for the sake of God, principles upon which "universa lex pendet et prophetae" (Matthew 22:40), and which constitute the tribute (Romans 13:7-8) or debt (Matthew 18:23-25) every Christian owes on pain of being "delivered to the torturers." The line expressing forgiveness in the Paternoster was conventionally thought to refer to this debt. It was thus no small matter.

The first line of the poem thus suggests strongly that the speaker will either express a charitable message or be as a "sounding brass." We do not have to wait long to decide between these alternatives, for he immediately tells us that he is to be esteemed above all Christians by virtue of a "palm" he has won. Since "charitas . . . non inflatur, non est ambitiosa, non quaerit quae sua sunt," this is clearly a "brassy" statement. Just how vain and empty it is we shall soon see, but first let us consider the "palm." Dronke describes it as a "Pauline metaphor,"[20] but the Scriptural palm of victory as distinguished from the Pauline "bravium" (1 Corinthians 9:24), which appears later in the poem, is derived from Apocalypse 7:9, where great multitudes in white robes bearing palms stand before the throne of the Lamb praising the Lord. As verse 14 explains, "Hi sunt, qui venerunt de tribulatione magna, et laverunt stolas suas, et dealbaverunt eas in sanguine Agni." Their fate is pleasant, as verses 16-17 assure us: "non esurient, neque sitient amplius; nec cadet super illos sol, neque ullus aestus; quoniam Agnus, qui in medio throni est, reget illos et deducet eos ad vitae fontes aquarum, et absterget Deus omnem lacrymarum ab oculis eorum."

Medieval readers (or listeners), being accustomed to the Scriptural palm, were undoubtedly anxious to discover the nature of this new palm, and to learn about the tribulations the speaker has suffered in order to win it. In his self-esteem, he sounds a little like the Pharisee of Luke 18:11. Moreover, the assertion of that self-esteem after the suggestion of charity in the first line is more than a little ridiculous and hence humorous. I do not mean that it produced loud laughter, but I am confident that it did produce a smile. A smile is a fleeting thing, difficult to recapture, but we shall find more such smiles in the poem.

The second stanza opens with an echo of the well-known Passion hymn of Fortunatus, which begins,

> Pange, lingua, gloriosi proelium certaminis
> et super crucis tropaeo dic triumphum nobilem
> qualiter redemptor orbis immolatus vicerit.

The speaker, however, wishes to record his own struggle and the glorious prize he has won for himself:

> 2.1 Pange, lingua, igitur,   causas et causatum.
> Nomen tamen domine   serva palliatum,
> ut non sit in populo   illud divulgatum
> quod secretum gentibus   extat et celatum.

I daresay that most medieval men, including students, not all of whom were able, like Abelard, to remain continent until their middle years, would have described their amorous achievements in less exalted terms. The terms the speaker uses here are not only in bad taste; they are illogical. For the expression "causas et causatum" would have reminded young students of something. The rare participle *causatus* (from *causo* rather than the usual Classical *causor*) used substantivally occurs prominently in only one familiar work: the translation of Aristotle's *Posterior Analytics* by Boethius. It appears in 1.7 toward the close in the clause "cum non ex causatis sciat causis,"[21] which forms part of an argument to show that demonstrative principles appropriate to one discipline cannot be used for demonstration in another discipline unless the axioms of the two are the same, or unless one discipline can be thought of as being logically subordinate to the other. In this instance, however, our lover does not hestitate to employ principles from Divinity (or the study of the Sacred Page) to the processes and, presumably, the results of seduction. Divinity and seduction do not have the same axioms, since it is an axiom of Divinity that fornication is forbidden. For the same reason Divinity cannot be subordinated to seduction. The two are incompatible, and our lover is speaking foolishly. The word *causatum* also appears in the Boethian version of *PA* 2.17, where it is shown that the same effect may appear in two unrelated subjects and proceed from entirely different causes. That is, the palm

Note on the Photograph (Copyright, the University of London, Warburg Institute) from the *St. Alban's Psalter*.

The text is Psalms 118:25-32, together with the initial and the opening of the section comprising vv. 33-40. The upper initial illuminates v. 28: "Dormitavit anima mea prae taedio; confirma me in verbis tuis." In the lower part, a figure holds a text of the opening of v. 37 of the next section, "Averte oculos meos, ne videant vanitatem; in via tua vivifica me," pointing at the same time to the lovers below. The scene forms the initial of v. 33: "Legem pone mihi, Domine, viam justificationum tuarum." The well-watered garden at the right in the lower initial is either a Paradise of earthly delights envisaged by the lover, or the Paradise of spiritual delights that rewards those who follow the "viam veritatis" (v. 30), or both, since the nature of the "garden" depends on the attitude of the observer. The ocular preoccupation with "vanity" in v. 37 is obviously seen as an aspect of the "sleep" in v. 28.

The illustration is relevant to both poems since it clarifies the kind of Venereal "sleep" that results from "sight." This theme, which has Ovidian as well as Scriptural sources, is common in later literature. Cf. the definition of "love" in Andreas Capellanus, *De amore*, 1.1.; *Purity*, line 706; Chaucer, *KT*, 1096, 1114; *Troilus*, 1.272-273; Shakespeare, *MV*, 3.2.63-107. These examples could be multiplied in both English and European traditions.

DE SIT RVM TIo
anima mea: uiuifica me
secdm uerbum tuum.
Vias meas enuntiaui
& exaudisti me :
doce me iustifica
tiones tuas.
Viam iustificationũ
tuarũ instrue
me: & exercebor in mirabilibz tuis.
Dormitauit anima mea pre tedio:
confirma me in uerbis tuis.
Viam iniqtatis amoue a me: & de
lege tua miserere mei.
Viam ueritatis elegi: iudicia tua nõ sũ obliť.
Adhesi testimoniis tuis dñe: noli me cõfunde.
Viam mandatoris tuois cucurri:
cũ dilatasti cor meum.

claimed by our speaker does not proceed from the same causes as the palm mentioned in the Apocalypse. To continue to suggest demonstrations or "causes" based on Divinity, as the speaker does, is thus foolish in another way. It remains to be seen, however, whether the lover's palm is "inanis." It may not be, in spite of his foolish language, since there is such a thing as a pagan or Classical palm of victory, achieved customarily after strenuous effort.

Our lover finds himself neither in a stadium nor on a playing field, but in a flowery garden (st. 3) doubting what to do, wondering whether he sows seed in sand, and despairing because he loves a "mundi florem." If this garden is like other similar gardens in medieval literature, it represents a state of mind, like that described in "Dum Diane vitrea" (st. 7), rather than an actual place. The flower he desires is denied him (st. 4) by "quandam vetulam" who permits the Rose, as he calls her, neither to love nor to be loved. The hag is worthy to be snatched into Hell, but she persists, so that the lover hopes that she may be struck by lightning (st. 5). He asks his audience to hear what he may have seen ("quid viderim"), in this event, while the hag remained stunned. It is important to understand that the thunderbolt never fell from above; it was merely desired. The remainder of the poem contains the recollections of the musings of the lover as he stood in his dreamlike *locus amoenus*. But the lover's speeches and the responses of the girl are imagined only, reflecting the speaker's befuddling warmth and concomitant delusions. As the students or clerks who read this poem were aware from works like the *De nuptiis Philologiae et Mercurii*, the proper solution to this kind of garden uneasiness is marriage, although the marriage may be figurative, like that between wisdom and eloquence said to be figured in the poem just mentioned. But the subject of marriage is not introduced, for what is desired is a simple Venereal relationship, as we soon discover.

The girl, as Wimsatt points out, is described in flower and star imagery strongly reminiscent of conventional praise for the Blessed Virgin (st. 6), and when the lover rushes to her and kneels before her (st. 7), he addresses her in terms that make this comparison unmistakable:

> 8.1 Ave, formosissima   gemma preciosa!
>   ave decus virginum   virgo gloriosa!
>   ave lumen luminum,   ave mundi rosa . . .

But this effusive greeting is promptly followed by an anticlimactic line revealing our day-dreamer's actual intentions:

> 8.4 Blanziflor et Helena   Venus generosa.

Although it is true that in the twelfth century after it became commonplace to see the bride in the Canticle as Mary, the attractiveness of her physical attributes was sometimes indicated in very frank terms, and love for her was often expressed in what is today startling imagery, no one would seriously have sought to combine the Blessed Virgin, Blanchefleur, Helen and Venus in the same person. To deny that the effect of this line is humorous seems to me to be insensitive. Whatever we may think of Blanchefleur, Helen had an unsavory reputation in the twelfth century; and it would hardly have been possible for a girl to be a "virgo gloriosa," which Helen certainly was not, and a "Venus generosa" at the same time. This is not to suggest that medieval people did not enjoy sexual pleasure, the gift of Venus, or that men (even students) did not employ flattery to obtain it. In this instance, however, the flattery is so self-contradictory and outrageous that it is laughable. We are reminded of similar literary techniques in the *De amore* of Andreas Capellanus.[22]

The speaker's dream-girl does not laugh (st. 9), but demurely expresses the hope that God will save her suitor. Her speech rather suggestively acknowledges God to be the ruler of all things, including violets, tokens of humility, and roses "in spina." The celestial rose suggested earlier in the Marian imagery bears no spines, but this one, like the thorny and transient roses of Venus (*MVIII* 11.1, Bode 1.228-229), evidently does. Her speech is, we should recall, imagined by the musing lover, so that any ironies suggested by the violets and roses are inadvertent on his part, like his persistent abuse of logic. But this should not prevent us from enjoying them. Evidently God was not the source of the lover's wounds, for he hastens to assure his friend, in terms reminiscent of Proverbs 6:24-26, that since she has wounded him, she ought to supply the remedy (st. 10). She promptly denies responsibility for his injuries, very properly, since it has always been clear to thinking persons that the kind of passion the lover endures arises from within. In the twelfth century Andreas Capellanus assured his readers of this truth, and indeed went to some pains to explain it (*De am.* 1.1). However, the girl very courteously asks that the plaintiff reveal his wounds. Then, she assures him, she will cure him with a simple remedy:

> 11.4   vis, te sanem postmodum   gracili medela.

The uncommon word *medela* probably recalled to the minds of twelfth-century students the little passage "De medico" in Ecclesiasticus 38:1-15, which begins,

Honora medicum propter necessitatem, etenim illud creavit Altissimus; a Deo est enim omnis medela, et a rege accipiet donationem. Disciplina medici exaltabit caput illius, et in conspectu magnatorum collaudabitur. Altissimus creavit de terra medicamenta, et vir prudens non abhorrebit illa.

Although God did not wound the lover, He, as the girl suggested earlier, will supply any real cure that is administered. As we shall see, the lover actually proves to be incurable because he seeks his remedy in the wrong place.

The lover explains (st. 12) that his wounds are obvious. He saw the girl dancing at a feast. Since that time, we are astonished to learn, he has been meditating on her beauty without satisfaction for almost six summers! The number six was associated with the sixth age beginning with the Redemption and hence generally with the coming of Christ,[23] so that we may hope that the miseries of the lover may soon be over. But literally speaking, a period of over five years is a very long time to wait for Venereal satisfaction once it has become an object of cultivated desire, and it is extremely doubtful that anyone in the twelfth century who hotly desired it and was not squeamish about gaining it would allow himself to go without it for so long a time. There were those who renounced it and put it from their minds, but our lover was not one among them. His patience under the circumstances is remarkable to say the least, and leads to disconcerting thoughts concerning the ordinarily innocent Ovidian proverb (*Her.* 5.115) echoed earlier in the poem:

> 3.3 Dubito quod semina   in harena sero.

In any event, the girl, our hero says, was when he saw her "cunctis . . . speculum et fenestra." The word *speculum* applied to a *persona* probably echoes Wisdom 7:26, where the personified Sapientia is described as being "speculum sine macula Dei maiestatis." This image, like other imagery in the surrounding context, was applied to the Blessed Virgin and echoed in the liturgy. It is repeated in Chaucer's description of Blanche, who was "A chef myrour of al the feste." (*BD* 974) Both poets probably reflect the same liturgical passage. The rather puzzling use of *fenestra* may also be Scriptural in origin, although its connotations are quite different unless we wish to think of Mary as a window through which we may discern God. But this is clearly not what the lover has in mind. Other connotations are summarized by St. Ambrose in his comment on Psalms 118:37: "Averte oculos meos, ne videant vanitatem," which produced a famous love scene in the St. Alban's Psalter:[24]

Si videris mulierem ad concupiscendum eam [Matthew 5:28], intravit mors per fenestram [Jeremiah 9:21]. . . . Claude ergo hanc fenestram, cum videris alienae mulieris pulchritudinem [Ecclesiasticus 9:8,11] ne mors possit intrare. Oculi tui non videant alienam, ne lingua perversum loquatur [Proverbs 23:33]. Tuam ergo fenestram claude, ne morti pateat intranti. Sed etiam alienam fenestram cave [Ecclesiasticus 21:26]. A fenestra enim domus suae intrat fornicaria.

St. Ambrose goes on to discuss the windows of words and kisses. Our present woman is both a "strange woman" and a "strange window," in Terentian terms (*Htm.* 3.1.481), a window "ad nequitiem." Although the original connotations of the language of the poem cannot be demonstrated with certainty, it seems likely that the expression "speculum . . . et fenestra" repeats the anticlimax we observe in 8, with the same humorous effect.

Stanzas 13-23 in which the lover sets forth his case contain a flattering and stylized description of the girl (st. 13-17), an account of the lover's suffering brought on by his seeing her (st. 18-21), and a plea for remedy (st. 22-23). A few details may be noticed here, although careful study would undoubtedly reveal much that needs comment. Helen and Venus reappear together in stanza 14:

> 14.3 unde dixi sepius,   deus, deus meus,
> estne illa Helena,   vel est dea Venus?

The pursuit of Helen, whatever Yeats or Camus may have made of it in modern times, was clearly imprudent and ultimately disastrous; and the mention of the two in the same breath strongly brings to mind the foolish judgment of Paris. As Horace put it (*Epist.* 1),

> quid Paris? ut salvus regnet vivatque beatus
> cogi posse negat.

Our speaker is courting trouble, for Venus as the mythographers tell us, following Fulgentius (*Mit.* 2.1), brings her followers to "shipwreck."

In stanza 17 the line

> 17.1 Forma tua fulgida   tunc me catenavit

suggests the plight of various figures like Mars, caught amusingly with Venus in "graciles ex aere catenas" (Ovid *Met.* 4.176), or Holofernes, concerning whom Judith prayed (Judith 9:13), "capiatur laqueo oculorum suorum in me," as indeed he was captured, losing his head literally as well as figuratively. Our hero has been so enmeshed that he has been unable to drink, eat or sleep (st. 20), presumably for over five years, and has had small solace from imaginary encounters with the girl at night (st. 21). Either he is exaggerating in this his imaginary address to his lady, or he has been very foolish indeed. In the course of his plea, however, he says that a recompense will exalt him like a cedar of Lebanon:

> 23.1 Quod quidem si feceris,   in te gloriabor,
>   tamquam cedrus Libani   florens exaltabor.

Although cedars of this kind (Rehder[2] 1.4.7.2) are hardly very floriferous, the source of "exalted" members of the species is either Ecclesiasticus 24:7 or Psalms 36:35–36. The former is a verse spoken by Sapientia, "Quasi cedrus exaltata sum in Libano," a figure transferred in the liturgy to the Blessed Virgin. Needless to say, the remedy our lover desires will not make him either wise or in any way like the Virgin. The verses from the Psalm offer another possibility: "Vidi impium superexaltatum et elevatum sicut cedros Libani; et transivi, et ecce non erat; et quaesivi eum et non est inventus locus eius." Here the humor lies in the contrast between the implied references, and in the comment on the speaker they suggest.

In the dialogue the girl maintains a rather proper surface attitude. After politely assuring her lover that she has suffered more than he has, an assurance that represents nothing more than the lover's hope in this imaginary encounter, she offers silver, precious stones, or any other recompense that she has available (st. 26). When he has made it clear that he has no desire for material wealth, which as was well known usually flows in the other direction in encounters of this kind, she courteously suggests that he take whatever he wants. The kiss and the delights of "Paradise" follow, at least in imagination, with the conclusion

> 31.1 Hic amplexus gaudium   est centuplicatum,
>   hic mecum et domine   pullulat optatum,
>   hic amantum bravium   est a me portatum,
>   hic est meum igitur   nomen exaltatum.

The hundredfold joy amusingly echoes Matthew 19:29, or, since the lover has expressed doubt about where he sows seed, more appropriately Luke 8:8. The latter verse is from the Parable of the Sowers. There seed fallen on good ground produces fruit a hundredfold, representing "qui in corde bono et optimo audientes verbum retinent et fructum adferunt in patientia" (Luke 8:15). Our lover has been deaf to the "verbum" echoed in his own language, although he has, so to speak, brought forth a rather odd kind of fruit in patience. He resembles those who sow seed among thorns, where, we remember, roses to his taste grow. These are those who "audierunt et a sollicitudinibus et divitiis et voluptatibus vitae euntes suffocantur et non referunt fructum" (Luke 8:14). Certainly the imaginary joys here envisaged hardly constitute much "fruit." Nor, for that matter, do the cones on cedars of Lebanon.

But we are assured that these joys do constitute the "bravium" of lovers. The word echoes 1 Corinthians 9:24-27, where the race is won through the exercise of another kind of patience:

> Nescitis quod ii, qui in stadio currunt, omnes quidem currunt, sed unus accipit bravium? Sic currite ut comprehendatis. Omnis autem qui in agone contendit ab omnibus se abstinet. Et illi quidem ut corruptibilem coronam accipiant, nos autem incorruptam. Ego igitur sic curro non quasi in incertum: sic pugno non quasi aërem verberans; sed castigo corpus meum et in servitutem redigo, ne forte, cum aliis praedicaverim, ipse reprobus efficiar.

If the reward of lovers is mere fantasy as it is here, their discipline before the race is indeed futile, and they do "beat the air" with words, as our poor speaker does. His "exalted name" made him worthy of a glorious palm indeed; and the spectacle of his proud triumph, holding the palm of victory in his hand after years of struggling with nothing but a day-dream to temper his despair constitutes a little comic masterpiece. Actually, he should say, as does Ovid's lover in *Amores* 3.2.82, who has at least been a spectator at a stadium, "palma petenda mea est."

With these considerations in mind we can fully appreciate the humor of the concluding stanzas. I need do no more than quote them for the reader's delectation (with the MS reading *amara* in 33.1 restored). They do not, of course, offer much encouragement to lovers, at least not to those who idolize their mistresses. A lover's hope is greater the more he is embittered, as anyone remembering this one ought to know.

32.1   Quisquis amat itaque   mei recordetur:
       nec diffidat illico,   licet amaretur;
       illi nempe aliqua   dies ostendetur
       qua penarum gloriam   post adipiscetur.

33.1   Ex amaris equidem   amara generantur;
       non sine laboribus   maxima parantur.
       Dulce mel qui appetunt   sepe stimulantur:
       sperent ergo melius   qui plus amarantur.

The forms of the rare verb *amarare* "to embitter" in 32.2 and 33.4, where the reader or listener might expect forms of *amare* constitute pleasant witticisms. On the whole, in fact, the poem displays a remarkable array of verb forms. Its original purpose may have been to serve as a grammatical exercise for students. If it was, the master who wrote it took care that the students had something else to attract them, and to entertain them as well, once they began their exposition. If the verb forms were not pedagogical, they nevertheless constitute a graceful exhibition of Latin eloquence in a smiling illustration of the vanity of idolatrous passion as it was understood in the Middle Ages, a theme that then constituted a kind of wisdom. Perhaps the author deserves Apollonian palms like those accorded Ovid (*AA* 2.1-3):

> Dicite "io Paean!" et "io" bis dicite "Paean!"
>   Decidit in casses praeda petita meos;
> Laetus amans donat viridi mea carmina palma. . . .

To conclude our examination of these two poems, it seems to me appropriate to say that it is very dangerous to read medieval Latin love lyrics in the light of artificial conventions of literary history like "courtly love." The secular Latin lyrics of the Middle Ages, if it is at all proper to call them that, are often witty where they have been taken seriously, and often orthodox where they have been assumed to represent some kind of "pagan" or personal revolt. The pagans with whom medieval clerks were familiar were usually very moral in outlook, and this remark applies to Ovid, as well as to writers like Cicero and Seneca, for Ovid customarily wrote with tongue in cheek and a witty gleam in his eye. He was always "alive," alert to the humorous possibilities of ordinary human foolishness. Our medieval poems need very close analysis in terms of their own cultural environment. They have not often received it. But when they do, the vigor and subtlety we find in them amply repay us for our efforts.

Five Poems by Marcabru

This article was essentially a reply to the conclusions of the late Father A. J. Denomy concerning Marcabru's songs, and, in a larger sense, part of a general effort to discredit theories of "courtly love." It is of some interest to notice that Dimitri Scheludko was adducing the "special Augustinian conception of the dual division of love" in connection with literary texts in 1937, when I was still occupied with interpretations of tragic catharsis. For an excellent recent discussion of "Fin' Amors," see Edmund Reiss, "Fin' Amors: Its History and Meaning in Medieval Literature." Medieval and Renaissance Studies, 8 (1979), pp. 71-99.

⸙

ARL APPEL'S conclusion that Marcabru celebrated a *fin'amors* which is "die Liebe, die um Gott ist und mit ihm selber eins wird,"[1] supported in a long series of articles by Dimitri Scheludko,[2] and in a recent book by Guido Errante,[3] has been seriously questioned.[4] The traditional position was perhaps best stated by Scheludko, who wrote concerning the content of the poems, "Was den Inhalt anbetrifft, so führte Marcabrun in die Trobadordichtung die christliche, spezielle Augustinische Konzeption von der Zweiteilung der Liebe ein." Further, he found the style of the poems to involve a use of scriptural symbols:

> Marcabrun besass eine bildhafte, symbolische Denkweise. Er gebrauchte sich der biblischen Parabel-Sprache nähernd, sehr gerne Symbole und Bilder mit fernliegenden Analogien, so dass der Sinn seiner Ausdrücke in vollem Masse nur dann erraten wird, wenn wir zuerst alle seine Begriffsassoziationen (die sich meistens im Kreise der biblischen und christlichen Vorstellungen bewegen) richtig festlegen.[5]

In the present paper, I wish to show through an analysis of five poems, in four of which objections to the traditional view have been raised, that Scheludko's position may be defended in preference to newer theories of "courtly love" and Arabic influence.[6]

Scriptural materials in *Al departir del brau tempier* (ed. Dejeanne) have been indicated by both Scheludko[7] and Errante,[8] but these materials have not been well integrated with the poem as a whole. In the opening stanza the poet observes, at the departure of winter, the broom, the broom heath, peach blossoms, the willow, and the elder. The last two plants, which contribute forcefully to the general impression of a disappointing spring, reappear as a kind of melancholy echo in the rest of the poem, where they are used to typify men whom the poet dislikes. Errante characterizes the willow as "l'albero della suprema tristezza," citing Psalms 136:1-2.[9] But the symbolic meanings of objects mentioned in the Bible are not always available simply by inspection. We may consult glosses, scriptural dictionaries, or moral encyclopedias to determine these meanings, since such sources yield commonplaces spread widely through sermons, doctrinal works, literary works, and through "folklore" built up by centuries of preaching and instruction based on the allegorical interpretation of the scriptural text. In the present instance, authoritative glosses reveal that willows represent men who are sterile in good works even though they proffer virtuous words (green leaves).[10] Marcabru's comparison between willows and men who neglect their obligations in favor of vain boasting thus reflects a traditional symbolic convention. Although the elder does not appear in the Bible, it is treated in moralized encyclopedias. Thus Alexander Neckam explains that the elder offers pleasant flowers but degenerates in fruit, and that in the same way some men begin well but degenerate "cum tempus expectationis adest."[11] Meanings parallel to those of the willow and the elder were probably suggested by Marcabru's broom plants.[12] The traditional symbolism which is consistent with the context also helps to illuminate the remainder of the poem.

The poet is concerned (st. 2) with a great garden in many parts of which are attractive plants with promising shoots and green fruit. Although they appear to have the foliage and flowers of fruit trees, at the time of fruiting they are merely elders and willows. Perhaps the peach blossoms of stanza 1 were a false hope. This description is followed by a superficially irrelevant observation: *E pus lo caps es badalucs,/ Dolens son li membr' estremier.* The garden is a very common symbol of the church, not of the ecclesiastical hierarchy but of the body of communicants,[13] and in Marcabru's version of it the trees, or members, flower as if to produce good works (cf. Canticles 7:12), but instead of producing fruit in season (Psalms 1:3), they are like the evil trees of Matthew 7:17. Much the same kind of imagery is employed in the *Chanson de sainte Foy*, where trees also represent men.[14] The decay of the garden seems to be due to the absence of a "head." As Paul says repeatedly, Christ is the head of the church,[15] and conventionally His place was occupied by the successors of Peter in the Papacy. During the first part of his literary career Marcabru's patron was Guilhem VIII, who supported Anacletus II against the claims of Innocent II, and for a time Poitiers was a center of activity for Innocent's opponents. As Prosper Boissonade has suggested, Marcabru's *Aujatz de chan* (9) and *Lo vers comens* (33) probably reflect an interest in Anacletus.[16] I suggest that the present statement that the "head" is void probably reflects Marcabru's feeling that the garden of the Church was, at the time of the schism, without a true gardener and that the supporters of Innocent among the noblemen were not worthy. If this assumption is correct, we should date the poem in the years preceding Guilhem's spectacular submission to St. Bernard.

In stanza 3 we find a contrast between *li bon arbre primier* and the present occupants of the garden who are mere twigs and straw. They are reluctant in bold enterprises but quick to make promises, wherein they show themselves to be willows and elders. These disappointing noblemen, who may represent those who abandoned the cause of Anacletus, are spoken of contemptuously by Marcabru and by other *soudadier*. Perhaps these are the "milites Christi" of St. Paul, whose spiritual qualities were thought to be a part of the obligation of knighthood, but whose battle was carried on by persons of all ranks.[17] Such persons would be sensitive to hypocrisy, which is the subject of stanza 4. The poet's enemies spend the night jousting with words and during the day they engage in boasting contests in the shade of the elder.[18] They resemble their ancestors about as much as Cazères and Carlux (very small places) resemble Toulouse and Montpellier.[19] The majority are elders, and he is fortunate who finds a laurel or olive among them. The laurel is a classical symbol which came to be associated with various virtues as well as with the obvious idea of "victory." For example, Neckam makes it a symbol of wisdom.[20] And the fruitful olive might represent wisdom also, by virtue of its association with Minerva, or, in scriptural terms it might stand for Christ or the just man.[21] It is difficult at this remove to determine exactly what virtues Marcabru intended, but since the laurel and olive are clearly opposed to the willow and elder it is obvious that they do represent virtuous persons of some kind, the rare good trees in Peter's garden.

The literal meaning of stanza 6 is obscure, although light has been shed on it by Kurt Lewent.[22] It implies that the gardener with his key-ring, who probably represents the Pope with his apostolic keys, downed by a wind, has fled the garden with his eyes shut so that no tenant remains. That is, no one now holds the garden as tenant under God. Referring to the gardener, the poet says, *Per esclavina e per trabucx /*

An laissat mantelh e caussier. The *sclavina* and *tribuci* suggest a monastic costume. Innocent was vigorously supported in his struggle against Anacletus by St. Bernard and by the order of Cluny. Perhaps Marcabru meant to imply that the Papacy was about to be taken over by monastic influence so that the Pope was transformed from a gardener of the Church to a recluse. But I offer this only as a very tentative suggestion.[23] The poem concludes with an exclamation against willows and elders who will become forever vagrants if they are not supported by king and count and duke—substitutes, perhaps, for the transformed gardener. Although it presents grave difficulties, the poem as a whole furnishes clear illustrations of the kind of stylistic technique ascribed to Marcabru by Scheludko.

Al son desviat, chantaire (5) contains a typical instance of the abstraction *Jovens.* Although the poem has been dated before the poet's prolonged visit to the court of Alfonso VII.[24] Denomy argues with convincing thoroughness that *Jovens* here and elsewhere in Marcabru's poetry represents an Arabic ethical ideal stemming from the cult of *futuwwa.* This view is attractive, but several objections may be raised to it, and it is possible to explain *Jovens* as a traditional scriptural symbol. The chivalric form of *futuwwa* was based on the saying, sometimes attributed to the Prophet, "No sword can match dhu-al-Faqār, and no young warrior can compare with 'Ali," a statement often inscribed on medieval Arabic swords.[25] The cult of *futuwwa* existed in two forms during the Middle Ages, one of which flourished among illiterate people who idealized noble and generous warriors for the faith, especially those who fought against crusaders; the other was associated with the Sufis and is not relevant to our purpose.[26] But it seems to me unlikely that a Spanish emperor like Alfonso VII whose hereditary duty was the restoration of Visigothic unity and the destruction of Moslem power in Spain, and whose chivalry found inspiration in the cult of Santiago, would look favorably on an ethical ideal based on the cult of Ali, or that a poet whose works show genuine crusading zeal would borrow a Moslem religious idea for purposes of exhorting Christian knights *in nomine Domini* to fight against the heathen.[27] In his famous *Pax in nomine Domini!* (35), probably written in 1137 partly as a memorial to Guilhem VIII,[28] Marcabru shows no tolerance for the Saracens and their ways. Failure to praise *Jovens* properly[29] is made responsible for the suffering of the Christian knights (st. 7), but the positive ideas among which this concept appears are very obviously Christian (ll. 5 ff., 28, 43, 65, 72). Much the same may be said of *Emperaire, per mi mezeis* (22), where *Jovens* appears among ideals which are clearly Christian. A Mohammedan ethical concept seems out of place in these contexts, if not heretical, and Marcabru was an enemy of heresy.[30]

The concept "youth" has conventional scriptural connotations which, characteristically, may be either "good" or "evil." Thus the *Allegoriae in sacram scripturam* contains the following: "*Juvenes*, intellige fortes, dicente apostolo Joanne: 'Scribo vobis, juvenes, quod vicistis malignum,' id est, vobis spiritualiter fortibus, quod superastis diabolum . . . *Juvenes*, lascivi, ut in Psalmis . . . *Juvenes*, leves. . . ."[31] Among definitions of *juventus* in this work the final one evokes a common and significant image in which youth and age are contrasted: "*Juventus*, reversio ad bonum, ut in Psalmis: 'Renovabitur ut aquilae vita tua,' id est, ad instar aquilae a prava vetustate."[32] This is put more positively in the *Distinctiones* of Alanus: "Juvenis, proprie, dicitur renovatus per gratiam."[33] The evil old age implied here is familiar in Romans 6:6, where the *vetus homo* is said to be crucified at baptism; or in Ephesians 4:22–23, where we are urged to put off the "Old Man" and to put on the "New Man." Lombard, following Ambrose, explains: "Homo itaque si vitia pristina sequitur, vetus dicitur; si autem in novitate vitae ambulat alienus a saeculi errore, novus dicitur." Again, following Haimo, he adds: "id est, assumite similitudinem novi hominis, id est, Christi."[34] In Colossians 3:6–17 this concept is developed further, so that it becomes apparent that youth represents the Image of God in man, which should be restored by putting down the "Old Man."[35] The original "Young Man" whom we are urged to imitate is Christ, who restored the loss perpetrated by the Old Adam. To follow Christ is to be young, to be renewed by grace; to follow the Old Adam in sensuality is to be old. Youth thus suggests Christ as an exemplar and reason or spiritual valor in Christians. Further connotations of youth and age appear in the tree images illustrating the *De fructibus carnis et spiritus* printed among the works of Hugh of St. Victor.[36] The evil tree which bears the vices is marked "Vetus Adam," and its highest fruit is *luxuria*. Its opposite which bears the virtues is marked "Novus Adam" and its crowning fruit is *caritas*. In the poems of Marcabru, *Jovens* is plainly opposed to *luxuria*[37] and is associated with another love which, according to Scheludko, is *caritas*. In his sermon *De cantico novo*, St. Augustine explains some of the more obvious implications of the contrast between the New Man and the Old Man, calling attention to the New Song, the New Law, the New Jerusalem, and their opposites.[38] He associates "newness" in man with the pilgrimage toward the Celestial City. A crusade is basically an armed pilgrimage reflecting the greater pilgrimage of the spirit, so that we should not be surprised to find a poet in the twelfth century recommending "youth" as a virtue to crusaders. It would thus be reasonable to think of Christ rather than Ali as the type of *Jovens* in Marcabru's poetry except for Denomy's objection that love in this poetry cannot be *caritas*.

The general import of the first six stanzas of *Al son desviat, chantaire* is clear: adultery is both foolish and deceptive.[39] There follows a lament that *Jovens* and *fin' Amors* no longer rule the world, a fact which encourages false love. When they ruled as *paire* and *maire*, *Proeza* was maintained *a celat et a saubuda* but now duke and king and emperor have defiled it. *Jovens* is here obviously a characteristic of those who are "fortes" in the struggle against the kind of false love typified by adultery, and there is no reason why it should not be associated with *caritas*. Adultery is a common figure for departure from the word of God, or for evil behavior generally,[40] and the figures *paire* and *maire* may have been intended to suggest Christ, the exemplar of "youth," and His spouse, the Church.[41] When they ruled, reason and love, which had been corrupted in the Fall,[42] were restored. And when they are neglected so that they do not rule, corruption thrives once more. In stanza 8 it is said that *Jovens* has faded away, so that *Amors* is lost in thought or dreaming.[43] That is, since reason has decayed, charity has lost its joy and is inactive. The use of the word *Jois* by the early troubadours has been examined in detail by Denomy,[44] whose collection of materials is invaluable to anyone studying this concept. He points out that the relationship between love and joy in the poetry suggests specifically that *Jois* is parallel with grace in theology, although the poetry uses a conceptual system quite different from that employed in theology. Several objections may be raised to these conclusions. As Denomy himself says, "So intimately do grace and charity cohere in the soul of the just that St. Augustine would seem to deny a real distinction between them."[45] This lack of distinction may be observed among theologians of the twelfth century. Peter Lombard, for example, equates charity in man with the Holy Spirit, implying that fraternal love is not something created.[46] And he further equates grace with the Holy Spirit.[47] If we wished to make a parallel between grace and the personified abstractions of Marcabru, therefore, it would be logical to make it parallel with *Amors* rather than *Jois*. *Fin' amors* was used elsewhere in the twelfth century to mean charity. In Simund de Freisne's *Vie de saint Georges*, for example, a queen who suffers martyrdom "vers Deu eut amur fine."[48] Joy, which existed in medieval theology as a concept quite distinct from grace, might accompany either this love or the opposite (adulterous) love of the world (*cupiditas*). There were thus two kinds of joy. To quote Simund de Freisne again: "Hom ne deit esgarder mie / Vers les biens ki sunt en tere / Pur la fause joie cunquere; / Mès deit esgarder en haut / Vers la joie ki ne faut."[49] "Joy" as a traditional theological concept has been discussed by Errante,[50] and it would be possible to accumulate a great many supporting references.[51] The parallels *Amors-Caritas* and *Jois-Gaudium* thus seem more reasonable than Denomy's *Jois-Gratia*. There remains the problem of the different conceptual systems said to operate in the poetry and in theology. It seems to me wrong to lump all troubadour poetry together with the assumption that it represents a uniform scale of values. Marcabru himself (37) attacks poets who celebrate false love, so that it is clear that not all poets wrote on the same subject. Scheludko assumed correctly, I believe, that not all poets who imitated Marcabru's language preserved his concepts.[52] But in the poem before us the statement that *Amors* is *de Joi deseretada* is not inconsistent with a lament concerning the decline of charity in the world. If the various noblemen Marcabru condemns have substituted the joy of the flesh, as the emphasis on adultery suggests, for the joy of the spirit, it is obvious that they have concomitantly deserted charity, which demands that the world be used rather than enjoyed for its own sake and that joy be directed toward the eternal.

Stanza 9 has given rise to two objections to the view that *Amors* in Marcabru's poetry is *caritas*. Denomy affirms that the birth of Divine Love is not "confined to the well-born," and that its growth is not restricted "to a leafy bower protected from cold and heat."[53] Literally, these arguments are unassailable, but it is possible that the poet's language is figurative. The stanza runs,

> L'amors don ieu sui mostraire
> Nasquet en un gentil aire,
> E·l luocs on ill es creguda
> Es claus de rama branchuda
> E de chaut e de gelada,
> Qu'estrains no l'en puosca traire.
> (49-54)

If the love Marcabru praises *nasquet en un gentil aire*, the false love which he condemns is associated with a base generation. In *Bel m'es quan son li fruich madur* (13, st. 6) he speaks of *l'Amistats d'estraing atur / Falsa del lignatge Caim / Que met los sieus a mal ahur*. And in *Pax in nomine Domini!* (35, st. 5) he says, *Probet del lignatge Caï, / Del primeiran home felho, / A tans aissi / C'us a Dieu non porta honor*. The noble generation in which true love is born is thus an opposite of the Generation of Cain, which is figurative. St. Augustine explains that the world of men may be divided into two generations: the generation of Cain, made up of those who live "according to man"; and the generation of Abel (or Seth) made up of those who live "according to God." The latter are associated with charity or grace and the former with cupidity.[54] The generation of Cain is associated with adultery both literally and figuratively in the person of Lamech.[55] In the Bible itself similar distinctions in generation may be found, as in I John 3:2, 9-12; 5:1-5, 18. The statement that love *nasquet en un gentil aire* is thus quite harmonious with patristic and scriptural conventions. Raimbaut d'Orange, in *Cars, douz,* which imitates Marcabru's style, says that Worth *per un fill pot reviure, / Vas cui m'atur, de bon aire.* Walter Pattison sees as a "secondary allegory" here a reference to Christ.[56] It was Christ who made possible a renewal of the generation of the just in charity.

Certain figurative potentialities of the garden imagery in the stanza have been noticed.[57] Aside from the possible reference to the *hortus conclusus* of the Canticum, one leafy tree which may be said to shelter love is the Tree of Life, frequently taken as a figure for Christ.[58] In the protection of this tree love may be said to grow sheltered from the heat of prosperity and the cold of adversity,[59] and to be protected from the depradations of the stranger, or Satan.[60] If we take the leafy bower in this way we can make some sense of the last two lines in the poem: *Desiderat per desiraire / A nom qui•n vol Amor traire.* This may reflect the language of the prophesy of Aggeus 2:8 *et veniet Desideratus cunctis gentibus.* That is, the desired one is called *Desiderat* by the desirer who wishes to bring forth love from the tree, or to share in the love brought to humanity by Christ.

Floral imagery appears once more at the opening of *Bel m'es quan son li fruich madur* (13), where conventions suggested in the preceding poems may be relevant. In connection with the first line Errante quotes Canticles 2:13: *Ficus protulit grossos suos.*[61] Honorius says concerning this verse, "Ficus profert fructum, scilicet, quisque fidelis bonum opus. . . ."[62] But the meaning "good works" for fruit does not necessarily depend on this verse of the Canticum. It would be possible to add many more scriptural references (e.g., Matthew 7:16-21, 12:33; Luke 6:43-45; Wisdom 4:1-6) in support of this convention, especially if we were to consult commentaries as well as the text itself. In the stanza as a whole the fruit and the renewed green growth of autumn suggest a moral atmosphere very different from that of the disappointing spring imagery of 3. Tentatively, if the fruit suggests the works of the just the renewed green implies a renewal of faith, and the singing birds may represent the faithful praising God[63] and avoiding the shadows of spiritual blindness or iniquity.[64] The contemplation of such things might well fill the poet with the joy which accompanies charity[65] and cause him to have renewed hope for his own salvation.

But, the poet says (st. 2), false lovers debase love and exalt crime. We should not imagine that love has deteriorated on this account, for it does not change its appearance. If *Amors* here is charity, Marcabru may have been reflecting 1 Corinthians 13:8, *caritas nunquam excidit.* The last two lines of the stanza, *Nuills hom non sap de sa valor / La fin ni la comensansa* may then refer to verse 9 of the same passage—*Ex parte enim cognoscimus*—with an additional allusion to passages like Isaiah 41:4, 48:12; Apocalypse 1:8, 22:13. Stanza 3 offers nothing inconsistent with this view. He who wishes may credit the foolish prophets who debase *Amors*, but the poet asks that God may protect him from changing his opinion. He has set himself toward a love which does not deceive, a characteristic which it may owe to 1 Corinthians 13:4, where it is said that charity *non agit perperam.*[66] His happiness is great in summer, in winter, and at Easter, he says, implying that his love pleases him in prosperity, in adversity, and in the contemplation of that Resurrection which promises the resurrection of the just. With a little assurance, his happiness will be much greater; that is, he can look forward to the fruition of his love but not with complete assurance.

Stanza 4 may be seen as a logical continuation of this train of thought. The poet may look forward to greater happiness because, whatever anyone may say to the contrary, a man becomes better through *Amors* just as wine comes from grapes.[67] Marcabru has never heard of anyone becoming worse through *Amors*,[68] and he has himself obtained greater worth through it. But he still lacks *un pauc de segwhen* (as anyone must who seeks spiritual reward) and he must not boast for fear of the one whose gifts he hopes for. Denomy objects to reading *caritas* for *Amors* in this stanza on the grounds that Divine love is not "fearful to boast of its possessions because of the possibility of loss thereby."[69] I do not understand this objection, for the principle reflected in the poem seems to be that of 1 Corinthians 13:4: *caritas . . . non inflatur.* Chrétien de Troyes (*Li contes del graal*, ll. 43-44) reflects the same source with an assertion that "Charité . . . de sa bone oevre / Pas ne se vante." In general, the positive element in this poem may be seen as an elaboration of principles in 1 Corinthians 13 and the negative element as an attack on those who fail to observe them.

Errante quotes Matthew 12:33 as a source for the imagery in stanza 5.[70] But very similar imagery appears elsewhere in the Bible, so that the poet may well have had in mind a generalized concept based on various passages rather than any one text. Taking Lewent's explanation that *recim* of line 34 is from *recimar*, "(re-)prendre cima,"[71] the first

three lines may be roughly translated. "It would indeed be difficult for
a fool to change his nature and for him not to continue enjoying his
folly, and for a foolish woman not to be intemperate."[72] The tree imagery, which contrasts with that of the opening, implies that an evil
tree grows from evil nourishment producing from an evil branch
flowers and fruit of evil thoughts. This happens whenever *Jois* does
not reign. In view of the obvious scriptural echoes in the imagery, it
seems reasonable to interpret this to mean that the absence of spiritual
joy like that suggested in 1 and 3 is characteristic of false love, which
produces the tree of cupidity with its evil flowers and fruit. The high
position given to *Jois* is not surprising since an unwillingness to abandon fleshly joy as a goal in itself is a strong deterrent to charity. Our
interpretation of the first five stanzas is confirmed in its general outline
by the context established in stanza 6, where it is said that the false love
of the Generation of Cain, which is certainly cupidity, leads its followers to misfortune. It prevents men from loving properly, fearing no
shame or blame, and puts the fool in such confusion that he would not
keep faith with those who would give him all of France.[73] That is,
cupidity is insatiable. If the false love Marcabru condemns is that of
the Generation of Cain, his *Amors* is probably the opposite of this love,
or charity, and *Jois* in this poem may well be not a "courtly love"
parallel to spiritual joy, but spiritual joy itself.

The opening of *Per savi·l tenc ses doptanssa* (37) is obscure.

> Per savi·l tenc ses doptanssa
> cel qui de mon chant devina
> So que chascus motz declina,
> Si cum la razos despleia,
> Qu'ieu mezeis sui en erranssa
> D'esclarzir paraul' escura.
>
> (1-6)

Errante observes, "Marcabru dichiara senza false modestie di ritenere
abilissimo colui che riesca a penetrare tanto il senso letterale che quello
nascosto dei suoi canti."[74] A doctrine of literary obscurity was popular
among medieval poets,[75] and the nature of Marcabru's poem certainly
suggests that he was familiar with it. Lewent argues that the last two
lines of the stanza do not mean that Marcabru did not know what he
himself was saying, but that he was disturbed in his effort to untangle
the confusion created by the false poets referred to in the following
stanzas.[76] These poets (st. 2) trouble the worthy and distort the truth,
deliberately using words in an evil way.[77] They write, perhaps, without Marcabru's *razo*, confusing true and false love (st. 3) or celebrating

a love Marcabru considers to be false. They misuse concepts and limit
the connotations of words because they overlook the true meanings
they should convey.[78] We may conjecture that a similar effect of limited connotation with similar damaging results might be obtained by
interpreting the Canticum as a glorification of fleshly desire. That this
kind of conceptual framework is not irrelevant is indicated by the remainder of stanza 3:

> Qu'ieu dic que d'Amar s'aizina
> Ab si mezesme guerreia;
> C'apres la borsa voianssa
> Fai fols captenenssa dura.
>
> (15-18)

The first two lines here express a theological commonplace based on
Galatians 5:7. False love intensifies an inner warfare which one wages
against himself. St. Augustine, for example, has this to say of it:
"Modo genus hoc belli ex apostolica Epistola legebatur: *Caro concupis-
cit adversus spiritum, et spiritus adversus carnem; ut non ea quae vultis,
faciatis. Et hoc grave bellum, et quod est molestius, internum. . . .
Etenim ex peccato divisus es adversum te.*"[79] When the fool who follows false love, Marcabru continues, finds his purse empty, *Amars*
becomes cruel to him.[80] That is, cupidinous desires become a torment
when one has no means of satisfying them.[81]

The remainder of the poem may be thought of as an elaboration of
the conflict between the flesh and the spirit, with a condemnation of
those who embrace the cause of the flesh. The poet is irritated (st. 4)
when he hears it said that *Amors* deceives and debases those who renounce *Amars*.[82] Those who say this lie, for the welfare of the followers of *Amors* consists of joy, patience, and temperance, which are, we
may observe, appropriate virtues to accompany charity. Through
them the two opposing kinds of desire are made harmonious and directed toward the same end. Such a parallel exists (st. 5) when one
does not try to walk in two ways. That is, the warfare mentioned in
stanza 3 does not exist when the flesh and the spirit do not form desires contrary to each other, or when the flesh is controlled by patience
and temperance. The figure may be from Ecclesiasticus 2:14: *Vae duplici corde et labiis scelestis et manibus malefacientibus et peccatori terram in-
gredienti duabas viis!* With *bon' Amors* a man has desires of both types
united for a single purpose, and a sure faith which is white, precious,
true, and pure.[83] This is probably the same "faith" which inspired the
poet's crusade poems. *Amors* is said to have *signifianssa de marcad' o de
sardina* (st. 6). Errante calls attention to the lapidaries which elaborate

Apocalypse 21:19-20 in this connection.[84] The gems have both "magical" and "moral" values, the first of which are frequently figures for the second. The green emerald conveniently symbolizes constant faith,[85] and the sard conveys the idea of martyrdom.[86] Both of these are logically connected with charity, the latter especially in the atmosphere of the crusades. *Amors* is called the root and crown of joy. Again, if *Amors* is *caritas* it is true that it produces spiritual joy and that it also represents the fulfillment of joy. *Amors*, the stanza concludes, reigns with truth and has sovereignty over many creatures. Since charity in man may be regarded as a participation in the harmony of the universe, and since that harmony, which extends from the angels to the lowest of created beings, may also be called "charity," it is true that charity has power over many creatures.[87] The exceptions are human, for man alone among earthly creatures, in theological terms, has reason and the free will which permits him to abandon both reason and love.

Stanza 7 contains the lines which are said to demonstrate that *Amors* cannot be charity in this poem:

> Segon dich, faich e semblanssa,
> Es de veraia corina
> Car se promet e·s plevina,
> Ab sol que·l dos no sordeia,
> E qui vas lieis no s'enanssa
> Porta nom de follatura.
>
> (37-42)

But this stanza may be taken as an elaboration of the idea of "truth" mentioned in the preceding stanza. According to word, deed, and appearance, *Amors* arises from a sincere heart. This is true provided that one does not defile its gifts. Love of the right kind, that is, pledges itself and manifests itself in word, action, and appearance unless the person involved breaks faith, or departs from the truth. If words, deeds, and appearances do not conform to thoughts, the result is conventionally a lie: "Ille mentitur, qui aliud habet in animo, et aliud verbis vel quibuslibet significationibus enuntiat."[88] The follower of *Amors* is thus a follower of truth because he pledges himself and maintains his pledge. Denomy argues that charity is "hardly a matter of self-promise,"[89] but all baptized Christians in the twelfth century, presumably, pledged themselves to forsake Satan and to live in imitation of Christ (Romans 6:1-11). In a sense that is not very obscure, therefore, charity is a matter of promise and pledge. However, it is true, as Marcabru indicates, that this pledge is not always kept. Without any pledge to follow the Old Man, there are many whose white robes are torn through departure from truth. He is a fool, Marcabru says, who does not rise to love.

Teaching and preaching, the poet continues (st. 8), are not valued at all by one whose heart is bound in folly.[90] The poet knows that when love is *Amars* it is mostly false and deceptive.[91] The fool (st. 9) or false poet repeats what he hears, not according to its true meaning but in such a way as to create confusion. His love originates in rapine. In this situation, love falls in love, *Constans* is constancy,[92] and false usage is justice. We should notice that the flame of physical love is inconsistent with *Amors*, a fact which tends to remove it from the realm of "courtly love." The poem concerns evil people (st. 10) kept in the dark by an evil star, for they take pride in foolishness without good action. The poet hopes that the thought on account of which they are puffed up may cause them an evil fortune. It is not without significance that *Amars* is characterized by pride, the first of the vices, and is thus opposed to charity, which does not inflate.[93] Looking back over the poem, we see that Marcabru condemns false poets who celebrate *Amars*, a vainglorious love, rather than *Amors*, which is associated with faith, truth, and sacrifice. Such persons contribute to the warfare between the flesh and the spirit, alienate their listeners from truth and harmony, subvert the pledge of baptism, and invert justice. The poem exhibits a clear and logical thematic development which leads to no self-contradiction if we consider *Amors* to be *caritas*.

It is asserted that *Amors* cannot be charity in *Pus mos coratges s'es clarzitz* (40) because charity does not "single out or reject an individual."[94] The idea of selection or rejection appears in the first stanza:

> Pus mos coratges s'es clarzitz
> Per selh Joy don ieu suy jauzens,
> E vey qu'Amors part e cauzis,
> Per qu'ieu n'esper estre manens,
> Ben dey tot mon chan esmerar,
> Qu'om re no mi puesca falsar,
> Que per pauc es hom desmentitz.[95]
> (1-7)

When the poet sees that *Amors* makes distinctions and chooses, he feels that he should be very careful in composing his song so that he may not be accused falsely. The specific source of his worry is probably that revealed in stanza 7. His poem is largely devoted to the severe castigation of others, and the poet does not wish to make his accusations if he is guilty himself. As we have seen, the theology of the twelfth century tended to disregard the distinction between grace and charity. In a state of grace man was thought to share in the substance of the Divinity in accordance with the import of texts like 1 John 4:12-13, 16, etc. But it is also obvious that God bestows grace on some and not on others. A statement that charity chooses or rejects individuals may thus mean simply that God chooses or rejects individuals, for *Deus charitas est.* The view that this is what Marcabru had in mind is supported by the remainder of the poem.

He who is chosen by *Amors* is joyful, courteous, and wise. On wisdom, we may compare a statement of Rabanus, "Nemo perfecte sapit, nisi is qui recte diligit."[96] But he who refuses love is destroyed, for he who blames *fin' Amors* is made an idle fool. Marcabru gives us a long list of such scorners (sts. 3-5) who are typically cupidinous. Among them are false judges, thieves, perjurers, prostitutes, homicides, traitors, simoniacs, magicians, lechers, usurers, drunkards, false priests, false monks, and so on. Hell will receive them with its flames because *fin' Amors* has promised that it will be so. We may observe that persons of this kind are usually said to be subject to the punishment described because they have scorned God's love and are hence of their own volition without grace.[97] In stanza 6, the language of which echoes Psalms 35:10-13, Marcabru asks for grace himself, praying for mercy that he may not suffer the pains of Hell and for protection that he may not remain there.[98] The image of the prison is conventional, appearing in Psalms 67:19 and in St. Paul's quotation in Ephesians 4:7-10. The gloss on the latter passage explains, "Captivitati ergo dicuntur quia capti, quia subjugati, sub leve jugum missi, liberati a peccato, servi facti justitiae."[99] But Marcabru blames himself more than others (st. 7), for he who wishes to blame another must first be sure that he is himself not guilty of the same crimes.[100] Only then may he blame and remain secure. *Qui sine peccato est vestrum,* etc. But he who is under the protection of *Amors* and can speak well may call attention to the sins of others. The doctrine here is correct: "Primo vos ipsi justitiam legis implete, et sic innocentes manibus, et mundo corde, ad lapidandam ream concurrite. Primo spiritualia legis edicta, fidem, misericordiam, et charitatem perficite, et sic ad carnalia judicanda divertite."[101] And the problem was a perennial one among medieval poets, for, as Salutati said many years after Marcabru's songs were composed, a poet, whose office is in part to blame others, must of necessity be a good man.[102] Altogether, the objection that *Amors* cannot be charity in this poem seems to me ill founded, and I see nothing in it to suggest "courtly love." This concept has been made to cover a multitude of very different things in the Middle Ages, but it seems unlikely that

Marcabru was moved by any of the attitudes associated with it. In *Dirai vos senes duptansa* (18) he claims to have been a man *Quez anc non amet neguna, / Ni d'autra fo amatz.* (st. 12) And he also says in the same poem, on scriptural authority, *Qui per sen de femna reigna / Dreitz es que mals li•n aveigna.* (st. 11) The impression created by these remarks and by others like them is evident in the criticism of the troubadour Raimon-Jordan, who thought that Marcabru had been unfair to women.[103] In any event, lest we generalize too abruptly, "courtly love" seems out of place in the five poems here examined, and these poems are not necessarily inconsistent with the theories of Appel and Scheludko concerning the poetry of Marcabru.

The Partitura Amorosa *of Jean de Savoie*

❧

On Pierre Bersuire, mentioned in the first note, see now Charles Samarin, "Pierre Bersuire," Histoire littéraire de la France, 39 (1962), 259-450. Chaucerians may be interested to notice that there was a manuscript of Bersuire's Ovidius moralizatus at the Hospital of St. Thomas of Acon in London in the fourteenth century. The poem itself is an excellent example of clerical wit, composed in the best traditions of medieval Latin humanistic verse. Its humor, allusiveness, and word-play are reminiscent of some poems in the Carmina Burana, and it is a fine specimen of what might be called "non-fraternal" late Latin poetry. Poems sharing its characteristics, both in Latin and in the vernaculars, have often been dismissed as "courtly love" lyrics.

❧

UNFORTUNATELY only a small part of the purely literary work produced in the circle of Philippe de Vitry has been preserved.[1] Among the few surviving poems is a Latin *partitura* by Jean de Savoie which develops the *quaestio*:

> An diligi debeat ocius
> Cupidinis experta jacula
> Sua pridem succensa facula,
> Vel penitus in ejus artibus
> Inexperta, ceteris paribus?[2]
> (5-10)

The respondent decides in favor of the inexperienced virgin, contrary to the judgment of the proponent. After some argument the two agree to place their quarrel before Philippe de Vitry, who renders a decision to the effect that "verus amans" should choose the virgin. The poem is addressed to Jean Campion, a chaplain of the cathedral of Tournai; and the sender was Jean de Savoie, "canonicus Sancti Benedicti Parisiensis et secretarius notarius Palatii."[3] Although the tone of the poem is obviously light and humorous, the particular question involved is a rather odd one for these clerical gentlemen to be considering, even as a joke. Perhaps, however, the joke may have involved a certain amount of wit in addition to its superficial ribaldry. In other words, the hu-

manists of the fourteenth century may not have been above creating
what Rabelais called *Sileni*.

A clue to this possibility is afforded by the language of the second
response to the question:

> Nam virginis delectabilius
> Spirat odor atque fragrantius,
> Et redolet quam rosa premula [*sic*]
> Quemadmodum et fumi virgula
> Que ascendit ex aromatibus
> Per desertum miris odoribus.
>
> (35-40)

The last three lines reflect Canticles 3:6: *Quae est ista quae ascendit per
desertum sicut virgula fumi ex aromatibus myrrhae et turis et universi pulveris
pigmentarii?* Pierre Bersuire, who like Jean de Savoie, was a friend of
Phillipe de Vitry,[4] observes concerning the Scriptural *fumus*: "Iste est
igitur quidam moralis fumus, qui est laudabilis & virtuosus."[5] To determine how this is true, we must consult a commentary on the Canticum. After the middle of the twelfth century it became fashionable to
substitute "Maria" for "Ecclesia" as the *sponsa* in the Canticum, so
that the respondent in the poem suggests a reference to the Blessed
Virgin and her virtues rather than to the hypothetical maiden of little
amorous experience. A typical interpretation of the verse quoted is afforded by Cardinal Jean Halgrin d'Abbeville:

> Ascendit siquidem beata Virgo. . . . *Ascendit per desertum*, id est per
> mundum, quem pro deserto habuit; nam contemnens mundum et
> ejus concupiscentias, spiritualibus adhaesit deliciis. Ascendit autem
> *sicut virgula*, propter rectitudinem intentionis et operis, propter
> gratiam humilitatis, propter perseverantiae soliditatem, propter ex-
> tenuationem carnis suae. . . . *Ex aromatibus*. . . . Beata enim Virgo
> omnium virtutum odore profudit Ecclesiam; ipsa enim habuit
> omnia aromata virtutum . . . Per myrrham . . . signatur jejunium, et
> aliae carnis macerationes. Per thus suavis odoris, orationum fragran-
> tia designatur. Per universum pulverem aromatum . . . designantur
> omnes virtutes conditae patientia et humilitate.[6]

The use of *odor* to signify virtue or its good influence was very old and
quite conventional at the time the poem was written,[7] although it
could also convey related concepts. Bersuire begins his discussion of
the subject by suggesting three meanings which are (implicitly)
anagogical, allegorical, and tropological variations of a single theme:
"Cum odor aliquando sumatur pro coelestis gloriae suavitate & fra-

grantia, aliquando pro bona fama & nominis redolentia, aliquando pro virtutum sanctitate et gratia. . . ."[8] When the respondent in the poem maintains that the virgin he has in mind is more fragrant than the new rose, like a pillar of smoke from aromatic spices, he means that the Blessed Virgin, burning with celestial love, is a better mistress than a young lady experienced in the works of Venus, "sua pridem succensa facula." A classic example of a new rose of the kind here rejected is, incidentally, afforded by the little bud in the *Roman de la rose*, who eventually succumbs after Venus has applied her torch.

The poem is not without suggestions which look forward to this ambiguity between the question intended by the proponent and the answer developed by the respondent. In the first line the respondent is addressed as a man "Ulixea fulgens facundia." On the surface, the "facundia" of Ulysses is exactly the kind of eloquence needed by a successful hunter of the doves or rabbits of Venus. Ovid recommends it, or pretends to recommend it, above the advantage of physical beauty itself (*Ars. am.* 2):

> Nec levis ingenuas pectus coluisse per artes
> Cura sit et linguas edidicisse duas.
> Non formosus erat, sed erat facundus Ulixes,
> Et tamen aequoreas torsit amore deas.
>
>   (121-124)

The "linguas duas" may have conveyed to medieval readers of Ovid an idea very much like that in Virgil's "Tyriosque bilingues," rather than an admonition to learn Greek as well as Latin. In any event, Ovid tells the story of Ulysses' departure from Calypso. And in the *Remedia amoris* (lines 249 ff.) we find him again departing, this time from Circe. Medieval commentators found Ulysses' eloquence to be directed against love rather than an instrument for its attainment. Thus, according to Arnulf of Orléans, Ulysses used his eloquence to free his companions of the love induced by Circe.[9] Bersuire describes Ulysses as a "vir justus & prudens." When his men came to Circe's island she offered them a "poculum" whose drink changed them into beasts. One interpretation, Bersuire tells us, makes Circe the Devil and her drink "mundi prosperitas vel deliciarum ebrietas vel malarum concupiscentiarum voluptas: que qui biberint fiunt porci."[10] He compares Circe's cup with the *calicem vini furoris* of Jeremiah 25:15 and with the *calix aureus Babylon* of Jeremiah 51:7. Ulysses wisely disdains this cup. The expression "Ulixea . . . facundia" thus affords an interesting example of *aequivocatio*,[11] for it can mean either (1) that kind of eloquence desirable in amorous pursuit, or (2) wise eloquence which is used to discourage fleshly love. In the poem the proponent evidently has the first meaning in mind, but the respondent proceeds to demonstrate eloquence of the second variety.[12]

The same ambiguity is evident elsewhere in the first stanza. The respondent is addressed as "Rabbi," or master. But this title, according to Matthew 23:7, is one coveted by the Scribes and the Pharisees, hypocrites who speak virtuously but act according to their selfish inclinations. Judas twice uses the epithet in addressing Christ. At the same time, however, the word is used in a very respectful way to address the Saviour (John 1:38, 49; 3:2, etc.). A man called "Rabbi" might thus be a cleric who could speak confidentially on the basis of experience about matters of lustful love, like the Pharisaical clerk in the *De amore* of Andreas Capellanus, or, on the other hand, he might be a man to discourage such love by both precept and example.[13] Our Rabbi is said to be one whose industry knows "Cupidinis acta retexere." There are two common meanings for the god Cupid, both of which are reflected in Bersuire's commentary on the *Metamorphoses*. There the god of love is either (1) "carnis concupiscentia" or (2) "amor carnalis filius voluptatis."[14] Although the second of these can be used as a figure for the first, they are literally very different. "Carnis concupiscentia" is a malady of the soul which was equated with original sin, or the source of all vices,[15] whereas "amor carnalis" is simply fleshly love. The verb *retexere*, "unravel," can mean either "relate" or "annul." On one level, therefore, the proponent suggests that the industry of the amorously eloquent hypocrite should be able to reveal or relate the acts of fleshly love. But, on another level, the industry of a man of wise eloquence should be able to annul the acts of concupiscence. "Industria" of the right kind is the opposite of sloth, the porter of the gates of worldly delight.[16] In the *quaestio* the lady "Cupidinis experta jacula" may be either (a) a lady who has experienced the stimulus of carnal love, or (b) a sinner moved by concupiscence. Her maidenly alternative is thus either (a1) a lady unfamiliar with carnal love, or (b1) a lady free from sin. The proponent refers to ladies (a) and (a1), but the respondent considers alternatives (b) and (b1). Since only one lady was free from sin, "a rose without spines," and she is obviously preferable to a sinner, he chooses the virgin. Since his choice cannot be made without a certain amount of renunciation, it is made with difficulty.

In the first response the choice of the Blessed Virgin is defended on the grounds that she is sweeter "naturali zelo" than the other alternative, "experta veneris actibus." The word *naturalis* like *Ulixea* and *Cupido*, is equivocal. For natura could indicate either the nature of man before the Fall or the corrupted nature of man after the Fall.[17] Thus Bersuire explains that "natura humana habet insitam quandam regulam naturalem, per quam cognoscit quid est faciendum & quid etiam omitendum." On the other hand, "pro statu naturae lapsae vitia sunt naturalia nobis."[18] The respondent in the poem thus says that the "virguncula," by whom he means Mary, is "naturally," or "virtuously," more enjoyable than the sinner. But the proponent, who takes his question to refer to a literal alternative between two kinds of women, understands only the demands of fallen nature in this connection and consequently objects to the effect that the virgin who is "tremula" and "querula" is, if anything, a nuisance to the prospective lover. The humor in the poem, as distinct from its ribaldry, arises from the fact that whereas the questioner maintains his literal alternatives, the respondent develops an answer based on a figurative interpretation of the question. In effect, the respondent rejects both of the literal alternatives and offers a solution to the problem of desiring either literal alternative. That is, love for the Blessed Virgin should destroy lust either for an experienced woman or for a virgin unfamiliar with the old dance of love. The respondent's answer undercuts the literal question completely.

The contestants decide to submit their dispute to the judgment of Philippe de Vitry,

> Musicorum princeps egregius,
> Orphealis heres eximius
> Cuius nomen vivat per secula.
> (45-47)

Again, the expression "Orphealis heres" means more than is literally implied by "musicorum princeps." What Bersuire has to say of Orpheus is singularly appropriate to the theme of our poem:

> Orpheus significat predicatorem & diuini verbi carminum distatorem: qui de inferis: id est de mundo veniens debet in monte scripture vel religionis sedere carmina & melodiam sacre scripture canere. . . . Mulierum copulam debet fugere & carnis amplexus penitus exhorrere & contra ipsarum malitias predicare.[19]

Orpheus is also a man whose soul, stung by the serpent, descends to Hell. It remains to be seen what kind of "Orphealis heres" Philippe is. He decides that the "virgineum florem" is the proper object of the true lover, who should approach it,

Pertractans hunc amicabilius
Ut consurgant simul ad oscula
Pregustantes amoris pocula
Absque eo quod in amantibus
Intrinsecis latet dulcoribus.[20]
(56-60)

At first glance, this decision seems to recommend love for a literal virgin, albeit with some qualification. The flower should be treated in
such a way that the lovers rise together to kiss. Incidentally, a kiss
could represent a mingling of spirits in the Middle Ages as well as in
the Renaissance.[21] However, the lovers taste beforehand from an
"amoris pocula," or philter. This expression is associated with magic
(Horace, *Epod.* 5.38) and recalls the cup of Circe which turned Ulysses' companions into swine. But the activities of the lovers are qualified in the phrase "Absque eo quod," etc. They are to be without that
which lies hidden with inner delights among lovers. That is, perhaps,
they are to be without the delights "malarum concupiscentiarum"
which turn people generally into swine.

But Philippe's decision has implications beyond the chaste love of a
literal virgin. The last two lines of the poem reflect a phrase which
occurs in Canticles 4:1 and 4:3. The first of these verses runs: *Quam
pulchra es, amica mea, quam pulchra es! Oculi tui columbarum, absque eo
quod intrinsecus latet.* Verse 3 repeats the phrase: *Sicut vitta coccinea labia
tua, et eloquium tuum dulce. Sicut fragmen mali punici, ita genae tuae absque
eo quod intrinsecus latet.* In these contexts *absque* does not have its most
obvious meaning "without," but conveys the notion "besides" or
"and in addition," as it does in Genesis 28:9.[22] In the commentaries,
the phrase *absque eo quod*, etc., means "and in addition those virtues
which are visible only to God," or "and in addition charity."[23] Reading the poem in the light of this parallel, which suggests the Blessed
Virgin again, we see that the lovers taste the cup of love with those
virtues which are visible only to God, or with charity. A *poculum* appropriate to this kind of tasting is mentioned in Canticles 8:2. It is
clearly an opposite of the *calicem vini furoris* said by Bersuire to be the
equivalent of Circe's cup: *Apprehendam te et ducam in domum matris
meae; ibi me docebis, et dabo tibi poculum ex vino condito et mustum malorum
granatorum meorum.* Jean d'Abbeville explains, "*Vinum* conditum dicit
charitatem melle devotionis, et aromatibus bonorum operum."[24] The
"poculum amoris" thus becomes a "poculum charitatis." Pre-tasting
this very special philter, the lovers rise together to kiss. Bersuire divides kisses into three main types: "charitatis, falsitatis, voluptatis."

One "osculum charitatis" represents union with God: "Sic verè Deus elongatur ab illis qui per peccatum ab eo se elongant, quia longe est Dominus ab impiis. Illis autem, qui per penitentiam sibi appropinquant, solet appropinquare, & usque ad osculum, i.e. vsque ad perfectae charitatis vinculum eis per gratiam copulari."[25] What Philippe decides, therefore, is that "verus amans" should choose the Blessed Virgin. And pre-tasting the charity which she, the well of grace, supplies, should rise together with her toward union with God.[26]

A commentary on the *Thebaid* which circulated in the Middle Ages asserts that although "hilares" and "jocundi" may lie on the surface of a poem, nevertheless, when the figures are explained, "utiles" and "idonei" may be discovered underneath.[27] To medieval humanists the production of literary works black to the outward eye and even ridiculous, but fair within, must have been an engaging pastime and in some measure a rather serious one. The truths of the faith shine, at times, more brilliantly than usual when they are seen gleaming from the fragments of an attractive but completely earthy shell which one has just removed with some difficulty. The poetic principle is vividly expressed by Richard de Bury in the *Philobiblon*, completed some five years before our poem was written. Some men, he says, are inclined to suffer tedium in study and to throw away the nut "prius quam testa soluta nucleus attingatur." But there is an ancient remedy for this difficulty: "Idcirco prudentia veterum adinvenit remedium, quo lascivium humanum caperetur ingenium quodammodo pio dolo, dum sub voluptatis iconio delicata Minerva delitesceret in occulto."[28] In the present instance, the poet provides an entertaining and delicately wrought *cortex* concealing not only some excellent doctrine but also a very graceful compliment to Philippe de Vitry, who, it is implied, was, in the best sense possible, an "Orphealis heres."

Chrétien's Cligés *and the Ovidian Spirit*

❧

This article is a revision of a paper delivered at a Modern Language Association meeting in Chicago. I believe that a rehabilitation of Ovid is a necessary step toward a real understanding of a great deal of medieval, Renaissance, and even Rococo literature. Readers may recognize Ovid's advice in "On Painting the Face," here quoted in part, as it is reflected in Clarissa's speech in The Rape of the Lock, *5. 9-34. For the two Venuses, see further Robert Hollan-der,* Boccaccio's Two Venuses *(New York, 1978). There have been some efforts to identify scriptural elements in Chrétien. See Tom Artin,* The Allegory of Adventure *(Lewisburg, Pa., 1974), and, for a non-satiric reading, Jacques Ribard,* Le chevalier de la charrette *(Paris, 1972).*

❧

THE indebtedness of Chrétien to the poetry of Ovid has long been evident. We know that he translated the *Ars amatoria* and the story of Philomelà from the *Metamorphoses*, and what he says at the beginning of *Cligés* may imply that he also translated the *Remedia amoris* and the story of Tantalus and Pelops. Foster E. Guyer has demonstrated that there are numerous reflections of Ovid's poetry in *Cligés, Lancelot,* and *Yvain*, and that the conception of love in these romances owes much to Ovid.[1] We have been reminded in an essay by Jessie Cross-land that imitation of Ovid played a large part in the development of love poetry from the time of Charlemagne to the sixteenth century,[2] so that Chrétien's indebtedness to Ovid is only what we should expect of a poet who wrote of love during a period which has been called the "Age of Ovid." There were other influences at work in Chrétien's poetry, some of them more important than the Ovidian influence, but a more definite conception of what Ovid meant to Chrétien should be at least of some help in the interpretation of his work. In the present paper I wish to suggest some of the problems involved in formulating a conception of this kind. If Chrétien and his contemporaries were guilty of basing conclusions on "Ovid misunderstood," as some have alleged, we should at least try to discover just how Ovid was "misunderstood."

The "Ovidian spirit," a term which I shall use to designate the wider implications of Ovid's attitudes and literary techniques, has not been by any means uniformly conceived in modern times. That is, there is still no very clear distinction between "Ovid understood" and "Ovid misunderstood." As one scholar who was dissatisfied with certain traditional attitudes toward Ovid put it, "Ovid died, for at least the third time, in the nineteenth century, and was buried deep under mountains of disparaging argument to make a throne for Virgil."[3] A mild example of this disparagement in a commonplace form may be found by consulting S. G. Owen's article in the eleventh edition of the *Encyclopaedia Britannica* (s.v. "Ovid") where it is said that the *Ars amatoria* is "perhaps the most immoral work ever written by a man of genius." Ovid is accused of being sensual, superficial, and unconcerned with serious ideas. On the other hand, E. K. Rand, in a memorable essay called "Ovid and the Spirit of Metamorphosis," insisted that "there is no pruriency" in the *Ars amatoria*. For Rand, Ovid was primarily a satirist. Referring to the *Ars*, he said that Ovid "left it for those who could detect his satire to find . . . that ridicule is a most potent remedy of love."[4] Since the poet was not prurient, in spite of his immoral material, "the Puritans of Ovid's day drew one false conclusion from his works, and the entourage of Julia drew another." If Ovid was a satirist, he must have had some sort of standard of values to use as a basis for his satire. Rand did not elaborate this point, but in a recent book called *Ovid: A Poet between Two Worlds* Hermann Fränkel contends that Ovid looked forward, at least emotionally, to the new world of Christianity.[5] For Fränkel Ovid's standard of values is more a matter of poetic feeling than of concrete doctrine, but he nevertheless makes it clear that such a standard exists. There is obviously a difference between the "Ovidian spirit" as seen by Owen and that envisaged by Rand or Fränkel, both of whom find serious undertones in Ovid's poetry. Our own predispositions in this respect necessarily affect our opinion of the kind of enterprise Chrétien was engaged in when he translated the *Ars amatoria* or when he made use of Ovid's poetry in his romances.

The kind of opposition that exists between Owen's "Ovidian spirit" and Rand's "Ovidian spirit" is at least as old as the early fifteenth century, and probably as old as the poetry of Ovid itself. Jean Gerson, famous for his attack on the *Roman de la rose*, and for his reforming zeal in other directions, recommended to his confessors that all copies of Ovid should be burned, condemning his poetry as a dangerous stimulus to lechery.[6] At about the same time Coluccio Salutati was defending Ovid on much the same grounds that Rand later used. Salutati thought that the *Amores* was an attack on vicious love, and that in the *Ars amatoria* Ovid's precepts show beneath the surface the evils of love's service to the end that it may be avoided.[7] In other words, Salutati thought that Ovid actually condemned love when he seemed to praise it; and we should not forget that to praise something when one means to condemn it is, according to a standard medieval definition, to use irony.[8] I suspect that Gerson and Salutati represent two fairly common medieval traditions. There have always been persons with a strong reforming spirit to whom the poetry of Ovid has been unacceptable. An atmosphere of reform grew more pronounced toward the end of the Middle Ages, especially under the influence of the friars, who were inclined to distrust all but the most obviously devotional or moralistic poetry.[9] Needless to say, Chrétien was not a reformer, and it is possible that his attitude toward Ovid resembled that of Rand and Salutati rather than that of Owen and Gerson.

It is undeniably true that extensive use of Ovid was made throughout the Middle Ages by persons of unquestionable piety who were, at the same time, not in any sense puritans. Thus Theodulf of Orléans observed that, although Ovid and Virgil may be frivolous on the surface, many truths lie hidden in their works.[10] We should notice here the perception of a difference between the surface and the underlying meaning of Ovid's poetry which was also evident to Rand and to Salutati. Jessie Crossland writes that "the prurient nature" of Ovid's poetry, which she takes for granted, "does not seem to have shocked even serious authors of the Carolingian period, who frequently incorporate passages from the *Ars amatoria* or the *Remedia amoris* into their didactic and moral works."[11] She goes on to point out that Alcuin used the *Ars amatoria* in his *Praecepta vivendi* along with quotations from Virgil, Horace, and the Old and New Testaments. Ovid influenced the poetry of Rabanus Maurus, who was obviously not interested in the cultivation of pruriency. Perhaps these writers were not shocked because they were able to observe useful truths beneath Ovid's surface immorality. In the twelfth century we may notice a parallel situation in the works of writers like John of Salisbury and Alanus de Insulis; in fact, Ovid became well enough acclimated to be quoted in scriptural commentaries, like that of Thomas the Cistercian on the Canticum (*PL*, 26, cols. 9-862). Evidence of this kind, of which a great deal could be adduced, tends to confirm the notion that the attitude expressed by Salutati represents an early and important medieval tradition.

We may well inquire concerning the nature of Ovid's appeal to serious authors in the Middle Ages. Certain incidental attractions occur to us at once, such as the parallels between the first book of the *Metamorphoses* and the Book of Genesis. Ovid is also full of wise saws and well-turned phrases on a wide variety of subjects. But, if we assume that the general attitude expressed by Salutati and Rand had some currency, there may have been also something attractive to medieval Christians in Ovid's theory of love. At the opening of the fourth book of the *Fasti*, Venus is invoked as the "mother of the twin loves." After the invocation Ovid refers in a jocular way to his earlier books on love, but indicates that his new project in the *Fasti* is more serious. Here Venus is described as a cosmic force which governs the earth, the sea, and the heavens, causes plants and animals to perpetuate their species, inspires the arts among men, and, as Venus Verticordia, preserves the chastity of wives. These activities are very different from those of the "mother of tender loves" who presides over the *Amores* and the *Ars amatoria*. The love described in these earlier works, although equally the product or "son" of Venus, has little to do with chastity. The observations of an anonymous eleventh-century commentator on the *Fasti* are thus not entirely fantastic:

> There are two Venuses, one chaste and modest who leads the way in virtuous loves . . . the other a voluptuous goddess of unlawful passion . . . There are thus two loves, one good and modest . . . the other shameless and evil. It is to be noted that there is one Venus literally called "Genetrix" by the Romans who is considered by Ovid to be the mother of both loves.[12]

The same description is used by Albericus of London (*Myth. Vat.*, III, 18) who attributes it to Remigius, so that it may have been as old as the ninth century. When Bernard Silvestris, commenting on Virgil, wrote of two Venuses, one of which represents "natural justice" or "mundana musica" and the other of which is the "mother of all fornication,"[13] he may not have been departing very far from one possible conception of the "Ovidian spirit."

The idea that there are two loves, one reflecting the harmony of created nature, and the other shameful, reprehensible, or ridiculous, was not unfamiliar in a purely Christian frame of reference during the twelfth century. It was held that good and evil are fundamentally matters of love, and that love springs like a fountain within the human breast which may turn either in the stream of charity, a love which is the source of all good, or in the stream of cupidity, a love which is the source of all evil.[14] The good love was said to be harmonious with the force which preserves the order in nature and makes nature fruitful, and this love was abandoned by man for the evil love in the Fall.[15] It is not, therefore, surprising that John the Scot, writing of the evil Venus, should identify her with original sin,[16] that is, with concupiscence of the flesh taken in a general rather than in a specific sense. Concupiscence was the "mother of all fornication" both physical and spiritual, but at the same time necessary so that fallen man, who could no longer reproduce himself reasonably, might perpetuate his race. There was thus an obvious parallel between the Ovidian concept of "twin loves" and the Christian concept of two opposing loves. Although we may not agree with what he says, we may perhaps see a certain historical reasonableness in the assertion of Arnulf of Orléans in the twelfth century to the effect that in the *Metamorphoses* Ovid set out to condemn irrational love, or the immoderate love of temporal things, and to encourage rational love, or love for the creator.[17] Ovid's conception of the creator (*Met.*, 1.20-87) was in some respects very different from that of Arnulf; nevertheless, the Christian commentator could find in the pagan poet surprising anticipations of his own attitude toward the dual nature of love.

In view of the uses made of Ovid's poetry by medieval writers and commentators, it seems to me probable that there flourished in the twelfth century, when Ovid achieved widespread popularity, a notion very similar to that expressed by Rand to the effect that ridicule is "a most potent remedy" of the wrong kind of love. Ovid himself spoke of his *Ars* as his book of "jokes" (*Trist.*, 2.237-238) and insisted that the work advocates nothing unlawful. He called himself "tenerorum lusor amorum" (*Trist.*, 3.3.73; 3.10.1), a phrase which may imply mockery as well as playfulness. If Ovid was thought to condemn cupidinous love in the *Metamorphoses*, moreover, an examination of the text will show that much of this condemnation, or supposed condemnation, involves humor. As Fränkel puts it, "There is no need to say much about the humor in the *Metamorphoses*, because it is one of its most obvious features."[18] With reference to Chrétien, it would be useful to know whether he regarded Ovid as a humorous mocker of a misdirected love which, in the Christian context of his romances, could be associated with cupidity. I do not propose to answer this question here, but to suggest that, if he did think of Ovid in this way, we should perhaps be more sensitive to humorous possibilities in his own work. In support of this suggestion, I wish to consider briefly a few tentative illustrations of Ovidian irony in *Cligés*.

When Cligés "in the flower of his age" (almost fifteen) appears at the court of the Emperor of Germany where he sees Fenice for the first time, Chrétien pauses to describe his beauty. He says that the boy is fairer than Narcissus, who died because he fell in love with his own image in a fountain and could not consummate this love—and also wiser. As Guyer points out, this passage is unmistakably a reference to the story of Narcissus in the *Metamorphoses*, a story which has certain very obvious connotations. Fränkel has this to say of it:

> The Ovid of the *Metamorphoses* is far from composing parables or preaching sermons; he merely tells fascinating stories; and yet, in so doing, he furnishes material for many a sermon. The medieval *Ovide moralisé* is mostly inept, but the idea was not so preposterous as it seems. The words in which Ovid expresses Narcissus' fatal predicament lead very close to a profound truth. Self-love is headed for self-destruction. Its thirst can never be quenched. . . .[19]

He goes on to say that Narcissus was changed into a flower "as fine and proud, as single and useless as he used to be." In the twelfth century Arnulf of Orléans says of the same story, "Narcissus is said to have loved his shadow, because he put his own excellence above all other things. . . . He was changed into a flower, that is, into a useless thing. . . ."[20] On the general implications of the Narcissus story the twelfth century and the twentieth are thus in agreement. Having made his point about Cligés "in the flower of his age," Chrétien shows his two young protagonists making eyes at each other, each falling hopelessly in love with the other's beauty, so that, without speaking, they come to have a common desire. In this sense their hearts are merged in one, a quaint device, we may observe, which arranges matters so that each in effect loves himself. Perhaps Chrétien intended his lovers to look a little foolish and reinforced this intention by referring to Narcissus.

Cligés and Fenice manage to avoid Narcissus' untimely end partly through the offices of an enchantress named Thessala. She claims to know more of charms and witchcraft than Medea, who was born in Thessaly, a country noted in Ovid, Lucan, and elsewhere for the practice of witchcraft. The comparison with Medea is not very propitious and certainly does not suggest that Thessala is a person whose enterprises may be considered to be at all virtuous. In *Heroides* 12 Medea confesses that her witchcraft can subdue dragons and wild bulls, but not her own passion. And in the *Metamorphoses* this passion is admittedly something contrary to justice, piety, and modesty (7.72).[21] The crimes to which love and witchcraft lead Medea are remembered once more in the *Tristia* (3.9), where Ovid uses the story of how Medea murdered and dismembered her brother to contribute to the unwholesome atmosphere of his place of exile. If Cligés is like Narcissus, and

Thessala, who helps him, is like Medea, Chrétien cannot have regarded their activities in a very favorable light. Among the specific devices Thessala uses is a potion or philter; as Fränkel points out, such means were repugnant to Ovid, who condemned them repeatedly.[22] Again, at one point in the story, Cligés suggests that Fenice leave her husband and go with him to Britain, where she will be received, he says, more joyfully than Helen was received at Troy when Paris took her there. As Foster Guyer suggests in his article cited above this passage probably reflects Paris' courtship of Helen as pictured in the *Heroides* (16.175). That the wooing of Helen was ill-fated and not very wise is sufficiently clear; but Ovid emphasizes this fact in the same epistle by making Paris assure his lady that she need not fear the warfare of the Greeks, who will not pursue them. And even if the Greeks are aroused, Paris says, he is a man of great power and deadly weapons. In this instance common knowledge of the outcome of Paris' enterprise provides the background for Ovid's irony. Meanwhile, the suggestion that Cligés is like Paris, famous for his bad judgment (cf. Horace, *Epist.*, 1.2.10-11), and that Fenice is like Helen, whose beauty leads only to misfortunes which she herself laments in the fifteenth book of the *Metamorphoses* (232-233), is not auspicious for our protagonists.

Guyer demonstrates that Ovidian ideas characterize both Alexander's courtship of Soredamors and Cligés' courtship of Fenice.[23] Love is a tyrannical power which tortures lovers, burns them, causes paleness, trembling, lack of appetite, sleeplessness, mental derangement, and so on. Although we are usually urged to accept these things as "conventions" without any particular meaning, if Rand's general attitude was correct they are a part of Ovid's design to make love ridiculous.[24] Chrétien does not lend them any greater dignity by adding yawning and sweating to the symptoms of lovesickness—the second of which Chaucer was to use for humorous effect in his picture of "joly Absolon." One of the most prominent features of love in Cligés is that it begins with the eyes. Thus Soredamors complains that she has been betrayed by her eyes; and her debate with herself, as Guyer shows, owes something to the inner debate of Medea, who has almost conquered her passion when the sight of Jason causes it to flare up again. Alexander confesses that he was wounded through the eye. Love's arrow, which he elaborates in such a way as to make it identical with the appearance of Soredamors, has passed through his eye to his heart. In this process it by-passes the understanding. To show how his understanding has been neglected in this process, Chrétien gives us a picture of Alexander in bed embracing and caressing a shirt which contains a strand of Soredamors' hair; at this point Chrétien openly calls him a fool. Again, Cligés and Fenice are, like Narcissus, betrayed by their eyes. It seems likely that Chrétien was just as aware as Ovid was (*De med. fac.*, trans. I. H. Mozley, 45–50) that "Love of character is lasting: beauty will be ravaged by age, and the face that charmed will be ploughed by wrinkles . . . Goodness endures and lasts for many a day, and throughout its years love securely rests thereon." We may recall similar ideas in Cicero's *De amicitia*, and that love through the eyes is regarded with disfavor in the Old Testament, where, for example, Holofernes is captured by his eyes when he sees Judith (Judith 10:17, 16:11). Love through the eyes is a kind of foolishness in both pagan and scriptural contexts; not to mention the context of ordinary common sense.

I do not mean to imply that Chrétien was sermonizing any more than Ovid was sermonizing; but it seems to me that his Ovidian references and "conventions," if we may call them that without emptying them completely of meaning, may have had an ironically humorous effect. If the obvious reflections of Ovid alone pointed in this direction, the evidence would be very tenuous, since it is probably impossible to demonstrate conclusively that Chrétien interpreted Ovid in any special way. But there are other evidences of light mockery in the romances, especially in *Cligés*. For example, Soredamors spends some very anxious moments seated by Alexander's side trying to make up her mind how she should address her prospective lover. She does not know whether to call him by his name or to address him with the word, "Friend." She is afraid that if she calls him "Friend" as she would like to do she might be telling a lie, since the two have never spoken. On the other hand, his name is so long that she might stumble over it and stop half way through. While she is meditating in stony silence on these awful possibilities, the Queen enters and very casually punctures Soredamors' reverie by addressing Alexander as "Friend." Again, and here the touch is a little more serious, when Cligés promises Fenice that, if she will go to Britain with him, she will be as well received as Helen was in Troy, Fenice replies to the effect that a move of this kind would injure her reputation. No one would then believe that she had never submitted to the embraces of her husband. To support this very virtuous posture she quotes St. Paul, who, she says, advised those who cannot remain chaste to keep themselves free from blame. The humor in this argument arises from the fact that what St. Paul says (1 Corinthians 7:9) is that "if they do not contain themselves, let them marry. For it is better to marry than to be burnt." But Fenice has not been using her marriage to avoid being burnt, and there may be some ironic significance in the fact that the plan she proposes on the basis of her scriptural authority results in her being burnt in yet another way. We may add that her resurrection from the ashes suggests another ironic inversion.[25] In any event, the authority she cites condemns the very position she seeks to support. At the same time it suggests the solution to love's difficulties which Alexander and Soredamors found on the good advice of the Queen. Serious considerations aside, there seems to me to be a certain humor in the disparity between what Fenice is seeking to justify by her authority and what her authority actually says.

At one point in the story the contrast between charity and cupidity, which, as we have seen, may be thought of as a Christian fulfillment of Ovid's "twin loves," is made explicit, but with a very light touch effected by the introduction of an Ovidian idea. In the course of Fenice's feigned illness, the Emperor who is her husband in name only wishes to bring a physician to examine her. Fenice says that only one physician can cure her and that her life or death is wholly in his hands. The Emperor and his companions think that she means God, as they very well might, since according to a very old convention Christ is regarded as the physician of the soul. But just as Oenone can be helped neither by herbs nor by a god, but only by Paris, and just as Medea cannot cure her malady by witchcraft but only with the help of Jason, Fenice, Chrétien tells us, actually meant Cligés when she mentioned a physician: "He is her god who can cure her and who can cause her to die." This remark reminds us at once of Ovid's lovesick ladies and of the Christian sin of idolatry. Love for Cligés is set against love for God, or cupidity in the typical form of sexual passion against charity. As a matter of fact, Fenice is not sick at all except for a certain self-induced warmth, and she needs spiritual attention rather than the offices of the learned gentlemen from Salerno. But these ideas are kept from being too serious and heavy-handed by the humorous incongruity between what Fenice is thinking and what the Emperor is thinking; and the humorous level is maintained in the subsequent events, which include the hilarious demise of the physicians at the hands of more than a thousand indignant ladies who have observed Fenice's "martyrdom" through a little crack in a door.

Ironic humor is perhaps one of the chief characteristics of the "Ovidian spirit" as it is viewed by Rand. In a sense the whole second part of *Cligés* develops toward an ironic conclusion. When Fenice first reveals her love for Cligés to Thessala, she describes her aversion to the situation typified by the love of Iseut and Tristan, of whom, she says, many idle tales are told. Again, she tells Cligés that she is not really a wife and that her body belongs to him exclusively, as well as her heart. No one, she maintains self-righteously, will learn to do villainous deeds by her example. Cligés will never be called Tristan nor she Iseut, for their honor would then be lost. On the basis of the same reasoning she refuses to run away with Cligés. If she did, men would say evil things about them and no one would believe that she had kept her body for him alone. As it turns out, the deceits and lies of the lovers and the charms and craft of Thessala and Jehan serve only to intensify Fenice's evil reputation. For at the very end of the romance we are told solemnly that there has not been an emperor of Greece since the time of the story, who, thinking of how Fenice deceived Alis first with the potion and then with the other ruse of her pretended death, did not fear his wife and keep her under lock and key away from the company of any men except those castrated in youth. I suggest that the references in the story to such characters as Narcissus and Paris, together with the conventions borrowed from Ovidian love poetry, also point toward the fact so eloquently revealed in the conclusion that Fenice and Cligés were a little deluded in their conception of honor.

To return once more to our central problem, the question of the significance of Ovid's influence on Chrétien, it must be admitted that it is possible to interpret Ovid in a number of different ways. If Ovid is essentially a prurient poet, it follows that he must have been misunderstood by a great many medieval writers from Alcuin to Salutati. And in that event either Chrétien misunderstood him or was a prurient poet himself. It is true that some of his critics have accused him of having only a superficial conception of morality. On the other hand, there is some reason for seeing Ovid as a satirist with some feeling for moral standards, a poet whose chief weapons were ridicule and humor. If we see him in this light, his influence on serious medieval authors is easier to understand and we have some basis for suspecting irony and humor in less-serious medieval vernacular authors who show substantial evidence of his influence. The humor of a distant generation in a society very different from our own is sometimes difficult to detect, and our philological methods are clumsy before a joke. But the conception of Chrétien as a mild satirist has, it seems to me, something to be said for it and is in some ways more consonant with what we know of the twelfth century than the conception sometimes presented to us that he was a slightly immoral romantic sentimentalist.

The Idea of Fame in Chrétien's Cligés

It seems to me that we shall not understand Chrétien very well until we have learned to read his text carefully, paying attention to deviations from conventionally accepted moral ideas, false logic, wordplay, and echoes of the scriptures and the classics, and considering what he has to say in the light of the rivalries, diverse local customs, and interests of his own time. For a good recent discussion of The Song of Roland, *see Gerard J. Brault,* The Song of Roland *(University Park and London, 1978), vol. 1.*

W E are often led to think that fame is a subject celebrated in Antiquity, neglected during the Christian Middle Ages, and revived in the Renaissance, when men, freed from the shackles of asceticism, turned once more to the pursuit of laurel crowns and immortal reputations. When fame is desired or praised in early medieval poetry, we are likely to think of that poetry as "pagan," and when fame is celebrated in a chivalric environment later on, we usually say that it is "secular." There may be a certain very limited truth in this view, but as Maria Rosa Lida de Malkiel has shown, fame was by no means neglected during the Middle Ages,[1] and it is quite possible that the differences between "religious" and "secular" views of fame may not be quite so great as has been supposed. Perhaps it would be best to say simply that the thinkers of the Middle Ages introduced a certain order into concepts of fame developed in Antiquity.

Some ancient writers, as Lida de Malkiel demonstrated, deliberately cultivated fame, while others scorned the praise of the crowd or commented on the fickleness of reputation. Both Virgil and Ovid, for example, describe the untrustworthiness of fame in vivid terms,[2] although Ovid concludes his *Metamorphoses* with the boast, "Wherever Rome's power extends over the conquered world, I shall have mention on men's lips, and, if the prophecies of bards have any truth, through all the ages shall I live in fame."[3] In *The Consolation of Philosophy*, a book revered throughout the Middle Ages and widely read during the Renaissance, fame is associated with Fortune, and the pursuit of it for its own sake is shown to be vain.[4] The New Testament

indicates a contrast between "worldly" fame and "eternal" fame in
Heaven, and Christian writers often insist on the futility of pursuing
the former, since it leads to vainglory, which opens the way for all the
vices. If we confine ourselves to this dichotomy, which is not, actually, without a certain precedent in Cicero,[5] many passages in medieval
literature seem oddly un-Christian. The fame of Scyld as it is described by the *Beowulf* poet, not to mention that of Beowulf himself,
looks suspicious; and Roland's reluctance to sound his horn seems
vainglorious.

But medieval ideas seldom fall easily into simple dichotomies, however much we may wish to force them into a Procrustean polarization.
The Bible itself urges, at the beginning of the forty-fourth chapter of
Ecclesiasticus, "Let us now praise men of renown," and the text proceeds at once to do so, including among its heroes one worthy who
"made a violent assault against the nation of his enemies." This sounds
fairly "secular." Could worldly reputation serve a good purpose, even
though it should not be pursued for its own sake? It could indeed, and
there is nothing "un-Christian" about the idea. In fact, it was widely
held that every Christian has an obligation to maintain a good reputation, and for good reasons.

This idea is vividly illustrated in a passage from Abelard's *History of
My Calamities.* The dejected philosopher, who had been in his youth
much concerned about his fame, and not a little vainglorious about it,
found himself in ill repute, practically exiled in the monastery of St.
Gildas de Rhuys. His fame was such that in spite of his eunuchry he
could not visit Heloise to assist her by preaching at the Paraclete without attacks from those who alleged that he did so only because of "a
certain delight in concupiscence." Detraction, that is, rendered him
powerless to do good, just as his wound had made him powerless in
another way:

> But what I endured much less from the wound, I was now made to
> suffer for a longer time through detraction, and I was tormented
> more by the diminution of my fame than by that of my body. For it
> is written, "A good name is better than great riches" (Proverbs
> 22:1). And as St. Augustine says in a certain sermon *On the Life and
> Manners of Clerks,* "He who trusting to his conscience neglects his
> fame is hard-hearted." And, as he says earlier in the same work,
> " 'Let us provide,' as the Apostle says (Romans 12:17), 'good things
> not only in the sight of God, but also in the sight of all men.' On our
> own account our conscience is sufficient for us. In our concern for
> others, our fame should not be polluted but should flourish in us.

Conscience and fame are two things. Your conscience is for you; your fame is for the benefit of your neighbor."[6]

One of the obvious exemplary lessons of Abelard's *History* is that fame sought for vainglorious ends is easily destroyed by some weakness arising from vainglory itself. The principle is clearly implied in the account of Abelard's enormous success as a teacher at Paris and his loss of fame after his lapse with Heloise:

> Whence in both kinds of study [logical and exegetical] my scholars multiplied, and my pecuniary rewards and glory were such that my fame cannot be hidden from you. But since prosperity always puffs up fools, and worldly tranquility enervates the vigor of the mind, which is easily destroyed by carnal attractions, just at the time I sought to excel all the world in philosophy and feared no disturbance from anyone, I began to relax the reins of libido, which I had previously grasped most continently. And the more I prospered in philosophy and the exposition of the Scriptures, the more I receded from philosophers and divines in uncleanness of life. For it is fitting that philosophers, not to mention divines . . . should chiefly triumph in the beauty of continence. When, therefore, I was laboring completely in pride and lechery, Divine Grace bestowed on me a remedy for both maladies, even though I did not wish it.

Divine Grace also deprived Abelard of his fame, a fact that at first injured only his vanity, as he tells us when he describes his reaction to his castration:

> The clerks especially and particularly my own students tortured me with their intolerable laments and wailings, and I suffered much more from their compassion than from my wounds, feeling the embarrassment more keenly than the injury, and being afflicted by the shame more than by soreness. There ran through my mind thoughts of how much fame I had acquired and of how easily and quickly this fame had been brought low, if indeed it was not extinguished, and of the just judgment of God in that I had been afflicted in that part of my body with which I had sinned.

This worldly shame, rather than devotion, caused him to take monastic orders. But even after the shame had passed his fame remained sullied and prevented him, as we have seen, from performing good works.

The passages from Abelard's *History* clearly involve two kinds of "worldly" fame: one that a man cherishes for himself, out of vanity, and another that he cherishes for others, out of charity. Fame of the first kind leads to vainglory and frequently to a loss of reputation, while fame of the second kind is often necessary to the performance of good works. There is no reason, moreover, to restrict the second kind of fame to clerks; anyone should be expected to maintain it, and it is obvious that the higher a man's station in society and the greater his responsibilities, the more he was obliged, in the hierarchical society of the Middle Ages, to cultivate this second kind of fame. It is, in fact, exactly this kind of fame that is exemplified by Roland. The author of the poem went to some lengths to make this fact clear, and there is no reason why we should quarrel with him. When Oliver asks Roland to sound his horn, Roland replies,

> Jo fereie que fols,
> En dulce France en perdreie mun los.
> (1053-1054)

Is the fame he cherishes for himself or for his compatriots? His reply to Oliver's second request is explicit:

> Ne placet Damnedeu
> Que mi parent pur mei seient blasmét,
> Ne France dulce ja cheet en viltét!
> (1062-1064)

The last denial of Oliver's request repeats this theme once more:

> Ne placet Damnedeu ne ses angles
> Que ja pur mei perdet sa valur France!
> (1089-1090)

We have no ground whatsoever for arguing with Roland about the manner in which he seeks to please God or to avoid displeasing Him. In the poem St. Gabriel and St. Michael show no hestitation about taking his soul to Paradise, and the Good Lord, in the Middle Ages, did not ordinarily send such Messengers to relieve the vainglorious. Nor did Roland lose his reputation among the French who were familiar with his story because they thought him to be vain. Perhaps our difficulties with the ethics of the poem will be assuaged somewhat if we cease to think of Roland as a "personality" and consider him for what he was clearly intended to be: an exemplification of certain ideals of "vasselage," among them that kind of fame that is maintained not for ourselves but for others.

We are left with two principal kinds of fame, "Heavenly," and "worldly." The second may be either vainglorious and selfish, or, on the other hand, unselfish and self-sacrificing. Perhaps the second kind of "worldly" fame may be thought of as an aspect of "Heavenly" fame because it is pleasing to God. The saints offer excellent examples of good fame, and there were in the Middle Ages saints in great variety so that anyone no matter what his rank or station could seek good fame by emulating the example of one or another of them. It should not surprise us that fame should become a subject for analysis by medieval poets, and I wish to suggest here that it is the subject of one of the romances of Chrétien de Troyes, *Cligés*. The evidence of the text shows, I think, that Chrétien was very much aware of the general distinctions we have examined. They are, after all, rather simple moral principles.

If Ovid could boast that his fame would spread throughout Roman territories and endure "through all the ages," Chrétien in turn could assert that his first Arthurian romance, *Erec*, would be remembered as long as Christianity endures:

> Des or comancerai l'estoire
> Qui toz jorz mes iert an memoire
> Tant con durra crestiantez;
> De ce s'est Chrestiiens vantez.
> (23-26)

It may be argued that he was thinking of the lesson he had in mind—

> Que cil ne fet mie savoir,
> Qui sa sciance n'abandone
> Tant con Deus la grace l'an done—
> (16-18)

a good Christian moral ensconced under the apparently worthless surface of a "conte d'avanture." Even if this is true, however, it cannot be denied that he shows an unmistakable interest in his own reputation.

This interest reappears at the beginning of *Cligés*, where he tells us at the outset it was he who wrote of Erec and Enide and of King Mark and Iseult, and who translated certain works of Ovid. On these accomplishments, we infer, his fame rests. Now he will tell us of a young Greek who "por pris et por los" went to England, then called Britain. The story comes, he says, from a very old book, and from such books one learns that chivalry and learning once flourished in Greece, then passed to Rome, and finally to France, where the honor of their cultivation now rests. Chrétien asks God that this honor may be welcomed in France and never depart. Of Greece and Rome, he says, no more is heard.

There is certainly nothing wrong with a desire to retain the honor or fame of chivalry and learning in France, and if Chrétien thought that he was helping to preserve it there by writing his tales and romances, his enterprise was, at least from a medieval point of view, a worthy one, and his reputation was an important asset. The disappearance of the fame of Greece and Rome (in a current rather than an historical sense) suggests an object lesson. That is, God has granted fame to France, but it may not remain there. Chrétien has told us that chivalry and learning passed from Greece to Rome and from Rome to France. He said nothing whatsoever about their ever having resided in Britain. Yet he will tell of a Greek, whose country has lost its fame, who went to Britain to gain fame. If we have read the prologue with any attention, certain conclusions are obvious: (1) the young Greek who went to Britain was misdirected, and (2) his pursuit of fame there must have been vain. Therefore, (3) the story Chrétien has to tell us will deal with false fame and the loss of fame, so that it will be, in effect, a warning to France. Meanwhile, it is also apparent that it was foolish to seek "pris et los" in Britain, so that we should expect the activities of those who did so to be at least potentially amusing. Even if we are inclined to avoid the logical implications of what Chrétien says in his prologue, on the ground, perhaps, that he was a naïve and loose-jointed writer who cannot be expected to make sense, it is clear that the prologue is largely "about" fame: the fame of Chrétien, the fame of Greece, Rome, and France, and the fame sought by the young Greek in Britain. It is not difficult to show that this subject is not abandoned in the romance itself.

We are introduced at once to Alexander, the son of the Emperor Alexander and the Empress Tantalis, and the elder brother of Alis, not without a rather playful hint of the common element "Alis" in all of these names. Our young hero is too "corageus et fiers" to seek honor in his own country and wishes instead to journey to Britain. For the purposes of his journey he asks his father for gold and silver. In Britain he can learn honor, he says, and "conquerre pris et los," devoting himself entirely to the pursuit of fame. His father, with remarkable generosity, grants him two barges full of gold and silver and urges him to practice generosity as the best source of fame. It is better, he says, than birth, courtesy, knowledge, nobility, wealth, power, chivalry, hardiness, seignory, beauty, or anything else, adding,

> Mes tot aussi come la rose
> Est plus que nule autre flors bele,
> Quant ele nest fresche et novele:

> Aussi la, ou largesce vient,
> Dessor totes vertuz se tient,
> Et les bontez que ele trueve
> An prodome, qui bien s'esprueve,
> Fet a cinc çanz dobles monter.
>
> (208-215)

The rose "fresche et novele," we may reflect, does not last very long, and neither does the kind of generosity that will multiply virtues so much last very long either, although the young Alexander's barges should enable him to emulate the fabled generosity of Alexander the Great for a considerable time. In any event, fame acquired in this way is unlikely to rest on a secure foundation, being closely allied with Fortune. This fact would hardly have escaped Chrétien's audience, who undoubtedly greeted the speech of the elder Alexander with a smile.

When he reaches Britain, Alexander does impress the court with his generosity, but like Abelard he is permitted by his prosperity to fall desperately in love. The object of this passion, who returns it, is Sir Gawain's sister, Soredamors, a golden-haired damsel who says that her name means "sororee d'amors." Alexander soon decides that he would rather have this gold than all the metallic gold in Antioch, and he becomes intensely interested in his fame as a means of obtaining it. The love story is developed with entertaining Ovidian irony,[7] and in the course of it a new theme is introduced: treason. At one point Chrétien says that God hates traitors most of all:

> Car traïtor et traïson
> Het Des plus qu'autre mesprison. . . .
>
> (1709-1710)

Treason is the greatest source of ill fame, although traitors like Judas and Ganelon are well remembered. The traitor in this instance, who is said to be worse than Ganelon, seizes the kingdom while Arthur is abroad, so that the King and his court must hasten home to confront him. Having become one of Arthur's knights and having successfully defeated the traitor, Alexander is still left with his love problem. No longer interested in gold, he gives up a trophy cup that would have brought him reward anywhere in the world. But the Queen intervenes in time, offering some memorable advice:

> "D'amor andotriner vos vuel;
> Car bien sai qu'amors vos afole.
> Por ce vos ai mis a escole,
> Et gardez ne m'an celez rien,

Qu'aparceüe m'an sui bien
As contenances de chascun,
Que de deus cuers avez fet un.
Ja vers moi ne vos an celez!
De ce trop folement ovrez,
Que chascuns son panser ne dit,
Qu'au celer li uns l'autre ocit:
D'amor omecide seroiz.
Or vos lo que ja ne queroiz
Force ne volanté d'amor.
Par mariage et par enor
Vos antraconpaigniez ansamble.
Einsi porra, si con moi sanble,
Vostre amors longuemant durer.
Je vos os bien asseürer,
Se vos an avez buen corage,
J'assanblerai le mariage."
                         (2290-2310)

As Abelard discovered, concealed love is no road to good fame; loving couples should join together "parenor" in marriage. This advice may sound a little curious coming from Guenevere, and it is quite possible that Chrétien placed it on her lips with jocular intent; it is nevertheless sound advice, as everyone in the audience would have seen. The marriage is duly celebrated, Alexander abandons his quest for fame, and the young couple have a son, Cligés.

Thus ends the first part of the romance, and in it Chrétien has set his themes. Good fame results more from good action than from wealth, especially when that action involves the overthrow of treason. The solution to the problem of fleshly concupiscence is marriage if honor is to be preserved. Meanwhile, treason is the worst of crimes, whether in feudal relations or in personal relations, and in either instance it destroys good fame. It is not unreasonable to assume that this preliminary narrative was composed not simply to provide an "historical" background for the protagonist, Cligés, but to develop these themes. However, the validity of this assumption must depend on the treatment of the subsequent narrative.

When Alexander returns to Greece after his marriage, he has some trouble with his brother Alis, who has taken over the realm in his absence. But a suitable arrangement is made: Alis will keep the name of Emperor while Alexander will exercise the real power. Alis swears never to marry, so that Cligés may succeed him without question, seeming content with the mere name of Emperor:

> Alis n'i a mes que le non,
> Que anpereres est clamez; . . .
>   (2588-2589)

This fact introduces a subsidiary theme: just as Alis has only the name of Emperor, so also will he have, when the time comes, only the name of husband. In both instances the name, which should carry with it a certain honor and repute, becomes empty, and the fame that inheres in the name is lost. As we shall see later on, Fenice has only the name of Empress or wife, and Cligés has only the name of a loyal vassal. We shall, that is, find Chrétien much occupied with the consequences of false pretense for the sake of fame.

Fortunately for Alis, his brother Alexander soon dies, and, misled by evil counsel, he decides to take a wife in violation of his oath. He chooses the very beautiful Fenice. Cligés makes no objection to this wrongdoing at the time, and shows no inclination to protest, especially after he has seen Fenice, with whom he falls desperately in love because of her beauty. Fenice suffers from the same malady at the mere sight of Cligés, but since she is acutely concerned about her fame, her malady poses a special problem. As she explains to her nurse Thessala, she does not wish to marry Alis because she loves his nephew. Moreover, if she were to take Cligés as a lover, her reputation would be lost:

> Miauz voldroie estre desmanbree,
> Que de nos deus fust remanbree
> L'amors d'Iseut et de Tristan,
> Don tantes folies dit l'an,
> Que honte m'est a reconter.
>   (3145-3149)

Fenice has no wish to give her body to two men when her heart belongs to one, for this would be to repeat the highly scandalous conduct of Iseult, whose fame, we gather, was not of the best.[8] She asks her nurse, therefore, to arrange matters so that she will not have to marry Alis. We should notice that her love is based only on the fact that Cligés is beautiful—"Mes n'an set plus que bel le voit"—or, in other words, that he appears to be an attractive source of satisfaction; and that her concern for family is entirely "for herself" and not at all "for others," involving no inclination toward self-sacrifice at all. These points would hardly have been lost on a twelfth-century audience who had not yet experienced the successive triumphs of sentiment, romanticism, and pious self-gratification that lie in our own background. The essential selfishness of our heroine's passion accounts for the fact that she readily accepts Thessala's solution. This involves a potion that will make Alis after his marriage think that he enjoys his wife, when, as a matter of fact, he does not, but only dreams of doing so. In this way Fenice will give her body only to the man she desires, while her husband will be deceived. We may reflect that this potion has certain advantages over that imbibed by Tristan and Iseut.

The potion is duly prepared and administered. It works beautifully:

> Ore est l'anperere gabez.
> Mout ot evesques et abez
> Au lit seignier et beneïr.
> Quant ore fu d'aler gesir,
> L'anperere, si come il dut,
> Avuec sa fame la nuit jut.—
> 'Si come il dut,' ai je manti,
> Qu'il ne la beisa ne santi . . .
> (3329-3336)

> . . . .

> Et cil la prie et si l'apele
> Mout soavet sa douce amie,
> Tenir la cuide, n'an tient mie;
> Mes de neant est an grant eise:
> Neant anbrace et neant beise,
> Neant tient et neant acole,
> Neant voit, a neant parole,
> A neant tance, a neant luite.
> Mout fu bien la poisons confite,
> Qui si le travaille et demainne.
> (3356-3365)

Poor Alis, we are told, never enjoyed other satisfaction than this vain imagination produced by the potion. As for Fenice, it is clear that she is no real wife, and that, in fact, she has connived in a kind of treason.

Meanwhile, the Duke of Saxony, to whom Fenice had been promised by her father, seeks to steal Fenice away, thus affording Cligés an opportunity to win fame in her defense. His heroic feats in this rather dubious cause, rendered dubious by the fact that the marriage involved violations of oaths by two emperors, are truly magnificent, if rather amusingly exaggerated; but the fame he seeks is selfish, for he wishes only to make an impression on Fenice, not to defend the interests of his countrymen. Although he finds an opportunity to tell Fenice of his love, he is afraid to do so, not only because he, who so easily conquered so many fierce adversaries, is afraid of her, but also

because she is, at least legally, his uncle's wife, so that he is embarrassed. Commenting on this situation, Chrétien says,

> Serjanz qui son seignor ne dote,
> Ne doit remenoir en sa rote
> Ne ne doit feire son servise.
> Seignor ne crient, qui ne le prisc,
> Et qui nel prise, ne l'a chier,
> Ainz se painne de lui trichier
> Et de la soe chose anbler.
>
> (3879-3885)

The lord in this instance is specifically Love, and Chrétien's comment
concerns the attitude of Cligés toward Love, which has mastered
him.[9] This love arose, as the narrative has explained, because Cligés
and Fenice were overcome, each at the sight of the other's beauty.
They mutually desire to possess each other; for each the other is an
extremely desirable beautiful object. The comparison between Cligés
and Narcissus (2761 ff.) in this connection is a clear indication that
what he wishes is his own satisfaction. And, as the passage just quoted
indicates, he is completely subject to this desire. But the words here
applied to Love are based on the analogy of the proper relation between lord and subject. They suggest a generalization that applies to
the lovers as well as to anyone else. Both Cligés and Fenice wish to
deceive Alis and should not "remenoir en sa rote." For them to do so
while wishing to deceive him is treasonable, since they are clearly
seeking to take away something that is his. That is, one cannot derive a
principle from one realm of application and apply it to another and
then turn around to say that the second application vitiates the first.
To do so is merely to destroy the entire argument. Herein lies the
humor of the passage quoted, a kind of humor characteristic of Chrétien that is frequently overlooked.

The final triumph of Cligés, undertaken ostensibly in the defense of
Alis, but actually to support his own interests in Fenice, is his personal
victory in single combat over the Duke of Saxony. The result is the
complete disgrace of the Duke, who, in his pursuit of Fenice, destroys
his fame. He seeks desperately to retain it, saying to his formidable
young adversary, who has been inspired to new vigor by an outcry
from Fenice,

> "Vaslez! jant et apert
> Te voi mout et de grant corage.
> Mes trop par ies de juene aage:

> Por ce me pans et sai de fi,
> Que, se je te vainc et oci,
> Ja los ne pris n'i aquerroie,
> Ne ja prodome ne verroie,
> Oiant cui regehir deüsse,
> Quë a toi conbatuz me fusse;
> Qu'enor te feroie et moi honte.
> Mes se tu sez quë enors monte,
> Granz enors te sera toz jorz
> Ce que solemant deus estorz
> T'ies anvers moi contretenuz.
> Or m'est cuers et talanz venuz,
> Que la querele te guerpisse
> Ne quë a toi plus ne chanpisse."
>   (4156-4172)

The Duke is unwilling to sacrifice himself in his cause, even though there is some justice in it, and as a result he suffers disgrace. For when he repeats the words above publicly, "Cligés ot l'enor et le pris," (4184), the falsity of the Duke's fame is apparent to all, so that he and his men go home in great sorrow:

> Li dus an Seissoingne repeire
> Dolanz et maz et vergondeus;
> Car de ses homes n'i a deus,
> Qui nel taingnent por mescheant,
> Por failli et por recreant.
>   (4194-4198)

But the "honor" of Cligés also rests on an insecure foundation, for he was not, as he seemed to be, actually protecting the interests of his lord. In fact, as we shall see, the pursuit of Fenice for selfish ends, so to speak, is not an appropriate way to win fame. The Duke of Saxony affords the first object lesson to this effect.

After he has returned to Greece, Cligés is still reluctant to tell Fenice about his love for her, partly out of shame. We must forgive our twelfth-century ancestors for not sharing our own views about the merits of immediate gratification, especially among the young. Cligés does remember his father's advice: to win honor he should go to Britain and engage in tournaments. With this pursuit in mind, he approaches Alis, explicitly calling attention to his youth and inexperience and alleging that

> An Bretaingne sont li prodome,
> Qu'enors et proesce renome.
> (4255-4256)

To associate with them, he says, would be honorable. Alis, with some reluctance, grants his wish, offering him instead of two barges of gold and silver, "plus d'un sestier" of these precious metals. (4274) Chrétien needed no further illustrations of Alexandrine generosity as a means of acquiring fame. Cligés takes leave of Fenice, weeping bitterly with averted eyes—"Si sanble que vergoingne an et." (4300) Fenice regards him in turn "come peoreuse et coarde." These attitudes, which involve secrecy, are contrary to the advice of Guenevere, but Cligés and Fenice have no prospect of honorable marriage. Cligés explains that

> ". . . droiz est, qu'a vos congié praingne
> Come a celi cui je sui toz."
> (4326-4327)

This remark tortures poor Fenice, who cannot determine whether it represents an amorous inclination or is simply an appropriate remark addressed to her as Empress. As her subject, Cligés owes her a debt of love—"courtly" or "courteous" love if you wish—but in this she has no interest at all:

> Pansive est an Grece venue:
> La fu a grant enor tenue
> Come dame et anpererriz;
> Mes ses cuers et ses esperiz
> Est a Cligés, quel part qu'il tort,
> Ne ja ne quiert qu'a li retort
> Ses cuers, se cil ne li raporte,
> Qui muert del mal, dont il l'a morte.
> (4343-4350)
>
> . . . .
>
> Mout li est po de son anpire
> Et de la richesce qu'ele a.
> (4360-4361)

It is clear that Greece now has an empress "in name only," to whom all legitimate praise is mere flattery.

Flattery is indeed a subject that occupies her meditations. Her heart, she says, is with Cligés, and she hopes that it will flatter him "si come an doit servir a cort":

> "Qui viaut de son seignor bien estre
> Et delez lui seoir a destre,
> Si come ore est us et costume,
> Del chief li doit oster la plume,
> Nes lors quant il n'an i a point.
> (4529-4534)

> . . . .

> Qui les corz et les seignors onge,
> Servir le covient de mançonge."
> (4561-4562)

In the same way, she says, her heart, which is with Cligés, must flatter him. Flattery creates a false fame in the mind of the person flattered, feeding his vainglory. Chrétien, as distinct from Fenice, is certainly not recommending that all courtiers practice flattery; rather he is satirically commenting on the prevalence of flattery in courts and incidentally saying something about Fenice herself, who has been quick to lie to her overlord, Alis. Even she has some inkling of the evil of flattery, for, after suggesting that her heart flatter Cligés and be obsequious, as is the custom, she adds that he is "si biaus, si frans, et si leaus" (4567) that her heart's praise of him will not constitute flattery. Cligés may be beautiful, but his candor and loyalty are open to question. As the poet says, "Einsi travaille amors Fenice." (4575) Her love leads to curious moral dilemmas and even more curious rationalizations. It is one of Chrétien's virtues that he is able to keep his principal theme—fame—alive and flourishing even when his ostensible topic is love.

In Britain Cligés is eminently successful. He has four horses—white, sorrel, fallow, and black—and obtains some colored suits of armor to wear with them. A tournament is held on the plain before Oxford. There Cligés on his black horse in black armor overcomes Sagremor. On his fallow horse in green armor he overcomes Lancelot; on his sorrel in red armor he overcomes Perceval. Finally, on his white horse in white armor he confronts Gawain and shows himself to be his equal until the two are separated by King Arthur. The stratagem of the colors, which form an effective disguise, enables him to win greater fame when, "vestuz a guise de François," (4990) he is recognized by those he had captured at the tourney. All proclaim his great worth:

> "Ce fustes vos, bien le savons!
> Vostre acointance chiere avons
> Et mout vos devriiens amer
> Et prisier et seignor clamer,
> Qu'a vos n'est nus de nos parauz.

Tot autressi con li solauz
Estaint les estoiles menues,
Que la clartez n'an pert es nues,
La ou li rai del soloil neissent:
Aussi estaingnent et abeissent
Noz proesces devant les voz;
Si soloient estre les noz
Mout renomees par le monde."
                    (5003-5015)

Thus is the fame of British chivalry dimmed by a young Greek. The great knights of Arthur's court have been overcome, not without Apocalyptic overtones suggested by the colored horses. Although there may be some consolation for the British in the fact that Cligés is Arthur's kinsman, it is nevertheless true that he has done nothing to glorify the reputation of Britain. His glory, as usual, is for himself.

When he returns to Greece, Cligés is welcomed with enthusiasm. The emperor is so abashed that he gives him all his land and treasure, but these gifts are of small worth to him, since he cares nothing for Greece but thinks only of his love, Fenice. When the lovers finally reveal their passion to each other, Fenice assures Cligés that she is not a wife, so that no one will learn any villainy from them as people do from Tristan and Iseut; their fame will be secure:

"A tort sui apelee dame;
Mes bien sai, qui dame m'apele,
Ne set que je soie pucele.
Neïs vostre oncles nel set mie,
Qui beü a de l'andormie,
Et veillier cuide, quant il dort,
Si li sanble que son deport
Et de moi tot a sa devise
Aussi come antre ses braz gise;
Mes bien l'an ai mis au defors.
Vostre est mes cuers, vostre est mes cors,
Ne ja nus par mon essanpleire
N'aprandra vilenie a feire;
Car quant mes cuers an vos se mist,
Le cors vos dona et promist,
Si quë autre part n'i avra.
Amors por vos si me navra,
Que ja mes ne cuidai garir
Ne plus que la mers puet tarir.

> Se je vos aim et vos m'amez,
> Ja n'an seroiz Trinstanz clamez,
> Ne je n'an serai ja Iseuz;
> Car puis ne seroit l'amors preuz."
>   (5240-5262)

How their love can be "preuz" in view of the deceit she describes is difficult to understand. However, she demands that Cligés remove her from Alis in such a way that he will not know where she is and neither of them will be blamed. Next day Cligés offers a solution. They can flee to Britain, where she will be welcomed more enthusiastically, he says, than Helen was welcomed at Troy when Paris took her there. The comparison is, to say the least, inauspicious, and is hardly a compliment to the British, who claimed to be descended from the Trojans and should have learned better than to welcome Helens of any kind. However, Fenice will not accept this solution. If they fled to Britain, her fame would be destroyed, for no one would know how she had deceived Alis, and everyone would think her to be as bad as Iseut:

> "Et je dirai:
> Ja avuec vos einsi n'irai;
> Car lors seroit par tot le monde
> Aussi come d'Iseut la blonde
> Et de Tristran de nos parlé,
> Quant nos an seriiens alé;
> Et ci et la, totes et tuit
> Blasmeroient nostre deduit.
> Nus ne crerroit ne devroit croire
> La chose si come ele est voire.
> De vostre oncle qui crerroit dons,
> Que je li sui si an pardons
> Pucele estorse et eschapee?
> Por trop baude et por estapee
> Me tandroit l'an et vos por fol."
>   (5309-5323)

Fenice implies that the world regards Iseut as a wanton and Tristan as a fool, but her reasons for this judgment are rather curious. They rest on the assumption that Iseut's only fault lay in giving her body to two men, whereas in fact Tristan and Iseut afford a bad example because they deceived King Mark and allowed their passion to transcend all other considerations of any kind. The proverbial *tristitia* of Tristan and the moral dilemmas into which he and Iseut fell were the results of their passion. Fenice's unfavorable comments on Iseut are thus actually unfavorable comments on herself and on the passion she cultivates. In the context of the poem, they are for this reason inadvertently humorous. Moreover, they constitute one further bit of satire on British chivalry and British traditions.

The stratagem finally adopted by the lovers, which results in the "martyrdom" of Fenice, the amusing behavior of more than a thousand women, the "resurrection" of Fenice, like the Phoenix, from her ashes, and the amusing discovery of the lovers in their iconographic "garden of delight,"[10] need not detain us here. The events allow Chrétien to develop his ironic treatment of a passion and to introduce once more the theme of treason. When Alis seeks to learn from the faithful servant of Cligés, John, the hiding place of the escaped lovers, John delivers a long speech on true fidelity, in which he says, with an echo of Roland's "vasselage":

> Car se je muir por mon seignor
> Ne morrai pas a desenor. . . .
> (6569-6570)

John is the only Greek in the poem who shows any such concern. Far from being willing to die for his overload, Cligés, who escapes with Fenice to Britain, seeks military aid against his own country at the court of King Arthur. His formal claim is to the effect that Alis has taken a wife in violation of his oath. Since Cligés did not protest at the time and indeed exerted himself strenuously to protect Alis from those who objected to the marriage, this claim is more than a little hollow. It is not rendered any more convincing by the fact that Fenice, in accordance with her own protestations, has never been a wife to Alis and could not possibly bear him an heir. However, Arthur, with what must be regarded in the poem as typical British stupidity, quickly assembles an army, vowing to destroy every Greek city that resists him. The forces of Britain are needlessly assembled, however, for the faithful John reports that Alis has died of grief and frustration.

Thus the lovers are united in their own country, where Cligés is emperor and Fenice is still not altogether a wife:

> De s'amie a feite sa fame,
> Mes il l'apele amie et dame,
> Ne por ce ne pert ele mie,
> Quë il ne l'aint come s'amie,
> Et ele lui tot autressi,
> Con l'an doit feire son ami.

> Et chascun jor lor amors crut . . .
> N'onques cil celi ne mescrut
> Ne querela de nule chose.
> > (6753-6761)

This sounds very enticing to the modern romantic imagination, and there are many who are inclined to think that Chrétien should have ended his story here. But, as we have seen, his subject was fame, and we have yet to see the final result of the quest of Cligés for fame and the desire of Fenice to acquire a good reputation:

> Onques ne fu tenue anclose,
> Si come ont puis esté tenues
> Celes qu'aprés li sont venues;
> Qu'ains puis n'i ot anpereor,
> N'eust de sa fame peor,
> Qu'ele le deüst decevoir,
> Se il oï ramantevoir,
> Comant Fenice Alis deçut
> Primes par la poison qu'il but
> Et puis par l'autre traïson.
> > (6762-6771)

Here Chrétien himself calls the potion and the feigned death "traison." Cligés and Fenice belong, actually, to the lineage of Ganelon, and they established a lasting custom in their country:

> Por quoi aussi come an prison
> Est gardee an Costantinoble,
> Ja n'iert tant riche ne tant noble,
> L'anpererriz, ques qu'ele soit;
> Que l'anperere ne la croit
> Tant con de cesti li ramanbre.
> Toz jorz la fet garder an chanbre
> Plus por peor que por le hasle,
> Ne ja avuec li n'avra masle,
> Que ne soit chastrez an anfance.
> De çaus n'est crieme ne dotance,
> Qu'amors les lit an son liien.
> Ce fenist l'uevre Crestiien.
> > (6772-6784)

Thus are Fenice and her lover Cligés, who is, in effect, replaced by *castrati*, remembered for their treason. The fame and renown for which

Cligés fought so fiercely are lost in the disgrace brought about by his selfish passion, just as the fame and renown of Tristan were destroyed by the same weakness; and the foolish conscience of Fenice has brought her a lasting ill fame worse than that of Iseut. Treason, that sin hated most by God, whether it appears in feudal relationships or in marriage, brings in this instance only infamy. It may not be irrelevant to recall that the most infamous of all men, in the twelfth century, were those belonging figuratively to the generation of Cain, whose love was typically adultery, or, in Marcabru's words,

> l'Amistats d'estraing atur
> Falsa del lignatge Caim
> Que met los siens a mal ahur.

There are, however, wider implications of Chrétien's poem. Chivalry and learning, he said, passed directly from Rome to France. The fame of a national group in the twelfth century rested largely on its chivalric leadership, so that the personal fame of members of feudal courts in effect constituted the fame of the group. The Germans, represented in the narrative by the Emperor of Germany and by his daughter Fenice, do not fare very well. The Greeks, as represented by Alis and Cligés, fare even worse, and it is not surprising that, as Chrétien says in his prologue, no more is heard of them. The Duke of Saxony, whose people represent a substantial part of English tradition, is disgraced completely. But Chrétien's most telling blows are directed against Britain. King Arthur's court not only finds its fame eclipsed by Cligés, whose memory is infamous, but it supports his treasonable activity, both personal and feudal. *Cligés* should probably be thought of not as an "anti-*Tristan*" but as a "super-*Tristan*"; for whereas King Mark is duped on the night of his marriage into accepting a substitute for his wife, he does enjoy the substantial favors of Brangien. Fenice leaves her husband with a mere dream. And this deceit brings a kind of infamous immortality to a kinsman of King Arthur. *Cligés* is not only a narrative essay on fame; it should probably be thought of as a witty and humorous attack on the kind of *pietas* fostered by Geoffrey of Monmouth's Arthur. It is quite possible that *Le chevalier de la charette*, which makes the flower of British chivalry a triumphant adulterer, is a further development of this theme.

Love Conventions in Marie's Equitan

The delightful Lais *of Marie de France are often puzzling, but this one seems fairly transparent.*

ALTHOUGH it is clear that Marie's *Lais* reflect a variety of attitudes toward love, and that she was concerned with love of various kinds, some of which are not easy to define precisely, her description of love in *Equitan* is specific enough to enable us to draw certain conclusions from it. In 1933 Ernest Hoepffner published a study of the poem in which he concluded: "Nous pensons qu'en le faisant Marie a entendu prononcer une condamnation sévère de cet amour qui n'est motivé par rien que par le simple désir sensuel. . . . Tel est donc l'amour qui entraîne les amants au péché et au crime."[1] Elsewhere, in the preliminary discussion, the conception of love which Marie condemns is associated with that developed by the troubadours.[2] But in 1944 Alfred Ewert objected that Marie's "didactic and moralizing intention was perhaps hardly as conscious and clear-cut as Hoepffner presents it." He observed, somewhat unhistorically, that Marie set forth "a conception which comes much closer to 'la passion' of Racine than to the 'amour courtois' of the Troubadours."[3] Leaving the question of the troubadours to one side, I wish to show here that both the characteristics of sensual love as Marie describes it in *Equitan* and her attitude toward that love are commonplaces of twelfth-century thought, so that Hoepffner's perception of a moral attitude in this *lai* was probably correct.

It has been pointed out that the prologue to Marie's *Lais* shows a considerable awareness of more or less learned traditions.[4] It is not unreasonable to assume, therefore, that she may have known something of clerical ideas concerning sensual love. During the latter part of the twelfth century by far the most popular learned discussion of human love was the *De spirituali amicitia* of Ailred of Rievaulx. The definition of sensual love in this treatise runs as follows:

> Verum amicitiae carnalis exordium ab affectione procedit, quae instar meretricis divaricat pedes suos omni transeunti, sequens aures et

oculos suos per varia fornicantes; per quorum aditus usque ad ipsam mentem pulchrorum corporum, vel rerum voluptuosarum inferuntur imagines: quibus ad libitum frui, putat esse beatum; sed sine socio frui, minus aestimat esse jucundum. Tunc motu, nutu, verbis, obsequiis, animus ab animo captivatur, et accenditur unus ab altero, et conflantur in unum: ut inito foedere miserabili, quidquid sceleris, quidquid sacrilegii est, alter agat et patiatur pro altero; nihilque hac amicitia dulcius arbitrantur, nihil judicant justius: idem velle, et idem nolle, sibi existimantes amicitiae legibus imperari.[5]

With only a few verbal changes this definition reappears in a condensation of Ailred's work which carried such authority in the twelfth century that it was attributed to St. Augustine.[6] Peter of Blois defines the same kind of love in much the same way, revealing an obvious indebtedness to Ailred:

Sane amor ex carne proveniens sequitur aures et oculos suos per varia fornicantes, atque per eorum aditus usque ad ipsam mentem rerum concupiscibilium imaginem introducit. Sic more meretricio divaricat pedes suos omniumque spiritum immundorum spurcitiae se exponit, productioris vitae sibi spatium pollicetur. Contemnit terribilia Dei judicia, et hoc solum vitae suae ascribit, quod indulget extraordinariae voluptati.

Sicque animus aspectibus impudicis, verbis et nutibus, et obsequiis illectus et attractus, in malum miserabiliter captivatur; dumque duae mentes quodam foedere foedo in una voluntate conflantur, quod odibilius est Deo et animae perniciosius operantes, se infelices omnia lege amicitiae facere arbitrantur.[7]

This love is not the fruit of serious deliberation, is not tested by judgment, and is not ruled by reason. It knows no measure but proceeds without discretion:

Haec itaque amicitia nec deliberatione suscipitur, nec judicio probatur, nec regitur ratione; sed secundum impetum affectionis per diversa raptatur; non modum servans, non honesta procurans, non commoda incommodave prospiciens; sed ad omnia inconsiderate, indiscrete, leviter, immoderateque progrediens.[8]

The essential elements in Ailred's definition reappear in the definition of love at the beginning of the *De amore* of Andreas Capellanus.[9] It is fairly certain, therefore, that the definition was a commonplace in clerical circles at the time Marie wrote.[10]

In the dramatic elaboration of the story of Equitan which may be considered as Marie's peculiar contribution to it,[11] reflections of ideas in these definitions of sensual love are not difficult to find. King Equitan is, in the first place, a man whose *affectio* is receptive to stimulation through the ears and eyes:

> Deduit amout e drüerie:
> Pur ceo maintint chevalerie.
> Cil metent lur vie en nuncure
> Que d'amur n'unt sen e mesure;
> Tels est la mesure de amer
> Que nul n'i deit reisun garder.
> (15-20)

He does not guide himself by reason or measure but uses his love of pleasure and sexual satisfaction as a source of "chivalry." In this context the idea of chivalry probably has much the same ironic implication that it has in the *Lai dou lecheor*, but Marie does no more than hint at what is there expressed with cynical forthrightness.[12] The king's ears are soon stimulated when he hears of the beauty of his seneschal's wife. Without seeing her, he responds eagerly to what he has heard:

> Li reis l'oï sovent loër.
> Soventefez la salua,
> De ses aveirs li enveia;
> Sanz veüe la coveita,
> E cum ainz pot a li parla.
> (38-42)

Once the image of the lady's "gent cors" and "bele faiture" is firmly implanted through the ears, Equitan becomes anxious to satisfy his eyes.[13] When he does so, he is wounded to the heart by the arrow of love. This is a figurative way of saying that the image of the lady's beauty passed from the eye into the mind, where it remained fixed. Having followed his ears and eyes, the king spends a sleepless night nursing his conscience and contemplating his proposed conquest.

Equitan's conscience is disturbed by one thought: the love he feels for his seneschal's wife is contrary to the love he owes his seneschal:

> Ceo est la femme al seneschal.
> Garder li dei amur e fei,
> Si cum jeo voil k'il face a mei.
> (72-74)

The king's lecherous inclinations are thus, as he realizes, contrary to his feudal obligations and to the second precept of charity.[14] What he proposes to do is, in Ailred's language, plainly "wicked" and "impious." And his rationalization to excuse it is, to say the least, cynical:

Si bele dame tant mar fust,
S'ele n'amast u dru̧ eüst!
Que devendreit sa curteisie,
S'ele n'amast de drüerie?
(79-82)

The lady is so beautiful that it would be a shame if she did not engage in an adulterous love. Moreover, she would have no "courtesy" unless she loved. The courtesy Equitan seeks in his lady is not that frequently ascribed to the Blessed Virgin and her imitators but rather that described in the "cortois e bon" *Lai dou lecheor* or in the *Du C.* of Gautier le Leu.[15] It is an appropriate companion to his own "chivalry." When the lady makes her first refusal on the grounds of social inequality, the king at once questions her courtesy (151-162). However, he promises that he will become her man and "ami," turning the feudal relationship between them upside down. And he will, of course, die if she refuses:

Ne me laissez pur vus murir!
Vus seiez dame e jeo servant,
Vus orguilluse e jeo preiant!
(174-176)

On the basis of these and similar "obsequia," which are typical of what has been called "courtly love," the two exchange rings and enter into a "miserable pact." As Ailred describes pacts of this kind, the participants consider nothing sweeter nor more just than their mutual satisfactions. When Equitan's subjects demand that he marry, therefore, he and his lady, in outright defiance of all justice, plan to murder the seneschal to get him out of the way so that they may preserve their sweet union. The extremely hot bath into which this plan leads them may be regarded as a poetically appropriate opposite of that cool bath in which impulses like those which motivate the lovers are supposed to be removed. Marie's conclusion refers not only to the murder trap but also to Equitan's love:

Ici purreit ensample prendre:
Tel purcace le mal d'autrui
Dunt le mals tut revert sur lui.
(308-310)

For, as Andreas says, love of this kind is not only displeasing to God; it also causes one to injure his neighbor: "Nam ex amore proximus laeditur, quem ex mandato divino quisque tanquam se ipsum iubetur diligere."[16] And when a man injures his neighbor in this way, he injures himself.

Marie's story reflects with some fidelity the conventional attributes of lecherous love as they are described in more or less learned works of her time. In view of this fact, and in view of her ironic treatment of the "chivalry" and "courtesy" which spring from this love, we may conclude that Hoepffner was justified in attributing to her a "didactic and moralizing intention." But the words *didactic* and *moralizing* have, in our time, certain unpleasant connotations so that we hesitate to apply them to admirable works of art. Perhaps it would be better to say that Marie shaped her story in such a way that it would illustrate in terms of concrete particulars familiar to her audience something she regarded as a respectable and useful philosophical idea. Ideas of this kind and their practical applications are difficult for laymen to comprehend when they are expressed abstractly, so that the unlearned are inclined to have ears and hear not. Philosophical principles are of little value if no one understands them. But Marie herself expresses this more vividly and forcefully than I can:

> Quant uns granz biens est mult oïz,
> Dunc a primes est il fluriz,
> E quant loëz est de plusurs,
> Dunc ad espandues ses flurs.

IV

The Pearl as Symbol

◆§

Sign would be a better word than symbol *in this title. As readers of Charles Moorman's confused remarks in the introduction to his edition of the poem,* The Works of the Gawain Poet *(Jackson, Miss., 1977), 32-37, are aware, interpretations of the meaning of* Pearl *are still by no means stable. The editor, seemingly unaware of the doctrinal principles involved, even suggests that the maiden may "overstate her case" for dramatic reasons. Although he says that the poem "abounds in scriptural and patristic allusions," he fails to annotate them, giving us no explanation, for example, of the expression "wythouten spot," repeated at the close of each of the first five stanzas. In my own discussion the word* levels *is probably inappropriate.*

◆§

I N discussions of *The Pearl* it has not been possible to formulate a consistent symbolic value for the central figure in the poem which would meet with more than temporary or qualified acceptance. A re-examination of some of the relevant Scriptural commentary may yield a satisfactory value. Usually when commentaries are consulted, the result is a confusing list of possible symbols, none of which seems entirely consistent with the poem.[1] J. B. Fletcher made the Pearl a symbol of innocence, the possessor of innocence, or the means and reward of salvation.[2] More recently, Sister Mary Hillman has said that the Pearl stands for a gem, the soul, or the kingdom of Heaven.[3] It may be shown, I believe, that both of these interpretations are in a sense fundamentally correct. It is stated clearly in the poem that the Pearl is among the hundred and forty-four thousand brides of the Lamb in the Celestial Jerusalem.[4] Her symbolic value should therefore be consistent with that of these brides.

In the set of homilies on the Apocalypse attributed to St. Augustine, the virgin brides are said to represent all members of the Church of pure faith, regardless of sex. It is explained on the authority of St. Paul that all good Christians should be chaste virgins prepared to marry Christ; that is, they should keep themselves free of the pollutions of heresy and worldly cupidity:

Hi sunt qui se cum mulieribus non coinquinaverunt, etc. (Apoc. 14:4), virgines hoc loco non solum corpore castos intelligamus, sed maxime omnem Ecclesiam, quae fidem puram tenet, sicut dicit Apostolos, *Sponsavi enim vos uni viro, virginem castam exhibere Christo* (2 Cor. 11:2): nulla adulterina haereticorum commixtione pollutam, nec in male blandis et mortiferis hujus mundi voluptatibus usque ad exitum vitae suae absque remedio poenitentiae infelici perseverantia colligatam.[5]

It is explained further that through baptism and penance one may attain the purity necessary to a bride of Christ:

Addit post hoc dicens: *Et in ore ipsorum non est inventum mendacium* (v. 5). Non dixit, non fuit; sed, *non est inventum*. Qualem enim invenit Dominus cum hinc evocat, talem et judicat: nam aut per Baptismum, aut per poenitentiam possumus in interiori homine et virgines effici et sine mendacio.[6]

Assuming that this interpretation is relevant, we may conclude that the Pearl represents those who are free of heresy and sin and are thus suitable brides of Christ. The validity of our assumption depends upon whether or not it is consistent with the poem. It is obvious at once that the interpretation elucidates the last stanza of the poem, where it is urged that all readers become "precious perleȝ" of Christ. The poet wishes all of his audience to become suitable brides of the Lamb, or, in other words, to prepare themselves for residence in the Celestial City.[7] But it is also obvious that the Pearl is something more than simply a good Christian.

A commentary on the Apocalypse by Bruno Astensis furnishes a means of classifying the various brides in the Celestial procession. Together they are said to represent "omnem Ecclesiae multitudinem." Their number, however, is symbolic, so that the various parts of the number indicate a division among the virgins:

Merito ergo beatus Joannes centum quadraginta quatuor millia cum Agno stantes vidisse describitur, ut per centum summam virginum perfectionem, per quadraginta vero, omnes peccatores ad veram poenitentiam conversos: per quatuor autem cunctos Evangeliorum observatores, qui quasi quadrati lapides, semper firmi et stabiles in fide perstiterunt.[8]

Some of the brides have never sinned and are in the highest state of virginal perfection; some are reformed sinners; and some are those who have been stable in the faith. Since the Pearl embraced the faith in infancy at the eleventh hour,[9] she must be placed in the first of these classifications. Other baptized Christians may be "pearls" too, as the last stanza of the poem indicates, but only if through penance they can approach the unspotted condition of the Pearl.

In the course of the poem it is emphasized that the Pearl is "wythouten spot," or, as it is phrased in the language of the Vulgate, *sine macula*. It is significant that all of the brides of the Lamb in the Apocalypse are said to be *sine macula* (Apocalypse 14:5). More positively, the condition of being *sine macula* is a necessary prerequisite to a place in the Celestial City. The doctrine is expressed positively in Psalm 14:

> *Domine, quis habitabit in tabernaculo tuo*
> *Aut quis requiescet in monte sancto tuo?*
> *Qui ingreditur sine macula. . . .*

The sacred mountain represents eternal life, or, as St. Augustine put it, "supereminentiam charitatis Christi in vita aeterna."[10] Quoting earlier authorities, Lombard glosses *sine macula* as "innocens."[11] In other words, a state of innocence, or freedom from spiritual blemish, is necessary to salvation.

As an infant who died shortly after baptism, the Pearl may be thought of as the archetype of innocence. That is, she represents the most clearly definable extreme of a condition which it is necessary for all Christians (in the Medieval sense) to attain before salvation is possible. In general, as Dante observed:

> Fede e innocenza son reperte
> solo ne' parvoletti; poi ciascuna
> pria fugge che le guance sian coperte.[12]

In adults, this childlike innocence must be restored, so that the soul is *sine macula*. The *Pearl* poet puts it, "þe innocent is ay saf by ry3t," a theme which he elaborates in stanza 61:

> Jesus con calle to hym hys mylde,
> & sayde hys ryche no wy3 my3t wynne
> Bot he com þyder ry3t as a chylde,
> Oþer elle3 neuer more com þerinne.
> Harmle3, trwe, & vndefylde,
> Wythouten mote oþer mascle of sulpande synne—
> Quen such þer cnoken on þe bylde,
> Tyt schal hem men þe 3ate vnpynne.
> Þer is þe blys þat con not blynne

> Þat þe jueler soȝte þurȝ perre pres,
> & solde alle hys goud, boþe wolen & lynne,
> To bye hym a perle watȝ mascelleȝ.
>
>   (721-732)

The "jueler" referred to is the *negotiator* of Matthew 13:45-46, who sold all of his jewels for a pearl of great price. In the next stanza, this Scriptural text is interpreted, and it is said in effect that the pearl of great price is the life in the Celestial City, for the sake of which we are advised to forsake the "worlde wode," or cupidity for temporalia. The Pearl herself possesses such a pearl which she wears as a token on her breast:

> ' "This maskelleȝ perle, þat boȝt is dere,
> Þe joueler gef fore alle hys god,
> Is lyke þe reme of heuenesse clere";
> So sayde þe Fader of folde & flode;
> For hit is wemleȝ, clene & clere,
> & endeleȝ rounde, & blyþe of mode,
> & commune to alle þat ryȝtwys were.
> Lo, euen in myddeȝ my breste hit stode!
> My Lorde þe Lombe, þat schede hys blode,
> He pyȝt hit þere in token of pes.
> I rede þe forsake þe worlde wode,
> & porchace þy perle maskelles.'
>
>   (733-744)

It should be observed that lines 733-735 do not represent a quotation or paraphrase of the Scriptural text, where the Kingdom of God is compared with the merchant. The lines state a conclusion or *sentence* based on the text. A similar interpretation is given by Bruno Astensis:

> Simile est igitur regnum coelorum, id est sancta Ecclesia, homini negotiatori, quoniam sicut ille unius margaritae desiderio omnia vendidit, et eam emit; ita et ista pro amore patriae coelestis et aeternae felicitatis, non solum ea quae habuit vendidit, verum etiam se ipsam servituti subjugavit, ut eam emere et possidere valeat. [13]

The members of the earthly church, that is, renounce what they have in this world in order to obtain the pearl "aeternae felicitatis." Basically, this is a traditional interpretation of the parable. [14]

The Pearl, who, as we have seen, may be considered to represent the archetype of innocence, wears on her breast the symbol of eternal life which was placed there by Christ. The appropriateness of this arrangement is obvious when we reflect that only through the Redemption may those who are *sine macula* attain the pearl of eternal felicity. The relation between the Pearl and the jeweller's pearl is clearly expressed in the opening lines of Psalm 14 already quoted. These lines say, in terms of the poem, that only those who are pearls (*sine macula*) will obtain the pearl of the celestial life. The Pearl thus not only typifies innocence; she typifies those who dwell in the Celestial City, or, since such folk determine the character of eternal life, she typifies that life also. We arrive at the conclusion, then, that the Pearl typifies both the characteristics necessary to life in the New Jerusalem and that life. The pearl of the parable and the Pearl of the poem are two aspects of one symbol.

Perhaps this conclusion may be clarified by applying it to the poem as a whole. At the beginning of the poem, the dreamer is described as one who has lost a pearl. The meaning of this situation is clear if we consider the dreamer to be not the poet but any typical adult. What he has lost is the innocence or spotlessness of childhood,[15] and concomitantly eternal life in the Celestial City. His vision of the Pearl is a device by means of which the poet may impress upon his audience, the members of which are in much the same situation as the dreamer, the necessity for regaining and maintaining a life of innocence. To this end he stresses what is for him the captivating beauty of innocence and of the Celestial City. The love of innocence and that of eternal life are corollary to the first precept of charity, which is a matter of the heart. Only when the will is turned toward charity is the individual capable of a state of grace. The beauty of the poem, which was intended to move the hearts of its audience toward charity, thus rests on a sound theological basis. To most Medieval thinkers, it is necessary for the reason to grasp a concept before the will can desire what that concept represents. This fact accounts for the elaborate doctrinal exposition in the poem. The poet wished his audience to understand the concept of innocence and that of the *denarius* awarded those who realize innocence. He also wished his audience to desire these things.

The symbol of the Pearl may be thought of on four levels. Literally, the Pearl is a gem. Allegorically, as the maiden of the poem, it represents those members of the Church who will be among the "hundred" in the celestial procession, the perfectly innocent. Tropologically, the Pearl is a symbol of the soul that attains innocence through true penance and all that such penance implies. Anagogically, it is the life of innocence in the Celestial City. The allegorical value presents a clear picture of the type of innocence; the tropological value shows how such innocence may be obtained; and the anagogical value explains the reward for innocence. To these meanings the literal value serves as a unifying focal point in which the other values are implied to one who reads the book of God's Work on the level of the *sentence*. The homiletic purpose of the poem to which Sister Mary Vincent Hillman has called attention results from the poet's emphasis on the tropological level. The author wished the members of his audience to learn how to become through Christ's Redemption "precious perle3 vnto his pay."

The "Heresy" of The Pearl

❧

The orthodoxy of the poem is now seldom questioned.

❧

T HE charge that *The Pearl* is heretical is a very grave one. Heresy was not something to be taken lightly in the fourteenth century; moreover, heretical doctrine seems especially strange in a work which emphasizes the importance of purity of spirit with evident sincerity. It has been said that the poet's interpretation of the Parable of the Vineyard includes the "heresy of Jovinian," to the effect that there is no differentiation in status in the celestial Jerusalem. Further evidence is available, however, in support of the view of J. B. Fletcher, R. Wellek, and others to the effect that there is no heresy in the poem.[1]

St. Augustine explains the parable at length in one of his sermons.[2] The general agricultural image is treated first. We cultivate God, and He cultivates us: "Colimus enim eum adorando, non arando. Ille autem colit nos tanquam agricola agrum."[3] In His labor of cultivation, God extirpates the seeds of evil from us and opens our hearts as with a plow in order to plant the seeds of the precepts, whose fruit is piety. Since God is in this sense a farmer, he planted a vineyard and called workers into it. The workers called at various times throughout the day are interpreted in two ways in the sermon. The second interpretation is relevant to *The Pearl*:

> Tanquam enim prima hora vocantur, qui recentes ab utero matris incipiunt esse christiani; quasi tertia, pueri, quasi sexta, juvenes; quasi nona, vergentes in senium; quasi undecima, omnino decrepiti: unum tamen vitae aeternae denarium omnes accepturi.[4]

Those who are called first are baptized infants; those called at the third hour are children, and so on. The fact that the Pearl is said in the poem to have died in infancy has made this interpretation seem irrelevant, since she says that she went to the vineyard "in euentyde."[5] In other words, she could not have gone into the vineyard in old age if she died in infancy.

In Medieval exegesis it was not unusual for early interpretations of Scriptural passages to become elaborated with the passage of time. A comment of a few lines in Augustine or Bede may fill a column by the twelfth century. In the process, the basic meaning or *sentence* remained with very little change, but there were frequently changes in detail. Let us compare the interpretation of Augustine just quoted with that of Bruno Astensis in the twelfth century:

Regnum coelorum, Ecclesia est; paterfamilias, Christus Dominus noster: ejus namque familia, et angeli et homines sunt: magna quidem est familia, quia magnus est et paterfamilias. Venit autem iste paterfamilias ut conduceret operarios in vineam suam. Vinea enim Domini Sabaoth, domus Israel est: vinea, Dei Ecclesia est: extra quam qui laborat, mercedem non recipit: in qua qui laborat, denarium suscipit. Ille enim denarius, remuneratio est aeternae beatitudinis: ideo unus denarius omnibus datur: unus primis, et unus novissimis. Et alii quidem primo mane laborare incipiunt: alii vero circa horam tertiam: alii autem circa sextam, et nonam horam: alii quoque circa horam undecimam. . . . Primo namque mane in vinea Dei laborare incipiunt, qui a primaeva aetate, id est a pueritia in Ecclesia Dei Domino serviunt: illi autem circa horam tertiam laborare veniunt, qui in adolescentia servire incipiunt: veniunt autem et illi circa sextam et nonam horam, qui vel in juventute, vel in senectute, ad poenitentiam convertuntur. Undecima vero hora illa est, quae in qualibet aetate fini appropinquat et morti proxima est. Hanc enim horam non solum juvenes et senes, verum etiam pueri habent.[6]

The general pattern and the basic meaning of the two interpretations are the same; but Bruno makes the eleventh hour, "in euentyde," an hour which can apply to persons of any age. Those who begin to labor in the church in the eleventh hour are those who go shortly before death. That this interpretation was widely accepted is attested by the fact that it survives as an English idiom, *at the eleventh hour*.[7] When the Pearl says that she went "in euentyde," therefore, she is simply stressing the fact that she did not labor in the vineyard of the church. That is, she was baptised only shortly before death.

The poet's general interpretation of the parable is thus not an "inversion" of St. Augustine's. Nor are his remarks concerning heavenly reward contrary to St. Augustine's. In his sermon, St. Augustine emphasizes the fact that in the reward which they receive for their labors, the workers in the vineyard are all equal, "unum tamen vitae aeternae denarium omnes accepturi." It is this doctrine which has been mistaken in *The Pearl* for the "heresy of Jovinian":

> Erimus ergo in illa mercede omnes aequales, tanquam primi novissimi, et novissimi primi: quia denarius ille vita aeterna est, et in vita aeterna omnes aequales erunt. Quamvis enim meritorum diversitate fulgebunt, alius magis, alius minus: quod tamen ad vitam aeternam pertinet, aequalis erit omnibus. Non enim alteri erit longius, alteri brevius, quod pariter sempiternum est: quod non habet finem, nec tibi habebit, nec mihi. Alio modo ibi erit castitas conjugalis, alio modo ibi erit integritas virginalis: alio modo ibi erit fructus boni operis, alio modo corona passionis. Illud alio modo: illud alio modo: tamen quantum pertinet ad vivere in aeternum, nec ille plus vivet illo, nec ille plus illo. Pariter enim sine fine vivunt, cum in suis quisque claritatibus vivat: et ille denarius vita aeterna est. Non murmuret ergo qui post multum tempus accepit, contra eum qui post modicum tempus accepit. Illi redditur, illi donatur; utrisque tamen una res donatur.[8]

In answer to the "murmuring" of the dreamer, who is astonished to find the Pearl among the blessed after little or no labor, she expresses precisely this doctrine:

> 'Of more & lasse in Godeȝ ryche,'
> Þat gentyl sayde, 'lys no joparde,
> For þer is vch mon payed inlyche,
> Wheþer lyttel oþer much be hys reward.'
> (601-604)

In other words, "in vita aeterna omnes aequales erunt," whether the reward is "lyttel oþer much"; or "quamvis enim meritorum diversitate fulgebunt . . . aequalis erit omnibus."[9] There is certainly no heresy here.[10] Just as St. Augustine and Bruno use the parable as a basis for warnings against despair and vain hope, the author of *The Pearl* uses it to show that anyone, no matter what he has done in the past, may through repentance regain sufficient purity of spirit to achieve his reward.[11] The phrase "in euentyde" simply emphasizes the fact that the Pearl, who died in infancy, had been baptized only at the eleventh hour. A re-examination of the evidence has shown that the interpretation and use of the Parable of the Vineyard in *The Pearl* are consistent with Medieval exegetical tradition.

The Question of Typology and the Wakefield Mactacio Abel

With reference to the use of contemporary costumes in the plays, p. 223 Mrs. Anita Schorsch, author of the delightful little book Pastoral Dreams *(New York, 1977), has demonstrated to me that Biblical characters in American popular art also appeared in contemporary dress. In the* Secunda pastorum, *here mentioned briefly, the Old Law atmosphere that prevails before the young shepherd's act of mercy was probably reinforced by the contrast between Mak's Wife and Mary, the one spinning to make money in the cloth industry, and the other spinning the garment of Christ's humanity while the husband knocks at the door. See the perceptive article by Gail McMurray Gibson, " 'Porta haec clausa erit': Comedy, Conception, and Ezechiel's Closed Door in the* Ludus Coventriae Play *of 'Joseph's Return,' "* JMRS, *8 (1978), esp. pp. 152-153, together with her earlier article, "The Thread of Life in the Hand of the Virgin," in* Sylvia Heyden: Recent Tapestries *(Durham, N.C., 1972), 9-15. Mak's knocking while he carries his own "lamb" should probably be regarded as a humorous comment on contemporary society, whose Maks have substituted ill-gotten material rewards for the Lamb they should discover. Cain's "mixed team" should have been described as a team of oxen and horses; such teams were not uncommon.*

RECENT studies of medieval mystery plays have demonstrated a growing interest in what is called "typology," conceived as a discipline in which Old Testament events are "figures" or "types" of events in the New Testament. The learned and convincing article by Rosemary Woolf, "The Effect of Typology on the English Mediaeval Plays of Abraham and Isaac"[1] did much to stimulate interest in the subject; V. A. Kolve sought to show the relevance of "typological" considerations to the general structure of the dramatic cycles;[2] and in her recent book Woolf has been careful to keep before us the "typological" relationships suggested by the plays.[3] With reference to "typology" generally, Woolf, whose acquaintance with the subject in the visual arts is impressive, observed that knowledge of the significance

of "types" was not recondite in late medieval England, and that, indeed, it formed a part of "the small stock of knowledge which the
common people might be expected to have received."[4] In the hierarchical society of the time we may suspect that the plays were heard by
persons of some responsibility, including masters of shops, merchants,
rectors of parishes and their clerks, municipal and manorial officials,
and even by local magnates and their followers, as well as by servants,
apprentices and laborers. Their "small stock of knowledge" probably
included a great deal of practical information consistent with the structure of the society in which they found themselves, and it is likely that
this information included some basis for making practical judgments
about their own conduct as well as about that of their fellows, subjects
and superiors. In most societies this kind of information is avidly
sought, and there is no reason to suppose that late medieval society
was exceptional in this respect. In fact, it is hard to imagine why
late-medieval craftsmen and guildsmen should have spent so much
time and effort maintaining their pageants, training or employing actors and minstrels, and generally supporting the plays if the benefits
had been purely theoretical.

The use of "typology" in the analysis of the plays may be criticized,
in fact, not on the ground that it is a recondite subject, but on the
ground that, as it is usually understood today, it is a severely limited
subject, theoretical rather than practical. The fact that Isaac and his
surrogate the ram may be viewed as types of or figures for Christ in
His Divinity and in His flesh, and that the sacrifice looks forward to
the Crucifixion and hence to the Sacrament of the Eucharist is of considerable theoretical interest, especially in that it illuminates an event
in the Old Testament, but in its practical implications it remains, in
and of itself, irrelevant to the ordinary concerns of the medieval spectator. The plays must have had some bearing on their daily concerns as
well as on their theoretical grasp of exegetical principles. In medieval
art, practical implications were often left unstated, or merely suggested, but the Wakefield plays elaborate them to an unusual degree,
as if the author wished to make sure that they were not overlooked. In
order to understand the nature of his achievement, however, it will
repay us to look more deeply into the question of "typology."

Although medieval artists traditionally made use of "types and antitypes" in their representations, and, in the later Middle Ages, lists of
them might be compiled for guidance, the word *typology* itself was not
a common medieval term, and the "system" it implies was not usually
regarded as an end in itself. Hence the strictures on the subject by our

most reliable authority on medieval exegetical practice, which, in view of the widespread current use of the term, are worth quoting at length:

> Nous ne confondrons pas davantage cette allégorie scripturaire, in-tégralement comprise, avec ce qu'on appelle aujourd'hui, d'un nom moderne qui depuis quelque temps fait fortune, "typologie." L'al-legorie scripturaire autorise la typologie, elle la fonde, elle la con-tient en elle. Mais si l'on ne voyait que la typologie, on n'aurait pas pénétré le fond de la doctrine traditionnelle concernant l'Écriture. Outre que la typologie, telle qu'on la définit d'ordinaire, n'a pas son fondement en elle-même, elle ne dit rien par elle-même de l'opposi-tion dialectique des deux Testaments, ni des conditions de leur unité. Elle ne suffit donc point à montrer dans toute sa force l'oeuvre accomplie par Jésus-Christ. . . . Elle n'exprime pas le lien de l'intelli-gence spirituelle avec la conversion personnelle et la vie du chrétien, la relation du "Testament nouveau" et de "l'Homme nouveau," de la nouveauté de l'intelligence nouveauté de l'espirit. . . . Elle arrête à mi-chemin l'élan spirituel.[5]

These remarks should be taken quite seriously, and not as so much rhetoric, especially the objection that "typology" taken in itself does not express the relationship between spiritual understanding and the life of the Christian.

Does this mean that the "types and antitypes" familiar in medieval art from very early times are essentially sterile, or that the mystery plays that exploit them employ a principle that "arrête à mi-chemin l'élan spirituel"? It certainly does not, and to think that it does is to misunderstand a great deal of medieval art and to impose on it a sterile literalism that would have appalled even large numbers of Woolf's not very knowledgeable "common people," who were accustomed to thinking of types and antitypes not in terms of "typology" but in terms of "spiritual understanding." A great deal of medieval art is enigmatic, and "types and antitypes" are no exception to this rule. They do not offer a stated lesson any more than does, let us say, a typi-cal Gothic Nativity in which the Infant rests on an altar in a church before the two beasts while Mary and Joseph stare off into a spaceless realm in apparent unconcern. The picture is not "about" the historical birth of Christ, but rather leads the observer to think of that Nativity that takes place within his own heart at the Sacrament of the Altar, when he and his fellows are united in a bond of love made possible by a sacrifice that he is obliged in one way or another to repeat. Participa-tion in Communion was customarily preceded by confession and penance, so that the nature of this sacrifice would have been obvious even to the illiterate. The picture is thus spaceless and timeless except in the sense that its space and time are the space of any Christian at any time he attends Mass. The "mystery" of the picture implies a relevance to the "personal conversion and life of the Christian."

TROPOLOGY

The word for this phenomenon most commonly used was "tropology," and its effect, which is far more important than the term, is to make events in both the Old and New Testaments immediately and practically relevant to the daily life of the observer. If Old Testament events are to be significant in this way, however, they must be, so to speak, "Christianized," or made relevant through their New Testament fulfillment. The burden of Isaac seen as the burden of the Cross is a forceful reminder that every Christian must also engage in self-sacrifice, setting aside the inclinations of the flesh inherited from the Fall (or the Old Man) in obedience to the New Law, which demands that every man not only love God, but love his neighbor as himself. In short, the juxtaposition of types and antitypes implies tropology,[6] a fact that is suggested in most representations by dressing the Old Testament figures in contemporary medieval costumes. Tropology releases Scriptural events from the limits of space and time and makes them perennial. There is nothing especially obscure or recondite about this sort of implication, for it was ingrained by centuries of Scriptural exposition. Thus St. Gregory, whose example as an expositor in the late Middle Ages was equalled only by that of St. Augustine, hastened over the "allegorical" sense in his expositions of the Gospels to arrive at the wider implications of tropology.[7] We should understand, however, that the "allegorical" sense which gives instruction in the faith is a necessary intervening step if the "tropological" sense is to be anything more than a simple moral lesson readily discernible from the history. In connection with the Old Testament, St. Gregory explained, "Audivimus ex historia, quod miremur; cognovimus ex capite, quod credamus; consideremus nunc ex corpore, quod vivendo teneamus. In nobismetipsis namque debemus transformare quod legimus."[8] The tropological sense proper is a moral or practical meaning vivified through faith in Christ and membership in the Church. As Henri de Lubac says, "C'est par le sens tropologique ainsi compris que l'Écriture est pleinement *pour nous* la Parole de Dieu, cette Parole qui s'adresse à chacun, *hic et nunc*, aussi bien qu'à toute l'Église, et disant à chacun 'ce qui intéresse sa vie.' "[9]

The early Gothic Nativity scene to which we have called attention

gradually changed during the course of the late Middle Ages: its figures became more "human" in appearance and attitude, and the spaceless gold leaf backgrounds were replaced by scenes shown in crude
perspective. By the fifteenth century the church interior had frequently been supplanted by a small shed, sometimes with a ruined
roof. The trend is sometimes lamented. Thus Émile Mâle wrote, "We
have far to go from this majestic conception, wholly theological in its
grandeur, to the picturesque crèches which appear at the beginning of
the fifteenth century and mark the end of great religious art."[10] What
happened is usually described as an "increasing realism," although the
word *realism* is perhaps best confined to Courbet and his successors,
who not only heralded it as a new concept, but lent it connotations
inappropriate to the study of medieval and Renaissance art. In any
event, the developing style involved greater verisimilitude in a contemporary rather than in an historical sense. That is, figures from the
past were treated as though they were contemporaries of the observer
and not as historical figures from an earlier era. The verisimilitude was
accompanied by a new appeal to feeling that manifested itself first in
Italy, inspired by the evangelical movements of the later Middle Ages,
especially by the Franciscans. I have elsewhere sought to characterize
this development in the arts not as "realism," but as "increasingly detailed exemplification" whose function was not to distract the observer from the "theological grandeur" of the subjects treated in
ecclesiastical art, but to make their implications more immediate in the
life of the observer.[11] Where "tropological" implications are left
largely to the understanding in Romanesque and early Gothic art, late
medieval and Renaissance artists sought to emphasize the *"hic et nunc"*
of spiritual understanding by means of an increasingly localized verisimilitude. The artist, in other words, gave to the "airy nothings," or
implied principles of early Gothic art a local habitation and a name.
Where Scriptural materials are concerned, verisimilitude serves as a
means of making tropological implications more forceful and explicit.
A certain "universality" is sacrificed for the sake of immediacy with
reference to a particular audience, perhaps somewhat more inclusive
and less well educated than that addressed in earlier art.

The plays of the Wakefield Master afford excellent examples of
tropological elaboration of Scriptural narrative, and they bear unmistakable signs that this is indeed their intended function. If we assume
that the actual subjects of their narratives are not a series of Scriptural
events *per se*, but rather a series of very significant events perennially
recurring by virtue of their Scriptural authority, described in terms of
the daily life of Wakefield at the time of the presentation, we shall find

them much easier to understand. The "characters" in the plays are often in effect the spectators themselves, most of them easily recognizable because of the author's skill at local verisimilitude; and the events these characters experience, although they are structured in patterns provided by the Scriptures, are events familiar to the audience in the practical conduct of their affairs. A full study of the plays would thus involve a careful examination of social conditions in England during the first half of the fifteenth century; however, some of the problems suggested by the plays may be examined without this more detailed analysis.

ANACHRONISMS

For example, the "anachronisms" that appear with special frequency in the plays of the Wakefield Master represent essentially the same technique that places the newly born Christ child upon an altar within a church in early Gothic Nativities. As Kolve points out, the settings and costumes were probably "contemporary" in all of the mystery plays,[12] but the Wakefield plays contain a large number of verbal anachronisms as well. Kolve's explanation involves the common medieval concept of the exemplary character of history and the contention that the events described were intended to be understood from the perspective of eternity rather than from the limited perspective of human temporality.[13] Both concepts are relevant, but they do not, as Kolve realizes, fully account for the peculiarities of the plays. It is true that the past, to use St. Augustine's words in the *De doctrina christiana* (2.28.44), was said to belong "to the order of time, whose creator and administrator is God," so that past history was thought to contain useful examples illustrating the operation of Divine Providence. A sharp distinction was made, however, between the historical time of the Old Law and that of the New, so that "examples" under the Old Law had to be treated with circumspection.[14] But this distinction becomes blurred in the spiritual life of the individual. Although it is true that every Christian formally puts off the "Old Man" who lives "by the law" at baptism (Romans 6:3-6), most nevertheless lapse (Galatians 4:17-24), failing to strip themselves of "the Old Man and his deeds" (Colossians 3:5f.). Hence there is, even under the New Law, something of the Synagogue as well as of the Church in every man.[15] The "anachronisms" in the plays, which keep the time of the New Law before us, are thus indicative of the fact that the author's concern was not with "history" as such, but with the spiritual life of his own contemporaries. The anachronisms provide, moreover, a means of avoid-

ing the embarrassment of Old Law "examples" taken literally. It cannot be emphasized too strongly that Old Law attitudes, among which
were considered to be vanity, selfishness and malice, together with a
general blindness to the Order of Providence, were regarded in the late
Middle Ages as the primary sources of what we should call social disorder, oppression and tyranny. The complaints of the shepherds at the
opening of *Secunda pastorum* are essentially complaints about the reign
of the Old Law, with its attendant inversions, in contemporary society. If we can recognize the fact that the real subject of the plays is the
spiritual life of the audience, the anachronisms as well as inconsistencies in literal geography, like the distance between Wakefield and the
scene of the Nativity, disappear.

Kolve's second argument concerns the distinction between time,
which is a feature of creation, and the timeless eternity of Heaven. In
accordance with a tradition stemming from Plato's *Timaeus* (37-38),
time is "the image of eternity." In the Middle Ages this image could
be seen in two ways. First, the cyclical character of temporal succession on earth obvious not only in seasons, months and days, but also
in the more or less regular "life-span" of all temporal things, was regarded as proof that time is a reflection of an immutable realm. This is
the idea expressed in Theseus' great speech on the death of Arcite in
Chaucer's Knight's Tale:

> "That same Prince, and that Moevere," quod he,
> "Hath stablissed in this wrecched world adoun
> Certeyne dayes and duracioun
> To al that is engendred in this place,
> Over the whiche day they may nat pace,
> Al mowe they yet tho dayes wel abregge . . .
> For it is preeved by experience,
> But that me list declaren my sentence.
> Thanne may men by this ordre wel discerne
> That thilke Moevere stable is and eterne."
>
> (2994-3004)

But this argument is not a derogation of present time, for, as William
of Conches explained in the twelfth century, "Duobus modis tempus
imitatur evum: vel quia per successiones continet omnia que evum
simul, vel in ea parte que presens est, ut ait Boetius: in ea enim sola
simile est eternitati."[16] The reference is to the final prose in *The Consolation of Philosophy*, which probably owes something to the discussion
of time in the eleventh book of St. Augustine's *Confessions*. There it is
explained that for the human mind "the past" is but a memory of the

past in the present, and that "the future" is an expectation of the future in the present, so that only the present may be said to exist in the temporal world. But for God the past, the present and the future as we see them constitute a simultaneous present. This consideration leads St. Augustine to a recognition of his own limitations and of the overwhelming majesty of God. Boethius has his Lady Philosophy say, "Atqui si est diuini humanique praesentis digni collatio, uti uos uestro hoc temporario praesenti quaedam uidetis, ita ille omnia suo cernit aeterno" (5 pr 6). She goes on to explain that God's vision violates neither man's freedom of choice nor his responsibility, conferring on him instead a "necessity for probity," since the Supreme Judge sees everything. That is, the recognition of eternity, which may be inferred from the cyclic character of temporal successions, imposes an obligation on everyone to use the little present of his own world well. To return to the plays, we may conclude that their relevance arises from their bearing on the present seen as a manifestation of events perennially recurring not in literal space and time but within the human heart.[17]

The tropological emphasis in the plays not only accounts for their anachronisms and spatial inconsistencies; it also explains what appear to be inconsistencies in their narrative development. To cite the single most celebrated example, *Secunda pastorum* is usually said to fall into "two parts" not altogether consistent in theme; but this incoherence disappears if the subject is seen to be not the actual but the perennial discovery of Christ, with special reference, it is true, to shepherds and to pastors of souls, the latter being suggested by the figurative meaning of "shepherds." But the lesson applies to anyone. When the shepherds, under the inspiration of the "youth" among them who shows from the outset glimmerings of wisdom, and whose charitable impulse leads to the discovery of the stolen sheep, are led to perform an act of mercy, substituting a toss in a blanket for the legal death penalty for stealing sheep after Mak has shown repentance (ll. 622-623), they have, in effect, implemented the New Law and are thus in a position to discover Christ. The third shepherd's response to Mary's injunction, "Tell furth as ye go," reveals the "time" of the action: "Forsothe, allredy it semys to be told / Full oft" (ll. 749-750). The message of charity, in which the tempering of justice with mercy to the penitent is not only the essence of the Redemption but a common practical application, is often told but seldom heeded. Its reward is a tropological Nativity with all the joys therein implied. Viewed in this way, the play does have a consistent thematic development unmarred by "two separate parts."[18] Moreover, the comic aspect of the behavior of the unconverted shepherds is entirely consistent with the medieval habit of finding irrational (or sinful) conduct laughable.

Wakefield Abel

These principles may be illustrated further in a more careful examination of the first of the Wakefield plays, *Mactacio Abel*,[19] sometimes regarded by modern critics as a play in which the "religious element" is slighted in favor of dramatic sympathy for Cain's rebelliousness. The play opens with a speech that calls attention forcibly to its tropological relevance. Garcio (or Pikeharnes) greets the audience with some obscene injunctions to silence (ll. 6–7), and observes to the audience concerning his master, Cain, "Som of you ar his men." This does not mean, of course, that some of them are plowmen,[20] but that they belong to what St. Augustine called "the generation of Cain," analogous with the Pauline "sons of Ishmael," made up of all those who live "according to the flesh" rather than "according to God."[21] Human beings are all sinners, but some show a kind of dedication to worldliness, and these are the "men" of Cain. Although some members of the audience may have been unfamiliar with this concept, the character of Cain in the play is sufficiently vivid to make its implications clear.

When Cain himself enters, he is driving a large mixed team that refuses to obey him. The team may be a reflection of Deuteronomy 22:10, "Thou shalt not plough with an ox and an ass together," which means, according to the *Glossa ordinaria*, "In bove et asino arat, qui recipit Evangelia cum Judaeorum observantia, quae praecessit in umbra."[22] However, such mixed teams of eight were commonly used for plowing large areas, and the implication may be either that Cain enjoyed a large holding, or that he was setting out to work on his lord's demesne. But we soon find Cain referring to Christ, although he maintains an Old Law attitude himself, so that he is clearly not an historical Cain but a perennial Cain. The disobedience of the animals is a clear indication that he has not subdued himself. In Genesis 1:26–30 God gave men "dominion over the fishes of the sea, and the fowls of the air and the beasts," a gift repeated in Genesis 9:1–2 to "Noe and his sons." In connection with these passages, John of Salisbury explains, "Cum uero primum sit excutiendus sensus historicus, quicumque animum uel ad fidem uel ad opera fidei, quae sunt boni mores, magis informat, laudabilior et plane utilior est." In the present instance, "cum in se ipso homo subiecerit, dominium sui aliorumque consequitur."[23] As Bishop Brinton put it in the fourteenth century, "just as man serves God, his superior, the earth and the elements ought to serve man, their superior." But when men are slothful, or derelict in the service they owe God, they lose control over those things below them, so that they become injurious.[24] The idea was commonplace; it appears, for example, in Shakespeare's *Othello*, where that worthy remarks,

> every puny whipster gets my sword,
> But why should honor outlive honesty?
> (V, ii)

Even Cain's boy refuses to serve him, striking back at his master and commanding the team to "let the plogh stand" (line 56). Cain's slothfulness in a spiritual sense and his lack of success with "the earth" in spite of his determined worldly wisdom are evident in the remainder of the play. When we first meet him he is already a victim of the curse (Genesis 4:12) "When thou shalt till it, it shall not yield to thee its fruit." This fact is not anticipation of things to come, but another indication that Cain as we see him in the play is not a literal historical figure.

When Abel enters with a friendly and charitable greeting, Cain replies with the remark that he should have waited until he was called, commands him to help with the plow, and interlards these uncivil greetings with obscenities—"Com kys myne ars!" "kys the dwillis toute!" and "Go grese thi shepe vnder the toute / For that is the moste lefe!" The "typology" of this play refers us to the Crucifixion, but the "crucifixion" of Abel does not simply "correspond" mechanically with the Crucifixion of Christ; it is, rather, the Crucifixion by "the World" of all those who earnestly seek to follow Christ. Cain's malice toward his brother is presented in local terms because the concern of the author was with the plight of the Cains and Abels in his audience, not with historical events for their own sake. Abel does not return malice for malice, a fact that considerably reduces the "dramatic" quality of the play from a modern point of view. Instead he patiently explains that both owe God a sacrifice. In fifteenth-century terms "tithing" is one outward manifestation of this sacrifice, but it is merely an outward compliance, useless unless made in the proper spirit. The *Glossa ordinaria*, quoting Isidore of Seville, explains in conjunction with Genesis 4:34 that "justus in omnibus quae agit per fidem et charitatem (de quibus caeterae virtutes oriuntur, et sine quibus nihil possunt) Deo placere contendit, quod significatur in adipibus oblatis."[25] No reference is made to the "fat" offered by Abel in the play, since its significance would probably have escaped the audience, but Abel is given a consistently faithful and charitable attitude. Every

Christian was thought to have an obligation to "pay what he owes."
Thus in *Piers Plowman* (ed. Skeat) Christ taught Dobest, giving God's
priesthood, or Piers, the power to assoil on one condition:

> Dobest he taughte,
> And gaf Pieres power   and pardoun he graunted
> To alle manere men   mercy and forgyfnes,
> Hym mygte men to assoille   of alle manere synnes,
> In couenant that thei come   and knowleche to paye,
> To Pieres pardon the Plowman   *redde quod debes.*
>
> (B 19.178-182)

The Latin tag is a reference to the parable of the servant in Matthew
18:23-35 where Christ promises strict justice to the uncharitable: "So
also shall my heavenly Father do to you, if you forgive not every one
his brother from your hearts." This is the debt owed, and the prerequisite for pardon under the New Law. The Wakefield author keeps
his characters consistent with this idea. If Cain is, actually, a thor-
oughgoing citizen of "the earth," familiar in every community, Abel
is the faithful and charitable man. Their use in this way is fully justified
in the *Glossa ordinaria*:

> Cain et Abel de una matre geniti, figura sunt omnium hominum qui
> de radice peccati in hanc vitam propagantur; et alii terrenam
> ciuitatem et mortiferas delicias sunt amaturi, et quantum in se est
> ambitione possessuri; quos significat Cain, qui interpretatur *posses-*
> *sio.* Alii futuram civitatem quaesituri, et de hujus habitationis mis-
> eriis lugentes, ad futuram gloriam toto desiderio transituri, quos
> significat Abel, qui interpretatur *luctus.* . . .[26]

The two cities grow up "mixed" in the human heart, as St. Augustine
explains,[27] so that there is something of Cain and something of Abel
in every Christian, or, in every member of the play's audience. It may
be objected that the audience had not read the *Glossa ordinaria*, which
was beyond their "small stock of knowledge." That may be, but the
play is clearly intended to add its lessons to that stock of knowledge by
elaborating them in its words and actions.

Thus Abel's concern for "future glory" is immediately revealed in
his reply to Cain's obscenities:

> And therfor, brother, let vs weynd,
> And first clens us from the feynd
> Or we make sacrifice;
> Then blis withoutten end

> Get we for oure seruyce,
> Of hym that is oure saulis leche.
>
> (78-83)

Lines 79-80 suggest the penance or self-sacrifice necessary to charitable action, the "ancient sacrifice" of "an humble and a contrite heart"; and the expression "oure saulis leche" is a clear allusion to Christ. But Cain compares this advice with the preaching of a hypocritical friar— "let furth your geyse; the fox will preche" (line 84),[28] engages in a further obscenity,[29] and reveals a reluctance to leave his plow for the sake of God, from whom, he says, he gets only "soro and wo." In spite of Abel's assurance, "God giffys the all thi lifyng," Cain refuses to understand. He has, he says, paid his tithes—"My farthyng is in the preest hand"—although the obvious possibility of wordplay on "farthyng"[30] casts some doubt on the spirit of his payment. He is reluctant to sacrifice because his "wynnyngs" are "meyn," and he has no confidence that Christ ("hym that me dere boght") will lend him anything. Cain can think only in terms of material things, and he refuses to understand that even those material things he has are, as Abel explains, "bot a lone." God, he thinks, has always been his "fo," so that his fields do not prosper like those of other men, and he has no desire to give his precious possessions either to God or to any man (ll. 134f.). The author makes Cain's preoccupation with *possessiones* unmistakable, as well as the frustration that accompanies this preoccupation. Cain's denial of brotherly love becomes overt in lines 159-166, and this, as we have seen, is what his unsatisfactory sacrifice implies.

The Comic

The comic scene in which Cain counts out his offering probably had its inspiration in the text of Genesis in the Latin version used by St. Augustine, Isidore of Seville, and, because of the latter, reflected in the *Glossa ordinaria.* The Vulgate version of Genesis 4:6-7 in the Douay translation reads in part: "And the Lord said to him: Why art thou angry? And why is thy countenance fallen? If thou do well, shalt thou not receive? But if ill, shall not sin forthwith be present at the door?" In the earlier version, which I quote as it appears in the Dods translation of *The City of God* (15.7), we find instead: "And the Lord said unto Cain, Why art thou wroth, and why is thy countenance fallen? If thou offerest rightly, but dost not rightly distinguish, hast thou not sinned?" St. Augustine explains that although the sacrifice is made "rightly" to the true God, Cain may be said to fail to distinguish because he follows his own will instead of God's in making his offering. The *Glossa ordinaria* adds from Isidore, "Si recte offeras, et non recte dividas, peccasti: quia etsi antea Judaei recte illa offerebant, in eo rei sunt quia novum Testamentum a veteri non distinxerunt" (*PL*, 113, col. 98). In order to make Cain's failure to distinguish between Old Law selfish malice and the charity of the New Law clear, the playwright has him carefully select an inferior sheaf for God while keeping the better nine for himself. Almost everyone sometimes falls into the same error, whether in actual tithing or in daily affairs, and some, like Cain, pursue it with vigor. The play's exploitation of the possible wordplay in "non recte dividas" by making the action a deliberate "dividing up" must have delighted the clerks in the audience, while the layfolk were undoubtedly amused by Cain's foolishness.[31] When Cain begins "dividing" the second group of ten sheaves, he shuts his eyes, claiming that he can thus "doy no wrong" (ll. 225-228). The theme of "spiritual blindness," which was common in the visual arts[32] as well as in literature,[33] and was often associated with the Synagogue or the Old Law, vividly reinforces the character of Cain's offering. It accounts for his attitude toward God, whom he regards in purely materialistic terms. He will not, he says, offer him any more than the one poor sheaf he has supplied, not even enough to "wipe his ars withall" (line 238). When he finally releases a second sheaf, having selected a poor one and remarked that he will give no more even though God may become his enemy (261-262), he finds that his offering stinks "like the dwill in hell" (283), as, indeed, it should, since it is offered in malice rather than in love.

This behavior is accompanied by a superstitious fear of God, which has, rather oddly, won him the admiration of certain modern critics. For when God addresses him, reprimanding him for his attitude toward Abel, which constitutes the real nature of his "tithing," he responds by calling Him a "hob ouer the wall" (line 297), and expresses a determination to hide: "On land then will I flyt" (line 303). The ambition to hide from God, which once motivated Adam and Eve, is, of course, foolish, and is in this instance, where God is reduced to a mere hobgoblin, laughable. Sustained malice implies a self-imposed exile from one's fellow men, but hardly a means of escape from that ultimate justice promised in Matthew 18:35. Hate is also a kind of murder in accordance with 1 John 3:15: "Whosoever hateth his brother is a murderer."[34] The murder of Abel in the play not only exemplifies this idea; it also illustrates a fate that those who follow Abel may suffer either literally or daily at the hands of the malicious. For his part, Cain is condemned to walk in fear of his neighbors and looks forward to an early burial "in Gudeboure at the quarell hede" (line 367); but this easy escape is denied him. In despair, like his Scriptural predecessor, he blasphemes against the Holy Spirit, denying that a request for mercy would help him:

> It is no boyte mercy to crave,
> For I do, I mon none haue.[35]
>
> (376-377)

As an exemplar of worldliness, Cain cannot seek the mercy available to the penitent; he must seek a worldly solution to his problem.

That solution is the one personified in the *Roman de la rose* as Bien Celer. Cain asks his boy to hide the corpse, but Pikeharnes, with his usual obedience, refuses to cooperate, expressing a fear of the bailiffs. There follows a comic scene which probably owes its contemporary relevance to the fact that murderers at the time, after being arrested by the bailiffs and jailed by the sheriff, were turned over to the local justice of the peace and his court. With unfortunate regularity such cases were referred to the King's Bench, which, also with unfortunate regularity, supplied pardons for the offenders.[36] In any event, Cain seeks to proclaim his innocence "in the kyngys nayme," while Pikeharnes simultaneously proclaims his guilt. Having eluded his master's wrath, Pikeharnes then warns the audience that they shall have the same blessing from God that Cain had. At the close of the play Cain recognizes that his place is with Satan and once more decides to hide, becoming "a fugitive and a vagabond . . . upon the earth" whose fate serves as a warning to those who substitute selfish malice for the debt of brotherly love they owe to God. In fifteenth-century England Cain's exile was a far more serious matter than it might be today in the anonymous societies of our great cities. As some of the modern critics of this play have demonstrated the malicious are in any event now treated with considerable sympathy. England was then in this respect more like the America described by Tocqueville: "In Europe, a criminal is an unhappy man who is struggling for his life against the agents of power, while the people are merely a spectator of the conflict; in America he is looked upon as the enemy of the human race, and the whole of mankind is against him." The small, tightly-knit communities of the fifteenth century, like some small communities in the south of Europe today, had small tolerance for criminals.

Far from neglecting the "religious element" in his material, or "secularizing" it, or moderating it by introducing distracting comic elements, the playwright has done his best to make the spiritual significance of his narrative immediately available to the audience before him in terms that they could readily understand. Too often today we regard what medieval men thought of as "the spiritual significance" of the Scriptural narrative as being something mystical, airy and highly theoretical. On the contrary, it was eminently practical. But the technique of the Wakefield Master has nothing in common with nineteenth-century "realism" whose social message was based on abstract political principles. Since the technique of the play was employed in a great deal of late medieval and Renaissance art, we should seek a more fitting term for it than *realism*. It was, in fact, a kind of tropological verisimilitude. With regard to the "social criticism" in the Wakefield plays, we should notice that it is directed against the malicious (or men of Cain) regardless of social rank. There are in the plays reflections of contemporary abuses, like the activities of royal purveyors, or, perhaps, the laxity of the King's Bench, or the blindness of ecclesiastical courts, but the criticism is essentially moral criticism to which all ranks in society are subjected. Cain is not pictured as a member of an oppressive aristocracy, and in *Secunda pastorum* the first shepherd treats his servant, the third shepherd, with a tyranny not unlike that under which he himself suffers. Herod, the exemplification of Old Law tyranny, rules everywhere, attacking the hundred and forty-four thousand of Apocalypse 14:3-5 (*Magnus Herodes*, ll. 487-489), who are the innocent, in guises of great variety, even in "Kemptowne." And the judgments of Caiphas the Bishop and Annas the Archdeacon in their ecclesiastical court reflect the judgments of the worldly everywhere, who can always find "tortores" or summoners to assist them. The author of the plays leaves his audience with the possibility of finding these characters in themselves and among their fellows, men whose "subjects" may range from communicants, citizens in towns, workers in shops and fields, to a wife and a brood of children. As Maurice H. Keen so aptly states it, "We shall deceive ourselves if we think of late medieval England in modern terms, with . . . social tensions centring round the competing interests of classes divided horizontally from one another."[37] The "common people" who witnessed the plays were not a homogeneous mass; they lived in small vertically structured communities. The spiritual message directed to them in the plays was a matter of practical concern to each of them, for under these circumstances malice could disrupt any hierarchy, bring tyranny to any small group, and isolate any man who failed in that love celebrated in the feast of Corpus Christi. In their skillful use of detailed verisimilitude for the development of traditional ideas these plays are comparable with the paintings of the great Netherlandish masters of the same century. We should, I think, respect them accordingly.

V

The Historical Setting of Chaucer's
Book of the Duchess

ঙ

It has recently been argued by John N. Palmer, "The Historical Context of the Book of the Duchess," *Chaucer Review, 8 (1974), 253-256, that Blanche of Lancaster died in 1368 rather than in 1369. However, if this revision turns out to be correct the essential argument of the article here printed remains unchanged. Palmer's remarks about the* terminus ad quem *for the publication of the poem seem to me unconvincing, since Chaucer would have described conditions at the time of Blanche's death. A very promising account of the form of the poem by Marc M. Pelen, "Machaut's Court of Love Narratives and Chaucer's* Book of the Duchess, *Chaucer Review, 11 (1976), 128-147, reinforces the general thematic ideas here suggested. For another argument dating the publication of the poem in 1374 see the appendix to John M. Hill, "The* Book of the Duchess, Melancholy, *and that Eight-Year Sickness," Chaucer Review, 9 (1974), 35-50.*

ঙ

CRITICISM of Chaucer's *Book of the Duchess*, the first major work of a young man who was to become England's most famous poet, has sometimes neglected not only the immediate historical setting of the poem and the most probable circumstances of its first publication, but also the *mores* of its audience. At the beginning of the year 1369 the most notable poet attached to the English court was Jean Froissart, who wrote under the patronage of Queen Philippa. Both Edward III and his Queen spoke French (rather than English) as their natural language, and the Queen in particular was quite evidently an admirer of literary fashions as they had developed in the French language. In this year, which marked a turning point in the fortunes of English chivalry,[1] King Edward's court was still the most brilliant in Europe. The glory of English victories earlier in the century and the prestige of the Order of the Garter were still intact. Chaucer himself went off campaigning in France.

Queen Philippa died of the plague on August 14, the Vigil of the Assumption. Chaucer, who had returned to England, was, on September 1, granted funds for mourning for himself and his wife. On September 12, Blanche, Duchess of Lancaster, also died of the plague. Her husband, John of Gaunt, was campaigning in Picardy, whence he did not return until November 3. England thus lost two of its noblest ladies within a few weeks. The effect of these losses in a society bound together by close personal relationships must have been profound. Froissart spoke of the Queen as "the most courteous, noble, and liberal queen that ever reigned in her time,"[2] and of Blanche he wrote,

> Aussi sa fille de Lancastre—
> Haro! mettés moi une emplastre
> Sus le coer, car, quant m'en souvient,
> Certes souspirer me couvient,
> Tant sui plains de melancolie.—
> Elle morut jone et jolie,
> Environ de vingt et deux ans;
> Gaie, lie, friche, esbatans,
> Douce, simple, d'umble samblance;
> La bonne dame ot à nom Blanche.[3]
>
> (241-250)

The Duke of Lancaster instituted a memorial service to be held for Blanche each year on September 12 at St. Paul's Cathedral,[4] a ceremonial which he continued to support for the remainder of his life. He arranged for an elaborate alabaster tomb to be erected by Henry Yevele, who was to become England's most distinguished mason.[5] An altar was erected near the tomb, and two chantry priests were engaged to sing masses there throughout the year.[6] In accordance with the explicit provision of his will, John was buried by the side of Blanche.

Concerning John of Gaunt's reaction, Armitage-Smith observes, "of the sincerity of the Duke's grief·there need be no question," adding that his gratitude to the memory of Blanche "never failed."[7] More recent writers, pointing, with appropriate disdain, to the Duke's relations with Katherine Swynford, who was the guardian of his children, and to his marriage to Constance of Castile, have been more cynical. But the alliance with Katherine indicates nothing except the fact that the two were thrown together by circumstance at a time when the Duke was still relatively young and vigorous in an age that was neither sentimental nor especially squeamish about sex. The marriage to Constance, which was made for political reasons, has no bearing on John's feelings for either Blanche or Katherine. For our purposes the Duke's feelings, for which we have little evidence, are not, in any event, important. What is important is the Duke's public posture. And there is nothing in that posture to cast doubt on Armitage-Smith's conclusion. The tomb, the altar, the chantry-priests, and the annual memorial service were all reminders of the inspiration Blanche had been, not only to John personally, but to all those who had known and loved her. Chaucer's *Book of the Duchess*, a work prepared by a young squire who was to receive very substantial favors from John of Gaunt in the future, should be considered as a kind of literary counterpart of Henry Yevele's alabaster tomb, a memorial to a great lady celebrating neither Chaucer's nor anyone else's intimate feelings and "psychological" reveries, but the kind of tribute a great lady, still "jone et jolie," suddenly destroyed by a terrible malady, deserves from all men of good will.

Perhaps it is futile to speculate about the unfulfilled potentialities of history. Nevertheless, it seems reasonable to suppose that if the Queen had not died, depriving Froissart of his position at the English court, we might very well have had a formal elegy for Blanche in French. Blanche's father, Henry of Lancaster, had been the author of a devotional treatise, the *Livre de Seyntz Medicines*, written in French. The fact that Chaucer wrote the elegy is an indication of the "Anglicising" of the English nobility during the second half of the century. It is also a tribute to the growing prestige of Geoffrey Chaucer. If Speght was right, and the "A. B. C." was actually written for Blanche during her lifetime, that poem may be regarded as further evidence indicating Blanche's preference for literature in English. It would serve at the same time as a foretaste of the serious attitudes to be expected from the young squire. But when Chaucer did begin his poem, he introduced it with an echo of a poem by Froissart, an echo which is at once a clue to the thematic content of the poem and a tribute to the French poet who was in a very real sense Chaucer's predecessor.

It cannot be emphasized too strongly that *The Book of the Duchess* is essentially a funerary poem, a poem designed to be delivered orally before an orthodox audience of noblemen, great men of London, ladies, and clerks, whose literary tastes were traditionally French. It is also true that medieval poems other than those written for private devotion or for evangelical instruction were "occasional" poems, composed for an audience assembled for some specific social occasion.[8] The gathering might be anything from a dinner to a festival of the Pui. We should think of Chaucer's poem as being "public," written neither to express the very private feelings of the author nor to inspire the very private reactions of anyone sitting alone in the silence of a study. The most probable occasion for its presentation would have been one of the memorial celebrations held each year on September 12, perhaps at supper at the Savoy, perhaps in the nave of St. Paul's, which was thought of as "belonging to the people" and used for a variety of lay activities. As we read *The Book of the Duchess*, then, we should try to image ourselves hearing it read as we sit (or stand) in an audience of fourteenth-century ladies and gentlemen assembled especially for the purpose of paying tribute to the memory of Blanche, Duchess of Lancaster, who had been one of the ladies of highest rank in the English court.

The men and women who sit around us as we listen to the poem are chivalric in outlook and orthodox in sentiment, attitudes that were by no means thought of as being inconsistent. The Duke of Lancaster was, throughout his life, a generous benefactor of ecclesiastics and of religious institutions. His later patronage of Wyclif had nothing to do with any lack of orthodoxy on his part,[9] and the status of Katherine Swynford as his mistress after 1372 neither made him a "pagan" nor caused him to be thought of by his peers as a "great sinner." The fulminations of politically hostile chroniclers should not be taken too seriously, no matter how much they may appeal to the ingrown Calvinism of certain modern historians. With reference to Chaucer himself, it is significant that some of his closest associates at court were Lollard knights, men who were Lollards not out of any lack of orthodoxy, but by virtue of the fact that the spiritual corruption of their church and society was a matter of grave concern to them.[10] Whatever we may think of either the Duke or the poet, however, *The Book of the Duchess* was a public poem, and since it was a public poem and not an expression of personal feeling, we may expect it to exhibit certain proprieties. There can be little doubt that Blanche of Lancaster was a lady who attracted much genuine affection in courtly circles. Her rank was great enough to inspire a certain devotion to begin with, and her youth and charm must have attracted many persons of importance in addition to Jean Froissart.

Considering the occasion of Chaucer's poem and its probable audience, there are then certain things we might expect of it in advance: a generally chivalric attitude; a tactful restraint with reference to the lady, her family, and her associates; a statement, either direct or indirect, of the conventional ideas associated with funerary consolation; and, finally, a fairly close adherence to the techniques and general attitudes of the popular French poetry of the time. At this point my literary friends will object: "It is unfair to go outside of the poem. One should begin with the text, without any presuppositions whatsoever." Let me reply that it is impossible to read anything "without any presuppositions," and that what has happened is that most critics of the poem have brought to it a great many post-romantic presuppositions concerning both the subject of the poem and its technique, which are entirely inappropriate to its cultural setting. In any event, let us consider the above points in reverse order.

To begin with, scholars have long since pointed out that Chaucer does indeed rely heavily on French sources for the materials of his poem. They have gleaned a number of parallel passages which are quite convincing, as well as some which are not so convincing.[11] What they have not done is to make useful comments on the significance of the borrowings. That is, the passages used have a contextual significance in the works from which they are derived, a significance of which Chaucer was certainly aware and of which many members of his audience were probably aware. As a consequence of this failure literary critics have frequently disregarded the parallel passages as constituting so much dusty and irrelevant information. And, indeed, in their present form, they are just that. The situation is made worse by the fact that there are hardly more neglected European poets anywhere than the poets of fourteenth-century France. When one looks for interpretations of their works, which are frequently allegorical in technique, one finds instead of interpretation a series of statements to the effect that the poems are "conventional." To say that a poem by Machaut or Froissart is merely an agglomeration of "conventions" is simply to say, with a certain professorial profundity, that one does not know what the poem is about. There are thus many details in *The Book of the Duchess* which must remain relatively obscure until serious studies of the French sources have been made.

It is possible to make a general statement about the French poetry Chaucer drew upon that has some bearing on the thematic content of *The Book of the Duchess*. That poetry shows a heavy reliance on themes from *The Consolation of Philosophy* of Boethius, a work that enjoyed increasing popularity during the course of the century and that Chaucer later undertook to translate into English. The *Consolation* has not fared well in modern times, having been victimized by literal-minded comments, by irrelevant analyses on the part of philosophers trained in nineteenth-century German metaphysics, and by a general failure to take its themes seriously or to assume that anyone ever did take them seriously. In the fourteenth century, however, the *Consolation* was a book regarded with genuine love by many, especially by those who had witnessed the devastations of the plague and suffered personal losses in those devastations; its themes appear not only in literary works but also in the visual arts of the time, penetrating even to country parishes. The book was thought of as being thoroughly orthodox, a fact that one modern authority fully appreciated, observing that "there is nothing in this work for which a good case might not have been made by any contemporary Christian theologian, who knew his Augustine."[12]

Since the commentaries of Guillaume de Conches and Nicholas Trivet on the *Consolation* have never been printed, perhaps the best short introduction to the work as it was understood in later Middle Ages is that provided by Jean de Meun for the translation he presented to Philip the Fair of France.[13] After identifying himself, explaining the reasons for his translation and the techniques he employed in it, Jean goes on to outline the thesis of the work. He points out first of all, with a rather elaborate argument, that all things tend toward the good. In this respect, however, man differs from other things, since his course is not predetermined (i.e., he has free choice). The true good of man lies in the intelligible, but sensible goods impress him first (i.e., those goods perceived by the senses rather than by the understanding) and he is misled into deserting his proper good in favor of those things which are sensible. He must therefore be taught to distinguish reasonably between the two kinds of good and to know what kind of good he should enjoy. Most men go astray in this respect, enjoying things of the wrong kind. And this causes their lives to be full of bitterness. For sensible things, which are transitory and mutable, cannot be enjoyed without sorrow. The *Consolation*, Jean says, is most useful in teaching the distinction between true and false good, in showing what things are to be enjoyed, and in demonstrating how other things are to be used.[14] Among all the books ever written, Jean assures his royal patron, this is the best one for teaching us to despise false and deceptive goods (later called "biens sensibles forains et fortunieux," or alien goods of Fortune) and to seek instead true and immutable goods that will lead us to happiness. Boethius, we are told, was wrongfully imprisoned, but he endured his misfortune well and wisely as a strong man of good heart. In his book, he is presented as a man divided into two parts: first, as a man cast down by "passions sensibles," and second, as a man divinely raised up to intelligible goods. That is, the figure "Boethius" in the book is the man cast down, while the other reasonable part of him is represented by Philsophy.[15] The actual Boethius, we assume, always endured his trouble patiently.

What relevance has all this to a funerary poem? An inkling of the answer to this question may be found in the pages of Dante, who tells us in the *Convivio* (2.13) that he was inconsolable after the death of Beatrice until he had read the *Consolation* of Boethius and the *De amicitia* of Cicero. In the *De amicitia* he would have found that true friendship, or true love of one human being for another, is based on virtue; and in the *Consolation*, that such friendship, or love, is not subject to Fortune. That is, the virtues of another human being are intelligible rather than sensible goods which, in a Christian context, are derived from God and do not perish. Moreover, the memory of the virtues of one who has died can act as an inspiration, just as the memory of a loved one as a physical being that has perished can bring a sense of acute loss.

If we turn our attention to *The Book of the Duchess*, it is apparent at once that one character in it, the Black Knight, regards the loss of Blanche as the loss of a gift of Fortune. He is introduced, much like the *persona* "Boethius" in the *Consolation*, in a condition of despair arising from the loss of Blanche as a sensible object, and this loss is attributed specifically to the operations of Fortune. In Boethian terms, this kind of sorrow, although it occurs spontaneously in all of us, is actually a kind of foolishness. Chaucer is careful to make his Knight a beardless adolescent who gave himself up to "love" in "idleness" before he ever saw Blanche.[16] He is obviously in need of the kind of instruction that, as Jean de Meun assures us, may be found best expressed in the *Consolation*. It must be emphasized that themes from this work were common in French poetry—perhaps the most obvious example being Machaut's *Remède de Fortune*, which Chaucer drew upon heavily—that they appeared in the visual arts, and even found a prominent place in highly "secular" works like Geoffrey de Charny's treatise on chivalry. That is, Chaucer's audience would have been in a position to realize fully the implications of losing a chess game to Fortune. Of the two principal "characters" in Chaucer's poem, one, the Knight, despairingly recounts his experience with reference to Blanche—his first sight of her, his conception of her person and character, his first unsuccessful approach, his acquisition of the lady's grace, and finally, the fact of her death. The other "character," the dreamer, acts as a confessor, pressing the Knight to reveal the whole course of his experience and offering a certain amount of wise advice, like that, for example, on the folly of suicide. The parallel between this general situation and that in the *Consolation* is obvious and would hardly have escaped Chaucer's audience. The plight of the Black Knight expressed in terms of Fortune would have suggested a more "proper" attitude, even if such an attitude were not otherwise indicated in the poem. As we shall see presently, however, the "proper" attitude is very definitely suggested.

As we have suggested earlier, a funerary poem, to avoid boorishness, might be expected to show considerable restraint in its implications concerning actual persons. The young poet would have been particularly careful not to offend John of Gaunt, no matter what his "private" feelings may have been, if indeed he had any as distinct from his "public" feelings about the Duke. If the poem, as a public memorial, had been offensive to the Duke, we should in all likelihood have no evidence of its existence today. However, in June, 1374, the Duke, as he put it, "by our special grace and for the good, and so on, that our good friend Geoffrey Chaucer has done for us" granted to Chaucer and to his wife "for the good service . . . performed for our very honored dame and mother the Queen, whom God pardon, and for our very dear friend and companion the Queen [of Castile]," a pension of ten pounds a year for life.[17] The sum is exactly half that granted Chaucer many years later by Richard II as a recognition for his services in the very distinguished office of Clerk of the King's works. It is not unlikely that the phrase "for the good, and so on" referred in part to *The Book of the Duchess* itself. The Duke was in England for the first time on September 12 in this year to attend the memorial service for Blanche in person. It is significant that he referred to this grant specifically on January 20 of the following year.[18] Under the circumstances, the traditional view that the beardless adolescent who appears in the poem as the Black Knight overcome by the loss of Blanche as a gift of Fortune was intended to represent John of Gaunt is absurd. Whatever we may think of the Duke, there is little doubt that he felt grief for the loss of Blanche, but there is also little doubt that any public representation of the Duke's grief contrived by a good friend would have shown him, like Jean de Meun's Boethius, suffering "tout sagement sa douleur comme homme fort et de grant cuer." The Black Knight shows a consistent blindness to the intelligible, even when it is suggested by his own words. There is no probability whatsoever that he was meant to represent literally anyone in Chaucer's audience, least of all John of Gaunt. He may well have represented, however, a certain aspect of almost everyone in the audience.

Much of the confusion concerning the poem has arisen from our inclination to see the grief of the Black Knight in a "psychological" context rather than in the moral and philosophical context familiar to the society of which Chaucer was a part. Efforts to demonstrate this distinction have met with rejoinders like "We are back again in an idealized Middle Ages peopled only with righteous Christians."[19] The fact that people thought of human conduct in "moral" terms during the Middle Ages does not mean that their behavior was "moral," especially from our point of view. We tend to think of human beings in

Tomb of John of Gaunt, Old St. Paul's Cathedral, London. Courtesy of the Marquand Library, Princeton.

"psychological" terms, but this fact does not imply that people in our own society are generally sane and well-adjusted. On the contrary, our literature shows a strong preoccupation with themes of isolation, *anomie*, and alienation. We seek as best we can to regard persons suffering from social maladjustment and psychological weakness with sympathy and understanding. Although this sympathy may sometimes imply criticism of society, it does not ordinarily imply any criticism of the "terms" of the psychology used to depict the suffering of the individual. For example, O'Neill's *Mourning Becomes Electra* reflects certain principles of Freudian psychology, but this fact does not imply any criticism of Freud.

Medieval men were also urged, as they are in the *Consolation*, to take pity on sinners, since a malady of the spirit is more serious than a malady of the flesh.[20] But this pity does not imply either that sinners are not sinners or that there is anything wrong with the conceptual system upon which the pity itself is based. If we look at the Black Knight (rather vaguely and without paying any attention to the connotations of the terms used to describe him) from a "psychological" point of view, his grief seems quite understandable and not reprehensible at all. If we look at him in the context of the moral philosophy of the fourteenth century, he appears, not as a "psychological entity," an individual like ourselves alienated in an absurd world, but as an exemplification of an understandable but errant attitude toward the lady that is not very complimentary to the lady. Had she, after all, no intelligible virtues? Was she mere flesh? Most frequently, the Black Knight has been seen romantically, with an attitude that has its roots in the cult of melancholy that grew up in the eighteenth century and that has been reinforced by various outgrowths like *ennui*, existential absurdity, ambiguity, and so on. Our "psychology" as it appears in literary criticism is, as a matter of fact, little more than an amorphous reflection of these attitudes. It is a product of a society in which the tightly-knit communities of the past have broken down so that the individual is left with a somewhat diminished and fragmented identity as a member of large and loosely organized groups in which the ties of organization do not form channels of personal satisfaction. Chaucer lived in no such society. He and his contemporaries would not have understood what we mean by "psychology," and, what is more important, would have felt no need for it. In any event, *The Book of the Duchess* is a public funerary poem that may be expected to reflect the most elevated public philosophy available for its conceptual framework.

The "anguish of a troubled heart" is something that we are inclined to regard with a certain reverence. The phrase brings to mind linger-ing fancies decked with wisps of autumnal melancholy we have heard echoing in the finest sonatas of Mozart, in the grand symphonies of Beethoven, in the graceful strains of Chopin's nocturnes, in the nos-talgic memories inspired by Brahms, or even if our tastes are more advanced, in those brief moments of tenderness in Webern, where the anguish is intensified by poignant feelings of alienation and despair. We know that Chaucer had not heard these things and was not famil-iar, indeed, in spite of his elegy, with the theory that the most beautiful and appropriate subject for poetry is the death of a beautiful woman. But, we assure ourselves, he was human, and so must have felt as we feel, but without the richness of association that we are able to bring to his poetry.[21] We are in a position to find much in it, quite legitimately, of which he had only a rudimentary apprehension. This line of argu-ment has a certain appeal, but it is, nevertheless, sheer nonsense.

In 1853 Delacroix wrote in his journal,

> Exquisite music at the house of charming Princess Marcelline. I especially remember Mozart's *Fantasia* [K. 475], a serious work, verging on the terrible, and with a title too light for its character; also a sonata by Beethoven which I already knew—but admirable. I really liked it exceedingly, especially the mournful imaginative pas-sages. Beethoven is always melancholy. Mozart is modern too; I mean by this that like other men of his time he is not afraid of touch-ing on the sad side of things.[22]

Although Delacroix was not an historian of music, his observation that "modern" music is distinguished by melancholy and sadness touches on a profound truth: the glorification of "the anguish of a troubled heart" as an aesthetically appealing theme to be revered in itself is relatively modern. Chaucer uses the phrase once, in his Par-son's Tale, where it is a definition of the sin of "accidie": "Thanne is Accidie the angwissh of troubled herte; and Seint Augustyn seith, 'It is anoy of goodnesse and Ioye of harm.' Certes, this is a dampnable synne."[23] The branches of this sin include sloth, despair, lassitude, and *tristicia*, "the synne of worldly sorwe." Its remedies are fortitude, magnanimity, sureness or perseverance, magnificence, and constancy, virtues which are distinctly chivalric.[24] Perhaps some will reply that Chaucer's humble and devout Parson, who taught "Cristes loore and his apostles twelve" after he had "folwed it hymselve" was an old Puritan, to whose strictures Chaucer, who was, after all, a great poet and hence "advanced," could have given small credence.[25] But this is to misunderstand both the Parson and his creator. With reference to the "Puritanism," we should recall that the Parson, although he was a learned man and a clerk, was also "to synful men nat despitous." This does not mean that he relaxed his principles. What it does mean is that the Parson employed "fairnesse" and "good ensample." He was, that is, no Pharisee who said one thing and did another. No one in the Middle Ages except for a few pious hypocrites who were condemned with equal severity by Jean de Meun, Petrarch, Boccaccio, and Chaucer, thought that "sinners" were "those others." Every man since the Fall was by nature a child of wrath, to paraphrase St. Paul; and no one expected any individual to refrain from sin altogether. Everyone was required to confess his "deadly" sins at least once a year. If society had been made up of the righteous, the ecclesiastical hierarchy might just as well have closed its doors and gone out of business. With reference to the *"accidie"* of the Black Knight specifically, it is obvious that it deprives him of virtues like magnanimity and magnificence and that we should consider his conduct to be unreasonable. His virtues have been turned to vices (ll. 598ff.), he seriously contemplates suicide (ll. 689-690), and he desires to do nothing worthwhile. This attitude is hardly, in fourteenth-century terms, a fitting tribute to a great lady in a chivalric society. In other societies it might have a certain appeal. Thus, if we accept for a moment Rousseau's account of the affair (whose verisimilitude is all that is important here),[26] when M. Grimm deliberately adopted a posture very similar to that of the Black Knight because he had been rejected by Mlle. Fel, he won for himself an enormous reputation as a prodigy of love and devotion and was warmly received by the best society of Paris. But Chaucer did not live in eighteenth-century Paris. The age of *sentiment* had not yet arrived. If we glance back at Froissart's remarks quoted earlier, we shall notice that the old poet shows no inclination to cultivate the melancholy he feels when he remembers Blanche, and that his sighs follow an exclamation that is vigorous and positive.

The Black Knight, like M. Grimm, is a lover; and this fact also should lead us to read Chaucer's poem with a certain caution. Some critics of the poem have written about it as though they were themselves spiritual descendants of Emma Bovary and expected everyone else, including Chaucer, to share the same general outlook. Perhaps nothing has been more characteristic of the past two hundred years than the violence and rapidity with which attitudes toward sexual relations and love between the sexes have changed.[27] There is no need to go into the history of these matters in detail here; it is obvious that the place of sexual relations and love in a society where feelings of loneliness, boredom, namelessness, and alienation are common, and environments created by an industrial society seem inhumane, should be very different from their place in a predominantly rural society where everyone had a more or less natural position in a small community. It is true that war and pestilence created dislocation in the fourteenth century. But the dislocated, in general, tended to become outlaws, not authors, especially in England. The Middle Ages had experienced none of the glorification of sentiment (the beginnings of which are apparent in Rousseau), the strong urge toward the brotherhood of all mankind (which led Baudelaire to think that prostitutes are holy, and has produced many golden-hearted whores since), the squeamishness of the Victorians, nor the crisis marked by the revolt of D. H. Lawrence and the observations of Freud, all of which, together with some more recent "revolutions," lie in our immediate background. Although in the Middle Ages contemplatives and, perhaps, apprentices, took vows of chastity, and priests were not encouraged to have concubines, and medieval manors supported many unmarried serfs, it is unlikely that many persons, especially among those of gentle birth, suffered long from sexual frustration. What we call "the facts of life" were not concealed from children;[28] they were not mysteries for adolescent fumbling; and no one felt any compulsion to be either "sincere" or sentimental about his miscellaneous sexual activities.

It is true, as churchmen disturbed by Albigensian errors insist throughout the later Middle Ages, that fornication was considered to be a "deadly sin." But so were getting drunk, eating too much or too delicately, envying your neighbor's goods, dressing yourself up proudly beyond your station, and, indeed, a great many other kinds of fairly common behavior "deadly sins" also. These were things that everyone was expected to fall into occasionally and which everyone was supposed to reveal to his confessor. No one was encouraged to do any of these things, but no one was especially surprised when anyone did. A vicious inclination to pursue sins of any given type, sexual or otherwise, was heartily discouraged, but the medieval ecclesiastical hierarchy did not pursue the subject in such a way as to encourage what we might call "Ruskin's Problem." Nor was there much need for "Rousseau's Solution." Sinning did not make anyone a "pagan," and no one thought that pagans enjoyed life more than Christians. Adultery was, naturally enough, another "deadly sin." In this matter the feudal Middle Ages maintained a "double standard" for social reasons. Feudal holdings were hereditary, and feudal tenants wished their holdings to descend to their own children, not to the children of intruders. But the ladies, although a few may have been misled by "the book of Launcelot de Lake," did not have their "psychological needs" stimulated by the kind of romantic picture books that fascinated little Emma Bovary, did not immerse themselves vicariously in novels, and did not, finally, live in a dull, postrevolutionary middle-class society. In the fourteenth century, in short, sex was neither a mystery nor a mystique. Although it was quite profitable for summoners, arch- deacons, and rural deans, it did not constitute a profound personal problem, especially among noblemen, who in general found "veni- son" plentiful. To use an example pertinent to our present discussion, the first child of John of Gaunt of whom we have any record was born when John was about eighteen, and the lady in question, one Marie de Saint Hilaire, was probably by no means his first love.[29]

If fornication was simply one among many "deadly sins," and adul- tery occasioned little surprise among the male nobility,[30] there was something else that was severely condemned by the ecclesiastical au- thorities and ridiculed by laymen because it led to impenitence spiritu- ally and to a foolish neglect of social obligations. And that was a single-minded and impenitent fixation on a single member of the op- posite sex as a means of enjoyment to be venerated above all other things. As this sort of passion is usually described, it has pleasure, not marriage, as its end; and it deprives the victim of the solaces of all other women except the one fixed upon. This kind of "idolatrous" love is not, in substance, of medieval origin. It is described by Lu- cretius.[31] In the Middle Ages it is illustrated in Abelard's *Historia calamitatum*, in the Tristan romances of Béroul and Thomas, in Chré- tien's romances of Cligés and Lancelot, in the *Roman de la Rose*, in Chaucer's *Troilus*, in *Celestina*, and, in the Renaissance, in Shake- speare's *Antony and Cleopatra*. Medical authorities described it as "heroic" love, an appellation in which the word *heroic* is pejorative. It is the same sort of thing that in Rousseau's account M. Grimm pre- tended to feel for his opera singer. We are naturally inclined in reading medieval texts of the kind just mentioned to react in much the same way that fashionable Paris reacted to Grimm's predicament, and to add to our sentiment a further veneer of Biedermeier sentimentality glossed with a dash of existential loneliness. From a medieval point of view, the great difficulty with a passion of this kind is that it leads al- most inevitably to frustration, or even death, and it deprives its victim of the mercy of the New Law.

It would be foolish to accuse John of Gaunt of any such impenitent passion. But the Black Knight in *The Book of the Duchess* seems to have been thrown by his grief into a condition very much resembling it. Without Blanche, he can do nothing constructive, and life itself seems worthless. When his interrogator suggests to him that he has, in view of his description of Blanche, had "such a chaunce as shryfte wythoute repentaunce," he can reply only that it would be treasonable for him to repent of his love. He has no notion of what his description of the lady has implied: the virtues of Blanche belong to the realm of the intelligible and are not subject to Fortune. The quest of the idolatrous lover is not a quest for virtue, but for his own "bliss." And it is this, the Knight assures us, that he has lost. Without it, death seems the only solution. His "shrift," in other words, has not led him to see the essential selfishness of his passion.

Turning now from the Black Knight to the description of Blanche, we find that scholars and critics have insisted, in spite of the fact that Chaucer's materials are clearly derivative, on seeing it as at least in part an actual description of the lady. In one sense it may be, but it is hardly a visual portrait. We know more, in so far as details of feature are concerned, about some of the characters in *The Canterbury Tales*. What does Chaucer, in fact, tell us? Blanche outshone the other ladies as the sun does the stars. She was of good stature, she maintained a steadfast countenance, and her demeanor was noble and friendly (ll. 817-847). She danced, sang, laughed, and played in an attractive way; she had golden hair, a steady glance, and an eye that seemed merciful (ll. 848-877). She was temperate in mood, neither too solemn nor too gay, and she loved charitably (ll. 878-894). She had a beautiful face, red and white, that was "sad, symple, and benygne" (ll. 895-918). She spoke softly, reasonably, and truthfully, without malice, flattery, or chiding (ll. 919-938). Her neck was round, fair, and straight. Her throat was like a round tower of ivory and of moderate size (ll. 939-947). She had fair shoulders, a long trunk, well-proportioned arms, white hands with red nails, round breasts, broad hips, and a straight, flat back (ll. 948-960). She outshone the other ladies in comeliness of manner, and was, like the Arabian Phoenix, unique (ll. 961-984). The description goes on to consider intangibles: Blanche's goodness, truth, and well-ordered love (ll. 985-1034). He who looks for an individualized "portrait" in these lines will look in vain. Did the lady have long lashes? What color were her eyes? Was her nose long or short, her chin slightly jutting or round and dimpled? Was her lip full?

We are told that Blanche was a beautiful, attractive, and well-mannered blonde, exceptionally well-shaped and with the coloration to be expected. In other words, the description is highly stylized and is not, in the modern sense, a "portrait" at all. If we look carefully at the description in the original we shall find it to contain much more emphasis on *invisibilia* than on *visibilia*. Moreover, it contains features like the ivory tower which are clearly iconographic, or, in other words, features that point to ideas rather than to things. The *invisibilia*, both stated and implied, moreover, all point to Blanche's virtues, so that ll. 895-1032 form a logical conclusion to the description. The emphasis on virtue in the description, which may be detected even without reference to conventional iconography (a subject which seems to irritate most of my fellow-Chaucerians about as much as virtue itself does), is hardly surprising in a funerary poem. What is surprising is that the Black Knight fails to see the wider implications of what he has said. He has been lamenting the loss of Blanche as a physical being, a gift of Fortune. But the virtues he has described have nothing to do with Fortune and cannot be destroyed by anything Fortune may do. This fact could hardly have escaped Chaucer's audience, and did not escape the Black Knight's interrogator, who remarked,

> Hardely, your love was wel beset;
> I not how ye myghte have do bet.
> (1043-1044)

A lady of such virtue is truly lovable.

Two "characters" in the poem remain to be discussed: the Emperor Octovyen, and the speaker. The usual notion that the Emperor or king (line 1314) is meant to represent Edward III is hardly very convincing. What, exactly, would have been the point of the dreamer's undertaking a hunt under the auspices of King Edward in which the king himself did nothing but ride toward the manor of Richmond after an unsuccessful day in the field? If Octovyen was meant to be Edward, we can conclude only that Chaucer must have succeeded very well in puzzling his royal master.

There remains the speaker, who acts also as interrogator in the questioning of the Black Knight. It is usually assumed that the dream in the poem is, in spite of the warnings in ll. 270-290, a literal dream experienced, or feigned to have been experienced, by Geoffrey Chaucer, our young squire. Let us picture the situation. Chaucer, a member of the court of comparatively low rank, rises at a memorial gathering for Blanche, and says, in effect, "I am in very low spirits, having suffered for the past eight years, and cannot sleep. But I read a tale about Ceys and Alcione and went to sleep. Then I dreamed about waking in an elaborately decorated chamber and taking part in a hunt, led by the Emperor Octovyen, where I met a Black Knight lamenting the death of a lady under a tree. He told me how much he loved Blanche, whom he described; but he refused to be consoled. As I woke up, I saw Octovyen riding to Richmond." If we are to believe the most recent critics of the poem, he added somewhere in this account a remark like the following: "Oh, I say. Life, love, and all that. Frightfully ambiguous, what?" The only reasonable reaction to all this would have been to send the poor squire to St. Bartholomew's. Nobody in the audience, unless Philippa Chaucer were there, could possibly have had any interest in the squire's personal feelings, or in whether he had been ill for eight years or twenty, or in what he might have dreamed. What is the Emperor Octovyen, or, if you prefer, Augustus Caesar, doing in the English countryside? It is small wonder that a distinguished literary historian finds the poem "crude," with a "story" that "drags," full of "hackneyed" conventions, and without "profound emotion" or "piercing thought."[32] As it is usually read today it is worse than this. It is a piece of foolishness which would have been an affront to the court and a disgrace to its author. Those who insist on clinging to "what the poem says literally" are only offering some justification for the usual connotations of the word *academic*. Do they also engage in disputes about the number of petals growing on the girl whom Burns describes as being "like a red, red rose"?

It is much more probable that the "I" at the beginning of the poem represents not Chaucer individually and specifically but the initial reaction of the mourners for Blanche generally, somewhat exaggerated for poetic purposes. The story of Seys and Alcione is not something he chanced to have read, but something of significance for all the mourners, who have set before them an example of someone who cannot endure a temporal loss "comme homme fort et de grant cuer," and cannot understand the consolatory implications of the message,

> Awake! let be your sorwful lyf!
> For in your sorwe ther lyth no red,
> For, certes, swete, I nam but ded, . . .
> (202—204)

There is only one sense in which the statement "I nam but ded" can be taken as a reason for not sorrowing, and, considering both the occasion for the poem and the nature of the audience, that sense would have been obvious. It can be found explained fully in the Epistle of the Mass for the Burial of the Dead, which begins, "Brethren: We will not have you ignorant concerning them that are asleep, that you be not sorrowful, even as others who have no hope; for if we believe that Jesus died and rose again, even so them who have slept through Jesus, will God bring with Him." Alcione, who looked up and "saw noght," is among those "who have no hope."

In the dream, as we have seen, there is an obvious parallel between the interrogator and Lady Philosophy in the *Consolation*, and between the Black Knight and the mournful "Boethius" of the same work. Every man, including every man in Chaucer's audience, has, as it were, two parts, one involved in the senses and the other capable of comprehending the intelligible. What is revealed in the Black Knight's long confession is the significance of an Alcione-like attitude, an attitude typical of that part of any man that is involved in temporal things. It is for this reason that Spenser names his "man in black" in the *Daphnaida*, who is certainly not John of Gaunt, "Alcyon." The attitude depends on our being overcome by idleness (or neglect of virtuous activity) in the first place, and by love for those things that may be apprehended by the senses. Then the object finally settled upon becomes, through desire, a gift of Fortune, the loss of which leads to "accidie" and despair. But at the promptings of the interrogator, the Black Knight, together with the audience, is led to dwell upon Blanche's virtues. If Blanche was as virtuous as the description implies, as noble, temperate, truthful, and charitable as the Black Knight indicates, then a despairing attitude like that of Alcione is neither necessary nor, in fact, complimentary to her. Aside from a few hints, like the observations on suicide, and a generally reasonable tone (sometimes described as "realistic" or inappropriately humorous), the interrogator leaves the positive side of his message unstated. It was stated openly in the Burial Service and in Commemorative Masses, but *The Book of the Duchess* is a poem, or, in other words, a work in which indirect statement may lead the audience to certain conclusions that are only suggested. Meanwhile, the Black Knight and the dreamer represent two aspects, not only of Geoffrey Chaucer, but of everyone who loved Blanche.

Whether the poem conveys "profound emotion" depends entirely on the reader's experience and training. The Burial Service can in itself be very moving, and the ideas in the *Consolation* of Boethius can be moving also. Whether the doctrines of St. Paul and of Boethius actually constitute "serious thought" I leave to the gentlemen who, a moment ago, were discussing the number of petals growing on the girl. In the past, some of them have complained loudly about the inadequacy of Pauline and Boethian doctrines, which fail somehow to cope with the rich ambiguity of life. However, there is no reason to imagine that there was much sniveling about "ambiguity" in the court of Edward III. Had there been peaches there, men would have dared eat them.

The chivalric character of the poet and of his audience remains for our consideration. It is manifested, first of all, in the pervasive shimmer of good humor that glances from the surface of the poem, a tone that we can detect, without too much difficulty, in the little lament from Froissart quoted at the beginning of this essay. In a famous letter to his brother Toby, Mr. Walter Shandy strongly urged him to have his beloved Widow Wadman read "devotional tracts" and to keep from her such authors as Rabelais, Scarron, or Cervantes. Their books "excite laughter," thus making them inappropriate, for "there is no passion so serious as lust." Mr. Shandy here hit upon a great truth. If he had lived in our age, he might have added that certain forms of aesthetics and psychology share the same seriousness, since they are not unrelated to the passion mentioned. Morality, except in its nineteenth-century guises, is not nearly so serious, a fact that has resulted in the destruction of much of Chaucer's humor at the hands of the aesthetically or psychologically inclined. In the fourteenth century specifically, young noblemen were discouraged from maintaining a solemn attitude in public, for "papelardie," or false holiness, was considered foolish and in bad taste.[33] The light tone of much of Chaucer's poem is not difficult to point out. For example, when the speaker introduces his book of "fables," he says that it spoke

> Of quenes lives, and of kinges,
> And many other thinges smale.
> (BD 58-59)

The bantering tone continues in the story itself. Alcione's grief is not always treated with great solemnity:

> Ful ofte she swouned, and sayd "Alas!"
> For sorwe ful nygh wood she was. . . .
> (103-104)

Again, the scene between Juno's messenger and Morpheus is openly humorous:

> This messager com fleynge faste
> And cried, "O, ho! awake anoon!"
> Hit was for noght; there herde hym non.
> "Awake!" quod he, "whoo ys lyth there?"
> And blew his horn ryght in here eere,
> And cried "Awaketh!" wonder hyë.
> This god of slep with hys oon yë
> Cast up, axed, "Who clepeth ther?"
> "Hyt am I," quod this messager.
> (178-186)

The light tone is marked in the dreamer's reaction to the story—in his elaborate promise to Morpheus "in game," and in his introduction to the dream that "nat skarsly Macrobeus" (284) could understand. Although the speeches of the Black Knight are serious in intent, his behavior as he describes it not infrequently borders upon the ridiculous, and, in any event, the reactions of the interrogator maintain a courteous but good-natured tone. His response to the final revelation of Blanche's death, for example, is one of detached but good-natured sympathy:

> "Is that your los? Be god hyt ys routhe!"
>
> (1309)

Most critics of the poem have been disappointed by the fact that this response is not more lugubrious. Its tone is not very different from Froissart's

> Haro! Mettés moi une emplastre
> Sus le coer. . . .
>
> (242-243)

In neither instance should the light tone be taken as an indication of lack of feeling. Chaucer was not attempting to encourage the serious, basically lustful attitude of the Black Knight. He had no desire to encourage grief. On the contrary, the serious, melancholy, slothful mood was exactly what he wished to discourage. He is saying, in effect, to all the mourners for Blanche, "let be your sorwful lyf!" When the light of reason is allowed to play on the scene, grief departs from those who have hope. Meanwhile, the general tone of the poem is aristocratic and good-humored, consistent with the predominantly chivalric nature of the audience.

In addition to presenting a contrast to a reasonable attitude toward Fortune, the Black Knight's behavior contrasts sharply with the current conception of chivalric love. In the little poem that Edward III is said to have written for the Black Prince, the poet says,

> Des femes venent les proesces
> Et les honours et les hautesces.

He refers to the fact that great ladies were frequently regarded as sources of chivalric inspiration to men who loved them for their nobility and virtue. Such love had little to do with lust or sentiment and did not have sexual satisfaction, readily available elsewhere, as its aim. It was basically similar to the kind of love any vassal owed to his overlord or any subject owed to his queen. In short, it was exactly the kind of love that Chaucer himself and the noblemen in his audience owed to Blanche, Duchess of Lancaster. In an age like ours when a long period of adolescent frustration, or semi-frustration, is common, and when love of any kind involving generosity of spirit is reported to be difficult,[34] we may find this convention hard to understand. But the attitude had been popularized in the fourteenth-century poems of Machaut, and it is illustrated in Chaucer's poem itself.

When the Black Knight first approaches Blanche, he feels that he will die if he does not speak to her (1188). He is so fearful that he can only grow pale and blush by turns (1215), and when he does finally speak, he can say nothing but "mercy!" (1219) The lady, who, as we have been told, "loved as man may do hys brother" (892), and "loved so wel ryght, she wrong do wolde to no wyght" (1015-1016), quite properly refuses to have anything to do with the Knight. His approach shows no virility, and, certainly, no chivalry. On the contrary, it reveals a merely selfish "sensible passion" without any virtue to commend it. The fact that the lady shows no resemblance to the Parisian ladies who, years later, were to be so overwhelmingly impressed by the antics of M. Grimm should surprise no one. "Another yere" (1258), when the Knight is able to desire nothing but the lady's "good," he receives a ring, and his inclinations become harmonious with hers. If the description of Blanche means anything at all, this harmony implies a virtuous and noble demeanor on the part of the Knight. In other words, Blanche was an inspiration to truly chivalric conduct to those who loved her reasonably. This, after all, is exactly the idea Chaucer wished to get across. If the virtues of the Duchess were an inspiration to reasonable and noble conduct in life, her memory should continue to inspire such conduct. Once this point has been made, or strongly suggested, the "characters" in the poem—the Black Knight and the dreamer—have served their usefulness and may be quickly dismissed. They are, of course, not "characters" at all in the modern sense, and what happens to them is not a "story." Their dismissal is a logical consequence of the poem's thematic development. The poem itself ends "abruptly" only if we read it in the same spirit that we read, let us say, "The Little Red Hen."

In conclusion, let us consider very briefly the poem "as a poem." At the time it was delivered, the memory of the young duchess was still fresh in everyone's mind. England was still free of the disillusionment that was to result from failures abroad and social unrest at home, justly confident of its place as a great European power. In the minds of the nobility, the inspiration afforded by noble ladies like the Duchess of Lancaster, gracious and beautiful in demeanor and steadfast in heart, was at least in part responsible for their success. What does Chaucer's poem, then, mean to us? It means nothing at all in so far as "emotional profundity" or "serious thought" are concerned unless we can place ourselves by an act of the historical imagination in Chaucer's audience, allowing ourselves, as best we can, to think as they thought and to feel as they felt. If we cannot take the themes of the *Consolation* of Boethius seriously, if the text of the Burial Mass leaves us unmoved, and, above all, if we insist on demanding romantic and post-romantic emotionalism in everything we read, there is small likelihood that Chaucer's poem will move us in any way. The poet was not seeking to create "purely literary"effects; and there is no virtue in poetry itself, in spite of certain recent notions of Frazerian-Jungian archetypes, operating by sympathetic magic in the enchanted mists of the collective unconscious, that will bring Chaucer's tribute to life for us in any other way. It would be better, indeed, not to read the poem at all unless we can, in imagination, picture Blanche, young, gay, and of humble cheer, suddenly lost to the family of the Duke and the court of the King, and exclaim with Froissart, "Haro!"

The Concept of Courtly Love as an Impediment to the Understanding of Medieval Texts

❧

The lecture on which this essay is based was delivered at a conference on the meaning of courtly love held at the Center for Medieval and Renaissance Studies at the State University of New York at Binghamton in March, 1967, presided over by my old friend, collaborator, and former colleague at Princeton, Bernard F. Huppé. There John F. Benton, who used historical data, and I criticized the prevailing concept of "courtly love." I remain still of the opinion that in spite of a very few expressions like the following from Flamenca *(lines 1197-1200; cf. 981-988) in medieval literature, the term as it is now used is essentially modern:*

> *E que faria s'us truans,*
> *Ques fenera d'amor cortes*
> *E non sabra d'amor ques es,*
> *L'avia messa en follia?*

Here the jealous old Archambaud, like the queen, has been misled by the king's courteous gestures, and nothing like the "courtly love" of modern criticism is implied.

Turning to the specific content of the essay, I should now like to add that it seems possible that the conventionally accepted date for the death of Blanche of Lancaster (12 September, 1369) should be set back a year. See John H. Palmer, "The Historical Context of the Book of the Duchess," *Chaucer Review, 8 (1974), 253-261. It should be noted also that Chaucer moved from Aldgate to Greenwich at about the time* Troilus *was being revised. Among the social conditions described as being relevant to Chaucer's attitude in that poem I should have called attention to the decline of English chivalry in the field, a subject of complaint by the Commons in 1377 and by the Lords in 1386. French attacks on the south coast were renewed in 1377, and the Scots attacked in the north. The English suffered from threats of invasion, which reached a peak of intensity in 1385, when a French invasion fleet was assembled. That is, New Troy was under siege when Chaucer wrote his poem. He would hardly have concerned himself with "courtly love" for its own sake at this time. He was closely associated with the royal Chamber, and it is reasonable to suppose that he and his friends at court, to whom he addressed himself,*

*should have been concerned with the contrast between chivalric leaders who
worked "to commune profit" with self-denial, and those who were "likerous
folk" interested primarily in self-satisfaction achieved through wordly wisdom
and deceit. That is, the central theme of* Troilus *in some ways resembles that
of* Hamlet *as it is described elsewhere in this volume.*

☙

I HAVE never been convinced that there was any such thing as what is
usually called courtly love during the Middle Ages. However, it is
obvious that courtly love does exist in modern scholarship and criticism, and that the idea appeals to a great many people today.

Our evidence concerning medieval people as it appears in court records, historical narratives, and other sources reveals them as being
severely practical within the limits of their knowledge, and not at all
sentimental. But what modern scholars have described as "courtly
love," a thing, I might add, that medieval scholars refrain from describing, is not only impractical but downright inconvenient. For
example, as a "courtly lover" I should be constrained to love someone
else's wife, unless, that is, I happened to live in England, where, some
authorities insist, I might on occasion practice the art with my own
wife.[1] The non-English situation is not only inconvenient for the lady,
but dangerous, since adultery on the part of a wife in medieval society,
as in modern Italy, was not taken lightly by law and custom. In fact,
during the late Middle Ages in some areas adultery on the part of the
husband was not always regarded with much tolerance either. In late
fourteenth-century London, for example, a man and woman taken in
adultery were required to be shaved, except for two inches of hair
around the head, taken to Newgate Prison, and thence paraded publicly through the streets accompanied by minstrels more than half way
across the City to be incarcerated in a small prison in the middle of
Cornhill called the Tun.[2] However, a further feature of "courtly love"
is that it was frequently "pure," so that wife or no wife what one got
for his pains, and these were considerable, was little more than anticipatory elation, presumably identical with a feeling described by the
troubadours as "joy." Although at least one modern scholar has described this, quite seriously, as "the highest earthly good," I have personally found no medieval counterparts of *Playboy Magazine*, nor indeed any sort of encouragements then of the kind of vicarious joys we
seem to pursue with such avidity today. I should imagine pure courtly
love especially inconvenient in England, where one might be a
"courtly lover" to his wife, although I should not be surprised to find

it adduced any day now to explain the merriment of Merry England and the curious lineage of the True Born Englishman.

We are told further that the lady involved should be of much higher station than the lover, that she should be located at a distance, that the lover should tremble in her presence, and that he should obey her slightest wish. He should, moreover, fall sick with love, faint when he sees a lock of the lady's hair, preserve his chastity, and perform great exploits to attract the attention of the lady. All this seems to me a terrible nuisance, and hardly the kind of thing that Henry II or Edward III would get involved in. But that is not all. The lover should also use all the techniques recommended in the *Roman de la rose*. That is, he should spend all his wealth, employ outrageous flattery, engage in blatant hypocrisy about what he wants, and convince the lady that she can accumulate great wealth and a kind of eternal youth by granting her favors. Of course, I realize that various forms of irrational conduct are now carried out with a "holier-than-thou" air, in the name of sophistication; but I doubt that many medieval noblemen could be persuaded to go so far as to become "courtly lovers," even for the sake of a superior social tone and that great ideal frequently attributed to them, and to modern real estate developments, "gracious living."

The advocates of "courtly love" in my audience are probably eager to point out by this time that I have generalized too hastily. Some will allege that "courtly love" is represented only by the troubadours, some will say that its secrets are revealed only in the pages of Andreas Capellanus, or, perhaps, in the romances of Chrétien de Troyes. Some will say that it is the ancestor of modern romantic love, while others will allege that modern romantic love has nothing to do with it. A few may state that it is a French invention, and that through it France taught the Western World how to appreciate women properly. This diversity of opinion about the nature of "courtly love" is matched by accounts of its origins, which include such things as Pictish matriarchal customs, Manichaean heresies, neo-Platonism, the scarcity of women in Provençal courts, and the Cult of the Blessed Virgin Mary. In spite of this enormous diversity of learned opinion concerning both the nature of courtly love and its origins, the fact remains that almost any medieval literary work that has anything at all to do with love will inevitably be said to show the "conventions of courtly love." Indeed, in most instances, these "conventions," carefully selected to fit the work in question, will be said to "explain" the work. Students will dutifully repeat this explanation, because students may be led to say almost anything, and those among them who grow up to become teachers will almost inevitably repeat it to their students.

At various times in the past I have sought to show that works presumably illustrative of "courtly love" like the *De amore* of Andreas Capellanus, or the *Lancelot* of Chrétien de Troyes, or the *Roman de la rose*, are, in fact, ironic and humorous.[3] The result of this effort has frequently been a reaction to the effect that the works in question may not advocate "courtly love," but at least they satirize it. That is, "courtly love" is like a see-saw: if a man pushes down hard on one end, the other end comes up, and, behold! it is still there. What is being satirized in the works in question is not "courtly love" at all, but idolatrous passion. Idolatrous passion is not a peculiarly medieval phenomenon. It appears in the Old Testament, for example in the stories of Ammon and Holofernes; it is condemned by Lucretius, who recommended visits to prostitutes to get rid of it; and Ovid wrote a whole treatise, the *Remedia amoris*, supplying techniques by means of which one might extricate oneself from its snare. It seems to be a chronic human weakness, although attitudes toward it change with changes in style. It was glossed over with sentiment by the late eighteenth century, glorified with rebellious individualism by the romantics, and thoroughly sentimentalized by the Victorians. Today it seems to be cherished as a manifestation of the deep needs of the personality, and is frequently greeted with what might be called profound psychological piety. In the Middle Ages, however, the classical attitude toward it remained, although it frequently looks "feudal" or "courtly" because it is described in a medieval setting, and it also looks fairly harmless when it is couched in the delicate conventions of the Gothic style. At that time it had overtones of meaning in Christian thought that made it highly significant as a vehicle for philosophical ideas. Christianity was then recognized as a religion of love, rather than as a cult of righteousness, so that aberrations of love were thought to have far-reaching implications in the conduct of everyday affairs. Because of the broad area of associations connected with it in theology and philosophy, idolatrous love was a useful vehicle for the expression of literary and poetic themes. But it was not regarded in terms of sentiment, romantic rebelliousness, sentimentality, or, that great criterion for aesthetic appeal in modern novels, plays, and television programs, stark psychological realism.

Medieval love poetry is extremely varied. There are poems expressing sexual desire, although these are usually not "lyrical" in the modern sense; poems sung in praise of great ladies; crypto-religious poems, written, like the Song of Songs, in terms of physical love; popular songs that do not differ much, except for a certain lack of sentimentality or crypto-sentimentality, from popular songs written today. Aside from the lack of lyrical subjectivity and sentimentality, medieval poetry sometimes shows what might be called frank physical optimism. The medieval troubadour was a Latin, and like some Latins today, he tended to regard women functionally, that is, with an eye to their potentialities either as bed companions or as childbearers. The required qualities are frequently identical. It was possible, moreover, to contemplate and even to celebrate these potentialities in a disinterested way, without feeling any deep personal urge to exploit them. Moreover, the ladies seem to have enjoyed being praised for the physical assets peculiar to their sex. Neither the troubadours nor their successors in the Middle Ages dwell much on sentimental attributes: locks of hair curling over the ear or forehead, little tilts of the nose, characteristic gestures, or other endearing individual traits. The general attitude extends frequently to the Blessed Virgin, and poems addressed to her often display what is to our psychologically sensitive ears a shocking concern for her red lips, white teeth, straight back, graceful shoulders, and so on.[4] But she was, after all, a woman, and, presumably, sufficiently beautiful to become the Mother of God.

Although medieval love poetry displays what is to us a certain lack of appreciation for the richness of the human personality, its variety is sufficiently great so that the label "courtly love" is hardly adequate to describe it. Indeed, there are times when the use of this label simply turns the poems upside-down, so that we have little chance of understanding them at all. To illustrate this process, I have chosen two examples from the poetry of Chaucer. Let us begin with an early work, *The Book of the Duchess*.

The standard interpretations of *The Book of the Duchess* all stem from the account of the poem developed many years ago by George Lyman Kittredge. There have been strong disagreements among scholars about the nature of the malady experienced by the speaker at the beginning of the poem, and about whether the dreamer in the poem is a naïve and inept fool or a skilful guide and counsellor. But almost everyone agrees that the Black Knight is at least in part a representation of John of Gaunt, Duke of Lancaster, and that, whatever else he may be, he is an ideal courtly lover, belonging to the sub-type: English courtly lover of his own wife. Although the portrait of Blanche, if it can be called a portrait, that appears in the poem is highly stylized, we are told that she is made to represent an ideal "courtly mistress." This is a dubious compliment. But, in any event, the poem as a whole is said to illustrate the transference of current French fashions about courtly love to English soil, where they were somehow made appropriate to an elegy for a great lady.

I think it is proper to ask what Kittredge's assumptions about love were when he wrote his interpretation of the poem. This is what he said:

> Now there is nothing new in the Black Knight's story, either in form or substance. The experience he describes is typical, and he speaks throughout in the settled language of the chivalric system. Love was the only life that became the gently nurtured, and they alone were capable of love. Submission to the god was their natural duty; in his grace and favor was their only hope; for no man's heart was in his own control.[5]

We are led to believe, that is, in rather touching language, that the English nobility subjected themselves to Cupid, and that their "only hope" lay in that god's favors. Medieval views on this subject were quite different. For example, in 1346 the distinguished Mertonian, Thomas Bradwardine, who was at the time Chancellor of St. Paul's and Master of the London schools generally, delivered a sermon celebrating English victories at Crécy and in Scotland. Of the conquered enemies of England, he said in part,

> Embracing a seventh error, they seem to emulate antique pagans worshiping Hymen or Cupid, the god of carnal love. Soldiering in Venus, associating themselves with the retinue of Aphrodite, they think the vigor of their audacity to be probity, victory, or triumph. But they say that no one can be vigorous unless he is amorous, or loves amorously, that no one can fight strenuously to excess unless he loves to excess. But how profane is this foolishness, how false, insane, and wild! . . . They labor strenuously in arms to make for themselves a name like the name of the greatest upon earth. . . . And why do they wish such a name? That they may be loved by foolish women. . . . And who gives them the payment and reward for their labors? Who, except for the god for whom they fight, to whom they devote themselves, and whom they worship? And what payment or reward do they get for their pride? Public and immense disgrace. And for their lechery? A stinking and intense burning.[6]

Bradwardine goes on to explain that devotion to Cupid or Venus is actually enervating, and that English restraint in this matter partially accounts for the victories of English chivalry.

It is obvious that our representatives of Harvard and Merton were not talking about the same thing. To begin with the first, Marshall McLuhan has assured us, and I think properly, that most of us look at the world through a rear-view mirror. I might add that this mirror does not give us a very distant view into the past, and, moreover, that it is frequently tilted upward toward the clouds. Both the god of love and the "gently nurtured" as they are alluded to by Kittredge clearly belong to the realm of romantic and Victorian fiction, and have nothing to do with the Middle Ages. He had in mind a sentimental passion only faintly and enticingly tinged with sex, a tinge made decorous by reference to the uncontrolled "heart." Bradwardine, on the other hand, regarded Cupid and Venus as figures for lecherous desire, pure and simple. His insistence, moreover, that lechery or amorous passion is destructive of chivalry is a commonplace of medieval thought from the twelfth century onward among both religious and secular writers on the subject. In so far as Chaucer is concerned, the references to Venus in his work are all consistent with the view expressed by Bradwardine. His two most famous descriptions of her temple, in the Knight's Tale and in *The Parliament of Fowls*, are derived largely from Boccaccio's *Teseida*, and Boccaccio himself informs us in his notes to that work that Venus represents irrational concupiscence.[7] It is hardly surprising that in this temple Palamon vows to make "werre alwey with chastitee" ("The Knight's Tale" I(A) 2236), and it would be difficult to describe this vow as being either very noble or very chivalrous.

To return to *The Book of the Duchess*, it should have been clear in the first place that the Black Knight could hardly be regarded as an admirable figure in the poem. He explicitly describes his loss as a loss to Fortune in unmistakably Boethian terms. Anyone who has read *The Consolation of Philosophy* with any care, and not simply as a source for more or less meaningless labels, knows that subjection to Fortune was regarded as a kind of foolishness brought on by too much concern for mere externals. The Black Knight is not only foolish in this respect; he is also very clearly suffering from sloth, a vice regarded during the Middle Ages as stemming from a lack of fortitude. No one in Chaucer's audience would have regarded lack of fortitude and subjection to Fortune as "chivalric" qualities. The fact that advocates of "courtly love" cheerfully embrace them as characteristics of the doctrine they advocate is simply another indication of the inherent absurdity of the doctrine itself. As for John of Gaunt, it may be that the grief he suffered at the death of Blanche in 1369 may have led him temporarily into an attitude somewhat resembling that of the Black Knight, but this does not mean that the Black Knight *is* John of Gaunt. John of Gaunt was a Duke, not a knight. To put this very simply, when the time for paying poll taxes came around, the Duke of Lancaster paid more than any other man in England.[8] Earls paid somewhat less, and mere knights still less. Chaucer did not put a Black Duke in his poem. There are other reasons for not associating the Black Knight too closely with the Duke, but in spite of these facts, preconceived notions of "courtly love" turned the Black Knight into a kind of romantic hero and exemplar of true chivalry. That is, the concept of "courtly love" has prevented generations of scholars from seeing that if the figure of the Black Knight makes any sense at all in the poem, it is intended as a criticism of an attitude toward the deceased Duchess of Lancaster. Those who grieved for her immoderately, like the Black Knight, were thinking of her as mere flesh and blood, an attractive object of desire forever lost. Needless to say, this attitude neglects the lady's more human qualities: her virtues and the value of her memory as an inspiration to chivalric conduct. And it is just these qualities that are celebrated in the poem.

If there was, during the Middle Ages, any such thing as "chivalric love," it was the medieval precedent for the kind of love any Englishman is still supposed to have, however faintly, for his King or Queen. Every subject was expected to love his overlord, man or woman, and his overlord's wife if the overlord happened to be a man. Great ladies like Blanche of Lancaster might have expected the love and devotion of all those in their households, and of many lords, knights, squires, and clerks in other households besides. Blanche of Lancaster specifically was a national figure, the greatest lady in England at the time of her death. But this love was a disinterested devotion, somewhat like that inspired by the Blessed Virgin during the Middle Ages.[9] It had nothing whatsoever to do with either sex or sentimentality, and could not be associated with Cupid or Venus in any way. We have become so preoccupied in recent years with "personality" and the "inner life" that this sort of thing has become very difficult to understand. Nevertheless, this is the kind of love that Chaucer undoubtedly felt and expected others to feel for Blanche. With the love of Sir Lancelot for Guenevere or the love represented as that of the dreamer in the *Roman de la rose*, a poem that ends with a thinly veiled description of sexual intercourse, it has nothing whatsoever in common.

For a second and final example of the kind of obfuscation that results from "explaining" medieval poems in terms of "courtly love" let us turn very briefly to *Troilus and Criseyde*. The protagonist belongs, of course, to another English sub-species of the type: he is a "courtly lover" of a widow. Nevertheless, Robinson assures us, he is an "ideal courtly lover."[10] Like other ghosts, the "ideal courtly lover" takes many forms. As the poem is usually described, its appeal is essentially romantic; it is a tragic and moving story of love in flower and love in frustration. It is consistent perhaps with that eternal pattern of dashed hopes so movingly described by Camus in *The Myth of Sisyphus*, a pattern with which all of us seem to acquire a certain experience. It is not difficult now, in fact, to talk about it in terms of "archetypes," another family of ghosts that clank their chains through modern academic halls. Now it is true that the obvious relevance of *The Consolation of Philosophy* to the thematic development of this poem should have prevented any such concept of it from arising, but "courtly love" is more pleasant to talk about than the philosophical intricacies of Boethius, and it is much easier to talk about it than it is to get students to read *The Consolation*.

Before we consider the poem itself, I think it might be proper to ask ourselves why Chaucer was interested in the story of Troy. The obvious answer, of course, is that the story was popular during the Middle Ages and that Chaucer read Boccaccio's *Filostrato* in some form, liked it, and wrote a poem based on it. But this does not answer our question very specifically. Chaucer probably finished *Troilus* in the latter part of 1386 or in 1387. He was living at the time above Aldgate in London in the apartments granted him by the Mayor and Aldermen of the City in 1374. In this connection, we should remember that the Mayor of London ranked as an Earl, the aldermen as barons or tenants-in-chief of the Crown, and Chaucer as a squire. Although the city of London itself enjoyed increasing prosperity, with some interruptions, during the later fourteenth century, England as a whole did not. There was, in the first place, a severe agricultural depression that created considerable uneasiness among the feudal nobility who were largely dependent upon agricultural production. At the same time, after 1369 the rivalry with France went badly for the English, so that by the end of the century the French court had replaced the English court as the center of European chivalry. The behavior of Edward III in his latter years was, to say the least, unedifying, especially in view of his neglect of the realm and his besotted concern for Alice Perrers, who, incidentally, had a sumptuous residence in London. King Richard was never able to live up to the promise he showed in confronting the rebels in 1381. The nobility was factious, and Parliament reflected their intrigues. The Parliament of 1386 indulged in fanciful accusations against the King's friends, and was probably instrumental in depriving Chaucer of his position at the Custom House. And in 1388 the Merciless Parliament proceeded to more or less wholesale judicial murder. Armed bands roamed the countryside; the court was sapped by intrigue and rumors of intrigue; brawling and disorder

broke out not only in the country and in the streets of the towns, but
even before the royal justices in the King's Bench. In short, the ties of
the old feudal hierarchy seemed to be breaking down in favor of self-
seeking, personal ambition, and greed. As Chaucer himself put it, in a
poem probably written at Aldgate,

> . . . in oure dayes nis but covetyse,
> Doublenesse, and tresoun, and envye,
> Poyson, manslauhtre, and mordre in sondry wyse.
>
> ("The Former Age," 61-64)

Under these circumstances it was natural that men should turn to the
traditions of the past to find inspiration for reform. Some of Chaucer's
friends were "Lollard Knights" who exhibited a remarkably serious
concern for traditional Christian moral doctrine.[11] Chaucer's old patron, John of Gaunt, was the patron and devoted friend of the famous
reforming mayor of London, John of Northampton.

Where would a Londoner, concerned about decay in the society
around him, look for the traditions of his city? In 1419 when Richard
Whittington was mayor, the Clerk of the City, John Carpenter, compiled a *repertorium* of city customs based on documents, some of them
very ancient, available at the Guildhall. This book became a standard
reference, known, because of its original binding, as the *Liber Albus*.
Carpenter was a man with whom Chaucerians should sympathize, for
he left a number of books in his will that we know were familiar to
Chaucer, including the *De planctu Naturae* and the *Anticlaudianus* of
Alanus de Insulis, the *De miseria humanae conditionis* of Innocent III, and
the *Philobiblon* of Richard de Bury. Incidentally, the tradition of
Richard de Bury's inspiration was quite strong at St. Paul's during the
later fourteenth century. Concerning the City of London the *Liber
Albus* tells us,

> In the year from the beginning of the World 4032, and before the
> Lord's Incarnation 1200, the city that is now called 'London,'
> founded in imitation of Great Troy, was constructed and built by
> King Brut, the first monarch of Britain, being at first called 'New
> Troy,' and afterwards 'Troinovant'. . . .[12]

Another passage, which may be an addition to the text but is said to be
based on "ancient books," elaborates this idea:

> Among the noble cities of the world which fame has rendered il-
> lustrious, the City of London is the one principal seat of the realm of
> England which diffuses far and wide the celebrity of its name. It is

happy in the salubrity of its climate, in the enjoyment of the Christian religion, in its liberties so well deserved, and its foundation at a most ancient date. Indeed, according to the testimony of the chronicles it is much older than the City of Rome; for, springing from the same more ancient Trojans, London was founded by Brut, in imitation of great Troy, before the foundation of Rome by Remus and Romulus; whence it is that, even to this day, it possesses the liberties, rights, and customs of the ancient city Troy, and enjoys its institutions.[13]

We may remember that the Merciless Parliament accused the then former Mayor of London, Nicholas Brembre, of wanting to change the name of London to "Petty Troy," to declare himself Duke, and to execute several thousands of his opponents. The charge was ridiculous, but the mention of the word *Troy* probably added to its initial plausibility. In any event, the judicial murder of Brembre duly ensued.

Troy, then, served as the great exemplar of the City of London specifically and of the realm of England generally, an idea that we can see operative in *Sir Gawain and the Green Knight*, although it is true that the purport of that work has been obscured by talk about "courtly love." The fall of Troy loomed as a warning to all Englishmen. It came about as a result of the choice made by Paris, who thought Venus, or the life of pleasure and self-satisfaction, more attractive than either Juno, the active life, or Pallas, the life of contemplation or wisdom. The result was the rape of Helen, a lady not venerated in the Middle Ages as she came to be in the pages of Yeats or Camus. The action was an insult to Pallas or wisdom, who had been, so to speak, a kind of patron saint of Troy. To understand the implications of these fabulous events, we should remember that wisdom was regarded throughout the Middle Ages as a royal virtue, proper to kings and princes, and in the individual the supreme control over the passions. Christ was conventionally called *Sapientia Dei Patris*, the Wisdom of God, and the Blessed Virgin was sometimes associated with Pallas, since she had brought Wisdom to mankind. As Raoul de Preslles says in his commentary on *The City of God*, so long as Minerva or *Sapience* ruled the city, Troy was full of virtue, but when she lost her *seignorie*, the city reverted to fleshly lusts and idolatry and thus became doomed to fall.[14]

Boccaccio's poem contained the story of a young prince of Troy who fell passionately in love with a young widow and lost her. His name, "Troilus" in English, suggested a Latin form meaning "Little Troy," so that it was not difficult to make the downfall of Troilus an analogue of the downfall of Troy itself. Just as Venus, or the cultivation of Venus, brought about the destruction of Troy, so also it brought about the destruction of Troilus. The general moral situation is clear enough in Boccaccio, but it had a specific applicability to London and to England as a whole that made it peculiarly suitable for Chaucer's use. Chaucer could refurbish the old object lesson in a new guise, and, with very little difficulty, use Troilus to typify the kind of individual action that brought about the downfall of the City. It does not matter especially whether Chaucer believed the Trojan origin of London literally; the story was well known, and its poetic implications were sufficient. It seems to me that the first step we should make in our understanding of the poem is a recognition of the fact that medieval poetry generally is functional in the society that produces it. It does not have a "reality of its own." Nor was Chaucer a detached historian of past events. The real subject of *Troilus and Criseyde* lies in the life around Chaucer and not in the remote Trojan past. No one in the fourteenth century thought of art as existing "for its own sake." Art was, rather, a vehicle for cherished ideas designed to be practical in its effects.

In the light of these considerations, the general purport of the poem becomes fairly obvious. However, it might be well to point out certain specific features that appear in it to suggest their general significance. In this very hasty account, I shall emphasize what might be called "social" considerations rather than those philosophical aspects of the poem that I have discussed in another place, although it is true that what we call social and political ideas were discussed in moral terms during the Middle Ages. The action of the poem begins at a festival of Pallas in Troy. Since Pallas is the deity of wisdom and what happened to Troy was the result of neglecting her, this scene has considerable thematic importance. Instead of paying any attention to the civic ceremonies, Troilus and his companions are wandering around

> Byholding ay the ladies of the town.
> (1.126)

That is, they are tempting Cupid instead of worshiping Pallas. The arrow flies and sends the young Prince of Troy to his chamber alone, where he begins to dream about Criseyde's *figure*. Very soon he is saying to himself

> "myn estat roial I here resigne
> Into hire hond."
> (1.432-433)

We should notice that it is his royal estate, not his person, that Troilus surrenders so quickly to a woman he does not really know. If we remember that there is a sense in which Troy is London, or the realm of England, what we are witnessing is an action typifying the beginning of that decay that Chaucer could see so well in the life around him. To make this idea clear, Chaucer adds that Troilus becomes very fearful, but not fearful concerning the condition of the city. He is afraid of not being able to win Criseyde:

> Alle other dredes weren from his fledde,
> Both of th'assege and his savacioun.
> (1.463-464)

He goes out to fight Greeks, not for the "rescous of the town" (1.478), but to win the kind of Venereal fame Bradwardine thought appropriate to defeated Frenchmen. The opening action of the poem is thus a thematic echo of the Judgment of Paris. Troilus has spurned Pallas and embraced Venus. At the same time, he has abandoned the interests of his community in favor of self-interest and self-satisfaction.

Perhaps I should pause briefly to emphasize the fact that I am not trying to make Chaucer a Puritan. No one expected medieval noblemen to observe strict chastity. But it is one thing to engage in occasional dalliance and quite another to abandon oneself completely to idolatrous passion. Any man in a position of responsibility who devoted himself entirely to any kind of self-interest could hardly be considered admirable. The fact that we are able to romanticize the behavior of Troilus is due to post-Renaissance cultural developments that Chaucer could not possibly have foreseen.

After Pandarus has promised to get Troilus anyone, even his own sister if that is desirable, he leads Troilus in a prayer to Cupid, asking forgiveness for his earlier jokes about love and lovers. He is soon praying also to "blisful Venus" (1.1014) and beseeching Pandarus on his knees to help him. All this "religious" activity has usually been rendered harmless by what has been called "the religion of courtly love." It is, of course, actually a bitter comment on the substitution of "covetyse" and "doublenesse" for the devotion that had made London "happy . . . in the enjoyment of the Christian religion." We see Troilus praying to Venus again in Book II after Pandarus has won a kind of qualified assent from Criseyde and has learned that what she is chiefly concerned with is her "honor," which means for her not the virtue itself, but worldly reputation. Incidentally, the anticipatory "joy" supposed to be characteristic of "courtly love" is here described, just as Bradwardine described it, as a fire. It grows warmer the closer

Troilus gets to his goal and is not extinguished after he has attained it. The "doublenesse" apparent in Criseyde's conception of honor is further emphasized in the technique used by Pandarus to bring the lovers together. That is, he lies to both Deiphebus and Criseyde. It is not accidental that the ruse he employs recalls the story of Ammon, whose affair led to civil war.

Medieval men had a strong sense of social hierarchy. Disturbances in society were thought of as violations of that hierarchy, and failures to maintain the integrity demanded by one's estate or degree were thought to be productive of social chaos. Chaucer plays amusingly on this theme in Book 3. At the opening, in the house of Deiphebus, Criseyde approaches Troilus as he lies in bed feigning sickness with a request for "lordship" and protection. But what she receives is a promise from Troilus that he will be under her "yerde." The phrase *sub virga*, which this promise reflects, was conventionally used to describe the condition of children, or, occasionally, of wives. Although this inversion is amusing on the surface, the implications for "New Troy" are hardly comic. We can see an analogy to this situation in the punishment for "common brawlers" decreed in the City of London by John of Northampton. A convicted "brawler" was to be led through the City with minstrelsy holding a distaff with tow on it in his hand and placed in the "thews" or stocks designed especially for women, the implication being that his unruliness deprived him of the worth proper to the masculine estate. The predicament of the "brawler" as he holds his distaff is amusing, but the implications of his presence are nevertheless serious. To call Troilus' desire to be under Criseyde's "yard" a manifestation of "courtly love" is a little like saying, quite seriously, that the distaff in the hand of the brawler is a sign of the irrepressible medieval reverence for women.

The theme of the inverted hierarchy is clear enough in Troilus' complete submission to Venus and to Fortune in Book 3. It receives an added emphasis on a social level in Book 4, where the Trojan Parliament is shown considering whether to turn Criseyde over to the Greeks in exchange for Antenor. Hector, who is an exemplar of chivalry in the poem, takes a firm attitude:

> "We usen here no wommen for to selle."
>
> (4.182)

But he is overcome by "noyse of peple" (4.183) as furious as a fire blazing in straw. The image is probably intended to recall the proverbial fire in the bed-straw and to emphasize the analogy between the fury of the people and the passion of Troilus. Chaucer had undoubtedly had plenty of experience with "noyse of peple" in London; and the scene, as others have pointed out, is probably a comment on English Parliaments, perhaps a specific reflection of the Parliament of 1386.[15] The passage looks forward to a similar one in the Clerk's Tale:

> O stormy peple! unsad and evere untrewe!
> Ay undiscreet and chaungynge as a fane!
>
> ("The Clerk's Tale" IV[E] 995)

In neither instance is the poet simply making an historical observation; he is calling attention to something very real in the life of his times. For Chaucer, who had not enjoyed the benefits of the French Revolution, passionate popular outbursts were an inversion of the natural order of sovereignty in the commonwealth. They boded ill for Great Troy and New Troy alike.

The decision of the Trojan Parliament emphasizes the helplessness of Troilus in the situation he has created for himself. He cannot, for shame, reveal his own connection with Criseyde, and he cannot, because of what she calls her "honor," take her away stealthily. He can only blame Fortune, whom he has always honored, he says, "above the goddes alle," and the god of love, who seems to have "repeled" his grace. The two go together, both in the individual and in the state. That is, if the state succumbs to the passions of the people, disregarding its ordered hierarchies in the pursuit of self satisfaction, it is, in effect, worshiping Venus and subjecting itself to Fortune. That is why Chaucer is able to say in Book 5,

> Fortune . . .
> Gan pulle awey the fetheres brighte of Troie.
>
> (5.1546)

A city or a realm can, like a man, give rein to its passions and subject itself to the whims of Fortune. It can also enjoy what Bradwardine calls the reward of Cupid, "a stinking and intense burning."

When Troilus has found his death on the battlefield, a death deliberately sought in despair and hence a form of suicide, and the city, having lost Hector, is dying also as a result of its own foolishness in abandoning Pallas, the poet adds a stanza that includes a reference to paganism:

> Lo here, of payens corsed olde rites,
> Lo here, what alle hire goddes may availle,
> Lo here, thise wrecched worldes appetites. . . .
>
> (5.1849-1851)

The "worldes appetites" and the "goddes" are essentially the same thing. Chaucer is not engaging in idle moralizing; he is condemning exactly the same kind of weakness that Bradwardine attributed to the conquered French in 1346, who "seemed to emulate antique pagans, worshiping Hymen or Cupid, the god of carnal love." Chaucer obviously felt that the English might be doing the same thing, so that New Troy stood in danger of suffering the fate of Great Troy, whose "liberties, rights, and customs" it preserved.

To call Troilus a "courtly lover" caught in the snares of a romantic universe, and to grow sentimental over his fate, is simply to disregard the text of the poem and to foster a kind of historical desecration. From a literary point of view, the "courtly love" interpretation takes all of the humor out of the poem, and, at the same time, substitutes lustful or, if you prefer, "psychological" seriousness for the poem's true serious purpose. We have done the same kind of thing with a great many other medieval works. Even Arcite in the Knight's Tale, who says that "positif lawe" is "broken al day for love" (I[A] 1167–1168), and excuses his own conduct on the ground that a lover simply has to have his beloved whether she is a "mayde, wydwe, or elles wyf" (I[A] 1171) has been turned into an ideal "courtly lover" and made a hero. Do my colleagues really believe that Chaucer had no moral or social responsibility? I think it is time we stopped teaching medieval texts to the tune of "Hearts and Flowers." The sophistication of the tune with things like pseudo-Albigensian heresies, pseudo-Platonic philosophies, or pseudo-Arabic doctrines does not conceal its true nature, nor do these wailing ghosts on the sidelines make it any more respectable intellectually. The study of courtly love, if it belongs anywhere, should be conducted only as the subject is an aspect of nineteenth and twentieth century cultural history. The subject has nothing to do with the Middle Ages, and its use as a governing concept can only be an impediment to our understanding of medieval texts.

Chaucer's Franklin and his Tale

✒

The word franklin *was ordinarily used to designate a prosperous freeholder, or an individual wealthy because he held extensive lands in free tenure. The Black Death had afforded many people opportunities to acquire land in freehold, and our Franklin has evidently been highly successful in using the profits of his offices to invest in land. We should understand that the lands in question are valuable for the income they produce, and, further, that they are "held" under a lord and not, in the modern sense, "owned." The statement that "justices of the peace were unpaid" needs qualification, since beginning in 1392 each one who sat could demand 4s per diem for his labors. Chaucer was himself named as an "associate" on a peace commission of 1385, probably to represent court interest for some case or series of cases. He was named directly on a commission of 1386, but there is no evidence that he attended sessions. Although those named were supposed to be reputable and substantial persons, some were of rather unsavory character. Since Chaucer was also knight of the shire for Kent in 1386 he had an opportunity to know many men whose careers resembled that of the Franklin. The abuse of language, since it often had practical consequences, was a matter for deep moral concern in the fourteenth century. This was still true in the Renaissance, as two articles by Margreta de Grazia forthcoming in* Journal of the History of Ideas *and* Spenser Studies *will demonstrate. See also her "Shakespeare's View of Language: an Historical Perspective,"* SQ, 29 (1978), 374-388.

✒

CLOWN. Give me thy hand. I will swear to the Prince thou art as honest a true fellow as any is in Bohemia.
SHEPHERD. You may say it, but not swear it.
CLOWN. Not swear it, now as I am a gentleman? Let boors and franklins say it, I'll swear it.

The Winter's Tale, 5.2.166-171.

A MONG the portraits in the General Prologue to *The Canterbury Tales* there are some whose significance is readily apparent today. The Parson, for example, is obviously compounded of a collection of ideal attributes, some of which comment rather bitterly on the character of many priests Chaucer and his contemporaries could see about

them in London; and for those today familiar with the rich body of
iconography generated by anti-fraternal propagandists from the days
of William of St. Amour onward there is nothing very obscure about
the picture of the Friar. At times we are assisted by deliberate contrasts
like that between the Knight and the Squire, or that between the Parson and the Pardoner; and the more we learn about Chaucer's immediate background, both intellectual and social, the more vivid and
often more humorous his little sketches become. We may well suspect
that the Prologue as a whole was, at the time it was first read, a comic
masterpiece, but that today it has lost a great deal of its humor along
with its satiric sting. Among the more obscure portraits is that of the
Franklin, who, we are told, rides along in company with the Sergeant
of the Law.

As I have suggested elsewhere,[1] it is probably helpful to regard the
pilgrims not as "personalities" or "realistic portraits," or even as
"types," if that word implies typical examples. They are better understood as collections of attributes exemplifying either the ideals or the
weaknesses of the groups to which they belong. The Sergeant and the
Franklin, as administrators of royal justice, have a great deal in common; moreover, actual Sergeants and men who held the various
offices occupied by the Franklin frequently encountered one another in
the conduct of their affairs. Royal justice was a profitable enterprise,
both for the Crown and for its agents, but it is probable that Chaucer,
many of whose friends exhibited a considerable interest in reform, regarded the abuse of office for personal profit on the part of those
agents much in the same way that he regarded the abuse of office for
personal profit on the part of friars and summoners. Greed and hypocrisy are not the special province of ecclesiastics. If the corruption of
justice for gain among ecclesiastical dignitaries seemed reprehensible
and thus subject to humorous attack, the corruption of justice for gain
among administrative dignitaries must have seemed equally reprehensible, and equally comic when it rested on false pretenses.

That the Sergeant of the Law is an object of satire in the Prologue
has long been clear, and efforts have been made to identify him with
one of Chaucer's personal enemies, Thomas Pynchbek, although
Chaucer's Sergeant is not described as having been chief baron of the
Exchequer, as Pynchbek was in 1388. His relations with Pynchbek do
indicate, however, that Chaucer knew something about sergeants. His
own Sergeant, often seen drumming up trade at the Parvys, probably
in the nave of St. Paul's, is a man of seeming wisdom, since "his
wordes weren so wise." He often served "in assise," which means that
he often travelled with one or two other justices to the counties to ad-

judicate disputes concerning the ownership of land, either by general commission to settle such cases, or by virtue of letters patent issued to specific plaintiffs. Justices in assize sometimes encroached on the powers of local justices of the peace in their sessions, and, as individuals, they were frequently named to sit with justices of the peace in their own sessions, especially when their legal knowledge was required to consider felonies. Our Sergeant has become enormously wealthy in fees, robes, and land, not, we infer, in the interest of strict justice. He talks as though he knew all the cases and judgments since King William's time, not to mention all the statutes (both wildly impossible tasks), so that he could readily bear down opposition with fictitious technicalities. His activities at the king's bench, to which serious cases from the counties were often referred, and which exercised continuous control over the activities of the justices of the peace, would have brought him into frequent contact with men like the Franklin. We might add that Sergeants regularly attended Parliament where they carried on a great deal of business behind the scenes; there also they would of course meet knights of the shire on many occasions.

That the Franklin is the Sergeant's companion does not suggest that he is a very trustworthy character, although the association between the two figures simply reflects the fact that such men were in real life closely associated. Chaucer begins his description of the Franklin in general terms, to which we shall return, and reserves his account of his career for the last six lines. He was a justice of the peace, often a member of the Commons in Parliament, and he had been a sheriff and a "contour," presumably in reverse order. It was not uncommon for members of the country gentry to serve at one time or another as J. P., sheriff, and knight of the shire.[2] The word "contour" is now nonspecific, but since it is coupled with "shirreve," we are perhaps safe in assuming that the Franklin began his career either as chief clerk or "receiver of moneys" in a sheriff's office, or as a sheriff's accountant. The "receiver" collected the ordinary farm of the county as well as summons, both for small debts and for the fines and amercements of the central courts and for the assizes. Again, the accounts of the bailiffs and those of the receiver were reviewed by an auditor before the sheriff made his presentation at the Exchequer. In any event, the Franklin's early activity seems to have been a profitable one, since it led to higher office.

The duties of the sheriff were complex, and it is difficult today to gain the kind of first-hand impression of his activities that Chaucer's audience must have had. He appointed bailiffs to act within his jurisdiction to assist him in making arrests and collecting revenues, and he presided over the county court and the hundred courts, where he could review petty offenses. He summoned jurors for the preliminary sessions of the justices of the peace. When accused persons pleaded not guilty, the sheriffs also summoned trial juries for the justices. "Thus," writes McKisack, "it was open to the sheriffs to empanel jurors to suit one of the parties, to procure wrongful indictments, and to make false returns."[3] When the power of local magnates was great, sheriffs not unnaturally became their instruments. Temptation was also open to them in their capacity as jailors, especially since prisoners paid for their keep and were, at the same time, subject to pressures of one kind or another to testify in accordance with the sheriff's interests. The sheriff was also responsible for executing writs of various kinds, including those writs directing him to arrange the election of two knights from each shire, two burgesses from each borough, and two citizens from each city to serve in Parliament. These elections were not, of course, popular elections in the modern sense but were carried out in the county courts by the sheriff and other substantial county officials. Finally, the sheriff was, as we have seen, a financial officer responsible for collecting royal revenues, including the fines and amercements mentioned earlier. He had to make biennial accountings for these revenues to the Exchequer, which meant that he had to keep very careful accounts, since Exchequer officials, whose sessions were attended by sergeants of the law, always suspected sheriffs of withholding funds. In general, it is safe to say that sheriffs were very important men in their counties, but that they had no great reputation for integrity. As McKisack puts it, "The corruptibility of the sheriffs was notorious."[4]

During the later fourteenth century, except for the year 1390, when they were selected in Parliament, justices of the peace were selected by the council, chiefly under the direction of the chancellor and the treasurer. Commissions of the peace were sent out to the "lord and sire" of the sessions, men like the Franklin, who would inform the members of the quorum, who were relatively few in number in comparison with the number of persons named, of their duty to attend. Those named in commissions included noblemen, lawyers, and members of the local gentry. Great noblemen, like John of Gaunt, who was often named, could not be expected to attend, but noblemen with strong local interests might wish to participate in sessions. Among the lawyers, whose presence was needed in cases of felony, men like Chaucer's Sergeant were frequently named. Efforts to keep sheriffs from being named were apparently not altogether successful, since the sheriff and the local J. P. often had many common interests, and sessions were often held in county courts. Apparently undersheriffs, bailiffs, and constables served, and knights of the shire sometimes appeared on commissions of the peace. In the course of Chaucer's lifetime the powers and duties of the justices of the peace varied. After the Peasant's Revolt, for example, they were replaced by special commissions. However, we can assume that they generally inquired into felonies, trespasses, and economic offenses, as well as into lesser offenses against the peace. In actual practice, although the justices usually had power to determine cases of felony, felons were convicted with comparative rarity, their cases being referred to the king's bench where they fairly regularly obtained pardons. The justices of the peace "very largely failed in dealing with felonies."[5] The profits available from pardons were too great to be ignored by medieval administrators. It should be added, perhaps, that justices of the peace were unpaid, and were expected in the ordinary course of things to obtain their rewards through their own activities.

The fact that the Franklin was "knight of the shire" does not mean that he was of noble birth, or that he was a belted knight; he might, indeed, be of very humble origin. Members of the Commons from the counties varied a great deal in background, and there is no reason why we should need to be more specific concerning a figure who is actually representative of a group. Where social rank was concerned, men in the counties were considered to be somewhat inferior to men of equivalent rank at court. However, the Franklin was a considerable figure in the shire. His services as sheriff and J. P. would have made him a likely candidate for the Commons. As we have seen, knights were elected in the county, and this means that local prestige, combined, perhaps, with the influence of local magnates, who were not above intervening forcibly in matters of deep concern to themselves, made election possible. As a member of the Commons, where Chaucer himself appeared in 1386,[6] the Franklin was in a distinctly subservient position to the Peers, who in the fourteenth century were still using the Commons as instruments of their own interests. This fact, combined with the probability that this local career depended on the desires of local magnates, may well account for the preoccupation that the Franklin shows with "Gentilesse" in his Prologue and Tale. Chaucer ends his portrait by saying, "Was nowhere swich a worthy vavasour," where the word *vavasour*, originally a word for "subvassal," indicates that he was a large landholder, like his friend the Sergeant.

The above sketch of the career of the Franklin and the character of the Sergeant leaves many details and possibilities unmentioned, but it does show that the two are natural companions, and that they are

closely related in a single administrative complex. Because of the
Sergeant's character, the relationship between the two is suggestive of
connivance, and this suggestion is reinforced by the fact of the
Franklin's great wealth. But the facts of the Franklin's career are colored even more strongly in negative terms by the characterization
with which they are introduced. The Franklin is described as an el-
derly man of sanguine complexion and highly developed Epicurean
tastes:

> Wel lovede he by the morwe a sop in wyn;
> To lyven in delit was evere his wone,
> For he was Epicurus owene sone,
> That heeld opinioun that pleyn delit
> Was verray felicitee parfit.
>
> (334-338)

In Chaucerian terms, as distinct from the literary historical fiction that
asks us to associate the Franklin with men like Sir Roger de Coverly,
these attributes should relate the Franklin in our minds with Januarie,
who also indulges himself with morning winesops (Merch. T. IV[E]
1843) and agrees with those clerks who hold "that felicitee stant in de-
lit" (2021-2022). The Franklin's appetites run more to food than to the
female flesh relished by Januarie, but they are no more admirable. If
we remember, moreover, that St. Julian gave up his wealth and social
position to feed and shelter the poor, the statement that the Franklin
was "Seint Julian . . . in his contree" is not without a certain irony,
which is hardly alleviated by the subsequent account of an abundance
of fine wine, flesh, fowl, fish, and carefully prepared sharp sauces.
There is no reason to suppose that these delicacies, resting on a "table
dormant" in the Franklin's hall (an ostentatious luxury that few could
afford), were provided for the poor of the county. Rather, we suspect
that they were available to influential men like the Sergeant, the
Franklin's friends among the gentry, the sheriff, the constable, and
others who could further his material interests. In general, Chaucer's
"ideal" portraits demonstrate interest in intangibles, so that the
Knight, for example, loves chivalry, truth, honor, generosity, and
courtesy; the Clerk is preoccupied with moral virtue; the Parson is
concerned with "hooly thought and werk," maintaining a "suf-
ficaunce" in little wealth, and avoiding the temptations of rigorous ti-
things and easy positions in London. If Chaucer had wished us to admire the Franklin, he would certainly have indicated some interest on
his part in justice; instead he emphasizes a consuming desire for self-
indulgence of a kind that only wealth can bring. With this fact in

mind, as we see him riding along wearing a defiant dagger and a bag of silk suggestive of avarice hanging from his white girdle, any suspicions we may have about his exercise of his various offices are fully justified. And we may conclude without hesitation that, morally speaking, he was riding in appropriate company.

In most instances it is not difficult to show that the tale told by each of the "characters" in the General Prologue actually consists of an elaboration of the attribute there described. As we might expect, the Franklin is strongly impressed by the superficial and empty rhetorical extravagances of the Squire,[7] which seem to him to demonstrate "gentilesse"; "thow hast thee wel yquit and gentilly," he says, going on to praise the young nobleman for speaking "feelingly" and with unsurpassed eloquence. A few lines later, however, we find him saying, with false modesty and obvious inconsistency, that he knows nothing of rhetoric, and, further,

> Colours of rethoryk been to me queynte;
> My spirit feeleth noght of swich mateere.
> (726-727)

It is clear that he admired the Squire not for any substance that may be found either in his person[8] or in his narrative, but for the superficial and empty splendor of his "array," both literal and verbal. He explains that he himself has a son who lacks the Squire's discretion, exclaiming

> Fy on possessioun,
> But if a man be vertuous withal. . . .
> (686-687)

It is true as both Boethius and the Parson explain that true "gentilesse" is based on virtue, rather than on inherited status or wealth, but the special vice in his son that disturbs the Franklin is one that touches a very tender spot—he spends and loses all of his money. To be virtuous (and hence "gentil") from the Franklin's point of view is to keep and increase one's "possessioun." The laughable absurdity of these observations only irritates our Host, who is not generally very astute, so that he is emboldened to reprimand a man much above him in station, exclaiming, "Straw for youre gentilesse!"

But the Franklin is not to be put down, and he proceeds at once to tell a tale told by "olde gentil Britouns,"[9] which will demonstrate, we infer, his own "gentil" tastes and manners. His hero is a knight, not a knight of the shire, but a nobleman, who loves a lady among "the faireste under sonne," but because of her "heigh kynrede" (not, we notice, her virtue), he is afraid to make his feelings for her known. She, however, taking note of his "obeysaunce" and what the Franklin amusingly calls "penaunce," takes pity on him and agrees to take him for her husband and her lord "of swich lordship as men han over hir wyves." Evidently the Franklin feels that the Pauline hierarchy in marriage is not generally popular, especially among the noble. It certainly does not appeal to the Franklin's hero and heroine, for the former swears at once to disregard it, disavowing any "maistrie," and agreeing to obey his wife like a lover,

> Save that the name of soveraynetee,
> That wolde he have for shame of his degree.
>
> (751-752)

We conclude that, even as a nobleman, the knight would have been an object of scorn if his subservient relationship had become known. It is probably true that whatever may have been said in modern discussions of "courtly love," men who subjected themselves to women except in formal feudal relationships were not highly regarded in the Middle Ages, and the learned might have recognized in the knight's position a kind of foolishness once renounced by the poet Ovid.[10] No one sought to excuse the subservience of King Edward III to Alice Perrers on the ground that he was simply a "courtly lover" of another man's wife. It is not irrelevant to observe also that our knight deliberately disavows the sacrament that made marriage a reflection of the relationship between Christ and the Church.

As a result of the knight's self-denial, the lady, exulting in "so large a reyne," a figure, incidentally, that recalls the rider and horse relationship used conventionally to suggest the hierarchies of spirit and flesh or husband and wife,[11] agrees to be a true wife, although this promise, in view of her husband's obedience, implies little more than an "appearance," like his "soveraynetee." But the Franklin hastens to defend the relationship thus established. His words have won him the reputation of being a great authority on marriage; in fact, he is often credited with solving the problem of the "marriage group" in *The Canterbury Tales*. According to the usual theory, the Wife of Bath advocates the sovereignty of the wife, the Clerk advocates the absolute sovereignty of the husband, and the Franklin solves the problem by making the two equal, thus allowing Chaucer to anticipate the present happy state of affairs, transcending his own time and outdistancing Shakespeare and Milton. This achievement seems highly unlikely, but it is even more unlikely when we consider the orthodoxy of King Richard's court generally and the character of Chaucer's friends. But there are more detailed objections. The Clerk says specifically that he does not mean that wives should behave toward their husbands as Griselda did (IV[E] 1142-1144); his story, he explains, concerns patience and obedience in the face of Providential adversity. If he is answering the Wife of Bath, as he obviously is, he is answering implications of her Prologue and Tale that concern literal marriage only incidentally. It may be argued, moreover, that the theme of marriage is introduced in the Knight's Tale, and that it is by no means neglected in the tales of the Miller, the Reeve, and the Man of Law. We should expect of the Franklin a literalistic attitude and an attempt at an Epicurean marital arrangement.

The Franklin does not disappoint this expectation, pointing out first that friends must obey each other if their friendship is to be maintained. He does not say, as others had said before him, that friendship should be based on mutual desires, or, to quote Cicero, that it is *nihil aliud nisi omnium divinarum humanarumque rerum cum benevolentia et caritate consensio*, but that friends must obey each other. A little reflection will show that this is a ridiculous proposition in terms of actual practice. If Friend A desires one thing, but realizes that Friend B desires the other, what are friendly A and B to do? What if A accedes to B, and B, in friendly fashion, accedes to A at the same time? Or if A commands B to do one thing in his company and B commands A to do something else? It would be best, perhaps not to define friendship in terms of obedience, but the Franklin, in this matter as in others, shows little penetration. He goes on to say, in a very famous echo of the words of that worldly wise and cynical character Amis in the *Roman de la rose* of Jean de Meun,[12] that love and "maistrie" are incompatible, a principle that if applied rigorously, would have undermined the entire structure of Chaucer's society, not to mention the Christian religion as it was then understood. However, the Franklin means love in a limited sense:

> Whan maistrie comth, the God of Love anon
> Beteth his wynges, and farwel, he is gon!
> Love is a thyng as any spirit free.
> Wommen, of kynde, desiren libertee,
> And nat to been constreyned as a thral;
> And so doon men, if I sooth seyen shal.
>
> (765-770)

If "the God of Love" is the same god that appears in the *Roman* (Cupid, or sexual desire), and there is no reason to assume that he is not, these lines express some commonplace themes of Christian morality, although these themes are not exactly favorable to the Franklin's general argument. That is, marriage is a sacrament, the first, in fact, to be established by Christ. Its function is to direct and control concupiscence, or the operations of the God of Love. Thus the Parson, a "lerned man" to whom Chaucerians might well pay more attention, adduces chastity (faithfulness) in marriage, which "maketh the hertes al oon of hem that ben ywedded, as wel as bodies" the first remedy against the vice of lechery, or in other terms the free activity of Cupid.[13] The levity, indiscretion, and fickleness of Cupid are proverbial.

It is true also that women "of kynde" desire liberty, a principle explained fully by the Old Woman in the *Roman de la rose*, who says, in Dahlberg's translation,

> "Moreover, women are born free. The law, which takes away the freedom in which Nature placed them, has put them under conditions. . . . Thus, when they are engaged, captured by law, and married in order to prevent quarreling, contention, and murder and to help in the rearing of children, who are their joint responsibility, they still exert themselves in every way, these ladies and girls, ugly or beautiful, to return to their freedom."[14]

And it is quite obvious that men who place their own pleasure above responsibility desire the same freedom. But the "kynde" or nature involved here is the nature St. Paul speaks of when he says (Ephesians 2.3) that "we were by nature children of wrath." That is, the fallen nature of man and woman does not readily acquiesce to the restraints of hierarchical marriage.[15] These implications of the Franklin's words would have been clear at once to most persons in Chaucer's audience. They do not bode very well for the mutually obedient relationship the Franklin has proposed, nor do they contribute to any impression that the Franklin himself is very astute.

He goes on to explain, however, that his lovers will have to be patient, and that they must learn to suffer a great deal. Since the argument still follows that of Amis in a general way, it will repay us to look very briefly at that worthy's exposition in the *Roman*. Having just recommended flattery and false courtesy to the lover, Amis turns to the subject of wealth and large gifts, concluding, with reference to the beloved, that "if she saw a great heavy purse, all stuffed with bezants, rise up all at once, she would run to it with open arms; women are not so maddened that they would run after anything except purses. Although formerly they had other customs, now everything is going into decline."[16] This consideration leads to a discussion of the Golden Age, which in the view of Amis was a time of free Epicurean delights when the "simple secure people led their carols, their games, and their idle, pleasant activities, free of all cares except to lead a life of gaiety in lawful companionship. . . . All were accustomed to being equal, and no one wanted any possessions of his own. They knew well the saying, neither lying nor foolish, that love and lordship never kept each other company nor dwelt together. The one that dominates separates them."[17] Amis finds that "it is the same in marriages," and proceeds at once with the Jealous Husband's famous attack on marriage. When this attack has been completed, Amis adds, "Yes indeed, without fail, whatever she says, he will not be loved by his wife if he wants to be called 'lord,' for love must die when lovers want lordship."[18] Thus a woman who has been loved by a man *par amour* and who subsequently marries him is usually disappointed, for, since the man who once jumped at her every wish now wishes to command, she is unhappy. Because the Golden Age has given way to an hierarchical society through greed, lovers should not be jealous. If a man finds his lady unfaithful, he should not criticize her but "pretend to be blind, or more stupid than a buffalo"; he should allow her to come and go as she pleases, never believe any evil of her, and never reproach her for her vices. Moreover, even if he is "beaten or reviled, even if she should pull out his nails alive, he must not take revenge but rather thank her." He should deny any unfaithfulness on his part, or if necessary claim to have been forced into it; and if she is sick, he should flatter and console her with false tenderness. But in spite of all this, Amis concludes, no woman is to be trusted and no woman is so loyal "that one could ever be certain of holding her, any more than if one held an eel by the tail in the Seine." This is not true of "good women," but, Amis says, "I never yet found any." He once more recommends flattery, for a woman, "however foolish she is, knows by her natural judgment that, whatever excess she commits, good or bad, wrong or right, or whatever you wish, she does nothing that she should not, and she hates whoever corrects her."[19]

The Franklin's knight, who believes that he who is most patient in love has the greatest advantage, thus lays himself open to some rather disconcerting possibilities. Those mentioned by the Franklin are sufficiently pregnant with potential adversity—wrath, illness, astrological influences, the effects of wine, sorrow, or alteration in complexion. If the husband is to have only the name of sovereignty and continue the "obeisaunces" and "penaunces" of his courtship, he will probably suffer a great deal. Under the circumstances, the lady can hardly be blamed for swearing that "nevere sholde ther be defaute in here," since her husband would never have anything about which to complain. In the event that both parties take the Franklin's little scheme

seriously, always obeying each other, the potentiality for two very literal patient Griseldas is obvious. When the Franklin seeks to ra-
tionalize the position of his wedded pair, the result is mere absurdity:

> Heere may men seen an humble, wys accord;
> Thus hath she take hir servant and hir lord,—
> Servant in love, and lord in marriage.
> Thanne was he bothe in lordshipe and servage.
> Servage? nay, but in lordshipe above,
> Sith he hath both his lady and his love;
> His lady, certes, and his wyf also
> The which that lawe of love acordeth to.
>
> (791-798)

In the context of a society in which hierarchical social relationships
were considered to be natural this passage simply makes no sense at all
except as an amusingly verbose flurry of illogicality. How can a man
be a lord and a servant at the same time? When is he "in lordshipe" and
when is he "in servage"? Far from solving the problems of an imaginary "marriage group," the Franklin has succeeded only in making
himself ridiculous and in exhibiting the kind of greed that prompted
old Januarie to try to make of marriage a haven for the pleasant exercise of concupiscence. The hierarchy of marriage was an integral part
of the society of Chaucer's time, firmly established in theology, canon
law, criminal law, and the prevailing political theory.[20] The idea that
Chaucer (as distinct from his Franklin) would have seriously attacked
it is absurd. The Franklin, whose eye is firmly fixed on externals, is
just the kind of man to be satisfied with an "appearance" if it seems to
imply pleasure for himself.

In the subsequent tale, the effects of the marital arrangement just described are far from happy. Arveragus, the husband, after "a yeer and
moore" of bliss decides to go to England for two years to exercise his
chivalry. Dorigen, his wife, does not exercise much patience, but begins to weep and sigh, according to the Franklin "as doon thise noble
wyves whan hem liketh," reassuring his audience of his expertise in
noble manners. She secludes herself and refuses all diversion until her
friends succeed in consoling her a little and Arveragus sends her letters
announcing his hasty return. On the seacoast she indulges herself with
a long complaint against the Providence of God, who has heedlessly
and unnecessarily placed rocks on the Breton coast that might en-
danger any ship bearing Arveragus on his return (865-893). Complaints against Providence, are, as both Boethius and the Parson explain, foolish and reprehensible, although the Franklin seems unaware
of this; and the special complaint about rocks in the sea has its own

iconographic overtones. For the pilgrimage of life is often a voyage on the sea of the world, and the rocks are the temptations, either of prosperity, when they form a resting-place for Sirens or Mermaids, or of adversity.[21] When these figurative rocks are covered up by sophistical arguments or by the seductive voices of the mermaids, they do not become less dangerous but more threatening. The efforts of the Franklin just described to make marriage a refuge for the God of Love affords a good example. If the Boethian philosophy underlying it is taken seriously, Dorigen's complaint becomes humorous, and there seems little doubt that Chaucer, who took the trouble to translate *The Consolation of Philosophy*, intended it to be so.

Among the diversions provided by Dorigen's friends is a garden, so curiously bedecked by May "with his softe shoures" and "by craft of mannes hand" that it seemed to be "the verray paradys." There everyone joins in song and dance except Dorigen, who is too sorrowful to participate in the festivities. The scene is familiar. Troilus prays to Cupid in such a garden (*TC* II, 505-539), Emelye roams about there singing in the Knight's Tale (I[A] 1033-1055), and old Januarie constructs it with great diligence (IV[E] 2021-2056). It is, that is, another version of the garden described by Guillaume de Lorris, whose delights are closed to Dorigen just as they are to "Sorowe" herself (*Romaunt*, 301-348). This locale, like most other "scenes" in Chaucer's work, is not actually a location in space and time. It is an appropriate place for the machinations of the God of Love, who in this instance inspires a young Squire, Aurelius, who closely resembles the Squire in the General Prologue. His vanity is displayed in his costume, for he is "jolyer of array . . . than is the month of May" and in his skill at song and dance. He is also young, strong, wealthy, and in the Franklin's estimation wise, not to mention being "servant to Venus" or like the Franklin himself a man bent on pleasure. After the usual preliminary hesitation, Aurelius makes his approach to Dorigen, concluding, "Have mercy, sweete, or ye wol do me deye!" This plea, like that of Nicholas in the Miller's Tale—"Lemman, love me al atones or I wol dyen"—is neither very noble nor very manful,[22] and of course Aurelius does not die upon the lady's refusal, which he receives immediately:

> "By thilke God that yaf me soule and lyf,
> Ne shal I nevere been untrewe wyf
> In word ne werk, as fer as I have wit;
> I wol been his to whom that I am knyt.
> Taak this for fynal answere as of me."
> (983-987)

She adds "in pley" a promise that if Aurelius will "remoeve alle the rokkes, stoon by stoon," from the Breton coast so that they do not hinder shipping, she will love him "best of any man." But this promise in so far as "entente" is concerned is merely a repetition of the first vow to be true to her husband, since it demands an impossible task. This fact is emphasized in Dorigen's reply to her suitor's request for "oother grace," a reply, incidentally, that exhibits a profound ignorance on her part of modern ideas of "courtly love":

> "No, by that Lord," quod she, "that maked me!
> For wel I woot that it shal never bityde.
> Lat swiche folies out of youre herte slyde.
> What deyntee sholde a man han in his lyf
> For to go love another mannes wyf,
> That hath hir body whan so that hym liketh?"
> (1000-1005)

But neither the refusal nor the advice makes much impression on Aurelius, who takes the remarks about the rocks with legalistic literalism, exclaiming that their removal would be impossible, and concluding with solemn absurdity, "Thanne moot I dye of sodeyn deth horrible." He proceeds at once to meditate on rock removal, but does not, of course, die.

This literal-minded reaction to the words rather than to the clear "entente" of Dorigen's playful remarks places Aurelius in company with other literal-minded figures in the preceding tales. The summoner in the Friar's Tale, for example, exhibits a literal-minded preoccupation with the "shap" and "bodies" of fiends, paying no attention at all to their powers and functions as instruments of God, so that he steadfastly refuses to repent, with devastating but just results. He takes the carter's curse literally without any heed to his "entente," which even the fiend can understand (II[D] 1543-1558). The friar in the Summoner's Tale is so hopelessly literal-minded that he becomes preoccupied with the problem of how to divide a fart into twelve equal parts, and the Wife of Bath herself shows a complete disregard for the "entente" of the Scriptural passages she quotes. The Franklin, preoccupied with satisfying externals, cannot be expected to do much better, and his characters, in this respect, turn out to be no better than he is. Aurelius hopes fervently for a very high "spryng flood," which might, indeed, cover up the rocks but would hardly make them less dangerous as hindrances to shipping, although Dorigen demanded that they be removed so that "they ne lette ship ne boot to goon."

Arveragus returns safely, and Aurelius instead of suffering death simply lies in bed for over two years unable to put his foot down because of his truly remarkable physical discomfort. His lamentable situation offers a further example of the Franklin's inadvertently humorous exaggeration. But Aurelius is aroused by his brother, who thinks that it might be possible to find a clerk in Orleans who could with "an apparence" make the rocks seem to disappear, using operations concerning the mansions of the moon. The Franklin here interrupts to display his own skepticism for, as he says,

> hooly chirches feith in oure bileve
> Ne suffreth noon illusioun us to greve.
> (1133-1134)

It is true that the mansions of the moon have nothing to do with the illusion that follows;[23] nevertheless, the Franklin's notion that Holy Church, whose teachings he has been blithely disregarding, protects him from illusion is laughable. If it were true, there would be no sinners in the Church, and no Epicureans among nominal believers to be misled by externals. The Franklin's Christianity is not very profound.

Aurelius and his brother do indeed find a clerk who entertains them with illusions involving hunting, jousting, and dancing before he enters a contract to "remoeven alle the rokkes of Bretayne" (1221) for a thousand pounds. The fact that the delightful and noble pastimes presented by the clerk are illusory should have served, perhaps, as a warning, but Aurelius persists, although he does not, as it turns out, have a thousand pounds. But he promises to deliver this enormous sum for the privilege of alleviating his physical distress on the person of Dorigen, and this in spite of the fact, as he well knows, that she is no longer interested in the rocks because Arveragus has returned. Needless to say, he is neither being very "gentil" nor even moderately considerate. He is, in fact, being very stupid. In the fourteenth century, not to mention Breton antiquity, if anyone thinks that to be relevant, a thousand pounds would have been sufficient to purchase the Venereal services of a variety of amiable and capable wenches for a number of years. It is true that the purchase of such services is not very noble, but, after all, that is exactly what Aurelius is seeking to do. His concentration on Dorigen, the wife of a knight reputed to be "of chivalrie the flour" can be attributed only to vanity. The magician sets about some sham calculations just before the high tide after the winter solstice,[24] so that through what the Franklin thinks of as "his magik" it "semed that alle the rokkes were aweye" (1296). We should notice that the clerk did not, as he promised, remove the rocks, and that, in so far as Aurelius is concerned, they were not removed stone by stone as Dorigen de-

manded. The fact that the tide is said to have lasted for a week or two
in the Franklin's account should probably be attributed, as Wood
suggests, to the Franklin's usual weakness for exaggeration.

After falling at the feet of his master, the clerk, to thank him and his
lady, Venus, Aurelius proceeds at once to inform Dorigen of her predicament. His approach is full of pious hypocrisy, since his prayer to
Venus has made his real aims very clear, and, at the same time, he
knows very well that Dorigen does not wish to be unfaithful to her
husband. Addressing her as his "righte lady," whom he loves best
"and lothest were of all this world displese," he asserts again that he is
about to die, reminds her of her promise, adding, before announcing
the disappearance of the rocks,

> Madame, I speke it for the honour of yow
> Moore than to save myn hertes lyf right now.
> (1331-1332)

The bold statement that his interest lies in Dorigen's honor when he
wants nothing but to dishonor her is not only ridiculous but laughable, not to mention being ignoble by any standards except those of the
Franklin, who places pleasure before everything else.

Dorigen is naturally most displeased. Remarking that the removal
of the rocks is "agayns the proces of nature," she begins to weep, wail,
and swoon. She complains bitterly, and foolishly, against Fortune, and
meditates at great length on a long series of exempla, some of them
ridiculous, involving maids and wives who have suffered death rather
than dishonor or led chaste lives in the face of tribulations. She deter-
mines finally, after a day or two of such unpleasant speculation, that
she must die. If Aurelius was foolish to take the words or the "appearance" of Dorigen's second oath seriously rather than its "entente,"
Dorigen is downright silly to do so.[25] But the Franklin's characters
are, in a sense, all little images of himself. Thus when Dorigen informs
her husband of her plight, he too is deceived by an appearance and
launches into a pious diatribe on "truth," which has won for him,
rather oddly, a reputation among critics as an exemplar of true
chivalry:

> Ye shul youre trouthe holden, by my fay!
> For God so wisly have mercy upon me,
> I hadde wel lever ystiked for to be
> For verray love which that I to yow have,
> But if ye sholde youre trouthe kepe and save.
> Trouthe is the hyeste thyng that man may kepe.
> (1474-1479)

The "truth" is that Dorigen's second promise was a denial; nevertheless, our noble knight, breaking into tears,[26] adds at once,

> I yow forbede, up peyne of deeth,
> That nevere, whil thee lasteth lyf ne breeth,
> To no wight telle thou of this aventure,—
> As I may best, I wol my wo endure—
> Ne make no contenance of hevynesse,
> That folk of yow may demen harm or gesse.
>   (1481-1486)

Our hero will thus be satisfied with an appearance of honor or "truth" in his marriage, just as he was satisfied with an appearance of husbandly status in the first place. He is, in effect, very adept at covering up rocks. Meanwhile, the threat to kill his wife if she does not commit adultery and keep quiet about it in the name of "truth" is hardly a manifestation of "gentilesse." The usual interpretations of this tale deprive it of its humor as well as of its basically serious "entente." It is true that Dorigen does not live up to the cynical expectations of Amis in the *Roman de la rose*. But the wedded pair, having followed the recommendations of Amis concerning marriage, are both made to suffer what in Jean de Meun were the trials of the husband only. Arveragus tearfully demands the unfaithfulness of his wife, and she, who has just contemplated suicide to avoid breaking the "truth" of her marriage, is now threatened with death if she does not do so cheerfully. Chaucer has thus gone a step beyond Jean de Meun, showing that even when women are virtuously inclined, they cannot keep faith if their husbands are sufficiently stupid, and that this is true especially when "mutual forbearance" has been substituted for the usual Pauline relationship. In defense of Jean de Meun, however, it might be added that his Jealous Husband was, after all, a sufficient manifestation of husbandly stupidity. Like the Franklin, he sought to make marriage a vehicle for pleasure.

Dorigen proceeds secretly to meet her lover in an appropriate garden, but when Aurelius learns of what the worthy knight has done, he decides to set aside his pleasure rather than perform a churlish act "agayns franchise and alle gentillesse." Actually, his vanity triumphs once more, so that, seeking to outdo the great virtue of Arveragus, he releases Dorigen from her promise, at the same time calling her "the treweste and beste wyf" he has ever known, in spite of the fact that she has just come to receive him as her lover. Impressed by this renunciation of that surpassing good, pleasure, the Franklin observes,

Thus kan a squier don a gentil dede,
As well as-kan a knyght, withouten drede.
(1543-1544)

Aurelius proceeds to the clerk, disturbed because he does not have the necessary thousand pounds and requesting the privilege of making payments in installments. At first, the learned gentleman is taken aback, inquiring whether or not he has fulfilled his side of the bargain. He has not actually done so, although Aurelius thinks that he has by magic caused the rocks to disappear. When the clerk learns that Arveragus out of "gentilesse" has made Dorigen keep the letter of her promise, and that Aurelius has taken pity on her and released her out of "gentilesse," he, being a proud man, decides that he is "gentil" also and releases the Squire. A basic attribute of "gentilesse" is generosity, so that the Franklin, at the close of his tale, inquires, "Which was the mooste fre, as thynketh yow?" Chaucer must have awaited with some amusement the reactions of his audience.

Generosity is a great virtue, but it is impossible to be generous with something to which one has no right. In the tale, Aurelius has no justification for taking Dorigen's second promise literally, and he does not, as he realizes, remove the rocks stone by stone from the coast, so that he has no claim on Dorigen's person at all and hence nothing to give up. Dorigen promised emphatically to be faithful to her husband, so that she has no right to give up her physical favors to Aurelius. The clerk does not "remove" the rocks as he promised to do. And Arveragus, having renounced all sovereignty over his wife, has no right to demand that she submit to Aurelius. If he gives up anything, as the source of this tale suggests,[27] it is his honor or "truth" in marriage, but this, after all, was a mere appearance. The Franklin's conception of "gentilesse" is consistent with his admiration for the Squire's rhetoric, with his Epicurean concern for externals, and with the kind of attitude we might expect on the basis of his career. Chaucer's interest was not, however, in the Franklin as a person. As we see him riding along with the wealthy and venal Sergeant, we are led to wonder about the state of royal justice in England if it rests in the hands of men whose weaknesses are exemplified by these self-deluded and pompous figures who cannot see beneath appearances either in the world itself or in words. Both, in fact, are skilled at using words to hide the truth.[28]

Some Disputed Chaucerian Terminology

✒️

I have been informed by Professor Norman Davis that the new text of The Book of the Duchess *being prepared under his direction and here covertly mentioned has been delayed. As I shall indicate in articles now in press (see bibliography), changes in fourteenth-century English society after the Black Death were probably deeply discouraging to Chaucer and were responsible for much of his humorous criticism of his contemporaries. With reference to changes in modern attitudes toward agrarian history, Ada Elizabeth Levett observed in 1927 in an article in* EcHR *that "The agrarian history of England appears to need re-writing almost every ten years." If anything, this observation is more incisive today than it was fifty years ago.*

✒️

CHAUCER'S language may be obscure to us for various reasons. There are, in the first place, words like *viritoot* in the Miller's Tale (3770)[1] that are etymologically obscure, so that aside from the evidence of the context and conjecture we lack any means of making a preliminary assessment of their meanings. Others are subject to occasional doubts, often unexpressed. For example, it has always seemed to me that *embosed* in *The Book of the Duchess* (353) would make more sense as a word based on OF *bos* "wood," meaning that the hart "so moche embosed" was protected by a retreat into a thick wood rather than that he was "flecked with foam," but this is not a point that I wish to argue at length. Again, the etymologies usually offered for *Eclympasteyr* in the same poem (167) strike me as being weak. The word looks a little like a corruption of a French nonce-word, *enclynposteir* "that slep and did noon other werk," but again I do not wish to make any formal defense of this conjecture. Both instances, as I have said, simply indicate an uneasiness of a kind that most Chaucerians probably feel about scattered words in the text. In these instances, a new edition of the poem currently in preparation may settle the questions in one way or another.

Words of this kind are fortunately not very numerous, so that they give less trouble than more ordinary words that are obscure because of gaps in our knowledge of fourteenth-century life and thought. At times their obscurity is concealed either because they seem obvious at first glance or because simple explanations for them appear in dictionaries, or in the notes and glosses that accompany our texts. The connotations of *curteisie*, for example, have recently been discussed once more,[2] and in Chaucer's work this word, like many others, is made confusing by its ironic use. Thus the Knight loved "curteisie," but that this "courtesy" is the same as that of the Squire—"curteis he was, lowely, and servysable"—or that of the Friar—"curteis he was and lowely of servyse"—seems very dubious, for we cannot easily envisage the Knight indulging himself in the self-seeking obsequiousness of the hypocritical Friar. The Squire also seems to be interested more in youthful self-indulgence than he is in the ideals revered by his father. But concrete words may deceive us also, not because we fail to grasp immediate meanings, but because the connotations of concrete words are often just as elusive as those of abstract words. For example, a number of Chaucer's characters may be described generally as "peasants," although as we are beginning to discover this is a hard word too. At least they are workers in the fields or inhabitants of the manors and villages of rural England. We actually know very little about agrarian life in the second half of the fourteenth century, and many of the generalizations current about it thirty years ago have been called in question by recent studies in local history, which reveal, in addition to a mass of useful detail, the fact that we have a great deal more to learn.

In the following pages I wish to explore some of the difficulties involved in evaluating Chaucer's portraits of humbler folk, largely to show that the difficulties are in fact there. Meanwhile, occasions will arise to comment on the connotations of a number of words, although, for reasons that will become apparent, these comments are preliminary in nature. At the outset, it is important to realize that Chaucer was not writing anything like "documentary realism," so that his own attitudes toward rural characters and their work are not clear unless we know something about what the groups they represent were actually like. An agrarian historian has, in fact, complained about the unsatisfactory conclusions reached by using Chaucer's work or *Piers Plowman* as evidence for actual conditions.[3] It would obviously make more sense to know something about actual conditions first and then to consider the significance of Chaucer's treatment of them.

Chaucer was a Royal Squire who, as Denholm-Young has recently reminded us, had been a "strenuous man" with a background of military service in the field.[4] He was thus undisputably a gentleman, at times a "country gentleman" about whom we know a great deal more than we do about most country gentlemen in his time, but as a royal servant he would outrank the Squire in the General Prologue, not to mention Aurelius in the Franklin's Tale. Moreover, he addressed himself to an aristocratic audience whose sympathies he clearly had no wish to alienate. It is a mistake, as well as a grievous oversimplification, to consider Chaucer as a member of the "middle class." Did he view those below him in the social hierarchy with contempt? Did he dislike peasants (a term here loosely used) simply because they were peasants? These and similar questions had perhaps best not be answered too hastily.

There are various features of rural life in England during Chaucer's mature lifetime that make any effort to be very precise about evaluating characters like the Yeoman, the Reeve, the Miller, the Plowman and their fellows difficult. The actual counterparts of characters just mentioned all usually belonged to the *familia* or staff of hired servants on a manor. We may include the Yeoman not because he is a yeoman but because he is a forester serving the Knight. Incidentally, Chaucer's position as deputy chief forester in a royal forest administered by Sir Peter Courtenay, brother of the archbishop of Canterbury and uncle of the earl of Devon, was a royal administrative post that does not make him resemble our Yeoman in any way. To return to the manor, we here encounter our first major problem. During the later fourteenth century a manor might have customs very different from those on a nearby manor, and manors of ecclesiastical lords, which were very numerous, might differ in various ways from manors held by lay lords.[5] If manors might vary in extent, complexity, and custom in a limited area, they varied even more in different parts of the country, partly because of variation in soil and climate, and partly because ancient local customs were both diverse and tenacious. Thus there were distinct differences between manorial life in Kent, where most peasants were "free,"[6] and that in Devon;[7] and rural life in Oxfordshire[8] might be very unlike rural life in Norfolk or in the north and west. The "classic manor" sometimes existed, but it was by no means the rule.

Not only was there considerable variation from place to place, but rural society was undergoing astonishingly rapid changes during Chaucer's lifetime, especially after the disruptions caused by the Black Death. Although it is possible to generalize about these changes over a long period of time, especially if we extend our view into the sixteenth century, in the fourteenth century developments were by no means uniform, so that an estate after about 1360 in one area might experience rapid changes that had already been taking place more slowly in the early years of the century, whereas similar changes might not appear elsewhere until after 1400. We are confronted, therefore, with an extremely varied "map," so to speak, shifting in different ways and at varying rates on separate manors. Moreover, most areas on our "map" are blank, awaiting the further detailed studies of local historians. It is also true that some villages were "free," experiencing little manorial jurisdiction. The only consolation afforded the Chaucerian by this situation is that Chaucer himself would have had to make his representations of rural life sufficiently general so as to be comprehensible to his audience. We may thus expect his substantive assumptions to be fairly traditional, but his attitudes might be highly colored by developments during his lifetime.

Let us consider as an example the Reeve. Traditionally, a reeve was a serf elected annually by his fellows in the manorial court to serve for a year to keep a record of income and expenditures on his manor. He collected rents, paid holders of manorial offices, bought and sold grain or livestock, looked after hedges and plow beasts, and generally supervised manorial husbandry, setting the time for plowing, sowing, harvesting, etc. It was important that he coordinate the efforts of his fellow workers. In his financial accounts, he was sometimes assisted by a clerk, or in some areas, his financial duties might be assumed by a bailiff. He might be assisted by a beadle who saw to it that tenants performed their customary services. Generally, his own customary services were remitted during the time of his office, and he was paid a stipend just a little more than that received by other regular servants like plowmen, carters (who might be responsible for harrowing as well as for carting), and dairy assistants. He was often supervised by a bailiff, an official who often had several manors on the same estate under his jurisdiction, and he was accountable to his lord or to his lord's steward or receiver. During the later fourteenth century when many demesne holdings were leased, the office of reeve became confused with that of bailiff, but the reeve was a bailiff of sorts in any event and could be called a bailiff. Chaucer's reeve still has a bailiff to supervise his activities. Some reeves became relatively wealthy during the later fourteenth century, since their experience gave them an advantage in the management of land that could be leased or purchased after the Black Death, and in the late fifteenth century and in the sixteenth we find persons of decidedly high estate acting as reeves, after the office had become a sinecure.[9]

It has sometimes been suggested that Chaucer's Reeve served in part as a steward (or seneschal), but in fourteenth-century terms this suggestion may be misleading. A steward was not, strictly speaking, a manorial servant, but a prominent member of the *curia* or *familia* of his lord, concerned with general estate management, and he might well be the highest ranking member of his lord's council.[10] His functions were judicial as well as administrative, so that he might preside over manorial courts and hundred courts, and he was frequently a man of legal training and considerable prominence. Thus Thomas Raymond, a lay steward of Tavistock Abbey, was a member of parliament six times during the later fourteenth century, was Recorder of Exeter from 1383, and Royal Escheator for Devon in 1401.[11] In Chaucer's description of the Manciple we learn that among his employees at "a temple" there were a dozen out of thirty so expert in the law that they were

> Worthy to been stywardes of rente and lond
> Of any lord that is in Engelond,
> To make hym lyve by his propre good
> In honour detteless (but if he were wood),
> Or lyve as scarsly as hym list desire;
> And able for to helpen al a shire
> In any caas that myghte falle or happe.
>
> (579-585)

As the example of Thomas Raymond shows, a steward might indeed serve in the shire. It is rather difficult to think of a village carpenter like the Reeve as a man of legal training, and if we make him his lord's steward, we shall have to think of that lord as a very impoverished man indeed. Those who take this view and wish to make the countess of Norfolk the reeve's lord will have to attribute to that lady a certain quixotic air.

Looking at our Oswald more closely, we learn that he was so expert at keeping his accounts of buying and selling that his auditor or receiver, who might in some instances be a special official and in others the steward, could find no fault with them. He was, moreover, thoroughly conversant with his lord's property on the manor and expert at estimating manorial productivity. His efficiency has won for him a long term of office, and his experience has taught him all the tricks and plots of any bailiff who may supervise him, as well as the sleights of shepherds and other workers, so that all are afraid of him, and he has managed to obtain a tree-shaded dwelling in a meadow, in Norfolk, suggestive of free status. So far, he seems a trusty and unusually efficient servant. But he has a store of goods fraudulently obtained, and, being a clever man, he knows how to steal from his lord and please him at the same time. With these revelations what appeared at first to be efficiency becomes petty tyranny, and Oswald emerges as an especially odious character. But he is not a "typical" reeve, even though his portrait may reflect in some ways commonplace complaints about reeves.[12] Some reeves were, like most of us, occasionally untrustworthy,[13] or negligent and inefficient. But this reeve is consistently lacking in fidelity or "trouthe" to his lord and is a wilful oppressor of his neighbors. Chaucer is not attacking reeves, but is demonstrating or exemplifying the weakness to which unscrupulous as distinct from inefficient reeves might be especially prone.[14] The basis of Chaucer's criticism is here, as elsewhere, moral; that is, the shallow shrewdness and lustfulness of the character revealed in his physiognomy and further emphasized in the prologue to his tale are consistent with the clever and unscrupulous self-indulgence exhibited in his actions.[15] To put this in a general way, at the risk of offending some of my readers, Oswald is thoroughly cupidinous and wise in the wisdom of the world. His efficiency serves to emphasize a moral weakness.

During the latter decades of the fourteenth century some areas of the agricultural community were enjoying a new prosperity,[16] although it was often achieved at the expense of social coherence on individual manors. Holdings both free and servile that fell vacant as a result of the Black Death were often leased or sold to more prosperous tenants who could afford them, and a reliance on private initiative for gain at the expense of community spirit often resulted, sometimes with a concomitant increase in crime.[17] Chaucer may have regarded this tendency with misgivings, and indeed, like the factionalism at court, it may be in part responsible for the bitterness he expresses at the close of "The Former Age":

> For in oure dayes nys but covetyse,
> Doublenesse, and tresoun, and envye,
> Poyson, manslauhtre, and mordre in sondry wyse.
>
> (61-63)

He clearly admired ideals of community service and was contemptuous of those who, like the Reeve, selfishly disregarded them. An excellent example of his idealism in this respect is afforded by the Plowman. A plowman in the fourteenth century was not simply a peasant with a plow, but a man elected or appointed to serve as plowman among the demesne servants of a manor. Next to the reeve, he was often the best paid of these servants. Chaucer's Plowman is a truly admirable character:

> A trewe swynkere and a good was he,
> Lyvynge in pees and parfit charitee.

God loved he best with al his hoole herte
At alle tymes, thogh him gamed or smerte,
And thanne his neighebor right as hymselve.
(531-535)

He gladly works at threshing and ditching for his neighbors without pay, and faithfully pays his tithes. It is clear that this is not meant to be either a "typical" plowman or an "individual," but a statement of ideals, just as the picture of the Reeve is a picture of the failure of ideals.[18] The selection of a peasant for this exemplification of the New Law probably does not represent an idealization of peasants any more than the picture of Oswald or that of the dishonest and contentious Miller represents a condemnation of peasants. It was appropriate to clothe the highest Christian ideal in humble guise. If we can take the learned and virtuous Parson literally as the Plowman's brother, he also is of peasant stock. Since these characters do serve as indirect criticisms of their actual counterparts, who often did not resemble them,[19] they may not serve very well as evidence for Chaucer's attitude toward peasants.

There can be little doubt that the Yeoman is treated with respect, even though we are not told much about him, and it is not exactly clear what a "yeoman" was. By the year 1600 "yeomen" had become a class to themselves, so that Thomas Wilson could write of five principal classes in the realm: (1) nobles, (2) citizens, (3) yeomen, (4) artisans, (5) rural workers.[20] But the word *yeoman* was a much looser term in Chaucer's day, and persons to whom it was applied in the countryside were not nearly so wealthy as some of those described by Wilson. Chaucer's yeoman, as his green costume and bow indicate, is a forester on an estate whose lord, the Knight, held hunting rights in his forest or forests. Some foresters were concerned only with the use of wood, especially important not only for carpenters but also for brewers or ale-wives and dairy assistants who burned it in their fires. Our forester thus "knew al the usage" of "woodecraft" as well as being a hunter. Roughly speaking, a country yeoman was a "peasant" who might be "free,"[21] but who had sufficient holdings and sufficient reliability to make him stand out clearly above his fellows. During the early fifteenth century, the words *yeoman* and *husbandman* might be used without distinction in southeast England[22] to indicate a "farmer" of relatively independent status. In other areas a fourteenth-century yeoman might be a peasant who held over thirty acres of land and was regarded as a leader in his community, often serving as beadle, ale-taster, or in some other official capacity.[23] We may thus think of the yeoman as a man whose good service and industry had won him a place of honor in his community, so that he deserved his position among the permanent manorial servants of his lord as forester.

In her classic study, *The English Yeoman under Elizabeth and the Early Stuarts*, Mildred Campbell concluded that the word *yeoman* was not a term used to designate status during the thirteenth and fourteenth centuries, since freemen beneath the gentle rank of Squire were then known as "franklins."[24] However, Chaucer's Franklin held offices in the shire rather than offices on a manor (unless his early position as "contour" was manorial), so that he belongs to a status that is not necessarily gentle, but is distinctly above that of a yeoman, although men like the Franklin might be of very humble origin.[25] That yeomen were thought of as having a special status in the agrarian society of the fourteenth century is quite evident from the ridiculous pretensions of the miller in the Reeve's Tale, "deynous Symkyn," who married the illegitimate daughter of the local parson whom he regarded as a girl of "noble kyn." She was also raised in a nunnery and hence a virgin suitable for a man of his own elevated estate:

> For Symkyn wolde no wyf, as he sayde,
> But she were wel ynorissed and a mayde,
> To saven his estaat of yomanrye.
> (3947–3948)

He is extremely sensitive about his status, which entailed "Greet sokene . . . of al the land aboute," actually a privilege enjoyed not because of his estate but because of his spectacular success as a thief. Thus when he hears Alayn's revelations concerning that enterprising clerk's treatment of his daughter, he thinks of the jeopardy in which his lineage has been placed at once:

> "A, false traitour! false clerk," quod he,
> Thow shalt be deed, by Goddes dignitee!
> Who dorste be so bold to disparage
> My doghter, that is com of swich lynage?"
> (4269–4272)

His wife has been "disparaged" in the same way, if we assume, that is, as the miller seems to do, that yeomen like himself belong to a higher estate than clerks. Chaucer is probably here trying to keep before the audience certain scriptural and ecclesiastical concepts of lineage suggested by the Reeve's prologue and elaborated at the beginning of the tale, which considerably enhance the humor of the situation. But if we keep our attention centered on the letter, which is amusing enough, since the mutual admiration between the miller and the parson with reference to lineage is ridiculous, it becomes evident that there are bad yeomen as well as good ones, and that comparative wealth in peasant society, as in any other, does not necessarily imply virtue in Chaucer's mind. This miller, like the Miller in the General Prologue, would ordinarily be ranked among the regular servants of a manor, or as a very humble servant of a lord who owned a mill, a man whose status was high only from a village point of view.

To return once more to the Knight's Yeoman, there has been some tendency to view him in relation to the *cursus honorum* at the royal court, which described the following ranks in ascending order: esquire, yeoman, knight-bachelor. But this system had no relevance to life in the countryside and was largely outdated at court in the later fourteenth century. As Denholm-Young points out, "the feudal squire did not become a yeoman, who was socially beneath him, nor did the yeoman become a squire."[26] In royal circles a yeoman might be a man of relatively high rank. Not only was the Black Prince's master cook a yeoman, but his steward in Devon and Cornwall could be called "the Prince's yeoman" also, although he was sheriff of Cornwall.[27] The Canon's Yeoman, to mention another yeoman in Chaucer, was probably a man of some substance among the humble, who had become the chief servant of the Canon. Thus the word *yeoman* meant different things in different contexts. In a similar way a sheriff is a "royal bailiff," although he appointed lesser "bailiffs" to serve him. Looking forward to the sixteenth century, the word *yeoman* came to be used as we have seen for important men beneath the rank of gentleman in the country, but this development probably took place because independent husbandmen had become more numerous and more prosperous. The forester in green who accompanies the Knight is a manorial servant, a "yeoman" by virtue of the fact that his industry and efficiency in faithful service have made him a man above his fellows. He could, we are told, "dresse his takel yemanly," a fact suggestive of a certain manual expertise. Local lords, as well as great ones, customarily affected great panoply and display in their travels, taking with them large and sumptuous household staffs. But the Knight has no steward, clerk, or other court official in his train:

A Yeman hadde he, and servantz namo
At that tyme, for him liste ride so.
(101-102)

The bow and arrows of his servant may be a reminder of the triumphs of English archers in the field, a memory that produced regulations encouraging the practice of archery among the people at large as late as

1388.[28] And the fact that the Knight rides with this modest retinue is a further testimony to his "meakness" or humility.

One of the more common regular servants on a demesne was the dairy assistant, who was usually, although not always, a woman. She was not a formidable character like a reeve, hayward, or reap-reeve, and Chaucer treats his exemplar, the "povre wydwe" of the Nun's Priest's Tale, with sympathy. She is a cottager, which means that she ranks among the poorer members of the peasant hierarchy, below virgaters or half-virgaters, although she is relatively well provided with three sows, three cows, a ewe, which probably furnished milk, and seven hens governed by a cock. Her "broun breed" may indicate that she had an allowance of rye or mixed grain from the manor as well as her stipend as a "maner deye" and her wages. The *daya* was often assisted by dairymaids, who may here be represented by the widow's two daughters. Aside from milking and, at times, looking after domestic fowl, the chief task she engaged in was the manufacture of cheese and butter, both of which were by modern standards heavily salted. Cheese was often among the commodities either used by the lord and his *familia* or sold by the reeve, and in some areas it formed an important item in manorial production, since English cheeses were much esteemed in the fourteenth century, even in France. In some areas, the *daya* not only managed the dairy but was responsible for winnowing. As late as the eighteenth century it was possible to see women winnowing in the fields of Devon, and in Chaucer's time they must have been a fairly common sight.[29] Those who wish to see the widow as a figure for the Church will be happy to know that one of her duties was to separate the chaff, which the Priest tells us to disregard, from the grain.

Chaucer seems to be especially impressed by the simple and temperate diet of his *daya*, which in his mind, combined with "exercise," afforded by the production of cheeses weighing about eight pounds and winnowing, protected her from the dangers of "reppleccioun" and "apoplexie." But the consumption of milk, coarse bread, "seynd bacoun," whatever that was, and an occasional egg or two without any kind of "poynant sauce" was not "typical" of peasant fare, which, among other things, included large quantities of ale supplied by village ale-wives. Chaucer is making a moral point as well as a dietary one, for his more admirable characters are, unlike that old gourmet the Franklin, abstemious. Thus another peasant, Griselda, a poor shepherdess, drank "ofter of the welle than of the tonne" (215) and worked hard from dawn to bedtime. Given aristocratic status, she becomes adept at settling disputes among her people (430-434), and even, in the absence of her lord, at pronouncing "juggementz" of "greet equitee" (439). Another poor cottager, once more a widow, appears in the Friar's Tale. The literal-minded and unscrupulous summoner who persecutes her, a petty and avaricious tyrant like the Reeve, seizes her "newe panne," which would have been among her most valuable possessions. Thus an inventory of the goods of a deceased Worcester peasant of 1346 valued his cart at 7d, his plow at 4d, but his brass pot was worth 2s 4d, and his brass pan 1s.[30] The stupidly vainglorious and avaricious parson of the Reeve's Tale, who "yaf many a panne of bras" to Symkyn with his daughter, was, in peasant terms, bestowing considerable wealth upon his "noble" son-in-law. Earthenware pots were cheap and plentiful, but a pan was valuable. In the Friar's Tale, Chaucer's sympathies are clearly with the widow, who succeeds finally in settling the fate of her tormentor.

If we look back on the evidence adduced above it becomes clear that Chaucer was not, in any modern sense of the word, "class-conscious." He judged his characters on the basis of their moral qualities and on their abilities to contribute to the coherence of community life with self-restraint and industry. The Reeve and the Miller are crude characters, but they are no worse than the Man of Law or the Franklin.[31] Meanwhile, much detailed study of agrarian life remains to be done, and when we leave the manors and villages to consider the shires and their lesser "gentry" we are even more in the dark. Chaucerians must wait upon historians to make the connotations of much of Chaucer's ordinary language vivid and meaningful. Without their works, we must rely on our own experience in a very different kind of society, with its own values and ideals, and this can do nothing but lead us astray, especially if we regard Chaucer's characters as being "realistic."

VI

Leonardo da Vinci, "Virgin of the Rocks." Alinari/Art Reference Bureau/
Editorial Photocolor Archives, Inc.

In Foraminibus Petrae: A Note on Leonardo's "Virgin of the Rocks"

❧

The commentary of William of Newburgh on the Canticum has now been edited by John C. Gorman, S.M. (Fribourg, 1960). For the relevant passage, see pp. 133-138. Although historians of art have generally been less reluctant than literary historians to consult exegetical sources, there are still those who think that almost any cultural product of the Renaissance is likely to be "pagan" or to contain "pagan mysteries."

❧

CRITICS have encountered considerable difficulty in explaining the setting of Leonardo's "Virgin of the Rocks." Thus Ludwig H. Heydenreich asserts, "Das Bild schildert kein Ereignis der biblischen Geschichte."[1] A background of apocryphal or legendary material has been postulated and denied.[2] Although biblical history offers no explanation for the rocks, a very simple and obvious source appears in conventional biblical exegesis. A convention arose in the twelfth century whereby the *Sponsa* in the Canticum could be taken as the Blessed Virgin as well as the Church, and this attitude persisted in Catholic countries well after the time of Leonardo.[3] Thus Canticles 2:13-14 was read as an injunction to the Virgin: *Surge, amica mea, speciosa mea, et veni, columba mea, in foraminibus petræ, in caverna maceriæ.*

As an example of the kind of analysis to be expected from commentators on these verses, I quote excerpts from that given by Martin Del'Rio, whose very full treatment of the Canticum was published in 1604.[4] His material on the passage is derived from the twelfth-century commentary of William of Newburgh[5] and therefore represents a tradition which began much earlier than Leonardo and persisted after his death. After explaining that *petra* is a sign for Christ, he continues,

> Abundat enim foraminibus, quibus omnes intrare volentes, suscipit, continet, & continendo implet: porro ipsa non impletur, quia si [Psalms 48:3] *omnes terrigenæ & filij hominum, simul in unum dives & pauper* vellent intrare, non deessent foramina quibus reciperentur,

imo & superabundarent. . . . Columbæ vt accipitrem effugiant, in petræ foramina se recipiunt, & ibi nidulantur. Inter has columbas spirituales MARIA est *columba* columbarum: illi quam cæteris, altior profundiorque nidus, seu cubile fuit in *petra*, quam ipsa peperit, quæ de ipsa fuit [Daniel 2:45] *sine hominis manu abscissa.* Sed quæ *maceria?* Vineæ Domini Zaboath ex lapidum congerie munimentum. *Vinea* hæc sunt electi, eorum *maceria* sunt custodes Angeli, de quibus Apostolus [Hebrews 1:14] *Omnes sunt administratorij spiritus, in minis- terium missi, propter eos qui hæreditatem capiunt salutis.* Verum ista *maceria* continua non est, sed multis interrupta locis, habet, propter angelicas ruinas, multiplicem *cauernam.* . . . Nullus vnquam mor- talium tot virtutibus insignis, tam dives meritis fuit, quam pia mater Saluatoris. Ipsa *in foraminibus petræ* habitauit propter se, ipsa *in cauerna maceriæ* propter alios. . . .[6]

The openings in the rock are refuges for the faithful in Christ, and the cavern or caverns are vacancies in the wall of the Lord's Vineyard. Both are said to be appropriate places for the Blessed Virgin, who is, in fact, specifically invited to appear there.

Although critics have sometimes been reluctant to find conven- tional Christian ideas in the painting,[7] it is probable that Leonardo's rocks like Lochner's rose arbor were deliberately contrived so that their departure from historical meaning would call the observer's at- tention to symbolic meanings.[8] There is no need to assume that Leonardo knew William of Newburgh's gloss; ideas similar to those it contains had been current for some time. Almost any interpretation which takes the *Sponsa* as the Virgin, glosses the rock as Christ. Other features of the picture are probably symbolic also. Thus the stream coming down from the mountainous rock in the distance and what appears to be a pool in the immediate foreground may well have been suggested by Canticles 4:15: *Fons hortorum, puteus aquarum viventium, quæ fluunt impetu de Libano.* Liban is usually taken to mean Christ, and the water is the Water of Life which has connotations like baptism, grace, and so on.[9] Its presence in this picture would certainly not be inappropriate, especially in view of the presence of St. John. In the pic- ture the Virgin has put down the Christ child and seems ready to take up John into her lap. As Kenneth Clark observes, John here "typifies the human race in need of protection."[10] While Christ holds up his hand in benediction, the angel looks toward the observer and points emphatically at John as if to suggest a relation between the two. All this combines to make a perfectly reasonable *sententia.* Having allowed Christ to go from her, the Virgin is ready to receive the observer if through baptism and the grace of Christ he will seek protection with her *in foraminibus petræ, in caverna maceriæ*. It should be remembered that the *Sponsa* is also the Church, and that the injunction *veni, columba mea, in foraminibus petræ* applies to individual members of the Church as well as to the Virgin.[11]

Sidney's Metaphor of the Ulcer

꘏

The quoted remarks of Puttenham, Nashe, and Heywood, not to mention Sidney's own observations, imply a belief in Divine Providence. They are relevant, I believe, to Shakespeare's tragedies, which, in accordance with both medieval and Renaissance conventions, demonstrate the ill consequences of the protagonist's subjection to Fortune.

꘏

IN the introduction to his *Elizabethan Critical Essays*, G. G. Smith indicates that "Sidney's metaphor of the ulcer discovers a trace of that Italian tradition which expresses the original medical sense of κάθαρσις."[1] The passage under consideration is a part of the famous defense of tragedy in the *Apologie for Poetrie*, where Sidney wrote:

> So that the right vse of Comedy will (I thinke) by no body be blamed, and much lesse of the high and excellent Tragedy, that openeth the greatest wounds, and sheweth forth the Vlcers that are couered with Tissue; that maketh Kinges feare to be Tyrants, and Tyrants manifest their tirannicall humors; that, with sturring the affects of admiration and commiseration, teacheth the vncertainety of this world, and vpon how weake foundations guilden roofes are builded. . . .[2]

It seems to me that the association of Italian Renaissance interpretations of catharsis with this passage is definitely misleading; Sidney's meaning can be explained much more conveniently in terms of conventional Elizabethan literary theory, without reference to obscure or remote sources.

One cannot be quite certain of what is meant by "the original medical sense of κάθαρσις,"[3] but it is possible to examine the discussions of the Italian interpreters who contributed to the so-called "medical" tradition. The first modern discussion of catharsis of which we have any record is that of G. B. Casalio which appears in his *De tragoedia et comoedia lucubratio*.[4] Since it utilizes the noun *purgatio* to render κάθαρσις, it may be loosely termed "medical."[5] Casalio explained the purgation as a threefold operation: (1) tragedy inures the spectators to calamity; (2) it teaches them what are the proper circumstances under which they should indulge in pity and fear; (3) it shows the common fate of all humanity and thus reconciles the spectators to their own misfortunes.[6] Exactly the same explanation occurs in the first modern commentary on the text of the *Poetics*, that of Robortello.[7] In his *Discorsi*, G. B. Giraldi Cintio held that tragedy, by means of the pitiful and the terrible, purges the spectator of vices and conduces to virtue.[8] What is supposedly one of the first instances of a "pathological" interpretation of catharsis appeared in Giovanni della Casa's great courtesy book, *Il Galateo*. Della Casa found that the lamentation inspired by tragedies is efficacious in healing grief.[9] An interpretation involving a purgation of the emotions themselves rather than of the spectator was advanced in Pietro Vettori's commentary on the *Poetics*. Vettori used the word *purgatio*; however, he did not mean by it a "clearing away" of pity and fear, but a moderation of these passions and of others which are evil only in excess.[10] One of the most frequently cited "medical" interpretations is that in A. S. Minturno's *Arte Poetica*,[11] but it should be observed that Minturno merely compared the effect of tragedy to a homeopathic medical treatment;[12] he did not explain the purgation in terms of the medical theories of his time but simply elaborated the first and third points of the process described by Casalio and Robortello, whom, incidentally, he refrained from mentioning.[13] A more plausibly "medical" explanation was offered in M. Antonio Scaino's edition of the *Politics*. Scaino assumed that the emotions were related to the humours in Aristotle's writings, and that the result of the tragic catharsis is a feeling of relief and calm. Tragedy is said to moderate the excess of the disturbing humour, but this effect is brought about "*col mezzo del soave parlare.*"[14] These are the most important "medical" explanations of catharsis before 1581. It seems impossible to me to read them, either individually or collectively in some sort of "tradition," into Sidney's statement that tragedy "sheweth forth the Vlcers that are couered with Tissue."

Before considering the literary theory underlying the metaphor of the ulcer, let us try to determine what the metaphor itself means. Fortunately, it occurs elsewhere in Elizabethan literature. Lyly's *Euphues* describes his warm but unrevealed love in the following words:

> Well, well, seeing the wound that bleedeth inwarde is most daungerous, that the fire kepte close burneth most furious, that the Oouen dammed vp baketh soonest, that sores hauing no vent fester inwardly, it is high time to vnfolde my secret loue, to my secrete friende.[15]

In this case the "wound" is Euphues' love, and it is the more painful for being concealed. Again, in the address "To the Gentlemen of the Inns of Court" which prefaces Lodge's *Alarum against Usurers*, the author, who is about to expose the secret devices of certain Elizabethan racketeers, remarks, "I thought good in opening the wound to prevent an ulcer."[16] In other words, he hoped to put a stop to a hidden evil by exposing it. Another relevant passage appears in the *Misfortunes of Arthur*:

> I neuer yet sawe hurt so smoothly heald,
> But that the skarre bewraid the former wound:
> Yea, where the salue did soonest close the skinne,
> The sore was oftner couered vp than cur'de:
> Which festering deepe and filde within, at last
> With sodaine breach grew greater than at first.
> What then for mindes, which haue reuenging moodes,
> And ne'r forget the crosse they forced beare:
> Whereto if reconcilement come, it makes
> The t'one secure, whiles t'other workes his will.
> Attonement sield defeates, but oft deferres
> Reuenge: beware a reconciled foe.[17]

All of these passages obviously stress the danger of concealed maladjustments. But in what sense does tragedy, opening the wounds and showing the ulcers within, reveal such maladjustments? And what are the evils Sidney had in mind?

The answers to these questions are to be found in the conventional Elizabethan conception of tragedy. Puttenham, in accounting for the origin of tragedy, tells us that in ancient times great men succumbed to "lusts and licentiousness of life," and that after they were dead and no longer to be feared

> their infamous life and tyrannies were layd open to all the world, their wickednes reproched, their follies and extreme insolencies derided, and their miserable ends painted out in playes and pageants to shew the mutabilitie of fortune, and the iust punishment of God in reuenge of vicious and euill life.[18]

Nashe wrote in his *Pierce Penilesse* that "Playes . . . shew the ill success of treason, the fall of hastie climbers, the wretched end of vsurpers, the miserie of ciuill dissention, and how iust God is euermore in punishing of murther."[19] And Thomas Heywood wrote that "if we present a tragedy, we include the fatall and abortive ends of such as commit notorious murders, which is aggravated and acted with all the art that may be to terrifie men from the like abhorred practises."[20] These selections are fairly typical, I think, of Elizabethan apology for the stage, according to which the chief function of tragedy is the exposure of the previously unknown criminal activities of the tragic personages and of their subsequent punishment, to the end that the spectators may be discouraged from pursuing such activities themselves.

Sidney's "wounds" are thus the crimes presented on the stage; and the metaphor of the ulcer refers to the content of tragedy, not to its effect. His remarks on the effect of tragedy immediately following the metaphor simply reflect, like those of Puttenham, Nashe, and Heywood, the commonplace notion that plays should act as *exempla*, an idea which Sidney himself dwelt upon in the course of his discussion of the relative merits of poetry and history. There he observed that "if euill men come to the stage, they euer goe out (as the Tragedie Writer answered to one that misliked the shew of such persons) so manacled as they little animate folkes to followe them."[21] Aristotle certainly never thought of the tragic stage as a gallery of rogues.

A Medievalist Looks at Hamlet

᳅

This essay is based on a lecture delivered from notes before an undergraduate audience. In writing it out I have kept the lecture form and maintained the general style, omitting extensive documentation containing elaborate references to both primary and secondary sources. With reference to the latter, for example, there are valuable materials in Eleanor Prosser's Hamlet and Revenge *(2nd ed., Stanford, 1971). My own views are more extreme than hers, and differ in detail, although I should like to commend her highly for her careful research in primary sources and for her willingness to take seriously what she found there. The attitude adopted here was first formed many years ago and is in part a reaction against popular views of* Hamlet *that seek to make the protagonist admirable, in spite of the fact that he is an obvious moral weakling and an unrepentant felon, or to make him sympathetically "understandable" as an innocent adolescent in search of "identity." Shakespeare would have been completely unable to understand the latter view, since it reflects a peculiarly modern problem; the former would have been grossly repugnant to his sensibilities and inconsistent with attitudes toward tragedy current in his time. It is unfortunate that the morality of Shakespeare's tragedies has often been misunderstood since the shortsighted and historically inaccurate observations of Dr. Johnson, and today we suffer also from a reaction against nineteenth-century literalism and hypocrisy that makes it difficult for us to understand, much less to sympathize with, the moral principles embraced, often with surprising enthusiasm, by our medieval and Renaissance ancestors in Western Europe. These were frequently classical in origin, although transformed by attitudes that were then thought to be distinctively Christian. Above all, we should be aware of the fact that such principles were then practical, not merely theoretical, and necessary to the preservation of a reasonably livable social environment, however they may differ from views about human nature and society fashionable today.*

᳅

I SHOULD like to say at the outset that I am a medievalist, not a Renaissance scholar, and that I have used only very obvious sources in support of what I have to say here. Perhaps because of my background, not to mention certain prejudices widely attributed to me,

Shakespeare's play looks very different to me from the picture of it usually developed by Renaissance scholars and literary critics. In the first place, the idea that a prince who is obviously a murderer and a schemer and whose actions allow his kingdom to fall into the hands of its traditional enemy should be made into a hero, even into a type of "modern man," suggests to me both a very un-Elizabethan sentimentality on the part of modern readers and some rather odd conclusions about "modern man." It is true that "modern man," as the news media daily reveal, is scheming and murderous enough, and that murders, unlike their Elizabethan predecessors, now go unhanged, their punishment being frequently mitigated for "psychiatric" reasons, or temporary insanity, which means that they were very angry at the time of the crime or did not know what they were doing. They are not even relegated to God's justice, which Elizabethans thought to be providentially inevitable in life and vividly illustrated in exemplary fashion in tragedies. Providence and God's justice are no longer much in vogue, but they were very much in fashion during Shakespeare's lifetime.

Moreover, Elizabethans were peculiarly sensitive about the integrity of their kingdom, and were very anxious to avoid civil strife of the kind vividly illustrated in the old tragedy of *Gorbuduc*, admired by Sidney, and in Shakespeare's *King Lear*. They were also fearful of foreign domination. Both seemed to threaten them continuously. They were, moreover, anxious and sensitive about the problem of succession, for the Queen had no heir and wisely refused to make known any decision she may have made about the matter in order to avoid dissent. Meanwhile, the specter of Spanish rule was raised once more by the disgruntled and rebellious Earl of Essex. In fact, Elizabethans were probably much more concerned about the fate of the Danish kingdom in the play, and much less concerned about what we are pleased to call the "personalities" of the characters, than we are.

At the opening of the play we are introduced to two rival kingdoms, Denmark and Norway, in both of which the king's nephew is heir to the throne. The Norwegian nephew, Fortinbras, is busily seeking to enlarge his dominions, while the Danish nephew has been studying at a university. We are in Denmark, and this is the kingdom whose fortunes we are to witness. The elder Hamlet of Denmark, we learn, had won a well-deserved reputation as a warrior. Not only was he successful against the Poles, but had enlarged his domain at the expense of the elder Fortinbras, whom he had killed in the process. Now the younger Fortinbras is seeking to regain these lost lands "by strong hand," or by force. Hence the careful watch at Elsinore, and hence the

uneasiness over the portent of the Ghost. Horatio thinks of portents in
Rome before the fall of Julius, although he recognizes the widely held
view that portents are the work of the Devil. In this connection, he
points out that the Ghost leaves at dawn, and he seconds the view of
Marcellus, at least tentatively, that unwholesome spirits cannot walk
during the nights before Christmas. Marcellus later fears that the
trouble may be "something rotten" in the state of Denmark itself, a
fear hardly alleviated by Horatio's reminder of Providence: "Heaven
will direct it." The Devil, as everyone knew, can do nothing contrary
to the will of God and serves only as a salutary testing agent, however
he may seek to inspire vicious conduct.

That something is indeed curious in Denmark is revealed immediately, for Claudius, the recently deceased King Hamlet's brother,
rather than his son, is King, and has, with the advice of the Council,
although with dubious propriety, married the natural heir's mother.
Since young Hamlet is obviously of age when we meet him, being
about thirty years old near the end of the play, we wonder why he was
not chosen King, and what he was doing still lingering at a university.
He is a somewhat suspicious character from the beginning. At the
close of the play, although young Fortinbras has long since abandoned
his attack on Denmark, the kingdom, like a rotten plum, falls into his
hands, without any effort on his part. Whose fault was that? I am sure
that the Elizabethans asked this question, and that we should ask it
ourselves. They would undoubtedly have been astonished, moreover,
by young Hamlet's obvious immersion in private problems and by his
clear lack of concern for the welfare of the state and for his future
subjects.

Before we consider the character of Hamlet I should like to digress
briefly on a number of topics. First of all, the modern concept of "personality" was completely unknown in the sixteenth century. The
Greeks had no such concept, and no word for it; in scholastic Latin,
personalitas, a word unknown in Classical Latin, meant simply the
quality of being a man as distinct from being an animal. During the
eighteenth century the word "personality" came to mean the sum of
the characteristics of an individual, and in the nineteenth century it became a reified abstraction with depths, force, and, eventually, the host
of problems, difficulties, and aberrations, which you, who have these
little things somewhere inside you, now know very well. Any psy-
chologist can tell you all about them. You may say, "Oh, but
Elizabethans had them, even if they didn't mention them!" I can assure
you that they belong to the world of words, not to the world of
things, and that Elizabethans were just as innocent of them as they

were of Newton's law of attraction, which was once applied to almost every conceivable subject by eighteenth-century intellectuals. The theories you entertain will pass too, unless the human mind stagnates and everybody believes what he is told.

What our ancestors had instead of personalities, which are, after all, "ghosts," were characters and immortal souls. You may think that the latter are "ghosts" too, but this attitude will not help you to understand your ancestors. Leaving souls aside, characters were combinations of moral qualities that manifested themselves in word and action. People did not then have "depths" or subconscious minds; you knew them in accordance with what they did and said. Their characters were determined, they thought, by the state of the humors or by the result of some kind of persistent activity, unless some physical injury rendered them incompetent. In considering *Hamlet* we should dismiss this last consideration from our minds, since no character in the play is hopelessly incompetent physically. To their way of thinking unbalanced humors or persistent habits of life, like too much study, were not excuses for irrational behavior; for every man is endowed with reason, the general remedy for original sin, which brought sickness into the world. The reason was the prince, so to speak, that ruled the appetites and passions, and princes had a greater obligation than other persons to be reasonable or wise, and to govern their appetites and passions well. The analogy between the human body and the commonwealth, both of which should be governed by reason, was common, and is reflected in Laertes' words of warning to Ophelia about Hamlet's obligations. When passion or appetite dominated reason in an individual, the result was what was called "division" or inner warfare, and exactly the same thing among individuals could produce "division" in a kingdom.

The general frame of reference within which these ideas were developed was the philosophy of Christianity as it was then understood. I do not mean "scholastic philosophy" specifically, for this is only one largely academic branch of Christian philosophy, not much relished by humanists like Petrarch, Ficino, and Erasmus, or even by Queen Elizabeth, a devout woman who, unlike her father, disliked legalistic-sounding discussions of Divinity. Her subjects either went to church, where they often listened to homilies she prescribed, or paid a fine. And she thought that non-Christians could not possibly be good citizens. Shakespeare, who showed no inclination to pursue fancy Italian "advanced" manners, or to become an "Italianate Englishman" as the phrase went, died a substantial and respected member of his church at Stratford. It is true that certain "pagan" writings were much relished by Elizabethans, especially those of Cicero and Seneca. But I suggest that those who think that this "paganism" meant something like being freely "human" as we understand that term and dancing merrily on the greensward dressed in cheesecloth in the Spring take a good hard look at Cicero *On Friendship*, *On Old Age*, or, above all, at *The Offices*, a copy of which Elizabeth's counselor Lord Burghley, whom she called her "Spirit," used to carry in his bosom. Or try Seneca *On Benefits*, a very influential work. The more advanced may find consolation among the Greeks, in Aristotle's *Ethics*, in Plutarch's *Moral Essays*, or in Plato. Elizabethans also liked Virgil, Horace, Juvenal, and, above all, Ovid, who because of his wit had not yet become the "dirty poet" the nineteenth century made out of him. But all these things, as well as others from Antiquity, were read with a keen eye to the New Testament, especially to St. Paul, so that readers might mine from them "Egyptian Gold" for the Lord as both St. Augustine and Erasmus, in his popular *Enchiridion*, recommended.

I think that no one familiar with commonplace Christian ideas can fail to recognize in Hamlet obvious symptoms of what was called Sloth, the first of the vices to follow Pride in her procession in Spenser's *Faerie Queene*, and the "nurse" of all the rest (1.4.18-20). "Idleness," wrote Burton, "is the evil genius of our nation," so that this is no trivial matter of small interest to Shakespeare's audience. Sloth was not mere laziness, although it could be that, but a vice with spiritual as well as physical manifestations. Chaucer's Parson, who will do as a reasonably conventional authority, defines sloth as "angwish of troubled herte," which sounds like melancholy, and it is indeed true that melancholy was an attribute of sloth. The slothful man, the Parson tells us, does not wish to do any good thing but falls into despair, an aspect of the irremissible sin against the Holy Spirit, or God's love, which was conventionally exemplified in the person of the suicidal Judas. Sloth, the Parson continues, leads to "rechelessness." It is, moreover, the "bilge" of all wicked and villainous thoughts, which result in babbling, trifling and "alle ordure." Finally, it produces "worldly sorrow" or *tristitia*, which slays a man, for he becomes "anoyed of his owene lif." Failure to perform good works was thought of as a kind of disobedience to God, and those who were thus disobedient were said to find God's creatures noxious and disobedient to them. I know that all this sounds strange, since "the anguish of a troubled heart" was intensely cultivated by the romantics, became a fashionable existentialist posture, and is still thought of frequently as being a mark of sensitivity and sophistication. But it was not highly valued by Elizabethan Christians, and Shakespeare's melancholy characters should all be regarded with suspicion. There is something wrong, not with their "personalities," but with their moral attitudes. Perhaps I should add at once that vicious persons were to be regarded with pity, since a malady of the spirit was thought to be far worse than a malady of the flesh. But a reasonable man did not want to "be like" a vicious person any more than he wanted to be like a man with a broken leg, a severed arm, or a terminal illness.

The remedy for sloth was fortitude, a virtue especially desirable in a prince. Our friend the Parson describes fortitude as an "affeccioun thurgh which a man despiseth anoyouse thinges." It leads to magnanimity, or the willingness to undertake great things wisely and reasonably, to faith, hope, sureness, magnificence, or the performance of great works for small reward, and to constancy or steadfastness. For further information on sloth and its remedy, fortitude, there are some useful materials in Rosemond Tuve's book, *Allegorical Imagery* (Princeton, 1966); and for the princely virtues attendant on fortitude, there are elaborate discussions in Sir Thomas Elyot's *Boke Named the Gouernour*, parts of which I shall quote later.

Is Hamlet slothful? When we first meet him, he is dressed strikingly in black, a little like Spenser's monkish vice, wishing he were dead. The world, he thinks, is an "unweeded garden," because his mother has married Claudius after mourning the death of the elder Hamlet for only a month. Claudius is justified in saying that extended mourning "shows a will most incorrect to heaven." But Hamlet is obviously much more concerned about his mother's marriage than he is either about his father's death or the welfare of the state of Denmark. In fact, he accuses her of lust, certainly a villainous (or perhaps, if there is a difference, Freudian?) thought that the Parson might well have characterized as "bilge," since it is consistent neither with the Commandment "Honor thy Father and Mother," with the reflection of that Commandment in the Elizabethan catechism, nor with the character of Gertrude as we see it in the play. She has acted with obvious innocence, but with questionable judgment, on the advice of her Council; and her chief weakness seems to be an unshakable affection for her son. As for Hamlet, the idea that he should die to escape the unweeded garden of the world, instead of getting busy with his hoe, hardly demonstrates any fortitude. Moreover, by traditional standards, those who think the garden of the world to be hopelessly unweeded probably need a little weeding themselves. Our "hero" is not a very attractive character at the outset, and there is no reason to think that Shakespeare wished to make him so.

Matters do not improve in the fourth and fifth scenes of the first act.

In his remarks on Danish drunkenness Hamlet points out that a natural defect, for which a man is not guilty, or a vicious habit, may ruin a man as well as a kingdom. This is true of a kingdom only if it is not ruled wisely, and of a man only if he abandons his reason. But Hamlet rashly proceeds to confront the Ghost, even if it be a "goblin damned," denying that it can influence his soul, not because his soul is rational, but on the dubious ground that it is immortal, as if there were no immortal souls in Hell. Horatio's warning that he might lose his "sovereignty of reason" is futile, probably because not much of this sovereignty exists in Hamlet. "Desperate with imagination," or without rational control, Hamlet approaches the apparition, which immediately calls for revenge. It accuses Claudius of murder and Gertrude of lust, rather temptingly suggesting that Hamlet leave her "to Heaven," since vengeful action against his own mother, who in any event does not appear to be very lustful, would be difficult, whereas a rather unattractive uncle might be easy prey. Hamlet takes the bait at once, but soon displays those symptoms of sloth that will make him a lackluster avenger as well as a lackluster Prince. Responding to the Ghost's "Remember me," he vows to forget all trivial records and "saws of books," and then, almost in the same breath, proceeds to draw forth his notebook to record the saw, "one may smile and smile and be a villain." And when we meet him again in the second scene of the second act he is reading a book. Although the Ghost demands a vicious course, revenge, Hamlet blithely and foolishly assures Horatio that it is "honest." The passion of revenge only confuses him, leaving him without the possibility of any rational action, and, at the close of the scene he can say only,

> The time is out of joint. O cursed spite
> That ever I was born to set it right!

If anything his slothful malady will now become worse than ever. Lest we seek to excuse him because of the power of the Devil, we should remember the principle that the Devil cannot test a man beyond his own power to resist. If that were not true no man would have freedom of choices, and that is something that only we can take away from ourselves.

Further very strong indications of sloth appear in Hamlet's most famous soliloquy, but before looking at it I should like to digress for a moment to quote a part of Sir Thomas Elyot's discussion of Fortitude (*Gouernour*, 3.9.):

"A man is called in latyne *Vir*, whereof, sayeth Tulli, vertue is named. And the moste propre vertue longynge to a man is fortitude, whereof be two excellent properties, that is to saye, the contempte of dethe and of griefe. But what very fortitude is he more plainly doth declare afterwarde ... sayenge, Thinges humane aught to be little estemed, dethe nat regarded, laboures and griefes to be thought tollerable. Whan this is ratifyed by iugement and a constant oppinion, than that is a valiaunt and stable fortitude. But there unto I wolde shulde be added, whiche oppinion and iugement procedeth of a reason, and nat repugnaunt to Justyce."

Incidentally, Elyot has already explained (3.4) that fraud, lying, including the pretense that something is true that is not, like Hamlet's "antic disposition," deceit, and violence are all contrary to justice, which should be maintained (3.5) even between mortal enemies. Thus, he continues, regarding fortitude, "And than it shal accorde with this sayenge of Aristotelle, A Valiaunt man sustaineth and dothe that which belongeth to fortitude for cause of honestie. And a little before he saieth, A man that is valiaunt as well suffereth as dothe that whiche agreeth with his worship, and as resoun commaundeth. So no violence or sturdye mynde lackynge reson and honestie is any parte of fortitude." Like the other virtues, fortitude is maintained by reason. One of its aspects is patience, which Elyot says (3.11) "is a noble vertue, appertayninge as well to inwarde gouernaunce as to exterior gouernaunce, and is the vainquisshour of iniuries, the suer defence agayne all affectes and passions of the soule, retayninge all wayes glad semblaunt in aduersitie and doloure." As for vengeance, he continues (3.12), "More ouer the best waye to be aduenged is so to contemne Iniurie and rebuke, and lyue with suche honestie, that the doer shall at the laste be therof a shamed, or at the leste, lese the frute of his malyce, that is to say, shall nat reioyce and haue glorie of they hindraunce or domage." This is not to say, of course, that wrongs cannot be righted by law, as indeed they should be.

Although Hamlet at the opening of his soliloquy is not yet sure that Claudius is guilty, having confessed shortly before that the spirit he has seen "may be a devil," he is overcome by *tristitia* and is again thinking about suicide. The alternatives he suggests are whether it is "nobler" to "suffer the slings and arrows of outrageous fortune" or "to take arms against a sea of troubles and by opposing end them." The "opposition" to fortune he has in mind is that favored by Chaucer's Troilus, suicide, evidently a noble action to his way of thinking were it not for the prospect of immortality, which makes him fearful. Nobody, he says, would bear the common burdens of life except for the "dread of something after death." Is it "cowardly" to face life's vicissitudes? On the contrary, as the passages from Elyot we have just read indicate, it is the part of a man to bear them well. There is nothing courageous about slothful despair, and the terms Hamlet uses would have called to mind at once the doctrines of *The Consolation of Philosophy* of Boethius, a work, partly translated by Elizabeth in her youth, whose ideas were widely current and are indeed adduced by Hamlet himself. For in the very next scene he tells Horatio that he is

> A man that Fortune's buffets and rewards
> Hast ta'en with equal thanks; and blest are those
> Whose blood and judgment are so well commeddled
> That they are not a pipe for Fortune's finger
> To sound what stop she please. Give me that man
> That is not passion's slave, and I will wear him
> In my heart's core.

Is he calling Horatio a coward because he suffers misfortune gladly? Horatio, as we shall see, is not quite the man Hamlet thinks he is, but the words serve as a kind of self-comment. His query, "Who would fardels bear?" would have brought to the minds of many in the audience images of Isaac with his faggots and Christ with his Cross. The thoughts in this most famous soliloquy, repeated with awe by a multitude of modern students, were in Shakespeare's time repulsive and deplorable. Christian writers from Minucius Felix onward had insisted that life is a testing in which we are all subjected by Divine consent to adversities that try us. Boethius held that virtue arises from difficulties overcome, and Burton says in his *Anatomy* (1.1.2.2.), "virtue is not virtue unless it has a foe by the conquering of which it shows its merit." Milton in his great defense of the liberty of the press wrote, "I cannot praise a fugitive and cloistered virtue unexercised and unbreathed, that never sallies out and seeks her adversary, but slinks out of the race, where that immortal garland is to be run for [1 Corinthians 9:24], not without dust and heat." He goes on to cite the example of Spenser's Guyon. But Hamlet would like to slink away, never having learned that "the uses of adversity" are "sweet."

Any vice leads to babble, or idle chatter, and sloth as the Parson indicates is especially conducive to babbling and trifling. The underlying idea comes from St. Paul, who said (1 Corinthians 13:1), "Thogh I speake with the tongues of men and Angels, and haue not loue, I am as sounding brasse, or a tinkling cymbal." The Geneva gloss explains, "If the Angels had tonges, and I had the vse thereof, & did not bestowe them to profite my neighbour, it were nothing but vaine babling." Hamlet's brazen notes have so affected those who mistakenly identify themselves with him, after the fashion recommended by nineteenth-century critics, or those who are swayed by empty rhetoric, that they miss the import of what he is saying. What Horatio calls his "wild and whirling words" have often seemed brilliant to the unwary. As Ophelia observes after listening to the loveless and fleering speeches enjoining her to seek a nunnery, his reason is like "sweet bells jangled, out of time and harsh." He is in fact "out of time" with that harmony of Creation Jessica was taught to appreciate in *The Merchant of Venice*.

Shakespeare emphasizes the point by having Hamlet condemn himself in his own advice to the players. How does Hamlet play his own part? He is offended "to the soul" he says, to hear some boisterous fellow "tear a passion to tatters, to very rags." Does he do this? The players, he says, should "suit the action to the word, the word to the action." Does he do this? Does he "strut and bellow"? Referring to the clowns, he says that "there be of them that will themselves laugh, to set some quantity of barren spectators to laugh too, though in the meantime some necessary question of the play be then to be considered." Hamlet, although not ostensibly a clown, certainly does this, not because of a humorous disposition, but because his sloth leads him to malicious sarcasm. Instances abound, including his tasteless barbs at Ophelia at the play, his inconsequential trifling with recorders and vain boasting afterwards, or his sallies at Polonius. He jests inconsequentially about Polonius after murdering him, and again on the same subject when the king is searching for the body. At the graveyard, which should remind him of the need to repent, he jests about painted ladies and speculates idly on the fate of Caesar's clay. At the funeral of Ophelia, far from showing any loving respect, he rushes forward idly boasting, "It is I, Hamlet the Dane!" and grapples with Laertes, claiming to have loved Ophelia better than he did and offering to out-rant him. In his confrontation with Osric, we wonder which fop is more despicable, the genuine one or the one who mocks him when there is "some necessary question to be considered." Hamlet's verbal victims are easy prey, either in person or because of circumstance, and his famed "wit" is a pretentious disguise for weakness, often in the form of malicious railing.

Sloth, as Spenser said, is the nurse of the other vices, and in this instance it makes Hamlet susceptible to wrath in one of its worst forms, the malicious passion for revenge. We are not sure that Claudius is guilty until he reacts near the beginning of the third act to Polonius' remark that "devotion's visage" and "pious action" may "sugar o'er" the Devil himself. Nevertheless, Hamlet, having heard (as Shakespeare may have heard in the story of Alexander Phereus in Plutarch) that tragedies "make mad the guilty and appal the free" so that tyrants proclaim their guilt, cries, "O Vengeance!" and prepares the play *The Murder of Gonzago.* The reaction of the King to this bit of indirection does not, of course, prove his guilt to the court, for in the play the nephew of the player king murders him, not his brother, and the audience generally, if they thought of it at all, had every right to conclude that the play was a veiled threat on Hamlet's part to murder his uncle. It is clear that Hamlet should have used open means to restore order in his kingdom. Elizabethan England, the frame of reference for the audience of Shakespeare's play, was by no means a primitive society ignorant of the kind of gifts bestowed upon Athens by Athena in the *Oresteia.* The English, as Fortescue amply demonstrates, were proud of their laws. The playlet is thus a merely malicious form of trifling, and is directed as much against the Queen as it is against Claudius. But she hardly reacts as a guilty person, for her first words to Hamlet afterward are "Hamlet, thou hast thy father much offended."

Malice was much more contemptible in the sixteenth century than it is today, when its expression is sometimes encouraged by psychiatrists, and it is deliberately fostered by political ideologists and other breeders of controversy. The source of Elizabethan ideas on the subject was St. Paul, whose remarks are worth quoting (Romans 12:16-21). He has just been exhorting his audience to love one another "without dissimulation," and not to be "slouthful to do service": "Be of like affection one towards another: be not hie minded: but make your selues equal to them of the lower sorte: be not wise in your selues. Recompense to no man euil for euil: procure things honest in the sight of all men. If it be possible, asmuche as in you is, haue peace with all men. Dearly beloued, auenge not your selues, but giue place vnto wrath: for it is written, Vengeance is mine: I will repaye, saith the Lord. Therefore, if thine enemie hunger, fede him: if he thirst, giue him drinke: for in so doing, thou shalt heape coles of fyre on his head. Be not ouercome of euil, but ouercome euil with goodness." We may recognize here the source of Elyot's remarks on vengeance, quoted above, and those who are curious may find a very similar idea in Plutarch. The basic principle was not neglected by Queen Elizabeth. Bacon observes that she "settled all matters of the church" during the first year of her reign. One thing she did was to have prepared a set of injunctions for all the churches, and one of these (No. 21) reads, "Forasmuch as variance and contention is a thing that most displeaseth God, and is most contrary to the blessed communion of the body and blood of our savior, Christ, curates shall no wise admit to receiving thereof any of their cure and flock which be openly known to live in sin notorious without repentance, or who hath maliciously and openly contended with his neighbor, unless the same do charitably and openly reconcile himself again, remitting all rancour and malice, whatsoever controversy hath been between them. And nevertheless their just titles and rights they may charitably prosecute before such as have authority to hear the same." This is a kind of echo of her father's last speech before Parliament, wherein he called attention to the love between himself and his subjects, and then castigated them for the lack of charity and concord among them, pointing out that Paul in 1 Corinthians 13 says that "Charity is not envious, Charity is not proud," and accusing them of uncharitable religious controversy. The Temporality, he said, "be not clear and unspotted of malice and envy." They should bring their complaints to "some of our Council," or even to himself. Finally, they should be "in charity with one another, like brother and brother." Hamlet obviously lacks the fortitude to bring his complaint calmly and openly before the Court, and Claudius, as we shall see, is clearly afraid that he might do just that.

Malice, incidentally, was considered to be a chief source of melancholy. Thus Burton, who was a student at Oxford at about the time *Hamlet* was written, having observed that hatred can "subvert whole kingdoms" (*Anatomy*, 1.1.2.3.8), continues,

"This hatred, malice, faction, and desire of revenge, invented first all those racks, and wheels, strappadoes, brazen bulls, feral engines, prisons, inquisitions, severe laws, to macerate and torment one another. How happy might we be, and end our time with blessed days and sweet content, if we could contain ourselves, and, as we ought to do, put up injuries, learn humility, meekness, patience, forget and forgive, as in God's word we are enjoined, compose such small controversies amongst ourselves, moderate our passions in this kind, *and think better of others*, as Paul would have us, *than of ourselves: be of like affection one towards another, and not avenge ourselves, but have peace with all men!* But being that we are so peevish and perverse, insolent and proud, so factious and seditious, so malicious and envious, we do by turns harass, maul and vex one another, torture, disquiet, and precipitate ourselves into that gulf of woes and cares, aggravate our misery and melancholy, heap upon us hell and eternal damnation."

That is an admirable piece of Baroque prose, and it makes its point well.

We should not forget that in Shakespeare's time Christianity was still a religion of love, not of righteousness, except perhaps among some extreme Puritans or other grim Old Testament literalists. Love reasonably directed is charity; love directed toward oneself or self-satisfaction through a creature is cupidity. Shakespeare's comedies for the most part cheerfully demonstrate the triumph of reasonable love, a theme consistent with what Jonson called his "open and free nature"; his tragedies exhibit the destructive powers of malice, which is inverted love, the worst part of any vice. I know that the tragedies have been called "pagan," and that their protagonists have turned into heroes; but "paganism" would have been both impossible and stupid in an Elizabethan context. Jonson says that Shakespeare's flights "did take *Eliza*," to whom either paganism or malice would have been anathema. Malice was commonly regarded as something to be at all costs avoided, even though some did not succeed. Thus William Fleetwood, Recorder of London, was expressing a very common opinion when he wrote to Lord Burghley, "I thank God from all my heart I have never used any man living with malicious dealing." Not all men succeeded in avoiding it, but at least they knew that they should try. Every subject learned in Elizabeth's catechism the line "To bear no malice nor hatred in my heart."

Is Hamlet malicious? His malice toward his mother is evident from the beginning, but he maliciously abuses almost everyone who crosses his path. Thus Ophelia reports that he came to her with jacket unlaced, hatless, his stockings falling down, his knees knocking, and then, as she says,

> He took me by the wrist and held me hard;
> Then goes he to the length of all his arm,
> And, with his other hand thus o'er his brow,
> He falls to such perusal of my face
> As he would draw it. Long stay'd he so.
> At last, a little shaking of mine arm,
> And thrice his head thus waving up and down,
> He rais'd a sigh so piteous and profound
> As it did seem to shatter all his bulk
> And end his being. That done, he lets me go,
> And with his head over his shoulder turn'd
> He seem'd to find his way without his eyes,
> For out o' doors he went without their help
> And to the last bended their light on me.

This sorry performance, a part of his "antic disposition," is a deliberate and malicious abuse of a woman he is supposed to love. His letter reported in the next scene to "the most beautified Ophelia" is even

worse, a "satirical" insult. He treats her with contempt after his soliloquy, greeting her.

> Nymph, in thy orisons
> Be all my sins remembered,

as though she were persecuting him and maliciously complaining
about his shortcomings to God. In the midst of a flood of abuse, he
says, "I did love you once." Did he? His jests at the play are hardly acts
of love. He will, of course, claim to love her again later, but poor
Ophelia is merely a pawn to his darker purposes. And this is not
"madness," for Hamlet is soon explaining to Guildenstern that he is
not actually mad.

His treatment of his mother is equally rash, maliciously inept, and
deliberately hypocritical:

> Let me be cruel, not unnatural;
> I will speak daggers to her, but use none.
> My tongue and soul in this be hypocrites:
> How in my words somever she be shent,
> To give them seals never, my soul, consent!

Can a man be deliberately cruel to his mother and not unnatural? I
hardly think so. When he so affrights her that she calls for help,
Polonius reveals his presence behind the arras, and Hamlet (with
princely courage, shall we say?) draws his sword and thrusts it
through a man who cannot see him and whose identity is unknown to
him. He was hoping to kill Claudius, but it should be understood that
through Hamlet's own negligence Claudius is still King, and that
Hamlet's act would have constituted treason. Our courageous and
noble prince proceeds at once to go to work on his mother, maligning
the father of his beloved Ophelia and seeking to demonstrate with the
aid of a picture that his natural father was a better-looking man than
Claudius and hence a more worthy object of her cupidity. He should
be concerned about the state, not about his mother's taste in male
flesh, which is not only irrelevant but not, in Gertrude, a great sin.
Sexual pleasure with a husband is ordinarily a venial, not a deadly sin,
and Gertrude is clearly no lusty young wench. But he succeeds in confusing her, denies emphatically that he is mad, and proceeds at once
with obvious relish to plot against the lives of his best friends, Rosencrantz and Guildenstern. He has, in effect, debased and dishonored his
Queen and mother by committing murder in her presence, by accusing her of indiscriminate lust, and by openly plotting a deadly and
malicious stratagem.

But this behavior is entirely consistent with what precedes it. For Claudius, thinking himself alone, tries to pray. The King, whatever else he may be, is not a complete fool. He knows that he has committed the sin of Cain by murdering his own brother, that, as a widely current saying attributed to St. Augustine had it, there can be no absolution without restitution, and that he cannot give up his kingdom and thus cannot repent. The New Law of Christ promises mercy to those who are repentant, but none to those who are not. Thus his prayers are mere words, and "Words without thoughts never to heaven go." Hamlet, who has been long at the university, should be equally aware of these principles, but, approaching Claudius from behind with his usual intrepid courage he thinks to kill him. The possibility that Claudius, caught in prayer, might go to heaven, however, stays his hand. And with almost unbelievable malice, he hopes to catch the King and kill him drunk, in rage, in bed with the Queen, or swearing at gambling, in order, he thinks, to send him straight to Hell. Decisions concerning the destiny of the soul are, of course, beyond human power, and Hamlet is being silly. But beyond this, his meditations show a callous disrespect for his mother and a contemptible and inveterate malice. Perhaps the Parson's word "ordure" is more appropriate here than "bilge."

The same malice exactly is directed against Rosencrantz and Guildenstern, his friends and unwitting pawns of the King. He sends them off to England to be killed, "not shriving time allowed." Thus he thinks to damn them. With his usual false heroics, he boasts to Horatio,

> Why, man, they did make love to this employment.
> They are not near my conscience; their defeat
> Does by their own insinuation grow.
> 'Tis dangerous when the baser nature comes
> Between the fell and incensed points
> Of mighty opposites.

Horatio, who, if he had been entirely honest, should have objected to this piece of obdurate malice, simply says, "Why, what a king is this!" What a king, indeed! A man who murders his best friends for no good cause, hoping to slay their souls as well, and then denies any repentance for his deed, certainly deserves something. Perhaps it is relevant to point out that impenitence is an attribute of sloth, and that it constitutes the worst sin of all, the irremissible sin against the Holy Spirit, or God's love.

Malice quite naturally leads to the stratagems of worldly wisdom, most strikingly illustrated by Shakespeare in the person of Iago, who knew well how to love himself, or thought he did, and tried to make the Will assisted by worldly wisdom the gardener of the body. But Iago has his cousins in *Hamlet*, and, in fact, no male character in the play with the exceptions of Rosencrantz, Guildenstern, and Fortinbras, is free of it. Francis Bacon, taking his title from St. Paul, "Of Wisdom for a Man's Self," has this, in part, to say of it: "Wisdom for a man's self is, in many branches thereof, a depraved thing: it is the wisdom of rats that will be sure to leave a house somewhat before it fall. It is the wisdom of the fox, that thrusts out the badger who digged and made room for him. It is the wisdom of crocodiles that shed tears when they would devour. But that which is especially to be noted is, that those which (as Cicero says of Pompey) are *sui amantes, sine rivali*, are many times unfortunate. And whereas they have all their times sacrificed to themselves, they become in the end sacrifices to the inconstancy of fortune; whose wings they sought by their self-wisdom to have pinioned." Readers of the essay would have easily recognized in Cicero's "sui amantes" a parallel with the "seipsos amantes" of 2 Timothy 3:2, to which I refer you, and would have seen in Bacon's "fortune" an instrument of Providence. The general idea was not obscure. Thus Burghley once wrote to the Cambridge humanist Thomas Smith, "I love wisdom and honor it, but when sleights and crynkes are joined therewith, as I am sorry sometime to see, commonly thereof followeth infinite incommodities both to the party that useth them, and to them who are therewith advised." He goes on, "God amend them, that meaning to make traps of malice, are for the more part trapped themselves."

Worldly wisdom is perhaps best described in *Hamlet* by Polonius, first in his famous instructions to Laertes to use worldly prudence and to be, like Iago, true to himself, and then, even more openly, in his instructions to Reynaldo:

> And thus do we of wisdom and of reach
> With windlasses and with assays of bias
> By indirections find directions out.

Characteristically, he falls into a "trap of malice" of his own and is the first victim of such a trap in the play. His demise is a kind of foreshadowing of what is to come. Claudius is, of course, a notorious offender in this respect, seeking first by indirections to discover the reasons for Hamlet's discontent and then by means of very elaborate stratagems to murder him. But Hamlet is if anything worse, for he sets to work at once with his "antic disposition." This leads to the downright abuse of Ophelia, and this, together with his rash murder of her father, to her own true madness and death beneath a willow. The location is poetically appropriate, for as Desdemona's song and American folksongs like "Keep Your Garden Clean" or "Down By A Willow Garden" indicate, the willow suggests that she loved a false young man. Hamlet loves her or does not love her at his own convenience. His stratagems include *The Murder of Gonzago*, the abuse of his mother for the wrong reasons, the cold-blooded murder of Rosencrantz and Guildenstern, his disrespectful and obnoxious ranting over the grave of Ophelia, and his final abuse of Laertes, to whom he insists, as he seeks to befriend him in the last act, that he murdered Polonius out of madness, when at the time he vehemently insisted that he was not mad. Just as he loves to suit his convenience, he is mad to suit his convenience.

Laertes begins well. His advice to Ophelia before his departure is reasonable and free from the malicious insinuations used by Polonius when he advises her. On his return he is naturally disturbed that his father's murderer is unpunished and appears leading a rebellious mob. Claudius explains that he was hesitant to bring Hamlet to public trial because his popularity might make any accusations, or "arrows," as he calls them, turn upon himself. Obviously, he fears that Hamlet, who seems to know too much, might reveal his own misdeeds before the court. Laertes, who is more courageous than either Claudius or Hamlet wishes, as he should, to "tell him in his teeth" what he has done. But he is soon persuaded by Claudius, who fears the consequences of open confrontation, to adopt the worldly-wise stratagem of the foils. Laertes, full of vengeful thoughts, not only agrees but thinks of poisoning the foil. And not to be outdone, Claudius devises the poisoned chalice. Laertes should have listened to Burghley, or to the fairly conventional cautions embraced in his remarks. As we approach the close of the play these elaborate "traps of malice" are about to spring on their inventors. Needless to say, this eventuality served only to fulfill the natural expectations of the Elizabethan audience.

But before considering the conclusion in more detail I should like to say a word about Fortinbras, who has been much maligned by critics seeking to elevate Hamlet. When Hamlet first encounters the Norwegian captain, he is impressed by the futility of fighting over "a little patch of ground," an attitude with which we today, familiar with the techniques of mass warfare and their consequences can readily sympathize. We should remember, however, that the Poles, whom Fortinbras was attacking, were a traditional enemy of Denmark, part of the elder Hamlet's reputation having arisen from the fact that he "smote the sledded Polacks on the ice." As he considers the example Fortinbras has set for him, Hamlet finally concludes,

> Rightly to be great
> Is not to stir without great argument,
> But greatly to find quarrel in a straw
> When honor's at the stake.

That is, the truly noble are not moved by trifles, but will move for the sake of honor, even if the material reward is small. This is Chaucer's Parson's virtue of magnificence, a part of fortitude, and it is clear that Fortinbras is exercising it. That Hamlet shows some confusion need not confuse us. Having observed that he has not been exercising his reason, he concludes, with a blind disregard for logic, "My thoughts be bloody or be nothing worth!" He is about the very noble business of arranging to have someone else murder Rosencrantz and Guildenstern. It seems to me indisputable that Elizabethans would have concluded at the close of the play that Denmark fell into good hands. Their own heroes were, after all, Henry V, who recovered lands in France, and their own Elizabeth, who, with much inferior resources but undaunted courage expressed in her famous speech at Tilbury, repulsed the might of Spain. The play closes, quite properly, with a peal of ordnance.

As the end approaches we are reminded of Providential justice once more in a speech that has won for Hamlet more sympathy than he deserves. "There is," he says, "a special providence in the fall of a sparrow." He continues, "If it be now, 'tis not to come; if it be not to come, it is now; if it be not now, yet will it come. The readiness is all." The echo of Matthew 10:29—"Are not two sparrowes solde for a farthing, and one of them shal not fall on the ground without your Father?"—implies, because of the Scriptural context that would not have been lost to most members of the audience, that men are more important than sparrows, so that they have an obligation, in spite of the enmity of father, mother, or other relatives, to take up their crosses. Has Hamlet taken up his cross with patience and fortitude, or has he sought to outwit fortune with lies and "assays of bias"? The banal remarks about the time of departure reflect mere fatalism, an aspect of slothful "rechelessness." A man is "ready" when he has been a faithful servant, not a servant who begins to "smite his fellows" (Matthew 24:42ff.; Luke 12:42ff.). A part of man's "cross," and, as everyone knew, an essential feature of his "readiness" is penance, but Hamlet has just announced proudly that the murder of his schoolfellows is not on his conscience, and he is about to excuse himself to

Laertes for the murder of Polonius. He was not to blame; his "madness" did it. This shows no contrition whatsoever, and Hamlet demonstrates no "readiness," either in word or in deed.

In the general slaughter of the last scene Laertes among the Danish men behaves much better than anyone else, setting a kind of standard. He recognizes that he is, as he says, "justly killed" by his own treachery and that his "foul practice" has turned upon himself. Horatio, not exactly standing at the bridge, offers to poison himself like an "antique Roman," perhaps forgetting for the moment Cicero's admonitions against suicide and the example of Judas. This is not a very noble reaction to a buffet of fortune. His farewell speech to his friend,

> Good night, sweet Prince,
> And flights of angels sing thee to thy rest,

which has brought tears to the eyes of modern audiences for the wrong reasons, exhibits the generosity of a gentleman; for however shallow Horatio may be, he is not a man to wish anything but salvation for another mortal. As for Hamlet, his murder of the King brings forth a general cry of "Treason!" as indeed it should, for although the play's audience knows of the King's unlawful usurpation, it has not been demonstrated to the court on the stage. Hamlet's only real concern is for his own worldly reputation. It is for this that he stays Horatio's suicidal impulse, hoping, with persistent "wisdom for himself" that he can save it. There are no signs that his "godlike reason" does not still "fust unused" within him. He shows no realization of the kind exhibited by Laertes, no contrition for his abuse of his mother and Ophelia, much less for his murders. He has forgotten that "Foul deeds will rise / Though all the earth o'erwhelm them, to men's eyes." And he can do no more than turn his kingdom over to the ancient enemy, Norway, against whom his father, whom he claimed to love but did not emulate, struggled with splendid valor.

Horatio, having regained his self-control, and denied that Claudius killed Rosencrantz and Guildenstern, according them a proper honor, sums up the play very well:

> So shall you hear
> Of carnal, bloody, and unnatural acts,
> Of accidental judgments, casual slaughters,
> Of deaths put on by cunning and forced cause.
> And, in the upshot, purposes mistook
> Fall'n on the inventors' heads.

Thus has Heaven directed the state of Denmark, not by intervening, but simply by allowing those "wise in themselves" to bring about their own destruction. There is no real "mystery" or "complexity" in the character of Hamlet as distinct from his mythical "personality." Personalities are, of course, always complex and mysterious, especially near their depths. But Hamlet did not have one of these convenient modern excuses for misconduct and self-indulgence. And Elizabethans did not regard befuddlement as a virtue, either personal, intellectual, "aesthetic," or moral. Hamlet faces no real "ethical dilemma," and there is no evidence whatsoever that he redeems himself. Malice, whether it proceeds from greed, ambition, sloth, jealousy, or frustrated appetite, spreads like a disease and can destroy a family or a kingdom as well as a man. This is what Shakespeare wished to demonstrate in his tragedies, and indeed demonstrated very well in this one.

Most of you are Americans, and should understand this, having a kind of traditional obligation to behave "with malice toward none, with charity for all." Indeed, Americans once had a general reputation for spontaneous good-nature, cheerful inventiveness in adversity, and a sincere regard for the physical and spiritual welfare of their neighbors. Elizabethans had never heard of Lincoln's Second Inaugural address. But they did have a Queen who knew well how to sacrifice private satisfaction for public good and who could say to her people on Nov. 30, 1601, "I do assure you that there is no prince that loveth his subjects better, or whose love can countervail our love. There is no jewel, be it of never so rich a price, which I set before this jewel: I mean your love. For I do more esteem it than any treasure or riches. . . ." In the following month, speaking of her dealings with the late King of Spain, whose soul, she said, "I trust be now in heaven," she stated that she had always acted out of simplicity, "remembering who it was that said 'The wisdom of the world was folly unto God,' and hope in that respect I shall not suffer the worse for it." Before the example of this "fair Vestal, throned by the West" the Hamlets, Othellos, Lears, Macbeths, and Antonys of the world are petty creatures indeed, hardly worthy of the name *Vir*. Shakespeare knew this, and so did most of his audience, who had no wish to see their England, renowned "For Christian service and true chivalry," make, like Hamlet's Denmark, "a shameful conquest of itself."

These at least are the conclusions of a medievalist, straying a little from his proper path.

Pope and Boethius

◆§

The fortunes of The Consolation of Philosophy *in the modern world roughly parallel the fortunes of a rigorous belief in Divine Providence. Much of the puzzlement evinced by modern critics concerning both Pope's* Essay *and Johnson's* Rasselas *might be alleviated by a careful study of Boethius. For* Rasselas, *see Boswell's Life, sub anno 1759. When "eternity" came to mean "infinite time" rather than an eternal present outside time, as it did for Dr. Samuel Clarke, in his celebrated controversy with Leibnitz, much of the argument in the* Consolation *became obscure.*

◆§

POPE'S interest in the *De consolatione philosophiae* of Boethius is attested by his partial translation of the ninth meter of the third book, completed, perhaps, "not later than 1710."[1] The translation involves only the first four and the last seven lines of the original meter, leaving the intervening seventeen lines unused. The meter itself is a kind of poetic summary of the beginning of Plato's *Timaeus,* although it is probable that Boethius was actually interested in the Christian implications of these materials. Pope's translation omits the obviously Platonic content of the meter, so that the result gives the impression of being a thoroughly Christian prayer. In the original the poem is an invocation to "the Father of all things." It begins,

> O qui perpetua mundum ratione gubernas
> Terrarum caelique sator qui tempus ab aeuo
> Ire iubes stabilisque manens das cuncta moueri,
> Quem non externae pepulerunt fingere causae. . . .

Pope translates:

> O thou, whose all-creating hands sustain
> The radiant Heav'ns, and Earth, and ambient main!
> Eternal Reason! whose presiding soul
> Informs great nature and directs the whole!
> Who wert, e're time his rapid race begun,
> And bad'st the years in long procession run:

> Who fix't thy self amidst the rowling frame,
> Gav'st all things to be chang'd, yet ever art the same![2]

The expression "perpetua . . . ratione," which emphasizes the idea that God continuously maintains a reasonable order in His guidance of the world, gives rise to Pope's more explicitly Christian epithet, "Eternal Reason." The use of Reason here rather than the more traditional Wisdom is faintly suggestive of an attitude toward the Deity somewhat like that expressed by Locke's "eternal cogitative being." Again, "terrarum caelique sator" produces the generalized "all-creating hands," and, in addition to heaven and earth, the "ambient main," added, perhaps, for the sake of rhyme. It is possible that Pope may have remembered the "fluctus auidum mare" of 2, met. 8.9. The original reflects the Platonic doctrine of the creation of time, familiar in the *Timaeus*, but Pope's "Who wert, e're time his rapid race begun" emphasized the eternity of God in a manner suggestive of conventional interpretations of the opening verses of the Gospel of John. Changes in emphasis in the translation of the last seven lines are not so marked. However, the original concludes with the lines,

> Tu requies tranquilla piis, te cernere finis,
> Principium, uector, dux, semita, terminus idem.

Pope substitutes the righteous for the pious, perhaps to suggest rational justice:

> In thee the righteous find
> Calm rest, and soft serenity of mind . . .

Finally, in the last line he once more emphasizes the idea of eternity:

> Our utmost bound, and our eternal stay!

Altogether, Pope showed little interest at this time in the expression of Christian ideas in Platonic language. His translation is an interpretation which leaves nothing puzzling or misleading for the "righteous" reader.

The editors of Pope's *Minor Poems* suggest a parallel between lines 3-4, 7-8 as they are quoted above and lines 267-270 of the first Epistle of *The Essay on Man*:[3]

> All are but parts of one stupendous whole,
> Whose body Nature is, and God the soul;
> That, chang'd thro' all, and yet in all the same,
> Great in the earth, as in th'aethereal frame. . . .[4]

Although Maynard Mack cites other parallels for this passage in the
notes to his edition of the poem which certainly indicate that the ideas
it contains were not uncommon, the lines may nevertheless be
thought of as a reflection of the Boethian meter. The second line
quoted above includes the Platonic concept of the "world-soul," a
concept which had been widely used for Christian purposes throughout the Middle Ages, especially after the middle of the twelfth century. The same concept appears in the portion of the meter which
Pope did not translate:

> Tu triplicis mediam naturae cuncta mouentem
> Conectens animam per consona membra resoluis.

This fact suggests that if Pope had the meter in mind when he wrote
his lines in the *Essay*, he was thinking of the original and not of his
translation. Be that as it may, there are other passages in the *Essay*
which may have been suggested by Pope's reading of Boethius.

For example, in 1.5.131ff., Pride, or the proud man, falls into "the
Absurdity of conceiting himself the Final Cause of the Creation":[5]

> Ask for what end the heav'nly bodies shine,
> Earth for whose use? Pride answers, "'Tis for mine:
> "For me kind Nature wakes her genial pow'r,
> "Suckles each herb, and spreads out ev'ry flow'r;
> "Annual for me, the grape, the rose renew
> "The juice nectareous, and the balmy dew;
> "For me, the mine a thousand treasures brings;
> "For me, health gushes from a thousand springs;
> "Seas roll to waft me, suns to light me rise;
> "My foot-stool earth, my canopy the skies."

With this we may compare *De cons.* 2, pr. 5.31ff.:

> An uos agrorum pulchritudo delectat? Quidni? Est enim pulcher-
> rimi operis pulchra portio. Sic quondam sereni maris facie
> gaudemus; sic caelum sidera lunam solemque miramur. Num te
> horum aliquid attingit? Num audes alicuius talium splendore glor-
> iari? An uernis floribus ipse distingueris aut tua in aestiuos fructus
> intumescit ubertas? Quid inanibus gaudiis raperis? Quid externa
> bona pro tuis amplexaris?

The heavenly bodies and the annual succession of Nature's bounties
display, as Pope says in his essay "On Nature and Death," the "Wisdom and Power of their Creator";[6] they are not the special property of
any single man. Pope goes on to condemn the proud, as he says in his

note, for "expecting that perfection in the moral world which is not in the natural." Just as there are plagues and earthquakes, deviations in nature, so also there are deviations in man:

> If plagues and earthquakes break not Heav'n's design,
> Why then a Borgia, or a Catiline?
>
> (155-156)

The proper attitude toward both forms of deviation is to submit:

> Why charge we Heav'n in those, in these acquit?
> In both, to reason right is to submit.
>
> (163-164)

We may find a similar attitude toward natural disasters and tyrants in *De cons.* 1. met. 4:

> Quisquis composito serenus aeuo
> Fatum sub pedibus egit superbum
> Fortunamque tuens utramque rectus
> Inuictum potuit tenere uultum,
> Non illum rabies minaeque ponti
> Versum funditus exagitantis aestum
> Nec ruptis quotiens uagus caminis
> Torquet fumificos Vesaeuus ignes
> Aut celsas soliti ferire turres
> Ardentis uia fulminis mouebit.
> Quid tantum miseri saeuos tyrannos
> Mirantur sine uiribus furentes?

Pope concludes that

> The gen'ral *Order*, since the whole began,
> Is kept in Nature, and is kept in Man.
>
> (171-172)

It is certainly Lady Philosophy's intention to demonstrate the Providential order in the affairs of men, and she has exactly the same problem to contend with that Pope faced later. For the disconsolate Boethius complains, 1. met. 5.25ff.:

> Omnia certo fine gubernans
> Hominum solos respuis actus
> Merito rector cohibere modo.

The first epistle of the *Essay* concludes with one of the most downright statements of the justice of Providence in English literature:

All Nature is but Art, unknown to thee;
All Chance, Direction, which thou canst not see;
All Discord, Harmony, not understood;
All partial Evil, universal Good:
And, spite of Pride, in erring Reason's spite,
One truth is clear, "Whatever *is*, is *right*."

(289-294)

Mack observes in a note to this passage that its second line is "the theme of Boethius's *De cons. phil.*"[7] More properly, it forms a part of the thematic structure of that work, just as it is a part of the argument stated in Pope's lines. The idea appears specifically in 5. pr. 1.18ff.:

"Si quidem," inquit, "aliquis euentum temerario motu nullaque causarum conexione productum casum esse definiat, nihil omnino casum esse confirmo et praeter subiectae rei significationem inanem prorsus uocem esse decerno. Quis enim coercente in ordinem cuncta deo locus esse ullus temeritati reliquus potest? . . . Quotiens," ait, "aliquid cuiuspiam rei gratia geritur aliudque quibusdam de causis quam quod intendebatur obtingit, casus uocatur, ut si quis colendi agri causa fodiens humum defossi auri pondus inueniat. Hoc igitur fortuito quidem creditur accidisse, uerum non de nihilo est; nam proprias causas habet quarum improuisus inopinatusque concursus casum uidetur operatus."

The harmony of creation is emphasized in 2. met. 8. Again, the idea that "partial evil" is actually good is stated in terms of Fortune in 4. pr. 7.2-3: "Omnem . . . bonam prorsus esse fortunam." Although Lady Philosophy does not say in so many words, "Whatever is, is right," she says something very similar (4. pr. 6.131ff.): "Hic igitur quidquid citra spem videas geri, rebus quidem rectus ordo est, opinioni uero tuae peruersa confusio." Moreover, she denies the possibility of evil (3. pr. 12.80ff.): "Malum igitur . . . nihil est, cum id facere ille non possit, qui nihil non potest."

The second epistle of Pope's *Essay* yields no very striking parallels with the *De consolatione philosophiae.* Epistle 3, however, contains a description of the "chain of Love" (ll. 7ff.) which, as Mack indicates in his note, has as one of its antecedents *De cons.* 2. met. 8. Again, both Boethius (2. met. 5) and Pope (ll. 147ff.) describe the Golden Age, but with rather different purposes in mind. In Epistle 4, after explaining that happiness does not lie "in Externals," Pope continues,

Fortune her gifts may variously dispose,
And these be happy call'd, unhappy those;

But Heav'n's just balance equal will appear,
While those are plac'd in Hope, and these in Fear;
Not present good or ill, the joy or curse,
But future views of better, or of worse.
   Oh sons of earth! attempt ye still to rise,
By mountains piled on mountains, to the skies?
                                        (67-74)

The idea that fortune creates hope and fear appears in the last meter of the first book of the *De consolatione*, ll. 20-28:

> Tu quoque si uis
> Lumine claro
> Cernere uerum,
> Tramite recto
> Carpere callem,
> Gaudia pelle,
> Pelle timorem
> Spemque fugato
> Nec dolor adsit.

Lady Philosophy here admonishes her pupil to avoid hope and fear based on externals. She had said earlier (1. met. 4.15-18),

> At quisquis trepidus pauet uel optat,
> Quod non sit stabilis suique iuris,
> Abiecit clipeum locoque motus
> Nectit qua ualeat trahi catenam.

Although Pope's initial point about the equalizing effects of hope and fear is not in Boethius, his admonition to the "sons of earth" makes essentially the same point that Boethius does. The "sons of earth" are, of course, those who set their hearts on earthly things and hope to achieve happiness from them. They need to learn, as Boethius says (4. met. 7.34-35) "superata tellus / sidera donat." Mack calls attention to a parallel between Pope's figure and the laguage of 2. pr. 6.1: "Quid autem de dignitatibus potentiaque disseram quae uos uerae dignitatis ac potestatis inscii caelo exaequatis?"[8]

Pope continues by asserting that the real pleasures of reason and the senses lie in "Health, Peace, and Competence," which are founded on virtue. The gifts of Fortune may fall either to the virtuous or to the vicious, but they cannot make the vicious happy:

> The good or bad the gifts of Fortune gain,
> But these less taste them, as they the worse obtain.

Say, in pursuit of profit or delight,
Who risk the most, that take wrong means, or right?
Of Vice or Virtue, whether blest or curst,
Which meets contempt, or which compassion first?
Count all th'advantage prosp'rous Vice attains,
'Tis but what Virtue flies from and disdains.

(83-90)

The idea that the wicked "take wrong means" in their pursuit of happiness and gain only that which the virtuous "disdain" is explained at length in *De cons.* 3. pr. 2 and 4. pr. 2. The latter passage concludes with the following observation concerning the wicked: "Faciunt enim quaelibet, dum per ea quibus delectantur id bonum quod disiderant se adepturos putant; sed minime adipiscuntur, quoniam ad beatitudinem probra non veniunt." They are truly happy, Pope says, who see and follow the scheme of Providence:

Oh blind to truth, and God's whole scheme below,
Who fancy Bliss to Vice, to Virtue Woe!
Who sees and follows that great scheme the best,
Best knows the blessing, and will most be blest:

It is clearly Lady Philosophy's desire to show her pupil this "great scheme" so that he may find happiness in following it.

As for worldly advantages, Pope explains at length that wealth, honors, titles, birth, greatness, fame, and superior parts do not bring true happiness. The discussion very roughly parallels that in *De cons.* 3, where the emptiness of a similar series of advantages is described. Specific arguments are sometimes similar as well. Pope's treatment of honors concludes,

Worth makes the man, and want of it, the fellow;
The rest is all but leather or prunella.

(203-204)

We shall look in vain for "leather or prunella" in Boethius, but in 3. met. 4 we learn that the costume of high office may adorn the wicked:

Quamuis se Tyrio superbus ostro
Comeret et niueis lapillis,
Inuisus tamen omnibus uigebat
Luxuriae Nero saeuientis.
Sed quondam dabat improbus uerendis
Patribus indecores curules.

> Quis illos igitur putet beatos
> Quos miseri tribuunt honores?

Boethius had also said (3. pr. 4.18ff.) that worth makes the man: "Inest enim dignitas propria uirtuti, quam protinus in eos quibus fuerit adiuncta transfundit." With reference to titles, Pope expresses some doubts about purity of lineage in noble families, but he concludes,

> What can ennoble sots, or slaves, or cowards?
> Alas! not all the blood of all the Howards.
>
> (215-216)

In other words, nobility lies in worth rather than in ancestry, an idea vividly expressed in *De cons.* 3. pr. 6, and met. 6. Summing up, Pope says,

> Bring then these blessings to a strict account,
> Make fair deductions, see to what they mount.
> How much of other each is sure to cost;
> How each for other oft is wholly lost . . .
>
> (269-272)

The idea that the pursuit of one false good can be made only at the expense of others appears in *De cons.* 3. pr. 9.50ff.:

"Qui diuitias," inquit, "petit penuriae fuga, de potentia nihil laborat, uilis obscurusque esse mauult, multas etiam sibi naturales quoque subtrahit uoluptates, ne pecuniam quam parauit amittat. Sed hoc modo ne sufficientia quidem contingit ei quem ualentia deserit, quem molestia pungit, quem uilitas abicit, quem recondit obscuritas. Qui uero solum posse desiderat, profligat opes, despicit uoluptates, honoremque potentia carentem gloriam quoque nihili pendit. Sed hunc quoque quam multa deficiant uides. Fit enim ut aliquando necessariis egeat, ut anxietatibus mordeatur cumque haec depellere nequeat, etiam id quod maxime petebat potens esse desistat. Similiter ratiocinari de honoribus, gloria, uoluptatibus licet."

Finally, the principle with which Pope concludes, "Virtue alone is Happiness below," is explained at length in *De cons.* 4. pr. 3.

In general, Pope's arguments are not quite so rigorous as those of Boethius, perhaps because he could expect his audience to fill in for him from the stock of commonplace Christian thought. He does not push their implications quite so far either, except, perhaps in the concluding lines of the first Epistle. Whether or not he actually had the *De consolatione* in mind when he wrote his *Essay* would be difficult to decide. The ideas and the figurative language of Boethius had been widely imitated for centuries at the time Pope wrote, so that he might easily have found both elsewhere. Nevertheless, the early translation of the meter does indicate that Boethius may have had a formative influence on Pope's thought. The fact that there are certain similarities between the *De consolatione philosophiae* and *The Essay on Man*, moreover, reinforces the conclusion long since established by students of Pope that the content of the *Essay* is essentially traditional.

Notes

INTRODUCTION—PAGES ix-xviii

1. See Mary J. Epstein's stimulating article, "*Ludovicus decus regnantium:* Perspectives on the Rhymed Office," *Speculum* 53 (1978), p. 289.
2. For example, see the summary report of observations made in a small Pennsylvania town, "The Americanization of Roseto," *Science News* (June 10, 1978), pp. 378-379, 382.

DOCTRINE OF CHARITY—PAGES 21-50

1. III, 16 (10), *PL*, 34, col. 72. Numbers in parentheses indicate chapters.
2. III, 15 (10), *PL*, 34, col. 71.
3. II, 8 (6), *PL*, 34, col. 39. Cf. Hugh of St. Victor, *Didascalicon* (ed. Buttimer), p. 55, where the principle is applied to non-Scriptural literature. The argument was still being used as a defense of poetic obscurity by Petrarch and Boccaccio. See C. G. Osgood, *Boccaccio on Poetry* (Princeton, 1930), pp. 61-62, 170, note 10, 171, note 16.
4. *Saint Augustine et la fin de la culture antique* (Paris, 1938), p. 489. I am indebted to B. F. Huppé for calling my attention to this work and for many other helpful suggestions.
5. *De doctrina*, II, 24 (16), *PL*, 34, col. 47.
6. G. Paré, A. Brunet, and P. Tremblay, *La renaissance du XIIe siècle* (Paris and Ottawa, 1933), pp. 233-237. The quotation is from Hugh of St. Victor, *ibid.*, p. 234, note 1.
7. *PL*, 107, col. 296. Cf. C. Spicq, *Esquisse d'une histoire de l'exégèse latine au moyen âge* (Paris, 1944), p. 41.
8. *Didascalicon*, p. 125.
9. *Op. cit.*, pp. xxxviii-xxxix.
10. St. Augustine, *De Gen. contra Manich.*, *PL*, 34, col. 203, St. Gregory, *Moralia*, *PL*, 75, col. 988, St. Bede, *Comm. in Gen.*, *PL*, 91, col. 203, *Expl. Apoc.*, *PL*, 93, col. 204, Bruno Astensis, *PL*, 165, col. 87, St. Martin, *PL*, 209, col. 413.
11. St. Augustine, *De Gen. contra Manich.*, *PL*, 34, col. 203.
12. *Ibid.*, 208.
13. Cf. the *Quaest. in Gen.* attributed to Bede, where Isidore is quoted to this effect, *PL*, 193, cols. 269-270.
14. See St. Augustine, *De Trinitate*, XIV, *PL*, 42, cols. 1035-1058.
15. Hom. IX in Eccles., *PL*, 175, cols. 171-172.
16. See St. Augustine on Ps. 1, *PL*, 36, col. 68 (partly quoted below), St.

Bruno of the Carthusians, *PL*, 152, col. 641, or St. Martin on Apoc 22.2, *PL*, 209, col. 413: *"Et folia ligni*, scilicet praecepta Christi quae tegunt et ornant fructum, id est verba praedicationis ejus sunt *ad sanitatem gentium*, gentilium videlicet conversorum si implentur. Christus ergo reddet fructum, et apostoli eorumque successores post eos praedicando, per universum mundum spargent folia, id est praecepta ipsius Christi."

17. The root of the good tree (rather than its crowning fruit) is sometimes *caritas*, and, conversely, the root of the evil tree is sometimes *cupiditas*, the *radix malorum*.

18. Honorius, *In Cant.*, *PL*, 172, col. 425.

19. St. Martin, *PL*, 209, col. 413.

20. Bruno Astensis, *PL*, 165, col. 87; cf. *ibid.*, 131-132, 180, etc.

21. St. Bruno of the Carthusians, *PL*, 152, col. 641.

22. This account is based on the description in B. Dickens and A. C. Ross, *The Dream of the Rood* (London, 1945), pp. 1-13.

23. In Ps. 64, *PL*, 191, col. 581. Cf. St. Augustine, *De civitate Dei*, xiv, 28. The references to Cain and Abel are not, of course, historical. Abel begins the generation of the just, to which all faithful Christians belong, regardless of physical parenthood. Cain begins the generation of the wicked, among whom must be included all those who love in cupidity.

24. Comm. in Ps. 79, *PL*, 191, col. 766. Cf. St. Augustine, *PL*, 36, col. 1026; or the *Summa sententiarum* (authorship disputed), *PL*, 176, col. 113, where Isidore is quoted.

25. *Opera* (Quaracchi, 1882 et seq.), vi, 4.

26. Ed. Wilmart, *Analecta reginensia* (Vatican, 1933), p. 183: "Et [quia] uere nullus tantus labor, nulla tanta miseria est in praesenti uita quam illicito et carnali amore capi et superari, et eius imperiis deseruire, quia aufert deum, aufert animam, cor et corpus a deo, idest in tantum ut non permittat hominem et mulierem sui iuris et sue potestatis esse; sed in seruitute miserabili detinentur, nec se de tali iugo possunt excutere, quando uolunt, sicut sciunt experti. At uero econtra, nichil dulcius, nil iocundius nichilque fructuosius est quam deum toto corde diligere et amoris eius obsequiis se assidue mancipare. . . . Ad contra, amor carnalis tam nobilium quam rusticorum, tam diuitum quam pauperum in immundicia terminatur et consummatur. . . . Sic seruiunt carnales amatores et amatrices in immunditia miserabili, et idcirco debemus ut possumus amorem carnalem et illicitum fugere et contempnere, et deo per perfectum amorem totaliter adherere."

27. Sermo clxii, *PL*, 38, col. 887: "Non solum fornicatio in sacris Litteris specialiter, sed etiam generaliter arguitur et nominatur . . . advertamus, illam esse generalem fornicationem animae humanae, qua non adhaerens quisque Deo, adhaeret mundo." Cf. *De sermone Domini in monte*, 36.

28. *PL*, 114, col. 162.

29. *PL*, 93, col. 127.

30. *PL*, 93, col. 12. Cf. St. Augustine, *PL*, 37, col. 1179; *Glos. ord.*, *PL*, 114, col. 671.

31. *PL*, 114, cols. 346-347; cf. Bede, *PL*, 92, col. 615.

32. Alanus de Insulis, *Distinctiones*, PL, 210, col. 932; cf. *Allegoriae in sacram scripturam* (twelfth century, authorship unknown), PL, 111, col. 1545.

33. See the references in note 32 and St. Gregory, *Moralia*, PL, 76, cols. 671-676, and *Gregorianum*, PL, 193, col. 298. Isidore of Seville, *Etymologiae*, xvii, vii, 47 (ed. Lindsay), associates the willow with sterility on other grounds.

34. See St. Gregory, *Moralia*, PL, 76, cols. 444-446, Bede, PL, 92, cols. 559-560, *Allegoriae*, PL, 112, col. 1053, and Alanus, *Distinctiones*, PL, 210, col. 964. Cf. Urban T. Holmes, Jr., *A New Interpretation of Chrétien's "Conte Del Graal"* (Chapel Hill, 1948), p. 22, note 12, and p. 32.

35. Rabanus Maurus, *De universo*, PL, 111, col. 513. This work not only contains a useful general discussion of the tree but a list of trees of various kinds together with their higher meanings. See also Rabanus on Ecclesiasticus 24, PL, 109, cols. 929-931.

36. *Sermones*, PL, 183, cols. 378-379.

37. PL, 109, cols. 930 and 1115.

38. For the significance of this term, see Gregory, *Hom. in Evan.*, ii, 38, PL, 76, cols. 1285-1286.

39. PL, 24, col. 417.

40. PL, 93, col. 12. Cf. St. Martin, PL, 209, col. 187.

41. PL, 36, 68. The Scriptural quotation is from a pre-Vulgate text of Isaiah 40:6-8.

42. A series of poems based on the contrast between the flower and the leaf was collected by George L. Marsh, "Sources and Analogues of 'The Flower and the Leaf,' " *MP*, 4 (1906-1907), 121-167, 281-387. Marsh concluded that in the ME poem the contrast represents a conflict between sensuality and reason. This conclusion is consistent with traditional Scriptural imagery.

43. St. Martin, PL, 209, col. 413, explains the somewhat puzzling location of the tree here as follows: "Vel citra fluvium, id est in hac vita, habemus lignum vitae, scilicet corpus et sanguinem Christi in quibus reficimur, et ultra flumen, videlicet in futuro habebimus ipsum praesentem."

44. For a suggestion that the river in Paradise flows from the tree, see St. Augustine, *De Gen. ad litt.*, PL, 34, col. 375. Cf. Bruno Astensis, *Expos. Apoc.*, PL, 165, col. 730.

45. Bede, *Comm. in Gen.*, PL, 91, col. 203, Rupert, PL, 167, col. 274, Strabo, PL, 114, col. 754. This water also appears in Ecclesiasticus 24:40 ff. Rabanus, PL, 109, col. 943, comments: "Ergo Christus sapientia Dei effudit in mundum flumina doctrinae evangelicae, quae abundantissime reficiunt et satiant avidas mentes electorum." Cf. note 50, below.

46. *De Gen. ad litt.*, PL, 34, col. 375.

47. E.g., see Bede on James 3:7, PL, 93, col. 28.

48. *Moralia*, PL, 76, col. 97. For the birds of St. Ambrose, see PL, 14, col. 237 f.

49. PL, 92, cols. 173-174.

50. Bede, PL, 91, col. 203, gives several alternative interpretations of the garden. Cf. Richard of St. Victor, *In Cant.*, PL, 196, col. 490. The river of wis-

dom in Ecclesiasticus 24:42 also waters a garden: "Dixi: Rigabo hortum meum plantationum, et inebriabo prati mei fructum." Rabanus, *PL*, 109, col. 944, comments: "Hortus enim plantationum sapientiae sancta est Ecclesia, quam ipsa Veritas [sc. Christus] suo dogmate semper irrigat et inebriat, ut fructum partus spiritalis quotidie proferat, in doctrina videlicet catholica et sacris virtutibus; et merito, quia illuminata a vera luce *quae illuminat omnem hominem venientem in hunc mundum* (John 1:9), a sole justitiae ipsoque oriente. . . ."

51. A concise but detailed summary of both allegorical and tropological meanings for this garden appears in a sermon by Hugh of St. Victor. I quote part of it, *PL*, 177, col. 1086, as an illustration: "Habet ergo sancta mater Ecclesia hortum per conversationem bonam, clausum per disciplinam, fontem per sapientiam, signatum per figuram. Habet paradisum malorum punicorum in passis martyribus, cyperos in praelatis rectoribus, nardum in subjectis humilibus, crocum in eruditis doctoribus, fistulam in compunctis poenitentibus. . . . Et istae sunt spirituales sanctae matris Ecclesiae divitiae. . . . Matrem Ecclesiam, charissimi nobis, in his omnibus imitemur, ut cum ipsa sponsum in decore suo videre mereamur, et cum sponsa in coelis gloriemur. Habeamus et nos paradisum malorum punicorum, adversa pro Christo saepius patiendo, et oppressis quotidie compatiendo cyperos, discrete nos regendo; nardum, nostris praelatis humiliter nos subdendo; crocum, luce sapientiae effulgendo. . . ." Although the various commentaries on the Canticum differ in detail, for the most part they are not actually inconsistent.

52. *PL*, 196, cols. 487 ff.

53. See Fr. Klaeber, *Beowulf*, pp. xlviii–li, civ, cxix, cxx–cxxiv.

54. *Ibid.*, note to l. 1357 ff., pp. 182–183.

55. *PL*, 91, col. 84 f.

56. This light should not be confused with the *fyrleoht* of the monster's den (1.1516), which comes from the flame of the wrong love.

57. *Beowulf*, p. 183.

58. See St. Gregory, *Moralia, PL*, 76, col. 510.

59. *Beowulf*, p. 185.

60. Bede's comment on Genesis 3:8 may furnish the basis for the description in the poem, *PL*, 91, col. 214: "Deambulat Deus in illis, non stabat, quia in praecepto illius non stabant. Et bene ad auram post meridiem, quia ab illis auferebatur lux illa ferventior veritatis, appropinquantibus errorum tenebris. *Absconderunt se*, et reliqua. In medio namque ligni se abscondit, qui versus a Deo, in erroris sui atque arbitrii voluntatibus vivit." Cf. Gregory, *Moralia, PL*, 76, cols. 671–676. This poem is examined more thoroughly in a study of Caedmonian poetry by B. F. Huppé, *Doctrine and Poetry: Augustine's Influence on Old English Poetry* (Albany, 1959).

61. *The Irish Tradition* (Oxford, 1947), pp. 62–63.

62. For the dew, see St. Gregory, *Moralia, PL*, 76, col. 132.

63. Ed. E. Trojel (Copenhagen, 1892), pp. 80–110. Page references to the *De amore* in the text are to this edition.

64. The marshy ground is described *ibid.*, 671–676.

65. See Genesis 39:6-7, Jeremiah 9:21, Ecclesiasticus 9:7-9, and Proverbs 23:33-34. The notion is repeated by writers of unquestioned piety as a warning. E.g., see the *Liber de modo bene vivendi*, *PL*, 184, col. 1241: "Oculi annuntii sunt fornicationis. Visio est prima occasio fornicationis. Mens enim per oculos capitur. Per oculos intrat ad mentem sagitta amoris."

66. See note 26, above.

67. *Récherches sur les sources latines des contes et romances courtois du moyen âge* (Paris, 1913), p. 372.

68. An indication of hypocrisy. It is not difficult to discern a very remarkable kind of hypocrisy in Fenice.

69. The tower is, I believe, the reverse of the Tower on the Toft at the beginning of *Piers Plowman*. That is, it is a reflection of the Tower of Babel, associated by the commentators with Babylon, and the opposite of the tower or tabernacle on Sion of Psalm 14. Only by erecting the Tower of Babylon in one's heart may one enter Amoenitas to enjoy its delights. The intruder, Bertran, does not enter the garden for this purpose and hence has no need for the tower.

70. Sleep is a common symbol not only for sexual embrace, which is probably implied here, but also for oblivion to the Word of God. See *Allegoriae*, *PL*, 112, col. 913.

71. The humor of Chrétien's treatment of the story is apparent on the surface in ll. 6016-6023 and ll. 6462-6463. When the actions of the characters are seen against the proper standard of values, the whole story becomes very lively. The theme of the two loves is introduced plainly in ll. 5706-5718.

72. The wall in the Canticum is usually interpreted to mean faith or discipline without which one cannot become a true member of the church. Perhaps the function of the wall in the *Roman* needs some explanation. The first figure on it is Haïne, whose presence demonstrates that one cannot hate a flower of the flesh and take joy in it at the same time. Near her is Felonie, suitable, perhaps, for those who wish to remain in the wet garden of Andreas but incompatible with true idolatry. Covoitise, which makes people wish to receive but not to give, centers attention on the acquisition of wealth and thus destroys love. For, as Andreas says (I, II), "In amantis ergo conspectu nil valet amoris actui comparari, potiusque verus amans cunctis exspoliari divitiis vel omni eo, quod humano posset excogitari ingenio, sine quo quis vivere non potest, penitus privari eligeret quam sperato vel acquisito amore carere" (p. 7). Beside Covoitise stands her relative, Avarice, the destroyer of the worldly display of fine clothing and the "largece" necessary to success in courtship. The first "rule" that the nobleman gets from the god of love in Amoenitas is "Avaritiam sicut nocivam pestem effugias et eius contrarium amplectaris." Envie follows, for she is not only subject to the same kind of limitations as is Covoitise, but is also incapable of looking anyone in the eye. The envious cannot make a necessary beginning with *concupiscentia oculorum*. Tristece and Vieillece are also there. The first can never know the society of Deduit, and the second has inadequacies which we have already seen in Andreas. The pretensions of Papelardie also keep one away from the garden. Finally, Povreté is

excluded because, to use the mock lament of Andreas, "Manifesto igitur experimento cognosco, quod ita superveniente inopia incipiunt fomenta amoris deficere" (p. 8). In general, the "virtues" attributed to the lover are worldly virtues stemming from pride.

73. Beauty of the flesh, simple-mindedness, sentimental pity, "villainous company," and sweet-looks all foster idolatry. Pride, fraud, shame, despair of consummation, and a wandering eye all tend to make the lover lose faith in his chosen goddess and seek satisfaction elsewhere.

74. See note 64 above. As in the *Liber de modo bene vivendi* the "arrows" of love are said in the *Roman* to enter through the eyes (l. 1694). True Christian love enters through the reason.

75. The literary influence of Guillaume de St. Amour is discussed by C. R. Dahlberg, "The secular tradition in Chaucer and Jean de Meun" (Princeton Ph.D. dissertation, 1953).

76. F. Petrarch, *Le familiari*, X, 4.

TERMINOLOGY—PAGES 51-72

1. "*Sans et matière*," *Romania*, 44 (1915), 14-36.

2. *Ibid.*, p. 22.

3. *Ibid.*, p. 36.

4. *Lancelot and Guinevere* (Chicago, 1930), p. 64. In Nitze's *Perceval and the Holy Grail* (Berkeley and Los Angeles, 1949), p. 228, *sens* is again defined as "interpretation."

5. *The Works of Sir Thomas Malory* (Oxford, 1947), I, lxv.

6. E.g., see *Civitas Dei*, 12, 19.

7. "*Sans et matière*," p. 16. He called attention to *junctura* in Horace, *Ars poetica*, 242. Cf. Cross and Nitze, p. 65, and *Perceval and the Holy Grail*, p. 286. The quotation from Philippe Mouskés seems to me irrelevant, since it is concerned with the elements of composition. Cf. the use of *junctura* in Quintilian. In "The Romance of Erec, Son of Lac," *MP*, 11 (1914), 488, Nitze made *conjointure* "probably equivalent to the word *roman*," but this is too much of a limitation.

8. *PL*, 210, col. 451.

9. See C. Spicq, *Esquisse d'une histoire de l'exégèse latine au moyen âge* (Paris, 1944), p. 14.

10. *De clericorum institutione*, *PL*, 107, col. 389. Cf. St. Augustine, *De doctrina Christiana*, III, 9 (5)-10 (6); Scotus, *Super ier. coel.*, *PL*, 122, cols. 170-171; Bruno Astensis, *Comm. in Matt.*, *PL*, 165, col. 252.

11. *De cler. inst.*, 389. Cf. *De doctrina*, III, 23 (15), 15 (10), 16 (10); I, 40 (36).

12. Ed. Curtius (Dresden, 1911), p. 5. Cf. "*Sans et matière*," pp. 25-26.

13. *Comm. in Gen.*, *PL*, 107, col. 605.

14. *PL*, 171, col. 1410.

15. *Super ier. coel.*, *PL*, 122, col. 146. The term *exercitatio* as it is used here is Augustinian. A very similar comparison is made by Petrarch, *Fam.*, X, 4.

16. *De doctrina*, III, 11 (7), *PL*, 34, col. 70. The implications of this passage are discussed at length in a forthcoming study of Old English poetry by Bernard

F. Huppé *Doctrine and Poetry: Augustine's Influence on Old English Poetry* (Albany, 1959).

17. *Contra mendacium*, 28 (13). (*PL*, 40, col. 538).

18. "De libris quos legere solebam," *MGH, Poetae*, I, 543.

19. *Comm. super sex libros Eneidos Virgilii*, ed. G. Riedel (Gryphiswaldae, 1924), p. 3.

20. *Ibid.*, pp. 50-51.

21. *PL*, 210, col. 454.

22. *Quaestiones in Numeros*, XLV, *PL*, 34, col. 739.

23. *Super ier. coel.*, *PL*, 122, col. 151.

24. *Etymologiae* (ed. Lindsay), I, 37, 26. Cf. St. Augustine, *De Trinitate*, XV, 9, 15. Similarly Peter Lombard, *Collect. in Epist. D. Pauli, PL*, 191, col. 1662, defines aenigma as "obscura allegoria."

25. *Etym.*, I, 37, 22.

26. Ed. C.C.I. Webb (London, 1909), I, 4 (p. 390c).

27. *Ibid.*, VIII, 24 (p. 816c).

28. *De arte prosayca metrica et rithmica*, ed. G. Mari, *RF*, 12 (1902), 928.

29. See the description of this work in E. Faral, *Les arts poétiques du XIIᵉ et du XIIIᵉ siècle* (Paris, 1924), pp. 42-46, and the edition of F. Ghisalberti (Messina, 1933).

30. *Anticlaudianus, PL*, 210, col. 491.

31. Phyllis Abrahams, ed., *Les oeuvres poétiques de Baudri de Bourgueil* (Paris, 1926), No. 216, pp. 649-650.

32. Ed. Wright, *Satirical Poets*, I, 11.

33. *Nun's Priest's Tale*, 3440-3443. Cf. *Man of Law's Tale*, 701-706. The nature and prevalence of the allegorical theory of poetry in the later Middle Ages are discussed by C. G. Osgood in the introduction to his *Boccaccio on Poetry* (Princeton, 1930).

34. *Didascalicon* (ed. Buttimer), pp. 96-97.

35. *Policr.*, VII, 12 (p. 666a).

36. II, 1 (1), *PL*, 34, col. 35.

37. I, 2 (2), *PL*, 34, cols. 19-20.

38. II, 24 (16), *PL*, 34, col. 47.

39. *De scripturis et scriptoribus sacris, PL*, 175, col. 11.

40. *De sacramentis, PL*, 176, col. 185.

41. *De script., PL*, 175, col. 21.

42. *De sacr., PL*, 176, col. 185.

43. Ed. Warnke, pp. 82-83.

44. *Op. cit.*, p. 56. "Etymologies" of this kind, which are not intended to be scientific philological observations, are common in Scriptural exegesis. To laugh at them for their scientific crudity is to fail to understand them.

45. *Ibid.*, p. 102.

46. *Ibid.*, p. 63.

47. See A. Maury, *Croyances et légendes du moyen âge*, ed. A. Longnon et G. Bonet-Maury (Paris, 1896), pp. 256-264.

48. See F.J.E. Raby, *A History of Christian-Latin Poetry* (Oxford, 1927), pp. 48-49, 363-375.

49. *PL*, 210, col. 487.

50. *Etym.*, VIII, 7, 10.

51. The fact that Scripture narrates a series of actual events, whereas a poem is concerned with fictitious events, may be responsible for Dante's distinction between the "allegory of theologians" and the "allegory of poets," most recently discussed by C. S. Singleton, "Dante's Allegory," *Speculum*, 25 (1950), 78-86. But Professor Singleton confuses this distinction with that between verbal allegory and the allegory of things. It seems obvious, moreover, that the *Divine Comedy* is a poem, not a history, and certainly not a new chapter in Scripture.

52. *Didas.*, p. 54. For what is said of philosophers here, cf. Marie de France, *Lais*, Prologue, 9 ff., where Priscian is cited.

53. See M. Grabmann, *Die Geschichte der scholastischen Methode* (Freiburg im Breisgau, 1911), II, 236-237.

54. *Didas.*, p. 58. For discussion see G. Paré, A. Brunet, and P. Tremblay, *La renaissance du XIIᵉ siècle* (Paris, Ottawa, 1933), pp. 116-117, and E. de Bruyne, *Etudes d'esthétique médiévale* (Brugge, 1946), II, 324-329.

55. *Ibid.*, p. 125.

56. *Comm.*, p. 36.

57. *De cler. inst.*, *PL*, 107, col. 382.

58. *De script.*, *PL*, 175, cols. 9-10.

59. *Policr.*, 7.11 (pp. 661a-661c).

60. "Marie de France, *Lais*, Prologue, 13-16," *MLN*, 64 (1949), 336-338.

61. *Lancelot and Guenevere*, p. 63.

62. *Wörterbuch zu Kristian von Troyes' sämptlichen Werken*, 2 Aufl. v. Breuer (Halle, 1933), p. 23.

63. *Policr.*, 2.16 (pp. 432c-433a).

OBSERVATIONS—PAGES 73-84

1. At the conference of humanistic scholars held November 5-6, 1965, at Princeton in connection with the series *Humanistic Scholarship in America: The Princeton Studies* the divergence between "critics" and "scholars" or their equivalents in a variety of fields became surprisingly evident. The "critics" seem in general to have fared better than the "scholars" on this occasion.

2. For an interesting discussion of this phenomenon, see Luis Díez del Corral, *The Rape of Europe*, trans. M. V. Livermore (New York, 1959), esp. Ch. 7.

3. Wölfflin's seminal study, available in English as *Principles of Art History*, was first published in German in 1915.

4. No adequate history of the Baroque style is as yet available. For the Rococo, there are suggestive observations in Arno Schönberger and Halldor Soehner, *The Rococo Age* (New York, 1960). Literary materials are used effectively in connection with the nineteenth century by Werner Hofmann, *The Earthly Paradise*, trans. B. Battershaw (New York, 1961). Efforts to distinguish the effects of Romanesque and Gothic styles in literature appear in Paul Zumthor, *Langue et techniques poétiques a l'époque romane* (Paris, 1963), and in

my *Preface to Chaucer* (Princeton, 1962). There are highly suggestive materials in the recent works of Marshall McLuhan.

5. J. H. van den Berg's most famous work, *The Changing Nature of Man*, is available in English, trans. H. F. Cross (New York, 1961). Certain of his other studies, notably *Het menselijk lichaam* (Nijkerk, 1959), are also relevant.

6. See the review article by R. van Caenegem, "Psychologische geschiedenis," *Tijdschrift voor Geschiedenis*, 78 (1965), 129-149.

7. For a brief account of the early development of structural linguistics, see Emile Benveniste, *Problèmes de linguistique générale* (Paris, 1966), Ch. 8. Levi-Strauss is best known to English readers for *The Savage Mind* (Chicago, 1966). The book reveals a fondness for outmoded Marxist polarities and is tinged with romantic neo-primitivism. Its author dislikes stylistic history. Nevertheless, some of the results are extremely useful. Foucault's relevant work is *Les mots et les choses* (Paris, 1966). His earlier work on madness tends to be sensationalistic and the scholarship is unreliable.

8. In 1950 in "Historical Criticism," pp. 8 ff., I wrote that the historical critic "looks with some misapprehension on the tendency of the literary critic to regard older literature in the light of modern aesthetic systems, economic philosophies, or psychological theories. He feels that such systems . . . do not exist before they are formulated." This statement was inspired by a reaction to some remarks by Percy W. Bridgman in *The Nature of Physical Theory* (Princeton, 1936), and was felt to be harmonious with views acceptable in the field of "general semantics," a subject that was then popular. However, the statement has frequently been deplored. I have not abandoned it, and the present essay may serve to make it more comprehensible.

9. *Chaucer's London* (New York, 1968), pp. 5-8, 68-69, 218-220.

10. The claim for Chaucer's "modernity" in this respect is usually made in connection with "The Franklin's Tale," but see my article pp. 272 ff.

11. See Jean Gimpel, *The Cathedral Builders*, trans. C. F. Barnes (New York, 1961), pp. 95-97.

12. Cf. *Chaucer's London*, pp. 5-7.

13. For changing attitudes toward time, see Georges Poulet, *Studies in Human Time* (New York, 1959). There are useful observations in Foucault, and in some of the writings of stylistic historians. Historians of the visual arts frequently treat changing attitudes toward space.

14. Modern thinkers often seek to objectify what are essentially subjective evaluations of space, as Martin Heidegger does in *Being and Time* (New York, 1962). On attitudes toward the past and the future, cf. Hofmann, *The Earthly Paradise*, p. 50, as cited in note 4, and my *Chaucer's London*, p. 120.

15. The romantic origin of the fundamental attitudes of modern criticism has been amply demonstrated by Meyer H. Abrams in *The Mirror and the Lamp* (New York, 1958).

16. The fact that empirical attitudes, for all their vaunted objectivity, imply the reality of the nervous system of the observer rather than that of anything observed is more often felt than faced squarely. The emphasis on the inner reality of the artist in modern art needs no special elaboration, since it is fairly

obvious. However, for significant observations on the subject, see, for example, Wallace Fowlie, *The Age of Surrealism* (New York, 1950), pp. 29-30; Marcel Brion, *Art abstrait* (Paris, 1956), pp. 25, 27, 93-94, 139.

THE ALLEGORIST AND THE AESTHETICIAN—PAGES 85-101

1. *Guide to Aesthetics*, trans. Patrick Romanell (New York, 1965), p. 9.
2. *Ibid.*, p. 10.
3. *Ibid.*, p. 25.
4. *Twentieth Century Painting*, trans. M. Shenfield (London, 1963), p. 2.
5. *Age of Surrealism* (New York, 1950), pp. 24-25.
6. From the basic principles stated in *De Stijl*, at least inspired by Mondrian, who adhered to them throughout his career. For a somewhat different English translation of the above passage, see Frank Elgar, *Mondrian* (trans. T. Walton, New York, 1968), pp. 93-94.
7. *Guide to Aesthetics*, p. 22.
8. *Ibid.*, p. 23.
9. *The Allegory of Love* (Oxford, 1936), p. 46.
10. For this and the following quotation, see *On Christian Doctrine*, trans. D. W. Robertson, Jr. (New York, 1958), pp. 37-38.
11. *Philobiblon*, 13. 1-25. For the quotations from Horace, see *Ars poetica*, 333, 343.
12. C. G. Osgood, *Boccaccio on Poetry* (Princeton, 1930), pp. 60-62.
13. *Age of Surrealism*, p. 29.
14. *The Cathedral Builders*, trans. C. F. Barnes (New York, 1961), p. 97.

MANNYNG'S—PAGES 105-113

1. Sermo IX, *PL*, 38, col. 76.
2. *Sermones*, Pars I, Sermo LXXXV, in Wm. of Auvergne, *Opera* (Orleans, 1674), II, 117.
3. *Collatio* II, 22 ff., *Opera* (Quaracchi, 1882-1902), V, 514-515.
4. Ed. J. Furnivall, *EETS*, *OS*, 119 (London, 1901).
5. Sermo CXXXIII, *PL*, 38, col. 738.
6. Sermo IX, *PL*, 38, cols. 76-77.
7. *Ennaratio super Deuteronomium*, Lib. I, Cap. XI, *PL*, 108, col. 862.
8. *Sententie*, ed. F. P. Bliemetzrieder, *Beiträge zur Geschichte der Philosophie des Mittelalters*, 18 (1919), part 2, 96.
9. *Institutiones in decalogum legis Dominicae*, *PL*, 176, col. 11. Cf. the *Summa Sententiarum*, no longer attributed to Hugh, *ibid.*, col. 121.
10. Lib. III, Dist. XXXVII, Cap. II, in Bonaventura, *Opera*, III, 810. The editors attribute the "mystic" interpretation to Isidore of Seville.
11. *Bibliotheca Casinensis* (Monte Cassino, 1873-1894), IV (Florilegium), 276.
12. *Op. cit.*, p. 96. Cf. the *Summa Sententiarum*, Tract. IV, Cap. IV, *PL*, 176, col. 122.
13. That is, the third commandment of the second table.

14. *Sententiae*, Lib. III, Dist. XXXVII, Cap. IV, *op. cit.*, III, 811. Lombard quotes St. Augustine.

15. See the Prologue, 1.9, and Gaston Paris, with reference to the *Manuel des Peches*, in the *Histoire Littéraire de la France* (Paris, 1865 ff.), XXVIII (1881), 182.

16. *Sententiae*, Lib. IV, Dist. XXVIII, Cap. IV, *op. cit.*, IV, 687.

17. Ed. B. Hauréau, *Notices et Extraits* (Paris, 1890-1893), I, 189.

18. *Decretum*, VIII, 90-97, *PL*, 161, cols. 603-604.

19. *Sententiae*, Lib. IV, Dist. XXXII, Cap. I, *op. cit.*, IV, 728-729.

20. *Etymologiae* IX, vii, 9, ed. Lindsay (Oxford, 1911). Cf. Rabanus Maurus, *De universo*, Lib. VII, Cap. V, *PL*, 111, col. 192.

21. Cf. G. H. Joyce, *Christian Marriage* (London and New York, 1933), pp. 58-61, 83-101. For the theology of child marriage, and the problems of consanguinity and affinity, which are reflected in this section of *Handlyng Synne*, see pp. 93-96, 505-520, 532-543.

22. *Sententiae*, Lib. III, Dist. XXVII, Cap. IV, *op. cit.*, III, 811. Cf. the *Summa Sententiarum*, Tract. IV, Cap. IV, *PL*, 176, col. 122.

23. That is, the fifth in the second table.

24. Lombard, *Sententiae*, Lib. III, Dist. XXXVII, Cap. V, *op. cit.*, III, 811.

25. Lombard, *Sententiae*, Lib. III, Dist. XXXVIII, Cap. III, *op. cit.*, III, 837.

26. Ll. 2654, 2664.

27. *Comm. in Lib. IV Sententiarum*, Dist. XVI, Pars II, Art. III, Quaest. I, *Opera*, IV, 409. Cf. Pierre of Poictiers, *Sententiae*, Lib. IV, Cap. VI, *PL*, 211, col. 1157.

28. *Sententiae*, Lib. III, Dist. XXXIX, Cap. VII, *op. cit.*, III, 859. Cf. Pierre of Poictiers, *Sententiae*, Lib. IV, Cap. VI, *PL*, 211, col. 1157.

29. See my "The Cultural Tradition of *Handlyng Synne*," *Speculum*, 22 (1947), 162-185.

PREACHING—PAGES 114-128

1. The phrases quoted are from J.H.R. Moorman, *Church Life in England in the Thirteenth Century* (Cambridge, 1945), p. 77, and H. S. Bennett, *Life on the English Manor* (New York and Cambridge, 1937), p. 33. Cf. G. C. Coulton, *Mediaeval Studies* (First Series, London, 1915), pp. 103-105, Margaret Deanesley, *The Lollard Bible* (Cambridge, 1920), pp. 198-199, and H. S. Bennett, *Chaucer and the Fifteenth Century* (Oxford, 1947), p. 91. In this article, I shall deliberately avoid a history of the current attitude. It is represented best in Moorman's recent study, where it is, however, only a relatively minor point in a work I have read with much profit.

2. A. Lecoy de la Marche, *La chaire française au Moyen Age* (2nd. ed., Paris, 1886), pp. 13-14; 23-24; 34; 220. The attitude here may need some qualification. See O. Dobiache-Rojdestvensky, *La vie paroissiale en france au XIIIe siècle* (Paris, 1911), pp. 173-175.

3. Cf. Lecoy de la Marche, p. 9, and R. Cruel, *Geschichte der deutschen Predigt im Mittelalter* (Detmold, 1879), pp. 46-47, 258.

4. Lecoy de la Marche, pp. 45-50.

5. See Dom A. Morey, *Bartholomew of Exeter* (Cambridge, 1937), p. 192 and note.

6. Moorman, p. 80.

7. Cf. Lecoy de la Marche, pp. 6, 271, 273.

8. *Divinarum sententiarum librorum Biblie ad certos titulos redacte collectarium.* I have seen the edition published at Paris in 1514.

9. Lecoy de la Marche, p. 275.

10. *Ibid.*, p. 276.

11. Hefele and Leclercq, *Histoire des conciles* (Paris, 1907-1938), v, 1340. The importance of this decree as a stimulus to popular preaching has long been recognized. See Lecoy de la Marche, p. 23; M. M. Davy, *Les sermons universitaires parisiens de 1230-1231* (Paris, 1931), pp. 29-30.

12. On his influence, see M. Gibbs and J. Lang, *Bishops and Reform, 1215-1272* (London, 1934), p. 108, and C. R. Cheney, *English Synodalia* (London, 1941), pp. 51, 62-89.

13. The twenty-seventh canon of the Lateran Council demanded that the priests be familiar with the sacraments.

14. The italics are mine.

15. Although sermons were usually written in Latin for preservation, they were delivered to the people in the vernacular. See Lecoy de la Marche, pp. 233 ff., L. Bourgain, *La chaire francaise au XIIe siècle* (Paris, 1879), pp. 169-196, Cruel, pp. 8-9; 214 ff., and A. Linsenmayer, *Geschichte der Predigt in Deutschland* (Munich, 1886), pp. 36-40. The verse from the Gospel or shorter "theme" was pronounced first in Latin, but the sermon as a whole was in the vernacular. Thus Honorius of Autun, *Speculum ecclesiae, PL,* 172, col. 829, wrote: "Ad omnes sermones debes primum versum Latina lingua pronunciare, dein patria lingua explanare." The necessity for making sermons understandable was clearly recognized. See Pierre of Poitiers, *Sententiarum libri quinque,* Lib. iv, Cap. v, *PL,* 211, cols. 1234-1235. R. W. Hunt, "English Learning in the Late Twelfth Century," *TRHS,* 19 (1936), 29-30, indicates a wide circulation of this work in England in the late twelfth century.

16. *Charters and Documents of Salisbury,* ed. W. D. Macray and W. R. Jones (Rolls Series, 1891), p. 130, and David Wilkins, *Concilia Magnae Britanniae et Hiberniae* (London, 1737), 573. Poore's decrees were issued, it is said, at Salisbury shortly after the Lateran Council and again at Durham between 1229 and 1237.

17. Moorman, p. 231.

18. *Charters of Salisbury,* pp. 130-131.

19. Wilkins, i, 573. The italics are mine. Cf. Hefele, v, 1324-1325.

20. *Charters of Salisbury,* pp. 135 ff., Wilkins, i, 574 ff.

21. This is the date employed by H. Weisweiler, S.J., *Maitre Simon et son groupe 'De sacramentis'* (*Spicilegium sacrum lovaniense,* fasc. 17, 1937), p. lxxv.

22. Hefele, v, 1356.

23. The statutes of Odo of Paris, which were one of the principal sources of Poore's statutes, mention only six sacraments. See Cheney, p. 55.

24. H. Rashdall, *The Idea of Atonement in Christian Theology* (London, 1925), pp. 381-382.

25. Gibbs and Lang, p. 110; cf. pp. 122-123.

26. Gibbs and Lang, p. 193.

27. On this division, cf. Cheney, p. 42. The text is printed in Wilkins, I, 640-646.

28. Wilkins, I, 642.

29. *Moralia*, Lib. XXXI, Cap. xlv, 87-88, *PL*, 76, cols. 620-621. Gregory's enumeration, rather than any of the other early formulations, was preferred by the scholastic philosophers, although they reduced the original eight sins to seven.

30. For statements of this distinction, see Hugh of St. Victor, *De sacramentis*, Lib. II, Pars XIII, Cap. I, *PL*, 176, col. 525; *Summa sententiarum*, Tract. III, Cap. xvi, *PL*, 176, cols. 113-114. Cf. in the thirteenth century William of Auvergne, *De vitiis et peccatis, Opera* (Orleans, 1673), I, 260; St. Bonaventura, *Comm. in Lib. II sententiarum*, Dist. XLII, Dubium III, *Opera* (Quaracchi, 1882-1902), II, 977. A list of "major" sins as distinct from vices may be found in the statutes of Richard le Poore, Wilkins, I, 577. Cf. *Concilium Trevirense* (1277), Mansi, XXIV, cols. 198-199. The phrase "seven deadly sins" is a misleading locution popularized in the late Middle Ages and again by more recent popular writers. For a discussion of the fact that the seven vices are not necessarily mortal, see the thirteenth-century *Compendium theologiae*, Tract. VIII, in J. C. Gerson, *Opera* (Antwerp, 1906), I, col. 347.

31. On the influence of these statutes, see Cheney, 90-91, 96-109.

32. Wilkins, I, 669.

33. *Ibid*. The treatise evidently does not survive.

34. Hefele, V, 1350.

35. Grosseteste, *Epistolae*, ed. H. R. Luard (Rolls Series, 1861), pp. xxi-xxii; A. G. Little, *Studies in English Franciscan History* (Manchester, 1917), p. 108. Cf. Bishop Quivil's remarks, Wilkins, II, 134.

36. It may be remarked that this is not the only instance of an English Bishop's effort to carry the Lateran decrees a step farther. Whereas Innocent III had demanded confession only once annually, Richard le Poore and the English bishops who utilized his decrees asked that their layfolk confess three times a year. See Gibbs and Lang, p. 123. Cf. the continental decree printed by Mansi, XXIII, col. 929, which instructed the priests to preach merely the necessity for annual confession. On the familiarity of thirteenth-century English bishops with the Fourth Lateran decrees, see Cheney, p. 85, note 4.

37. A more accurate estimate of its influence will be possible after the appearance of the new edition of the *Concilia*.

38. *Epistolae*, ed. Luard, p. 155; Cheney, p. 121. Cf. the statement in the sermon "Ad pastores ecclesiae persuasio," in E. Brown, *Fasc. rerum expetendarum* (London, 1690), II, 260.

39. Wilkins, I, 731-732; Cheney, pp. 125-136.

40. *Vetus liber archidiaconii eliensis*, ed. C. L. Feltoe and E. H. Minns (Cambridge Antiquarian Society, 1917), p. 9. Cf. Cheney, pp. 136-138. It should be noticed that the decree is followed immediately by materials on confession.

41. Wilkins, I, 704; Cheney, pp. 138-141.

42. *Registrum Johannis Pontissara* (Surrey Record Society, IV, 1915), p. 237; Cheney, pp. 138-141.

43. Wilkins, II, 143-144.

44. *Registrum Johannis Pontissara*, *loc. cit.*

45. Wilkins, II, 144.

46. On the use of authorities for the development of a sermon theme, see Th.-M. Charland, O.P., II *Artes praedicandi* (Publications de l'institut d'etudes mediévales d'Ottawa, VII, 1936), pp. 195 ff. Cf. E. Gilson, *Les idées et les lettres* (Paris, 1932), pp. 156-158.

47. Wilkins, II, 162.

48. Moorman, p. 231.

49. Cf. "The Cultural Tradition of Handlyng Synne," *Speculum*, 22 (1947), 169 ff.

50. See "A Note on the Classical Origin of 'Circumstances' in the Medieval Confessional," *SP*, 43 (1946), 6-14.

51. For an account of the various degrees of consent, see Peter Lombard, *Sententiae*, Lib. II, Dist. XXIV, Pars II, Cap. vi-xiii, in Bonaventura, *Opera* (Quaracchi, 1882-1902), II, 551-553.

52. Hefele, p. 1350.

53. On the activity of the Dominicans in producing confessional manuals, see P. Mandonnet, O.P., "La Summa de poenitentia m. Pauli," *Beitrage z. Geschichte d. Phil. u. Theol. des Mittelalters*, Supplementband 3 (1935), 531-532.

54. Various relevant matters were mentioned by Richard le Poore, Wilkins, I, 576-577. Cf. the Synod of Exeter, Wilkins, II, 134, and, on the continent, Mansi, XXIII, cols. 29, 1082, 1200.

55. *Opera* (Orleans, 1674), II, 219-247.

56. *MBP*, XXV, 352-358.

57. The treatise is described briefly in "The Cultural Tradition of *Handlyng Synne*," *Speculum*, 22 (1947), 180-182.

58. See my note, "The *Manuel des péchés* and an English Episcopal Decree," *MLN*, 60 (1945), 439-447. This article does not make adequate use of the materials on English synodalia published by C. R. Cheney, but its principal argument is not invalidated by this fact. The popularity of the *Manuel* is attested by the fact that it survives in some twenty-five manuscripts. See C. G. Laird, "Manuscripts of the *Manuel des Péchés*," *Stanford University Studies in Language and Literature* (1941), p. 99. The confesssional treatise described by Paul Meyer, *Romania*, 32 (1903), 95, may also be relevant here.

59. *English Synodalia*, Appendix II, pp. 149-152.

60. Gibbs and Lang, pp. 195-198.

61. Cheney, pp. 149-150.

62. *Ibid.*, p. 150.

63. Davy, p. 33.

64. Cheney, p. 151.

65. *Ibid.*, pp. 151-152.

66. Wilkins, II, 54.

67. *Ibid.*, pp. 54-56.

68. See Burchard of Worms, *Decretum*, *PL*, 140, col. 666.

69. Cf. Hefele, VI, 279, note. For the theological distinction between the two systems of dividing the creed, see the editorial note in St. Bonaventura, *Opera*, III, 539.

70. *Registrum epistolarum*, ed. C. I. Martin (Rolls Series, 1885), III; 949.
71. Ed. F. N. Davies (Lincoln Record Society, 1915), p. 12.
72. *Ibid.*, p. 174.
73. Moorman, p. 78, and note 1.
74. *Rotuli*, pp. 25, 38, 189, 208, 215, 258-259, 265.
75. Wilkins, II, 145-146.
76. For conjectures concerning the date and authorship of these statutes, see Gibbs and Lang, p. 109.
77. Wilkins, I, 661-662.
78. Wilkins, II, 145.
79. Cheney, p. 143.

BURANA—PAGES 131-150

1. *Medieval Latin and the Rise of European Love-lyric* (Oxford, 1965), vol. 1, pp. 306-313. The statement (pp. 306-307) that "no one since Schmeller in 1847 has even bothered to print the complete poem" neglects the text (Schmeller) and translation in George Whicher, *The Goliard Poets* (New York, 1949), pp. 30-35. Whicher's "translation" is an entirely new poem.
2. *Carmina Burana*, ed. Schmeller (Stuttgart, 1847), poem 37, pp. 124-125; *Carmina Burana*, ed. Hilka and Schumann (Heidelberg, 1930), poem 62, pp. 19-23.
3. *Remigii Autissiodorensis Commentum in Martianum Capellam* 2.70.11, ed. Lutz (Leiden, 1962), p. 191. Cf. *MV* III 7.3-4 (Bode 1.198-199).
4. The arguments adduced are impressive, although Orpheus is not customarily associated specifically with the sounds of evening. Further indications of his appropriateness in this poem appear below.
5. The mill in Dronke's quotation from Hildegard (p. 310) serves a very different purpose from that of the mill in the poem. The connection between them seems to me dubious.
6. The virtues of this translation were suggested to me by Thomas La Farge during a seminar discussion.
7. This is a special case of the Boethian principle (*Cons.* 2.m.2) that any kind of cupidinous desire is insatiable. This one in particular is said to lead to transitory pleasure and to leave a sting (3.pr.7 and m.7). But, as John of Salisbury explains, *Pol.* 8.6.724c, desire returns.
8. Dronke translates "joyous reins," but the Terentian proverb "Without Ceres and Bacchus Venus freezes" was well-known in the Middle Ages (e.g., *MV* III 1.7 Bode 1.155), and it was widely recognized that Venereal inclinations, as well as a certain somnolence, are stimulated by excesses of drinking and eating. The "vapor" here described is thus probably gastric in origin. Cf. *MV* III 11.2 (Bode 1.229): "ob vini petulantium libido excitari solet," or Proverbs 23:31-35.
9. *MV* III 8.4 (Bode 1.201). Moreover, Apollo was devoted to the laurel, a symbol of chastity. See Alanus de Insulis, "In Natali Sancti Augustini" (d'Alverny 206).
10. See the discussions of the story of Orpheus and Eurydice by William of

Conches and Arnulf of Orléans in John B. Friedman, *Orpheus in the Middle Ages* (Cambridge, Mass. 1970), pp. 106, 119. Cf. *MV* III 8.20-21 (Bode 211-213).

11. For the two Venuses, see *Remigii Autissiodorensis . . . in Martianum* 1.37.1, 1.8.7-8 (pp. 135-136, 79), as cited in footnote 3; William of Conches, *Glosae super Platonem* 111 (ed. Jeauneau, p. 202); Alexander Neckam, *Super Marcianum* Bodl. MS Digby 221 f. 37; Bernard Silvestris, *Comm. super sex libros Eneidos Virgilii* (ed. Riedel, p. 9); E. H. Alton, "The Medieval Commentaries on Ovid's *Fasti*," *Hermathena* 44 (1926), p. 136.

12. See *A Preface to Chaucer* (Princeton, 1962), pp. 408-410.

13. See Joseph Sauer, *Symbolik des Kirchengebäudes* (Freiburg im Breisgau, 1902), p. 225; Hugo Rahner, *Griechische Mythen in Christlicher Deutung* (Zürich, 1945), pp. 203-224. As Rahner points out, the moon was also associated with the Blessed Virgin Mary. For a discussion including both see Alanus de Insulis, *Distinctiones: PL*, 210, col. 842.

14. For an extended discussion of "ros coelestis gratia" see Alanus de Insulis, *Sermones Octo: PL*, 210, cols. 215-216. Cf. his comment on Canticles 5:2: *PL*, 210, col. 85. On sleep, see his sermon "Ad somnolentos" in the influential *Summa de arte praedicatoria: PL*, 210, col. 195D: Est somnus, quando quis rapitur ad contemplationem coelestium." It would be possible to extend these references, but Alanus should suffice for the relevant period.

15. The discussion of Orpheus in *MV* III 8.20 (Bode 1.211-212) begins: "Fuit autem Orpheus, ut pauxillulum expatiemur, vir maximus tam ingenii claritudine quam eloquentiae suavitate praefulgens. Sacerdos dictus est, quia et theologus fuit, et orgia primus instituit. Ipse etiam homines irrationabiliter viventes rhetorica dulcedine ex feris et immanibus mites reddidit et mansuetos, et ex vagis durisque composuit. Unde et bestias quaslibet, volucres et fluvios, saxa et arbores dicitur movisse." Ideas of this kind led to an easy association between Orpheus and the good preacher. See "The 'Partitura Amorosa' of Jean de Savoie," p. 166.

16. Vol. 1, p. 318, as cited in footnote 1. The text of the poem (ed. Schmeller, poem 50, pp. 141-145; ed. Hilka and Schumann, poem 77, pp. 53-58; as cited in footnote 2) is re-edited by Dronke in a note, pp. 319-322. The "translation" by George Whicher, *The Goliard Poets*, pp. 51-63, as cited in footnote 1, is an altogether different poem. Modern languages do not carry the connotations of the Medieval Latin vocabulary, so that translation is virtually impossible.

17. "Chaucer and the Canticle of Canticles" in *Chaucer the Love Poet*, ed. J. Mitchell and W. Provost (Athens, Georgia, 1973), p. 82. Not all of the Scriptural parallels adduced in this article are repeated here. The poem needs thorough annotation, preferably in an edition.

18. Hugh of St. Victor, *Didas.* 3.8, 6.8-12.

19. See Gabriel Nuchelmans "Philologie et son mariage avec Mercure jusqu'à la fin de XIIe siècle" *Latomus* 16 (1957), pp. 84 ff.

20. Vol. 1, p. 320, as cited in note 1.

21. TLL *s.v. causo*. The word also appears in PA 2.17 (Boethius). Boethius

1.7 corresponds with 1.9 in modern texts. For the relevant passages, see *PL*, 64, cols. 721 and 758 or *Libri logicorum* (Paris, 1520), fols. 171r and 205r. In the first passage Aristotle envisages a universal science whose truths apply everywhere: "Erunt enim illa omnium principia, et scientia eorum domina omnium, et namque scit magis ex superioribus causis sciens, ex prioribus enim scit, cum non ex causatis sciat causis; quare si magis scit, et maxime, et scientia illa erit magis, et maxime." That is, his knowledge would be based on causes not derivative of other causes. The second passage begins, "De causa autem, et cujus causa est dubitabit aliquis, nunquid cum causatum est, et causa est, ut si folia fluunt, aut deficit luna, et causa deficiendi, vel folia cadendi erit, ut si hujus est lata habere folia, deficiendi autem terram in medio esse. Si enim non, aliqua alia erit causa ipsorum, si vero causa sit, et causatum simul, ut si in medio est terra, deficit, aut, si latum est folium, folia fluunt; si autem sic est, simul utique erunt, et demonstrabuntur per invicem." The expression "causas et causatum" means roughly demonstrative causes together with that which is caused by something else and acts as a cause to account for the palm. Taking this literally, since the palm turns out to be "empty" as a result of a cause deriving from other causes not mentioned, the expression is ironic even without the context I have presented.

22. I have sought elsewhere to describe the humorous effects in the dialogues presented in this work. See *A Preface to Chaucer*, pp. 392-448. Some scholars are still not amused, but in my opinion they have not studied the text carefully, and I have not been impressed by their objections.

23. The general idea is a commonplace. A convenient recent discussion appears in V. A. Kolve, *The Play Called Corpus Christi* (Stanford, 1966), pp. 88-92. For a casual example applied to "hours" rather than "ages," see *Glossa ordinaria* (on John 4:6): *PL*, 114, col. 371.

24. For a discussion of the illustration, reproduced in Otto Pächt, C. R. Dodwell and Francis Wormald, *The St. Alban's Psalter* (London, 1960), Plate 77, see *A Preface to Chaucer*, pp. 191-192. The quotation is from *Expositio in Ps. 118: PL*, 15, col. 1328. See p. 143 below, for a photograph of the illustration.

MARCABRU—PAGES 151-165

1. "Zu Marcabru," *ZRP*, 43 (1923) 454. On Marcabru's style, see pp. 441 ff.
2. "Beiträge zur Entstehungsgeschichte der altprovenzalischen Lyrik," *AR*, 15 (1931), esp. pp. 178-191; "Religiöse Elemente im weltlichen Liebeslied der Trobadors," *ZFSL*, 59 (1935), esp. pp. 414-415; "Zur Geschichte des Natureingangs bei den Trobadors," *ZFSL* 60 (1936), esp. p. 280; "Anlässlich des Liedes von Raimbaut d'Aurenga *Cars douz*," *AR*, 21 (1937), esp. pp. 287-288; "Über die Theorien der Liebe bei den Trobadors," *ZRP*, 60 (1940), esp. pp. 198-206.
3. *Marcabru e le fonti sacre dell'antica lirica romanza* (Florence, 1948). This is a revision of the author's earlier *La lirica romanza delle origini* (New York, 1943).
4. See Theodore Silverstein's review article, "Andreas, Plato, and the Arabs," *MP*, 47 (1949), esp. pp. 120-121.

5. "Anlässlich des Liedes von Raimbaut d'Aurenga *Cars douz*," p. 288, as cited in note 2.

6. See Alois R. Nykl, *Hispano-Arabic Poetry* (Baltimore, 1946), pp. 371 ff., and, for more detailed discussion, Alexander J. Denomy, *"Fin' Amors*: the Pure Love of the Troubadours," *MS*, 7 (1945), esp. p. 147; "Jovens: the Notion of Youth among the Troubadours," *MS*, 11 (1949), pp. 1-22; and *"Jois* Among the Early Troubadours," *MS*, 13 (1951), pp. 177-217. Father Denomy's principal conclusions are summarized in "Courtly Love and Courtliness," *Speculum*, 28 (1953), pp. 44-63. These articles contain an enormous amount of useful material assembled with great care and thoroughness.

7. "Beiträge zur Entstehungsgeschichte," p. 180, as cited in note 2.

8. *Marcabru*, pp. 212-213, as cited in note 3.

9. *Ibid.*, pp. 212-213.

10. Augustine's gloss on the psalm referred to by Errante, *Opera* (Paris, 1836-1838), vol. 4, col. 2160A-B, reads in part: "Salices ligna sunt infructuosa . . . Rigantur haec ligna de fluminibus Babylonis, et nullum fructum ferunt. Sicut sunt homines cupidi, avari, steriles in opere bono; ita cives Babyloniae, ut etiam ligna sint illius regionis, ex istis voluptatibus rerum transeuntium pascuntur . . . quaeris fructum, et nusquam invenis." Gregory the Great, whose *Moralia* is a veritable treasure-house of conventional scriptural imagery, wrote, *PL*, 76, col. 676D: "Qui scilicet more salicum fructus non ferunt, sed in foliis viridescunt, quia ea quae gravia ad dicendum non sunt, aliquando honestatis verba proferunt, sed nullum vitae pondus ex bonis operibus ostendunt." Cf. Rabanus, *De universo*, *PL*, 111, col. 519. For further discussion, see Scheludko, "Beiträge zur Entstehungsgeschichte," p. 181, as cited in note 2, and "The Doctrine of Charity in Medieval Literary Gardens," pp. 28-29.

11. *De naturis rerum*, ed. Wright (London, 1863), p. 173. Cf. the note following.

12. Marcabru's broom plants are probably those represented by ML *genesta* and *scopa*. I have found no twelfth-century discussions of the symbolism of these plants, but Bersuire, who frequently reflects conventions as early as Rabanus, associates the *genesta* with sin, *Repertorium* (Cologne, 1730-1731), 2. 492: "Genesta vel myrica, est frutex crescens in terris desertis, & occultis, cujus praesentia infoecundam terram esse indicant, in qua crescit. . . . Talis frutex est peccatum, quia verè in terra inculta per poenitentiam, & deserta à Deo & sanctis, id est, in homine, qui est impius, & peccator, crescit, & generatur, & sterilitatem spiritualem in eo denotat." The *scopa*, Bersuire says, *ibid.*, 2. 526, has delicate white bark when young, but when it becomes older the bark grows black and hard. Its fruit is useless. It has thin light leaves, easily moved by winds. In the same way many men are moved to light words either boastful or wrathful. They appear virtuous when young, but as they grow older they are seen to be evil and infamous. His remarks on the elder, *ibid.*, 2. 522, support the idea found in Neckam: "Sambucus habet flores odoriferos, sed fructus habet nigros, foetidos, & deformes, duplicem etiam corticem dicitur habere. Sic hypocritae, & falsi homines duplicem habent corticem, quia tales pleni sunt duplicitate, contra illud Ecclus. 2. Vae duplici corde. Et pro certo

licet flos conversationis redoleat, & sit bonus; fructus tamen suae operationis foetet, niger est, & infamis, & malus. . . . Vel expone simpliciter de luxuriosis . . ." In the later Middle Ages the elder was said to be the tree on which Judas hanged himself.

13. Errante, *Marcabru*, p. 212, as cited in note 3, furnishes the equation "gardino-mondo," which, I believe, is approximately correct. Cf. "The Doctrine of Charity," pp. 31-32 and notes 50, 51, p. 48. See further Augustine, *Sermo* 304, *Opera*, vol. 5, col. 1818, or almost any gloss on Canticles 4:12 which takes "Ecclesia" as the bride. The headnotes in the modern King James Bible (Oxford, 1897) still indicate that the "garden enclosed" is the Church.

14. See "St. Foy among the Thorns," *MLN*, 67 (1952), 295-299, where references to standard glosses are given. On trees and men, cf. Rabanus, *De universo*, *PL*, 111, col. 509.

15. 1 Corinthians 11:3; Ephesians 1:22, 4:15, 5:23; Colossians 1:18.

16. "L'histoire dans l'œuvre de Marcabru," *Romania*, 48 (1922), pp. 215-216.

17. See Alanus de Insulis, *De arte praedicatoria*, *PL*, 210, cols. 186-187.

18. For possible connotations of "shade," see "St. Foy among the Thorns," p. 299, as cited in note 14.

19. On the interpretation of the text here, see Kurt Lewent, "Beiträge zum Verständniss der Lieder Marcabrus," *ZRP*, 37 (1913), p. 316.

20. *De naturis rerum*, p. 170, as cited in note 11: "Laurus viroris gloria nec in hieme nec in aestate destituitur, nec coruscantis aeris fulgure uritur. Hinc est quod haec arbor amicissima Jovi perhibetur, eo quod insidias aeris non sentit. Pheobus etiam eam amasse fingitur, eo quod per ipsam designatur sapientia, quae nec in adversitate fortunae laeditur injuriis, nec in prosperitate vincitur illecebris. Per hiemem namque accipimus adversitatem, per aestatem designari solet prosperitas." Cf. Bersuire, *Repertorium*, 2. 495-496. These general ideas are familiar to students of Petrarch.

21. See Alanus, *Distinctiones*, *PL*, 210, col. 881C-D, and Bersuire, *Rep.*, 2. 504-505.

22. "Beiträge zum Verständniss," p. 316, as cited in note 19. He suggests that *clavier* of l. 41 is a key-ring, not a porter, and that *An* of l. 44 should be emended to *A ·n*.

23. The *mantelh* might be the Papal mantel, but woolly robes were worn by persons other than monks. See Urban T. Holmes, *Daily Living in the Twelfth Century* (Madison, 1952), p. 165.

24. See Appel, "Zu Marcabru," pp. 413-415, as cited in note 1; Errante, *Marcabru*, p. 290, as cited in note 3.

25. Philip K. Hitti, *History of the Arabs* (New York, 1951), p. 183; *Encyclopaedia of Islam* (London, 1943), *s.v. Futūwa*; *Shorter Encyclopaedia of Islam* (Leiden, 1953), *s.v. futuwwa*.

26. See Franz Taeschner in *Der Islam*, 24 (1937), p. 68. But suggested parallels between *futūwa* and western chivalric conventions should be viewed with caution. See Gerard Salinger, "Was *Futūwa* an Oriental Form of Chivalry?" *American Philosophical Society Proceedings*, 94 (1950), 481-493. Salinger concludes that *futūwa* "has nothing to do with the chivalry of the European Mid-

dle Ages." I am grateful to Bayly Winder for this reference. The article contains a very full bibliography.

27. It is not difficult to conceive of the members of Alfonso's court borrowing technical procedures from their hereditary enemies or taking over some of the material features of their civilization. In the same way, it is not unreasonable to conjecture that Provençal poets may have borrowed melodies or verse forms from their Arabic contemporaries. Arguments that they did have been advanced by Nykl, *Hispano-Arabic Poetry*, pp. 371 ff., as cited in note 6, and by Ramón Menéndez Pidal, *Poesía árabe y poesía europea* (Havana, 1937). This view has been vigorously contested, and no certain conclusions seem possible at present. The borrowing of ethical ideals, however, is quite another matter. On the connotations of the title "imperator" in Spain, see Ramón Menéndez Pidal, *El imperio hispánico y los cinco reinos* (Madrid, 1950), esp. p. 158. On the cult of Santiago, see pp. 126, 148. It is significant in this connection that Marcabru's early patron Guilhem VIII died on a pilgrimage to Compostella, where he had set out to do penance for barbarisms committed during his campaign in Normandy. It is not likely that Marcabru would substitute Ali for St. James, or that Alfonso would have looked with favor on anyone who attempted to do so.

28. See Boissonade, "L'histoire," p. 219, as cited in note 16.

29. In terms of the scriptural symbolism explained below, failure to praise *Jovens* properly is failure to praise Christ and to maintain reason as opposed to lechery.

30. See Boissonade, "L'histoire," pp. 239-240.

31. *PL*, 112, cols. 974-975.

32. *Ibid.*, 975.

33. *PL*, 210, col. 825.

34. *Glossa major*, *PL*, 192, cols. 204, 205.

35. The contrast between the "Old Man" and the "New Man" is analogous with that between the "exterior man" and the "interior man." The exterior man represents the flesh or the sensuality, which man is said to have in common with beasts; the interior man represents the spirit or the reason, which is said to be the distinguishing characteristic of redeemed humanity. See Peter Lombard, *Sententiae* (Ad Claras Aquas, 1916), 2.24.4.

36. *PL*, 176, cols. 107-110. Cf. Scheludko, "Beiträge zur Entstehungsgeschichte," p. 180, as cited in note 2.

37. E.g., see *Soudadier, per cui es Jovens* (44), ll. 1-8; *Pax in nomine Domini!* (35), sts. 6-7; *Assatz m'es bel del temps essuig* (8) ll. 1-10.

38. *Opera*, Vol. 6, cols. 989-1000.

39. For clarification of specific points, see Lewent, "Beiträge zum Uerständniss," pp. 318-319, as cited in note 19. Errante's scriptural parallels, *Marcabru*, pp. 203, 246, as cited in note 3, seem to me relevant only in a very general way.

40. For wider meanings of "adultery," see St. Augustine, Sermo 9 or Sermo 318, *Opera*, vol. 5, cols. 73, 1876; Gregory, *Moralia*, *PL*, 75, col. 1156.

41. During the twelfth century *Maria* was sometimes substituted for *Ecclesia*

as the spouse in the Canticum, so that *maire* may have suggested Mary as well as the Church.

42. See St. Augustine, *Enchiridion*, 24, *Opera*, Vol. 6, cols. 358-359; Hugh of St. Victor, *De sacramentis*, 1.7.25-38, *PL*, 176, cols. 293-306.

43. Cf. the striking image in the *Peterborough Chronicle* under the year 1137: Warsæ me tilede, þe erthe ne bar nan corn, for þe land was al fordon mid swilce dædes and hi sæden openlice ðat Crist slep and his halechen."

44. "*Jois* Among the Early Troubadours," as cited in note 6.

45. *Ibid.*, p. 214.

46. *Sententiae*, 1.17.2. The authority used is Augustine. But this point was disputed by theologians in the thirteenth century. See the "Articuli in quibus magister sententiarum non tenetur communiter ab omnibus," printed *ibid.*, I, lxxviii.

47. *Glossa major*, *PL*, 191, col. 1361.

48. *Oeuvres*, ed. Matzke, *SATF* (Paris, 1909), p. 106, line 1366.

49. *Le roman de philosophie*, *ibid.*, p. 24, lines 640-644. Fin' amors, like "joy," "courtesy," "gentilesse," etc., could be used either in a worldly or a spiritual sense. The worldly use of these terms is frequently ironic. Cf. "Love Conventions in Marie's *Equitan*," p. 202.

50. *Marcabru*, pp. 247 ff., as cited in note 3.

51. E.g., see the General Index in Augustine, *Opera*, Vol. 11, cols. 1336-1337. For a vivid twelfth-century description of spiritual joy, see Alanus, *Summa de arte praedicatoria*, *PL*, 210, col. 180.

52. "Anlässlich des Liedes Raimbaut d'Aurenga *Cars douz*," p. 289, as cited in note 2. Cf. "*Amors de terra lonhdana*," *SP*, 49 (1952), 568.

53. "*Fin' amors*," p. 147, as cited in note 6.

54. *De civitate Dei*, *Opera*, Vol. 7, 14.27, and 15.1,17,18.

55. See *Glossa ordinaria*, *PL*, 113, cols. 101-102.

56. *The Life and Works of the Troubadour Raimbaut d'Orange* (Minneapolis, 1952), p. 71.

57. Errante, *Marcabru*, p. 185.

58. See "The Doctrine of Charity in Mediaeval Literary Gardens," p. 23.

59. Cf. note 20, above.

60. E.g., Gregory, *Moralia*, *PL*, 75, col. 1005, "Quis vero alienus nisi apostata angelus vocatur?" Cf. *Allegoriae*, *PL*, 112, col. 857.

61. *Marcabru*, p. 228.

62. *PL*, 172, col. 393. He also gives a meaning "in malo," col. 392.

63. "The Doctrine of Charity," pp. 31, 36, as cited in note 10.

64. See Gregory, *Moralia*, *PL*, 76, col. 494. In his treatise on the Epistle of John, *Opera*, Vol. 3, col. 2490, Augustine associates shadows with the Old Man, light with the New Man.

65. Errante, *Marcabru*, p. 248, discusses *Jois* in this stanza.

66. The theme of the deceitfulness of sensual love is a commonplace emphasized by Marcabru's disciple Bernart Marti. See Ernest Hoepffner's edition, *CFMA* (Paris, 1929), vii-ix.

67. The *Allegoriae*, *PL*, 112, col. 1079, reflects a convention according to

which the fruit of good works produce the wine of "laetitiam ex amore vero."
68. Cf. Lewent, "Beiträge zum Verständnis," p. 328, as cited in note 19, where *no n'auzim* is substituted for Dejeanne's *non auzim*.
69. *"Fin' amors,"* p. 147, as cited in note 6.
70. *Marcabru,* p. 239.
71. "Beiträge zum Verständnis," p. 328.
72. Marcabru associates "measure" *(temperantia)* with courtesy in *Cortesamen vuoill comenssar* (15) and with *Sofrirs (patientia)* in *Per savi · i tenc ses doptanssa* (37).
73. In this stanza I have not followed Lewent's interpretation, "Beiträge zum Verständnis," p. 329, where *los sieus* (line 43) is said to refer to the followers of *Jois.* Since Lewent's observations are usually acute, I regard my interpretation here as very tentative.
74. *Marcabru,* p. 189.
75. See "Some Medieval Literary Terminology," p. 51.
76. "Beiträge zum Verständnis," p. 441. Cf. Errante, *Marcabru, loc. cit.*
77. Cf. Lewent's suggestions, "Beiträge zum Verständnis," p. 441.
78. Errante, *Marcabru,* p. 186, cites Isaiah 5:20 in connection with this stanza.
79. Enn. in Ps. 163, *Opera,* Vol. 4, cols. 2280-2281. For a medieval vernacular parallel, see *Le chevaler Dé,* ed. K. Urwin, *RLR,* 68 (1937), pp. 163 ff., lines 809-834.
80. Cf. Lewent, "Beiträge zum Verständnis," p. 442.
81. Cf. *L'inverns vai e·1 temps s'aizina* (31), st. 4. See also "The Subject of the *De amore,"* *MP* 50 (1953), pp. 156-157.
82. Cf. Lewent, "Beiträge zum Verständnis," p. 442. He questions *rencia* in line 22.
83. Errante's comparison, *Marcabru,* p. 255, with Genesis 2:24 seems to me irrelevant without further explanation.
84. *Marcabru,* pp. 223-224. Cf. Scheludko, "Ueber die Theorien der Liebe," p. 201, as cited in note 2.
85. E.g., Rabanus, *De universo, PL,* 111, cols. 466, 470; Marbod, *PL,* 171, col. 1773.
86. *De universo, PL,* 111, cols. 467, 470; Marbod, *PL,* 171, col. 1773.
87. See "The Subject of the *De amore,"* pp. 148-149, as cited in note 81.
88. St. Augustine, *De mendacio, Opera,* Vol. 6, col. 712.
89. *"Fin' amors,"* p. 147, as cited in note 6.
90. The figurative language of ll. 45-46 is obscure. For a suggestion, see Lewent, "Beiträge zum Verständnis," p. 443, where there is also an interpretation of lines 47-48.
91. Cf. note 66, above.
92. *Constans* is a term of opproprium. See Pattison, *Raimbaut d'Orange,* p. 70, as cited in note 56.
93. On proud boasting cf. Bernart Marti, *D'entier vers far ieu non pes,* stanzas 9-11, pp. 17-18, as cited in note 66.
94. *"Fin' amors,"* p. 147, as cited in note 6.
95. See Lewent, "Beiträge zum Verständnis," p. 445, where Dejeanne's *mi* in the sixth line is emended to *m'i.*

96. De cler, inst., PL, 107, col. 382. Cf. Augustine, De fide et symbolo, Opera, Vol. 6, col. 274.

97. Cf. Errante's discussion, Marcabru, pp. 204-207.

98. Cf. Lewent, "Beiträge zum Verständnis," p. 446, and Scheludko, "Ueber die Theorien der Liebe," p. 202, as cited in note 2.

99. Glossa major, PL, 192, col. 199.

100. Lewent, "Beiträge zum Verständnis," p. 446, substitutes ieys for lieys in line 48.

101. Bede, In Ion., PL, 92, col. 736.

102. De laboribus herculis, 1.13,1, ed. Ullman (Zurich, 1951), Vol. 1, p. 68.

103. See No·m posc mudar no diga mon veiaire, 3, ed. Kjellman (Uppsala, 1922), p. 62: "E ja nuls hom que sia de bon aire / No sufrira qu'om en diga folor [i.e., the follies of women], / Mas cilh que son vas amor tric e vaire / Se·n anon e·s tenhon ab lor; / Qu'En Marcabrus, a lei de predicaire, / Quant es en gleiza oz denant orador, / Que di gran mal de la gen mescrezen, / Et el ditz mal de domnas eissamen, ..." On Marcabru's attitude toward women, see Scheludko, "Beiträge zur Entstehungsgeschichte," pp. 185-186, as cited in note 2.

PARTITURA—PAGES 166–172

1. We especially miss the work of Philippe de Vitry, who was known as the foremost of French poets. See Arthur Piaget, "Le Chapel des Fleurs de Lis," Romania, 27 (1898), 55-92, where the "Chapel" and the "Dit de Franc Gontier" are printed; A. Coville, "Philippe de Vitry, notes biographiques," Romania, 59 (1933), 520-547; Edmond Pognon, "Ballades mythologiques de Jean de Le Mote, Philippe de Vitry, Jean Campion," Humanisme et Renaissance, 5 (1938), 385-417; "De nouveau sur Philippe de Vitry et ses amis," ibid., 6 (1939), 48-55. Perhaps the most distinguished member of the group was Pierre Bersuire, who, like Philippe, was a friend of Petrarch. Much of his work survives. See Fausto Ghisalberti, "L'Ovidius moralizatus de Pierre Bersuire," Studi romanzi, 23 (1933), esp. 15-25; Joseph Engels, Etudes sur l'Ovide moralisé (Groningen, 1945), pp. 23 ff. Bersuire commented on Ovid and the Bible, compiled an encyclopedia of moralized natural history and a Scriptural or exegetical dictionary, and translated Livy into French. On Jean de Le Mote, see M. Aquiline Pety, La voie d'enfer et de paradis . . . by Jehan de Le Mote (Washington, D.C., 1940), pp. 2-13.

2. The text is printed by Pognon, "De nouveau sur Philippe de Vitri," pp. 53-55, as cited in note 1.

3. Quoted by Pognon, "Ballades mythologiques," ibid., p. 404.

4. See the introductory remarks to the Ovidius moralizatus, ed. Ghisalberti, p. 89, as cited in note 1, where Bersuire expresses his indebtedness for certain moralizations in French verse given him by "magister Philippus de Vitriaco vir utique excellentis ingenii, moralis philosophie et historiarum antiquarum zelator precipuus, et in cunctis mathematis factis eruditus."

5. Repertorium (Venice, 1583), 2.156.

6. PL, 206, col. 361. This commentary was completed in 1233. Its influence

is attested by the fact that it was printed in 1521 by Jodicus Badius Ascensius at Paris. For further substantiation of the ideas expressed in it, however, we may refer to Alanus de Insulis, *In Cant.*, *PL*, 210, cols. 74-75: "Bene quasi virgula fumi, quia gracilis et delicata, quia divinis extenuata disciplinis, et concremata intus in holocaustum incendio pii amoris et desiderio charitatis. *Ut virgula*, inquit, *fumi ex aromatibus*; nimirum quia multis erat repleta virtutum odoribus."

7. The pattern of Jean d'Abbeville's discussion is evident in St. Gregory's treatment of the same verse, *PL*, 79, cols. 504-505, although Gregory applies it to *Ecclesia*. For the *odor*, cf. Gregory, *Hom. in Ezech.*, *PL*, 76, col. 830; *Moralia*, *PL*, 76, col. 775; Rabanus, *PL*, 107, cols. 589-590. The spiritual odor is sometimes as it is in the last of these references, the odor of spiritual flowers.

8. *Repertorium*, 2.617.

9. Fausto Ghisalberti, *Arnolfo d'Orleans* (Milan, 1932), p. 227. A fourteenth-century annotator, quoted by Ghisalberti in a note, observes, "In rei veritate Circe erat meretrix pulcherrima que mutabat homines s. suos amatores. . . . Ipsa vero non mutavit Ulixem quia ipse habebat florem sibi datum a Mercurio qui flos dicitur moly. Per Ulixem intelligitur sapiens. Per florem qui dicitur moly eloquencia intelligitur. Qui bene dicitur dari a Mercurio quia ipse deus eloquencie. Moly dicitur habere nigram radicem quia illa que proponunt sapientes nigra sunt et obscura donec veniant ad conclusionem."

10. The quotations from Bersuire's account of Ulysses and Circe are from *Metamorphosis Ovidiana* (Paris, 1515), Lib. 14. In his article in *Studi romanzi*, as cited in note 1, Ghisalberti does not set out to print a complete text. He does include valuable materials not in the early printed editions.

11. This is a well-known device in medieval logic. See Petrus Hispanus, *Summulae logicales*, ed. I. M. Bochenski (Turin, 1947), pp. 68-70.

12. The combination of Christian wisdom and eloquence suggested in the medieval comments on Ulysses was an important humanistic ideal throughout the Middle Ages. In the western tradition, it stems from Cicero, *De inventione*, 1.1.1, whence it was adapted for Christian purposes by St. Augustine, *De doctrina christiana* 4.5.7-8. In the *Comm. in. Somnium Scipionis* of Macrobius (1.9), the ideal is attributed to Virgil and in turn used by Bernard Silvestris, *Comm. super sex libros Eneidos Virgilii* (ed. Riedel), p. 1, as a justification for studying the Roman poet. The respondent in the poem thus takes what humanistic readers would have regarded as a very admirable course of action. But wisdom and eloquence are illustrated even more forcefully in the decision of Philippe de Vitry at the close of the poem.

13. The clerk in Andreas, *De amore* 1.6.G (ed. Trojel), p. 188, openly identifies himself with the Scribes and the Pharisees: "Et hoc est, quod evangelica clamat auctoritas; videns enim Dominus, suos clericos iuxta humanae naturae infirmitatem in varios lapsuros excessus, ait in evangelio: 'Super cathedram Moisi sederunt scribae et pharisaei; omnia, quaecunque dixerint, vobis servate et facite, secundum autem opera illorum nolite facere' [Matthew 23:2-3], quasi dicat: 'Credendum est dictis clericorum quasi legatorum Dei, sed quia carnis tentationi sicut homines ceteri supponuntur, eorum non inspiciatis opera, si eos contingerit in aliquo deviare.' Sufficit ergo mihi, si altari assistens meae

plebi Dei studeam verbum annuntiare. Unde, si ab aliqua petam muliere amari, sub clericali me non potest praetextu repellere. . . ." This gentleman is a typical "Rabbi" in the bad sense of the word. Andreas means, of course, to satirize hypocritical clerks, not to set up an ideal of "courtly love" as applied to clerks.

14. *Metamorphosis*, fol. viii.

15. See Peter Lombard, *Sententiae* 2.30.8-10.

16. On sloth, cf. "The Doctrine of Charity in Mediaeval Literary Gardens," pp. 42-43.

17. See Peter Lombard, *Sententiae* 3.20.2.

18. *Repertorium*, 2.552.

19. *Metamorphosis*, Lib. 10.

20. Pognon's text reads *adoscula* in line 57.

21. See Jean d'Abbeville, *PL*, 206, col. 27: "Nam persona quae osculatur aliam, spiritum suum spirat ad illam. . . . Habetur quoque in osculo dulcis et delectabilis duorum conjunctio."

22. Cf. *TLL*, 1.186-187.

23. Thus Gregory, *PL*, 79, col. 509, comments: "Sed quamvis magna sint quae extrinsecus apparent, majora tamen in occulto retinent, quae divini oculi soli vident." Alanus, *PL*, 210, col. 77, explains, "Latet quidem hominibus, Deo aurem patet." Honorius, *Sigillum B. Mariae*, *PL*, 172, cols. 505-506, is more specific: "*Absque eo quod intrinsecus latet*, scilicet charitate. . . . Absque eo dulci affectu qui intrinsecus latet, in Dei solius conspectu." Jean d'Abbeville's explanation is similar, *PL*, 206, col. 410: "*absque eo . . . soli* Deo cognitum, nemini manifestum." Honorius, *In cantica*, *PL*, 172, cols. 412-413, plays on the two meanings of *absque*. The fragments of pomegranate are those who follow the apostolic life. They are chaste and furnish good example (unlike Andreas' clerk) "absque eo quod intrinsecus latet, scilicet absque ["and in addition"] charitate quae in corde latet, vel absque ["without"] fomite peccati [i.e. concupiscence] quod in membris latet."

24. *PL*, 206, col. 785.

25. *Repertorium*, 2.647.

26. The decision on this level does not exclude chaste love for a literal virgin. In fact, love of this kind was to become a common poetic stepping-stone toward love for the Blessed Virgin and ultimately love for God.

27. Fulgentius, ed. Helm, p. 180.

28. Ed. Thomas, Cap. 13. Cf. Petrarch, *Invective contra medicum*, ed. Ricci (Rome, 1950), p. 37: ". . . poete, inquam, studium est veritatem rerum pulcris velaminibus adornare, ut vulgus insulsum . . . lateat, ingeniosis autem studiosisque lectoribus et quesitu difficilior et dulcior sit inventu."

CLIGÉS—PAGES 173-182

1. "The Influence of Ovid on Chrestien de Troyes," *Romanic Review*, 12 (1921), pp. 97-134, 216-247.

2. "Ovid's Contribution to the Conception of Love Known as 'L'Amour courtois,' " *MLR*, 42 (1947), pp. 199-206.

3. T. F. Higham, "Ovid: Some Aspects of his Character and Aims," *Classical Review*, 48 (1934), p. 105. A notable contribution to the reinstatement of Ovid as a poet is the essay by A. G. Lee, "Ovid's 'Lucretia,' " *Greece and Rome*, ser. 1, 22 (1953), pp. 107-118.

4. *Harvard Essays on Classical Subjects* (Cambridge, Mass., 1912), p. 229.

5. Berkeley and Los Angeles, 1945. In one sense resemblances between Ovid's paganism and Christianity indicate only that he was a man of his age. Commenting on the history of ideas of immortality, Franz Cumont observes (*After Life in Roman Paganism*, New Haven, 1922, p. 1): "These ideas became more and more like the conceptions familiar to us as gradually their time grows later, and those generally admitted at the end of paganism are analogous to the doctrines accepted throughout the Middle Ages." That Ovid was influenced strongly by such ideas, especially as they appeared in Neo-Pythagorean contexts has been shown by Augusto Rostagni, *Il verbo di Pitagora* (Turin, 1924), especially pp. 248 ff. Although it is usually said that the Pythagorean discourse in *Met.*, 15 is a kind of afterthought, recent evidence tends to show similar influences at work in Ovid's earlier poetry. For example, Jérôme Carcopino, *La Basilique pythagoricienne de la Porte Majeure* (Paris, 1944), especially pp. 377-383, has shown striking resemblances between details of a stucco relief in the apse of a Neo-Pythagorean church and *Heroides*, 15. Ovid was a careful student of the poetry of Virgil, whose Neo-Pythagorean tendencies have been brilliantly demonstrated in Carcopino's *Virgile et le mystère de la IVe églogue* (Paris, 1943). See further Clemens Haselhaus "Metamorphose-Dictungen und Metamorphose-Anschauungen," *Euphorion*, 47 (1953), p. 124. Some notion of Neo-Pythagorean ideas may be obtained by consulting the documents collected by Louis Legrand, *Publius Nigidius Figulus* (Paris, 1931). We may add that Ovid seems to have thought highly of Asclepius (*Met.*, 15.626 ff.), whose cult resembled Christianity in many ways and consequently caused more difficulty to early Christians than that of any other classical deity. See Emma and Ludwig Edelstein, *Asclepius* (Baltimore, 1945), especially vol. 2, pp. 132-138.

6. *Opera* (Hagae Comitum, 1728), 3.923. Gerson quotes Ovid as an authority against lechery in the very sermon in which the condemnation occurs.

7. *De laboribus Herculis*, 1.13, ed. B. L. Ullman (Zürich, 1951), vol. 1, p. 69.

8. See Isidore, *Etymologiae*, 2.21.41.

9. Mussato, Boccaccio, and Salutati were all forced to defend their admiration for poetry against attacks by friars. Franciscans were generally opposed to secular learning, although there were exceptions. Some Dominicans, influenced by St. Thomas, *Summa theol.*, 1.1.9 ad 1; 1-2.101.2 ad 2, denied the utility of poetry.

10. *MGH, Poetae*, 1.543. For bibliographies covering Ovid's medieval reputation generally, see Edgar Martini, *Einleitung zu Ovid* (Brunn, 1933), pp. 92-96, and Friedrich Lenz, "Ovid. 1928-1937," in Bursian's *Jahresbericht*, No. 264 (1939), pp. 120-126. A useful survey is that by Otto Gruppe, *Geschichte der*

klassischen Mythologie und Religionsgeschichte, a supplement to Roscher's *Lexikon* (Leipzig, 1921), pp. 1-35.

11. "Ovid's contribution," p. 199, as cited in note 2.

12. See E. H. Alton, "The Mediaeval Commentators on Ovid's *Fasti*," *Hermathena*, 44 (1926), p. 136.

13. *Comm. super sex libros Eneidos Virgilii*, ed. Riedel, p. 9.

14. See the quotations in "The Subject of the *De amore* of Andreas Capellanus," *MP*, 50 (1953), p. 149, note 27. The ideas are commonplace and could be identified in various forms in many other sources.

15. See Ailred of Riveaulx, *De spirituali amicitia*, *PL*, 195, col. 667. Cf. the same author's *Speculum charitatis*, *PL*, 195, cols. 524-525 and Boethius, *De cons.*, 2, met. 8.

16. *Annotationes in Marcianum*, ed. Lutz, p. 13.

17. Fausto Ghisalberti, *Arnolfo d'Orleans* (Milan, 1932), p. 181.

18. *Ovid*, p. 85, as cited in note 5; see also the very discerning note 42, p. 215.

19. *Ibid.*, pp. 83-84.

20. Ghisalberti, p. 209.

21. We should notice that the loss of these virtues characterizes the beginning of the iron age, *Met.*, 1.127-150, where justice is represented by Astrea, the Virgo of Virgil's Fourth Eclogue. It is thus probable that Ovid regarded these virtues rather highly.

22. *Ovid*, pp. 62 and 203, note 27.

23. See the list of Ovidian characteristics in Fränkel, pp. 124-125.

24. It is noteworthy that some of these "conventions" are listed as disadvantages of love by Albertanus of Brescia, *Dei trattati morali di Albertano da Brescia*, ed. F. Selmi (Bologna, 1873), pp. 211-214.

25. The name Fenice suggests the Phoenix, a traditional symbol of the resurrection of Christ and of the just. See Lactantius' *De ave phenice*, and the study by Emanuele Rapisarda, *Il carme "De ave phoenice"* (Catania, 1946). For the twelfth century, see Alexander Neckam, *De naturis rerum* (London, 1863), p. 85.

IDEA OF FAME—PAGES 183-201

1. *La Idea de la Fama en la Edad Media Castellana* (Mexico, 1952), and the translation by Sylvia Roubaud, *L'idée de la Gloire dans la Tradition Occidentale* (Paris, 1968). This work contains a systematic, if brief, survey of classical and medieval ideas of fame.

Quotations from Chrétien in the present article are from Wendelin Foerster's editions.

2. See B. G. Koonce, *Chaucer and the Tradition of Fame* (Princeton, 1966), pp. 32-39.

3. 15.877-879, Loeb Classics tr. by F. J. Miller. Cf. *L'idee de la Gloire*, p. 44.

4. See Koonce, *Chaucer*, pp. 23-32.

5. *Ibid.*, p. 33.

6. Cf. St. Thomas Aquinas, *Summa theol.* 2-2.73.2: "inter res temporales

videtur fama esse pretiosior, per cuius defectum impeditur homo a multis bene agendis. Propter quod dicitur Eccli. 41, 15: *Curam habe de bono nomine; hoc enim magis permanebit tibi quam mille thesauri magni et pretiosi.*"
7. Cf. "Chrétien's *Cligés* and the Ovidian Spirit," p. 173.
8. It is unfortunate that Chrétien's version of the Tristan story does not survive and that the early French versions are fragmentary. However, it is probably that Iseut was not, in the twelfth century, regarded as an admirable or pathetic romantic heroine.
9. This theme is developed in the *Roman de la rose*, where it is used to suggest idolatry. See John V. Fleming, *The Roman de la Rose: A Study in Allegory and Iconography* (Princeton, 1969), pp. 96-97.
10. Cf. "The Doctrine of Charity in Medieval Literary Gardens," pp. 41-42. The humor of the device itself and of its specific use should have received greater emphasis.

EQUITAN—PAGES 202-206

1. "Le Lai d'*Equitan* de Marie de France," *A Miscellany of Studies . . . Presented to L. E. Kastner* (Cambridge, 1932), p. 301. Hoepffner calls attention to a similar unfavorable attitude toward sensual love in Chrétien and in Marcabru. These comparisons, I think, are just, although their validity has been obscured by recent generalizations concerning "courtly love."
2. *Ibid.*, p. 298. It seems to me unwise to include the varieties of love treated by the troubadours under a single type. See my article "*Amors de terra lonhdana,*" *SP*, 49 (1952), p. 567, note 9. Hoepffner himself makes an exception of Marcabru, p. 302.
3. Marie de France, *Lais* (Oxford, 1944), note on pp. 168-169. It is possible that Ewert's attitude toward Marie's intention might have been altered somewhat if he had been able to use Leo Spitzer's article, "The Prologue to the *Lais* of Marie de France and Medieval Poetics," *MP*, 41 (1943), pp. 96-102. See Ewert's note at the bottom of p. 163. Quotations from Marie in the present article follow Ewert's text.
4. See the article by Spitzer referred to in note 3 and "Marie de France, *Lais*, Prologue, 13-16," *MLN*, 64 (1949), pp. 336-338.
5. *PL*, 195, col. 655C-D. The word *affectio* in the first sentence should be translated "state of mind" rather than "affection," which has connotations in English not implied in the Latin.
6. See *PL*, 40, col. 833. Peter of Blois attributes this work to Augustine. See Marie M. Davy, *Un Traité de l'amour du XII siècle* (Paris, 1932), pp. 140, 142.
7. Davy, p. 130. In general, Peter of Blois depends heavily on Ailred's *De spirituali amicitia* and on his *Speculum caritatis*. Cf. ibid., p. 34, note 2.
8. These are Ailred's words, *loc. cit.* The other two treatises follow them closely, so that it is not necessary to quote them also.
9. See the *De amore*, ed. Trojel, p. 3. Ailred says that love has its origin in a state of mind; Andreas calls it "innata." In Andreas' definition, as in Ailred's, love proceeds from the stimulation of the senses. Then the lover forms an

image or series of images of his beloved in his mind. Finally, the lovers are joined in a desire to fulfil the "laws of friendship" or the "precepts of love." Except for the expression "immoderata cogitatione," Andreas does not use Ailred's condemnatory language, but the pattern of his definition unmistakably resembles that of Ailred's definition.

10. Ailred's work as a whole was designed to form a Christian counterpart to Cicero's *De amicitia*. It is not improbable that ideas quite similar to those expressed by Ailred became associated with Cicero's essay in medieval academic circles.

11. Cf. Hoepffner, p. 195. It is not necessary to confine Marie's contributions to lines 1-190. Perhaps rather she made whatever alterations were necessary to form of her original materials "une mout bele conjointure."

12. See Gaston Paris, "Lais inédits," *Romania*, 8 (1879), 65-66. For the ideal underlying the social satire in this poem, see John of Salisbury, *Policraticus* (ed. Webb), 6.11; *Carmen de bello Lewensi* (ed. Kingsford), lines 165 ff. An element of literary satire as well as social satire in the *Lai dou lecheor* has been suggested by Mortimer J. Donovan, *Romanic Review*, 43 (1952), 81-86. This theory is especially helpful in accounting for some of the formal elements in the poem.

13. Love as a result of mere description is a folk-tale motif (T 11.1), but authors of Marie's sophistication do not usually use materials of this kind without purpose, or simply for the sake of preserving a story. In beginning with the ears Marie was probably following Ailred's description of carnal love or some later description based on it.

14. Feudal amity between lord and vassal had been traditionally associated with divine love. E.g., see François L. Ganshof, *Qu'est-ce que la féodalité?* (Brussels, 1947), pp. 49-51. What was implied by "faith" is described, ibid., pp. 103-104. Cf. Marc Bloch, *La Société féodale: la formation des liens de dépendance* (Paris, 1939), pp. 354-361. The discussion in John of Salisbury, *Policraticus*, 4.3, is relevant here. In Carolingian times, adultery with a vassal's wife was considered an act of treason and it was probably still so regarded in the twelfth century. See Ganshof, p. 46. A king especially was supposed to forego personal satisfaction in order to maintain a bond of charity with his people. See *Carmen de bello Lewensi*, lines 909 ff.

15. The latter poem is printed by Charles H. Livingston, *Le Jongleur Gautier Le Leu* (Cambridge, Mass., 1951), pp. 238-249. The editor's remark, pp. 237-238, that this poem is "une expression singulière de la philosophie de la nature traitée amplement par Jean de Meung dans le *Roman de la Rose*" shows, it seems to me, an insensitivity to Gautier's ironic humor and may also be too severe on Jean de Meun. Since he took the trouble to translate Ailred's *De spirituali amicitia* Jean de Meun must have had at least some regard for its principles. On true and false courtesy, cf. Dante, *Convito*, 2.11. The use of false courtesy as a veil for irregularities is amusingly illustrated in Chaucer's description of Symkyn the miller: "For therbiforn he stal but curteisly, / But now he was a theef outrageously." ("Reeve's Tale," 3997-3998). Cf. "Chaucerian Tragedy, " *ELH*, 19 (1952), p. 18.

16. *De Amore*, p. 316, as cited in note 9.

PEARL AS SYMBOL—PAGES 208-214

1. Such a list may be found in Professor Osgood's note to ll. 735-742, on pp. 82-83 of his edition (London, 1906).

2. "The Allegory of The Pearl," *JEGP*, 20 (1921), 1-21, esp. pp. 2, 12, 14.

3. "Some Debatable Words in *Pearl* and its Theme," *MLN*, 60 (1945), 243.

4. Stanzas 66, 73; Apocalypse 14:1. The "inaccuracy" of the number in stanza 66 represents, I believe, a sort of poetic license. It was possible to suggest a familiar Scriptural passage or devotional text merely by hinting at it, or by quoting it incompletely. The technique is familiar in sermons.

5. *PL*, 35, col. 2437.

6. *Ibid.* Note that "lying" is used figuratively.

7. There is nothing "mystical" about this desire, or about the process of becoming a bride of Christ. To the Medieval mind, one becomes either a bride of Christ or a servant of Satan; there is no alternative.

8. *PL*, 165, col. 680.

9. See D. W. Robertson, Jr., "The 'Heresy' of *The Pearl*," p. 215.

10. *PL*, 36, col. 143.

11. *PL*, 191, col. 168.

12. *Paradiso*, 27.127-129.

13. *PL*, 165, col. 192.

14. Cf. Bede, *PL*, 92, col. 69, where the pearl is the celestial life; Rabanus, who quotes St. Gregory, *PL*, 107, col. 953. The authority of Gregory, Bede, and Rabanus is certainly sufficient to establish a tradition. Of the passages cited by Professor Osgood, pp. 82-83, not all refer to this parable.

15. It should be stressed that this lost innocence is not necessarily sexual.

Pearl "HERESY"—PAGES 215-217

1. Fletcher's article, "The Allegory of *The Pearl*," *JEGP*, 20 (1921), 1-21, is still one of the most fruitful studies of the poem. On heresy, see especially pp. 17-18. Although Wellek denies the existence of heresy in the poem, *Studies in English by Members of the English Seminar of the Charles University* (Prague, 1933), pp. 20-26, he seems to find some self-contradiction in the doctrine.

2. Sermo LXXXVII, *PL*, 38, cols. 530-539.

3. *PL*, 38, col. 530.

4. *PL*, 38, col. 533. The first interpretation involves the ages of mankind rather than the ages of man.

5. Osgood's ed. (London, 1906) 1.582. See his note, p. 75.

6. *PL*, 165, col. 237.

7. *NED*, *s.v. eleventh.*

8. *PL*, 38, col. 533.

9. Cf. the doctrine which Fletcher, pp. 17-18, found in St. Thomas: "Just as one man can get more good out of a penny than another, so one spirit in the presence of God can realize him more fully than another."

10. In stanza 38 it is said that in the celestial city everyone is "quen oþer

kyng." This is not heresy either, but a reference to the symbolism of the denarius. Rabanus comments, *PL*, 107, col. 1028-1029, "Denarius figuram regis habet. Recepisti ergo mercedem quam tibi promiseram imaginem et similitudinem meam." In the celestial city where the distorting forces of cupidity do not operate, the human soul is the true image of God, the King.

11. See stanza 56 and the final stanza of the poem.

Typology—Pages 218-232

1. *Speculum*, 32 (1957), 805-825.
2. *The Play Called Corpus Christi* (Stanford, 1966), Ch. 4.
3. *The English Mystery Plays* (Berkeley and Los Angeles, 1972). Like her earlier work on the lyric, *The English Religious Lyric in the Middle Ages* (Oxford, 1968), this book must be ranked as a major contribution to English medieval studies.
4. "The Effect of Typology," p. 825, as cited in note 1.
5. Henri de Lubac, *Exégèse médiévale* (Paris, 1959-1964), Pt. 1, Vol. 1, pp. 352-353. In this passage the expression "opposition dialectique" is perhaps slightly inaccurate, since the New Law is a "fulfillment" of the Old rather than something in dialectical opposition to it. But Father de Lubac was undoubtedly seeking to emphasize the idea that the contrast between the Old Testament and the New leads dynamically to spiritual implications.
6. Cf. my *A Preface to Chaucer* (Princeton, 1962), pp. 189-190.
7. *Exégèse médiévale*, Pt. 1, Vol. 2, p. 551.
8. Quoted from the *Moralia, ibid.*, p. 555.
9. *Ibid.*, p. 566.
10. *Religious Art* (New York, 1949), p. 78.
11. *A Preface to Chaucer*, Ch. 3.
12. *The Play Called Corpus Christi*, p. 106, as cited in note 2.
13. *Ibid.*, pp. 106-110; 116-122.
14. Cf. *A Preface to Chaucer*, pp. 325-326.
15. Cf. my *The Literature of Medieval England* (New York, 1970), pp. 3-4.
16. *Glosae super Platonem*, ed. E. Jeauneau (Paris, 1965), 96, p. 180.
17. We may compare, if we wish, the underlying attitude here with modern structuralist depth analysis, which seeks to discover the deep structures of the human personality and the recurrent structures of human behavior, thought and expression that result from them. The idea appeared, for example, in Vilfredo Pareto's "residues" and "derivations," although it has been refined and elaborated in recent years and has led to a great deal of pedantic "analysis" of literary texts. It often leads to a kind of cultural "anthropomorphism" based on current conditions, to sentimental neo-primitivism, and to generalizations about the past that ignore the elementary facts of cultural history. Those who would dismiss the subject of tropology as "mysticism" in a derogatory sense should recall that its aims were operational. Structuralism is not only "mystical" in its assumptions, but is operationally inconsequential, a fact that may account for its academic popularity.

18. Cf. *A Preface to Chaucer*, pp. 301-302.

19. The text followed is that of A. C. Cawley, *The Wakefield Pageants in the Towneley Cycle* (Manchester, 1958).

20. Cf. Muriel Bowden, *A Commentary on the General Prologue to the Canterbury Tales* (New York, 1948), p. 241, where Chaucer's Plowman, by virtue of his trade, is called "a descendant of 'Caym.' "

21. *De civ. Dei*, 15.1-2.

22. *PL*, 113, col. 476. Cf. David Lyle Jeffrey, "Stewardship in the Wakefield *Mactatio Abel* and *Noe* Plays," *ABR* 22 (1971), 69.

23. *Policrat.*, 7.10.659 A-B. Cf. Jeffrey, p. 69.

24. Cited in my *Chaucer's London* (New York, 1968), p. 67.

25. *PL*, 113, col. 98.

26. *PL*, 113, col. 98. The word *figura*, which, in spite of modern efforts to sophisticate it, was a very general term, is here used to refer to members of the Church Militant and not simply to the New Testament.

27. *Enn. in Ps.*, 64.2.

28. For the figure in the visual arts, see Mary D. Anderson, *Misericords* (Harmondsworth, 1954), pp. 21-22; and in popular verse, see "The False Fox" printed by Rossell H. Robbins, *Secular Lyrics of the Fourteenth and Fifteenth Centuries* (Oxford, 1952), no. 49, especially ll. 10-14.

29. The word "hay" in line 88 probably implies "flesh."

30. Cf. Chaucer, "Summoner's Tale," line 1967, and the subsequent problem.

31. As I have pointed out elsewhere, irrational or sinful behavior was often regarded as being comic in the Middle Ages. See *Abelard and Heloise* (New York, 1972), pp. 110-112. This kind of comedy often appears in "religious" contexts.

32. See Erwin Panofsky, "Blind Cupid," in *Studies in Iconology* (New York, 1962), pp. 95-128; Mary D. Anderson, *Misericords*, p. 18.

33. E.g., "Second Nun's Tale," 488-504.

34. The principle was well-known. Cf. Chaucer, "Parson's Tale," line 564. The parallel with "Summoner's Tale," ll. 2009-2010, indicated in Robinson's note is, however, false, since the latter passage is literal.

35. Cf. *Glossa ordinaria, PL*, 113, col. 99: "Peccata peccatis adjiciens desperat, nec credit se veniam posse adipsici, quod est blasphemia in Spiritum sanctum, quae non remittitur in hoc saeculo nec in futuro." This principle was conventionally explained by confessors to their pentitents, so that it would not have escaped even the unlearned in the audience.

36. See Bertha Haven Putnam, *Proceedings Before the Justices of the Peace in the Fourteenth and Fifteenth Centuries* (London, 1938), p. cxxviii.

37. *England in the Later Middle Ages* (London, 1973), p. 31.

BOOK OF DUCHESS—PAGES 235-256

1. The war with France was resumed in this year, the enemy now being the astute Charles V rather than the chivalrous King John. John of Gaunt's ven-

ture into Artois and Picardy met with little success, and the invasion of Robert Knowles in the following year was a failure. Edward fell under the influence of Alice Perrers, a woman hardly of the type to inspire chivalric idealism, leaving the guidance of the realm to others. England faced a period of decline, marked by financial crises, social and political unrest, and general decay.

2. *Chronicles*, trans. T. Johnes, Book 1, Ch. 272.

3. *Le joli buisson de jonece, Oeuvres*, ed. Scheler (repr. Geneva, 1977), Vol. 2, lines 241-250.

4. The services were elaborate. For that held in 1371 the Duke allowed Sir William Burghbrigg of his council £38 18s, a considerable sum. See *John of Gaunt's Register*, ed. S. Armitage-Smith (London, 1911), no. 943. For information about the first service attended by the Duke in person (1374), see N. B. Lewis, "The Anniversary Service for Blanche, Duchess of Lancaster, 12 Sept., 1374," *Bulletin of the John Rylands Library*, 21 (1937), pp. 176-192.

5. On June 8, 1374 (*Register*, no. 1394), we find the Duke ordering alabaster for "new work" on the tomb. He was especially concerned to find material suitable for the effigies. On Jan. 26, 1375 (*Register*, no. 1659), arrangements were made to pay Yevele for his work.

6. For all of these arrangements, see Sydney Armitage-Smith, *John of Gaunt* (repr., New York, 1964), pp. 75-78.

7. *Ibid.*, pp. 76, 77.

8. This point has been well made with reference to the lyric especially by John Stevens, *Music and Poetry in the Early Tudor Court* (Lincoln, 1961). See especially Ch. 10, and the remarks about "applied" or "practical" art on p. 235.

9. See *John of Gaunt*, Ch. 8. The Duke may have been more concerned about ecclesiastical abuses than these pages indicate, although it is probable that he thought of them as being personal rather than institutional. The revolutionary character of Wyclif's thought was not due merely to the fact that he attacked abuses, for the abuses he attacked were deplored also by many persons whose inclinations were essentially conservative. His desire to reform the organization and theology of the Church was revolutionary.

10. There is a good discussion by Derek Brewer, *Chaucer in His Time* (London, 1963), pp. 226-237. The quotation from Clanvowe on p. 226, however, is not a condemnation of "courtliness" or "chivalry," but of worldly wisdom, which is a different matter entirely.

11. See most recently J. Burke Severs, "The Sources of 'The Book of the Duchess,' " *Mediaeval Studies*, 25 (1963), 355-362.

12. E. K. Rand, *Founders of the Middle Ages* (New York, 1928), p. 178.

13. Ed. V. L. Dedeck-Hery, *Mediaeval Studies*, 14 (1952), 165-275. Jean's Preface, here briefly summarized, appears on pp. 168-171.

14. Jean is here reflecting the Augustinian distinction between use and enjoyment. See Peter Lombard, *Sententiae*, 1.1.3.

15. This idea may also be found in Trivet's commentary. See *A Preface to Chaucer* (Princeton, 1962), p. 359.

16. Lines 759-804. In effect, the Black Knight tells us that he entered the

Garden of Deduit as it is described in the *Roman de la rose*. Although we may expect this to have been a fairly common procedure, it was nevertheless a foolish one, leading to what Chaucer calls in the Prologue to *The Legend of Good Women* (F 472, G 462) "falsnesse" and "vice." The early reputation of the *Roman*, which was not attacked on moral grounds "in its own century," is discussed by John V. Fleming, "The Moral Reputation of the *Roman de la Rose* before 1400," *RPh*, 18 (1965), 430–435.

17. *Register*, no. 608, as cited in note 4.

18. *Register*, no. 1662.

19. Donald R. Howard, *Speculum*, 39 (1964), p. 541.

20. *Cons.*, 4.pr.4 and m.4. For the manner in which these passages were understood in the fourteenth century, see Chaucer's translation.

21. Cf. H. S. Bennett's discussion of the word *alone* in connection with the "pathos" of Arcite's farewell to the world ("Knight's Tale," line 2779), *Chaucer and the Fifteenth Century* (Oxford, 1947), p. 83. It has, he says, "little of the evocative effect that it has for us with centuries of association behind the word 'alone'—associations magnificently called on by Coleridge in

> Alone, alone, all, all alone,
> Alone on a wide wide sea . . ."

Chaucer, it is said, had to rely on "cumulative effect" rather than association. It may be objected in the first place that the word *alone* had, in the fourteenth century, associations which had been gathering for some centuries since the text of Ecclesiastes 4:10 became available in the West. Moreover, at the risk of being accused of "literary insensitivity" once more, let me add that the passage in question is not "pathetic" at all. We shall do better to forget Coleridge, except for purposes of contrast, when we read Chaucer.

22. Trans. Lucy Norton (London, 1951), p. 192. The great painter was troubled by feelings of multiple personality and loneliness. E.g., see pp. 15, 40, 214. He speaks, p. 97 (1849), of an "unbearable sense of emptiness" to his friend Chopin, who was suffering acutely from "boredom."

23. "Parson's Tale," line 677.

24. Magnanimity, for example, is defined as "greet corage," which "maketh folk to undertake harde thynges and grevouse thynges, by hir owene wil, wisely and resonably." (X [I]731) The virtue of magnificence appears "whan a man dooth and perfourneth grete werkes of goodnesse." (X [I]735) It is not difficult to think of these virtues in connection with the Knight as he is described in the General Prologue.

25. The more "advanced" figures in the General Prologue to *The Canterbury Tales*, like the Monk and the Pardoner, are not treated with much sympathy.

26. *Confessions* 2.8 (1750–1752). It is possible that this story is colored by Rousseau's later hostility to Grimm.

27. For some hints of this change, see Jan H. van den Berg, *The Changing Nature of Man* (New York, 1961), Ch. 3. For the nineteenth century in particular, see the brilliant study by Werner Hofmann, *The Earthly Paradise* (New York, 1961), especially Ch. 10.

28. Medieval houses, even among the wealthy, afforded little bedroom pri-

vacy. In this connection, see also Philippe Ariès, *Centuries of Childhood* (New York, 1962), pp. 100ff., and p. 128.

29. See *John of Gaunt*, pp. 460-462, as cited in note 4.

30. In 1396 the Duke and Katherine petitioned the Pope to sanction their marriage, stating as one of the impediments the fact that they had lived in adultery during the lifetime of Constance. In connection with "sin" itself, we should be aware of the fact that the connotations of the word have changed enormously since the Middle Ages. The intense introspective concern for the subject exhibited by Bunyan in *Grace Abounding* would have then seemed unnatural, and Arnold's feeling that sin is "a positive, active entity hostile to man, a mysterious power" would have seemed Manichean, smacking a little of devil-worship. Arnold's further view that "the true greatness of Christianity" lies in "righteousness," a view that seems to be taken for granted by many modern writers, would have been regarded as Pelagian. Perhaps it would be better to translate "sin" in most medieval contexts as "unwise conduct." Christ was conventionally regarded as the "Wisdom of God," and His message was love, not righteousness, which was the message of the Old Law.

31. *De rerum natura* 4.1058-1072.

32. *Chaucer and the Fifteenth Century*, p. 36, as cited in note 22.

33. See *A Preface to Chaucer*, p. 461.

34. E.g., by such diverse witnesses as T. S. Eliot in *The Cocktail Party* and Camus in *The Stranger*.

COURTLY LOVE—PAGES 257-272

1. E.g., see John Lawlor, "The Pattern of Consolation in *The Book of the Duchess*," *Speculum*, 31 (1956), pp. 626-648.

2. *Liber Albus*, trans. H. T. Riley (London, 1861), p. 396.

3. E.g., in *A Preface to Chaucer* (Princeton, 1962), pp. 195-203, 391-452.

4. See the interesting discussion by James I. Wimsatt, "The Apotheosis of Blanche in *The Book of the Duchess*," *JEGP*, 66 (1967), pp. 26-44. A good example is described by Charles Schmidt, "Gottfried de Hagenau," *Revue d'Alsace*, 24 (1873), esp. pp. 164-165.

5. *Chaucer and His Poetry* (Cambridge, Mass., 1927), p. 63.

6. *Sermo Epinicius*, ed. H. A. Oberman and J. A. Weisheipl, *Archives d'histoire doctrinale et littéraire du moyen age* (1958), pp. 323-324.

7. Ed. A. Roncaglia (Bari, 1941), p. 417.

8. Reginald R. Sharpe, *Calendar of Letter-Books . . . of the City of London: Letter-book H* (London, 1907), p. 129, note 2.

9. On this feature of Marian devotion, see Jean Leclercq, *La liturgie et les paradoxes chrétiens* (Paris, 1963), pp. 200-204.

10. *The Works of Geoffrey Chaucer* (Cambridge, Mass., 1957), p. 387.

11. See Derek Brewer, *Chaucer in His Time* (London, 1964), pp. 226-30.

12. *Liber Albus*, p. 427, as cited in note 2.

13. *Ibid.*, p. 54. Among the "ancient books" were obviously Fitzstephen's description of London and Geoffrey's *Historia*.

14. (Abbeville, 1468), I, Sig. A viii recto. I owe this reference to John V. Fleming. On the tradition of a moral cause for the fall of Troy and on the relationship between Troy and Troilus suggested below, see John P. McCall, "The Trojan Scene in Chaucer's *Troilus*," *ELH*, 29 (1962), pp. 263-275.

15. See John P. McCall and George Rudisill, Jr., "The Parliament of 1386 and Chaucer's Trojan Parliament," *JEGP*, 58 (1959), pp. 276-288.

FRANKLIN—PAGES 273-290

1. See *Preface to Chaucer*, p. 249.

2. E.g., see the list included for Nottinghamshire sessions of 1393-1396 in Bertha Haven Putnam, *Proceedings Before the Justices of the Peace in the Fourteenth and Fifteenth Centuries* (London, 1938), p. 149, or the description of M.P.'s in May McKisack, *The Fourteenth Century* (Oxford, 1959), pp. 188-189.

3. McKisack, p. 206.

4. *Ibid.*, p. 206.

5. Putnam, p. cxxviii.

6. His experience there was unfortunate, and it is unlikely that he had much respect for members of the commons who readily submitted to great magnates like the Duke of Gloucester, who dominated the session. See John P. McCall and George Rudisill, Jr., "The Parliament of 1386 and Chaucer's Trojan Parliament," *JEGP*, 58 (1959), 276-288.

7. Cf. Robert S. Haller, "Chaucer's *Squire's Tale* and the Uses of Rhetoric," *Modern Philology*, 62 (1965), 285-295; and John P. McCall, "The Squire in Wonderland," *Chaucer Review*, 1 (1966), 103-109.

8. On the character of the Squire, see Alan Gaylord, "Chaucer's Squire and the Glorious Campaign," *Papers of the Michigan Academy of Science, Arts, and Letters*, 45 (1960), 341-361.

9. It has been suggested that since the Franklin's Tale is overtly a Breton lai, the pagan standards of the lai should be applied to it. See Kathryn Hume, "Why Chaucer Calls the *Franklin's Tale* a Breton Lai," *Philological Quarterly*, 51 (1972), 365-379. We know nothing of actual Breton lais, but they must have flourished at the court of Brittany during the late eleventh and early twelfth centuries. The Dukes of Brittany at the time, Hoel, Alain Fergent, and Conan III, were not by any stretch of the imagination men of "pagan" inclinations. The surviving lais in French and English are subject to a variety of interpretations. But the members of Chaucer's audience had no purely "literary" concerns and no inclination to take detached and objective views of the past. They undoubtedly judged Chaucer's tales by their own standards, regardless of the presumed dates of the events described. They did not have what Hume describes as "bourgeois moral attitudes," but this does not mean that they did not have any moral attitudes at all. The Franklin, as a matter of fact, comes closer to having what might be called "bourgeois moral attitudes" than any other character in the Prologue.

10. See Richard L. Hoffman, *Ovid and the Canterbury Tales* (Philadelphia, 1966), pp. 165-168.

11. See *A Preface to Chaucer* (Princeton, 1962), pp. 253-254, and fig. 6. Horses were in much more frequent use in Chaucer's time than they are now, and the folly of giving them too much freedom to exercise their own inclinations was more apparent.

12. Jean amusingly misapplied some lines from Ovid, *Metamorphoses* 2. 846-847. The most thorough and illuminating discussion of this passage available is that in Hoffman, pp. 63-67, and the accompanying notes.

13. Cf. the discussion in Peter Lombard, *Sententiae* 4.26.2.

14. *The Romance of the Rose by Guillaume de Lorris and Jean de Meun* (Princeton, 1971), p. 238.

15. On the distinction between two kinds of "nature" where human beings are concerned, see John V. Fleming, *The Roman de la Rose: A Study in Allegory and Iconography* (Princeton, 1969), 194-195, and on "natural love," see p. 131.

16. Dahlberg's translation, p. 154. The idea is a reflection of the ironic statement in Ovid, *Ars amatoria* 2.161-162: "Non ego divitibus venio praeceptor amandi: / Nil opus est illi, qui dabit, arte mea."

17. *The Romance of the Rose*, pp. 155-156.

18. *Ibid.*, pp. 169-170.

19. *Ibid.*, p. 178.

20. Cf. *A Preface to Chaucer*, pp. 374-375. For further elaboration, see Henricus de Segusio, *Summa* (Lyon, 1537), fol. 41, which contains a full-page diagram, and a discussion, fols. 41 verso-43. With reference to the present tale it may be of some interest to notice that under canon law a man who consents to the adultery of his wife is to be denied Holy Communion perpetually. See *Thomae de Chobham Summa Confessorum*, ed. Rev. F. Broomfield (Louvain, 1968), pp. 339-340. The analogy between marriage and the relationship between a prince and his dominions was still being used by Bacon. See "The Wisdom of the Ancients," in *Works*, ed. Spedding *et al.*, vol. 6, pp. 702-703. In fourteenth-century criminal law a wife who murdered her husband was said to be guilty of "petty treason," but no treason was involved if a husband murdered his wife.

21. See *A Preface to Chaucer*, pp. 144, 305-306, 400-401. The theme has most recently been discussed with reference to Chaucer by D. M. Burjorjee, "The Pilgrimage of Troilus's Sailing Heart," *Annuale Mediaevale*, 13 (1972), 14-31. For the Franklin's Tale, cf. R. P. Miller, "Allegory in The Canterbury Tales," in Beryl Rowland, *Companion to Chaucer Studies* (Toronto, New York, London, 1968) p. 285, who remarks justly concerning the rocks that "the desire to remove them, as well as their 'magical' disappearance, are both emblematic of the Epicurean imagination."

22. Cf. *A Preface to Chaucer*, pp. 46-47.

23. See the very careful and detailed discussion by Chauncey Wood, *Chaucer and the Country of the Stars* (Princeton, 1970), pp. 266-267.

24. *Ibid.*, pp. 245-249.

25. Alan Gaylord demonstrates fully in "The Promises in The Franklin's Tale," *ELH*, 31 (1964), 352-357, the prevalence of a commonplace ethical principle that rash promises leading to wrongful action are not to be kept.

Dorigen should not have been inclined to keep her promise about the rocks even if that promise had been serious. Since it was made "in pley" she has no obligation whatsoever to abide by it.

26. The allegation, sometimes made, that Arveragus knows in advance that his wife will be released is hardly supported by this outburst of weeping.

27. See Miller, p. 284.

28. On the shallowness of the Sergeant as he appears in his tale, see the brilliant essay by Wood, "Astrology in the Man of Law's Tale," *Chaucer and the Country of the Stars*, pp. 192-244.

CHAUCERIAN TERMINOLOGY—PAGES 291-301

1. The text used in this article is *Works*, ed. F. N. Robinson, 2nd ed. (Boston, 1957).

2. W. O. Evans, " 'Corteysye' in Middle English Literature," *Mediaeval Studies* 29 (1967), 143-157.

3. Edwin B. DeWindt, *Land and People in Holywell-cum-Needingworth* (Toronto, 1972), p. 3.

4. *Country Gentry in the Fourteenth Century* (Oxford, 1969), p. 24.

5. Cf. N. Denholm-Young, *Seignorial Administration in England* (Oxford, 1937), p. 1. Most of the material in this book, unfortunately for Chaucerians, is concerned with the thirteenth century.

6. For rural society in Kent, see most recently F.R.H. Du Boulay, *The Lordship of Canterbury* (New York, 1966).

7. See the remarkably fine study of H.P.R. Finberg, *Tavistock Abbey* (Cambridge, 1951).

8. See P.D.A. Harvey, *A Medieval Oxfordshire Village: Cuxham* (Oxford, 1965).

9. For a general description of a reeve, see Edward Miller, *The Abbey and Bishopric of Ely* (Cambridge, 1951), pp. 252-254. Cf. J. A. Raftis, *Warboys* (Toronto, 1974), pp. 242-243.

10. For an account of stewards in the thirteenth century, see Denholm-Young, *Seignorial Administration*, pp. 66-85.

11. Finberg, *Tavistock Abbey*, p. 238.

12. Cf. Muriel Bowden, *A Commentary on the General Prologue to the Canterbury Tales* (New York, 1948), pp. 251-252.

13. For accusations brought against an actual bailiff and an actual reeve see Marjorie Morgan, *The English Lands of the Abbey of Bec*. 2nd ed. (Oxford, 1968), pp. 65-66.

14. We may compare the treatment of the Friar. See my *Chaucer's London* (New York, 1968), p. 195.

15. There is obvious irony in the fact that the Reeve concludes his tale by saying, "A gylour shal hymself bigyled be."

16. The stimulating essay by A. R. Bridbury, *Economic Growth: England in the Later Middle Ages* (London, 1962), serves as a corrective to older views concerning this matter. Cf. Du Boulay, *Lordship of Canterbury*, pp. 140-141.

17. DeWindt, *Land and People*, pp. 163-267, 275; J. A. Raftis, "An English Village after the Black Death," *Mediaeval Studies* 29 (1967), 163-165, and *Warboys*, pp. 219-221. The device of leasing holdings so that some peasants, either in this manner or through purchase, acquired relatively large tenements appeared in some other areas well before 1349; in other areas demesne leasing did not become common until the fifteenth century. In some places demesnes were leased to members of the gentry or to wealthy merchants, but this practice seems to have been exceptional. On the estates of the duchy of Cornwall ordinary manorial holdings were leased at auction every seven years. There merchants, clerks, and even minor noblemen might hold tenements in a manor. See the admirable study of John Hatcher, *Rural Economy and Society in the Duchy of Cornwall 1300-1500* (Cambridge, 1970), pp. 75, 86-87. Under the wise and generous administration of the Black Prince the manors of the Duchy suffered comparatively little economic disruption as a result of the Black Death. It is true that high-ranking noblemen might occasionally hold small portions of manors elsewhere, however. Thus the large holdings of the countess of Pembroke included "a messuage and a virgate of land held of Robert Dyngelegh, as of his manor of Fytelton" in Wiltshire. See *Calendar of Inquisitions Post Mortem*, xvi, 7-15, Richard II (London, 1974), no. 19, p. 8. Cf. no. 909, p. 357.

18. The tendency to see the Plowman as a "symbolic" or iconographic character is probably correct, but there is a sense in which the other characters in the Prologue are iconographic in the same way. It makes little sense to single out one very virtuous character as being "symbolic" and to say that the vicious characters are "realistic." The statement about tithes may be another instance of Chaucer's criticism of the friars, some of whom apparently held that tithes were contrary to the law of God. E.g., see Dorothy Owen, *Church and Society in Medieval Lincolnshire* (Lincoln, 1971), p. 89. The instance here, however, dates from 1424. Cf. David L. Jeffrey, "Franciscan Spirituality and the Rise of English Drama," *Mosaic* 8 (summer, 1975), 38, on the sermons of the Franciscan William de Melton, also from the fifteenth century. Were Franciscans preaching against tithes in the fourteenth century?

19. For the Parson, cf. *Chaucer's London*, pp. 109-110. A picture of a vicious parson appears in the Reeve's Tale, but this does not mean that Chaucer thought all country parsons to be mercenaries.

20. *The State of England*, Camden Soc., 3rd ser., 52 (1936), p. 17.

21. The social distinction between "freemen" and "serfs" became blurred during the later fourteenth century, since prosperous peasants of free status might acquire land that demanded villein services, and prosperous serfs, on the other hand, might have "free" servants and occupy land formerly held in free tenure. Manorial yeomen were traditionally servile.

22. Du Boulay, *Lordship of Canterbury*, p. 162.

23. DeWindt, *Land and People*, pp. 159-161.

24. Reprint (New York, 1968). Appendix i, pp. 389-394.

25. For examples of relatively humble families among whose members one rose to become Knight of the Shire, see Marjorie Morgan, *English Lands*, pp. 115-117.

26. *Country Gentry*, p. 25.
27. *Ibid.*, p. 27.
28. *Chaucer's London*, p. 117 and note.
29. For dairy assistants in different areas, see Harvey, *Village*, p. 75, and Finberg, *Tavistock Abbey*, pp. 135-137. At Tavistock the *daya* did not winnow until about 1390. But see Dorothea Oschinsky, *Walter of Henley and Other Treatises on Estate Management and Accounting* (Oxford, 1971), p. 425.
30. R. H. Hilton, *A Medieval Society* (London, 1966), p. 104. This book is clear and well organized, but it is unfortunately marred by a naive Marxism combined with the usual concomitant cynicism and distortion of emphasis.
31. See "Chaucer's Franklin and his Tale," p. 273.

VIRGIN—PAGES 305-307

1. *Leonardo* (Berlin, 1943), p. 50.
2. See *The Virgin of the Rocks in the National Gallery* (London, 1947), p. 12. Cf. Kenneth Clark, *Leonardo da Vinci: an account of his development as an artist*, 2nd. ed. (Cambridge, 1952), p. 43.
3. The two alternatives were not considered to be mutually exclusive, but were regarded as equally valid and fruitful ways of reading the text. Thus Honorius Augustodunensis wrote commentaries illustrating both approaches. See *PL*, 172, cols. 347 ff. and 495 ff.
4. *In Canticum Canticorum Salomonis commentarius literalis, et catena mystica* (Paris, 1604). Each passage considered is interpreted separately under each of the following rubrics: "Littera," "Tropologia," "Mixta interpretatio, sev de Deipara," "Anagoge." The "allegorical" interpretation applying to the Church is omitted. The authorities used, which are listed on fols. 12v-14r, make up a very representative tradition from the time of the Fathers to recent writers like Luis de Léon.
5. See the note on "Guilhelmus Parvus," p. 13v, and for confirmation, Friedrich Stegmüller, *Repertorium Biblicum*, no. 3009.
6. *In Canticum*, fols. 91r-92r. On 86v Alanus de Insulis (12C) is quoted to the effect that the *foramina* are the wounds of Christ. A similar interpretation, fol. 89r, is attributed to St. Gregory the Great: "Talis anima bene dicitur *in foraminibus petræ & in caverna maceriæ*, degere . . . quia dum in crucis recordatione patientiam CHRISTI imitatur, dum ipsa vulnera propter exemplum in memoriam reducit, quasi columba in foraminibus, sic simplex anima in vulneribus, nutrimentum quo conualescat, inuenit."
7. E.g., Antonina Vallentin, *Leonardo da Vinci* (New York, 1938), p. 98, imagines the god Pan among the rocks and finds "more . . . of a heathen god than a heavenly messenger in the angel." This paganism, like that of many other critics of Renaissance art, belongs to the era of Walter Pater and Pierre Louys and has nothing to do with the supersititions of antiquity.
8. This was the technique attributed to scripture itself. See St. Augustine, *De doctrina christiana*, 3.5.9ff., 4.8.22; St. Gregory, *In Canticum*, *PL*, 79, cols. 471-474. Similar principles were applied to poetry. E.g., see Petrarch, *Invective*, ed. Ricci (Rome, 1950), pp. 69-70.

9. See Del'Rio's citations of Honorius, William of Newburgh, and others, fol. 160r. For "mixed" interpretations see pp. 160v–161v. E.g., Alanus is quoted as follows: "Merito o virgo tali arborum & aromatum decore decoraris, quia in te est *fons saliens in vitam æternam.* Qui fons *puteus* est, id est, inexhaustibilis & profundus propter scientiæ profunditatem. Nec tamen ex te fluunt aquæ viuæ, sed de *Libano*, id est CHRISTO, qui omnium virtutum decore candidatus est, & dicit: *si quis sitit, veniat ad me & bibat.*" The water is said by some commentators to emerge from the wounds of Christ, which, as we have seen, are symbolized by the clefts in the rock.

10. *Leonardo*, p. 43, as cited in note 2.

11. The extreme youth of St. John does not preclude a symbolic association with the observer. See Matthew 18:3.

SIDNEY—PAGES 308–311

1. *Elizabethan Critical Essays* (Oxford, 1904), I, lxxxvi.

2. *Ibid.*, I, 177.

3. The controversy over the meaning of the last clause in Aristotle's definition of tragedy has by no means been settled. Cf. the discussions of the subject in Ingram Bywater, *Aristotle on the Art of Poetry*, Oxford, 1909; D. S. Margoliouth, *The Poetics of Aristotle*, London, 1911; Augusto Rostagni, *La Poetica di Aristotle*, London, 1911; Augusto Rostagni, *La Poetica di Aristotele*, Turin, 1934; and Alfred Gudeman, *Aristoteles* ΠΕΡΙ ΠΟΙΗΤΙΚΗΣ, Berlin and Leipzig, 1934. Gudeman admits, *op. cit.*, p. 172, that we are ignorant of the psychological process Aristotle had in mind when he mentioned "catharsis"; and he believes, moreover, that we are not likely to know more about it in the future.

4. The exact date of the work is unknown. See Lane Cooper and Alfred Gudeman, *A Bibliography of the Poetics of Aristotle* (New Haven, 1928), p. 51.

5. Recent commentators frequently class interpretations of catharsis under two headings: (1) those which employ words meaning "purge," which are called "medical" or "pathological"; (2) those which employ words meaning "ˌ ˌrify" or "cleanse," which are called "ethical." See, for example, Bywater, *op   .* 152. This distinction, however, is not exact, for some interpretations do ˌot fˌll in either category, and some, like Scaino's, which is discussed beˌ ˌv ˌrˌolve a moderation rather than a purgation but are at the same time early ˌmedical."

ˌ. Casalio's work was printed in Jacobus Gronovius, *Thesaurus graecarum antiquitatum*, Leyden, 1697–1702. For the above discussion see vol. VIII, col. 1600.

7. *Francisci Robortelli Utinensis in librum Aristotelis de Arte poetica explicationes*, 2nd ed. (Basel, 1555), p. 46.

8. *Scritti Estetici* (Milan, 1864), II, 12. He explained that this process takes place because the spectator avoids imitating the vicious actions of the tragic personage for fear of coming to a like end. This, as we shall see below, is the position taken by Sidney. But the notion that tragedies function as exempla is not particularly Aristotelian and certainly not peculiarly Italian. Moreover, it is not implicit in the metaphor of the ulcer.

9. See Ingram Bywater, "Milton and the Aristotelian Definition of

Tragedy," *Journal of Philology*, 27 (1901), 274. The idea here expressed, however, may well be a non-Aristotelian commonplace. It is found also in the passage from Timocles, *Athenaeus*, VI, 233, and in Marcus Aurelius, *Meditations*, x, 6, where it is not now generally considered to be of Peripatetic origin.

10. *Commentarii in primum librum Aristotelis de Arte poetarum*, 2nd ed. (Florence, 1573), p. 54.

11. The *Arte Poetica* was an Italian elaboration of an earlier Latin *De Poeta*. In the *De Poeta*, Minturno used the verb *expio* to translate the idea of catharsis, thus introducing religious rather than medical connotations. He explained that tragedy acts as a warning against vicious passions. For his translation of the catharsis clause, see Bywater, *Aristotle on the Art of Poetry*, p. 361. The interpretation is discussed by J. E. Spingarn, *Literary Criticism in the Renaissance* (New York, 1908), p. 70.

12. *Arte Poetica* (Naples, 1725), p. 76. Cf. Spingarn, *op. cit.*, p. 80.

13. *Arte Poetica*, pp. 76-77.

14. Quoted by Bywater, "Milton and the Aristotelian Definition," p. 271.

15. John Lyly, *Works*, ed. R. W. Bond (Oxford, 1902), I, 210.

16. *An Alarum against Usurers*, ed. David Laing, Shakespeare Society (London, 1853), vol. 48, p. 36.

17. III, i, 109-120 in *Early English Classical Tragedies*, ed. J. W. Cunliffe (Oxford, 1912), p. 259.

18. *The Arte of English Poesie*, I, xv in Smith, *op. cit.*, vol. 2, p. 35.

19. *Works*, ed. R. B. McKerrow (London, 1910), I, 213.

20. *An Apologie for Actors*, Shakespeare Society (London, 1841), vol. 3, p. 53.

21. Smith, *op. cit.*, I, 170.

POPE—PAGES 332-340

1. *Minor Poems*, ed. Norman Ault and John Butt (London, 1954), 73. The note on the title refers to "*De Consolatione Philosophiae*, lib. 3, metrum I." The reference should read, "metrum IX." In this article the text of Boethius is quoted from the Loeb edition.

2. *Minor Poems* 73.

3. *Ibid.*, 74.

4. Quoted from the Twickenham edition of Maynard Mack (London, 1950).

5. Pope's note as quoted by Mack, *ibid.*, p. 31.

6. *The Prose Works of Alexander Pope*, ed. Norman Ault (Oxford, 1936), p. 137.

7. *Op. cit.*, p. 50.

8. *Ibid.*, p. 135.

Bibliography

BOOKS

(with B. F. Huppé) *"Piers Plowman" and Scriptural Tradition* (Princeton: Princeton University Press, 1951)

St. Augustine, *On Christian Doctrine*, translated with an introduction (New York: The Liberal Arts Press, 1958)

A Preface to Chaucer (Princeton: Princeton University Press, 1962)

(with B. F. Huppé) *Fruyt and Chaf: Studies in Chaucer's Allegories* (Princeton: Princeton University Press, 1963)

Chaucer's London (New York: John Wiley & Sons, 1968)

The Literature of Medieval England (New York: McGraw-Hill, 1970)

Abelard and Eloise (New York: Dial Press, 1972)

ARTICLES

Sidney's Metaphor of the Ulcer, *MLN*, 56 (1941), 56-61

Buzones, an Alternative Etymology, *SP*, 42 (1945), 741-744

The *Manuel des Péchés* as an English Episcopal Decree, *MLN*, 60 (1945), 439-447. See also letter in *MLN*, 61 (1946), 144

Certain Theological Conventions in Mannyng's Treatment of the Commandments, *MLN*, 61 (1946), 505-514

The Cultural Tradition of *Handlyng Synne*, *Speculum*, 22 (1947), 162-185

Frequency of Preaching in Thirteenth Century England, *Speculum*, 24 (1949), 376-388

Marie de France, *Lais*, Prologue, 13-16, *MLN*, 64 (1949), 336-338

The "Heresy" of *The Pearl*, *MLN*, 65 (1950), 152-155

The Pearl as a Symbol, *MLN*, 65 (1950), 155-161

Historical Criticism, *English Institute Essays 1950* (New York: Columbia University Press, 1951), 3-31

The Doctrine of Charity in Medieval Literary Gardens: a Topical Approach through Symbolism and Allegory, *Speculum*, 26 (1951), 24-49

Some Medieval Literary Terminology, with Special Reference to Chrétien de Troyes, *SP*, 48 (1951), 669-692

Cumhthach Labhras an Lonsa, *MLN*, 67 (1952), 123-125

Chaucerian Tragedy, *ELH*, 19 (1952), 1-37

St. Foy among the Thorns, *MLN* 67 (1952), 295-299

Amors de terra lonhdana, *SP*, 49 (1952), 566-582

The Subject of the *De amore* of Andreas Capellanus, *MP*, 50 (1953), 145-161

Love Conventions in Marie's *Equitan*, *Romanic Review*, 44 (1953), 241-245

In Foraminibus Petrae: a Note on Leonardo's "Virgin of the Rocks," *Renaissance News*, 7 (1954), 92-95

Why the Devil Wears Green, *MLN*, 69 (1954), 470-472

Five Poems by Marcabru, *SP*, 51 (1954), 539-560

The "Partitura Amorosa" of Jean de Savoie, *PQ*, 33 (1954), 1-9

Chrétien's *Cligés* and the Ovidian Spirit, *CL*, 7 (1955), 32-42

A Further Note on *Conjointure*, *MLN*, 70 (1955), 415-416

Pope and Boethius, *Classical, Medieval and Renaissance Studies in Honor of Berthold Louis Ullman*, edited by Charles Henderson, Jr. (Rome, 1964), 505-513

Chaucer, *American People Encyclopedia*, 1965 edition, 468-470

The Historical Setting of Chaucer's *Book of the Duchess, Medieval Studies in Honor of Urban Tigner Holmes, Jr.*, edited by John Mahoney and John Esten Keller (Chapel Hill: University of North Carolina Press, 1965), 169-195

The Book of the Duchess, Companion to Chaucer Studies, edited by Beryl Rowland (London: Oxford University Press, 1968), 332-340

The Concept of Courtly Love as an Impediment to the Understanding of Medieval Texts, *The Meaning of Courtly Love*, edited by F. X. Newman (Albany: State University of New York Press, 1968), 1-18

Some Observations on Method in Literary Studies, *New Literary History*, 1 (1969), 21-33. Reprinted in *New Directions in Literary History* (London: Routledge and Kegan Paul, 1974), 63-75

The Idea of Fame in Chrétien's *Cligés*, *SP*, 69 (1972), 414-433

Chaucer's Franklin and his Tale, *Costerus*, n.s. 1 (1974), 1-26

The Question of "Typology" and the Wakefield *Mactacio Abel, American Benedictine Review*, 25 (1974), 157-173

Two Poems from the *Carmina Burana, American Benedictine Review*, 27 (1976), 36-60

Some Disputed Chaucerian Terminology, *Speculum*, 52 (1977), 571-581

LECTURES

The Allegorist and the Aesthetician, first delivered at York University, England, 1967

A Medievalist Looks at *Hamlet*, first delivered at Princeton, 1974

IN PRESS

"And for my land thus hastow mordred me?": A Note on Land Transactions in Wife of Bath's Prologue

Chaucer and the "Commune Profit": The Manor

Simple Signs from Everyday Life in Chaucer

Index

Abelard, Peter, 139, 141, 184-185, 190, 248; Heloise, 184-185
Abrahams, Phyllis, 347
Abrams, Meyer H., 349
aenigma, 16, 56-58, 67, 71; *see* allegory
Aeschylus, 91, 322
aesthetics, 4, 74, 81-82, 85ff., 253, 260
affectio, 204, 368
Ailred of Rievaulx, 202-205, 367, 368, 369
Alain Fergent, Duke of Brittany, 376
Alanus de Insulis, 8, 9, 52, 56, 57, 58, 63, 64, 65, 139, 155, 175, 266, 343, 347, 355, 356, 359, 361, 364, 365, 380, 381
Albericus of London, 176
Albertanus of Brescia, 367
Alcuin, 30, 175
Aldermen, 265
Aletaster, 297
Ale-wives, 297, 300
Alexander Neckham, 152-153, 356, 358, 359, 367
Alexander Phereus, 321
Alexander Stravensby, Bp. of Coventry, 118, 121
Alfonso VII, Emperor of Spain, 154, 360
Alfred, King of England, 94
Ali, 156, 360; cult of, 154
alieniloquium, 50, 57, 71; *see* allegory
Allegoriae in sacram scripturam, 155, 344, 345, 361
allegory, 3, 7, 11, 19, 22-23, 26, 31, 42, 50, 53-54, 56-59, 61-62, 63, 64, 67, 71, 85-101, 108, 152, 158, 167, 213, 221, 344, 347, 348, 380; anagoge, 3, 7, 26, 31, 33, 36, 53, 59, 62, 63, 167, 213-214, 380; *littera*, letter, *historia*, 9-10, 22-23, 37, 53-54, 63, 66-67, 69, 72, 108, 170, 213, 220, 223-224, 227, 380; literalism, literal-minded, 281, 286, 288, 290, 301, 312, 324; *sensus*, sense, 9-10, 23, 37, 38, 51-52, 66-67, 69-72; *sententia*, sentence, 9-10, 16, 18, 23, 37, 38, 49, 66-67, 68-69, 70, 71-72, 212, 214, 216, 306; signs, 8, 9,

10-11, 15, 18, 59, 60, 62, 63, 209; *tropologia*, tropology, 3, 7, 22-23, 25, 26, 31, 53, 59-62, 63, 71, 167, 213-214, 220-223, 225, 226, 232, 344, 371, 380. *See also aenigma*, *alieniloquium*, *conjunctura*, *cortex et nucleus*, fruit and chaff, *integumentum*, *involucrum*, nut, *paille et grains*, *pallium*, shell and kernel spirit and letter, *tegmen*, typology
Alton, E. H., 356, 367
St. Ambrose, 31, 138, 146-147, 155, 343, 357
America, 218, 231, 331; Pennsylvania, 341
amour courtois, 131, 202; *see* courtly love, *fin amors*
anachronisms, 223-226
Anacletus II, 153-154
Andalusia, 40
Anderson, George, xiv
Anderson, Mary D., 372
Andreas, Capellanus, 21, 43, 46, 47, 49, 203, 205, 259, 345; *De amore*, 37-41, 45, 145, 142, 169, 260, 344, 364, 365, 368-369
angels, 29, 44, 162, 307, 320
animal spirits, 135
Annas the Archdeacon, *see* Wakefield plays
Anselm of Laon, 108, 109
Antioch, 189
Appel, Carl, 151, 165, 359
Arabic influence, 151, 154, 272, 360
Archambaud, *see* Flamenca, *Roman de*
archetype, 89, 211, 212, 256, 265
Ariès, Phillippe, 375
Aristotle, xii, 82, 94, 95, 142, 308-309, 311, 316, 319, 357, 381, 382
Armitage-Smith, Sydney, 236, 373
Arnold, Matthew, 375
Arnulf of Orléans, 139, 168, 177, 356
Art, American, 218; function of, 268; medieval, xiv, 11, 18, 26, 85-86, 98, 219-220, 221-222, 232; modern, 88-89, 98-

Art, American (*cont.*)
100; Renaissance, 304-307; visual,
73-74, 79-80, 83, 218, 241, 259, 372
Arthur, King of England, 187, 189, 196,
197, 199, 201
Artin, Tom, 173
artistic consciousness, 79-80, 85
asceticism, 183
Aucassin, 14
auditor, 295
St. Augustine, xi, xiii, xviii, 4, 8, 10, 12,
13, 24, 27, 30, 31, 35, 51, 53, 55, 56, 89,
96, 105, 107-108, 113, 115, 138, 151,
156, 157-158, 161, 203, 209, 211, 215-
217, 221, 226, 228, 240, 245, 326, 341,
342, 351, 358, 361, 368, 373; *Confessions*,
224-225; *Contra mendacium*, 347; *De cantico novo*, 155; *De civitate dei*, 6, 32, 229,
230, 267, 342, 361, 372; *De doctrina christiana*, 6, 22, 23, 53, 59-60, 92-94, 223,
341, 346, 364, 380; *De Gen. ad litt.*, 343;
De Gen. contra Manich, 341; *De mendacio*, 362; *De Sermone Domini in monte*,
342; *De Trinitate*, 341, 347; *Enchiridion*,
361; *Enn. in Ps.*, xvi, 64, 372; *Enn. in Ps.*,
136, 362; *On the Life and Manner of
Clerks*, 184; *Quaestiones in Numeros*, 347;
Sermo 9, 350, 360; *Sermo 87*, 370; *Sermo
133*, 350; *Sermo 162*, 342; *Sermo 304*,
359; *Sermo 318*, 360
Augustus Caesar, 251
Ault, Norman, 382
Ave, 115-116

Bach, 81
Bacon, Francis, xvi, 327, 377
bailiffs, 275-277, 294, 295, 299, 378
Baker, Carlos, xiv
St. Bartholomew's Church, 251
Baudri de Bourgueil, 57
Baumgarten, A. G., 86-87
beadle, 294, 297
beauty, abstract, 91-92; feminine, 29-30,
146, 204-205, 245, 261, 268; physical,
17-18, 25, 168, 178, 179, 180, 188, 249,
261; true, 32-33; of continence, 185; of
innocence, 213
Bede, the Venerable, 10, 12, 15-16, 28, 30,
31, 34, 45, 216, 342, 343, 344, 370;
Comm. in Gen., 341, 343; *De die judicii*,

35; *Expl. Apoc.*, 341; *Hexaemeron*, 33; *In
Ion*, 363; *James, S.*, 13; *Quaest. in Gen.*,
341
Bennett, H. S., 351, 374
Benton, John F., 257
Benveniste, Emile, 349
Beowulf, 11, 21, 33-36, 37, 49, 96;
Beowulf, 33-35, 45, 184; Grendel, 14,
33-35, 38; Grendel's mere, 33-35, 43,
50; Grendel's mother, 33; Scyld, 184
Bergson, Henri, 87
St. Bernard, 20, 28, 38, 95, 109, 153-154,
343, 350
Bernard of Chartres, 20
Bernard Silvestris, 9, 11, 55-56, 62, 66, 67,
139, 176, 347, 348, 356, 364, 367
Bernard Marti, 361, 362
Beroul, 45, 248
Bernini, 99
Bersuire, Pierre, xiv, 166-172, 358, 359,
363, 364
Bible
  general
    Catholic epistles, 16; Epistles, 15,
    19; Gospels, 221; New Testament,
    32, 139, 175, 183, 218, 221, 230,
    316, 371, 372; Old Testament, 7,
    32, 139, 175, 180, 218-219, 221,
    260, 324, 371; Parables, 8, 9, 23, 52,
    63, 69, 115-116, 152, 159, 212-213,
    363; of the grain of mustard seed,
    31; of the servant, 228; of the sow-
    ers, 69, 148; of the vineyard, 10,
    215-217; Prophets, 32, 63; Wisdom
    books, 139
  figures
    Abraham, 60, 218; Amnon, 260,
    270; Apostles, 25, 153, 245, 365;
    David and Uriah, 70; Herod, 232;
    Holofernes, 147, 180, 260; Isaac,
    218, 219, 221, 320; Jacob, 60;
    Jacob's rods, 54; Joseph, 111, 218,
    220; Judas, 169, 189, 316, 330, 359;
    Judith, 147, 180; Lamech, 158;
    Noah, 226; Peter, 152-153;
    Pharisees, 141, 246; Scribes and
    Pharisees, 169, 364; Seth, 158;
    Sion, 345; Solomon, 12; Zac-
    chaeus, 28
  individual books and passages

Apocalypse, 197, 210; *1-8*, 159; *7*, 141-144; *14:1*, 370; *14:3-5*, 36, 159, 210, 232; *14:15*, 211; *22:1-2*, 30, 38, 342; *22:13*, 159; *Aggeus, 2:8*, 158; *Canticum*, 9, 19, 21, 31, 32, 41, 43, 49, 93, 145, 158, 161, 167, 175, 260, 305, 344, 345; *2:13-14*, 158, 305-306; *3:6*, 167; *4:1,3*, 171; *4:12*, 359; *4:15*, 306; *5:2*, 356; *7:12*, 152; *8:2*, 171; *Colossians, 1:18*, 359; *3:5-17*, 155, 223; *1 Corinthians, 7:9*, 180; *9:24*, 141, 149, 320; *11:3*, 359; *13, 323*; *13:1*, 140, 320; *13:4-8*, 140, 159; *2 Corinthians, 11:2*, 210; *Daniel, 2:45*, 306; *Deuteronomy, 22:10*, 226; *Ecclesiastes*, 14, 27; *4:10*, 374; *Ecclesiasticus*, 2, 359; *2:14*, 161; *9:7-9*, 345; *9:8*, 11, 147; *21:26*, 147; *24*, 343; *24:7*, 148; *24:42*, 344; *28:14*, 29; *38:1-15*, 145-146; *38:4*, 120-121; *44*, 184; *50:8*, 29; *Ephesians, 1:22*, 359; *2:3*, 282; *4:7-10*, 164; *4:15*, 359; *4:22-23*, 155; *5:22-24*, 111, 359; *Exodus, 15:25*, 60; *20*, 108; *Galatians, 4:17-24*, 223; *5:7*, 161; *Genesis*, 9, 30, 31, 32, 41, 176; *1:26-30*, 226; *2:24*, 362; *3:8*, 24, 344; *4:6-7*, 229; *4:34*, 227; *6:4*, 33; *9:1-2*, 226; *22:13*, 60; *28:9*, 171; *28:11*, 60; *39:6-7*, 345; *Hebrews, 1:14*, 306; *Isaiah*, 30; *5:20*, 362; *40:6-8*, 15, 29, 343; *41:4*, 159; *James, 1:10-11*, 30; *3:7*, 343; *5*, 13; *Jeremiah, 9:21*, 147, 345; *25:15*, 168; *51:7*, 168; *John, 1:1ff*, 333; *1:38*, 49, 169; *3:2*, 169; *4:6*, 357; *4:12-16*, 30, 64; *8:44*, 24; *1 John, 3:2*, 9-12, 158; *3:15*, 230; *5:1-5*, 158; *Jude, 1:12*, 28; *Judith, 9:13*, 147; *10:17*, 180; *16:11*, 180; *Luke, 6:43-45*, 158; *8:8*, 148; *8:14*, 149; *8:15*, 148; *12:42ff*, 329; *18:11*, 141; *19:4*, 28; *23:31*, 28; *Matthew*, 31; *5:28*, 147; *7:16-21*, 152, 158; *10:29*, 329; *12:33*, 158, 159; *13:19*, 69; *18:3*, 381; *18:23-35*, 140, 228, 230; *19:29*, 148; *23:2-3*, 364; *23:7*, 169; *24:32-33*, 28; *24:42ff*, 329; *Numbers, 21:27*, 56; *1 Peter, 2:11*, 26; *Psalms*, 30, 32, 372; *1*, 341; *1:3*, 30, 152; *14*, 211-212, 345; *32:3*, 36; *35:10-13*, 164; *36:35-36*, 148; *42*, 34; *48:3*, 305; *64*, xiv, 342; *64:2*, 372; *67:19*, 164; *79*, 342; *118:25-32*, 142; *118:28*, 131; *118:37*, 146; *136*, 362; *136:1-2*, 152; *Proverbs, 6:24-26*, 145; *23:31-35*, 136, 147, 345, 355; *Romans, 6:3-6*, 13, 155, 223; *12:17*, 184; *12:16-21*, 322; *13:11-14*, 131, 138; *2 Timothy, 3:2*, 327; *Wisdom*, 2, 44; *2:8*, 29; *4:1-6*, 158; *7:26*, 146

Biedermeier style, 248
Black Prince, 254, 299, 379
Blanche of Lancaster, 235-238, 242, 250, 254, 255, 257, 263-264, 373; tomb of, 236-237, 373 (illus. 243)
Blessed Virgin Mary, 18, 29, 31, 49, 111, 144-145, 146, 148, 167-168, 169-172, 205, 218, 220, 225, 261, 264, 267, 305-307, 356, 360, 365; cult of, 259
Blickling Homilies, 33
Bliemetzrieder, F. P., 350
Bloch, Marc, 369
Boccaccio, Giovanni, ix, 47, 95, 96, 97, 173, 246, 263, 265, 267-268, 341, 366
Bochenski, I. M., 364
Boethius, x, xiv, 6, 12, 13, 40, 94, 100, 136-137, 142, 183, 224-225, 239-244, 251, 252, 256, 263, 265, 279, 284, 285, 320, 332-340, 355, 356, 367, 382; Lady Philosophy, 225, 240, 251, 335-338
Boissonade, Prosper, 153, 360
St. Bonaventura, 6, 27, 106, 112-113, 350, 351, 353, 354
Bond, R. W., 382
Bonet-Maury, G., 347
Boswell, James, 332
Bourgain, L., 352
Bovary, Emma, 246, 247
Bowden, Muriel, 372, 378
Bradwardine, Thomas, Bp., 262, 263, 269, 271-272, 375
Brahms, Johannes, 245
Brault, Gerald, J., 183
brawlers, 270
Brewer, Derek, 373, 375
brewers, 297
Bridbury, A. R., 378
Bridgman, Percy, W., 349
Brinton, Thomas, Bp. of Rochester, 226

Brion, Marcel, 350
Britain, 179-180, 187-189, 194-199, 201,
    279; *see* England
Broomfield, F., 377
Brown, E., 353
Brunet, A., 341, 348
Bruno Astensis, 210, 212, 216-217, 341,
    342, 343, 346
St. Bruno of the Carthusians, 342
Brut, Founder of London, 267
de Bruyne, E., 348
Bulgaria, 40
Bunyan, John, 375
Burchard of Worms, 354
burgesses, x, 276
Burghbrigg, Sir William, 373
Burjorjee, D. M., 377
Burns, Robert, 95, 251
Burton, Robert, xvi, 316, 320, 323
Butt, John, 382
Buttimer, Charles H., 347
Bywater, Ingram, 381, 382

Caedmonian poetry, 344
St. Caesarius of Arles, xii
Caiphas the Bishop, *see* Wakefield plays
Caligare, as medical term, 134
Campbell, Mildred, 298
Camus, Albert, 147, 265, 267, 375
Carcopino, Jerome, 366
Carmen de bello Lewensi, 369
Carmina Burana, 131-150, 166, 355
Carpenter, John, 266, 375. *See Liber Albus*
carpenters, 295, 297
carters, 294
Casalio, G. B., 308-309, 381
Castiglione, Baldassare, 21
catechism, 317, 324
catharsis, tragic, xii, 151, 308-309, 381,
    382
Cawley, A. C., 372
Cecil William, Lord Burghley, 316, 324,
    327, 328
Celestina, 248
Cervantes, Miguel, 253
Charland, Th.-M., 354
Charlemagne, King of France, 115, 173
Charles V, 372
Chaucer, ix, x, xi, 6, 9, 43, 58, 74, 78, 80,

96, 105, 110, 166, 235-236, 242, 246,
    250-251, 265, 266, 273, 277, 280, 282,
    285, 291-301, 374
  Works
    ABC, 237; *Book of Duchess*, 11, 146,
    235-256, 261-264, 291; *Canterbury
    Tales*, xi, 11, 105, 249, 280, 284
  Individual tales of
    Clerk, 271, 280; Franklin, 273, 277,
    280-290, 293, 349, 376; Friar, 286,
    301; General Prologue, 99-100,
    273, 274, 279, 285, 293, 299, 374,
    376, 379; Knight, 142, 224, 263,
    272, 281, 285, 374; Man of Law,
    281, 347; Melibee, 18; Merchant,
    21, 47-50; Miller, 21, 281, 285, 291;
    Nun's Priest, 47, 300, 347; Parson,
    14, 245, 372, 374; Reeve, 281, 298,
    369, 378, 379; Second Nun, 372;
    Summoner, 286, 372; Wife of
    Bath, 281; "The Former Age,"
    266, 296; *Legend of Good Women*,
    18-19, 374; *Parlement of Fowles*, 263;
    Troilus and Criseyde, 101, 142, 248,
    257-258, 264-272, 285; "Truth," 14
  Characters
    Absolon, 179; Antenor, 270; Ar-
    cite, 224, 272, 374; Arveragus, 284,
    286, 287, 289, 378; Aurelius, 285-
    290, 293; Harry Bailey, 47, 279;
    Black Knight, 241-246, 248-250,
    252, 254, 255, 261, 263-264, 373-
    374; Blanche, 146, 241, 246, 248-
    250, 252, 254-255, 261 (*see* Blanche
    of Lancaster); Book of the Duchess
    Speaker, 250-252, 254, 255, 261;
    Ceyx and Alcyone, 11, 251-253;
    Chauntecleer, xiii; Clerk, 278, 280;
    Criseyde, 268-271; Damyan,
    47-49; Deiphebus, 270; Dido, 11;
    Dorigen, 284-290, 378; Emelye,
    285; Franklin, 274-282, 288, 298,
    300, 301, 376; Friar, 99, 274, 292,
    378; Friar (Summoner's Tale), 286;
    Griselda, 280, 283, 301; Hector,
    270, 271; Januarie, 47-49, 278, 285;
    Knight, 274, 278, 292, 293, 297,
    299-300, 374; Magician, 286-287,
    289-290; Manciple, 295; May,

47-49; Miller, 293, 297, 299, 301; Monk, 374; Nicholas, 285; Emperor Octovyen, 250-251; Palamon, 263; Pandarus, 269-270; Pardoner, 14, 274, 374; Parson, 49, 100, 245-246, 273-274, 278, 279, 282, 284, 297, 316, 317, 320, 326, 329; Parson (Reeve's Tale), 298, 301, 379; Plowman, 293, 296-297, 372, 379; Reeve (Oswald), 293-297, 301, 378; Sergeant of the Law, 274-276, 290, 301, 378; Squire, 274, 278, 285, 290, 292, 293, 376; Summoner (Friar's Tale), 286, 301; Symkyn, 298-299, 369; Theseus, 224; Troilus, 267-272, 285, 319; Wife of Bath, xvii, 111, 280-281, 286; Canon's Yeoman, 299; Knight's Yeoman, 293, 297-299 Words
ecylmpasteyr, 291; embosed, 291; viritoot, 291
Chaucer, Philippa, 251
Cheney, C. R., 122, 352, 353, 354, 355
Le chevaler Dé, 362
Chivalry, xvii, 154, 183, 187-188, 197, 199, 201, 204-206, 235, 238, 245, 246, 252, 254-255, 257, 265, 278, 284, 287, 288, 331, 359, 373
Chopin, Fréderic, 245, 374
Chrétien de Troyes, ix, 51-52, 71, 259, 345, 367, 368; *Cligés*, 15, 41-42, 173-182, 183, 187-201, 248; *Conte del Graal*, 69, 159, 343; *Erec*, 9, 52, 64-65, 71, 187; *Lancelot*, 51, 69-71, 173, 248, 260; *Yvain*, 14, 173
Characters
Alis, Emperor, 181, 182, 188, 190-194, 196-199, 201; Alexander, 179-180, 188-191; Bangien, 201; Bertran, 42, 345; Cligés, 177-182, 190-201; Countess, 70-71; Duke of Saxony, 192; 193-194; Emperor Alexander, 188-189; Emperor of Germany, 177, 201; Empress Tantalis, 188; Enide, 187; Erec, 187; Fenice, 15, 41-42, 43, 177-182, 191-201, 345, 367; François, 196; Sir Gawain, 189, 196; Guenevere,

189-190, 195, 264; Iseut, Yseut, 15, 42, 45, 182, 187, 191-192, 197-199, 368; Jehan, 15, 41-42, 43, 49, 182, 199; King Mark, 187, 198; Perceval, 196; Sagremor, 196; Soredomors, 179-180, 189-190; Thessala, 178-179, 181-182, 191-192; Tristan, 42, 45, 48, 182, 191-192, 197-199, 201, 368; Yvain, 14
Christ, 10, 12, 17, 19, 22, 25, 28, 29, 31, 32, 33, 35, 50, 53, 62, 69, 96, 111, 122, 138, 146, 152, 153, 155-156, 158, 181, 209, 214, 218, 219, 225, 226, 228-229, 245, 251, 280, 306-307, 320; birth of, 220, 223; burial of, 13; bride of, 209-210, 370; *Christus Irrigans*, 30; Imitation of, 26, 35, 162; *Milites Christi*, 153; resurrection of, 159, 169, 367; second coming of, 28; wisdom of, 92, 267; wounds of, 380, 381
Christianity, 4-6, 11-13, 22, 32, 92, 114-115, 154-155, 187, 281, 312, 315, 323, 332-333, 364, 366
Christian life, 24, 26, 34-35, 62, 138, 140-141, 155, 209-211, 220-221, 228, 331; Christian heroism, 37; Christian warfare, 12, 161; inner warfare, 161; *Milites Christi*, 153-154
The Church, 7, 14, 19, 31, 49, 59, 93, 111, 138, 152-154, 156, 209, 213, 221, 223, 280, 287, 300, 305, 307, 345, 359, 361, 373, 380; Church Militant, 372; *Ecclesia*, 169, 210, 359, 360, 364
Cicero, 121, 150, 184, 281, 318, 327; *De amicitia*, 180, 240-241, 316, 330, 369; *De inventione*, 364; *De officiis*, 316; *De senectute*, 316
Cintio, G. B. Giraldi, 309, 381
Clanvowe, Sir John, 373
Clark, Kenneth, 306, 380
Clarke, Dr. Samuel, 332
cloth industry, xvii, 218
Cluny, 154
Coffman, George R., xi-xii
Coleridge, Samuel Taylor, 98, 374
Comar, Cyril, xvi
comedy, 308, 324
Commandments, Ten, 105, 113, 115-116, 119, 120, 124; First, 38, 105-106; Sec-

Commandments, Ten (*cont.*)
   ond, 106-108; Fourth, 317; Fifth, 108-
   109; Sixth, 109-112; Seventh, 112;
   Eighth, 112-113; Ninth, 39
Commissions of the peace, 276, 277
Compendium Theologiae, 353
Conan III (Duke of Brittany), 376
Confessors, Confession, 114, 118-121,
   125, 174, 220, 247, 353
Conjunctura, conjointure, 9, 52, 64-65,
   70-72. *See* allegory
conscience, 184-185, 201
constables, 277, 278
Constance of Castile, 236, 375
Conte d'avanture, 65, 187
contemplation, 138, 159
contour, 275, 298
convenientia, 76. *See* "Commun profit"
   under Virtues and Vices
cortex et nucleus, 8-9, 14, 53-55, 57-58,
   62-66, 69-72, 172. *See* allegory
cottager, 300, 301
Coulton, G. C., 114, 351
Council, Fourth Lateran, 1215, 6, 116-121,
   125, 352, 353
Countess of Pembroke, 379
Courbet, Gustave, 99, 222
Courtenay, Sir Peter, 293
courtesy, false courtesy, 188, 205-206,
   278, 282, 361, 362, 369; curteisie, 292;
   courteous, 145, 148, 164, 195; courtesy
   book, 309; *cortoise bon*, 205
courtiers' behavior, x, 37, 46, 196, 201,
   236-238, 373
Courtly Love, xvi-xvii, 39-40, 50, 70-71,
   150, 151, 164-165, 166, 195, 205, 257-
   272, 280, 286, 365, 368. *See also amour
   courtois, fin amors*
Coville, A., 363
Criticism, New, 85
Croce, Benedetto, ix, 80, 81-82, 85, 87-90,
   101, 350
Cross, Tom Peete, 51, 70, 346
Crossland, Jessie, 173, 175
Cruel, R., 351
crusaders, crusade, 154-156, 161, 162
Cumont, Franz, 366
Cunliffe, J. W., 382
Curia, 295

Cursus honorum, 299
Curtius, E. R., 346
Custom House, 265
Cyril of Alexandria, Bp., 115

Dahlberg, Charles R., 21, 282, 346, 377
dairy assistants, 294, 297, 300, 380
Dante, ix, 21, 23, 45, 211, 240-241, 348,
   369, 370; Beatrice, 240
Darby, H. C., xvii
Davies, F. N., 355
Davis, Norman, 291
Davy, Marie M., 352, 354, 368
daya, 300, 380
Deanesley, Margaret, 351
"Debate of the Body and the Soul," 5
De cervo ad fontem, 62
de Coverly, Sir Roger, 278
Dedeck-Hery, U. L., 373
De die judicii, see Bede
De Fructibus carnis et spiritus, 25, 26, 27, 39,
   49
de Grazia, Margreta, 273
Dejeanne, J.M.L., 151, 362
Delacroix, Eugène, 99, 245, 374
della Casa, Giovanni, 309
de Lubac, Henri, 92, 219-220, 371
de Malkiel, Lida, 183
demesne holdings, 294
demesne leasing, 379
Denholm-Young, N., 249, 378
Denomy, Alexander J., 151, 154, 156-157,
   162, 358
Desiderat, 158. *See* courtly love
de Tocqueville, Alexis, 231
DeWindt, Edwin, B., 378, 379
diachronic studies, 76, 82-83
Dickens, B., 342
Divinity, 142, 144, 164, 315
Dobiache-Rojdestvensky, O., 351
doctrine, doctrinal theology, 4, 9, 10, 22,
   27, 29, 30, 31, 32-33, 39, 40, 52, 68,
   71-72, 105, 113, 118, 139, 152, 164, 172,
   209, 211, 213, 216-217, 266; perversions
   of, 40, 47
doctrine of service, 40
Dods, Marcus, 229
Dodwell, C. R., 357
Dominicans, 6, 121, 354, 366

"Doomsday," 35
Donovan, Mortimer J., 369
drama, the stage, 82, 218-232, 310-311
"Dream of the Road," 26
Dronke, Peter, 131-132, 133, 134, 141, 355, 356
Du Boulay, F.R.H., 378, 379
Duke of Gloucester, 376
Duns Scotus, 8, 346
Dyngelegh, Robert, 379

Earl of Essex, 313
ecclesiastical courts, 232
Edelstein, Emma and Ludwig, 366
Edward III, 235, 250, 252, 254, 259, 265, 280, 373
elections, 276
elegy, 236-237, 240-241, 244, 245, 250, 261
"Elegy in a Country Churchyard." *See* Gray, Thomas
Elgar, Frank, 350
Eliot, T. S., 88, 375
Elizabeth I, Queen of England, 94, 315, 322-323, 324, 329, 331
eloquence, 137-138, 139, 140, 144, 150, 168-169, 364; false eloquence, 57, 279, 320-321
Elyot, Sir Thomas, 317, 318-319, 322
Encyclopaedia Britannica (11th ed.), 174
Engels, Joseph, 363
England, English, x-xvii, 114-128, 142, 219, 231, 235-236, 237, 239, 247, 255, 257-258, 261, 262, 269, 272, 284, 290, 292, 300, 322, 324, 331, 335, 353, 373, 376; Aldgate, 257, 265-266; Cambridge, 327; Canterbury, 14, 293, 379; Cornhill, 258; Cornwall, 299, 379; Coventry, 118, 122; Devon, 293, 295, 299, 300; Durham, 117, 120, 352; Ely, 120, 378; Exeter, 118, 120, 122, 295, 354; Greenwich, 257; Kent, 273, 293, 378; Lincoln, 122, 125; Lincolnshire, 114, 379; London, 166, 258, 262, 265-272, 273, 375; Norfolk, 293, 295; Norwich, 120; Nottinghamshire, 376; Oxford, 122, 196, 323; Oxfordshire, 293, 378; Richmond, 250; Salisbury, 117, 352; Tilbury, 329; Wakefield, 222, 224; Wilt-shire, 379; Winchester, 120; Worcester, 114, 119
epic, 49, 82
Epicurean, 281-282, 287, 290, 377
Epstein, Mary J., 341
Erasmus, 315, 316
Errante, Guido, 151-152, 157, 158, 159, 160-162, 358, 359, 360, 361, 362, 363
etymologies, 291, 347
Eucharist, *see* Sacraments: Holy Communion
Evans, W. O., 378
Ewert, Alfred, 202, 368
Exchequer, 274, 276
excommunication, 120
exegesis, 6-11, 22-23, 51-72, 92-96, 152, 216, 219-220, 286, 305. *See also* allegory; Bible, symbols
exempla, 52, 123, 311, 381
Existentialism, 98, 101, 244, 248, 316
Expressionism, 88-89, 97

fables, 52, 57, 58, 59, 62, 64, 65, 68, 94, 253
Fabliau, 47, 49
Fall, 18, 23, 24, 32, 46, 48, 156, 169-170, 176-177, 221, 282
"False Fox, The," 372
fame, 183, 201-269; *see* honor, reputation
Familia, 293, 295, 300
Faral, Edmund, 41, 347
feeling, feelings, 87, 90, 94-95, 97, 100; intuition, 87-88, 89-90; personal emotion, 140
Mlle. Fel., 246, 248, 255, 374
Feltoe, C. L., 353
Ficino, 315
Fielding, Henry, xv, xvi, 100
Figura, 372
figures, 7-8, 10-11, 15, 63; *see* allegory
Fin'amors, 27, 131, 156-164, 361; *see amour courtois*, courtly love
Finberg, H.P.R., 378, 380
Fitzstephen, William, 375
Flamenca, Roman de, 257; Archambaud, 257
Fleetwood, William, 324
Fleming, John V., 21, 114, 368, 374, 376, 377
Fletcher, J. B., 215, 370

Florilegium, 109
Flower, Robin, 36
Foerster, Wendelin, 367
Forester, 293, 297-298, 299
Fortescue, Sir John, C.J., 322
Fortunatus, 141
Foucault, Michel, 75-76, 77, 349
Fowlie, Wallace, 88, 98, 350
France, French, 114, 116, 160, 186, 187-188, 235, 237-239, 241, 257, 259, 261, 265, 269, 272, 291, 300, 329, 363, 368, 372, 376; Artois, 373; Brittany, 284-285, 376; Carlux, 153; Cazeres, 153; Crecy, 262; Louvain, 6; Montpellier, 153; Normandy, 360; Old French, 11; Orleans, 287; Paris, 115, 121, 185, 246, 248, 255; Picardy, 235, 236, 373; Poitiers, 153; Provençal, 259, 360; The Seine, 283; Toulouse, 118, 153; Tournai, 166
Franciscans, 3, 6, 114, 122-123, 124, 222, 366, 379
Frankel, Hermann, 174, 177, 178, 366
Frankl, Paul, xv
franklins, 273-276, 298
freedom, 40, 138, 282
freemen, 379
free will, 24, 40, 162; free choice, 240
French Academy, 98
French Revolution, 99, 271
Freud, Sigmund, xvi, 79-80, 101, 244, 247, 317
Freudian criticism, 80, 101, 244
friars, 10, 46, 99, 114, 120, 175, 229, 273-274, 366, 379
Friedman, John B., 356
Froissart, Jean, 235-239, 246, 253, 254, 373
fruit and chaff, 8-9, 47, 58, 72. *See* allegory
Fulgentius, 147, 365
Furnival, J., 105, 350
Futuwwa, futuwa, 154, 359-360

St. Gabriel, 186
Ganshof, François L., 369
Gautier, Théophile, 87
Gautier le Leu, 205, 369
Gaylord, Alan, 376, 377
genre studies, 82-83
gentry, 276, 278, 292, 301
Geoffrey of Monmouth, 201, 375

Gerard of Liege, 27, 40, 342
Germany, xiv, 11-12, 14-15, 97, 201, 237
Gerson, Jean, Bp., 174-175, 353, 366
Ghisalberti, Fausto, 347, 363, 364, 367
Gibbs, M., 352, 353, 354, 355
Gibson, Gail McMurray, 218
St. Gildas de Rhuys (Monastery), 184
Gilson, Etienne, 354
Gimpel, Jean, 98, 349
Glossa Ordinaria, x, xiv, 10, 28, 101, 226, 227, 228, 229-230, 342, 357, 361, 372
God, 39, 40, 50, 89-90, 92, 97, 145-146, 215, 225, 226, 227, 229-230, 300, 310, 332-333; Blessing of, 231; Book of, 22, 23, 214; Image, 15, 21, 24, 29, 33, 47, 92, 155, 371; Grace of, 17, 25, 31, 138, 155, 156, 158, 164, 172, 213, 306-307; Justice of, 13, 16, 18-19, 25, 28, 30, 33, 36, 38, 44, 225, 228, 230, 313; Kingdom of, 212; Love of, 32, 138-139, 157, 164, 316, 326, 369; Voice of, 58; Will of, 314; Word of, 15, 16, 18-19, 22, 25, 26, 29-30, 60, 69, 221, 345; Works of, 24, 60; Wrath of, 36, 45, 68
Godefroid de Fontaines, 6
Gorboduc, 313
Gordon, R. K., 12
Gorman, John C., 305
Grabmann, M., 348
graduate study, 83
Granovius, Jacobus, 381
Gratian, 112
Gray, Thomas, 133
Greece, 82, 91-92, 179, 182, 187-188, 194-195, 197, 199, 201, 269-270, 115, 316; Thebans, Athenians, Lacedemonians, 57; Athens, 322
Gregorianum, 343
St. Gregory the Great, 10, 12, 13, 21, 31, 118, 221, 341, 343, 344, 353, 358, 360, 361, 364, 365, 370, 371, 380
Grimm, Friedrich Melchoir, Baron von, 246, 248, 255, 374
Grosseteste, Robert, Bp. of Lincoln, 120, 125-127, 353
Gruppe, Otto, 366
Gudeman, Alfred, 381
Guildhall, 266
Guilhelm VIII, 153-154, 360

Guilhelmus Parvus, 380
Guillaume de Conches, 139, 224, 240, 355, 356, 371
Guillaume de Lorris, 45-46, 285. See *Roman de la rose*
Guillaume de Saint Amour, 46, 346
Guyer, Foster, 178, 179

Haimo, Bp. of Auxerre, 155
Haines, R. M., 114
Haller, Robert, 376
Harvey, P.D.A., 378, 380
Haselhaus, Clemens, 366
Hatcher, John, 379
Haunsard, John, 125
Haureau, B., 351
Hayward, 300
Hefele, C. J., von, 352, 353, 354
Hegel, 73, 78, 79
Heidegger, 90, 100
Helm, R., 365
Henricus de Segusio, 377
Henry II, King of England, 259
Henry V, King of England, 329
Henry of Lancaster, 237
Heresy, 12, 29, 33, 40, 43, 55, 67, 71, 72, 123, 154-155, 209, 215-217; Albigensian, 241, 272; Dualism, 40; Jovinian, 215, 217; Manichaean, 259, 375; Pelagian, 375
Heydenreich, Ludwig, H., 305
Heywood, Thomas, 308, 310-311, 382
Hierarchy, of being, 21, 226-227; Christian, 62; ecclesiastic, 152, 246, 247; of men and women, marriage, 110, 270, 280, 282-284, 289; of reason, 24; divine order, 137; feudal hierarchy, ix-xi, xvii, 39, 40, 48, 140, 186, 188, 190, 191, 201, 204-205, 219, 223-224, 231-232, 244, 246-248, 260, 265-267, 270-271, 273-278, 280-281, 284, 290, 291-301, 369, 373
Higham, T. F., 366
Hildebert, 54, 66
Hildegard of Bingen, 131, 355
Hilka, A., 355, 356
Hill, John M., 235
Hillman, Mary, Vincent, 209, 214
Hilton, R. H., 380
historia. See allegory: *littera*

historical archaeology, 80, 175
historical criticism, 3-20
historical geography, xvii
historical sociology, xvii
history, agrarian, xvii, 291-301; economic, xvii; local, xvii; see specific entries in general index
history, psychological, xiv, 4, 75, 76, 97
history of ideas, 3, 76
Hitler, 101
Hitti, Philip K., 359
Hoel, Duke of Brittany, 376
Hoepffner, Ernest, 202, 361, 368, 369
Hoffman, Richard L., 376, 377
Hoffman, Werner, 348, 349, 374
Hollander, Robert, 173
Holmes, Urban T., xii, 343, 359
Holy Days, Christian feasts, 114-115, 116, 125-127; Annunciation, 29; Corpus Christi, 232; Easter, 159; Nativity, 220, 221-222, 223-224, 225, 314; Vigil of the Assumption, 235
Holy Spirit, 8, 30, 31, 156, 231, 316, 326; divine inspiration, 8
Homer, 91, 92
homilies, 33, 115, 118, 120, 209, 214, 315
honor, 182, 190, 194, 269, 270, 271, 278, 289-290, 329. See reputation, fame
Honorius of Autun, 158, 342, 352, 365, 380, 381
Horace, 94, 95-96, 147, 171, 175, 179, 316, 346
Howard, Donald R., 374
Hugh of St. Victor, 34, 38, 42, 58, 60-61, 66-68, 92, 108, 343; *De fructibus*, 25; *De sacramentis*, 6, 347, 353, 360; *De scripturis*, 347, 348; *Didascalicon*, 6, 23, 37, 64, 66, 341, 347, 348; *Hom. ix in Eccles*, 341; *Institutiones*, 350
humanism, 5, 46, 50, 166, 172, 315, 327, 364
human nature, 75, 76-77, 79, 82, 312
Hume, David, 78
Hume, Kathryn, 376
humor, 16, 18, 37, 39-41, 44, 46, 48-49, 138, 141, 145, 147, 148-150, 166, 170, 172, 177, 180, 181, 182, 190, 193, 225-226, 229-231, 260, 272, 274, 285, 287, 289, 291, 299, 345, 357, 372

Hundred courts, 295
Hunt, R. W., 352
Huppé, B. F., xiii-xiv, 16, 257, 341, 344, 346
husbandman, 297
Husserl, Edmund, 75, 90
hymns, 138, 141

iconography, 63, 86, 199, 249-250, 284-285, 379. *See* symbols
Innocent II, 153
Innocent III, 117, 118, 119, 266, 353
Integumentum, 9, 55-58, 72. *See* allegory
Involucrum, 9, 55-58, 72. *See* allegory
irony, 37, 39, 42, 44, 49, 145, 175, 177, 179, 180, 181, 182, 189, 204, 260
Isidore of Seville, 56-57, 63, 111-112, 227, 229-230, 341, 342, 343, 347, 348, 351, 366
Italy, 222, 258, 308, 315, 381
Ivo of Chartres, 111, 351

Jaffe, Hans, L. C., 88
jailors, 276
St. James, 360
Jaufre Rudel, 58
Jean Campion, 166
Jean de Le Mote, 363
Jean di Meurn, 6, 46, 50, 94, 240, 241-242, 246, 281, 289, 369, 373. *See Roman de la rose*
Jean Halgrin d'Abbeville, Cardinal, 167-168, 171, 364, 365
Jean de Savoie, 166-173
Jeauneau, E., 356, 371
Jeffrey, David Lyle, 114, 372, 379
St. Jerome, 15, 21, 29, 45
Jodicus Badius Ascensius, 364
John, King of England, 372
St. John, 4, 47, 306, 381
John Gervais, 120
John of Garland, 57
John of Gaunt, 236-237, 238, 242, 248, 252, 261, 263, 260, 276, 372, 373, 375
John of Northampton, 266, 270
John of Salisbury, 10, 15, 57, 59, 68, 70, 94, 175, 226, 347, 348, 355
John the Scot (Scotus Erigenus), 54-55, 56, 86, 177, 346, 347; *Annotationes in Marcianum*, 367 (p. 177)

Johnes, T., 373
Johnson, Dr. Samuel, 99, 312, 332
Jones, W. R., 352
Jonson, Ben., 324
Joyce, G. H., 351
"Judgement Day II," 35
judgment of Paris, 147, 269; *See* symbols: Paris
judgments, justice, 163, 178, 179, 203, 219, 225, 232, 274-276, 278, 283, 290, 301, 317, 319; discretion, 203, 279; false judges, 164; indiscretion, 282-283; justice of Providence, 332, 335
Julia, 174. *See* Ovid.
St. Julian, 278
Julius Caesar, 314
Jung, C. G., 256
the just, 16, 28, 153, 156, 158-159, 342, 367
justices in assize, 274-275
justices of the peace, xi, 273, 275-277, 376
Juvenal, 316

Kant, 78
Kaske, Robert E., 21, 105
Keen, Maurice H., 232
Kieckers, Ernst, 76
King's Bench, 232-233, 266, 275, 277
Kingsford, C. L., 369
Kittredge, George Lyman, 261, 262, 263
Kjellman, Hilding, 363
Klaeber, Friedrich, 34, 35, 344
knight of the shire, 273, 275-277, 379
knight-bachelor, 294
knighthood, obligation of, 153-154
Knowles, Robert, 373
Kolve, V. A., 218, 223-224, 357
Koonce, B. G., 367

Lactantius, 367
La Farge, Thomas, 355
Laing, David, 382
Laird, C. G., 354
Lang, Jane, 352, 353, 354, 355
Langland, William, *Piers Plowman*, 4, 5, 6, 9, 10, 14, 96, 228, 292, 345; Dobest, 228; Piers, 228
Laslett, Peter, xvii
Last Judgment, 13-14, 26, 35, 37, 38
Launcelot de Lake, Book of, 196, 247, 264
Lawlor, John, 375

Lawrence, D. H., 247
laws, 224, 231, 258, 266–267, 270, 274–277, 284
lawyers, 276
Leclercq, 352, 375
Lecoy de la Marche, A., 351, 352
Lee, A. G., 366
Legrand, Louis, 366
Leibnitz, 332
Lenz, Friedrich, 366
Leonardo da Vinci, 305–307
Levett, Ada Elizabeth, 291
Lévi-Strauss, Claude, 75, 91, 349
Lewent, Kurt, 153, 159, 160, 359, 360, 362, 263
Lewis, C. S., 90
Lewis, N. B., 373
Liber de modo benevivendi, 345, 346
Libri logicorum, 357
Lincoln, Abraham, 331
Lindsay, W. M., 347, 351
lineage, 299
Lippi, Fra Filippo, 29
Lisenmayer, A., 352
Little, A. G., 353
"The Little Red Hen," 255
liturgy, 123, 138, 146, 148. *See* The Mass
Livingston, Charles H., 369
Livre de Seyntz Medicines, 237
Livre des reis, 54, 58, 66
Livy, 363
Lochner, Stephan, 306
Locke, John, 333
Lodge, Thomas, 310
Lollards, 238, 266
Longnon, A., 347
Loüys, Pierre, 380
Luard, H. R., 353
Lucan, 178
Lucretius, 248, 260, 375
Luis de Leon, 380
Luis Diez del Corral, 348
Lutz, Cora E., 366
Lyly, John, 309, 382
lyric, 82, 260–261, 373

Machaut, Guillaume, 235, 239, 241, 255
Mack, Maynard, 334, 336, 382
Macray, W. D., 352
Macrobius, 253, 364

Mactacio Abel, 218, 226–232; Garcio (Pikeharnes), 226, 231; *see* Wakefield plays
magic, 106, 123, 162, 164, 171, 287, 290, 377
Magnus Herodes, see Wakefield plays
"The Maid of the Moor," 3, 16–18
Major gloassatura; *Glossa major*, 363
Mak, Mak's wife, *see* Wakefield plays
Mâle, Emile, xiv, 222
Mandonnet, P., 354
Mannyng, Robert, xii, 105–113
manor, 293–301
manorial courts, 295
Mantelh, 359
Manuel de peches, 122, 351, 359
Marbod of Rennes, 362
Marcabru, xvii, 151–165, 357, 362, 368; Jovens, 154–156, 360
Marcus Aurelius, 382
Margoliouth, D. S., 381
Mari, G., 347
Marie de France, xvii, 9, 62, 69, 202–206, 248, 368, 369; *Lais*, 348
Marie de Sainte Hilaire, 248
Marrou, H.-I., 22
Marsh, George L., 343
Martianus Capella, 139, 144
Martin, C. I., 355
St. Martin, 341, 342, 343
Martin del'Rio, 305, 380, 381
Martini, Edgar, 366
martyrdom, 17, 29, 41, 140, 156, 162, 181, 199
The Mass, 88, 115, 119, 220–221; burial of the dead, 251–252, 256; commemorative, 252; creed, 115–116, 119; epistle, 115; gospel, 115, 119, 352; Lord's prayer, 115–116
Matzke, J. E., 361
Maurice de Sully, Bp. of Paris, 115
Maury, A., 347
Mayor of London, 265–267
McCall, John P., 376
McKerrow, R. B., 382
McKisack, May, 276, 376
McLuhan, Marshall, 262, 349
medela, 145
Meillet, Antoine, 76
melancholy, 98, 133, 152, 235, 245–246, 254, 316–317

memory, 24, 47, 135
Menendez Pidal, Ramon, 360
Metamorphosis Ovidiana, 364; *see* Ovid
Meyer, Paul, 354
St. Michael, 186
middle class, 293
Migne, J. P., 25
Miller, Edward, 378
Miller, F. J., 367
Miller, R. P., 377, 378
Milton, John, ix, 12, 80, 280, 320
Minns, E. H., 353
Minturno, A. S., 309, 382
Minucius, Felix, 320
Mitchell, J., 356
Misfortunes of Arthur, 310
Mondrian, 89
Moorman, Charles, 209
Moorman, J.H.R., 351, 352, 354, 355
Moralium dogma Philosophorum, 139
Morey, A., 351
Morgan, Marjorie, 378, 379
Moslems, 154, 155
Mozart, 245
Mussato, Albertino, 366
Mussolini, 101
myth, 88-89, 91
Mythographus Vaticanus Tertius, 145, 176,
    355, 356

Nashe, Thomas, 308, 310, 311
Natura, 95, 169-170, 282, 377
Neo-Positivists, Oxford, 78
Netherlands, 232
Newgate Prison, 258
Newton, 314
Nicholas Brembre, 267
Nicholas Trivet, 240, 373
Nietzsche, 88
Nitze, William A., 51-52, 54, 70, 346
Nigellus Wireker, 57-58, 65
Norton, Lucy, 374
Nuchelmans, Gabriel, 356
nut, 172; *see* allegory
Nykl, Alois, R., 358, 360

Oberman, H. A., 375
Odo of Paris, 352
O'Neill, Eugene, 244
Order of the Garter, 235

Ortega y Gasset, José, 80, 98
Oschinsky, Dorothea, 380
Osgood, Charles G., xiv, 23, 341, 347,
    350, 370
Ovid, 11, 57, 63, 138, 140, 150, 168, 280,
    316, 363; *Amores*, 125, 149; *Ars amatoria*,
    150, 173, 174, 175, 176, 177, 377; *Fasti*,
    176; *Heroides*, 146, 178, 179, 366; De
    med. fac., 180; *Metamorphoses*, 136, 137,
    147, 169, 173, 176, 177, 178, 179, 183,
    366, 377; *On Painting The Face*, 173;
    Remedia amoris, 168, 173, 175, 260; *Tristia*,
    177, 178
Ovide moralisé, 11, 15, 178, 62
Owen, Dorothy, 114, 379
Owen, S. G., 174-175
"Owl and the Nightingale," 15-16

Pacht, Otto, 357
paille et grains, 54, 66, 72. *See* allegory
pallium, 9, 57-58, 66, 72. *See* allegory
Palmer, John N., 235, 257
Pange lingua (passion hymn), 141
Panofsky, Erwin, 372
papacy, 152-153, 154, 375; papal mantel,
    359; *see mantelh*
Paraclete, 184
Paré, G., 341, 348
Pareto, Vilfredo, 371
Paris, Gaston, 351, 369
Parliament, 275-276, 297, 323; House of
    Lords, House of Peers, 257, 277; House
    of Commons, 257, 277; Merciless Parliament
    of 1388, 265, 267; Parliament of
    1386, 265, 271; Trojan Parliament
    (Troilus), 270-271
Pater, Walter, 380
Paternoster, 140-141
partitura, 166
Patrologia latina, xiii, xiv; *see* Migne
patronage, patron, 152, 235, 237, 238, 240,
    242, 265, 360
Pattison, Walter, 158, 362
St. Paul, 13, 45, 53, 58, 89, 96, 97, 140,
    141, 180, 152-153, 209, 226, 252, 280,
    282, 289, 316, 320, 322, 323, 327. See
    Bible
St. Paul's Cathedral, 236, 238, 262, 266,
    274
Pearl, 209-214, 215-217; *see* symbol

peasants, 292-301
Peasant's Revolt, 277
Pecham, John, 114, 115, 123-125, 352, 355
Pelan, Marc M., 235
penitentiaries, penitential manuals, 110,
    121; confessional manual, 354
Pépin, Jean, 92
Peraldus, William, 106, 350
period study, 79, 83
Perriers, Alice, 265, 280, 373
personality, 79-80, 91, 100, 260-261, 264,
    274, 314-315, 317, 331; *Personalitas*, 314
personified abstractions, 42
Peter Lombard, 26, 27, 40, 109-110, 111-
    112, 113, 155, 156, 211, 347, 360, 361;
    Sententiae, x, 6, 10, 108, 117, 118, 351,
    354, 360, 361, 365, 373, 377
Peter of Blois, 203, 368
Peter Quivil, Bp. of Exeter, 120, 122,
    126-128, 353
Peterborough Chronicle, 361
Petrarch, ix, 8, 96, 246, 315, 341, 346, 359,
    363, 365, 380
Petrus Hispanus, 364
Pety, Aquiline, 363
phenomenological psychology, 75, 90-91
Philip the Fair of France, 94, 240
Philippa, Queen of England, 235, 237, 242
Philippe de Vitry, 166-167, 170-172, 363,
    364
Philippe Mouskés, 346
Phillip of Alsace, 69
Piaget, Arthur, 363
Pictish matriarchal customs, 259
pictura, 9, 53, 63-64, 71-72. *See* allegory.
Pierre of Poictiers, 351, 352
plague, ix, xi, xvii, 236, 239, 273, 291,
    293-294, 296, 379
Plato, 91, 92, 95, 224, 316, 332-333, 334
Platonists, 92; neo-Platonism, 259;
    Pseudo-Platonic, 272
Playboy Magazine, 258
Pliny, 62
plowmen, 294, 296-297
Plutarch, 316, 321, 322
poetic license, 67, 370
Pognon, Edmond, 363
poll taxes, 263
Pope, Alexander, ix, xvi, 74, 78, 99, 173,
    332-340

Porphyrio, 59
Potion, Philter, 129, 182, 192, 200, 171
Poulet, Georges, 349
praise, 195, 158, 260, 360
preachers, preaching, 31, 114-128, 138,
    152, 163, 184, 356
Priscian, 348
private chapels, 125
prophecy, prophets, 140, 158-159, 154
The Prophet, 154
Prosser, Eleanor, 312
prostitutes, 164, 247, 260
Providence, 13, 223, 224, 281, 284, 308,
    313, 314, 327, 329, 332, 335, 338
Provost, W., 356
Prudentius, 23, 63
Psalter, St. Alban's, 142,
    146, 357 (illus. p. 143)
psychology, xv, xvi, 242, 244, 253, 260,
    272, 313-314
Pui, Festival of the, 237
Purgatio, 308-109. *See* catharsis
Purity, 142
Putnam, Bertha Haven, 372, 376
Puttenham, George, 308, 310, 311, 382
Pynchbeck, Thomas, 274
Pythagoreans, 92; Neo-Pythagorean, 366

quadrivium, 8, 22, 23, 60-61, 62, 71
quaestio, 107, 166, 169
Quintilian, 346

Rabanus Maurus, 6, 8, 10, 22-23, 29, 31,
    53-54, 59, 60, 63, 67, 108, 164, 175, 343,
    344, 346, 348, 350, 351, 358, 359, 362,
    364, 370, 371
"Rabbi," 169, 365. *See also* Robertson,
    D. W., Jr.
Rabelais, 166, 253
Raby, F.J.E., 347
Raftis, J. A., xvii, 378, 379
Rahner, Hugo, 356
Raimbaut d'Orange, 158
Raimon Jordan, 165, 363
Rand, E. K., 174-175, 176-177, 179, 181,
    373
Raoul de Preslles, 267
Rapisarda, Emanuele, 367
Rashdall, H., 352
Raymond, Thomas, 295

reality, realism, naturalism, 50, 77, 80, 87, 94, 96, 98, 99, 222, 232, 252, 260, 274, 292
reap-reeve, 300
reason, rational, 5, 24, 43, 46, 47, 92, 135, 156, 162, 177, 203, 315, 318-319, 329, 330, 333, 337, 343, 346, 360; irrational conduct, 117, 225, 263, 372
receiver, 275, 294, 295
recorder, 295
redemption, 23, 25, 146, 213, 214, 225; salvation, 26, 28, 159, 209, 211
reeve, 294-296, 300, 398
Reiss, Edmund, 151
Remigius of Auxerre, 176, 355, 356
Remus and Romulus, 267
reputation, 180, 182, 183-186, 187, 191, 200, 269
Retexere, 169
Ribard, Jacques, 173
Ricci, P. G., 365, 380
Richard II, King of England, 265, 280
Richard de Bury, 95, 99, 172, 266
Richard le Poore, 116-118, 125, 352, 353
Richard of St. Victor, 31, 343
ridicule, 41, 138, 176-177, 179, 182
Riedel, G., 347, 356, 364, 367
Riley, H. T., 375
Robbins, Russell H., 372
Robert de Sorbon, 110-111, 122
Robertson, D. W., Jr., *Abelard and Heloise*, xv, 372; Chaucer's London, 349, 372, 378, 379, 380; *On Christian Doctrine, see* St. Augustine; *Fruyt and Chaf*, xiii; *The Literature of Medieval England*, 371; *Piers Plowman and Scriptural Tradition*, xiii; *A Preface to Chaucer*, xv, xvii, 21, 349, 356, 357, 371, 372, 373, 375, 376, 377; "Amors de terra lonhdana," 361, 368; "Cultural Tradition of *Handling Synne*," 351, 354; "Chaucer's Franklin's Tale, 349, 380; "Chaucerian Tragedy," 368; "Doctrine of Charity," 358, 359, 361, 364, 368; Heresy of Pearl, 370; "Historical Criticism," 349; "Love Conventions in Marie's *Equitan*," 361; "The Manuel des Peches," 354; "Partitura amorosa," 356; "St. Foy among the Thorns," 359; "Some Medieval Literary Terminology," 362; "Subject of *De amore*," 362

Robinson, F. N., 264, 372, 378
Robinson, John A. T., Bp., 80, 89, 97
Robortello, Francesco, 309, 381
Roger Weseham, Bp. of Conventry, 114, 122-123, 124
romances, 9, 14, 41, 51, 69, 174, 177, 187-188, 190, 248, 259
Roman de la rose, x, 9, 21, 42-47, 48, 168, 174, 231, 248, 259, 260, 264, 281-282, 374, 386; *Amis*, 281-283, 289; *Avarice*, 345; *Biautez*, 44; *Bien Celer*, 231; *Cortoise*, 44; *Covoitise*, 345; *Dame Cortoisie*, 44; *Deduit*, 15, 43, 47, 48, 345; Garden of, 374; *Douz Regarz*, 44; *Envie*, 345; *Felonie*, 345; *Franchise*, 44, 47; *Genius*, 43, 46; *Haine*, 345; Jealous Husband (*Le Jaloux*), 283, 289; *Jonece*, 44; *Largece*, 44; *Leece*, 44; *Oiseuse*, 43, 44; Old Woman, *La Vieille*, 282; *Papelardie*, 47, 253, 345; *Povreté*, 345; Reason, 46; *Richece*, 44; *Sorowe*, 285; *Tristece*, 345; *Vieillece*, 345
Rome, 176, 183, 187-188, 267, 364
Roncaglia, A., 375
Roosevelt, F. D., 101
Ross, A. C., 342
Rostagni, Augusto, 366, 381
Roubaud, Sylvia, 367
Rousseau, J. J., 98, 246-247, 248, 374
Rowland, Beryl, 377
royal escheator, 295
royal purveyors, 231
Rudisill, George, Jr., 376
Rupert of Deutz, 343
Ruskin, John, 247
Russell, H. K., xi
Ruthwell Cross, 26

sacraments, 5-6, 19, 78, 88, 116-121, 219, 280, 282; sacramental grace, 124-125; baptism, 13, 30, 93, 162-163, 210, 211, 215, 217, 223, 306-307; Holy Communion, 219, 220, 337; penance, 5-6, 118, 121-122, 210, 211, 213, 220, 229, 231, 280, 283, 329; impenitence, 248, 326
saints, 18, 93-94, 115, 119, 187. *See* names of individual saints
Salinger, Gerard, 359
Salisbury Constitutions, 117

Saltair na Rann, 36-37, 43
Salutati, Coluccio, 95, 164, 174-176, 363, 366
Samarin, Charles, 166
Sapientia, 15, 23-25, 32, 62, 67, 144, 146-148, 267-268, 375; Wisdom, 16, 27, 28, 30, 91-92, 137-138, 139-140, 153, 164, 225, 333, 364
Saracens, 154
Satan, 7, 10, 12, 34, 46, 158, 162, 231; Devil, 168, 314; servant of Satan, 370
satire, 37, 50, 174, 182, 199, 260, 274, 369
Sauer, Joseph, 356
Savoy, 238
Scaino, M. Antonio, 309, 381
Scarron, Paul, 253
Schapiro, Meyer, xv
Scheler, A., 373
Scheludko, Dimitri, 151-152, 154, 155, 157, 165, 358, 360, 362, 363
schism, 153
Schlegel, Friedrich von, 88
Schmeller, J. A., 132, 355, 356
Schmidt, Charles, 375
Schonberger, Arno, 348
Schorsch, Anita, 218
Schumann, O., 132, 133, 355, 356
scientia, worldly wisdom, 24-25, 28, 32, 36, 42, 226, 258, 296, 327, 336, 373
Scots, 257, 262
secrecy, 136, 190, 195, 271, 289, 309-310
Secunda Pastorum, 218, 224, 225-226, 232. See Wakefield plays.
Selmi, F., 367
Seneca, 150, 316
seneschal, 204, 294, 295
sensory knowledge, 86, 87, 94, 204, 240-241, 343, 360, 368
sentimentality, 5, 46, 47, 50, 99, 100, 182, 191, 236, 246, 248, 258, 260-261, 263-264, 272
serfs, 379
sergeants of the law; 273-276, 298
Severs, J. Burke, 373
Shakespeare, ix, 74, 78, 80, 142, 227, 248, 258, 273, 280, 308, 312-331; Antony, 331; Claudius, 314, 317, 319, 322, 325-328, 330; Desdemona, 328; Fortinbras (the younger) 313, 314, 327, 328-329;

Fortinbras (the elder), 313; Gertrude, 317, 324-325; Guildenstern, 325-330; Hamlet, 314-315, 317-331; Hamlet (the elder), 313, 317, 328-329; Horatio, 314, 318, 320, 330; Iago, 327; Jessica, 321; Laertes, 315, 321, 327, 328, 330; Lear, 331; Macbeth, 331; Marcellus, 314; Ophelia, 315, 321, 324-325, 328, 330; Osric, 321; Othello, 331; Polonius, 321, 325, 327, 328, 330; Reynaldo, 327; Rosencrantz, 325-330
Sharpe, Reginald R., 375
shell and kernel, 8-9, 32-33, 35, 52-55, 95, 172
sheriff, 275-278, 299; under sheriff, 276
shires, 301
Sidney, Sir Philip, 308-311, 313, 381
Silverstein, Theodore, 357
Simon of Exeter, Bp., 118
Simoniacs, 164
Simund de Freisne, 156-157, 361
sin, 14, 19, 27-28, 35, 38, 105-113, 115, 118-121, 124, 164, 169, 170, 210, 225, 226, 229, 244, 245, 246, 247, 316, 323, 325-326, 353, 372, 375; Original Sin, 177, 315 (*see* Fall)
Singleton, C. S., 348
Sir Gawain and the Green Knight, 267
Sisam, Kenneth, 17
Skeat, W. W., 228
Smith, G. G., 308, 382
Smith, Thomas, 327
social disorder, 224, 270-271
social inequality, 205
social position, nobility, noblemen, aristocratic, 125, 153-154, 157, 188, 191, 248, 253-256, 259, 265, 269, 277, 279 (*see* courtiers' behavior)
Socrates, 91
Soehner, Halldor, 348
Solzhenitsyn, Aleksandr, xvi
The Song of Roland, 183; Ganelon, 187, 200; Oliver, 186; Roland, 184, 186, 199
sophistry, 40, 285
soul, 118, 170, 209, 211, 213, 225, 315, 318, 326, 371
space, 80, 220-221, 225, 285
Spain, 154, 313, 329, 360; Cult of Santiago, 154, 360

Spedding, J., 377
Spenser, Edmund, ix, 23, 80, 252, 316, 317, 320, 321; Guyon, 320
Spicq, C., 346
Spingarn, J. E., 382
spirit and letter, 22, 53-54, 57. *See* allegory
Spitzer, Leo, 368
squire, esquire, 250, 265, 299; Royal Squire, 292
Stalin, 101
Statius, 138, 172
Stegmuller, Friedrich, 380
Stephen Tempier, Bp. of Paris, 37, 40
Sterne, Laurence, 100, 253
Stevens, John, 373
steward, 294, 295, 299, 398
Stockhausen, Karlheinz, 81
Stoicism, 13
Stravinsky, Igor, 81
Streitberg, Wilhelm, 76
structural linguistics, 75-78, 349, 371
stylistic history, xi, xii, xiv, xv, 74-77, 80, 86, 90, 91, 97, 101, 349
Sufis, 154
Summa sententiarum, 342, 350, 351, 353
summoners, 232, 248, 274
superstition, 14, 50, 105-106, 230
Surrealism, 88, 98
survey courses, 83
Swynford, Katherine, 236, 238, 375
symbolism, 209
symbols and mythological figures. Alceste, 18-19. *See* Ovid. animals, 23, 26, 137, 140, 168, 218, 226; Apollo, 62, 99, 137, 150, 355; arrow, 44, 179, 204, 268, 346; Asclepius, 366; Astrea, 367; Athena, *see* Minerva; autumn, *see* seasons; Babylon, 5, 25, 26-27, 32, 33, 38-39, 42, 45, 168, 345; *see two cities*; Bacchus, 355; bag of silk, 279; bark, 358; *see* shipwreck. birds, 26, 31, 36, 43. blindness, 38, 39, 48, 134, 135, 158, 230, 232, 242; Bower, 16, 17, 18, 158; branches, 25, 31, 42, 160; brass, 141; bride, 145, 156, 167, 209-210, 305-307, 359, 361, 370; of the lamb, 209-211; buds, 28, 45, 47, 168; broom, broom heath, 152, 358-359; calix, *see poculum*. Calypso, 168; carbuncle, 45, 47; cavern,

306-307; cedars of Lebanon, 148, 149; city, 26, 27, 32, 36-37, 155, 210, 211, 212-213, 370-371; *see* Babylon, Jerusalem. Ceres, 355; Ceyx and Alcyone, 11, 251-252; Circe, 168, 171, 364; clouds, 132, 135; cold, 14, 34, 37, 42, 158; *columba*, dove, 306-307; cross, 23, 25, 31, 221, 227, 320, 329; crown, 19, 29; crystal, 45, 47; cup, *see poculum*. Cupid, 45, 56-57, 169, 261, 263-264, 268, 269, 271, 272, 281-282, 285; *see* God of Love. dagger, 279; daisy, 18-19; dance, old, 44, 170; darkness, 14, 16, 17-18, 24-25, 30, 31, 32, 33, 35, 37, 38, 42, 46, 47, 153, 158, 163, 359, 361; dawn, 13, 17; day, 17; deafness, 69, 148, 204; debt, 18, 140-141, 195, 228; *denarius*, 213, 217, 371; dew, 36, 47, 138; *ros coelestis*, 356; Diana, 131-133, 135-136; distaff, 270; door, 43, 48, 218; porter of, 169, 359. Eden, *see* Paradise. Egyptian gold, 316; eleventh hour, 10, 211, 216; elm, 28; emerald, 162; eunuch, 182, 184-185, 200; Eurydice, 355; evening, 215-217, 355; exile, 5, 12, 230-231; faggots, 320; farthing, 229. Fate, *see Fortuna*. Fen, 37-38, *see Beowulf. Fenestra*, *see* window. fig. 28; fire, 269, 270, 309; in the bed straw, 270-271; flood, 14, 33; flowers, 15-16, 18-19, 28, 29-30, 31, 36, 44, 45, 47, 144, 148, 152, 158, 160, 171, 178, 345, 364. *Flosfoeni; flos feni*, *see* flowers. flower and leaf, 18, 30, 343; fortuna, fate, 12, 13, 39, 94, 100, 183, 189, 240-241, 249-250, 252, 254, 263, 270-271, 288, 308, 310, 319, 327, 336-337; fountain, 31, 37, 38, 42, 45, 46, 176; fox and geese; 279, 372. fragrance, *see* odor. Frost and ice, 10, 12, 16, 34, 36, 38, 43; fruit, 24, 25-26, 28, 36, 37, 38, 49, 93, 149, 152-153, 155, 158, 160, 215, 226, 362, 342; *fumus*, 135, 167, 355; gardener, 153-154, 327; *Hortulanus*, 32; garden, 9, 15, 21-50, 135, 142, 144, 152, 153, 158, 285, 289, 317; *hortus conclusus*, 31, 47, 48, 158; hortus de liciarum, 31, 37, 38, 48, *see* two gardens. Garment, 218; putting off of, 223. Genesta, 358, *see* broom. Giants, 14, 33; god of Love, 37-38, 39, 43, 46, 193, 262-263, 271,

281, 282, 285, 345; *see* Cupid. Gems, 161-162, 209, 213; gold and silver, 148, 188-189, 195; Golden Age, 282-283, 336. Grass, 15-16; *see flos foeni*. Green, 15-16, 25, 28, 30, 48, 152, 162; costume of forester, 297, 299; greenrobe, 19; *see* leaf. Groves (of trees), 23, 24, 36, 43; hair, 179; blonde, golden, 43, 189, 198; hart, 34, 62-63, 291; head, 152-153; Helen, 144-145, 147, 179-180, 198, 267; hesperus, 132-133, 135, 137; horse, 62, 196, 377; rider and horse, 280; *hortus conclusus*, *see* garden, Blessed Virgin Mary. *Hortus deliciarum*, *see* garden. hounds, 34; hunt, 137, 250; Hymen, 262, 272; intemperance, 160; Iron Age, 367; ivy, 15; Jason, 181; Jerusalem, xvi, 5, 7, 12, 14, 25, 26-27, 31, 209, 213, 215, 228; *see* two cities. Jewels, jeweller, 212, 213; June, 253, 267; Jupiter, 19; keyring, keys, 153, 359; kisses, 147, 171-172; labor, laborers, 215, 217; Labors of the Months, 100; Lamb, 50, 93, 141, 218; *see* bride. laurel, 47-48, 153, 155, 355; leaf, 15-16, 25, 27, 28, 30, 36, 152, 158, 358; Liban, 306; *see* Bible: Canticum *4:15*. Lamp, 25, 33, 131-132, 138, 361; Light of the World, 17; lightning, thunderbolts, 144; lilies, 17, 29; lion, 7, 50. Living water, *see* water. Lucifer, 137; Marsh, 37-38, *see Beowulf*. Mars, 147; Medea, 178-179, 181; maladies, 81, 121, 169, 185, 191, 244, 261, 317, 318; love sickness, 47, 147-148, 179, 181, 191, 259, 270, 286-287; maladjustments, 309-316; *see* ulcer, wounds. medical terminology, 133-135, 308-309, 381, 382; *see* maladies, wound. mermaids, 285; Minerva, 16, 95-96, 153, 172, 267-268, 269, 271, 322; mirror, 146-147; moly, 364; monsters, 14, 34, 96; moon, 131-132, 138, 356, mansions of, 287; Morpheus, 133, 253; mountain, 211, 306; *mundana musica*, 176; Narcissus, 45, 178-179, 182; New Law, xiii, 4, 22, 50, 53-54, 69, 155, 221, 223, 225, 228, 230, 248, 297, 326, 371; New Man, 155, 221, 360, 361; *see* Christ. Newness, *see* Adam, Christ, Jerusalem, New Law, song. Night, *see* darkness. nightingale,

15, 41, 42, 43, 49; Novus Adam, 25, 155; *see* New Man *vetus Adam*. Numbers, 23, three, 7; six, 146; seven, 7, 17; eight, 7, 17; nine, 17; hundred, 213; hundredfold, 148; one-hundred forty-four thousand, 209, 232, 370; *Odor*, 167-168, 364; Oenone, 181; Oldness, *see* Adam Babylon, Old Law. Old Law, 4, 17, 22, 54, 72, 218, 223-224, 226, 230, 232, 371, 375; Old Man, 155, 163, 223, 360, 361; *see Vetus Adam*. olive tree, 46, 153; orchard, 42; Orpheus, 133, 135, 138, 170, 172, 355, 356; owl, 15, 18; Palm, 16, 28, 29, 141, 142-144, 149, 150; Pallas, *see* Minerva. Pan, 380; Paradise, 24, 31, 38, 39, 49, 142, 148, 186, 285, 343; Paris, 147, 179, 181, 182, 198, 267, 269; *Pastor bonus*, 43, 46, 218, 224, 225-226, 232, 295, 300; Peach blossoms, 152; *see* flowers. Pearl, 19, 209-214, 370; pear tree, 49. Petra, *see* rock. Philomena, 15, 136, 173. Phoenix, 199, 249, 367; physician, 121, 181; pilgrim, pilgrimage, 5, 12-14, 18, 26, 40, 100, 155, 285, 360; pine tree, 15, 42, 46, 48; plowing, plow, 226, 227, 229, 329, 372; *poculum*, 168-169, 171; pomegranate, 365; pool, 33-35, 48, 306; Priapus, 48; primrose, 3, 17; prison, 164; bondage, 4, 45, 53, 147; ram, 219; reins, 185, 280. River, *see* water. Rock, 23, 31, 33-34, 45, 148, 305-307, 377, 381; root, 25, 342; rose, 3, 17, 29, 44, 45, 49, 95, 144, 145, 149, 168, 169, 251, 306; sand, 144; sard, 162; *Scopa*, 358; sea, 12, 62, 68, 284-285; seasons, 15, 16, 18, 19, 28, 33, 152, 158, 159; seed, sowing, 31, 69, 144, 148-149, 215; Serpent, 170. Shade, shadow, *see* darkness. Sheep, 93, 225. Shepherd, *see Pastor bonus*. Shipwreck, 147, 284-286; wandering bark, 136. Silver, *see* gold and silver. *Sine Macula*, 211-213, *see* Pearl. sirens, 285; sleep, 10, 131-133, 135-136, 138, 142, 345, 356; smoke, *see fumus*. Song, 15, 31, 36; New Song, 155; spinning, 218; Sparrows, 329. *Sponsa*, *see* Bride. Spouse, *see* Bride. Spring, *see* seasons. Stars, 137, 138, 144, 163. Stones, *see* rock. Storm, 14-36; strangers, 14, 26, 147, 158; straw, 153; *see*

symbols and mythological figures (*cont.*) fire. stream, *see* water. Summer, *see* seasons. Sun, 16, 18, 19, 25, 28, 33, 36, 37, 38, 42, 132; swine, 8, 10, 55, 96, 171; sword, 33, 154; sycamore, 28, 49; *see* Bible: Zacchaeus. Teeth, 93; Tereus, 136; Theseus, 62; Thessaly, 178; thirst, 34, 46, 178; thorns, spines, 37, 38, 145, 149, 169; thrones, 38, 141; Tithonia, 138; tower, 41, 42, 249, 345; tree, 23-34, 37, 38, 42, 43, 44, 46, 49, 152-153, 155, 158, 160, 343, 359; tree of knowledge of Good and Evil, 23-24, 35, 38, 49; tree of Life, 15-16, 23, 25, 26, 28, 30, 31, 36, 158; Troy, 179-180, 198, 265, 266-272, 376, New Troy, Troinovant, 257, 266, 270, 271, 272; Petty Troy, Little Troy, 267; turtle, 49; twigs, 153. two cities, *see* Babylon, Jerusalem. Two fears, 5, 27; two gardens, 31, 36, 41; *see* garden. Two generations, 157-158; *see* Bible: Cain and Abel. Two kinds of Fame, 185-187; two kinds of Joy, 156; two kinds of Nature, 377; two loves, xvi, 5, 26-27, 176-177, 151, 345; two Trees, 31-32; two Venuses, 173, 176, 356; *see* Venus. Ulcer, 308-311; *see* wounds. Ulysses, 168-169, 364. Vapor, *see fumus*. Veil, 8, 22, 49, 54-57, 60, 71, 92-93, 95-96, 160, 341; *see* allegory. Venus, 134, 137-138, 144-145, 147, 168, 176-177, 262, 263-264, 267-271, 285, 288, 355; *Genetrix*, 176; *Verticordia*, 176; Militia of, 137-138; Veneral pursuits, 135-137, 142, 144, 146, 269, 287; *see* two Venuses. *Vetus Adam*, 25, 38, 49, 155; *see* Bible: Adam. Vineyard, 215-216, 306; violet, 17, 145. *Virga, see* yard. Virgo, 367; voyage, journey, 5, 12, 26-27, 35, 100, 285; wall, 42, 43, 306, 345; warmth, heat, 25, 32, 34, 37, 38, 135, 158; water, 17, 28, 30-31, 33, 34, 37, 38, 44, 46, 47, 142, 306, 343-344, 381. Water of life, *see* water. Weeds, 31, 32, 317; wells, 30-32, 44, 45, 47, 49; Well of Life, 31, 45, 172; white robes, 141, 163; willow, 28, 152-154, 328; wind, 153, 358; wine, 159, 362; window, *fenestra*, 146-147. Winter, *see* seasons. Woods, 36, 38, 42, 44, 48, 291, 297; worm, 10; wounds,

145-146, 179, 184, 204, 309-311; yard, *yerde*, 270; youth and age, 155-156, 225, 259, 381; Zeus, 91, 92; Zephyrus, 132
Synchronic studies, 77
"Systems Analysis," 76

Tabernacle, 345
Taeschner, Franz, 359
Tantalus and Pelops, 173; *see* Ovid.
Tavistock, Abbey, 295
Tchaikowsky, P., 81
tegmen, 9, 55, 72; *see* allegory.
Terence, 147, 355
Theodore of Tarsus, 121
Theodulph of Orleans, 9, 55, 175
Theology, pastoral, 6, 105, 112, 113
Thomas, *Tristan*, 248
Thomas, E. C., 365
St. Thomas Aquinas, 6, 10, 118, 366, 367, 368, 371
St. Thomas of Acon Hospital, 166
Thomas of Chobham, *Summa Confessorum*, 377
Thomas the Cistercian, 175
Timocles, 382
tithing, 227, 229-230, 278, 296, 379
tournaments, 194, 196
tragedy, 49, 82, 151, 308-311, 312-313, 324, 331, 381
Tremblay, P., 341, 348
Trinity, 7, 24, 46, 121; Divine inspiration, 8
trivium, 8, 22, 60-61, 62, 71
Trojan horse, 62
Trojel, E., 344, 364, 368
Troubadours, 202, 156-157, 165, 257, 259, 261, 368
The Tun, 258
Tuve, Rosemond, 317
typology, 218-232. *See* allegory.

Ullman, B. L., 363
understanding, 135
Unwin, K., 362

Vallentin, Antonia, 380
Van Caenegem, R., 349
Van den Berg, Jan Hendrick, xv, 75, 97, 374
vassalage, 186, 191, 193, 199, 254, 277, 369

vavasour, 277
verisimilitude, 99, 222-223, 232
Vettori, Pietro, 309, 382
Vetus liber archidiaconii eliensis, 353
victory, 141, 149, 153, 262
View of Frankpledge, xi
villages, 294, 301
Vinaver, Eugene, 51-52
virgater, 300; half-virgater, 300
Virgil, 8, 9, 11, 15, 55-56, 59, 62, 63, 66,
174, 175, 176, 183, 316, 364, 366, 367
Virtues and vices, 5, 25, 95, 246, 279, 309,
317, 337; vices, 29, 31, 78, 118, 163, 169,
184, 263, 316-317, 321, 353; virtues, 26,
30, 47, 94, 119, 124-125, 152, 153, 155-
156, 167, 169-171, 241, 249, 250, 252,
255, 267, 278, 289, 290, 319, 320, 339,
346; *accidia*, 43, 47, 245-246, 252; Adultery, 15, 20, 156-158, 201, 204-205, 247,
258, 289, 360, 369, 375, 377; almsgiving, 140; avarice, 279; blasphemy, 231;
boasting, 152, 153, 159, 338, 362. Charity, caritas, 3, 4, 10, 17, 21-50, 51, 53-54,
66-70, 71, 140-141, 155-159, 162, 171,
176, 181, 185, 204, 213, 225-228, 230,
323-324; chastity, 176, 180, 137, 209,
247, 259, 269, 282, 288, 355, 365;
churchbreaking, 112; common profit,
258, 269; concupiscence, 176, 184, 190,
263, 282, 284; *Concupiscentia carnis*, 38,
43, 45, 169; *concupiscentia oculorum*, 39,
44, 45, 47, 345; constancy, *constans*, 163,
245, 317, 362; continence, 185, 138;
cupidity, 3, 4, 12, 13, 22, 23, 26, 27, 28,
30, 32, 51, 53-54, 156, 158, 160, 176,
209, 211, 295, 324. Deception, 30, 156,
159, 163, 240, 361; deceit, 25, 258; doublenesse, 269-270; fraud, 319; despair,
28, 149, 217, 230, 241, 245, 252, 271,
316; forsaking God, 105, turning away
from God, 24. detraction, 109;
drunkenness, 164, 247, 318; envy, 247;
fear, 5, 27, 39, 309, 337; fear of God, 21,
27, 230; flattery, 145, 147, 195-196, 259,
282, 283; folly, 8, 14, 28, 40, 42, 47, 49,
142, 150, 156, 158, 160, 163, 164, 178,
179, 188, 201, 230, 241, 253, 261, 262,
263, 271, 280, 283-284, 331; forgiveness,
140, 228; *fornicatio*, 27, 38-39, 176, 177,
247-248; mother of, 176-177. Fortitude,

245, 263, 317-319, 329; friendship, 180,
241, 281, 369; generosity, 188-189, 195,
278, 290; gentilesse, 277, 278-279, 289,
290, 361; gluttony, 247, 278; good
works, 25, 28, 62, 152, 158, 185-186,
163, 316, 362; Goodness, 180, 240, 241;
greed, 284; hate, 230; hope, 25, 158,
317, 337; false hope, 152; vain hope,
217; humility, 17-18, 25, 145, 300;
hypocrisy, 28, 38, 40, 42, 153, 169, 229,
246, 259, 288, 292, 365; idolatry (including idolatrous love), 27, 29, 32, 38, 39,
42, 44, 45, 46, 49, 181, 149-150, 248-
249, 260, 267, 269, 345, 346, 368; *immoderata cogitatione*, 39, 47, 49, 369; industria, 169. Innocence, 19, 29, 99, 209,
211-214, 231-232, 370; joy (*jois*), 148,
156-157, 159, 160, 161, 159-162, 164,
225, 257, 269, 361; kidnaping, 112; love
of God, 4, 38, 140, 177, 181, 221; loyalty, 196; *largece*, 345; lassitude, 136,
245; laziness, 8; lechery, 29, 38, 39, 44,
174, 185, 204-206, 142, 164, 262-263,
282, 360; luxuria, 25, 27, 45, 62, 155; lying, 8, 24, 58, 64, 71-72, 106-107, 112-
113, 162, 164, 319, 370; magnanimity,
245-246, 317, 374; magnificence, 245-
246, 329, 374; malice, 224, 227, 230-232,
319, 321-327, 331; mercy, 124-125, 164,
218, 225, 231, 248; modesty, 178; false
modesty, 279. Murder, homicide, 108-
109, 164, 205, 230-231, 310, 313, 318,
321, 325-326, 327, 329-330, 377; oaths,
107, 190, 192; obscenity, 227-230; patience (*patientia*), 13, 146, 149, 161, 281,
282, 284, 319, 329, 362; perseverance,
245; piety, impiety, false piety, 11, 28,
31, 33, 175, 178, 201, 204, 215, 246, 284;
317; Pity, 244, 290, 309; pride (*superbia*),
24, 25, 92, 163, 185, 247, 262, 316, 334-
335, 346, 362; Pride of life, 45; pruriency, 174-175, 182; purity, 17, 29,
209-210, 215, 217; rape, 112, 136, 267;
rapine, 163; repentance, 217, 225, 249,
323; *see* sacraments. revenge, vengeance, 318-319, 321-322, 328; righteousness, 260, 323, 375; false holiness, 253;
sacrilege, 112; self-denial, 258, 280; renunciation, 169, 212; Self-sacrifice, 191,
221, 229; selfishness, 169, 186, 191-192,

virtues and vices (*cont.*)
194, 224, 230-231, 255, 292; self-esteem,
141; self-indulgence, 138, 278, 292;
self-love, xvi, 5, 24, 32, 40, 178; self-
satisfaction, 258, 267, 271. Shame, 160,
176, 185, 194, 201, 271; sloth, 43, 169,
227, 245, 254, 263, 316-318, 320, 321,
322, 326, 329, 365; idleness, 24, 44, 164;
sorrow (*tristitia*), 13, 16, 245, 264, 284-
285; *stultitia*, 25; suicide, 241, 246, 252,
271, 289, 319, 330; swearing, 113; false
swearing, 107; *see* oaths, lying. Temperance (*temperantia*), 161, 362; temptation, 14, 34, 135, 285; theft, 112, 164,
225; Treason, 164, 189-190, 192, 193,
199-201, 310, 330, 369, 377; *tristitia, tristicia, tristezza*, 152, 198, 245, 316, 319;
usury, 112, 164; vainglory, 163, 184,
186, 196; *see* gluttony, avarice. Vanity,
24-25, 185, 140, 141, 142, 150, 152, 224,
289; wrath, 321-322, 358
Visigoths, 154
Von Beethoven, Ludwig, 245
vulgar tongue, 115, 118; vernacular, 352

Wagner, Richard, 11, 88
The Wakefield Master, 222, 228, 232;
Wakefield plays, 218-232, 372; *Magnus
Herodes*, 232; *Mactacico Abel*, 218, 226-
232; *Secunda pastorum*, 218, 224, 225-
226, 232
Walafrido Strabo, 343
Walter de Cantilupe, Bp. of Worcester,
119-122
Walter de Kirkham of Durham, 120
"The Wanderer," 11-15
Warnke, K., 347
Webb, C.C.I., 347, 369
Webern, Anton, 81, 245
Weisheipl, J. A., 375

Weisweiler, H., 352
Weitzmann, Mrs. Kurt, xv
Weld, John, xiv
Wellek, René, 215, 370
Wetherbee, Winthrop, 131
Whicher, George, 134, 355, 356
Whittington, Richard, Lord Mayor of
London, 266
Wilkins, David, 352, 353, 354, 355
will, 14, 24, 26, 47, 213, 327
will (testament), 236, 266
William, King of England, 275
William Brewer, Bp. of Exeter, 118
William de Melton, 379
William of Auvergne, Bp. of Paris, 121-
122, 350, 353
William of Conches, *see* Guillaume de
Conches
William of Newburgh, 305-306, 381
William of St. Amour, 6, 274
Wilson, Thomas, 297
Wimsatt, James I., 21, 139, 144, 375
Winder, Bayley, 360
wisdom, *see sapientia*
witchcraft, 105-123, 178, 181
Wolfflin, Heinrich, xv, 74
Wood, Chauncey, 288, 377, 378
Woolf, Rosemary, 218, 220
word play, 166, 183
Wordsworth, William, 98
Wormald, Francis, 357
Wright, Thomas, xv, 347, 358
Wyclif, 238, 373

Yeats, W. B., 147, 267
yeoman, 293, 297-300, 379
Yevele, Henry, 237, 373
"Young Grammarians," xv, 76

Zumthor, Paul, 348

THIS BOOK HAS BEEN COMPOSED AND PRINTED BY
PRINCETON UNIVERSITY PRESS

DESIGNED BY BRUCE CAMPBELL
EDITED BY MARJORIE C. SHERWOOD

TYPOGRAPHY: BEMBO
PAPER: WARRENS 1854 TEXT

EDITORIAL ASSISTANTS:
JOHN V. FLEMING
GAIL M. GIBSON
JULIA BOLTON HOLLOWAY
HARRY J. SOLO

INDEX COMPILED BY
ANNETTE CAFARELLI

Library of Congress Cataloging in Publication Data
Robertson, Durant White.
  Essays in medieval literature.
  Bibliography: p.
  Includes index.
  1. Literature, Medieval—History and criticism—
Addresses, essays, lectures.   I. Title.
PN681.R55   809'.02   80-13130
ISBN 0-691-06449-0
ISBN 0-691-01375-6 (pbk.)